Harrison Birtwistle's Operas and Music Theatr

Music Since 1900

GENERAL EDITOR   Arnold Whittall

This series – formerly Music in the Twentieth Century – offers a wide perspective on music and musical life since the end of the nineteenth century. Books included range from historical and biographical studies concentrating particularly on the context and circumstances in which composers were writing, to analytical and critical studies concerned with the nature of musical language and questions of compositional process. The importance given to context will also be reflected in studies dealing with, for example, the patronage, publishing and promotion of new music, and in accounts of the musical life of particular countries.

Recent titles in the series

J. P. E. Harper-Scott
Edward Elgar, Modernist

Yayoi Uno Everett
The Music of Louis Andriessen

Ethan Haimo
Schoenberg's Transformation of Musical Language

Rachel Beckles Willson
Ligeti, Kurtág, and Hungarian Music during the Cold War

Michael Cherlin
Schoenberg's Musical Imagination

Joseph N. Straus
Twelve-Tone Music in America

David Metzer
Musical Modernism at the Turn of the Twenty-First Century

Edward Campbell
Boulez, Music and Philosophy

Jonathan Goldman
The Musical Language of Pierre Boulez: Writings and Compositions

Pieter C. van den Toorn and John McGinness
Stravinsky and the Russian Period: Sound and Legacy of a Musical Idiom

Harrison Birtwistle's Operas and Music Theatre

David Beard

CAMBRIDGE
UNIVERSITY PRESS

CAMBRIDGE
UNIVERSITY PRESS

University Printing House, Cambridge CB2 8BS, United Kingdom

Cambridge University Press is part of the University of Cambridge.

It furthers the University's mission by disseminating knowledge in the pursuit of
education, learning and research at the highest international levels of excellence.

www.cambridge.org
Information on this title: www.cambridge.org/9781316641989

First published 2012
First paperback edition 2016

A catalogue record for this publication is available from the British Library

Library of Congress Cataloguing in Publication data
Beard, David, 1971–
Harrison Birtwistle's operas and music theatre / David Beard.
p.   cm. – (Music since 1900)
Includes bibliographical references and index.
ISBN 978-0-521-89534-7 (hardback : alk. paper)   1. Birtwistle, Harrison – Criticism and
interpretation.   2. Birtwistle, Harrison Operas.   I. Title.
ML410.B605B43   2012
782.1092 – dc23   2012023152

ISBN 978-0-521-89534-7 Hardback
ISBN 978-1-316-64198-9 Paperback

To my wife Danijela, my parents, grandfather,
and in memory of my grandmother
Marjorie Grace Merrett

Contents

Plates

Acknowledgements

Many individuals and institutions have provided invaluable assistance in the production of this book. Arnold Whittall, as series editor, has given unstinting support, expert advice and encouragement throughout the writing process, and his guidance over many years has been inspiring. I am grateful also to Philip Rupprecht, David Schiff, and the anonymous reviewers for Cambridge University Press and the Arts and Humanities Research Council (AHRC) for their advice on proposals at an early stage. Vicki Cooper and Rebecca Taylor at Cambridge University Press were supportive but also flexible and understanding when the project's scope expanded significantly. This happened when Harrison Birtwistle put swathes of recently completed sketches at my disposal and informed me that his son, Silas, also had a large collection of undocumented material dating back from 1989 to the mid 1940s. I am deeply indebted to Harry and Silas for their passion, insight, hospitality and humour, which vastly enriched my research experience. Others who illuminated the way with first-person accounts include Alison Chitty, David Harsent, Stephen Langridge, Michael McCarthy, Stephen Plaice, Patrick Wright and Peter Quartermain. Of my colleagues at Cardiff University, Kenneth Gloag and Anthony Powers gave generously of their time to read drafts of early chapters, David Wyn Jones and Charles Wilson offered advice and information, and Nicholas Jones (with help from his son Hywel) set the music examples with impressive efficiency and patience. I am especially grateful also to Pat Harper for her thorough and thoughtful copy-editing.

My work is indebted to Michael Taylor who very generously shared his knowledge of Birtwistle's sketches when I visited him in Dublin back in the mid 1990s. Peter Franklin has been a constant friend and source of encouragement throughout, and I owe much to his guidance from the days of my doctoral research onwards. Others have contributed in ways too numerous to list here, but my sincerest thanks go to: Robert Adlington, Rupert Bergmann, Seth Brodsky, Edward Campbell, Rachel Cowgill, Jonathan Cross, Christopher Dromey, Björn Heile, Christopher Mark, Malcolm Markovich, Nicholas Marston, Roger Parker, Klaus Scherer, Emanuele Senici, Mary Ann Smart, Jean-François Trubert, Jérémie Wenger, and the anonymous reviewers for *twentieth-century music* and *Cambridge Opera Journal* who I should have thanked before.

In compiling research material I have been greatly assisted by numerous individuals: Felix Meyer, Robert Piencikowski, Tina Kilvio and Henrike Hoffmann at the Paul Sacher Stiftung, Basle; Rebecca Dawson, Kieran Morris and Bettina Tiefenbrunner at Universal Edition; David Allenby, Sally Cox and Pippa Patterson at Boosey & Hawkes; Nicholas Clark at the Britten and Pears Archive, Aldeburgh; Neil Jarvis and Clare Colvin at English National Opera; David Ogden at the Archive of the Royal Opera House, Covent Garden; Julia Aries at the Glyndebourne Opera Archive; Gavin Clarke at the Royal National Theatre Archive; Peter Brown and Amanda Wrigley at the Archive of Performances of Greek and Roman Drama, Oxford University, Classics Faculty; Laura Berman at Bregenzer Festspiele; Barbara Preis at Neue Oper Wien; and staff at Music Theatre Wales. I would also like to thank Anna Lacy for sending me her plan of the stage layout of *The Io Passion* on which Figure 7.1 is based.

I am extremely grateful to *Music & Letters* for an award to present research at a North American British Music Studies Association conference in Vermont, to the BBC for the opportunity to take part in a study day on *The Second Mrs Kong*, attended by the librettist Russell Hoban (who sadly died in 2011), and to the following universities for invitations to present papers on aspects of the book: Aberdeen, Belgrade, Bristol, Cambridge, Cardiff, Geneva, Huddersfield, Lancaster, Oxford and Sussex. A two-year small research grant from the British Academy facilitated early trips to Basle, and subsequent visits were funded by generous awards from Cardiff University. An AHRC Research Leave Award combined with a semester sabbatical from the School of Music, Cardiff University, also assisted enormously; my thanks go to the assessors who granted these awards, and to the School of Music for covering the costs of permissions. During this project I have had many rewarding experiences but I learned an immense amount from two workshops in particular: one on emotion communication in *Punch and Judy* at the Grand Théâtre, Geneva (my thanks to members of the cast: Gillian Keith, Jonathan May, Mark Milhoffer, Lucy Schauffer and Bruno Taddia); the other 'Making Yourself Heard: Drama for Change', run by David J. Evans at the ATRiuM, Cardiff School of Creative and Cultural Industries, University of Glamorgan.

Finally, this project has inevitably affected the lives of others, often because of my prolonged periods of absence. For their patience and forbearance, I am eternally grateful to Danijela, Ankica, my parents, and my grandfather. *Neizmjerno sam vam zahvalan.*

All score extracts are reproduced by kind permission from the publishers, as follows:

Tragoedia. © Copyright by Universal Edition (London) Ltd, London. Reproduced by permission. All rights reserved.

Punch and Judy. © Copyright by Universal Edition (London) Ltd, London. Reproduced by permission. All rights reserved.

Down By the Greenwood Side. © Copyright by Universal Edition (London) Ltd, London. Reproduced by permission. All rights reserved.

Bow Down. © Copyright by Universal Edition (London) Ltd, London. Reproduced by permission. All rights reserved.

The Mask of Orpheus. © Copyright by Universal Edition (London) Ltd, London. Reproduced by permission. All rights reserved.

Yan Tan Tethera. © Copyright by Universal Edition (London) Ltd, London. Reproduced by permission. All rights reserved.

Gawain. © Copyright by Universal Edition (London) Ltd, London. Reproduced by permission. All rights reserved.

The Second Mrs Kong. © Copyright by Universal Edition (London) Ltd, London. Reproduced by permission. All rights reserved.

The Last Supper. Music by Harrison Birtwistle. Libretto by Robin Blaser. © Copyright 2000 by Boosey & Hawkes Music Publishers Ltd. Reproduced by permission.

The Io Passion. Music by Harrison Birtwistle. Libretto by Stephen Plaice. © Copyright 2004 by Boosey & Hawkes Music Publishers Ltd. Reproduced by permission.

The Corridor. Music by Harrison Birtwistle. © Copyright 2009 by Boosey & Hawkes Music Publishers Ltd. Libretto by David Harsent. © Copyright 2009 by David Harsent. Reproduced by permission.

The Minotaur. © Copyright 2008 by Boosey & Hawkes Music Publishers Ltd. Libretto by David Harsent. © Copyright 2008 by David Harsent. Reproduced by permission.

Score extracts of music for *Tamburlaine the Great*, stored at the National Theatre Archive in London, are reproduced by kind permission of Harrison Birtwistle.

Facsimiles from the fair copy of *Lorca* and sketch pages from *The Mask of Orpheus*, *Gawain*, *The Second Mrs Kong* and *The Last Supper* are reproduced by kind permission of the Paul Sacher Foundation, Basle.

Permission to describe unpublished manuscripts belonging to Silas Birtwistle has been kindly granted by Silas Birtwistle.

The quotation from Benjamin Britten's undated letter to Birtwistle is used by kind permission from the Trustees of the Britten-Pears Foundation.

The cover image, from rehearsals for *Bow Down* at the National Theatre, London, in 1977, has been reproduced with kind permission of the photographer Nobby Clark.

Versions of Chapters 5 and 6 were previously published as follows: 'The Shadow of Opera: Dramatic Narrative and Musical Discourse in *Gawain*', *twentieth-century music*, 2/2 (September 2005), 159–95 (republished in Margaret Notley (ed.), *Opera After 1900*, vol. VI of The Ashgate Library of Essays in Opera Studies (Farnham: Ashgate, 2010), 319–55); and '"A Face Like Music": Shaping Images into Sound in *The Second Mrs Kong*', *Cambridge Opera Journal*, 18/3 (November 2006), 273–300.

Arts & Humanities
Research Council

A note on the text

Many of the works discussed in this book employ different internal referencing systems. The systems I adopt vary according to the one used in the work in question. In *Yan Tan Tethera*, for example, there are no rehearsal figures or even bar numbers, therefore I refer to page numbers. Elsewhere, as in *Gawain* and *The Second Mrs Kong*, I use the term 'Fig.', often with suffixes to designate a particular bar either after the rehearsal figure (e.g. Fig. 1^{+2}, which means the second bar after Figure 1, including the bar in which the figure itself appears), or before a figure (e.g. Fig. 1^{-2}, which means two bars before Figure 1). For *Down by the Greenwood Side* I employ the same system but with Letters (e.g. A^{+2}). In works with more than one act, figures begin from '1' at the start of each act. For this reason I refer mostly to page numbers in *The Mask of Orpheus* as these run continuously from the start of Act I to the end of Act III. In *The Minotaur* the barring begins from '1' in each scene, whereas *The Last Supper* and *The Io Passion* (both in one act) are barred continuously from start to end, but with no figures.

Page numbers in the main text refer to pages in a score not a libretto; page references for libretti and all other texts appear in the footnotes. In nearly all cases I refer to the full score. However, I make a distinction in Chapter 2 between pages and bars in the full score (FS) and in the vocal score (VS) of *Punch and Judy*. Scores published by Boosey & Hawkes are available to order, whereas many of those published by Universal Edition are mostly photocopies of handwritten fair copies used in performances; such scores may be available on request but are more expensive as they need to be specially prepared.

When referring to pitches in specific registers, this book uses the Helmholtz notation system, as follows:

Number series appear throughout this book. The text will explain the function of these numbers, which may refer to: ordering systems in the sketches; durations; unordered pitch intervals (treated the same whether ascending or descending), where 1 = a semitone, 2 = a tone, and so on; or contour patterns. The latter are indicated by the use of arrowheads, which indicate an ordered sequence, for example: <1, 4, 2, 3>, where 1 is the lowest position and 4 the highest.

A note on spelling. In the score and libretto for *Orpheus*, and in the score of *Mrs Kong*, Euridice is given in the Italian form. In the libretto for *Mrs Kong* and in the score and libretto of *The Corridor*, however, her name is spelled Eurydice. Unless quoting from Peter Zinovieff's libretto for *Orpheus*, all references in this book use the more common form: Eurydice.

A number of abbreviations are used for books, as listed below:

Hall, *HB*	Michael Hall, *Harrison Birtwistle* (London: Robson Books, 1984)
Hall, *HBIRY*	Michael Hall, *Harrison Birtwistle in Recent Years* (London: Robson Books, 1998)
Cross, *HB: MMM*	Jonathan Cross, *Harrison Birtwistle: Man, Mind, Music* (London: Faber and Faber, 2000)
Adlington, *MHB*	Robert Adlington, *The Music of Harrison Birtwistle* (Cambridge University Press, 2000)

Two institutions are abbreviated, as follows:

NTA	[Royal] National Theatre Archive, London
PSS	Paul Sacher Stiftung, Basle

All extracts from unpublished sketches, drafts and fair copies have been transcribed by the author after consulting the original manuscripts. When editorial changes or annotations have been made by the author these are given in square brackets. All microfilm references relate to the Sammlung Harrison Birtwistle of the Paul Sacher Stiftung in Basle. When microfilm numbers are given it indicates that the sketches referred to belong to the collection for the work that is the subject of that particular chapter or sub-section. Otherwise, further information is provided to indicate which part of the Sammlung Harrison Birtwistle the sketch is from. For example:

PSS 0540-0431; Musikbeispiele für Kurse.

This indicates the roll of film (0540), the specific page (-0431) and the title of the work or folder in the Sammlung Harrison Birtwistle (Musikbeispiele für Kurse).

Although I am aware that the convention in sketch studies is to cite the title of the collection that a sketch page belongs to and possibly a page number – if there is one, or if the page belongs to a sketchbook – and also, in certain instances, to give the dimensions of a page, I have decided to identify pages by microfilm numbers. However, in a few instances, notably in Chapter 5, the sketch material was consulted before it went to microfilm. Here the reference system lists the folder number, followed by the page number (although the page itself may not be numbered). There is a possibility that the sketches and drafts will be re-filmed. It is therefore important to note that the microfilms referred to here are from the first set of films, which were made before 2009. Given the volume and size of Birtwistle's sketch materials (he mostly works with A2-size manuscript paper with sixteen staffs), visitors to the Paul Sacher Stiftung will find working from microfilm considerably easier, although this is no substitute for working from the originals. Much work has been undertaken by Robert Piencikowski and Michael Taylor to identify pages in works up to *The Second Mrs Kong*. This information is provided within the manuscript folders but not always in the microfilms.

Finally, when I began this project it was not my intention to seek answers to questions directly from the composer or others. Since the period of writing coincided with the premiere of *The Minotaur* and the composition and premiere of *The Corridor*, however, opportunities arose to speak with Birtwistle and David Harsent, the librettist for both works. This inevitably shaped Chapters 7 and 8, in which these pieces are discussed. As these conversations shaped my thought on the other works discussed in Chapters 7 and 8, I decided to approach Patrick Wright and Peter Quartermain, who assisted Robin Blaser in his work on *The Last Supper* (Blaser sadly passed away in 2009), and Stephen Plaice, Stephen Langridge and Alison Chitty, who collaborated with Birtwistle on *The Io Passion*. While these chapters are therefore inconsistent with approaches adopted in earlier chapters, they are not inconsistent with the underlying premise of this book, which is to adopt different strategies in each chapter. That said, information gleaned from my conversations with Birtwistle is distributed throughout the book.

1 The roots of Birtwistle's theatrical expression: from *Pantomime* to *Down by the Greenwood Side*

With six major operas, around eight music dramas, and a body of incidental music to his name, Harrison Birtwistle has made a significant contribution to contemporary opera and music theatre during a period that spans more than forty years. This study is concerned not only to reflect the importance of these stage works by examining them in some detail but also to convey their varied musical and intellectual worlds. Previous studies have rightly focused on Birtwistle's perennial concerns, such as myth, ritual, cyclical journeys, varied repetition, verse–refrain structures, instrumental role-play, layers and lines.[1] These characteristics highlight consistency throughout Birtwistle's oeuvre and are a mark of his formalist stance. By contrast, this book is motivated by a belief that the stage works – in which instrumental and physical drama, song and narrative are combined – demand interpretation from multiple, inter-disciplinary perspectives. While not denying obvious or important relations between works, what follows is rather more focused on differences: Birtwistle's choice of contrasting narrative subjects, his collaborations with nine librettists, his varied pre-compositional ideas and working methods, his experience with different directors, producers and others, all distinguish one stage work from another. A recurring theme is therefore a consideration of ways in which Birtwistle's initial concepts are informed, altered or conveyed differently in each case. Moreover, as ideas evolve, from the composer's musical sketches to the final production, multiple meanings accrue that are particular to each drama. Original intentions and priorities change, become compromised or are jettisoned altogether, leading to tensions and contradictions that are instructive and distinctive to each work.

Despite the focus on differences, each chapter is guided by a central question: what is the relationship between the genesis and abstract musical processes of Birtwistle's operas and music theatre works, on the one hand,

---

[1] See Michael Hall, *Harrison Birtwistle* (London: Robson Books, 1984) and *Harrison Birtwistle in Recent Years* (London: Robson Books, 1998) – hereafter Hall, *HB* and *HBIRY*, respectively; Jonathan Cross, *Harrison Birtwistle: Man, Mind, Music* (London: Faber and Faber, 2000) – henceforth Cross, *HB: MMM*; and Robert Adlington, *The Music of Harrison Birtwistle* (Cambridge University Press, 2000) – subsequently Adlington, *MHB*. For an analytical review of these monographs see David Beard, 'The endless parade: competing narratives in recent Birtwistle studies', *Music Analysis*, 23/1 (2004), 89–127.

and the representational demands and 'real world' concerns of his libretti, narratives and plots, on the other? To consider this question, emphasis is given to close readings of sketches and scores as and when they intersect with broader aesthetic and cultural themes.[2]

Birtwistle is a prolific sketch writer. While researching this book I have studied well over 4,000 sides of sketches and drafts, and around 2,500 sides of unpublished drafts and annotated typescripts of libretti by different authors. The musical manuscripts vary from verbal jottings, through tables of pitches, charts with numbers or graphs, to skeleton and continuity drafts. This study is the first sustained consideration of all of the unpublished manuscripts associated with the stage works, the vast majority of which have not been discussed previously.[3] Such creative processes may appear to be entirely independent of the 'work' itself – that is to say, from the piece as it is staged, with costume, lighting, direction, singers, mime artists, and action. However, a key contention here is that the dialectical relationship between musical sketch and performance is central to an interpretation of Birtwistle's operas. When placed in context and interpreted as an intellectual concept or visual metaphor, even the most abstract sketch page may provide a clue to a work's governing rationale or dramatic narrative.

This opening chapter provides a context for the detailed examinations of stage works that follow. The chapter's first half deals with methodological issues and other questions relevant to the study as a whole. These include questions of genre, the notion of an avant-garde dilemma, Birtwistle's idea of the theatre, and the concepts of metaphor and presence. Drawing on unpublished sources and interviews, the second half explores Birtwistle's formative experiences, an unpublished piece of juvenilia titled *Pantomime*, stage works for schoolchildren, and a previously undocumented score for a music drama titled *Lorca*. The chapter concludes with a brief examination of *Down by the Greenwood Side* (1968–9) as a case study in the composer's attitude to the relationship between music, mime and drama.

---

[2] This approach follows the notion that 'texts are worldly, to some degree they are events, and, even when they appear to deny it, they are nevertheless a part of the social world, human life, and of course the historical moments in which they are located and interpreted'. Edward Said, *The World, the Text, and the Critic* (London: Vintage, 1991), 4.

[3] The majority of the sketches consulted are stored at the Paul Sacher Stiftung in Basle, Switzerland (henceforth abbreviated to PSS). However, I am extremely grateful to the composer for allowing me to study manuscripts that had not been sent to Basle at the time of writing, and also to the composer's son Silas for permitting me to examine an extensive collection of manuscripts that were given to him by his father prior to the composer's agreement with Paul Sacher in 1989. The research in this book also builds on my unpublished 'An analysis and sketch study of the early instrumental music of Sir Harrison Birtwistle, c. 1957–77', D.Phil. thesis, University of Oxford (2000).

Genre

> I remember people saying *Punch and Judy* is not an opera. So what? It is what it is.[4]

Distinguishing between music theatre and opera is not always easy, and in Birtwistle's stage music such categories are continually blurred and contested.[5] Moreover, as the above quotation suggests, generic distinctions are not necessarily important to Birtwistle. During this book, I often adopt the term 'stage work' as the most convenient catch-all phrase for a variety of pieces, nearly all of which resist their putative labels. Birtwistle's first major stage work, *Punch and Judy* (1966–7) is described in the score as an 'Opera in One Act'. However, its demotic subject and subtitle ('a tragical comedy or a comical tragedy'), chamber scale, baroque-titled subsections (including Aria and Passion Chorale) and fragmented form suggest a range of generic affiliations. One of *Punch*'s possible allegiances is to early twentieth-century music theatre works by Schoenberg and Stravinsky, which, like the stage works of Brecht and Weill, drew on popular entertainment, including cabaret, melodrama and dance. However, as will be discussed in Chapter 2, the irresolvable ambiguity of *Punch*'s generic identity – which mirrors Punch's own capricious nature – is fundamental to its meaning.

Birtwistle's first unambiguous use of the term 'opera' was applied to *Gawain* (1989–91; rev. 1994 and 1999); it was subsequently applied to *The Second Mrs Kong* (1993–4) and *The Minotaur* (2005–7), works that, to some extent, reveal an interest in operas by Wagner, Mussorgsky and Debussy. Yet *Gawain* followed a series of self-styled stage works, including 'dramatic cantata' *The Mark of the Goat* (1966), 'dramatic pastoral' *Down by the Greenwood Side* (1968–9), 'lyric tragedy in three acts' *The Mask of Orpheus* (1973–83) and 'mechanical pastoral' *Yan Tan Tethera* (1984). Nor did the apparent turn to opera in 1991 mark a clear break from self-styled forms: *The Last Supper* (1998–9) is described as a series of 'dramatic tableaux', and *The Corridor* (2008) as a 'scena for soprano, tenor and six instruments'; *The Io Passion* (2003–4) bears no descriptor but is styled as a chamber opera by its publishers. Birtwistle's stage works are not easily defined, either, by considering the institutions that commissioned them: *The Last Supper*

---

[4] Birtwistle in conversation with Beard at the composer's home in Mere, Wiltshire, on 18 November 2008.

[5] The reference to 'music theatre' in the title of this book is shorthand for 'experimental' or 'new' music theatre. However, British examples of this genre are often more closely bound to textual meaning than their continental European contemporaries. For more on generic definitions see Björn Heile, 'Recent approaches to experimental music theatre and contemporary opera', *Music & Letters*, 87/1 (2006), 72–81.

was premiered at the Deutsche Oper, Berlin. Nor, as Robert Adlington has pointed out, is scale a reliable indicator of genre.[6] *Orpheus* remains the most large-scale and ambitiously complex of the stage works. Opera is 'present' in this work, in the form of arias and recitative-like sections, and in the association of Orpheus with the birth of opera. Yet *Orpheus* is the composer's most experimental piece, with electronics, mime artists, puppets and non-linear narrative. *Gawain*, *Mrs Kong* and *The Minotaur*, by contrast, are more obviously indebted to operatic convention in terms of clearer narratives, greater characterisation and expressive devices. Yet here, too, an experimental approach is evident in the relationship between orchestra and text. Questions of genre are therefore useful, but only to the extent that Birtwistle's stage works may be compared to earlier models: to insist on a neat fit is potentially misleading.

What does exist in the composer's mind is a distinction between the kinds of detail possible in Grand Opera, on the one hand, and 'something that is more intimate and small' that explores an idea in 'close-up', on the other.[7] To this may be added a common distinction between emphasis on a libretto in opera and resistance or avoidance of textual meaning in music theatre. Yet even within these terms Birtwistle conspires against easy classification. *Io*, for example, mixes mime with speech, half-song and aria. Moreover, *Io* establishes a tension between stylised, artificial drama and a more natural sense of realism. As such, this work exploits and questions the possibility of distinguishing between opera as realism and music theatre as anti-realism.[8] Conscious that the characters in his 'kind of theatre' might become cardboard cutouts, Birtwistle has commented that such a thing 'is to be avoided at all costs, because more than anything else I want my characters to have blood in their veins and sex in their loins'.[9] Tensions between artifice and naturalism are fundamental to Birtwistle's concept of theatre. Brechtian distancing, Stravinskyan formalism, a focus on the *techniques* of theatre and a belief that 'the story can never be separated from the way it is told' *do* often have the upper hand.[10] But they do not rule outright. This is most clearly

---

[6] Robert Adlington, 'Music theatre since the 1960s', in Mervyn Cooke, ed., *The Cambridge Companion to Twentieth-Century Opera* (Cambridge University Press, 2006), 228.

[7] David Beard, 'Beauty and the beast: a conversation with Sir Harrison Birtwistle', *Musical Times*, 149 (Spring 2008), 24.

[8] The distinction is suggested by Adlington, 'Music theatre', 229.

[9] Birtwistle in 'Behind the mask: perspectives on the music of Harrison Birtwistle', a television documentary broadcast on Channel 4 in 1987. It is possible that this remark reflects Birtwistle's shift towards more conventional opera, but even in workshops during the 1970s he wished to avoid what he termed 'the Dalek effect' (a reference to a breed of remorseless mutated robots in the BBC television series *Dr Who*), in which stylised declamation is stripped of natural inflection; see Chapter 7.

[10] Adlington, *MHB*, 15.

exemplified by a duality in *Down by the Greenwood Side* between stylised pantomime, on the one hand, and an expressionist setting of the Ballad of the Cruel Mother, on the other, as will be discussed at the end of this chapter. In this and other stage works the Stravinskyan and the Schoenbergian jostle and vie with one another.

The avant-garde dilemma

In the 1950s and 1960s opposition grew towards opera and other forms of musical representation, particularly among high-modernist circles in Darmstadt. Most notably, Theodor Adorno and Pierre Boulez spoke out against opera, considering it to be costly, outmoded, irrelevant and bourgeois.[11] A dilemma therefore arose for those who pursued autonomous musical forms and abstract compositional techniques but were interested in theatre or opera. Given such opposition, how was a concern for abstract structures and experimental processes to be reconciled with an 'urge to engage with drama'?[12] This is a question that applies to many composers besides Birtwistle, and it is an issue that lies at the centre of this book. In certain instances, such as instrumental pieces by Karlheinz Stockhausen, theatricality was a by-product of an exploration of new notational devices, sounds and performance techniques: the virtuosic skills required to perform certain works ultimately drew attention to the idea that 'all music is by nature theatre, that all performance is drama'.[13] But many composers, such as Luigi Nono, Luciano Berio, Mauricio Kagel, György Ligeti, Henri Pousseur and George Aperghis, consciously developed new forms of experimental music theatre as a means of distinguishing themselves from prevailing formalist trends.[14] Birtwistle's parallel development is highlighted by a work such

[11] See Pierre Boulez, 'Opera Houses? Blow them Up!' *Opera*, 19/6 (1968), 440–50, and Theodor Adorno, 'Bourgeois opera', in David J. Levin, ed., *Opera through Other Eyes* (Stanford University Press, 1994), 25–44 (Adorno's article was originally published in 1955). It would be misleading to suggest that Boulez was unambiguously opposed to opera or music theatre, however, given his experience as an opera conductor, his involvement with the theatre company Renaud-Barrault (see Peter O'Hagan, 'Pierre Boulez and the project of "L'Orestie"', *Tempo*, 241 (2007), 34–52), and evidence that throughout the 1960s he had an operatic project, or 'scénographie musicale', in mind, which influenced his purely instrumental music (see Luisa Bassetto, 'Marginalia, ou *L'opéra-fantôme* de Pierre Boulez', in Jean-Louis Leleu and Pascal Decroupet, eds., *Pierre Boulez: Techniques d'écriture et enjeux esthétiques* (Geneva: Contrechamps Editions, 2006), 255–98).

[12] Adlington, *MHB*, 5. The dilemma stems from the problem that 'musical theatre is in many ways intrinsically at odds with the aesthetics of the avant-garde. The referentiality of staged enactions compromises the autonomy that avant-garde composers like to claim for their music'; Adlington, 'Music theatre', 233.

[13] Paul Griffiths, *Modern Music and After* (Oxford University Press, 2010), 191.

[14] Adlington has observed that music theatre was attractive to certain avant-garde composers because it allowed 'a re-engagement with dramatic enaction in a form that explicitly refuted bourgeois theatrical conventions'. Following such 'subtle critiques', other composers, notably

as *Verses for Ensembles* (1969), with its spatial separation of instrumental groups, choreographed movements for instrumentalists across the stage, and forms of instrumental role-play.

To align Birtwistle too directly with the continental avant-garde would be incorrect: his models were predominantly pre-war modernists, particularly Stravinsky. Moreover, the cultural context in post-war Britain differed from that in continental Europe: Britain actually witnessed a resurgence of interest in opera in the 1950s and 1960s. Yet within this context Birtwistle approached opera obliquely. As discussed in Chapter 2, *Punch* is a complex, ambiguous work that is not clearly positioned pro or contra opera. Moreover, in Britain at the time, *Punch*'s musical language was considered radical enough to be dubbed 'avant-garde', despite the fact that Birtwistle's direct experience of the European avant-garde was limited.

That said, Birtwistle did attended Darmstadt briefly in 1956, and his close contemporaries Peter Maxwell Davies, Alexander Goehr and John Ogdon kept him informed of developments there in the mid to late 1950s, when abstract, autonomous compositional systems were encouraged.[15] Birtwistle's use of expanding chromatic wedges – an especially important compositional tool from his first published work *Refrains and Choruses* (1957) until the early 1970s – dates from this time. In fact, evidence suggests that Birtwistle derived this technique from his study of Nono's *Canti per tredici*, which was premiered in Darmstadt the year Birtwistle attended.[16]

More recently, commentators have begun to appreciate the diversity of approaches adopted by composers at Darmstadt.[17] Similarly, Birtwistle has spoken of the importance of John Cage's arrival there in 1958 and of his own sense that serialism represented a dead end.[18] Another important

---

Hans Werner Henze and Louis Andriessen, developed forms of music theatre in opposition to the avant-garde; Adlington, 'Music theatre', 231 and 234.

[15]   According to an undated letter stored in Darmstadt, Birtwistle attended the Internationale Ferienkurse für neue Musik from 11 to 15 July 1956. Goehr's Fantasia Op. 4, for orchestra, and Richard Rodney Bennett's Four Pieces for Orchestra were premiered on 12 and 13 July, respectively. In 1957, Wolfgang Steinecke, the founding director of the summer course, invited Birtwistle to perform clarinet in Berg's Chamber Concerto for piano, strings and wind ensemble, but there is no record of Birtwistle's attendance.

[16]   A handwritten piano reduction of Nono's piece with pencil annotations indicating the use of an expanding chromatic wedge on A and mirror forms was in Birtwistle's possession and is currently owned by Silas Birtwistle.

[17]   See: Paul Attinello, Christopher Fox and Martin Iddon, eds., 'Other Darmstadts', *Contemporary Music Review* 26/1 (2007); Martin Iddon, 'Darmstadt schools: Darmstadt as a plural phenomenon', *Tempo*, 256 (2011), 2–8; Björn Heile, 'Darmstadt as other: British and American responses to musical modernism', *twentieth-century music*, 1/2 (2004), 161–78.

[18]   Birtwistle in conversation with David Beard at the composer's home in Mere, Wiltshire on 29 October 2008. For a broader perspective on British modernism and responses to Darmstadt in the 1950s, see Philip Rupprecht, '"Something slightly indecent": British composers, the European avant-garde, and national stereotypes in the 1950s', *Musical Quarterly*, 91/3–4 (2008), 278–325.

factor to consider is Birtwistle's experience while he was a Harkness Fellow at Princeton University in 1966–7: it seems likely, for example, that his awareness of Milton Babbitt's *Philomel*, for soprano and electronics, informed the opening of *Orpheus*, as discussed in Chapter 3.

Birtwistle's concept of theatre

> Birtwistle's re-thinking of the medium of opera is . . . radical. He doesn't "set" an opera libretto in the usual sense; he looks for a subject and for a way of handling it which together mirror the processes inherently at work in his own music.[19]

This quotation perfectly captures an idea handed down by Birtwistle himself, which seems to offer a way out of the avant-garde dilemma. If it can be argued that the drama is an expression of purely musical processes, then abstract, formalist principles remain paramount and aspects such as text, characterisation and narrative are secondary. Birtwistle has also often stressed the notion that he prefers to work with familiar narratives because the story will then not detract from what *he* wants to say.[20] A possible consequence of this approach is that the narrative and textual demands of a libretto may contradict the abstract concerns of the score.[21] Yet to reach a verdict on this question it is necessary to consider the level of interaction between composer and librettist. What I seek to explore throughout this book is evidence that Birtwistle is not a slave to his preconceived musical ideas – that, on the contrary, there is a reflexive relationship between text and music.

The notion that Birtwistle's musical ideas take priority also runs up against a problem when it is considered that numerous commentators have insisted on the theatrical nature of all Birtwistle's music. Witness Jonathan Cross's reference to 'the inherently dramatic nature of Birtwistle's musical thought' and Nicholas Snowman's remark that 'a sense of theatre pervades all his scores'.[22] Birtwistle himself has expressed a desire to get to the 'roots

---

[19] Malcolm Hayes, 'Pandas mate at last', *Sunday Telegraph*, 26 May 1991. This idea clearly informed David Freeman's direction of the original production of *Orpheus*, as revealed by his remark: 'The way that the theatre speaks has to match the way that the music speaks'; David Freeman, 'Composer and producer speak', in programme booklet for the English National Opera production of *Orpheus*, May–June 1986.

[20] Hall, *HB*, 148.

[21] Irene Morra, *Twentieth-Century British Authors and the Rise of Opera in Britain* (Aldershot: Ashgate, 2007), 53.

[22] Cross, *HB: MMM*, 79, and Nicholas Snowman, 'Birtwistle the dramatist: some reflections', in programme booklet for the first production of *Gawain*, Royal Opera House, Covent Garden, May–June 1991 [n.p.].

of theatrical expression', a sentiment that mirrors experiments by theatrical groups in the 1960s, such as Jerzy Grotowski's Laboratory Theatre and Peter Brook's Theatre of Cruelty.[23] According to this logic, dramatic ideas inform the music, which then determines the structure of the stage works. Yet it has also been argued that 'the theatrical credentials of Birtwistle's music overall are sometimes more presumed than proven':

> We arguably sell it short by unthinkingly insisting on the affinity. A willingness to negotiate with comprehensibility remains an important part of Birtwistle's make-up, one that doesn't sit altogether comfortably with the idea that his music presents an arena wherein to behold a spectacle.[24]

As mentioned above, Birtwistle's tendency to think in visual and spatial terms is highlighted in certain works, particularly by the choreographed movement and spatial arrangement of players in *Verses for Ensembles* and *Secret Theatre* (1984). 'The reason I did [this]', Birtwistle has commented, 'was to make it seem that *that* music happens here, in *this place*, and it doesn't happen in another place. It's a sort of visual clarification ... That's what happens in *Punch and Judy*: the murders all happen in one place; Choregos only sings in one place and so on.'[25] Such spatial consciousness recalls Antonin Artaud's dictum that 'the stage is a concrete physical space which asks to be filled, and to be given its own concrete language to speak', the thoughts of which 'are beyond the reach of the spoken language'.[26] In other words, such movements draw attention to the physical and aural *presence* of the performers in a manner that need not imply a specific meaning (a more detailed consideration of Artaud and the body is presented in Chapter 7).

To insist on the formalist aspects of Birtwistle's stage works also misses the importance of his references to older theatrical traditions. Recognising this leads Cross to observe an apparent contradiction 'at the heart of... Birtwistle's theatre':

> On the one hand, an examination of the historical contexts for Birtwistle's experiments with different kinds of theatre emphasizes both the contemporaneity and originality of his achievements. This is a process in which the composer himself has attempted to participate, aligning himself

23 Birtwistle in an interview with John Drummond, broadcast on BBC Radio 3 on 13 January 1988. During this interview Birtwistle also discussed his interest in David Lynch's film *Blue Velvet*, describing its 'strange world' and 'terrifying violence,' its images of unrealistic flowers and stuffed birds, combined with a concentration on 'very basic emotions.'

24 Robert Adlington, 'Summary justice' [review of Harrison Birtwistle festival, Southbank Centre], *Musical Times*, 137 (July 1996), 34.

25 Andrew Ford, *Composer to Composer: Conversations about Contemporary Music* (London: Quartet Books, 1993), 58.

26 Antonin Artaud, *The Theater and Its Double*, trans. Mary Caroline Richards (New York: Grove Press, 1958), 37.

with the high modernist enterprise of the post-war years in which the likes of Boulez were arguing for an abandonment of the past, for the destruction of all opera houses and so on . . . On the other hand, his ongoing interest not only in classical subject-matter but in the very forms and techniques of Attic tragedy, of baroque opera, even of Wagnerian music drama, shows a composer acutely aware of and responding to past traditions. In practice, Birtwistle's theatres seem to strike a fascinating balance between these two tendencies . . . Herein lies [their] originality and expressive power.[27]

One such past tradition is pastoral, a genre that Birtwistle explores most obviously in *Yan Tan Tethera*. It is frequently argued that, following Stravinsky, Birtwistle downplays subjectivity in his stage works, reducing individuals to archetypes that deflect attention away from character on to the dramatic situations in which they operate. Following William Empson, Cross has compared this flattening of subjectivity to similar effects in pastoral.[28] Chapter 4, however, explores *Yan Tan Tethera* in the context of other pastoral theories and reveals a more equal relationship between scene and agent, which arguably highlights subjectivity.

A representative sample of the critical reception of Birtwistle's stage works reveals a fair amount of consensus regarding his effective handling of music and drama. On attending performances of *Punch* and *The Minotaur* in 2008, Arnold Whittall remarked that the experience 'confirms that Birtwistle is the most creatively post-Wagnerian, post-Stravinskyan (that is: post-Verdian) dramatic composer of our time'.[29] The conductor Elgar Howarth has noted Birtwistle's 'superb sense of timing and proportion', which is 'essential to a composer working [. . .] in theatre time'.[30] The critic Andrew Clements has observed that Birtwistle 'has consistently demonstrated his understanding of the roots of drama'.[31] David Harsent, the librettist for *Gawain*, *The Minotaur* and *Corridor*, has spoken of his admiration for Birtwistle's 'colossal sense of theatre', stating that 'he understands theatricality – what it should do, and how it works'.[32] Arguably, what moved Harsent to make these comments is Birtwistle's ability to recognise key moments in a narrative and to enact responses that maximise dramatic effect.

Set against this conventional sense of dramatic timing, pace and climax, however, is Birtwistle's interest in what he terms 'emblematic theatre'.[33] It is

[27] Cross, *HB: MMM*, 83–4.
[28] William Empson, *Some Versions of Pastoral* (London: Penguin, 1995).
[29] Whittall, 'First performances. London, Royal Opera, Covent Garden: Birtwistle's *The Minotaur*', *Tempo*, 246 (2008), 50.
[30] Howarth, 'The Mask of Orpheus', *Opera*, 37/5 (1986), 492.
[31] Andrew Clements, 'Birtwistle unmasked', *Financial Times*, 17 May 1986.
[32] David Harsent in conversation with Beard, 21 January 2008.
[33] Birtwistle in conversation with Beard, 18 November 2008.

unclear precisely what Birtwistle means by this term, although it suggests an oblique approach to narrative in which more abstract concepts take precedence over the literal depiction of events in real time. Moreover, this idea resonates with what Michael Hall describes as an 'appositional way of thinking' that has inevitably drawn Birtwistle 'to a form of theatre where holistic presentation takes precedence over linear plot'.[34] Hall cites Martin Esslin on the Theatre of the Absurd: 'it is a theatre of situation as against a theatre of events in sequence, and therefore it uses a language based on patterns of concrete images rather than argument and discursive speech ... The formal structure of such a play is, therefore, merely a device to express a total image by unfolding it in a sequence of interacting elements'.[35] However, although relevant to the more experimental stage works, such as *Punch*, *Orpheus* and *Bow Down* (1977), this observation is by no means universally applicable. As Cross notes, there is nearly always a sense of movement in Birtwistle's stage works towards a moment of recognition and reversal.[36]

Hall's observations, however, *do* explain a general avoidance of dialogue and of attention to subtle emotional detail. This tendency has drawn criticism from some who view opera as a means to explore human nature in more realist terms.[37] Yet such criticism represents a somewhat restricted view of opera: is realism the only way to examine human emotion and communication? Moreover, realism itself is a problematic category, since it is *constructed* – and in very different ways by, for example, Mozart, Verdi, Janáček, Britten or Berg. Clearly, Birtwistle finds realist approaches too restrictive, since he is attracted to a form of theatre in which 'everything is possible'.[38] Ultimately, the incorporation of elements of realism into Birtwistle's emblematic or appositional concept of theatre results in fascinating tensions between artifice and realism, which become its *raison d'être*.

Metaphor

Birtwistle often thinks of his music in visual terms. As he has remarked: 'There's no actual separation to me between the things that I make and the things that I see.'[39] This sounds remarkably like the conclusion of

---

[34] Hall, *HB*, 119.   [35] Hall, *HB*, 119–20.   [36] See Cross, *HB: MMM*, 76–8.

[37] For example, Rupert Christiansen argued in a review of *The Minotaur* that Birtwistle 'can't do real people or subtle feeling' ('Enthralling, hypnotising – and unloveable', *Daily Telegraph*, 17 April 2008), while Alex Ross, reviewing *Mrs Kong*, suggests Birtwistle 'is not a man of quick dramatic instincts'; http://www.therestisnoise.com/2006/08/london_1995.html (accessed 22 August 2011). However, it is interesting to consider the extent to which opera as a genre is conducive to subtle emotions or (whatever this term means) quick dramatic instincts.

[38] Birtwistle in Beard, 'Beauty and the beast', 20.

[39] From 'A couple of things about Harry', a BBC2 *Art on Two* television documentary broadcast on 4 April 1971. The programme was directed by William Fitzwater.

metaphor theorist Mark Johnson who has observed that 'our understanding *is* our mode of "being in the world"... Our more abstract reflective acts of understanding... are simply an extension of our understanding in this more basic sense of "having a world"':

> human understanding involves metaphorical structures that blend all of the influences (bodily, perceptual, cultural, linguistic, historical, economic) that make up the fabric of our meaningful experience. Metaphor reaches down below the level of propositions into this massive embodied dimension of our being.[40]

While Birtwistle concedes that the languages of visual and aural media are very different – an issue considered in Chapter 6, in relation to *Mrs Kong* – he continually associates his purely musical thought with the material world.[41] For example, he has compared his musical processes to geological strata, street processions, objects in nature, and the turning of the seasons. This not only provides a useful comparison for his audiences; it also suggests that his pre-compositional ideas are rooted in his own *physical experience* of the world.

Birtwistle has remarked that a work may begin as 'a formal position [or] elaborate schemata... that you can call your idea'.[42] Such schemata are discussed throughout this book, as revealed by the sketches. Yet the sketches also illustrate how these schemata are adapted, developed, distorted or abandoned as a consequence of a range of processes involving number schemes, rotation, permutation and selection. Regarding such operations, Stephen Walsh has commented:

> Behind them all there looms something highly particular: an Image towards which the composer gropes or out of which he endeavors to materialise an object for the delectation of others. Birtwistle's music has the same quality of reification – the actualisation in time of a momentary impression – which one senses in Stravinsky... And perhaps the mechanical, the arbitrary, the deliberately 'irrelevant' patterns come off simply because the method of extension is less important than the fact of it, and perhaps also because 'irrelevant' procedures are less likely to corrupt the Image than conscious modifications.[43]

---

[40] Mark Johnson, *The Body in the Mind: The Bodily Basis of Meaning, Imagination, and Reason* (London: University of Chicago Press, 1987), 102 and 105.

[41] On painting and music, Birtwistle has spoken of differences in perception (taking in an entire painting at once in contrast to hearing a piece of music through time), and composition (how a painter has an immediate relationship to a painting unlike a composer whose ideas are realised in performance). See Ross Lorraine, 'Territorial rites 1', *Musical Times* 138 (October 1997), 4–8, and 'Territorial rites 2', *Musical Times* 138 (November 1997), 12–16.

[42] Birtwistle, cited in Hall, *HB*, 145.

[43] Stephen Walsh, review of Hall, *HB*, *Soundings*, 12 (1985), 77–8.

Walsh's remarks draw attention to the question of the relationship between Birtwistle's idea or image of a piece and his compositional method. A key proposition of this book is that the composer's methods are, like metaphor, 'a model or a picture of something to which we can never have direct access'.[44] George Lakoff has remarked that 'The locus of metaphor is not in language at all, but in the way we conceptualize one mental domain in terms of another . . . Metaphor is fundamentally conceptual, not linguistic in nature.'[45] By extension, it may be argued, to know something about Birtwistle's compositional processes is to know something about his image of the 'work', and vice versa. This observation provides a hermeneutic window onto Birtwistle stage works, since meaning is metaphorical, in that 'it suggests itself to the listener precisely at the moment of intersection of two incongruous languages'.[46] This is illustrated by the composer's own words:

> I always feel that everything's a compromise with an idea. You have a truce and a compromise. The idea you can feel as crystal, as a very potent thing, it's the seed. But the realisation of it – where you come up against the technique and the instruments, and so on – suddenly starts to become something else, which you can't bend back. You can't retrace it. It's like a stick, which has some sort of life in it and there's no . . . the only thing you can do is throw it away and start again.[47]

These remarks highlight Birtwistle's sectional approach to composition: he continually devises new schemes as he moves through a work, usually in the order that appears in the final score. Moreover, each opera begins with a different compositional premise. In some instances, a fund of material or schema conditions a large span: for example, expanding chromatic wedges operate throughout *Punch* (Chapter 2), instrumental lines generate harmonic fields in *Gawain* and *The Minotaur* (Chapters 5 and 8), and a table of modes governs Act II of *Orpheus* (Chapter 3). New schemata may be devised in the middle of sections, perhaps prompted by an aspect of the drama, for example at Hannah's lament in *Yan Tan Tethera*, during the projection of a film scene in *Mrs Kong*, and during the table-building scene in *The Last Supper* (Chapters 4, 6 and 8). Despite the highly abstract nature of these

---

44   Michael Spitzer, *Metaphor and Musical Thought* (London: University of Chicago Press, 2004), 1–2.

45   Cited in Robert Adlington, 'Moving beyond motion: metaphors for changing sound', *Journal of the Royal Musical Association*, 128/2 (2003), 302.

46   Philip Rupprecht, review of Anthony Pople, ed., *Theory, Analysis and Meaning in Music* (Cambridge University Press, 1994), *Journal of Music Theory* 41/1 (1997), 163.

47   Birtwistle in conversation with Beard, 18 November 2008.

schemes, they shadow or amplify themes specific to each opera. As such, they operate as metaphors for the dramas depicted on stage.

Metaphor brings the material properties of Birtwistle's music into contact with the physical world. It therefore provides a means to relate the composer's abstract sketching processes to the narrative and rhetorical aspects of his stage works. If metaphor is at the heart of Birtwistle's aesthetic, then that aesthetic can be said to concern the relationship 'between the physical, proximate, and familiar, and the abstract, distal, and unfamiliar'.[48] Yet this process is bidirectional – that is to say, it flows from Birtwistle's compositional methods, on the one hand, and from the listener, or decoder, on the other.[49] In other words, metaphorical meaning emerges when sketch study, music analysis and contextual enquiry *intersect*. More precisely, the significance of Birtwistle's abstract compositional processes is revealed when the sketches are examined in the context of critical and cultural theories that are relevant to each work, such as theories of parody, narrative, pastoral, film, body, and community.

Presence

Emphasis on metaphor implies a search for meaning. A contrasting approach that has informed this book, however, is suggested by the cultural theorist Hans Ulrich Gumbrecht. Although not entirely opposed to aesthetic interpretation, Gumbrecht argues that we should pay closer attention to what he terms 'the production of presence', that is, aesthetic experiences that have no semantic system and therefore no meaning. He contrasts this with the dominant cultural viewpoint, or 'the production of meaning', whereby aesthetic experience is continually read and interpreted from a text. In short, Gumbrecht wishes to see an end 'to the dominant, *exclusive*, paradigm of interpretation, semiotics, and hermeneutics, which is entirely unchallenged in humanities departments'.[50] In fact, this approach does not necessarily conflict with metaphor theory, since such theory stresses ways in which so-called *rational* thought processes are conditioned by our *physical* experience of the world – how the body 'works its way up into the mind'.[51]

It has already been remarked by other commentators that an important part of Birtwistle's aesthetic resists the production of meaning. Adlington, for example, describes how 'Birtwistle's constructional procedures are

[48] Spitzer, *Metaphor and Musical Thought*, 4. [49] Ibid.
[50] Hans Ulrich Gumbrecht, 'Production of presence, interspersed with absence: a modernist view on music, libretti, and staging', in Karol Berger and Anthony Newcomb, eds., *Music and the Aesthetics of Modernity: Essays* (Cambridge, MA: Harvard University Press, 2005), 347.
[51] Johnson, *The Body in the Mind*, xxxvi–xxxvii.

driven not so much by the desire to say things of a new refinement and complexity', as with other composers, but, rather, 'by the wish "to make things in ignorance of what they are"'.[52] He adds that 'there is an important element of Birtwistle's music that falls altogether outside the realm of the communicative and the meant', an aspect that 'holds something in reserve that prevents the complete grasp, the containing interpretation'.[53] This is reflected by the composer's own view that he is not in complete control of the creative process: 'there's always this idea that the creator is absolutely in control and can answer everything all the way down the line. I don't think that's so. [...] I sort of create, if you like, an imaginary "auralscape". And then I move into it and discover things in it that I didn't imagine.'[54] This resonates with Gumbrecht's remarks that 'the relation between presence effects and meaning effects [is not] a relation of complementarity, in which a function assigned to each side in relation to the other would give the co-presence of the two sides the stability of a structural pattern. Rather, we can say that the tension/oscillation between presence effects and meaning effects endows the object of aesthetic experience with a component of provocative instability and unrest.'[55]

While the thrust of this book is interpretative, it will not ignore those moments that resist or evade interpretation. These moments may arise, for example, from the non-alignment of musical layers or harmonic blocks (Chapter 8), physical actions or extreme vocal gestures (Chapter 7), or musical gestures that suggest some kind of secret instrumental theatre (Chapter 5). Gumbrecht argues that opera is a prime example of the production of presence, in which 'the aspect of spatiality... must be emphasized over that of temporality'.[56] Birtwistle's concern for this distinction is illustrated by an account from Di Trevis, who directed the original production of *Gawain*. According to Trevis, she spoke endlessly to Birtwistle 'about storytelling, how music is concerned with time while theatre is concerned with space, and we looked at how you can play with those two things in theatre. And I urged him not to solve theatrical problems but to pose them.'[57]

[52] Adlington, *MHB*, 195; the quotation is from Theodor Adorno, 'Vers une musique informelle', in *Quasi una Fantasia: Essays on Modern Music*, trans. Rodney Livingstone (London: Verso, 1992), 322.
[53] Adlington, *MHB*, 196 and 197.
[54] Birtwistle in Andrew Ford, *Composer to Composer: Conversations about Contemporary Music* (London: Quartet Books, 1993), 55.
[55] Hans Ulrich Gumbrecht, *Production of Presence: What Meaning Cannot Convey* (Stanford University Press, 2004), 108.
[56] Gumbrecht, 'Production of presence', 343.
[57] Di Trevis, quoted by Ann McFerran in 'Knights to remember', *Weekend Telegraph*, [n.d.] January 1991, 48.

The central reference point of what Gumbrecht terms 'presence culture' is the body, as opposed to the mind in 'meaning culture' (although metaphor theorists would dispute this distinction). Consequently, Gumbrecht argues, events occur within the context of an 'unchanging cosmological regularity'.[58] This is highlighted in Birtwistle's stage works by an emphasis on day/night cycles, clock time, and passing seasons, as in *Punch, Orpheus, Yan Tan Tethera, Gawain,* and *Io.* Gumbrecht also remarks that in presence culture, 'time is reversible – and for precisely this reason magic and re-presentation (making present again) appear to be possible. Presence culture is constituted around rituals of making-present-again, of re-incarnation.'[59] Birtwistle's obsession with the myth of Orpheus, and with re-presentations of the loss of Eurydice and other episodes from that myth, fits with this concept neatly, as do the cycles of death and rebirth in *Down by the Greenwood Side, Bow Down, Gawain, Mrs Kong, The Last Supper* and *The Minotaur.*

Also relevant to this study is Gumbrecht's observation that precisely at the moment that theatre began to reflect a Cartesian emphasis on reason – specifically, in plays by Pierre Corneille (1606–84) and Jean Racine (1639–99) – forms of staging, such as the *commedia dell'arte,* based on body artistry and opera, started to appear.[60] A similar bifurcation is embodied in Birtwistle's *Punch* and *Down by the Greenwood Side,* in which high art abstraction and slapstick pantomime, inspired by the *commedia dell'arte* and the medieval mummers' play, mirror similar tensions in music by other composers, notably Kagel and Ligeti. Arguably, much post-1945 opera and music theatre has helped undermine meaning culture, shifting attention on to presence effects.

Pantomime and early stage works

Birtwistle's interest in the theatre dates back to his childhood in the 1940s, to his participation in musicals and to his construction of a stage set, 'without any reference to what went on in[side] it'. It was, he claims, 'a natural thing'.[61] At the age of eleven he composed a piece entitled 'Pantomime: A Choreographic Sketch for Three Mime Artists and Unaccompanied Clarinet', which was the archetype 'for everything that has followed'.[62] The title was inspired by Ravel's subtitle for *Daphnis et Chloé:* 'symphonie chorégraphique'. Whether Birtwistle had some idea of the

---

[58] Gumbrecht, 'Production of presence', 347.   [59] Ibid., 346.
[60] Ibid., 349.   [61] Birtwistle in Beard, 'Beauty and the beast', 13.
[62] Birtwistle in conversation with Beard, 18 November 2008; the quotation is from Norman Lebrecht, 'Knights at the opera', *Independent,* Magazine section, 18 May 1991, 58. This unpublished piece appears on two sides of manuscript owned at the time of writing by Silas Birtwistle. The pages are undated, but Birtwistle believes he composed the piece *c.*1945.

choreography for his piece is unclear, as the extant score comprises the clarinet part alone. However, frequent changes of metre and rhythmic pattern
(simple and triple time are continually alternated) create an improvisational
feel and strongly suggest that the music is a response to an image of physical
movement, rather than any preconceived musical structure. Marked 'very
slow' at the start, the music gradually unfurls with an emphasis on minor
thirds (notably E–G and B–D), while trills and arabesques lend ornamental
colour. Centred on E, with a suggestion of E minor, the music is highly
gestural with frequent literal or subtly varied repetitions of one- or two-bar
phrases. A climax occurs near the end with a rapid rising chromatic scale
through three octaves (from *e* to *e'''*), which acts as a dramatic release of
tension following six accelerated repetitions of a short five-note phrase. This
fascinating early work illustrates the connection in Birtwistle's mind, from
a very early age, between physical movement and music, explored further
in Chapter 7. Moreover, it suggests that his interest in varied repetition was
a response to the subtle variations of pantomime, rather than pre-existing
musical conventions. The result is remarkably prescient of the solo clarinet
part in *Io*.

From the age of thirteen Birtwistle played clarinet at his local theatre, the
Hippodrome, in Accrington, Lancashire. 'My world was amateur theatre.
We used to do *Bless the Bride* and *The Gondoliers*, and then a wonderful thing
happened. The amateur opera was just before Christmas and I was asked to
stay on and do the pantomime.'[63] This experience has clearly persisted, for
even when he appeared to embrace opera in *Gawain* a key inspiration was
his vision of the Green Knight entering on a pantomime horse.[64] The group
that met in the Hippodrome each year, from November through January,
was the Accrington Amateur Operatic and Dramatic Society. Birtwistle's
involvement with this group appears to have lasted from 1947 until 1955;
for the last four years of that period he is listed in production notes as 'Advertising Manager'.[65] His involvement therefore continued during the period

---

[63] Birtwistle, quoted in Wright, 'The mystery of the kiosk composer', *Guardian*, 3 September
      1992. *Bless the Bride* (1947) was a musical with lyrics by A. P. Herbert and music by Vivian
      Ellis. Other works performed included: *The New Moon* (1928), lyrics by Oscar Hammerstein,
      Frank Mandel and Laurence Schwab with music by Sigmund Romberg; *The Arcadians* (1909),
      a 'fantastical musical play' in three acts by Mark Ambient and Alexander M. Thompson with
      lyrics by Arthur Wimperis and music by Lionel Monckton and Howard Talbot; and *Carissima*
      (1948), with lyrics by Eric Maschwitz from a story by Armin Robinson, and music by Hans
      May.
[64] Birtwistle's interest in pantomime horses also gave rise to the percussion piece *For O, For O, the
      Hobby-Horse Is Forgot* (1976). This work was inspired by the Dumb Show in Shakespeare's
      Hamlet, Act III scene 2; the title is a line spoken by Hamlet immediately before the dumb show,
      which re-enacts his Father's murder. The 'hobby-horse' is thought to refer to the omission of a
      pantomime horse in traditional Morris dances and May Games, but Hamlet uses it as a
      metaphor for his Mother forgetting his Father.
[65] See www.accringtontg.co.uk/mainmenu.htm (accessed 21 November 2008 but since removed).

that he studied clarinet at the Royal Manchester College of Music (1952 to 1955), and concluded only one year before he travelled to Darmstadt.[66] This commitment to what, by 1952, must have seemed a distinctly amateur context, is remarkable.[67] As Birtwistle himself explains:

> As the weeks went by, the orchestra got smaller and smaller, and at the end it was just me with a saxophone, a pianist, and a percussion player. And then when the pantomime finished there was variety. And in the end, because we weren't playing from parts, we played everything from memory. And there's a whole process, which must have been a way of dealing with the theatre; they had a series of numbers, which functioned in a particular way, and the music director would shout, and you'd play it – to get people on and off. It's called 'tabs'. One of them was called 'Happy' [sings: 'I wanna be ha-ppy'] and that's just to get them on. And there were several things like that, which were called out, and you played them, as well as the numbers, or songs, that people sang.[68]

The 'big' numbers in the variety shows, like 'Happy', were an invitation to the audience to join in a form of communal song, which contrasted with the solo acts in between. It is fascinating to speculate whether this was the origin of Birtwistle's interest in verses, refrains and choruses.

Birtwistle's earliest stage works were composed for children in the early 1960s when he taught music at schools in Wiltshire and Dorset.[69] These pieces anticipate many of his later concerns, including dualities – between natural and stylised movement, speech and song – and his interest in masks, mime, and ritual. This is illustrated by 'Mime', an unpublished work for pupils at Cranborne Chase Girls School in Wardour Castle, first performed on 17 June 1961 and based on a scenario Birtwistle devised himself.[70] The

---

[66] Hall, *HB*, 5.

[67] Birtwistle is listed as 'Honorary Advertising Manager' for productions of *Countess Maritza* in 1954, and *Wild Violets* in 1955. The latter was performed in Accrington Town Hall and reviewed in the *Accrington Observer*: 'The orchestra of ten instrumentalists under the direction of Mr Harry Ashworth of Rosegrove, the new musical director, are effective without being over prominent.' http://www.accringtontg.co.uk/reviews/wildviolets.htm (accessed 19 November 2008) [webpage since removed].

[68] Birtwistle in conversation with Beard, 18 November 2008. One of the variety acts was 'Randle's Scandals' by the Wigan-born comedian Frank Randle, who Birtwistle describes as 'a very notorious, *very* funny comedian, who was banned from the BBC.'

[69] Hall, *HB*, 23.

[70] An incomplete version of this unpublished work occupies twenty-six sides of a bound manuscript book owned by Silas Birtwistle. This is one of five books that include parts for sacred vocal pieces, some of which are annotated by the composer, and Birtwistle's own arrangements of works by Giovanni Gabrieli and sixteenth-century English keyboard pieces from the Mulliner Book, presumably for performances by schoolchildren. In addition to school exercises, many of the spare pages are filled with unpublished pieces and sketches for published works, including *Music for Sleep* (1963), *Narration: A Description of the Passing of a Year* (1963), *Tragoedia* (1965), and *Punch*. A sketch for Punch's Lullaby, from the start of the opera, follows on immediately from *Mime*. This raises the intriguing possibility that some of

scoring comprises two clarinets, two flutes and percussion (xylophone, woodblocks, bass drum, tambourines, cymbals and gongs), with short windows for players to improvise during a central fight scene. There are four mimes: the Green Man, the King (who also has some speech), the Evil One (also referred to as the Bad One) and the Good One. The work begins with the Green Man who dances on stage then exits. The King then enters and offers his daughter for marriage. Good and Bad suitors enter and fight; the former is killed and the latter dances a tango over his body three times, the music repeated on each occasion. The Green Man then re-enters, followed by the King (announced by cymbal and woodblock).[71] The themes of combat and rebirth evident in this scenario mark the work as a form of mummers' play that anticipates *Down by the Greenwood Side*. That this association was explicit in Birtwistle's mind is revealed by a comment he later made regarding the *Gawain* poem: 'The poem's been with me for a long time. Earlier than *Narration*[: *A Description of the Passing of a Year*] I did a piece for schoolkids – a kind of mummers' play – which I later realised had been based on ideas that are in the poem, too.'[72] Extant sources also reveal that around the same time Birtwistle sketched music for a Noh play, and later, in 1963, *Music for a Play*.

The following year, Birtwistle inaugurated and became music director of the Wardour Castle Summer School of Music, which met on 15–23 August 1964 and 15–21 August 1965; its president was Michael Tippett.[73] No doubt with opera on his own mind, Birtwistle chaired a session at the first meeting entitled 'Opera Today'; the panel members were Tippett, then writing *The Knot Garden* following the success of *King Priam* (1962), Davies, who had begun *Taverner*, and Goehr, then working on *Arden Must Die*.[74] A year later, Birtwistle secured a commission from the English Opera Group to compose *Punch*. Yet his initial response to that commission was

the music for the opera was composed as early as 1961, because the text that is set ('Dancy baby diddy / What shall daddy do widdy') exists in published transcriptions of the Punch and Judy puppet show and might therefore have been selected by Birtwistle before the libretto was written. There is also a drawing of the baby in *Punch*, which Birtwistle has dated c.1960.

[71] The score becomes a draft at this point, with no more stage directions; presumably another copy was prepared for performance.

[72] Hayes, 'Pandas mate at last'.

[73] In 1965, the school presented performances of music by numerous composers, from Dunstaple, Gibbons, Mozart, Bach and Handel to Cornelius Cardew, Hugh Wood, David Bedford, Robin Holloway, Roger Smalley, Boulez, Babbitt, Cage, Stockhausen and Subotnik. Other activities included instrumental tuition, rehearsals and performances by a choir, orchestra and other ensembles (Byrd's four-part mass was directed by Davies), lectures and seminars on composition, analysis, and twentieth-century music by Goehr, and a lecture on 'Schoenberg's Sketchbooks' by Leonard Stein.

[74] The panel took place on 19 August 1964. Birtwistle has revealed that he saw Tippett often during this period as they lived nearby; from conversation with Beard, 18 November 2008.

to compose *Tragoedia*, which received its world premiere at the 1965 summer school. Birtwistle declared that his intention when writing this seminal piece, which marks a decisive turn to an expressionist style, was to 'bridge the gap between "absolute music" and theatre music'.[75] This declaration highlighted Birtwistle's personal desire to approach opera obliquely. It may also have resulted from a perceived need to distance himself from the more 'realist' dramas of Britten, the leading British opera composer at the time.

In 1966, Birtwistle began to work fully on *Punch* and he moved with his wife and three children to Princeton on a Harkness Fellowship. Yet in the same year he also completed two other stage works and incidental music for a play. Composed for children but now withdrawn, *The Visions of Francesco Petrarca* (1965–6) was an hour-long setting of seven sonnets by the medieval poet Petrarch.[76] The piece was based on an alternating Sonnet–Vision (or verse–chorus) scheme: each sonnet was sung by a baritone (dressed as the poet) from the church pulpit, accompanied by a chamber ensemble of nine schoolchildren, then reinterpreted in mime by student dancers, accompanied by a thirty-strong school orchestra with a large array of percussion. Both forms were combined in the final section, where the poet's subject position is asserted more directly. The sonnets portray the violent loss of innocence: a hind is killed by two hunting dogs; a ship is hulled by a submerged rock; a laurel tree full of singing birds is destroyed by lightning; a pastoral scene is broken by an earthquake; a phoenix immolates himself; a 'faire ladie' is – like Eurydice – poisoned by a snake; another lady's beauty is lost in death.

The *Times Educational Supplement* described the work as 'a new kind of musico-dramatic experience'.[77] Although the use of speech, song and mime reflected a pragmatic need to provide varied roles for children with different abilities, the result anticipates more sophisticated techniques in *Orpheus*.[78]

---

[75] Birtwistle, from the original programme note to *Tragoedia*, cited in Hall, *HB*, 173. For more on this piece, see Chapter 2.

[76] Subtitled 'An allegory for baritone, mime, chamber orchestra and children's orchestra', the piece was commissioned by Archbishop Holgate's Grammar School and performed during the York Festival, at St Michael-le-Belfrey church, on 15, 16 and 17 June 1966. Birtwistle used Edmund Spenser's translations in George Kay, ed., *The Penguin Book of Italian Verse* (London: Penguin, 1958). The score was withdrawn for revision. However, a fair copy is held by the Paul Sacher Stiftung.

[77] [Anon.], 'Petrarch's sonnets set to music', *Times Educational Supplement*, 19 June 1966. Another critic referred to 'a strong musico-dramatic sense and very great creative ability'; also noted was the use of metal 'anvils', 'designed by Birtwistle and struck with gusto and shattering power'. Ernest Bradbury, review of the York Music Festival, *Musical Times*, 107 (August 1966), 696.

[78] Adlington, *MHB*, 15.

Often, however, the music was conventionally pictorial: there are woodwind cuckoo calls in Sonnet III, nine different bird songs in Vision III, a pastoral flute solo and staccato oboe 'babbling brook' effect in Vision IV. More experimental features include independent tempi, the use of expanding chromatic wedges to generate the baritone solo, and a choice of notes in the percussion in Vision IV, which anticipates the kind of 'mobile' textures later used in *Verses for Ensembles* in which the players move through the same set of pitches but in different registers so that a static 'object' is heard from different perspectives.

Less characteristic is the thirty-five-minute 'dramatic cantata' *The Mark of the Goat* (1966), commissioned by BBC Schools Programmes with a text by Alan Crang. Birtwistle has stated that he had no control over the choice of writer or the play's subject, which was 'too complicated'.[79] The narrative is certainly untypical of his stage works: a conflict is presented between a tyrannical dictator, Capran (nicknamed the 'Goat') – who kills his political opponent, Lucus – and a group of peaceful protestors who wish to bury Lucus but are fired on by soldiers (a note in the score recommends suitability for children aged thirteen to fifteen). Birtwistle's authorial presence is possibly evident in the existence of a turning point: the soldiers become transfixed by Lucus's symbol, the sun, and the body is removed.[80] There is also a distinction made between narrative, delivered in stylised speech, and drama, conveyed through action, speech and music. The scoring is flexible but recommends three clarinets, three players at one piano and a principal percussion section; additional percussion, including referee whistles, football rattles and sand blocks, is played by the soldiers who also sing and speak.[81]

Most of Crang's text is spoken by the Small Crowd, which narrates the action in the manner of a Greek chorus, their lines alternating between individuals and the entire group. This approach anticipates Peter Hall's production of the *Oresteia* (1981), which Birtwistle worked on from 1976 to 1981.[82] As in Hall's *Oresteia*, there are clarinet laments, partially improvised percussion continuums, and a concluding procession into the audience as Lucus's body is carried out by a chorus that sings an anthem. Moreover, the score's recommendation that rhythmic exercises be used in rehearsal, particularly for the soldiers who must play and speak simultaneously, raises issues to do with the combination of speech, music and movement that

[79] Birtwistle in conversation with Beard, 18 November 2008.   [80] Cross, *HB: MMM*, 76.
[81] See Harrison Birtwistle, *The Mark of the Goat* (London: Universal Edition, 1966), UE 14193.
[82] See David Beard, '"Batter the doom drum": the music for Peter Hall's *Oresteia* and other productions of Greek tragedy by Harrison Birtwistle and Judith Weir', in P. Brown and S. Ograjensek, eds., *Ancient Drama in Music for the Modern Stage* (Oxford University Press, 2010), 369–97.

Birtwistle later confronted directly in workshops with actors at London's National Theatre, and which culminated in his most radical piece of music theatre, *Bow Down* (see Chapter 7).

An unpublished draft stored at the Paul Sacher Stiftung in Basle reveals that in the same year Birtwistle also worked on a music drama titled *Lorca* (1966).[83] A dramatisation of the life and work of the Spanish poet and playwright Federico García Lorca, written by John Calder and Bettina Jonic, this stage work was performed during the Edinburgh Festival, at the Gateway Theatre, in September 1966.[84] The scoring comprises two sopranos, flute (doubling piccolo), clarinet, percussion (including xylophone and vibraphone), guitar and cello. A sketch for Judy's Aria, written on the back of the final draft page for *Lorca*, suggests that Birtwistle was quite far into *Punch* when he composed this piece.[85]

Lorca is especially revealing: it provides the first example of Birtwistle's turn to parody, his first use of pre-recorded music, and the first evidence of a more expressionist style, through allusions to Schoenberg's *Pierrot lunaire* (this has particular relevance to *Punch*, as discussed in Chapter 2). The *Pierrot* references include clarinet arabesques in both a 'Gypsy scene' and a section titled 'Moon music', which employs the eerie combination of piccolo and bass clarinet. Birtwistle's varied approach also extends to Spanish colouring (guitar and castanets), blues music in a nightclub, and a military march (which resembles the opening of *Punch*). Many features anticipate later stage works, including the use of question-and-answer formulas, verse–refrain structures, a lullaby, a nightmare, a bullfight, and the doubling of

[83] This unpublished work is not listed in any existing Birtwistle studies. The extant material comprises two sides of sketches, 1 draft, 43 sides of fair copy and 5 title pages; Birtwistle Samlung, PSS. Although the manuscript is undated it has been listed as 1965 by the Sacher Stiftung. However, the date of the performance (September 1966) suggests that the bulk of the work would have been undertaken in 1966. This is confirmed by correspondence held by Silas Birtwistle. John Calder wrote to Birtwistle on 11 August 1966 to formalise the commission: Birtwistle was to engage the musicians, compose and conduct the music in seven performances, from 6 to 10 September. Another letter, from Basil Horsfield Management, dated 5 August 1966, refers to a conversation between Calder and Birtwistle two weeks earlier, in which Birtwistle mentioned that he still needed to find a Spanish revolutionary song and two other items.

[84] Bettina Jonic began her career as an international opera singer in the 1950s. She became an established interpreter of Brecht, collaborated with Peter Brook, and founded her own actor/singer performance research centre following work at the Royal Opera House, Covent Garden. Marriage to the publisher John Calder in 1960 introduced her to Beckett and other avant-garde figures, which prompted her own poetry, play writing and experimental theatre for actors and musicians. The latter included *The Wheel*, a collaboration with David Bedford premiered on 11 May 1972 at the Roundhouse, London, billed as 'an attempt to build a free-wheeling tower of words, notes, sounds, shapes, movements, lights, colours'. http://bettinajonic.com/press-archive/ (accessed 25 June 2011).

[85] PSS microfilm 0530-0549; the page comprises a sketch with oboe d'amore and harp and Judy's opening line: 'Be silent'. (Henceforth, all references to microfilm pages will be indicated by 'PSS' plus the relevant four-digit microfilm reference number and four-digit slide number.)

Plate 1.1 Use of stabbing chords at the start of the Prologue and the
Epilogue to *Lorca*. PSS, Sammlung Harrison Birtwistle, *Lorca*

parts (Lorca and a male gypsy are each doubled by a singer). There are also four so-called Projections. Whether these were moving images or slides and what they comprised is unclear, but they presumably functioned as commentaries on the drama. As such, this is an antecedent of the many interpolated scenes in Birtwistle's later stage works: the Interstices in *Monodrama* (1967), toccatas in *Punch*, mime interludes in *Orpheus*, and so on. Each Projection is accompanied by a different ensemble in which the flute is always present.

An association with the reference to Greek tragedy in *Tragoedia* is also established in *Lorca* by the presence of a Prologue and Epilogue (as in *Punch* and *Monodrama*, also). Yet here these sections have an explicit dramatic purpose: in both scenes Lorca is subjected to interrogation by an agent of Franco's fascist state. Moreover, during the Prologue and Epilogue Birtwistle reuses a stabbing chord idea from *Tragoedia*, which is also used to accompany the murders in *Punch* (see Plate 1.1). Heard in the piccolo, clarinet and xylophone, the stabbing gesture's expressionist effect clearly hints at Lorca's imminent torture and demise. Further evidence of a turn to expressionism occurs in a central Nightmare section, during which the ensemble plays alongside a tape part for voice, piccolo and clarinet, with very high, sustained notes.[86] Here a slow waltz parody for cello and saxophone is combined with song. The waltz idea eventually culminates in a triple *forte* version for vibraphone, guitar and cello, with screeching woodwind on the tape.

This is the earliest evidence of a kind of polystylism that typified later works by Davies and that became associated with the Pierrot Players ensemble, which Birtwistle and the clarinettist Alan Hacker founded in 1967. Birtwistle's interest in parody culminated in *Medusa* (1969), which he subsequently withdrew because it felt like 'a lie'.[87] In truth, Davies had overshadowed Birtwistle, and the latter left the Pierrot Players to pursue alternative projects. Further evidence of Birtwistle's proximity to and distance from Davies in the late 1960s, but more important his desire to re-explore the 'roots' of theatrical expression, is revealed in *Down by the Greenwood Side*.

Down by the Greenwood Side

> It's the same way that I encountered *Punch and Judy*. I did a bit of research, and there it was. And I remember going to the Cecil Sharp House [in London] where they've got a bit of an archive, and there are some images

---

86 PSS 0530-0541.   87 Birtwistle, cited in Hall, *HB*, 147.

there, and old photographs, probably from the early nineteenth century, of
things that are absolutely extraordinary. And at the time nobody had heard
about mummers, when I used to talk about it. And I was fascinated by the
two traditions – the juxtaposition of this woman, who's for real in a way, and
[the mummers' play, which is a stylised, comic pantomime].[88]

Scored for soprano, four spoken parts, one mime and nine instrumentalists,
Down by the Greenwood Side, which lasts around forty minutes, alternates
sung verses from the traditional Ballad of the Cruel Mother with episodes
of speech and action based on versions of the English mummers' play, 'the
traditional dumb-show which took place at Christmas yet celebrated the
coming of spring'.[89] Clearly, this is a reworking of *The Visions*, in which
sung verses were alternated with mime. In Michael Nyman's libretto for
Down by the Greenwood Side, however, the ballad and pantomime present
differing perspectives on the topics of death and rebirth. These themes –
which are explored through acting styles that are 'stylised, non-realistic;
strongly-gestured pantomime' – are common to the many versions of the
mummers' play.[90] As Alan Brody observes:

> There are only two elements that we can safely say all the hundreds of texts
> and fragments collected so far have in common. They are all seasonal and
> they all contain a death and resurrection somewhere in the course of their
> action.[91]

A fundamental characteristic of the mummers' play, therefore, is varied
repetition:

> Except for some basic differences which can help separate them into three
> fairly distinct classes [the Hero-Combat, Sword Play and Wooing Ceremony]
> every one has the same, easily recognisable shape. Yet no two are exactly
> alike.[92]

Nyman's version of the mummers' play fits the Hero-Combat category, in
which combat, death and resurrection are consistent elements. According

---

[88] Birtwistle in conversation with Beard, 18 November 2008.
[89] Hall, *HB*, 67. The piece was commissioned by the Brighton Festival and premiered by
Music Theatre Ensemble on 8 May 1969 in the Festival Pavilion, West Pier, conducted by David
Atherton and directed by John Cox. The instrumentation is based on the ensemble associated
with the Cornish Floral Dance.
[90] [Anon.], 'Directions for Performance' in Harrison Birtwistle, *Down by the Greenwood Side: A
Dramatic Pastoral* (London: Universal Edition, 1971), UE 15321.
[91] Alan Brody, *The English Mummers and Their Plays: Traces of Ancient Mystery* (London:
Routledge and Kegan Paul, 1969), 3. Brody builds on E. K. Chambers's pioneering study *The
English Folk Play* (Oxford University Press, 1923), which is cited in the published score of
Down By the Greenwood Side.
[92] Brody, *The English Mummers*.

to Brody, there are four major sections in the Hero-Combat: Introduction, Combat, Cure, and Quête – the latter involves a collection of characters in a ceremony or procession at the play's conclusion. As indicated in the right-hand column in Table 1.1, Nyman and Birtwistle treat the Combat and Cure as a unit that is repeated, not unlike the Melodramas in *Punch*. These sections typically comprise boasts, challenges, counter-challenges, a 'hand-to-hand clash', and a lament for the fallen victim.[93]

Similarly, there are multiple variants of the Cruel Mother ballad. Yet common to these is a basic narrative in which a mother bears two illegitimate children whom she takes to a remote part of a forest and murders. On her return she sees two boys playing in the woods and tells them that if they were hers she would care for them and dress them in finery. They reply that they *are* her children and that she has dressed them in her 'own heart's blood'. In other words, *Down by the Greenwood Side* juxtaposes 'comic' and 'tragic' perspectives on the themes of death and rebirth.

The mummers' play is enacted within a central circle; to enter this space each character must declare 'In comes I'. The four speaking actors are Father Christmas, who acts as master of ceremonies, the protagonist St George, his antagonist Bold Slasher (a variant of the more traditional Turkish Knight), and Dr Blood, who revives St George. Jack Finney, who doubles as the Green Man, is played by a silent mime.[94] A production televised in 1972, however, included additional mimes played by two boys who handed out props, helped the main characters into the acting circle (a raised circular platform, lighter in colour), and represented Mrs Green's children.[95] This innovative production, overseen by Birtwistle, featured bright costume designs, moving cameras (with split screen, thermal imaging and goldfish-bowl lens effects), and audience participation (with cheers, boos and laughter).

A summary of the work's structure is given in Table 1.1. Until ballad 3 (the drama's still, lyrical centre), there is no obvious interaction between Mrs Green and the mummers' play.[96] This reflects Nyman's claim that the duality was inspired by a Romanian peasant icon on which the Virgin and Child was placed on one side and Saint George and the Dragon on the

---

[93] Ibid., 47–8.

[94] With the exception of one off-stage line: 'My name is not Jack Finney, it is Mr. Finney.'

[95] Produced by London Weekend Television in 1972, this production was broadcast again by Channel 4 in 1987. Stage production was by the composer, direction by Barrie Gavin, and the costumes, although different from those used in the first production, were by the original designer Anthony Denning. One of the young mimes was played by Keith Chegwin, later known as a children's television presenter.

[96] Ironically, the thinner accompaniment, slow pace and smooth vocal line in ballad 3 draw attention to Mrs Green's disturbing description of infanticide.

Table 1.1 *The formal layout of* Down by the Greenwood Side

	Ballad (song)	Mummers' play (speech & mime)	
1	Mrs Green, verses 1–3: 'There was a lady...' <u>sung refrain:</u> 'Low so low and so lonely' (×3) *Sprechgesang* <u>refrain:</u> 'Down by the greenwoods of Ivry' (×3)	enter Father Christmas enter St George enter Bold Slasher Fight St George killed	(Introduction) (Combat 1)
2	Mrs Green, verses 4–6: 'As I went out...' Sung/*Sprechgesang* <u>refrain:</u> 'All day long I love you all / Down by the greenwood sideyo' (×3)	Father Christmas calls for a doctor; enter Doctor Blood St George revived Fight St George killed	(Cure 1) (Combat 2)
3	Mrs Green, verses 7–10: 'I loved him well...' *Sprechgesang* <u>refrains:</u> 'Fine flowers of the valley' (×4) 'And the green leaves they grow rarely' (×4)		
Transition	Mrs Green, verses 11–13: 'O babes, O babes...' *Sprechgesang* <u>refrain:</u> 'Fine flowers...' *Sprechgesang* <u>refrain:</u> 'And the green leaves...'	Father Christmas: 'Let us sing a tune for him...' 'Seven years...to card and spin' 'Seven more...to serve in hell'	
3 (cont.)		Father Christmas: 'Call for Jack Finney' enter Jack Finney St George revived	(Cure 2)
4 **Ballad &** **play** **combined:** **all dance in** **the central** **circle**	Mrs Green <u>refrain</u> only: 'Fair-a-lair-a-li-do' Music in final section recalls ballad 2	Father Christmas: 'There was a lady drest in green...Off to prison you must go / And that was the end of Mrs Green'	(Quête)
Exit music	Six independent layers / musical objects and 'large sombre bell'	'The characters slowly file off'	

other.[97] However, after ballad 3, the two worlds begin to interact as Father Christmas responds to Mrs Green in a series of short exchanges. This is reflected in the instrumentation: initially, the ballads are accompanied by strings (violin and cello), woodwind and percussion, and the mummers' play by brass, woodwind and percussion; during the transition these groups are combined.

The first of Father Christmas's interjections suggests a kind of lament for the dead children (he intones: 'Let us sing a tune for him'). However, the tone is satirical (the strings play 'intensely but sweetly'), then denunciatory (against a repeated tritone in the piccolo – an idea that recurs at the end of the piece – it is declared that Mrs Green will 'serve in hell').[98] Brody suggests that the mummers' play lament relates back to the *threnos* (lament) in Greek tragedy, which immediately precedes the *anagnorisis*, the moment of discovery or recognition. Indeed, in the final section Mrs Green is acknowledged by the mummers' troupe and welcomed into the acting circle. Father Christmas narrates her tale and she depicts the murder of her children, but the context is a celebratory dance; even the description of her interrogation and arrest by the police is accompanied by a slow but 'sickly sweet' dance, in keeping with the Quête. In this way, the tragic and the comic dimensions of the work are held in meaningful tension.

In addition to her frequent use of *Sprechgesang*, Mrs Green is often instructed to adopt certain facial expressions. Over a short twenty-bar stretch, for example, her modes of expression include 'sad, as if singing to herself', 'smiling but as in a trance', 'with sad face', 'happily', and 'increasingly "wild in the eye"'. This suggests a high degree of instability in Mrs Green's character but also the influence of *Pierrot lunaire* from which comes an interest in madness explored more thoroughly in Davies's *Eight Songs for a Mad King* (1969), premiered one month before *Down by the Greenwood Side*. Elsewhere, Father Christmas is instructed to follow the general contour of the bassoon line. By this means, the music directs the actor to retain a kind of vocal intonation within the context of stylised declamation – a

---

[97] Nyman cited in Adlington, *MHB*, 17. In the televised production from 1972, Mrs Green holds a doll in her arms in a manner that resembles the pose of the Virgin and Child. Cross, however, following William Empson, argues that the mix of comic and tragic perspectives on the same 'situation' (death and rebirth) is a marker of the pastoral genre in which the 'situation is made something valuable in itself, perhaps for reasons hardly realized; it can work on you like a myth.' Empson, *Some Versions*, 50; cited in Cross, *HB: MMM*, 137.

[98] This judgement is anticipated by Mrs Green herself in the second ballad where, citing the children she saw in the woods, she sings: 'In seven years you'll hear a bell / in seven years you'll be in hell' (from letter N). This line is remarkably similar to Tony Harrison's libretto for *Yan Tan Tethera*, in which Alan is shut inside a hill for seven years, and where bell sounds are an important element in the so-called 'music of the hill' (see Chapter 4).

concept of 'lyrical formalism' that is especially relevant to *Orpheus*, as discussed in Chapter 3.[99]

As in *Pantomime*, Birtwistle's music during the mummers' sections is *suggestive* of actions, but there is no explicit choreography. Whether the music was an attempt to portray concrete images in the composer's mind is unclear. There is much scope for interpretation by the actors, particularly when St George is revived by Mr Finney. Here, however, Birtwistle has provided suggestive musical gestures including a descending scale in the flute marked 'liquid', a rising and falling scale that passes from the bass clarinet to the flute and back, and 'slapstick' percussion that alternates with very low and very high notes in the bass clarinet. This approach is relevant to the later stage works: in the original production of *The Minotaur*, for example, the choreography during the chase-and-kill scenes developed in response to the music.[100] This principle must also have applied to the hunt scenes in *Gawain*, the fight episodes in *Mrs Kong*, and the extended mime sequences in *Io*.

Down by the Greenwood Side exemplifies the turn away from opera to forms of music theatre that combine relatively simple ritualistic gestures with an experimental musical language. During Father Christmas's introduction, for example, the instrumentalists are given a choice of notes, contours, tempi and dynamics. Yet Birtwistle is prepared to parody such avant-garde tendencies: when Father Christmas is drowned out by the clatter produced by so many independent parts he shouts for the orchestra to stop. Elsewhere, experimental techniques relate directly to the drama. A moment of Webern parody, for example, in which a jagged line is passed between single notes in different instruments, produces a disjointed effect that underscores St George's boast to 'cut' and 'stew' his adversary.

Down by the Greenwood Side is Birtwistle's first systematic examination of the relationship between music, gesture and physical movement. Birtwistle's interest in this problem reflected a wider concern for ritualistic theatre in the late 1960s, one that Brody has related directly to a revival of interest in the mummers' play:

> The question of the relationship between actor and audience, the nature of the playing area, the very purpose of the performance itself, in terms of immediate or imaginative change – all these questions so central to an

---

[99] The use of nonsense verse, by Father Christmas and Dr Blood, also recalls the kind of modernist play on language typified by Stravinsky's *Pribaoutki* (1914).

[100] See Rhian Samuel, 'Birtwistle's *The Minotaur*: the opera and a diary of its first production', *Cambridge Opera Journal*, 20/2 (2008), 222–4.

Example 1.1 Walking rhythm at the opening of *Down by the Greenwood Side* (full score, UE 15321), bb. 1–3 (extract)

* These first three measures may be played as many times as are needed for the entry of Mrs Green. The alto flute part must only be played in its entirety the last time through […].

understanding and appreciation of the mummers' play, are precisely the questions we are challenged with by companies such as The Living Theater, Jerzy Grotowski's Theater Laboratory of Poland, Eugenio Barba's *Odin Teatret* in Norway, and the Bread and Puppet Theater in New York.[101]

Birtwistle's concern to examine the relationship between music and move-ment is revealed at the very opening when Mrs Green walks slowly onstage. Here the rhythm of her steps is notated in the score.[102] As shown in Example 1.1, the steps, which include a shuffle on the left foot, occur against a diminishing rhythmic pattern in the bass drum but are shadowed precisely by the alto flute.[103] The pastoral-sounding flute also unfolds a phrase based on an expanding chromatic wedge on B. The flute's first three notes (B, C, B) and repeated Ds in the lower woodwind and cello together form a [0,1,3] set that is prevalent throughout the work.[104] This set is a hallmark

101 Brody, *The English Mummers*, viii.
102 Other examples of this device include the limping triple time accompaniment to Punch's laughter when he enters in *Punch*, and the notation of Gawain's footsteps in *Gawain* at the end of Act I, at the start of Act II, and at Fig. 33, in association with his journey.
103 Mrs Green's dance movements in the lead into ballad 3 are also notated, as is the rhythm of her stabbing motions in the final combined mummers' and ballad scene, when she mimes her children's murder.
104 The flute's B, C, B opening is an early sign of a rising, falling semitone figure Birtwistle uses often but which he later associated with John Dowland's 'In darkness let me dwell', cited by the composer in relation to *The Shadow of Night* (2001) and utilised in *Semper Dowland, semper dolens: Theatre of Melancholy* (2009).

Example 1.2 B as symmetrical pitch centre in Mrs Green's vocal line, ballad 1 refrain, bb. 19–21

of Birtwistle's music that reflects his early fascination with expanding chromatic wedges, all of which begin with a semitone step up or down, followed by a tone in the opposite direction (e.g. B, C, B♭). B is also a pivot in Mrs Green's vocal line, as shown in Example 1.2.

Chromatic wedges were fundamental to Birtwistle's compositional processes throughout the 1960s and early 1970s, and they are particularly important in *Punch*. These were not just a convenient way to generate pitch material: they functioned as an image, or governing schema. The few extant sketches for *Down by the Greenwood Side* suggest that different expanding chromatic wedges were sometimes used simultaneously in symmetrical schemes based on a common interval cycle.

The clearest example of this schema is a 14-bar block for brass and woodwind heard in the first fight scene and repeated identically in the second fight (letters K and Q, respectively). This six-part section comprises fast moving parts, mostly in rhythmic unison; the result is a varied homophonic texture that moves in and out of focus. The sketches reveal that this section is based on expanding chromatic wedges arranged as a cycle of fifths, from the lowest part up as follows: F♯, C♯, G♯, D♯, B♭, F – these apply to the euphonium, trombone, cornet, bassoon, clarinet and piccolo, respectively.[105] From these expanding twelve-note sets Birtwistle selects a combination of four-, five- and six-note segments. He then reorders the internal content of each segment and, finally, redistributes the notes in different octaves to create a more disjointed effect. An extract of this process is shown in Example 1.3.[106]

The symmetrical schema is broken, however, during the transition. Here, when Father Christmas offers to 'sing a hymn' for the murdered child, a euphonium solo is played 'with "brass band" vibrato'. It is apparent from the sketches that the solo is based on an expanding chromatic wedge on F. The euphonium is therefore estranged from the other wind instruments (trombone, cornet, double bassoon, bass clarinet and alto flute), since it is not

---

[105] PSS 0528-0075. There are just eleven sides of sketches for *Down by the Greenwood Side* and seventy-seven sides of fair copy.

[106] Several errors occur in the transition from sketch to score, usually as a result of misread clefs (for example, the second pitch in the bassoon should be D♯, not F♯).

Example 1.3 Sketches for wind instruments during the two fight scenes, Letters K and Q. PSS 0528-0075

Example 1.4 Euphonium and Mrs Green in the transition, Letter T⁻⁷ to T (extract)

contiguous with their wedges along the cycle of fifths: they are based on A, E and B.[107] Irrespective, the rumbustious euphonium continues throughout the ballad – a gesture that relates back to Father Christmas's introduction, where he also danced to a euphonium theme. In other words, comic irony *intrudes* into Mrs Green's tragic narrative. This is especially evident when Mrs Green adopts the voices of her children yet the euphonium plays 'with vibrato', then jauntily as she 'turned as virgin home' (see Example 1.4). During the Quête, when Father Christmas declares 'She had a penknife in her hand', there is unabashed merriment in the euphonium, marked *forte* 'solo!' Here Mrs Green mimes her children's murder, yet the gravity of her crime is completely undermined by the music's counter-narrative.

[107] Two contiguous statements of the B wedge are divided into seven segments according to the palindromic sequence: 3, 4, 5, 6, 5, 4, 3 (where each number refers to the number of notes in each segment). A similar process is applied to the E wedge, although the palindromic scheme is an inversion of the one used for the B wedge: 6, 5, 4, 3, 4, 5, 6. Three-note selections are then made from each segment in the E wedge, which are reordered internally; for the B wedge, the original segments are retained but their contents reordered. By contrast, the segmentation scheme for the euphonium is asymmetrical: 4, 4, 4, 5, 4, 5, 4. PSS 0528-0073.

Example 1.5 Euphonium, Mrs Green and Father Christmas during the Quête, Letter W

Example 1.5 shows the tail end of this process, where the euphonium's jaunty syncopations provide a grotesque underscore to the image of Mrs Green walking off to wash the blood from her hands. In each of these examples, therefore, the music evokes bodily movements that are an ironic commentary on the text.

Overlap between the ballad and the mummers' play actually begins slightly earlier, at the lead into ballad 3, where the opening is revisited from a different perspective. When St George is killed the second time, Mrs Green enters and performs a silent dance to a rhythm notated in the score, against the diminishing bass drum rhythm from the start of the piece. At the same time Dr Blood 'feels St George's nose and his big toe and shakes his head', then declares: 'HE IS DEAD'. Mrs Green's dance and Dr Blood's examination are accompanied by a series of trichords in the woodwind and

Example 1.6 The presence of [0,1,3] sets in woodwind and string chords and Mrs Green's vocal line at the transition into ballad 3, Letter R^{-3} to R^{+2}

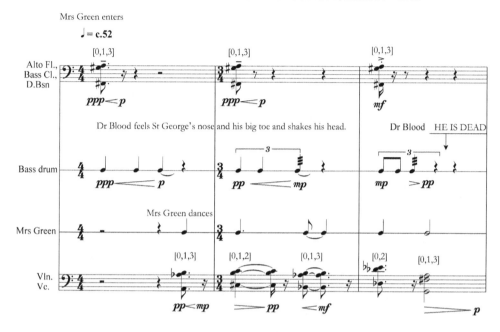

strings, most of which form set [0,1,3]. This harmony forms the basis of the accompaniment to ballad 3 and is also reflected in Mrs Green's vocal line, which is repeated literally in verses 7–13. In fact, the series of sets in the strings is replicated almost exactly in the vocal line, as shown in Example 1.6.

The work's conclusion is another demonstration of the close relationship between experimental device and dramatic content. Here the ragtag collection of characters 'slowly file off' the stage. They do so to a musical procession of apparently unrelated objects, played in independent tempi: a musical-toy-like cornet fanfare, associated with St George; the piccolo's tritone figure, associated with Mrs Green's journey to hell; angular limping

Example 1.7 The characters exit in procession, from Letter Z

dyads in the cello and a more regular tread in the violin, which relate back to ballad 3; a spiky clarinet version of the euphonium theme associated with Mrs Green going to the well to wash off the blood; a slow line in the double bassoon; a 'large sombre bell'. The splintered, fragmented ending, in which multiple images are held in tension, is common to several later stage works, notably *Orpheus*, *Mrs Kong* and *The Corridor*. Yet many of the musical objects at the end of *Down by the Greenwood Side* are actually related by the presence of [0,1,3] sets, as shown in Example 1.7. In this way, an important aspect of the music's underlying schema (the first two intervals of an expanding chromatic wedge) is brought to the surface in a manner that relates directly to a theatrical convention (the exit). The conclusion therefore comprises a compelling metaphorical intersection of two radically different languages: an abstract musical schema and physical theatre.

2 *Punch and Judy*: parody, allusion and the grotesque

> Not long ago there was a young composer who had a first performance of an opera not far from here [Birtwistle's *Punch and Judy*]. And at the same time there were other operas being performed in the neighbourhood. I know it was probably because of the tightness of time, and the absorption in his own job, but it seemed to me very strange that he didn't want to go and see how Mozart solved *his* problems. If he were setting out, from here to Newmarket, to drive, naturally, he would use maps to get there. Why, if he used maps to get to Newmarket, didn't he use maps which show how to write an opera?[1]

Speaking a year after the premiere of Birtwistle's *Punch and Judy*, Benjamin Britten seemed perplexed by Birtwistle's apparent lack of interest in, and awareness of, established operatic practices. Britten's observations and his alleged walkout from the first performance of *Punch* suggest that Birtwistle's work was somehow radically divorced from earlier operatic traditions.[2] But what *was* Birtwistle's attitude towards opera? Was *Punch* a subversive attack on the conventions of opera, or a constructive reconfiguration of the genre? Britten's remarks gloss over the fact that Birtwistle had been approached by Britten's opera company, the English Opera Group, when they heard he was working on an opera.[3] Britten, who knew Birtwistle's music, found the synopsis 'exceedingly' interesting and commissioned Birtwistle right away.[4]

---

[1] Benjamin Britten in an interview with Donald Mitchell for the Canadian Broadcasting Corporation, February 1969, in Paul Kildea, ed., *Britten on Britten* (Oxford University Press, 2003), 329.

[2] The anecdote of Britten walking out from the first performance of *Punch and Judy* is often repeated but I have been unable to substantiate the claim. John Tooley, who commissioned the work, states that Britten and Peter Pears 'left hurriedly at the end, apparently appalled by what they had heard' (John Tooley, *In House: Covent Garden, 50 Years of Opera and Ballet* (London: Faber and Faber, 1999), 79). Birtwistle himself is unclear what happened and claims not to know what Britten thought of the piece; from Birtwistle conversation with Beard, 28 November 2008.

[3] Tooley, *In House*, 79.

[4] From a letter dated 5 November 1965 stored in the correspondence file of the Sammlung Harrison Birtwistle, PSS. Around the same time, in a reference for Birtwistle's Harkness Fellowship application, Britten remarked: '[Birtwistle's] reputation as one of the most gifted of the younger composers in this country is growing steadily. I have heard some of his music, which to my mind confirms the justice of this reputation. He has more to say than most of his young contemporaries, and is feeling his way towards a very personal expression of his ideas. . . . we immediately encouraged him to go ahead [with his proposed opera] and gave him a commission for it. We feel sure he will produce something striking and provocative, but yet serious and sincere.' Letter stored at the Britten-Pears Foundation Archive, Aldeburgh. The letter is undated but was certainly written in 1965: the commission for *Punch* was confirmed by John Tooley on 3 November 1965 and the deadline for the fellowship was December of that year. Tooley's letter is stored in the PSS Sammlung Harrison Birtwistle correspondence file.

However, between the commission and the performance of *Punch*, Birtwistle shifted away from the gentle lyricism of his early music, as exemplified by *Entr'actes and Sappho Fragments* (1964), to the harder-edged, overtly dramatic style of *Tragoedia* (1965), an important companion piece to *Punch*. Birtwistle later explained: 'I very deliberately looked for a dramatic style because I knew that I was going to write an opera. It came out to be very hysterical, and loud, and it had a strong rhythmic sense about it.'[5] The result, according to one commentator, was 'a pure fury of gesture'.[6] Clearly, this shift to a more visceral sound proved too provocative for some.[7] Yet, when recently reminded of the rebellious climate of the late 1960s – the student protests, social and political revolutions – Birtwistle stated that *Punch* was not 'anti- anything'. Rather, it was more about 'a kind of formal theatre' than opera.[8]

Further questions arise, however, when statements made by the work's librettist, Stephen Pruslin, are taken into account. Pruslin made ambitious and ambiguous claims for *Punch*. He explained that the form of the Punch and Judy puppet show had provided a springboard to the exploration of other kinds of ritualistic theatre, and he referred to the 'invisible' theatre of Bach's *St Matthew Passion* as a model. However, Pruslin also stated that 'we wanted the quintessence of all the components and conventions of opera'. He described *Punch* as 'an opera in quotation marks', and he alluded to operas by Mozart, Beethoven and Monteverdi as models. Pruslin also stated that the intention had been to create 'a source opera' that would give 'the illusion of having been written before' all known operas.[9] This counterintuitive idea reads like an attempt by Pruslin to reconcile his personal interest in opera with Birtwistle's apparent lack of concern for the genre. As such, the collaboration was founded upon an uneasy tension between, on the one hand, a 'quasi-metaphysical search for origins and essences' and, on the other hand, a parodic, possibly ironic approach towards opera.[10]

Curiously, in a letter Birtwistle sent to Britten, dated 22 November 1965, he stated that he intended to spend his time at Princeton writing 'an opera based on the Elisabethan [*sic*] alchemists "Kelly and Dee"'. Letter stored at the Britten-Pears Archive.

[5] From 'A couple of things about Harry', BBC 2, 4 April 1971.

[6] Griffiths, *Modern Music and After*, 197.

[7] In his review of the first performance, Michael Nyman noted that some of the audience 'found their old appetites savaged – violence on the stage is admissible only if motivated by melodramatic passion, it seems, and the music was too loud'; 'Harrison Birtwistle's "Punch and Judy"', *Listener*, 10 October 1968, 481.

[8] Birtwistle in Beard, 'Beauty and the beast', 13.

[9] Stephen Pruslin, from the programme note to the Edinburgh International Festival performances of *Punch and Judy* in the King's Theatre, 22 and 24 August 1968. For a revised and expanded version, see Stephen Pruslin, 'Punch and Judy', liner note to CD recording of *Punch and Judy*, Etcetera KTC 2014, 1989.

[10] Nicholas Till, '"I don't mind if something's operatic, just as long as it's not opera." A critical practice for new opera and music theatre', *Contemporary Theatre Review*, 14/1 (February 2004), 20.

How are we to interpret such apparent contradictions and incongruities? To consider the question, this chapter proposes that an answer is to be found in the opera's relationship to other music and texts, through parody and allusion. This approach is most obviously suggested by the titles of the work's numerous short sections, as shown in Figure 2.1.[11]

Several of these titles evoke baroque forms, such as Sinfonia, Toccata, Passion Chorale, Passion Aria, Recitative, and Da Capo Aria. Here and elsewhere there are baroque-like obbligato doublings of voices with woodwind instruments.[12] The score also reveals the presence of a gavotte, minuet, and gigue, which Birtwistle has compared to Bach's orchestral Suites.[13] Many sections evoke a single mood or emotion, such as love, terror, or melancholy, which alludes to the baroque concept of *Affektenlehre*. These moments, such as the sadly tender Morals, suggest that emotions are assumed by the characters, like masks.[14] By contrast, static, tranquil scenes entitled Weather Reports and Travel Music mark the passing of time and present the opera as a kind of astrological clock that, in each cycle, faces East, West, North then South. Further cycles introduce demotic music that teases with riddles and short, repetitive themes – these motifs include the gigue and gavotte mentioned earlier, as shown in Example 2.1. A sense of purpose is also generated by the idea of a quest for Punch, the central character, conveyed by a series of Serenades. Overall, therefore, *Punch* generates considerable energy and colour by playing 'high' art against 'low'.

Other styles are parodied, too: Adlington lists parodies of plainsong, Webern and Stravinsky, to which may be added Boulez, and Babbitt (A Little Canonic Prelude to Disaster).[15] Birtwistle's debt to Stravinsky is especially evident in a series of so-called Passion Chorales, the use of additive

[11] All score references to *Punch and Judy* are either to the vocal score (London: Universal Edition, 1968), 14191L (henceforth VS), or the full score (henceforth FS): this is a photocopy of the fair copy in the hand of Birtwistle and other copyists, prepared by Universal Edition. It is dated 'Jan. 1966 – Jan 8th 1967'.

[12] Jonathan Cross, 'Lines and circles: on Birtwistle's *Punch and Judy* and *Secret Theatre*', *Music Analysis*, 13/2–3 (July–October 1994), 218–19.

[13] Birtwistle, from an interview with Ivan Hewett for the BBC Radio 3 broadcast of the English National Opera (ENO) production of *Punch and Judy* on 21 June 2008. It was apparently Birtwistle's idea to introduce these rhythmic allusions. The gigue and gavotte are shown in Example 2.1. It is unclear where the minuet is located but Punch's first entrance is marked 'tempo di waltz', and Serenades II and III are described as an 'allemande' and 'pavan' respectively.

[14] For a revealing discussion of the Morals and Morale, in which emotions are evoked by conventional means (sadness by soft sparse accompaniment with melismas on the word 'weep', and happiness by Scotch-snap rhythms in the horn), see Cross, 'Lines and circles', 205–12.

[15] Adlington, *MHB*, 11. In a pre-concert talk given in April 2008, Birtwistle stated that the Little Canonic Prelude to Disaster was intended as a parody of Milton Babbitt. See http://vodpod.com/watch/784015-harrison-birtwistle-and-stephen-pruslin (accessed 23 August 2011). The Boulez allusion occurs at the start of Punch's Serenade II: VS, p. 81, bars 122–5.

Figure 2.1 Sections in *Punch and Judy*

Prologue
Melodrama I
Punch's Lullaby [*verse-refrain* (×4)], War Cry I, Homage to Judy, Judy's Lullaby
Word-Game (×4)
Murder Ensemble I: Proclamation I, Passion Aria I, Couplets I, War Cry II,
    Resolve I
Toccata 1a
Passion Chorale I
Toccata 1b
Quest for Pretty Polly I
Travel Music I, Weather Report I, Prayer I, Punch's Serenade I, Pretty Polly's
    Rhapsody I, Moral I, Sinfonia
Melodrama II
Accusation, Principle I, Rule I
Riddle Game (×3): [*ritornello*] Formula I, Paradox, Principle II
Murder Ensemble II: Proclamation II, Couplets II, War Cry III, Resolve II
Toccata IIa
Passion Chorale II
Toccata IIb
Quest for Pretty Polly II
Travel Music II, Weather Report II, Prayer II, Punch's Serenade II, Pretty Polly's
    Rhapsody II, Moral II, A Little Canonic Prelude to Disaster
Melodrama III
Parody and Paraphrase, Rule II, Morale
Gebrauch[s]musik (×3): Roundel, Preyer, Coronation-Scene, Dithyramb; Paean
Recitative and Passion Aria II
Murder Ensemble III: Proclamation III, Couplets III, War Cry IV, Lament,
    Exorcism and Lullaby
Travel Music III, Weather Report III
Nightmare
Prognosis, (Fortune-Telling:) Formula II, Rule III
Tarot-Game: Draw (×3)
Black Wedding: Alarm, Definition, Black Wedding Procession [*on a ground*], Pretty
    Polly's Black Rhapsody, Quartet
Scourging: Condemnation-Principle, Rule IV, Cries, Adding-Song (Couplets
    IV-refrain ×6 and coda), Fainting-Spell
Quest for Pretty Polly III
Weather Report IV, Travel Music IV, Punch's Serenade III, Moral III
Toccata IIIa
Passion Chorale III
Toccata IIIb
Melodrama IV
Resolve III, Gallows-Song, Rule V
Interview-Game: First Sitting, Reply I, Second Sitting, Reply II, Tease, Death March
Execution: Couplets V, Aside, Couplets VI, War Cry V, Triumph
Punch Triumphans
Apotheosis, Love-Duet, Apostrophe
Epilogue

Example 2.1 Punch's gigue and gavotte in *Punch and Judy*, Melodrama I (vocal score (VS), UE 14191L), pp. 28–9, bb. 354–6 and 367–70

techniques, ostinatos, motoric rhythms, the use of a narrator, even the choice of subject matter. Such characteristics suggest links back to Vsevolod Meyerhold's interest in the *commedia dell'arte*, Stravinsky's *Petrushka* (Petrushka being the Russian version of Punch) and the neoclassical *Pulcinella* (named after the Italian forerunner of Punch). Birtwistle's *Punch* is also related to the highly stylised chamber theatre of *The Soldier's Tale* and *Renard*, the focus on archetypes in *Les Noces*, and the stylistic plurality and ceremony of *Oedipus Rex*.

Previous studies have correctly emphasised the importance of Stravinsky to Birtwistle. However, this chapter will focus on a specific source that has not been considered before: namely, Schoenberg's song cycle *Pierrot lunaire* (1912). As will be revealed, *Pierrot* and the texts it was based upon offered a conceptual and thematic map for Pruslin, which in turn presented certain possibilities to Birtwistle. It will be seen that *Pierrot* provided an important source of allusion and parody, but also a more subversive vein of ironic and grotesque imagery that suggests ways of thinking about the work's relationship to opera.

After examining Pruslin's libretto in some detail, this chapter will consider Birtwistle's pre-compositional ideas for *Tragoedia* and *Punch*. There are virtually no extant sketches for *Punch*.[16] However, a handful of sketches for *Tragoedia* suggest ways in which the two works are related at an abstract level, as well as intersections with Pruslin's libretto and source texts. The final part of the chapter focuses on the murder of Choregos, one of the work's

---

16 The extant material at the Paul Sacher Stiftung comprises around eight hundred sides of fair copy for the vocal and the full scores.

Figure 2.2 *Punch and Judy*, overall design (after Cross, *HB: MMM*, Fig. 2.1, 74)

Prologue

Melodrama I   Passion Chorale I   Quest for
                                          Pretty Polly I

Melodrama II   Passion Chorale II   Quest for
                                          Pretty Polly II

Melodrama III

                                                              Nightmare

                                          Quest for
                                          Pretty Polly III

                  Passion Chorale III

Melodrama IV

Punch Triumphans

Epilogue

principal characters. This emerges as a key turning point and a moment that sheds light on *Punch*'s subversive relationship to opera. The discussion then broadens to consider the wider ramifications of parody, allusion and the grotesque in *Punch*, with particular reference to Jacques Attali's concept of music as a simulacrum of ritual murder.

Signs of *Pierrot*: Pruslin's libretto

An important source text for Pruslin's libretto was the first recorded script of the Punch and Judy show, *The Tragical Comedy or Comical Tragedy of Punch and Judy*, first published in 1828. Scripted by John Collier and illustrated by George Cruickshank, this book (clearly the source of the opera's subtitle) was based on Giovanni Piccini's version of the puppet show performed in 1827. Basing his argument on the situation and rank of Punch's victims, and the order in which they are murdered, Robert Leach has argued that Collier's text comprises three 'movements' – domestic, social, and legal – followed by a coda, in which Punch murders the devil.[17] Pruslin retains these divisions (although he omits the coda), and he parodies the murders.

The structural pillars of Pruslin's plot are summarised in Figure 2.2.[18] Punch's murders are presented in each Melodrama, as follows: Punch's baby and Judy; a lawyer and doctor; Choregos; Jack Ketch. After each of the murders the characters remain on stage to form a chorus.

[17] Robert Leach, *The Punch and Judy Show: History, Tradition and Meaning* (London: Batsford Academic and Educational, 1985), 154.

[18] For a more detailed synopsis see Andrew Clements, 'Punch and Judy', in Stanley Sadie, ed., *The New Grove Dictionary of Opera*, vol. III (London: Macmillan, 1992), 1,176–7.

Most of the victims – the baby, Judy, the doctor and Jack Ketch the hangman – are derived from Collier's text. However, Pruslin introduces two new victims. The first of these, the lawyer, suggests the 'legal' movement of Collier's text, but Pruslin introduces him during the 'social' Melodrama II. Choregos, who is murdered in the 'legal' Melodrama III, is both an adaptation of, and exception to, Collier's text. Choregos is the master of ceremonies who introduces and presides over the performance. In one sense, therefore, he has some official standing, but as a narrator he is a servant to the plot. Moreover, his name recalls the title given to the person who sponsored and trained the chorus in Greek tragedy. Literally and symbolically, Choregos is both outsider and anomaly – an important point that I will return to later.

Another notable departure from Collier's text is Pruslin's extension, in order to offset Punch's evil deeds, of Punch's desire for Pretty Polly into a quest. From Birtwistle's perspective, the contrast of a love quest and recurring murders was a perfect match for his interest in verse–refrain forms, which dates back to *Refrains and Choruses* (1957). It is also likely that Birtwistle was attracted to the puppet show because its formal concerns mirrored his own. The stock-in-trade of the Punch and Judy show is cyclic repetition, as demonstrated by its many riddles, rhymes, punning games, and question-and-answer formulas, as well as the large- and small-scale patterning of its scenes in groups of three-plus-one, with an alteration or reversal in the added section. Consequently, Pruslin's libretto is based on cycles of recurrence and symmetry, ideas that, as Jonathan Cross has shown, extend to the music.[19] Birtwistle's sketches add appreciably to our understanding of this process, however, and this topic will be considered in some detail in the next section.

As Figure 2.2 reveals, Pruslin's principal building block consists of a Melodrama, where Punch's murders are committed, followed by a Passion Chorale, in which the chorus comments on Punch's actions, and a Quest, where Punch sings a lyrical Serenade to Polly who rejects him with an acidic Rhapsody. These units are further subdivided into over 120 sections, from which various other cycles are formed, including a series of instrumental Toccatas.[20] Linear direction towards the pivotal Nightmare section is combined with a constant turning back to re-explore the same dramatic situations from different perspectives. The Nightmare section does not exist in Collier's text, but it does parallel other versions of the Punch and Judy show in which Punch is frightened by a ghost. Cross interprets the central Nightmare as Punch's moment of recognition, or *anagnorisis*. During this section

---

[19] Cross, 'Lines and circles', 203–25.
[20] Birtwistle has suggested that the emphasis on opera numbers reflected Pruslin's fascination with Mozart's *Così fan tutte*; conversation with Beard, 28 November 2008.

Judy, disguised as a fortune-teller, 'reveals' her true identity to Punch, which prompts a reversal in the work's structure, or *peripeteia*.[21] This appears to be a functional device, however, rather than one in which Punch can be said to have gained knowledge, or any of the other connotations associated with the term *anagnorisis*. (As will be discussed later, Punch's atonement is far from convincing, and it actually occurs before the Nightmare.) Following the Nightmare, the Melodrama / Passion Chorale / Quest sequence is reversed and Punch wins Pretty Polly. By the end of the opera, a whole calendar year has passed, from Summer through to Spring. In the Epilogue, Pruslin departs from Collier's text once again, introducing a dance around a maypole to celebrate renewal and rebirth.

In addition to structural parody, Pruslin also mimics the doggerel of Collier's verse, although he develops his own elaborate style of wordplay. The bulk of Pruslin's text is his own, but some lines were taken from Collier's text. These lines include Choregos's Prologue, Punch's Resolve, 'Right toll de riddle doll', and Punch's opening Lullaby, 'Dancy baby diddy / What shall Daddy do widdy', to which Pruslin added 'Step on its back and watch it crack'.[22] Pruslin also added a fourth stanza, in which the baby is thrown into the fire (in Piccini's version it is thrown off the stage). Pruslin's additions to the Lullaby intensify the grotesque and macabre dimensions of Piccini's show and Cruickshank's illustrations, aspects that were more typical of Punch and Judy during the eighteenth and nineteenth centuries than they are today. Such intensification reflects the guiding influence of an arguably more important source text, one that has not been recognised by other commentators. This text is rarely parodied directly. Rather, it lurks behind the face of *Punch*, a hidden source of conceptual ideas that guides Pruslin's own inventive adaptation of the Collier–Cruickshank edition.

The source in question is actually a series of texts: Otto Erich Hartleben's 1911 German version of Albert Giraud's 1884 cycle of fifty poems, entitled *Pierrot lunaire*, on which Arnold Schoenberg based his eponymous song cycle. The debt here is more one of content than of style, and it reflects the fascination that Pruslin, Birtwistle, Peter Maxwell Davies and others in Britain shared for Schoenberg's *Pierrot lunaire* in the mid to late 1960s. This culminated in their formation of the Pierrot Players in 1967, an ensemble based on the instrumentation of Schoenberg's *Pierrot* – that is, a quintet of flute doubling piccolo, clarinet doubling bass clarinet, violin, viola and

---

[21] Cross, *HB: MMM*, 76. See also Hall, *HB*, 15–16 and 35.
[22] Punch's War Cry ('Roo-it-too-it-too-it-too-it-too-it') was also derived from a source in the British Library; Pruslin, CD liner note [n.p.].

cello, plus piano.[23] The group's first concert, performed in London's Queen Elizabeth Hall on 30 May 1967, comprised *Pierrot* (with soprano Mary Thomas) alongside the world premieres of Davies's *Antechrist* and Birtwistle's music theatre piece *Monodrama*.

Although *Monodrama* was composed after *Punch*, it was performed before the opera, then immediately withdrawn; dedicated to Davies, it was based on a libretto by Pruslin.[24] As Table 2.1 indicates, the formal design of *Monodrama* recalls *Punch*, which may explain why it was withdrawn: it fails to break new ground. The scenario is a parody of Greek tragedy, with an opening Parodos; the form is cyclic with *Punch*-like section titles (especially Cryptogram, Catastrophe, and Triumph); the soprano has several roles (she is the Protagonist, Prophetess, and Herald); the other vocal part – an off-stage male who speaks or shouts through a megaphone – is named Choregos; the libretto is filled with alliteration and rhyme schemes that are almost identical to those in *Punch* (for example, 'Only the heart of the vision will heal this incision in my visionary heart'), which prompts very similar musical responses to those in the opera (such as recurring fanfares, pulsating claves, and spiky clarinet and piccolo refrains). Yet, within the text there are explicit traces of *Pierrot*, in particular its repeated references to the moon.

Monodrama draws several key features from *Pierrot*, including the use of solo soprano (the only singing role), varied instrumental combinations based on Schoenberg's ensemble, and sectional form: as in Schoenberg's *Pierrot*, there are twenty-one sections in total, as shown in Table 2.1. Schoenberg's instrumentation is expanded in *Monodrama* and comprises flute (doubling piccolo and alto flute), B♭ clarinet (doubling A♭, E♭ and bass clarinet), violin, viola, cello, and percussion. Although the instrumentation is varied from section to section, as in *Pierrot*, the cello, flute, violin and clarinet – each of which perform solos in a series of four Interstices – form a core group that recurs in the Parodos, Transformula I, Incantation and Chant, and Triumph. This quartet also recurs in the three Cryptograms, which mark the three main cycles of the drama (a likely allusion to Schoenberg's division of *Pierrot* into three groups of seven songs); here the quartet is joined by the xylophone, possibly as a substitute for the absent piano. Additional similarities include the use of melodrama, *Sprechgesang*, and other expressionistic devices (in particular exaggerated string glissandi in the Incantation and Chant).

[23] The Pierrot Players were formed by Birtwistle and Alan Hacker – they auditioned the players, invited Davies to become joint artistic director, and organised the first concert. See Hall, *HB*, 50.

[24] No published score exists, but a complete fair copy is stored in the Sammlung Harrison Birtwistle, PSS. A recording is stored in the British Library Sound Archive (1967 broadcast: NP1131W BD 1).

Table 2.1 Monodrama, *overall design*

Parodos	Oracle I	Cryptogram I	Soliloquy I	Interstice I Interstice II	Transformula I	Interrogation I
(*)		Cryptogram II	Soliloquy II	Interstice III	Transformula II	Oracle (*) & Interrogation II
						Incantation & Chant
				Interstice IV		
		Cryptogram III				
						Catastrophe Triumph Exodos

At some point in the mid to late 1960s, Birtwistle plotted the instrumentation of *Pierrot* in a handwritten chart.[25] It seems likely that this chart relates to *Three Lessons in a Frame* (1967), which Birtwistle dedicated to Pruslin. Besides the absence of a voice, this chamber work is more faithful to *Pierrot* than *Monodrama* had been: it is scored for flute (doubling piccolo), clarinet, violin, cello, piano and percussion. *Three Lessons* was first performed by the Pierrot Players in their second concert, conducted by Davies at the Cheltenham Town Hall, on 17 July 1967. The work was withdrawn, but the fair copy used by Davies is stored in Basle.[26] In addition to various conductor's markings, the score includes additional information that suggests *Three Lessons* incorporated mimed action and other theatrical devices, namely: 'P[ierrot?] descends ladder' and 'Columbine Dummy'. Lesson II is marked 'Pierrot's farewell'.

Returning to *Punch*, there is a direct link between the opera's central character and Pierrot: both were stock characters in the *commedia dell'arte*, where, as Pulcinella (anglicised to Punchinello), Punch appeared alongside Pierrot.[27] Pierrot may be docile in appearance, but he possesses similar destructive tendencies to Punch. Conversely, Pierrot's desire for Columbine is mimicked by Pruslin's introduction of Punch's quest for Pretty Polly. Pruslin's Punch even describes himself as a 'moon-beam sweeper', which elides him with the moon-fixated Pierrot of Giraud's poems.[28] Pruslin's prominent references to 'Melodrama' in his libretto suggests Schoenberg's *Pierrot*, with its hybrid mixture of melodrama and cabaret. Schoenberg's interest in canons, as in Parodie, is reflected in *Punch*, notably in The Little Canonic Prelude to Disaster. There are structural parallels also: the brevity of Schoenberg's movements and the tripartite organisation of the poems he selected resonate with Pruslin's scheme. Moreover, the 'altogether more discomforting atmosphere' of Part II of Schoenberg's *Pierrot*, which deals with 'topics of extreme ritualistic violence and punishment', is mirrored in *Punch*'s central Nightmares.[29]

More telling, however, are the traces of Giraud's imagery in Pruslin's text. These include the moon references (as in the Travel Music sections), and the blend of the sacred and the secular. The latter is exemplified by Choregos's reference, in Proclamation I, to 'the holy sacrament of murder',

---

[25] This is handwritten on a piece of blue card; PSS 0540-0431, Musikbeispiele für Kurse.

[26] The copy bears Davies's initials, 'PMD', on the title page.

[27] Leach has also indicated that early versions of the Punch and Judy show included Pierrot. See Leach, *The Punch and Judy Show*, 162.

[28] Another allusion occurs here in the libretto: the questions in the Interview-Game (Your name? Your age? Your profession?) recall Claggart's questions to the three press-ganged recruits in Act I scene 1 of Britten's *Billy Budd*.

[29] Jonathan Dunsby, *Schoenberg: Pierrot lunaire* (Cambridge University Press, 1992), 47 and 44.

his description of Punch as the 'high priest of pain', as well as the Latin psalm singing during Jack Ketch's scene. Pruslin's Black Wedding evokes the sacrilegious Rote Messe; moreover, there is a Gallows Song (Galgenlied) and Serenade in both texts. *Pierrot*'s imagery is also reflected in the opera's stage directions: the needles referred to in Galgenlied and Parodie become a hypodermic syringe and a quill in *Punch*, implements used to murder the doctor and the lawyer. The *Pierrot* poets' association of bleeding wounds with 'den Altar meiner Verse' in Madonna – the concept of the poetic verse as a sacrificial altar (an idea revisited in Rote Messe and Kreuze) – is reflected in the presence of an 'Altar of Murder' in *Punch*, to which each of Punch's victims is led. This may also have influenced the direction to hang each of Punch's victims after they have been murdered.

Most significantly, the idea of Pierrot's journey homeward (Heimfahrt), with the moonbeam as his rudder and a 'friendly following wind' at his back, relates directly to Punch's quest for Pretty Polly, in which he journeys east, west, north, then south.[30] Both Pierrot and Punch end their journeys in a southerly direction. When Pierrot reaches Bergamo, he sees glimmers of the sun rising 'in the east' on 'the green horizon'. This explains Pruslin's reference to colours in Punch's Serenades, in particular Punch's longing for green in Serenade I, when he travels east:

> The world is blinded by lightning of green.
> Silence and sounds and song of flaming green.
> Greenness of sun and greenness of moon.
> Green, how I long for you flaming in green.

This text was not Pruslin's first version. Presumably at Birtwistle's request, either for more words or for a more elaborate verse, Pruslin altered what had been a simpler verse, as revealed by an early draft of the libretto:

> Green, how I want you, green!
> Green silence, green sounds,
> And song of flaming green.
> Sun on the sea and moon on the mountains:
> Green, how I want you, green![31]

Here, the repetition of the opening line at the stanza's end is an allusion to Giraud's and Hartleben's strict adherence to the rondel form, in which the opening phrase forms a refrain at the end of the second and third stanzas.[32]

---

[30]   The English translations of Hartleben's text in this chapter are by Andrew Porter, as cited in Dunsby, *Pierrot lunaire*.

[31]   PSS 0535-1078.

[32]   Roger Marsh notes that Giraud's references to green were a typically decadent *fin-de-siècle* allusion to absinthe. Pruslin's choice of colour references during Punch's Serenades, and the

Example 2.2 Punch's vocal line and clarinet with arabesque, Serenade III (full score (FS)), p. 340, bb. 870–6

Birtwistle's music suggests that he understood Pruslin's subversive allusion to *Pierrot lunaire*. His use of canons and palindromes mirrors Schoenberg's interest in such procedures, and his decision to pair Punch with the clarinet mirrors Schoenberg's use of the clarinet during sections in which Pierrot is named. Similarly, arching arabesques in the clarinet during Punch's melancholy Serenades recall Schoenberg's use of such figurations in *Pierrot*, which accompany Punch's sadly lyrical line, with yearning, upward leaps at the end of each line (see Example 2.2). A contrasting version of this idea occurs in Punch's Lullaby, in which the clarinet becomes ever more frenzied in each verse (faster tempo and more distorted melodic contour) and higher in register: Punch is paired with bass clarinet in the first two verses, then B flat clarinet in the third verse, and finally a 'screaming' E flat clarinet in the fourth verse when the baby is thrown into the fire. More instructive parallels between *Punch* and *Pierrot* will be discussed later, in

direction to spotlight Pretty Polly in green, red, blue and white, respectively, may also have been influenced by the colour symbolism in Giraud's poems, which focus in particular on 'red (sunset, opulence, blood), white (the moon, purity, Pierrot), and green (ocean waves, nature, and, importantly, absinthe)'. Roger Marsh, '"A multicoloured alphabet": rediscovering Albert Giraud's *Pierrot Lunaire*', *twentieth-century music*, 4/1 (2007), 112 and 116.

relation to the death of Choregos. However, such parallels are also to be found at an abstract, conceptual level. To explore this more abstract relation between *Punch* and *Pierrot*, it is first necessary to examine Birtwistle's sketches for *Tragoedia*.

Tragoedia into *Punch*: 'System for Goat-Song'

In his study of Schoenberg's *Pierrot*, Jonathan Dunsby identifies a single recurring motif, which he refers to as 'the "principal rhythm" of seven equally spaced notes (or chords)'.[33] He suggests that this was 'a flexible musical "idea" to be resorted to again and again in the melodramas: it could be repeated, expanded, contracted, added to, truncated, counterpointed against itself, and – what is most important – set either to repeated pitches or to any number of pitch "shapes"'.[34] The sketches for *Tragoedia* reveal that Birtwistle had been thinking in similar – though not identical – terms, and that he carried these ideas through into *Punch*.

Birtwistle's 'flexible musical "idea"' was a symmetrical chromatic wedge shape, an idea that evokes a suitably grotesque metaphor: like a needle inserted into a body, it penetrates and expands to fill the vacant space. The importance of this idea is revealed by a series of pages the composer sketched entitled 'System for Goat-Song'.[35] This system represents a conceptual principle or schema from which a composition could be generated. The 'Basic set' is a chromatic wedge that begins on B, followed by a downward chromatic step (henceforth labelled B˘): see group 'I' in Example 2.3.[36] This set is subdivided into four six-note 'cells'. Birtwistle labels these cells, he explains, after the 'four winds' used in Mahjong – in other words, after the four cardinal directions (North, South, etc.). The East and West winds are formed from the first and last six notes of the Basic set, respectively. North and South are formed by selecting notes that are either odd- or even-numbered (when B is counted as 1, B♭ as 2, C as 3, and so on). Each six-note cell has what the composer describes as 'a different identity': a rising chromatic; a falling chromatic; an expanding chromatic of small intervals; an expanding chromatic of larger intervals. For some reason, which is not explained, Birtwistle labels the rising and falling chromatic cells 'positive', and the expanding cells 'negative'. Essentially, Birtwistle uses these terms

---

[33] Dunsby, *Pierrot lunaire*, 28.   [34] Ibid.

[35] PSS 0540-0420, Musikbeispiele für Kurse. Birtwistle translated *Tragoedia* as 'goat dance', and it seems likely that he simply mis-remembered this translation when he wrote the title to his system.

[36] In the discussion that follows I use the symbol ˘ to indicate an expanding chromatic wedge that begins with a rising semitone, and the symbol ˘ for a wedge that begins with a falling semitone.

Example 2.3 'System for Goat-Song', PSS, Musikbeispiele für Kurse, side 6

Figure 2.3 Positive and negative cells

Positive = stepwise
Rising or falling chromatic
Either odd (North wind) or even
   (South wind) numbers
    from the Basic set
(Unidirectional)

Negative = bifurcated
Expanding chromatic
Either 1–6 (West wind)
   or 7–12 (East wind)
    from the Basic set
(Bidirectional)

to differentiate between two types of contour, or shape. This division is summarised in Figure 2.3.

Birtwistle then devised a circular system, by which each of the chromatic cells could be 'transformed into each other'. This was achieved by transposing the Basic set downwards through a series of minor thirds. The resulting circle of thirds (B, A♭, F, D) led to the chart shown in Example 2.3, which is divided into four groups (labelled I to IV). Note that Birtwistle maintains the position of each 'wind' (i.e. the specific pitch-class content) of I in all subsequent groups. Birtwistle then observed that the positive and negative cells all move one position in an anti-clockwise direction: for example, North I = West II = South III = East IV. He then noted that group III is the retrograde of I, and IV the retrograde of II. This means that there is 'only one real transposition', that of II, 'which is a minor 3rd below' the Basic set – that is, A flat. Finally, Birtwistle states that 'there is no logical reason for the second note to begin a semitone down', but that it could instead begin with a step up (i.e. B˅). He calls this a 'logical transposition'. This results in one pitch alteration in each 'wind'. For example, in group I, the West form of B˅ is B–B♭–C–A–C♯–A♭, whereas the West form of B^ is B–C–B♭–C♯–A–D. Therefore, the order of the pitches is altered, and A♭ is replaced by D.[37]

The few extant sketches for *Tragoedia* give some insight into how this system was used in the piece. They also confirm the central importance of B˅, B˅, and the 'one real' transposition of the 'logical transposition' A♭^ (or B^ IV). Exceptions to this are the opening Prologue and the central Stasimon movements, neither of which is based on sets from the system.[38] This is explained by the position of these movements outside the work's central scheme, as shown in Figure 2.4.

The division of the ensemble into two groups of four instruments (wind and string quartets), plus horn and harp, results in numerous tetrachords.

---

[37] It should also be noted that the transposition levels alter as follows: B˅II begins on D; B˅III on F; B˅IV on A♭.

[38] In the Prologue, the harp part is derived from three seven-note sets. The Stasimon is based on a C♯˅ chromatic wedge.

Figure 2.4 The formal structure of *Tragoedia* (after Cross, *HB: MMM*, Fig. 2.1, 74)

Prologue
        Parodos
                Episodion (Strophe I
                        Antistrophe I)
                                Stasimon
                Episodion (Strophe II
                        Antistrophe II)
        Exodos

Example 2.4 Stabbing tetrachord in *Tragoedia* (UE 14179), Fig. 4

For this reason, perhaps, Birtwistle often uses four-note selections from the six-note cells.

The sketches reveal that Birtwistle did not limit himself to the cells in the system, but that he partitioned his sets in other ways also. This is illustrated by the first nineteen bars of the Parodos. These bars announce the opening of the first structural pillar of the piece, and they lead to the work's most distinctive motif – a stabbing tetrachord in the woodwind, at Fig. 4, shown in Example 2.4. This violent gesture is the paradigm for a further nine related stabbing chords in *Tragoedia*, which are parodied in the opera when Punch murders the baby, Judy, the Doctor and Lawyer, and Jack Ketch – although not Choregos (this important exception will be discussed later). Birtwistle's concern with symmetry is also underlined by the fact that the woodwind chord at Fig. 4 is literally symmetrical, with an interval of fifteen semitones between each note.

A summary of the chords that lead up to this moment is provided in stages 1 to 12 of Example 2.5. These chords are either shared or passed between the woodwind and string quartets. As can be seen, the selections are drawn from B♭, the 'logical transposition' of the Basic set. In the first four stages, selections of adjacent notes fan outwards from the centre of the

Example 2.5 Analysis of Parodos chords up to Fig. 4 (stages 1–12) and stabbing chords beyond Fig. 4 throughout *Tragoedia* (stages 13–21)

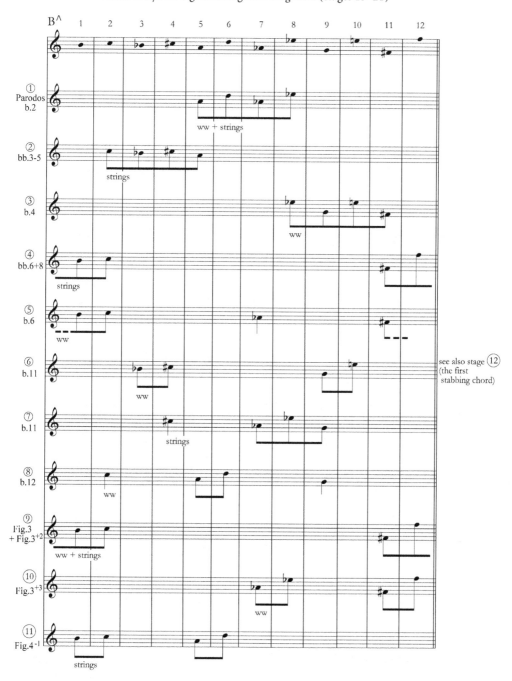

Example 2.5 (*cont.*)

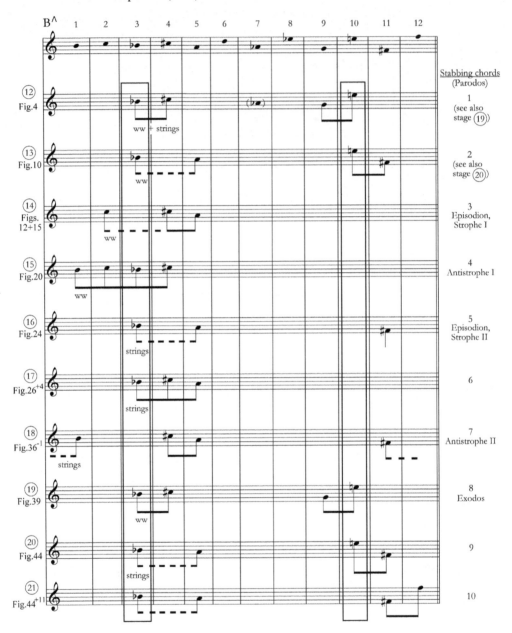

set, with the first and last notes of each selection acting as pivots. In stages 5 through to 11, more varied selections are made, nearly all of which are regular or symmetrical (the exceptions are 5 and 7). It is now possible to see that the stabbing chord at Fig. 4, which is literally symmetrical in the score,

Example 2.6 Analysis of stabbing chords during the murders in *Punch and Judy*

is also symmetrical within the scheme (with the exception of the grace note Ab). Moreover, its 'outer' notes, Bb and E, are a tritone apart. Stages 13 to 21 in Example 2.5 show all subsequent occurrences of the stabbing gesture in *Tragoedia*. This reveals that stages 12 and 13 are repeated in the Exodos, as stages 19 and 20. Both chords share Bb and E, although the second chord (stages 13 and 20) is irregular. This fits with Birtwistle's overall concern in *Tragoedia* with 'non-literal symmetry'.[39] A similar sense of imbalance is formed by the fact that in versions 12 to 21 the pitches are clustered around Bb and E, but the gravitational pull of Bb is stronger.

In *Punch*, this imbalance shifts to the second half of the Bˆ set, with an emphasis on E, F♯ and F. This is shown in Example 2.6. Unlike the situation in *Tragoedia*, here the selections are mostly irregular, although the majority of the notes in each chord are placed in a high register. The resultant high clusters recall the final stabbing chord in *Tragoedia*, as well as those in Strophe II (Figs. 24 and 26^{+4}). In fact, the stabbing chord heard at the Triumph, when Jack Ketch is murdered, is a variant of the final stabbing chord in *Tragoedia*: as shown in Example 2.7, both chords are played quadruple *forte*, in 2/4, and include *bb'''* and *f♯'/gb'*.

Another characteristic feature of the opera, which originates in *Tragoedia*, is the realisation of the wedge idea as an audible motif. At such moments,

[39] Birtwistle, cited in Hall, *HB*, 175.

Example 2.7 Final stabbing chords in *Tragoedia* (Fig. 44^{+11}) and *Punch and Judy* (VS, p. 223)

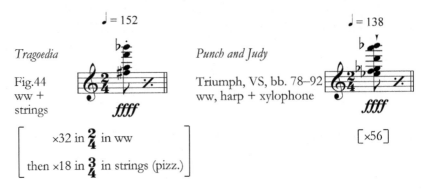

the abstract wedge idea is exposed: a cerebral process becomes a physical, dramatic presence. Attempts to disguise the underlying compositional process are abandoned, and the flexible musical idea becomes inflexible. As in *Punch*, there are two sides to this process. The raw, visceral side is heard in Strophe II at Figs. 24 and 26, played by the work's two principal protagonists, the horn and cello. At Fig. 26 this pair hammers out expanding wedges in a form of aural combat that amounts to a form of grotesque parody (see Example 2.8). Abstraction is marched to the gallows. Similarly, in *Punch*, various audible wedges accompany Punch's Word-Game, where Pruslin's text refers to 'a net unwound, a net unfurled'.[40] (As will be seen, the net is actually winding around Choregos, whose line in this section 'a sound that sings and sounds a thousand wounds' returns in Melodrama III). None of the wedges here belong to the particular cycle of thirds used in the Goat-Song system. This suggests that the system has been expanded in the opera to include the two other possible cycles: C, A, F♯, E♭, and C♯, B♭, G, E.

The audible realisation of Birtwistle's underlying scheme in *Punch* culminates in a parade of fifteen audible wedges in the Black Wedding Procession, the part of the Nightmare section when Punch is led away to be condemned. This section draws on all three cycles of thirds, although in a sequence that suggests a random order selection process has been applied. Over a repeated bass pattern, between one and three wedges are heard at any one point, which suggests they are intended to shadow the three mime dancers on

---

[40] An indication that Birtwistle associated the audible wedges with needles and incisions is suggested by his use of two such wedges in the middle of Proclamation II, at Choregos's words 'into incisions of eternity'.

Example 2.8 Audible wedges in *Tragoedia*: Episodion, Strophe II, Fig. 26

Example 2.9 Black Wedding Procession, *Punch and Judy*, FS, pp. 278–9, bb. 556–60

stage. Emphasis is placed on the two-voice compound melody that charac-terises the 'negative' contour. The result is a grotesque canonic pantomime that illustrates well the transformation that occurs when ideas from *Trageo-dia* are parodied in *Punch* (see Example 2.9). The result is ironic inversion: the stabbing chord is compared to 'a clockwork toy' when the Doctor and Lawyer are killed; the audible wedge becomes an accompaniment to verbal rhymes and comic pantomime.

The opposite, more reflective side of the audible wedge motif is exem-plified in *Tragoedia* by the opening of Strophe I.[41] This section begins with gently repeated *d′* pedals in the harp and a softly unfolding wedge in the horn that begins on *f′*. Suspicion that the horn wedge is B♭III, from the Goat-Song system, is supported by an analysis of the string section that accompanies

[41] The stabbing chord is also modified in this section: it is reduced to three detached chords. This gentler version recalls the three chords at the end of 'Columbine' in *Pierrot lunaire*, which are associated with 'the moonlight's pallid blossoms'.

Example 2.10 B' wedge and analysis of strings and horn in *Tragoedia*: Episodion, Strophe I, Fig. 11

the horn, from Fig. 11 to Fig. 12. Example 2.10 reveals that this section comprises four-note selections from B' – that is, the 'logical transposition' of the Basic set. This results in a non-literal symmetry between the horn and the strings, since B'III is the retrograde of the Basic set, which differs only marginally from B'.

Significantly, this string passage is one of only two ideas that are literally quoted in *Punch*, despite Birtwistle's misleading claim that *Tragoedia* appears 'practically note for note' in the opera.[42] (The other literal quotation is the harp cadence from Strophe II, and the end of the Parodos and Exodos sections, which is heard when Punch hangs his final victim, Jack Ketch). The string quotation occurs in the first two Travel Music sections of *Punch*. These begin with an allusion to Strophe I, with soft d' pedals in the horn and trumpet, before the string quotation at bar 447 (VS, p. 35). The significance of the string quotation is suggested by the dramatic context: Punch rides Horsey on his quest for Pretty Polly and, in Travel Music I, Choregos informs us that Punch travels 'eastwards'.[43] Logically, therefore, the first four notes heard in the first violin (e''', g'', eb'', $f\sharp''$) belong to the cell identified in the Goat-Song system as the East 'wind': D–G–Eb–F♯–E♮–F♮. This is also felt in Choregos's vocal line, which shadows the pitch content of the first violin (e', eb', g, f, etc.). One might expect the quotation to change in the second Travel Music section, when Punch rides 'westward', but it is unaltered. However, in line with Cross's observation that Melodrama III 'breaks away from the regular cycles of events so far established', and in anticipation of the fact that Punch eventually breaks free from his earlier cycle of quest and rejection, the quotation is removed from the third and fourth Travel Music sections.[44] In Travel Music III, the string section plays repeated pulses on claves. This is an ironic inversion of *Tragoedia*, in which members of the woodwind quartet play claves. Finally, in Travel Music IV, the strings play arching arpeggios. These are highly reminiscent of the rippling waters under Pierrot's waterlily boat as he journeys home to Bergamo, in Schoenberg's Heimfahrt. They also serve as a reminder that Punch's journey ends in the same direction as Pierrot's: southwards.

This returns us to Birtwistle's distinction between 'positive' and 'negative' cells. According to his system, the odd- or even-numbered cells, which are the North and South 'winds' in his Basic set, are positive. These cells form either rising or falling lines, in stepwise direction. They are unidirectional. We might have expected, therefore, to find them during the Travel Music scenes, but neither the string quotation from *Tragoedia* nor the music for claves or the arching arpeggios conform to this idea. There is some evidence elsewhere in the opera, however, that Punch's break from his cycle of quest and rejection is mirrored by a shift from negative to positive cells.

---

[42] Birtwistle, cited in Hall, *HB*, 175.

[43] The stage direction that Punch is seen 'in a picture frame', with its implication of a moment from the past, may also have prompted Birtwistle's decision to use a musical quotation at this point in the opera.

[44] Cross, 'Lines and circles', 210. In Daniel Kramer's 2008 production for ENO the notion of Punch breaking free of the work's cycles was dramatised by the removal of his make-up and costume following the Nightmare scenes. When he then serenaded Polly for the third time it was as the singer/actor himself. At the end of the production, however, Punch appeared to have resumed his old ways.

East and West 'negative' winds are prominent in the early part of the opera, which reflects Punch's journey east in Melodrama I and west in Melodrama II. This is illustrated by the Sinfonia, fragments of which appear as ritornellos throughout Melodrama II. This pointillist, post-Webern style parody, with leaps of over three octaves in places, is divided antiphonally between the pit orchestra and the stage band. The former group is based on the West wind of B♭, while the latter draws mainly on the East wind of B♭. Halfway through the Sinfonia the winds begin to merge and they are fully exchanged at bar 617 (VS, p. 45). A shift to the 'positive' North and South winds is signalled by the Little Canonic Prelude to Disaster, the Babbitt parody, which forms a short overture to Melodrama III, in which Punch travels north. Example 2.11 reveals how the melodic line passed between the instruments in the stage band is based on the North wind from B♭ (with the exception of the final note in the bassoon). Beneath this, the line in the pit orchestra is based on the South wind (with some minor exceptions).

Shortly after this comes the Morale section. This marks an important stage in the opera's cycle of Morals, which follow Pretty Polly's rejection of Punch. The Morale is unusual: it does not follow Punch's rejection, and Choregos's text changes. In the first two Morals, Choregos's text is identical ('Weep, my Punch . . . / It is impossible'), but in the Morale the text is parodied with ironic inversion ('Leap, my Punch . . . / it is yet feasible, so, fearless, fly'). As Cross notes, the earlier accompaniment – a mechanical series of recurring elements based on regular durational cycles – is replaced by a 'loud, vigorous and wild' solo horn line.[45] Example 2.12 reveals that the horn line is based on reordered versions of the 'positive' North and South winds in B♭. (The repetition of pitches indicated by the boxes corresponds to the last line of the text, which recapitulates the first word of the opening line: 'Leap'.)

Near the end of the opera, Punch and Pretty Polly sing a Love Duet to symbolise their union. Their duet concludes with a parody of a couplet refrain that was previously always sung by Punch and one of his victims prior to their murder: 'The bitterness of this moment is unendurably sweet/ The sweetness of this moment is unendurably bitter.' In the Love Duet, the meaning is inverted: 'The bitterness of this moment can never be bitter / The sweetness of this moment can only be sweet.' Earlier refrains are all set

---

[45]   Cross, 'Lines and circles', 210. A more regular solo bassoon line was introduced to the accompaniment in Moral II, but this is replaced in the Morale by the horn solo. In Moral III, the horn line is retained from the Morale, but now played to a slightly looser rhythm marked 'relaxed'. In this way, as Cross argues, the music in the final Moral reflects the sense of a journey of self-discovery for Punch.

Example 2.11 Analysis and score extract of A Little Canonic Prelude to Disaster, Melodrama III, *Punch and Judy*, FS, p. 172, bb. 925–7

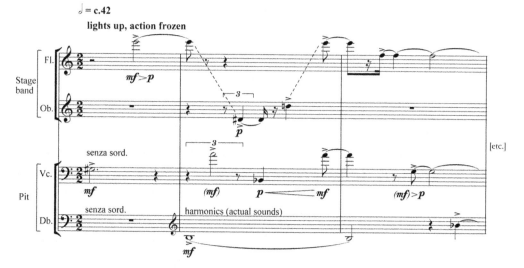

to a different accompaniment. This version is unusual, however, as it alludes directly to Figs. 16–17 of *Tragoedia* (the Anapaest section of Strophe I). In both instances, a single line is passed between horn and cello. In *Tragoedia*, this marks a rare moment of harmonious exchange between the work's protagonists, which is symbolised by the overlap and symmetrical division of their pitch material, as summarised in Figure 2.5.

In the Love Duet, the situation is rather different. There the partitioning of the melodic notes between the horn on the stage and the cello in the

Example 2.12 Analysis of horn solo, Morale, *Punch and Judy*

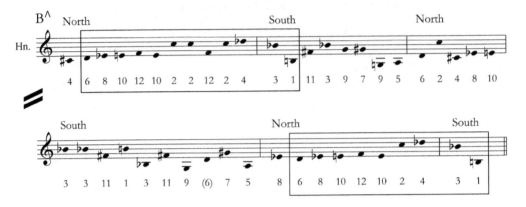

Figure 2.5 *Tragoedia*, Figs. 16–17, horn and cello pitch content

Set: BˆIII
Vc. = notes 1–7; hn. = notes 4–10

                                  <   hn.   >
Summary (shared pitches in bold):   1 2 3 **4 5 6 7** 8 9 10
                                    <   vc.   >

pit does not map directly onto the scheme that determines the pitch content. The pitch scheme is summarised in Example 2.13. This reveals two
retrograde motion cycles of the South wind (and the beginning of a third
cycle), interrupted by random order selections from the North wind. This
complicates the apparently straightforward concept of 'positive' cells. The
regular element does not progress forwards but continually turns back on
itself, and, in the process, it is interrupted by an irregular element.

    This ambivalent situation, which blurs Birtwistle's 'positive' / 'negative'
terminology, resonates with Pruslin's remarks about the opera's conclusion:

> The triumph of Pretty Polly is a photographic double-image which could
> then lead to Tamino-Pamina or Florestan-Fidelio as the 'positive' and to
> Nero-Poppea as the 'negative'. This relates to our interest in the Mozartian
> phenomenon of an ending which makes the gesture of a moral, but really
> leaves one with a question, an ambiguity, or an irreducible duality.[46]

Pruslin's distinction between the lovers of *Die Zauberflöte* and *Fidelio*, on
the one hand, and of *L'incoronazione di Poppea*, on the other, highlights
a contrast between love that is instrumental in upholding justice, in the

---

[46] Pruslin, programme note to *Punch and Judy*.

Example 2.13 Analysis of horn and cello in the Love Duet, VS, pp. 231–33, bb. 172–88

former, and love that contravenes social mores, in the latter. Arguably, the 'gesture' of a moral in *Punch* is precisely that – a functional device performed by the first two Passion Chorales and the Nightmare, in which Punch's actions are condemned. Yet Punch's murders continue and there is no clear indication why Pretty Polly decides to accept him.[47] Arguably, Birtwistle's pitch scheme for the horn and cello melody captures this ambiguous state of affairs, in which a point of formal closure, which reflects the completion of a calendar year from Summer to Spring, is marred by the absence of a clear moral outcome.

In the concluding section that follows, further intersections between Birtwistle's and Pruslin's conceptual ideas will be discussed, with specific reference to the death of Choregos in Melodrama III. The function and symbolic status of Choregos and his rejection by Punch will be considered. This sheds light on the relationship between *Punch* and opera and opens the discussion to a wider framework of intepretation.

The death of Choregos

> *Noise is a weapon and music, primordially, is the formulation, domestication, and ritualization of that weapon as a simulacrum of ritual murder.*[48]

> Indeed, we would go further and suggest that opera itself was invented and sustained to tame and domesticate . . . music by subjecting [it] to figurative narratives, human psychology and social gesture.[49]

Although the pattern of recurrence in *Punch* is broken by the Nightmare section, the real turning point occurs in Murder Ensemble III, when Punch murders Choregos.[50] Music, plot, parody and allusion all converge on this point. This is evident from the very first line, sung by Punch: 'a sound that sings and sounds a thousand wounds'. These words were first sung by Choregos in the Word-Game, at the start of the opera. They are therefore associated with the moment when audible wedges were first heard in the opera, and the idea of 'a net unwound, a net unfurled'. That net is about to encircle Choregos, and his repeated line alludes to the fact that he is murdered by music, or, rather, by noise. Ushered into a person-sized bass viol case, Choregos is bowed to death by Punch.

Choregos differs from Punch's other victims: as narrator and master of ceremonies, he is both inside and outside the action; he is present throughout

---

[47] Hall suggests that Pretty Polly accepts Punch because the devil within him is vanquished when Jack Ketch is killed, since Punch cries 'Huzzah, huzzah! The Devil's dead!' when Ketch dies. Yet this raises the question of why Ketch is used and not the devil (as in Collier's text), and why no real evidence is provided that Punch has actually changed, which would make the point indisputable. See Hall, *HB*, 63.

[48] Jacques Attali, *Noise: The Political Economy of Music* (Minneapolis and London: University of Minnesota Press, 2006), 24. Italics in the original.

[49] Till, "'I don't mind if something's operatic'", 18.

[50] Hall also sees this moment as the opera's turning point. See Hall, *HB*, 15–16.

the opera and links the sections; he does not belong to the traditional puppet show but has links to Greek tragedy and the use of narrators in Stravinsky's *Soldier's Tale* and *Oedipus Rex*.[51] He also receives a more elaborate and prolonged execution than any other victim in the opera, and his murder prompts the Nightmare section, in which Punch's misdemeanours are visited back on him. Given the manner of his death, it also seems that there is something specifically music-related about Choregos. His death scene is preceded by a cycle of three Coronation-Scenes, during which Choregos is 'crowned' with various musical instruments (trumpet, cymbal and drum), which are banged over his head. Moreover, each cycle is announced by a 'Gebrauchmusik' [*sic*] section (based on the opening fanfare from Choregos's Prologue), during which Punch collects the coronation instruments. In light of these musical associations, Meirion Bowen has suggested that Choregos represents 'music itself', while Adlington has remarked that Choregos resembles the character of Music in the Prologue to Monteverdi's *Orfeo*.[52] This would imply that Punch's rejection of Choregos symbolises the rejection of music in some way – the rejection of a certain kind of music, perhaps, or an attitude towards it. One key towards understanding that symbolism is to recognise that Choregos's musical death scene alludes to the Serenade in *Pierrot lunaire*, for, according to the stage directions, Punch bows Choregos to death with a 'serenade'.

The line 'a sound that sings and sounds a thousand wounds' is clearly an allusion both to Punch's imminent bow strokes and to Pierrot's 'grotesken Riesenbogen' (or 'D'un grotesque archet dissonant', as it appears in Giraud's original poem).[53] As Dunsby observes, Schoenberg chose a cello for his setting, rather than the viola indicated in the text, since he conceived 'of a monstrous viola, not a real one'.[54] The choice of a bass viol in *Punch* is therefore one step further along the line of grotesque parody. It also suggests that Pruslin was aware of Giraud's original poem, which refers to a viol ('viole'), which Hartleben, perhaps deliberately, mistranslated as 'Bratsche' (viola).[55] Further evidence for the idea that Pruslin alludes to the French poem, rather than Hartleben's, is provided by the fact that Giraud's

---

[51] Hall compares Choregos to 'both chorus and Evangelist' in Bach's *St Matthew Passion*. Hall, *HB*, 65. Bowen describes Choregos as 'both showman-commentator and the alter-ego of Punch himself'. Meirion Bowen, 'Harrison Birtwistle', in Lewis Foreman, ed., *British Music Now: A Guide to the Work of Younger Composers* (London: Elek, 1975), 68.

[52] Bowen, 'Harrison Birtwistle', 68, and Adlington, *MHB*, 10. This association was actually first suggested by Michael Nyman who observed that 'in a splendid conceit he [Choregos] represents music itself'. Nyman, 'Harrison Birtwistle's "Punch and Judy"', *The Listener* (October, 1968), 481.

[53] Marsh, '"A multicoloured alphabet"', 109.   [54] Dunsby, *Pierrot lunaire*, 24.

[55] Marsh, '"A multicoloured alphabet"', 109.

Pierrot 'Streaks the intruder's paunch' ('Zèbre le bedon du gênant'), rather than his bald head.[56] As Roger Marsh observes of Giraud's poem:

> the instrument on which Pierrot scrapes grotesquely is a seventeenth-century instrument, probably a bass viol, played between the legs like a cello. For when the elderly, frequently mistreated Cassander objects to Pierrot's serenade, Pierrot replaces the instrument with the old man, fingering his cravat and bowing his belly (not as Hartleben would have it, his bald head).[57]

In effect, this is precisely what Punch does. The bass viol case (one of several baroque references in this section) is a virtual body that is violated by Punch's bowing. It is also violated by the music, which has a saw-like motion, rather than the 'dreamy' bowing of Schoenberg's setting.[58]

The musical sketches indicate that the instruments of Choregos's death are not only the physical and musical gestures of Punch's bow strokes, but also expanding chromatic wedges – in other words, the flexible musical 'idea'. In this sense, the death of Choregos is the ultimate realisation of those moments in *Tragoedia* when the composer's abstract musical processes ruptured the surface. Example 2.14 illustrates the scheme used to derive the pitches of the cello and double bass parts in Proclamation III, when the Doctor and Lawyer sing, 'with downbows of destruction and ponticelli of pain' – the moment when Punch's bow strokes begin. The wedge here (B♭') is unrelated to the Basic set. Three-, four-, five-, six- and seven-note selections are made from the set, which are then reordered internally by random numbers (although the six-note selection is not used). Example 2.15 reveals the genesis of the cello and double bass parts in the Couplets and War Cry sections, when Choregos is killed. This begins at Choregos's line 'In cosines of sight and sawteeth of sound'. Here the set is B'IV. Birtwistle makes five-note selections, and moves forward through the set one note at a time a total of ten times. The cells are then reordered according to the same number scheme: 41352.

An indication of Birtwistle's sense of the importance of this moment, and also his ideas about its interpretation, have been highlighted by Michael McCarthy, who directed productions of *Punch* by Music Theatre Wales in 1997 and 2008. McCarthy has remarked that when Birtwistle attended a rehearsal in 1997, he 'saw the section where Choregos is bowed to death by Punch and immediately started giving me notes about how much more sexually and aggressively charged it needed to be'.[59] If Choregos is deemed in some sense emblematic of opera, this statement suggests an attitude towards

56 Translation by Kay Bourlier, in Marsh, '"A multicoloured alphabet"', 109.
57 Ibid.   58 Dunsby, *Pierrot lunaire*, 69.
59 Michael McCarthy in email to Beard, 18 November 2008.

Example 2.14 Sketch and score extracts for Murder Ensemble III, Proclamation III. PSS 0535-0238 and FS, pp. 225–6, bb. 245–8

[Selected and reordered to form:]

Final version, bb. 245–8, at 'with downbows of destruction and ponticelli of pain':

* = slight deviations; either deliberate alterations or unintentional slips.

the genre that is based on attraction and repulsion. In most productions, Choregos is roughly treated during this scene – pushed, poked and generally bullied by all the characters. Yet he receives a relatively gentle death: he is not stabbed. Rather, the instruction to bow him to death requires a certain intimacy, as Punch must take Choregos in his arms: he must embrace Choregos.[60]

[60] Birtwistle has expressed his concern when these particular instructions are ignored (conversation with Beard, 18 November 2008). For example, in a Netherlands Opera production, premiered on 9 January 1993, there was no bass viol case, and many other directions were ignored. Instead, Choregos crawled beneath a table. Punch, standing on the table, dangled a noose for Choregos to place his head inside. There was therefore no bodily contact between Punch and Choregos.

Example 2.15 Sketch and score extracts for Murder Ensemble III, Couplets. PSS 0535-0240 and FS, p. 227, bb. 257–61 and bb. 281–2

[B^IV]

Rearranged to form the following at 'In cosines of sight and sawteeth of sound':

Further evidence that Birtwistle considered Melodrama III important is provided by a draft of the libretto, annotated by Pruslin and the composer, and by a final draft of the score. The libretto draft reveals that several alterations were made to the structure in the lead-up to Choregos's murder. These alterations, which are written in Pruslin's hand, constitute extremely rare examples of changes to Pruslin's original scheme.[61] Moreover, in the

---

61 PSS 0535-1072–93. On this document, pencil markings with American spellings are presumably those of Pruslin. The handwriting of the pencil markings appears to match that of annotations in black pen (although these are often capitalised), while occasional pen marks in red are by Birtwistle (these include musical notation, such as rhythms written above text, and the word 'canon?' beside the 'bitterness/sweetness of this moment' couplet in Murder Ensemble I). Certain character names have also been underlined in red pencil, possibly by Birtwistle (there are also blue crayon marks by Birtwistle, and blue and red pen marks by Pruslin). Pruslin appears to have added numerous stage directions in pencil after typing the text. This suggests that the directions were either dictated by Birtwistle, or agreed upon collaboratively. The pen annotations are mostly to clarify the number of repetitions of sections ('1', '2', '3', etc.), or to introduce new section headings.

Figure 2.6 Sections in Melodrama III, final version

Parody and Paraphrase (*Punch turns suddenly to Choregos*)
Rule II
Morale ('Leap, my Punch')
Gebrauch[s]musik: Roundel, Preyer, Coronation-Scene, Dithyramb [×3]
Paean (*The dancers dance their Bacchanal*)
Recitative and Passion Aria II (*Punch ushers Choregos into bass viol case*)
Murder Ensemble III (*Punch bows a serenade on the bass viol*):
    Proclamation III, Couplets III, War Cry IV
Lament, Exorcism and Lullaby

score draft, the direction is added that during the Little Canonic Prelude to Disaster, which immediately precedes the start of Melodrama III, 'the characters and the action must remain frozen and on no account must the curtain be dropped'.[62] The decision was also taken to delay the single 'Gebrauchmusik' [*sic*] section until after the Morale (it was originally positioned after the Parody and Paraphrase section), and to repeat it three times at the head of each Coronation-Scene cycle. The idea that Punch should collect an instrument and later bang it over the head of Choregos was also added to the libretto draft. The final form is given in Figure 2.6.

Originally, the Preyer section ('Let the winds be gentle / Let the seas be calm') was spelt 'Prayer', but the spelling was altered by pen in the draft libretto. This was presumably to reflect the fact that the refrain is sung here, for the first time, by Punch who preys on Choregos. Finally, the section titles Proclamation, Couplets, War Cry and Resolve were also added.

The repeated 'Gebrauchmusik' [*sic*] sections and Coronation-Scenes allude directly to the Collier text and to *Pierrot*. Both of these texts deal with attitudes towards music, its role in society, and the association of noise with violence and murder. In the 'social' movement of Collier's text, Punch walks through the streets loudly ringing a hand bell. This prompts a servant to reprimand Punch on behalf of his master who objects to 'Dat nasty noise'. 'Do you call music a noise?' asks Punch, who then plays a word game with the servant. He claims that the bell is an organ, fiddle, drum, then trumpet: 'Do you like that music better than the other? – This is my bell, [Hits.] this my organ, [Hits.] this my fiddle, [Hits.] this my drum, [Hits.] and this my trumpet, [Hits.] there! a whole concert for you.'[63] Similarly, in *Pierrot lunaire*, Pierrot's scraping Serenade disturbs Cassander, who remonstrates

---

[62] PSS 0535-0399.

[63] John Payne Collier, *Punch and Judy, with Illustrations Drawn and Engraved by George Cruikshank*, 2nd edn (London: S. Prowett, 1828), 24.

with Pierrot to stop. In all three examples, musical instruments become weapons, and music becomes a means to control.[64]

On this subject, Jacques Attali has argued (following Adorno and René Girard) that music is a simulacrum of ritual murder. This argument is based on the belief that music, at its origin, constituted 'the collective memory' and that its principal function was to regulate society: it was integral to the day-to-day activities and rituals of society, which included pre-Christian sacrifice.[65] Music is therefore a vestige, or relic, of such events. In this sense, he argues, it is a simulacrum of murder. Choregos is actually murdered twice, for he returns later in the form of Jack Ketch. This underlines the representational, purely symbolic function of Choregos and the theme of ritual murder in the opera, which is the sense in which Attali uses the term *simulacrum*.

During the Coronation-Scenes, the singers play toy instruments. The result is a purposeless, child-like sonic disruption, which climaxes in a riotous Paean. These boisterous sections evoke the carnival, a form which, according to Mikhail Bakhtin, expresses 'the right to be free from all that is official and consecrated', and that is 'outside of and contrary to all existing forms of the coercive socioeconomic and political organization'.[66] The Paean is halted, however, when Judy gestures for the music and action to stop. This resonates with Attali's observation that '*noise is violence*: it disturbs'.[67] This disturbance creates a need for resolution, or the reassurance that order will be restored. Through history, Attali argues, music has channelled noise, first through sacrifice (that is, through its use in rituals), then through representation (whereby music is domesticated for a bourgeois audience), and finally through repetition (when music becomes a product for consumption). The juxtaposition of the carnivalesque Coronation-Scenes and Judy's gesture for them to stop may be compared to Attali's analysis of Pieter Brueghel the Elder's painting *Carnival's Quarrel with Lent*. In the painting, music is associated with the re-enactment of ritual sacrifice, staged by peasants in the

---

[64] Questions of musical taste and the idea of music as a weapon are topics visited elsewhere in the Collier text. For example, Scaramouch, Punch's first victim, enters with a stick that he claims is a fiddle. When Scaramouch's head is eventually knocked from his shoulders, Punch taunts: 'How you like that tune, my good friend? That sweet music, or sour music, eh?' Collier, *Punch and Judy*, 6.

[65] Attali, *Noise*, 30. As Douglas Collins points out, Attali, following Girard, returned to a discussion of 'the centrality of ritual sacrifice that had been opened during the 1930s by the members of "Le Collège de socologie," in particular George Bataille and Roger Caillois'. Collins, 'Ritual sacrifice and the political economy of music', *Perspectives of New Music*, 24/1 (Autumn–Winter 1985), 16.

[66] Mikhail Bakhtin, *Rabelais and His World* (Bloomington and Indianapolis: Indiana University Press, 1984), 257 and 255. Kramer's vibrant 2008 ENO production fully captured the carnivalesque aspect of *Punch*, with a brightly coloured set and costumes, and a mime troupe of mischievous Punches, which is not in the libretto.

[67] Attali, *Noise*, 26.

foreground of a carnival scene. Popular carnival elements, in the foreground and to the left-hand side of the painting, are juxtaposed against sacred acts, which occupy the opposite diagonal space. Music accompanies the pagan ritual in the foreground, but its absence from the sacred part of the painting symbolises Christianity's suppression of sacrifice. In the Christian world, music becomes domesticated.

For Attali, opera is a symbol of the domestication of music. Moreover, 'One or two decades after its invention', he argues, the musician was 'economically bound to a machine of power, political or commercial, which paid him a salary for creating what it needed to affirm its legitimacy.'[68] Clearly, the relationship between opera, patronage and domestication is more complex than Attali implies; in her 'Afterword' to the English translation of Attali's book, for example, Susan McClary points out that the plots of the earliest operas 'repeatedly involve the subversion of the inherited social hierarchy', while the style itself was based 'on the improvisatory practices of contemporary popular music'.[69] Nevertheless, Attali's view of opera reflects a discourse that held some sway in the twentieth century, as discussed in Chapter 1. His argument therefore raises the possibility that Punch's rejection of Choregos symbolises the rejection of opera as a potent symbol of social control.

This returns us to the moment when Judy stopped the noisy Coronation-Scene cycle and Paean. Judy's gesture creates a space in which she pleads for Choregos's life, and, in doing so, she invokes Gumbrecht's spatial notion of the production of presence discussed in Chapter 1. What follows is widely regarded to be the most beautiful moment in the opera: Judy's Da Capo Passion Aria.[70] The fact that this is the clearest moment of operatic parody in *Punch*, preceded by the only real example of recitative, adds weight to the idea that Choregos symbolises opera. In her Recitative, Judy begs the avenging Gods to witness 'My Choregos, in stringent suffering strung', while to Punch she pleads: 'Have mercy, Murderer! / Unstring your bow, which, like an arrow, pierces my heart.' The stylised text and baroque *Affekt* of the number does not undermine the function of Judy's Recitative or the charm of her Aria ('Be silent, strings of my heart'). Judy's request for silence is matched by the calm repose of her Aria, and in most productions she is spotlighted, centre stage, while the other characters freeze, or recede to darkened parts of the stage. (In the 2008 Music Theatre Wales production, a large stage curtain was draped beneath Judy to form a long flowing dress).

---

[68] Ibid., 17.   [69] McClary in Attali, *Noise*, 155.

[70] Hall describes Judy's Passion Aria as 'the most poignant moment' in the opera (*HB*, 65); Adlington refers to it as a prominent and 'beautiful' example of the lyrical side of *Punch* (*MHB*, 11); Cross describes it as 'one of the most beautifully lyrical numbers of the entire opera' ('Lines and circles', 218), but also as 'an aria in quotation marks, an aria "made strange"' (*HB: MMM*, 69–70).

At the very moment opera faces a death sentence, Birtwistle's music pleads convincingly for the defence. This situation resonates with Linda Hutcheon's argument that parody is not always at the expense of the parodied text.[71] Rather, she argues, parody 'is fundamentally double and divided; its ambivalence stems from the dual drives of conservative and revolutionary forces that are inherent in its nature as authorized transgression.'[72] Appropriately, in the context of Judy's Aria, Hutcheon observes that the etymological root of parody is the Greek word *parodia*, meaning 'counter-song'. However:

> *para* in Greek also means 'beside', and therefore there is a suggestion of an accord or intimacy instead of a contrast. It is this second, neglected meaning of the prefix that broadens the pragmatic scope of parody in a way most helpful to discussions of modern art forms[.][73]

The fact that the plea to save Choregos comes from Punch's wife supports the idea that, in this instance, the prefix *para* – 'beside' – is intended. True, Choregos, and by implication opera, is killed. But he is reborn, first in the Nightmare section (where he is masked), then as Jack Ketch, and finally as Choregos once more. 'Opera' is endlessly regenerated. Yet when the characters take their revenge on Punch in the Nightmare, the tone is highly ambivalent. For example, in the operatic Quartet, Pretty Polly sings of Punch: 'He's a wretch and a traitor, yet I want him still.'[74] Moreover, when revenge comes, in the Adding Song, the style is folk-like, rather than operatic.

This suggests that the 'dual drives of conservative and revolutionary forces' are fundamental to *Punch*. Hall observes that once Choregos is dead, Punch unconsciously realises that 'there is nothing for him to react against. He is impotent.'[75] This observation goes some way towards explaining Punch's strangely hollow admission of guilt – the only form of guilt he expresses in the opera – in the Lament that follows Choregos's death:

> O Gods, this vile disfigured sight
> Opens an abyss of agony in my soul.
> The ears throb, the taste sours,
> The eyes drown in a sunset of blood.
> The lights of the world go out
> And I am alone with the beating of wings.

---

[71] Linda Hutcheon, *A Theory of Parody: The Teachings of Twentieth-Century Art Forms* (Urbana and Chicago: University of Illinois Press, 2000), 6.

[72] Ibid., 26.   [73] Ibid., 32.

[74] This line in particular, and Polly's inexplicable devotion to Punch in general, are reminiscent of Anne Truelove's commitment to Tom Rakewell in Stravinsky's *The Rake's Progress*, in which Anne sings 'He loves me still'.

[75] Hall, *HB*, 16.

The score instructs that this text is to be delivered in a parlando style, without any change in contour (it is notated entirely on *b♭*), 'senza espressione'. In performance, however, effects have ranged from irony and emptiness to anguish.[76] Although the score suggests that no irony or genuine emotion is intended, the mismatch between the performance directions and the text creates a deliberate ambiguity. A similar situation occurs in the first two Morals, where Choregos's lines of sympathy for Punch are marked 'tenderly with expression', yet the accompaniment is regular and mechanical.

Such ambivalence serves as a reminder of Birtwistle's indifference to opera elsewhere in the work. As Adlington has remarked, *Punch*'s 'compulsive short-windedness' reflects the work's indifference to 'the larger continuities central to operatic tragedy from the middle of the nineteenth century to well into the twentieth'.[77] Rather, *Punch* is indebted to reassessments of opera by Stravinsky, Bartók and Schoenberg, especially their use of the grotesque to critically reinterpret genres that had 'become a cliché, or historically exhausted'.[78] *Punch* conforms to many of the accepted markers of the grotesque: it inhabits the margins or 'gap of ambivalence and ambiguity';[79] it conflates opposites (e.g. 'negative' and 'positive') and has a 'deeply paradoxical nature' (e.g. the pairing of pleasure and pain in the Couplets);[80] it implies the collision of different idioms and nouns (e.g. opera, ritual theatre, Passion), and 'the impossibility of finding a synonym';[81] it expresses the typically nineteenth-century grotesque themes of hybridisation and 'the agglomeration of a multitude of fragments';[82] it reduces human life to puppets and masks; it alludes to the dance of Death or *danse macabre* (e.g. Punch's Lullaby); and it involves the 'free play of comic and gruesome moments' by play with established musical protocols, and the projection of human emotional states, 'such as weeping, groaning and laughter' on to the music.[83] Moreover, the music is based on a concept – the Goat-Song system – that is coherent, unified and circular (the 'shape most ideal'), against

[76] An ironic interpretation is suggested by Stephen Roberts in the London Sinfonietta recording (Etcetera, KTC 2014), made in 1989. Gwion Thomas, however, delivered the lines without any emotion in the Music Theatre Wales production at the Linbury Studio in London, in 2008, while in the 1993 Netherlands Opera production Robert Poulton suggested fear and genuine regret.

[77] *MHB*, 11.

[78] Julie Brown, *Bartók and the Grotesque: Studies in Modernity, the Body and Contradiction in Music*. Royal Musical Association Monographs 16 (Aldershot: Ashgate, 2007), 136. This is a reference to Gabriele Beinhorn, *Das Groteske in der Musik: Arnold Schönberg's 'Pierrot lunaire'* (Pfaffenweiler: Centaurus-Verlagsgesellschaft, 1989).

[79] Geoffrey Galt Harpham, *On the Grotesque: Strategies of Contradiction in Art and Literature* (Princeton University Press, 1982), 8.

[80] Brown, *Bartók and the Grotesque*, 5.   [81] Harpham, *On the Grotesque*, 3.

[82] Liszt, cited in Brown, *Bartók and the Grotesque*, 31.

[83] Brown, *Bartók and the Grotesque*, 136.

which 'a civil war of attraction/repulsion' is enacted. Like many forms of the grotesque, therefore, *Punch* is marked by the co-presence of 'the normative, fully formed, "high" or ideal, and the abnormal, unformed, degenerate, "low" or material'.[84]

The grotesque elements in *Punch* also evoke the antithetical status of the antimasque. According to Julie Brown, the term *grotesque* was first used in England in 1639 with reference to characters in the antimasque section of a play, 'characters who were probably costumed in the manner of the French Harlequin'.[85] As Murray Lefkowitz explains: 'In contrast to the serious matter of the main masque (allegory, mythology, *deus ex machina*) the themes of the antimasques concentrated on mundane humour and the bizarre: the low-class comedy of beggars, cripples and drunkards, housewives and shopkeepers.'[86] Michael Nyman seemed to sense a link to such earlier theatrical traditions when he suggested that there are three alternating idioms in *Punch*: the violent, the lyrical, and the banal.[87] It should also be noted that the Punch and Judy show arose in England between 1760 and 1820 for 'audiences of the poor and exploited', in places, such as fairgrounds and carnivals, 'where popular culture was being reshaped and reinvigorated in a new, specifically working class image'. It was therefore aligned 'with the lower class experience of life'.[88] Moreover, Leach argues, there was a satirical dimension to the puppet show, which targeted the dominant class's attempts to control the poor through marriage, religion, the rule of law and hanging.

Finally, there is Punch himself. Few other characters in traditional mythology possess such impressive subversive credentials: his low status and belligerence; his existence beyond social conventions and his freedom from the need to conform; but also, as Leach remarks, his potential to 'evoke a specific kind of response – dangerous, pleasurable, anti-social and perhaps necessary'.[89] That Birtwistle realised this is demonstrated by his setting of Punch's first entrance. Punch's laughter – his grotesque tag, added by Birtwistle – marks his hybrid status (part shaman, court jester, clown, holy fool and shadow figure), while the limping waltz accompaniment, played at extreme ends of the orchestra's registers (in the double bass, double bassoon, violins and piccolo), evokes a wheezing breath and deformed appearance (the hooked nose, hunched back, bloated stomach, limp and squawking voice); see Example 2.16. Bodily degradation is suggested by 'alienated

84 Harpham, *On the Grotesque*, 9.   85 Brown, *Bartók and the Grotesque*, 7.
86 Murray Lefkowitz, 'Antimasque', in Stanley Sadie and John Tyrrell, eds., *The New Grove Dictionary of Music and Musicians*, 2nd edn, vol. I (London: Macmillan, 2001), 735.
87 Nyman, 'Harrison Birtwistle's "Punch and Judy"', 481.
88 Leach, *The Punch and Judy Show*, 32 and 29.   89 Ibid., 175.

Example 2.16 Punch's Lullaby, Melodrama I, VS, p. 5, bb. 54–8

CURTAIN UP (slow) revealing Punch moving to music round baby.

sounds that are at once "false" and comic',[90] which, in turn, implies the deformation of opera. Punch's laughter, like carnival laughter, is merry and triumphant, but also mocking and deriding: 'It asserts and denies, it buries and revives.'[91] The memorable tunes and folk-like elements in *Punch* also invoke the carnival, a medium that people have used for millennia 'to express their criticism, their deep distrust of official truth, and their highest hopes and aspirations'. Yet, like folk humour, in which 'Bare negation is completely alien,' Punch's laughter is ambivalent.[92] Moreover, the folk carnival posited the very social and ecclesiastical traditions that it sought to invert – as exemplified by the coronation trope depicted in *Punch*. As Hutcheon notes: 'The recognition of the inverted world still requires a knowledge of the world which it inverts and, in a sense, incorporates.'[93]

Attali argues that 'Noise only produces order if it can concentrate a new sacrificial crisis at a singular point, in a *catastrophe*, in order to transcend the old violence and recreate a system of differences on another level of organization.'[94] Arguably, that 'singular point' in *Punch* is the death of Choregos. Yet although the music and libretto provide signs of 'another level of organization', as symbolised by the shift from East and West to North and South winds, and a break from the earlier cycles of recurrence,

---

[90] Brown, *Bartók and the Grotesque*, 137.   [91] Bakhtin, *Rabelais*, 12.
[92] Ibid., 269, 12 and 11.   [93] Hutcheon, *Parody*, 74.   [94] Attali, *Noise*, 34.

the opera continues to balance criticism and ambivalence, on the one hand, with operatic gestures (such as the Love Duet), on the other. Ultimately, *Punch* may lack what Hutcheon refers to as a 'subversive edge', that is, a particular 'attitude or feeling', which is a defining feature of irony.[95] But this is because it adopts multiple attitudes towards opera, and those attitudes remain unresolved. Perhaps Britten disliked *Punch* because he felt that, like parody, it 'appeared to subvert the dignity of art'.[96] The evidence suggests that the subversive tendencies of *Punch* are indeed strong. However, such tendencies are balanced by ambivalence and ambiguities in Pruslin's claims for the work, in Birtwistle's musical elaboration of his underlying concepts, and in the opera's many allusions.

[95] Linda Hutcheon, *Irony's Edge: The Theory and Politics of Irony* (London: Routledge, 1995), 39.
[96] Hutcheon, *Parody*, 77.

3 *The Mask of Orpheus*: 'lyrical formalism', time and narrative

> I wanted to invent a formalism which does not rely on tradition in the way that *Punch and Judy*, my first opera, relied on tradition. There I used forms such as the chorale, toccata and gavotte. I injected them into my work just as Berg injected formal ideas into *Wozzeck*. In *The Mask of Orpheus*, I didn't want to hark back any more; I wanted to create a formal world that was utterly new.[1]

> All opera is Orpheus.[2]

Birtwistle's high-modernist ambition for his second opera, the three-act 'lyric tragedy' *The Mask of Orpheus*, was clearly stated. Difficulties in bringing *Orpheus* to the stage, and the many hours of labour invested in the work by Birtwistle, his librettist Peter Zinovieff,[3] and the electronic music composer Barry Anderson, all testify to *Orpheus*'s monumentality.[4] However, the

---

[1] Birtwistle, in Michael Hall, 'Composer and producer speak', in the programme booklet for the English National Opera premiere of *The Mask of Orpheus*, May 1986.

[2] Adorno, 'Bourgeois opera', 33.

[3] Peter Zinovieff worked with Birtwistle on a number of projects before *Orpheus* was finalised. In 1969, Zinovieff founded the Electronic Music Studios, London, in which capacity he collaborated with Birtwistle on *Four Interludes for a Tragedy*, the second version of *Linoi*, and *Medusa* (all 1969), *Signals* (1970), *The Offence* (a film score) and *Chronometer* (both 1972), and *Chanson de Geste* (1973). He also provided the text for *Nenia: the Death of Orpheus* (1970). It is clear from Zinovieff's diary entries in summer 1976 that he had begun work on the electronic music for *Orpheus*, but this was neither completed nor used in the final production. See http://sites.google.com/site/werdaviesrichard/p-zinovieff (accessed 31 August 2011).

[4] A detailed account of the opera's protracted commission history is given by Jonathan Cross (*Harrison Birtwistle: The Mask of Orpheus* (Aldershot: Ashgate, 2009), 33–8), but some details can be added. The opera was officially commissioned by John Tooley, general director of the Royal Opera House, Covent Garden, on 28 October 1969. In his letter to Birtwistle, stored at the Paul Sacher Stiftung, Tooley requested an opera for the 1972–3 season with conductor Colin Davis and director Peter Hall. Zinovieff was not the intended librettist. The letter states: 'The idea of collaboration with a major dramatist has already been put to you and I gather that you would be happy to go ahead with this.' This may refer to W. H. Auden who Birtwistle is reported to have met in 1968 but declined to work with. Birtwistle's initial proposal, with a libretto by an unnamed Greek librettist, was rejected by the Royal Opera in December 1969. He then planned an opera on the Chronos myth, working through 1970–1 on a project titled *Kronia*, the Greek word for 'time'. (Silas Birtwistle's collection includes a scenario for an opera on this subject, plus extracts from a libretto with a character named Kronia by another (unnamed) author, possibly Pruslin.) Meanwhile, an earlier commission to write an opera on Orpheus for the opening of London Weekend Television (LWT), with Hall as director and Pruslin as librettist, fell through (Pruslin's involvement is documented in the programme note to the premiere of Birtwistle's *Eight Lessons for Keyboards*, performed in the Purcell Room, London, on 13 January 1970, at which time the LWT Orpheus opera was clearly still a possibility). When Hall did not take up the role of co-director at Covent Garden in 1971, their commission lapsed. Undeterred, Birtwistle turned to the subject of Faust, which he worked on with Zinovieff. In the meantime Hall encouraged Glyndebourne to take up the commission and in May 1973 they agreed on an opera about Orpheus. This commission lapsed in June 1975,

idea that *Orpheus* would not rely on tradition was qualified by Birtwistle – it would not do so, he stated, 'in the way that' *Punch and Judy* had done. In other words, it would relate to tradition in other ways. As Birtwistle commented in 1975, 'I'm trying to take a fresh look at established musical forms, such as the recitative and aria, and see what new roles they can be made to accomplish.'[5] He continued that the distinction between recitative as the description of action and aria as a reflection on the moment is retained throughout the work but articulated in a new way: mime artists undertake physical actions, while singers express 'the poetics of the moment'.[6] Even Birtwistle's insistence on the creation of a new formal world was an Orphic rearward glance to the early seventeenth century, to the *Seconda pratica* and to the birth of opera itself.[7] The composer appeared to make this connection himself when, again in 1975, he remarked: 'When Monteverdi made that first musical statement about the theatre [*Orfeo* (1607)] he changed everything.'[8]

What follows is an examination of the relationship between the dramatic forms and themes of *Orpheus*, on the one hand, and Birtwistle's compositional processes, on the other. The chapter draws extensively on Birtwistle's musical sketches and related manuscripts, not least since there are more of these for this work than for any other he has composed: there are more than 2,000 sides.[9] These unpublished documents provide a unique opportunity to examine the composer's working methods in what is arguably his most ambitious and important work.

Central to both the libretto and the music is a highly formalist approach, yet the music often smoothes over the sectional divisions of the libretto to

however, owing to funding restraints. English National Opera then 'purchased' the opera in 1976 at a cost to the British Arts Council of £8,000; the intended director was Terry Hands. Yet by this time Birtwistle had agreed to other commitments (in addition to accepting new commissions he became Director of Music at the National Theatre in 1975). He did not resume the opera until 1981 when additional finance and a more realistic timetable for completion had been secured. The premiere ran for eight performances, from 21 May to 26 June 1986 (director David Freeman, designer Jocelyn Herbert). There were two semi-staged concert performances at the Royal Festival Hall on 11 and 12 April 1996 (director Stephen Langridge, designer Alison Chitty); the BBC broadcast of this production was subsequently released commercially by NMC Recordings (NMC D050). Act II was performed during the BBC 'Endless Parade' Birtwistle Festival at the Barbican on 10 January 1988, and at the BBC Proms on 14 August 2009.

5   Birtwistle in John Higgins, 'Harrison Birtwistle: the composer and the stage', *The Times*, 10 December 1975.
6   Birtwistle in Hall, 'Composer and producer speak'.
7   William Mann made a similar observation in his review of the premiere: 'Obwohl Birtwistles Partitur im Detail wenig Verbindung zu Mozart oder Verdi hat, knüpft es durch sie dennoch an die expressive Vokallinie von Monteverdis Helden.' *Opernwelt* 27/8 (August 1986), 47.
8   Birtwistle in Higgins, 'Harrison Birtwistle'.
9   In addition to fifteen folders of musical manuscripts, four folders of typescript relating to the libretto, and a complete fair copy of the score, held at the Paul Sacher Stiftung in Basle, there are around four hundred sides of musical sketches from the earliest stages of composition, owned, at the time of writing, by Silas Birtwistle.

build large, extended structures. The result is a tension between continuity and discontinuity that is comparable to Stravinsky's *Rite of Spring*. In this sense, *Orpheus* is a rejection of *Punch*, a clear move away from *Punch*'s breathless and impatient short-termism. Why this change of direction? It is possible that the stylistic shift reflects Birtwistle's increased awareness of the diegetic role of music in Wagner's operas following conversations with the theatre and opera director Peter Hall, with whom Birtwistle first discussed the idea of an Orpheus project. Birtwistle may also have been aware of recent trends in opera among his contemporaries, which reflect the avant-garde dilemma described in Chapter 1 – that is, the need to reconcile post-war interest in musical abstraction with the real world concerns and representational demands of opera. Davies's *Taverner* (1962–8; partly reconstructed 1970) and Henze's *The Bassarids* (1964–5), for example, develop through-composed textures in dialogue with formal archetypes: Davies incorporates aspects of the sixteenth-century fantasia and the mass, and both Davies and Henze work with symphonic form.[10]

Birtwistle may not have been motivated as strongly as Henze had been to break away from the perceived shackles of Darmstadt serialism, but he was nonetheless concerned that his opera would integrate graceful, rather than belligerent, song with formal innovation. This intention is captured in the phrase 'lyrical formalism', which appears in the margins of sketches for a work Birtwistle composed during a break in composition on *Orpheus*. This concept, which glosses the opera's subtitle 'lyric tragedy' (implying a tragedy that is more reflective and expressive than violent, epic, or heroic), underpins the opera as a whole and embodies two aspects that are central to the Orpheus myth. The first is song: Orpheus uses song to enter the Underworld, and his feelings, following the loss of Eurydice, are expressed through melancholic lament. The second is a dialectic between reason and intuition: Orpheus fails to restrain his instinctive urge to look back at Eurydice, despite the Oracle's warning that if he does so Eurydice will be lost to him forever. These ideas are combined to form a dialectic in *Orpheus* between formalist design and lyrical intent: the central second act, for example, is constructed from a series of seventeen song-like structures.[11]

---

[10] See Stephen Downes, 'Hans Werner Henze as post-Mahlerian: anachronism, freedom, and the erotics of intertextuality', *twentieth-century music*, 1/2 (2004), 179–207, and David Beard, '*Taverner*: an interpretation', in Nicholas Jones and Kenneth Gloag, eds., *Peter Maxwell Davies Studies* (Cambridge University Press, 2009), 79–105.

[11] This is comparable to Downes's description of Henze's *Bassarids*: structured as four symphonic movements (sonata, scherzo, slow movement – including fugue – and passacaglia finale), 'Henze wished to contrast his musical processes and structures with Wagnerian leitmotivic techniques and "endless melody": instead "there is the symphonic form", but "done in a very analytic, psychoanalytic way, with closed forms interpolated into it all the time".' Downes,

The concept of lyrical formalism will be discussed in more detail shortly, after certain general aspects of the opera have been outlined, but it is important to underline the dialectical nature of this concept, in which 'lyrical' suggests some kind of freedom, and 'formalism' denotes strictness. It therefore implies a dialectic between artificial form and structuralism, on the one hand, and freer creative processes or lyrical expression, on the other – in other words, a very modernist tension between 'expressive impulse and structural control'.[12] With this definition in mind, the bulk of the chapter is given over to a detailed examination of Birtwistle's compositional techniques and their relation to Zinovieff's libretto. This is followed by a concluding section in which some of the opera's principal issues and themes – namely, narrative, time and space – are interpreted in light of Jonathan Cross's suggestion that '*Orpheus* articulates the anxieties of a newly emerging post-industrial, post-imperial, post-modern age'.[13]

Useful overviews of *Orpheus* exist elsewhere.[14] However, certain key points will be outlined here in order to situate the more detailed observations that follow.

Context and scenario

Orpheus reflects the composer's interest in time, narrative and the exploration of myth. These topics are explored through the opera's central themes of language, memory, loss and love. Despite its surface complexity, *Orpheus* imparts a relatively straightforward narrative. The opening is concerned with the birth of Orpheus, language and music. Act I presents the wedding ceremony of Orpheus and Eurydice (scene 1), Eurydice's seduction by Aristaeus (scene 2), and Eurydice's funeral ceremony, followed by the Oracle's advice to Orpheus on how to rescue Eurydice from the Underworld (scene 3). In Act II, Orpheus dreams his descent to Hades, which is represented by a journey through seventeen arches. Act III is concerned with Orpheus's sacrificial death and his transformation into myth.

The resultant cycle of birth, loss and rebirth represents Orpheus's transition from human to hero to myth, an interpretation that reveals Zinovieff's debt to Ovid's *Metamorphoses*, although the libretto also draws on Virgil's

---

'Hans Werne Henze', 199 (the Henze quotation is from Paul Griffiths, 'Hans Werne Henze talks to Paul Griffiths', *Musical Times*, 115 (1974), 831).

[12] David Metzer, *Musical Modernism at the Turn of the Twenty-First Century* (Cambridge University Press, 2009), 171.

[13] Jonathan Cross, *The Mask of Orpheus*, 137.

[14] See 'Mask of Orpheus, The', in Stanley Sadie, ed., *The New Grove Dictionary of Opera*, vol. III (London: Macmillan, 1992), 249–51; Paul Griffiths, 'The twentieth century: 1945 to the present day', in Roger Parker, ed., *The Oxford History of Opera* (Oxford University Press, 1996), 231; Amanda Holden, ed., *The New Penguin Opera Guide* (London: Penguin Books, 2001), 86–7.

Georgics.[15] Parallel schemes are those of the ceremonies, arches, and tides: these topics characterise each act, respectively, although the ceremonies are also an important feature of Act III, and references are made to the arches in the outer acts. Such tripartite schemes pervade the opera, reflecting the importance of the number three in Orphic cosmology. This is exemplified by the triplicate presentation of the three main characters. In the libretto these are represented as Man/Woman (singer), Hero/Heroine (mime) and Myth (singer). In the score, the Man/Woman forms are described as singers (for example, O_s = Orpheus Singer), and the Myth forms as puppets (O_p = Orpheus Puppet). The latter are sung offstage by amplified singers. On stage, the Man/Woman singers wear half masks, and the Hero mime artists appear in full masks. At various times the central characters are also represented by dolls and large puppets with enormous masks. The other characters include three Women, three Furies, and three Priests. As in *Punch*, there are over 120 sections – or rather 'parts', as they are described in the libretto – arranged into 42 groups of three (for example: three Songs of Magic, three Duets of Love, and so on). Unlike *Punch*, however, not all the parts are musical (many relate to the mime action), and at times two or three may run concurrently. Nor is the arrangement always chronological; events from the past, present and future are reordered and repeated.

The opera's focus on multiple perspectives of events highlights the instability and variability of myth and memory – hence Orpheus's repeated refrain, 'I remember', which suggests the entire opera may be Orpheus's recollection of his own past.[16] As with other oral traditions, myths are retold. They therefore evolve into different versions and accrue new meanings. Consequently, the deaths of Orpheus and Eurydice are depicted in various contrasting versions throughout the opera. As in Greek tragedy, emphasis in the libretto is placed on the telling of the tale, rather than the narrative itself. Further complexity is added by the use of an invented Orphic language (in Act III), and electronic music realised at IRCAM by Barry Anderson in 1982–3.[17] Again, the principle of triplicate division is applied. There are

---

[15] The principal sources are: Books X (vv. 1–85) and XI (vv. 1–65) of Ovid's *Metamorphoses*, and Book IV (vv. 453–527) of Virgil's *Georgics*.

[16] Hall, *HB*, 117.

[17] Barry Anderson (1935–87) was a British composer, born in New Zealand. In 1979 he co-founded and became chair of the Electro-Acoustic Music Association of Great Britain. Anderson worked on the electronic music for *Orpheus* at IRCAM in Paris in 1981–2. Although he worked tirelessly to realise Birtwistle's ideas, the results are equally reflective of his own skills and invention in the studio, as discussed by Robert Samuels in 'The Mask of Orpheus', *Tempo*, 158 (1986), 41–4. This article draws on Anderson's sketches, which reveal the use of number matrices and permutational procedures, similar to those used by Birtwistle, to generate pitches and rhythms. In a BBC Radio 3 interview with Stephen Montague, broadcast in 1987, Birtwistle stated that he had prepared a 'complete score' of the electronic music, which Anderson realised. This score is owned by Silas Birtwistle, and for the most part it prescribes

three types of electronic music: drones, or Auras; vocal interjections by Apollo; music to accompany six mime interludes (three so-called Passing Clouds of Abandon and three Allegorical Flowers of Reason).[18]

The Auras are resonant sound spectra produced from a digital synthesiser. To some extent, these sounds substitute for the lack of a string section in the orchestra, although the wind instruments and percussion are also balanced by ensembles of plucked strings, including harp, mandolin and electric bass guitar, which evoke Orpheus's lyre. Apollo's vocal interjections are based on the invented language. They comprise formal commands, such as UI FÌ ('turn'), and 'lyrical' statements, such as RU FÌ ('love').[19] The sounds were created using the CHANT program, designed to recreate the human voice. Owing to difficulties producing consonant sounds, however, Apollo's voice is limited to a small number of phonemes; Birtwistle's ambitions for extended electronic vocalise were also abandoned as the results were deemed inappropriate.[20] The music for the mime interludes is the most complex, based on the spectral analysis of four harp sounds. The mimed interludes accompanied by the electronic music depict two kinds of story, both based on Ovid's account of the Orpheus myth. The Passing Clouds are associated with Dionysos, whose religion Orpheus opposed, whereas the Allegorical Flowers are related to Apollo, who instructed Orpheus in the art of music.

A sense that the music and libretto come together in the final act reflects the composer's formal, pre-compositional design, mentioned earlier.[21] However, there is also a corresponding shift in style that is attributed to a break in composition that occurred in the mid 1970s. Following remarks Birtwistle made to Hall, it was assumed that Act I and most of Act II were composed between autumn 1973 and spring 1975, at Swarthmore College in America, at New York State University, Buffalo, and on the remote Scottish island of Raasay.[22] However, the sketches reveal that Birtwistle actually began work on the opera in March 1973. It was previously believed that Act II, scene 3, and the whole of Act III were composed between autumn 1981 and summer 1983, mostly in Paris. However, there is evidence that

rhythms for the electronic music in some detail. Other extant sketches in Birtwistle's hand relate to the voice of Apollo, which mostly went unrealised, and skeletal scores that lack strictly notated rhythms or pitch, some of which appear in the final score. See also Nigel Osborne, 'Orpheus in Paris', in the programme booklet for the English National Opera premiere of *The Mask of Orpheus*, May 1986.

[18] The term Passing Clouds also appears in the sketches for *The Triumph of Time* (1971–2) to describe a recurring mobile; PSS 0538-0900 and 0538-0929–31.

[19] These statements are described as 'lyrical' in Barry Anderson's sketches.

[20] Samuels, 'The Mask of Orpheus', 43.   [21] Hall, *HB*, 145.

[22] Birtwistle reported to Hall that when he stopped work on the piece he 'hadn't quite finished the second act'; Hall, *HB*, 133. The sketches reveal that Birtwistle was in Swarthmore from September 1973 to May 1974.

parts of Act III were sketched as early as March 1974.[23] The sketches also shed further light on the break in composition, but the evidence is not conclusive.

David Freeman, the producer of the original production, memorably described *Orpheus* as 'a musical concept in search of a story line'.[24] The following section considers what that concept is, and why the Orpheus myth provided a suitable home.

Lyrical formalism

Lyricism and reason are key components in the Orphic myth: Orpheus works his magic through lyrical song and has an Apollonian desire for order. When Orpheus ignores the Oracle's advice and turns to look back at Eurydice he surrenders his reason to instinct with disastrous consequences. As Daniel Chua observes, 'Orpheus's voice works its magic only to lose the objects it desires'.[25] Birtwistle had intended to base his opera on Faust, another story in which reason is surrendered to intuition with the result, in Johann Spies's *Volksbuch* (1587), that the protagonist is torn apart. Both Orpheus and Faust are ambitious, aspiring individuals. They triumph in their quest for knowledge, but 'the man falters'.[26] Orpheus the poet-artist, like Faust, plays God and challenges death by his construction of language, music and an Orphic religion. Ultimately, Orpheus's body is dismembered and his oracle destroyed. Yet his song lives on, albeit in a further dialectical relationship between source and echo, eternity and decay.[27]

'Lyrical formalism' is an expression that appears in the sketches for *Melencolia I* (1976), for solo clarinet, harp and double string orchestra, one of the key *Orpheus*-related works composed immediately after Birtwistle suspended work on the opera.[28] The concept is not explained anywhere by the composer, and it is not mentioned specifically in the *Orpheus* sketches. Yet

---

[23] Sketches for *Orpheus* owned at the time of writing by Silas Birtwistle include a page titled '16.4.74. Act III Scene 2 Ceremony'; the page comprises workings on instrumentation and rhythm.

[24] David Freeman, cited in Patrick Carnegy, 'Mythopoeic decisions', *Times Educational Supplement*, 9 May 1986. Freeman had founded Opera Factory Sydney in 1973 and Opera Factory London in 1981.

[25] Daniel K. L. Chua, 'Untimely reflections on operatic echoes: how sound travels in Monteverdi's *Orfeo* and Beethoven's *Fidelio* with a short instrumental interlude', *Opera Quarterly*, 21/4 (Autumn 2005), 574.

[26] Andrew Porter, 'Another Orpheus sings', *New Yorker*, June 1986, 84.

[27] For example, Carolyn Abbate argues that Orpheus's song grows stronger, whereas Daniel Chua, following Adorno, argues for decay. Zinovieff's libretto describes the Exodos as a 'gradual decay'. Carolyn Abbate, *In Search of Opera* (Princeton University Press, 2001), 5–6; Daniel Chua, 'Untimely reflections', 579; Zinovieff, 'Explanatory document', PSS 0533-0117.

[28] Specifically, Birtwistle refers to 'Hard-edged lyrical formalism'. PSS 0534-0135; *Melencolia I.*

the association of lyrical formalism with the wistful solo clarinet melody in *Melencolia I* suggests that this is Birtwistle's way of describing lament, or lamentation, which is a topic that is central to *Orpheus*. As Cross has suggested, *Orpheus* is an allegory on loss, which is 'a key characteristic of melancholia first identified by Freud'.[29] The concept is therefore closely related to what David Metzer has termed 'modernist lament', in which the 'newest of sounds and an anarchic cry of sorrow' build a 'common ground'.[30]

Of particular relevance to *Orpheus*, Metzer notes that: 'To thrash in sorrow is not to lament. Intense feeling must be mediated through, become obedient to, prescribed means of expression, like a set formal structure or ritual pattern. It is only when the speaker subordinates his or her emotions to those means that a lament begins.'[31] There are strong parallels between this idea and Orpheus's lament in Act II and its division into seventeen sections. Metzer also argues that a 'strong conflict emerges' in the modernist lament 'between the force of personal expression and the fixity of the governing forms' to the extent that sounds may reach 'points of extravagant sonic metamorphosis', for example when song disintegrates into a wail. This actually happens towards the end of *Melencolia I* and in the second act of *Orpheus*.[32] Birtwistle's idea of lyrical formalism, therefore, implies intense expressions that are somehow in conflict with or restrained by regulating systems.

Other evidence suggests that Birtwistle's concept of lyrical formalism dates from the inception of his *Orpheus* project. For example, the opening of an abandoned version of *The Triumph of Time*, one of the opera's many satellite pieces, begun in 1970, is marked '*dolce* but cool'. This instruction relates to the start of an expansive melody passed between the soprano saxophone, horn and trumpet.[33] While working on a revised version of *The Triumph of Time* Birtwistle appeared in a television documentary on his music, broadcast in 1971. During a discussion of his childhood he referred to the town's 'encroachment' near his parents' farmstead as a 'rape of the landscape', yet also remarked that there was 'a terrific lyrical quality' about the altered scene.[34] Other evidence reveals the concept in Birtwistle's dramatic

[29] Cross, *Harrison Birtwistle: The Mask of Orpheus*, 142.

[30] David Metzer, 'Lament', in *Musical Modernism*, 145. Metzer explores laments in music since 1980, in particular by Ligeti, Kaija Saariaho, György Kurtág and Boulez. He suggests that the lament 'can be heard as part of the turn to a more directly expressive idiom that began [among modernists] in the 1980s' (162), although with Birtwistle it began at least a decade earlier in *The Triumph of Time*.

[31] Ibid., 146.

[32] In *Melencolia I* the clarinet's wailing occurs between letters S and T where it plays in the highest register 'as loud as possible' against extremely soft chords in the strings. Metzer notes that pedals or drones are traditionally present in musical laments, and these, too, are a feature of the final arch in Act II and the Songs of Magic in Act III of *Orpheus*.

[33] PSS 0538-0807; *The Triumph of Time*.

[34] Birtwistle in 'A couple of things about Harry', BBC broadcast in April 1971.

thought: one of the earliest conceptual sketches for *Orpheus* includes an abandoned idea that the opera should employ 'some sort of mimed percussion on stage', which would involve 'v. beautiful stylized gestures . . . (the[y] must not be percussion players but actors)'.[35]

A further aspect is suggested by Birtwistle's comment, made in 1983, concerning Piero della Francesca's *The Flagellation*: 'The lyricism, mystery and formalism it contains are qualities I've always wanted to emulate.'[36] Clearly, this raises the difficult question of how a painting may be considered lyrical. The painting's formalism is its architectural symmetry and linear perspective. Its mystery is the decision to place the subject (Christ's flagellation) in a covered courtyard in the background on the left, while an apparently unrelated group of three anonymous men, in earnest conversation, is situated outdoors in the foreground on the right. An ambiguity is therefore created between the painting's title and the picture's content. Birtwistle suggests that 'The essence of the painting lies beyond its subject. It's about something else.'[37] Yet importantly the ostensible subject is Christ's suffering. Intense personal feeling – the lyrical dimension – is therefore contained within, or restrained by, the painting's formal symmetries. For Birtwistle, therefore, the lyrical formalist 'essence' of *The Flagellation* lies in this tension between structure and emotion.

In *Orpheus* this tension results in a form of (de-)constructed song.[38] There is an historical precedent for this idea in Monteverdi's portrayal of Orfeo's agony and tragic loss. As Susan McClary has observed:

> in the laments [of *Orfeo*], it is Monteverdi rather than the orator who carefully constructs the signs of Orfeo's temporary insanity – the disorienting fluctuations in modal center, the rapid changes in rate of declamation, the discontinuous melodic lines, and so on. . . . now the gestures that once persuaded us have become unglued from their sustaining logic. He [Orfeo] can no longer assemble those shards and fragments rationally, and the illusion of secure reality his oratory had previously created is literally deconstructed before our ears.[39]

In Monteverdi's hands, Orfeo's laments seem instinctive and natural, yet they are carefully constructed and controlled by the composer. This

---

[35] PSS 0530-0592. A page in Silas Birtwistle's collection also refers to 'poetically exaggerated dumb sign language' for the Act I Love Duet.

[36] Birtwistle, cited in Hall, *HB*, 148.   [37] Ibid.

[38] Arnold Whittall similarly observes that one of the opera's 'most powerful effects is the sense it creates of song (with harp accompaniment) being deconstructed, in ways which cannot quite be "utterly new" . . . and which lend an ironic aura to its recurrent, spoken phrase, "I remember"'. Arnold Whittall, 'Orpheus – and after', *Musical Times*, 139 (Winter 1998), 55.

[39] Susan McClary, *Feminine Endings: Music, Gender, and Sexuality* (Minneapolis and London: University of Minnesota Press, 1991), 46.

situation is mirrored in *Orpheus*, in which the protagonist's efforts are directed, from the start, at preserving his memories in song, yet the libretto's broken syntax often militates against coherent lyrical expression. This is comparable to Cross's observation about Birtwistle's *Nenia: the Death of Orpheus* (1970), for solo soprano and small ensemble, in which 'the work becomes about itself, that is, it is about lament, about the materials of lament, about *performing* lament'.[40] Moreover, Zinovieff explains that his plot is concerned 'over and over again with the state of mind of Orpheus', but his highly unconventional libretto, which he describes as a 'graphic film script', is rigorously formalist: text, action, plot device, structure and character type are exhaustively detailed, tabulated and catalogued, with split-second timings for events.[41]

The musical sketches for *Orpheus* suggest a level of investment in pre-compositional plans and number schemes that far exceeds anything else Birtwistle has composed. Yet how closely do Birtwistle's schemes mirror Zinovieff's? Birtwistle has suggested that he invented a substructure in *Orpheus* that is 'not analogous with the text', that there is a musical level and a dramatic level 'and they don't start coming together until the last act'.[42] Adlington, however, argues that Birtwistle 'adheres only fitfully to the formal niceties of his libretto'.[43] By 'fighting shy of the extreme sectionality of the libretto' the music becomes more involved in the action and less ironically detached or concerned with 'the act of telling' than the composer would care to admit. Continuous musical textures 'maintain the unbroken theatrical spell' while Birtwistle 'frequently takes a stake in the raw drama of the narrative'.[44]

The concept of lyrical formalism is useful, in this respect, for it highlights Birtwistle's ability 'to think and feel beyond system', and the 'British love of paradox and compromise'.[45] What emerges from a study of Birtwistle's sketches for *Orpheus* is that systems and plans are important but they rarely survive intact. *Geometria* does not endure without access to the sketches. As Whittall argues, this is not to dismiss system, 'but to locate it in either superstructure or substructure: not – classically – in both'.[46] Another perspective is offered by Zinovieff, who remarked in an early version of the

---

[40] Cross, *Harrison Birtwistle: The Mask of Orpheus*, 24.
[41] Zinovieff, 'Explanatory document', PSS 0053-0028.
[42] Birtwistle, cited in Hall, *HB*, 145. Zinovieff had a slightly different conception: in his 'Explanatory document' he refers to music 'accompanying or punctuating the action' in Act I, and music 'more or less independent of the action' in Acts II and III. PSS 0533-0024.
[43] Adlington, *MHB*, 19.   [44] Ibid., 20.
[45] Whittall, 'Modernist aesthetics: some analytical perspectives', in James M. Baker, David W. Beach and Jonathan W. Bernard, eds., *Music Theory in Concept and Practice* (Rochester, NY: University of Rochester Press, 1997), 174.
[46] Ibid.

libretto that it is in 'the struggles, transformations and transitions *between* the levels [of the drama] that the originality of the Opera lies'.[47] However, a general distinction should be drawn between Zinovieff's tendency to construct systems and structures, on the one hand, and Birtwistle's tendency to dismantle and deconstruct them, on the other – although the important point here is that this requires Birtwistle to engage directly with the detail of Zinovieff's plans.

To consider this point in greater detail it is necessary to explore the work's genesis through the numerous extant manuscripts.

The extant manuscripts and early concepts

The musical sketches, early drafts of the libretto and other manuscripts for *Orpheus* are extensive. There are at least four main versions of the libretto, as summarised in Figure 3.1.[48]

The second of these documents offers some insight into Birtwistle's input into the drama. Many elements of the final version were in place in this version, such as the idea that the first two scenes of Act II would depict Orpheus's forward and return journeys, respectively. However, there was no mention of an arches structure, which raises the possibility that this was Birtwistle's idea. Rather, the act was divided into three distinct scenes. The emphasis in this version was on the obstacles that Orpheus (his back to the audience) would have to pass, such as the ferryman, Charon. Most of these obstacles are retained in the final version, with the exception of 'the terrible three-headed dog, Cerberus', which was replaced by the three Furies.[49] The curtain was to have fallen at the end of the second scene, with the sound of Eurydice's screams 'repeating and repeating' (in the final version, Arch 15 ends softly, the stage darkening after Orpheus's line 'The King stands highest').[50] In the third scene, Orpheus would try to persuade Charon to allow him to return to Hades (this was replaced by the sixteenth arch); refused permission, he would have lamented by the riverside, until deciding (as in Arch 17) to hang himself. In Act III scene 2, a key component,

---

[47] Zinovieff, Act I libretto, n.d., PSS 0533-0137. Italics added.

[48] The first document in Figure 3.1 is a simpler version of the final scenario, which notably includes a speaking Announcer who narrates the plot; for more on this see Cross, *Harrison Birtwistle: The Mask of Orpheus*, 32, fn. 69. The fourth document, which at the time of writing is held by Silas Birtwistle, comprises three pages of undated typescript (marked 1, 3 and 9). Two of the pages have pencil annotations by the composer; the pages are unbound but there are staple marks in the top left-hand corners. It is unclear when the final full title that appears here was adopted, but this document suggests it may have been earlier than previously assumed.

[49] Zinovieff, '"Orpheus": a lyric tragedy. An introductory document', unpublished document, 1973, 81–2. In one of his early conceptual sketches, Birtwistle noted Zinovieff's subsequent omission of Cerberus: 'The dogs are missing (my God!).' PSS 0530-0592.

[50] Ibid., 85.

Figure 3.1 Versions of the libretto

1   'Opera for the Village Hall', completed at 'Fearns, Isle of Raasay. New Year, 1972'. A *c.*60-page typescript held by Peter Zinovieff.

2   '"Orpheus": A Lyric Tragedy. An Introductory Document'. Dated 1973, with colour illustrations by Zinovieff's daughter, Sofka. At least four copies were made; one is held by Zinovieff and another by Universal Edition. This differs in important respects from subsequent versions, most notably in Act II.

3   Four volumes of an early libretto, titled 'Orpheus', stored in the Paul Sacher Stiftung (PSS 0533-0001–0636). These total 632 sides and comprise: (i) an 'Explanatory Document', dated 1974; (ii) libretto and scenario for Act I, undated, but likely to be 1974; libretto for Act II, dated September 1974 (contains a 'Graphic Scenario'); libretto for Act III, dated Easter 1975 (also with charts to show precise timings). The numbers of the parts in these libretti relate to most of those used in the final score.

4   Fragments of an undated typescript, titled *The Mask of Orpheus*, with text for Act I. This is most likely a document Birtwistle worked from in 1973–4.

5   A revised, 71-side libretto for the entire opera, dated 1978, but clearly edited and abridged for publication by Universal Edition in 1986. The part numbers in this version differ from earlier versions of the libretto, although there is some consistency with the final score for Act II scene 3, and more with Act III.

6   The original, unedited version of 5 (see above), dated 1978. This occupies 136 sides of a CD booklet that accompanies the NMC recording, published in 1997.

later omitted from the libretto, was Orpheus's instruction of men and young boys and a ceremony in which a masked woman would approach Orpheus three times asking him to marry her, 'but he rejects all women'.[51]

It is clear from the third document that both Birtwistle and Zinovieff were agreed on the central importance of asynchrony, that is, the principle that the music, text and action need not follow a one-to-one relationship.[52] (However, this principle is not explicitly stated in the second document, which suggests that it only fully crystallised at Birtwistle's behest.) As Zinovieff noted, 'something more than the orchestral score is needed if the most important principle of asynchrony is to be adhered to'.[53] Nevertheless, Zinovieff was open-minded about the feasibility of his stage directions, and many of his ideas were not realised in the original production. Some

[51] Ibid., 95. This sequence is not included in the final version.
[52] Zinovieff, 'Explanatory document', PSS 0533-0049. Here Zinovieff states that: 'Hitherto it has always been the case that the music, words and action are concommitent [*sic*], that they are interdependent at any one moment. In "Orpheus" this is not the case and there are times when the action must take place whatever the music … and, naturally, the reverse must also be the case. In an extreme example it should not matter to the visual aspects whether the orchestra got lost and became silent.'
[53] Ibid., PSS 0533-0026.

of the concepts are relatively straightforward, such as a moveable sun and vertical screens to symbolise the rivers. However, one of the more ambitious requirements is for a divided stage with a moveable rear portion that can be elevated and tilted, and this was not realised in the first production. Another challenge to producers is Zinovieff's eclecticism, which, at times, rivals Kagel's *Staatstheater* (1967–70). Amid the hieratic ceremonial scenes, for example, which evoke a pre-historic or non-Western rite, Zinovieff calls for a baroque-sounding 'Golden Carriage of Mirrors',[54] while the wedding ceremony in Act I is positively Wagnerian:

> One keeps looking for Hymen to the right, but he actually appears from above. An enormous spear in silver is first seen. It reaches right across the stage. Suddenly it can be made out to be a torch. It is smoking furiously, and attached to Hymen, who is represented as a large mask suspended on ropes and manipulated by the priests.[55]

Aspects of *Punch* are also recalled. During the wedding, the 'troupe of ceremony' takes out and arranges clothes and crowns, even opening 'a chest full of toys'.[56] (Although they have been overlooked by existing studies, childhood and the loss of innocence are important recurring themes in *Orpheus* that lend the opera an air of fragile vulnerability, in stark contrast to *Punch*). Zinovieff also calls for some kind of vehicle in which to enact the mime interludes; it was to be moved from one side of the stage to the other, either suspended from ropes or rolled on wheels. This was not realised in the original production, but it predicts the 'Place of Memory' in *Mrs Kong*, a transparent cube in which Vermeer paints Pearl's portrait (see Chapter 6).

Whether or not Birtwistle had anticipated the 'new type of opera document' that Zinovieff provided him with is unclear; certain indications suggest it came as a surprise.[57] To many composers, the libretto would surely seem overly prescriptive. On this subject, Birtwistle has remarked:

> In a way, the libretto seems so rigid, but the latitude for interpretation is also enormous. It has those two aspects to it. I see it as a kit. If you come to the score, and it starts with something, you follow it through, and then you go

---

[54] By contrast, Hall compares this to 'the *Flugwerk* used by the three boys in *The Magic Flute*'. Hall, *HB*, 121.

[55] Act I libretto, PSS 0533-0174. The original is italicised.   [56] PSS 0533-0175.

[57] PSS 0053-0026. A note in the possession of the composer's son, Silas, reveals Birtwistle's surprise at a 'production conception' for an opera that 'changes my all [*sic*] concept of writing the piece', and he asks whether 'the idea of the opera will always be in this form [?]'. This suggests that the note may have been written in response to receiving an early version of the libretto for the first act of *Orpheus*. Further evidence includes the following unidentified handwriting on the cover page of the undated libretto for Act I: 'When are we going to get Act II & is it going to be as extensively & exhaustively (exhaustingly) prescribed [?] as Act I?' PSS 0533-0128.

back to the libretto and you think, well, what's the subtext of this? What is this, what is this? A lot of it is strange, hieroglyphical – a smokescreen, if there is such a thing. It's Peter Zinovieff's way . . . But, in the end, it is what it is because of that way of thinking. It wouldn't be so fascinating if somebody had just done it normally.[58]

Clearly, the libretto acted as a stimulus to composition, rather than a hindrance, but Birtwistle did not feel compelled to follow it to the letter. To gain a more detailed appreciation of Birtwistle's relationship to the libretto's formal schemes it will be necessary to examine the musical sketches.

At the time of writing, 1,100 sides of musical sketches and drafts, 322 sides of Birtwistle's original fair copy, and over 600 sides that relate to the libretto are held in Basle. A substantial amount of additional material is also held by the composer's son, Silas. The early drafts and fair copy differ from the final score in several important respects. One such difference relates to the lead male vocal parts. According to the 'Explanatory Document', dated 1974, Orpheus's part was to be written for a high baritone and Aristaeus (called The Shadow) for a tenor.[59] Yet this was an alteration from the two earliest versions of the libretto, dated 1971 and 1973, in which Orpheus is listed as a tenor and Aristaeus as a baritone. Moreover, the sketches and fair copy for the first scene of Act I indicate that Birtwistle did begin to write Orpheus's part as a tenor, as his part is written in the treble clef. From Act I scene 3 onwards, however, Orpheus's lines were composed in the bass clef.[60] The explanation for this is that the performers Birtwistle was composing for changed: the original tenor role was written with either Robert Tear or Nicolai Gedda in mind; this changed to baritone when the lead role was likely to be given to either Thomas Allen or Benjamin Luxon.[61] Later still, Orpheus's bass clef lines were transposed into the tenor range, presumably when the title role passed to Philip Langridge.[62] This most likely did not happen until after 1983, since the alteration is not noted by Michael Hall. To summarise: Orpheus's part began as a tenor, changed to high baritone, then returned (in revised form) to tenor.

Michael Taylor has suggested that 'the [final] revision of the score and the libretto were presumably undertaken when the work was scheduled for

---

[58] Birtwistle in conversation with Beard on 18 November 2008.

[59] Orpheus is listed as high baritone and The Shadow as tenor in the 'Explanatory document' (PSS 0533-0007), in the 1978 version published in 1997, and in Birtwistle's fair copy.

[60] PSS 0532-0363.

[61] This is detailed in an ENO internal memo from Rosemarie Cave to Lord Harewood, dated 16 August 1976. Moreover, in a letter to ENO dated 18 August 1976, Birtwistle's agent, Andrew Rosner, states that according to Birtwistle the role of Orpheus is 'quite definitely' a baritone; ENO Archive.

[62] A revised fair copy in Birtwistle's hand is not extant; the final score is the work of more than one copyist.

performance in 1986',[63] although he suggests that only Acts I and II were overhauled.[64] Actually, the final score reveals that even in Act III the vocal parts of Aristaeus and Orpheus were altered: the newly transposed lines are written in a different hand to the other parts and pasted over the final score. (There is even a slip on pages 363–4, where Orpheus's original vocal part is mistakenly retained.) When he resumed composition after the break, Birtwistle had simply continued to compose the vocal parts as before, in the bass clef. Yet, as will be discussed later, the transpositions are not consistent (that is, the lines are not always transposed by the same interval), and several parts of Orpheus's line from Acts II and III were actually rewritten, presumably when the parts were transposed. The evidence suggests that Birtwistle broke off composition somewhere in Act II scene 2, but it is not possible to pinpoint the moment precisely. From Act III scene 2 onwards the fair copy becomes increasingly skeletal, with frequent instructions to the copyist to repeat sections from earlier in the opera. While this reflects the structural need for increased repetition in Act III, it may also indicate Birtwistle's preoccupation with the electronic music in 1981–3.

In the sketches and early drafts, the opening of the opera was rewritten several times, including Orpheus's vocal line. It is not uncommon for Birtwistle to rework the start of a piece, after which his compositional processes generally lead directly to the final score. In the original version of Act I, there was a wider range of 'exotic' sounds. In all early versions, the first act begins with four psalteries (a medieval zither with flat wooden sound box and strings played with a plectrum), and these were retained in the first fair copy alongside the Noh harp. Bamboo pipes were also used throughout the opening (these do not appear in the final score until pages 65–9);[65] the first fair copy even included an organ (from Fig. 13).[66] The text for Orpheus Puppet, which was to be spoken freely by an offstage singer, included lines that are not in the final version: '. . . Exhausted . . . We touched land at Thy[m]nias[?]. Tiphys' [. . .]. Exactly at day brea[k].'[67] Clearly, Birtwistle exercised discretion and either requested new text from Zinovieff (libretto version 2 supports this idea, as it has less text than the final version), or edited the text. Moreover, a comparison of the published versions of the libretto with the score for the opening scene reveals that

[63] Michael Taylor, 'Narrative and musical structures in *The Mask of Orpheus* and *Yan Tan Tethera*', in Hermann Danuser and Matthias Kassel, eds., *Musiktheater heute: Internationales Symposium der Paul Sacher Stiftung Basel 2001* (Mainz: Schott Musik International, 2003), 177.

[64] Taylor states: 'it may be surmised that Birtwistle amended a copy of the original score, rewriting Orpheus' music for tenor and "overhauling" . . . the parts of the opera that were almost ten years old [i.e. Act I and part of Act II] in the light of the recently completed third act'. Ibid., 177, fn. 7.

[65] PSS 0530-0902 and 0530-0906–22.   [66] PSS 0532-0244.

[67] PSS 0530-0967. The sketch pages for the opening are mouldy and hard to read in places.

Figure 3.2 The earliest dated sketch page. Transcribed from PSS 0530-0945.

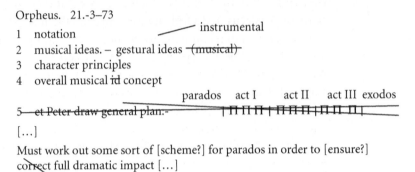

Orpheus.   21.-3–73

1   notation   ⟋ instrumental
2   musical ideas. – gestural ideas ~~(musical)~~
3   character principles
4   overall musical ~~id~~ concept
                                      parados   act I   act II   act III exodos
5   ~~et Peter draw general plan.~~
[…]
Must work out some sort of [scheme?] for parados in order to [ensure?]
correct full dramatic impact […]

Birtwistle took the text apart, reordering the lines for Orpheus Puppet and
breaking down those for Orpheus Singer into fragments and phonemes.
Although he became more interventionist from *Gawain* onwards, as will be
discussed in Chapter 5, it is clear from this evidence, and from Chapter 2,
on *Punch*, that Birtwistle has always exercised control over his libretti.

Further insight into Birtwistle's initial thoughts, and confirmation of
the date he began work on the opera, is provided by the sketch shown in
Figure 3.2. Of particular interest here is category 4, the 'overall musical
concept'. It is not clear what this was, but it is surprising that it comes so far
down the list, after 'musical ideas' (presumably a reference to the raw materials, such as pitch and rhythmic charts). The concern to devise an effective dramatic opening in the Parados was eventually overlooked; this section
is very short in the final version (Act I scene 1 begins on p. 2 of the score).[68]

Following this conceptual stage, Birtwistle marshalled his compositional
tools. Several hundred A4-size pages were filled with rhythms, pitch sets
(or 'modes'), and dynamic markings. These were then subjected to various
numerical reorderings and consulted at later stages in composition. Similar
tables, including whole series of pitch collections, were also prepared later in
the process, as and when they were required. As an early sketch makes clear,
it was Birtwistle's intention that some techniques would remain constant,
while others would be invented on the spot, to fit particular contexts.[69]
In other words, Birtwistle was already thinking in terms that Hall later
described as 'the sanctity of the context'.[70]

[68] All page number references in the main text of this chapter are to the final score, which was
      prepared by several copyists and reproduced by Universal Edition for the original production
      in 1986.
[69] On PSS 0530-0727, Birtwistle writes: 'al[l]ot certain procedures to specific areas[.] certain
      procedures in common'.
[70] Michael Hall, 'The sanctity of the context: Birtwistle's recent music', *Musical Times*, 129
      (January 1988), 14–16.

Figure 3.3 Act I, synopsis

Parados	The birth of pitch
Scene 1	Orpheus learns speech and song; he meets and marries Eurydice
Scene 2	Eurydice's seduction by Aristaeus; Eurydice's death
Scene 3	Eurydice is buried; Orpheus consults the Oracle on how to rescue Eurydice from the Underworld

What follows is a detailed examination of the compositional processes and their relationship to the libretto and the opera's dramatic themes. The discussion is not consistently chronological. However, it is intended that this approach will illuminate the dialectical relationship between drama and music, which lies at the heart of the opera.

Formal structures

From an aural perspective Acts I and II are relatively continuous, in contrast to the sectional libretto. The libretto's disjunctions only really become apparent in Act III, in which there is both a closer relationship between the music and the libretto, and a tension between relatively stable lines and disruptive vertical blocks.

Act I

Act I is ordered in terms of a basic linear trajectory, as summarised in Figure. 3.3.

For the most part, these events are arranged chronologically. Yet, at times, especially in scene 3, events becomes layered. The libretto and music are guided by a topical approach to narrative, as opposed to a synoptic approach – that is, the focus is on the overall dramatic mood or character of key narrative elements, rather than on their specific content. As Zinovieff comments (and Birtwistle underlines): 'it is with the mood and state of mind that the music is concerned'.[71] These *topoi* are alternated and revisited in verse–refrain patterns that are familiar from *Punch*, as illustrated in Table 3.1.

What for Adlington is an 'awkward, sprawling construction', with 'crude juxtapositions and mannered dramatic presentation', may be perceived, alternatively, as a regular see-sawing contrast, each dramatic topic (although not necessarily the parts) clearly marked by a change of voice, tempo, text, action or scenic device.[72] Further punctuation is provided by the mime

---

[71] Zinovieff, 'Explanatory document', PSS 0533-0107.   [72] Adlington, *MHB*, 20.

Table 3.1 *Act I, formal layout (chronological sequence is indicated by the rows, read from left to right, from the top of the page down; the columns indicate the cyclic structure)*

Parados	1st Orphic Hymn	1st Mystery			
Scene 1	1st Poem of Reminiscence	1st Mystery	**1st Duet of Love**	1st Passing Cloud	
			(cont.)		
	Wedding Ceremony 1st Exchange 'Answer!'	1st Complicated Question verse 1	short silence		**1st Love Duet Ext. 1**
	(cont.)				
	2nd Exchange	1st Complicated Question verse 2			**1st Love Duet Ext. 2**
	(cont.)	(cont.)			
	(cont.)		silence		
	3rd Exchange				**1st Love Duet Ext. 3**
	(cont.)	1st Complicated Question verse 3			
	(cont.)	verse 4	long silence (Apollo tape)		
					1st Song of Magic & 1st Immortal Dance

Scene 2	1st Cry of Memory	2nd Passing Cloud	1st Allegorical Flower	1st Look of Loneliness (Aristaeus Singer) verses 1–3				
	(cont.)							
	(fragment)			1st Look (verse 3: 'What memories. What tears…')				
Scene 3	1st Time Shift/ 1st Human Lie (Aristaeus puppet)	1st Whisper of Change	**Funeral Ceremony 1st Exchange** 'Answer!'	**1st Song of Failure** (Os aria)				
			(cont.) & (*)			1st Hysterical Aria (i)		(*) 2nd Immortal Dance
			(cont.)		2nd Complicated Question verse 1		**1st Love Duet Ext. 4**	
			(cont.)					
			2nd Exchange 'These coins…'		2nd Complicated Question verse 2	1st Hysterical Aria (ii)		2nd Immortal Dance

(cont.)

Table 3.1 (*cont.*)

+ orchestra divides

				1st Love Duet Ext. 5		**1st Spoken Argument** (Os recitative) +
(cont.)						
3rd Exchange 'Stars fall …' & (*)					(*) (cont.)	
		2nd Complicated Question verse 3	1st Hysterical Aria (iii)	**1st Love Duet Ext. 6**		
	2nd Statement of Reason +					
(cont.)			1st Hysterical Aria verse 2 (iv)			
	1st Magic Formula					
(cont.) 'Answer!'			1st Hysterical Aria (v)			
			1st Hysterical Aria (vi)			**1st Shout of Gratitude**

+

interludes and Apollo's commands, and space is made to highlight certain key dramatic events, such as Eurydice's unaccompanied marriage vow: 'I will'. A consideration of Act I in these terms highlights moments when Birtwistle chooses to ignore the divisions in Zinovieff's libretto, preferring instead to follow his own scheme. Yet there is also evidence that Birtwistle's music was conceived in direct relation to the action (for example, there are sketch pages headed 'beg[inn]ing of walk I', 'beginning walk II', and 'They make love').[73]

The three principal topics in Table 3.1 – the Duet of Love, the Ceremony Exchanges, and the arias and recitatives by Orpheus Singer (all marked in the table in bold) – structure the outer scenes in Act I. The opening Love Duet is divided in two and has nine further extensions: 1–3 occur during the wedding ceremony; 4–6 interrupt the funeral; 7–9 are woven into the 3rd Ceremony, in Act III.[74] The vocal lines for the duet sections in Act I were originally conceived as a continuous section, written across three A2-size pages.[75] The plan was subsequently divided up and redistributed, although there are numerous alterations and deviations (the resemblance is close enough in places to suggest that extensions 1–6 are drawn from the third page of the plan). The sketches consist of a line for Orpheus and another for Eurydice, each of which was subsequently divided in two. The vocal lines are based on two chromatic modes, with a span of interval 14 for Orpheus (from e to $f\sharp'$), and interval 18 for Eurydice (from d' to $g\sharp''$): both are symmetrical around pitch class B. Three- to seven-note selections were made for Eurydice and four- to six-note selections for Orpheus; each set corresponds to a complete utterance of one of the lovers' names, and each has at least one note in common with the opening set in Orpheus's line: F♯, G, A, B♭.[76] Similar selections generate the accompaniment. However, the accompaniment in extensions 4–6 and 7–9 was sketched later and generated by different systems.[77] Therefore, although the impression is created of a continuity that is fractured, this does not entirely reflect the way in which the music was constructed.

The Love Duet is the most conventionally lyrical material in the opera; when reviewing the first production, Robert Henderson described

[73] PSS 0531-0245, -0247 and -0251 respectively.

[74] This cut-and-paste approach was developed earlier in Birtwistle's instrumental piece *An Imaginary Landscape* (1971), in which five different types of material were sketched independently, as continuous drafts, then parsed and distributed through the piece. Aspects of this work were also based on the MUSYS computer program developed by Zinovieff. See Beard, 'An analysis and sketch study', 168–81; see also Adlington, *MHB*, 138–9.

[75] PSS 0531-0028–32.   [76] PSS 0531-0028–32. This early version is superseded by 0531-0036.

[77] The accompaniment in extensions 4–6 was determined by a process controlled by contours. PSS 0530-0785–6.

Eurydice's part in the duet as 'music of a ravishingly sensual vocal allure'.[78] Through a sustained aria, Birtwistle responds to Zinovieff's suggestion that Orpheus 'tries to preserve as a memory the static situation of loving Euridice';[79] hence, as Cross has observed, the melancholy failure of the voices to move beyond Orpheus's opening four-note set.[80] The duet consists of two vocal strands. One strand is melismatic song for the Orpheus and Eurydice singers, based on the names of the two lovers. The other consists of offstage, parlando statements by the Orpheus and Eurydice puppets, the text emphasising the pair's love through their remembrance of sights, sounds and touch.[81] The accompaniment is characterised by soft, high, sustained woodwind lines (at crotchet = c.56), with prominent piccolo, which was generated in a similar manner to the vocal parts: it comprises a series of four-note sets that alter very gradually.[82] As such, the music evokes the pathetic fallacy, whereby the lovers' states of mind are reflected in their surroundings.

The music for the wedding ceremony is a deliberate contrast. First announced by the distinctive sound of conch shells (later trombones), this has a faster tempo (crotchet = c.72), motoric rhythms in the percussion, and a stylised, declamatory text for male voices with formulaic statements, questions and answers. Zinovieff refers to 'the mysticism of primitive rites', and 'secret ritualistic dances' that 'together form one long ritual which is a sacrifice', or sacrificial murder. The wedding and funeral are 'rehearsals' for the final sacrifice in Act III, when Orpheus is torn apart.[83] The ritual nature of the exchanges, each of which is led by a Caller and three Priests, is underlined by Zinovieff's suggestion of a division into 'recitative–major aria–ceremony–silence–major song', concluding with a dance that 'takes place around the imaginary limbs of a horizontal tree of life'.[84] Strictly speaking, this is the portrayal of a ritual, rather than ritual itself. However, the libretto's scheme recalls the sectional analysis of rituals by structural anthropologists such as Lévi-Strauss.[85] Yet, at times, Birtwistle ignores Zinovieff's sectional

---

[78]   Robert Henderson, 'The Mask of Orpheus', *Daily Telegraph*, 23 May 1986.
[79]   Zinovieff, 'Explanatory document', PSS 0533-0183. The original text is italicised.
[80]   Cross, *The Mask of Orpheus*, 52.
[81]   The so-called 'puppet' forms of the central characters comprise off-stage singers combined with onstage mime artists. These roles are distinct from the use of actual puppets, masks and dolls, which constitute a third level of representation.
[82]   PSS 0531-0512–15.
[83]   Zinovieff, 'Explanatory document', PSS 0533-0110 and -0112, and Act I libretto, 0533-0198.
[84]   Peter Zinovieff, *The Mask of Orpheus: An Opera in Three Acts* (London: Universal Edition, 1986), UE 17683L, 46.
[85]   Victor Turner, for example, describes everyday rituals in pre-industrial societies in terms of 'the full sequence of stages[:] breach, crisis, redress, restoration of peace through reconciliation or mutual schism'; *From Ritual to Theatre: The Human Seriousness of Play* (New York: PAJ Publications, 1982), 111.

scheme. The start of the 1st Complicated Question (p. 25), for example, is not marked by a change of texture.

The duet and ceremony textures are absent from scene 2, which is focused instead on Aristaeus and the death of Eurydice and is mostly concerned with music and mime. In one mime Eurydice is raped, but in another she resists Aristaeus. Scene 3 continues the darker mood. The calming Love Duet persists but is undermined by new ceremony music that passes at the slow heartbeat pulse of crotchet=60; as Zinovieff remarks, 'Everything was slow and hushed,' each statement delivered 'in whispers'.[86] This clearly informed Birtwistle's approach; when setting the Caller's line 'Reach into darkness / While through these slits / Dark shadows', for example, Birtwistle wrote 'muffled drums?', followed by a sketch for four congo drums and temple blocks. A new, more frenzied topic is also introduced to represent the Oracle's wild pronouncements.

Birtwistle responded to Zinovieff's schemes by translating them into his own graphs and formal charts. For Act I scene 3 he prepared a chart that comprises three horizontal lines labelled, from the top down, 'Oracle', 'Orpheus Songs' and 'Ceremony'.[87] The most important musical events are then plotted on these lines. A fourth line at the bottom of the chart marked 'Journey', which relates to Eurydice's journey to the Underworld, is left empty. The absence of any attempt to map Eurydice's journey in music relates to the principle of asynchrony, whereby certain actions are not supported musically. Zinovieff requests that the stage should be divided into three separate areas, in which unrelated dramas are enacted:

- lower stage front: Eurydice's transformation from human to puppet to symbolise her journey to the Underworld (enacted in the Golden Carriage of Mirrors);
- upper stage left (raked): the funeral ceremony, where Eurydice's death is also re-enacted;
- upper stage right: the Oracle and the entrance to the Underworld.

Orpheus, on the upper stage, 'unconsciously' follows the carriage, which leads him from the funeral to the Oracle.[88] Both he and the carriage weave back and forth several times. Orpheus's songs are therefore the 'binding' layer. Moreover, Zinovieff suggests that the 'dialogue of recitative and aria' between each of Orpheus's sections expresses the 'struggle between life and death'.[89]

---

[86] Act I libretto, PSS 0533-0262 and -0269. Original text italicised.
[87] PSS 0531-0360.   [88] PSS 0533-0265.   [89] PSS 0533-0269.

Figure 3.4 The internal structure of the arches

Orpheus's journey recalls Punch's Travel Music. In Act II, for example, Orpheus journeys from the land of the living in the east to the land of the dead in the west. The emphasis, however, is on Orpheus's physical senses, as illustrated by the 2nd Statement of Reason (Act I scene 3, pp. 114–15):

> I see the sky line clear.
> I hear the battering of the horizon.
> I feel the air from the melting north.
> North is my freedom.[90]

According to the libretto, North is the past, South the future.[91] In other words, Orpheus believes that 'freedom' exists in his past, in his memories of Eurydice, rather than in his life without her.

Act II

> The echo's objectification of the voice turns it into a dead object. As Orphic detritus, the echo is both a dream and a nightmare.[92]

The idea that there is no escape from the labyrinth for Orpheus, that any sense of teleological journeying is actually a constant return to the centre of a maze, is most clearly expressed by the arches structure in Act II. Although we witness Orpheus's journey to the Underworld, the arches represent Orpheus's dream of a journey, which leads only to his despair and, ultimately, suicide.

Zinovieff's plan for the arches structure is the most prescriptive in the opera, with precise durations for the subdivisions of each arch. There are four stages to each arch: fact (aria); fantasy (recitative); distortion (speech); awakening. In Birtwistle's setting, the final stage is usually marked by a pause or held notes, so effectively there are three sections. Over this scheme, Zinovieff imposes another layer comprising dream and nightmare, which overlap at the fantasy. The relationship between these schemes is summarised in Figure 3.4.

---

[90] The word 'North' in this line is an alteration from the libretto, which reads: 'It is my freedom.'
[91] Zinovieff, *The Mask of Orpheus*, 49.   [92] Chua, 'Untimely reflections', 577.

In Arch 1, Zinovieff presents the durations (in minutes and seconds) as follows:

Dream = 2′20
fantasy = 0′14
Nightmare = 0′30
Total duration of Arch 1 = 2′36

To calculate the duration of the fact portion, it is necessary to deduct the fantasy from the Dream, i.e. 2′20 – 0′14 = 2′06. Similarly, to calculate the length of the distortion, the fantasy portion must be deducted from the Nightmare, i.e. 0′30 – 0′14 = 0′16. The total duration of the arch is therefore fact 2′06 + fantasy 0′14 + distortion 0′16 = 2′36. As the arch structure progresses, Orpheus's journey is one of decreasing fact and increasing distortion. This process culminates in Arch 15, in which the fact portion is reduced to 0′01 and the distortion increased to 1′47. The fantasy portions follow a different scheme. These expand from 0′14, at the start, to 0′48 in Arch 10, then decrease to 0′06 in Arch 15. By contrast, the fantasy portions in Arches 16 and 17 are the longest in the entire structure. The total duration of each arch decreases by three seconds absolutely regularly, from 2′36 in Arch 1 to 1′48 in Arch 17. This foreshortening of the arches clearly contributes to a sense of direction towards the musical and dramatic climaxes, which occur across Arches 14 and 15, when Orpheus awakens from his dream – an idea that symbolises the moment that he turns. After this, however, in Act II scene 3, the mood shifts to a sense of resignation. The turn is therefore not marked by a sudden and dramatic reversal. Rather, it represents the culmination of a long-range musical process that, once it climaxes, is followed by a gradual decline.

When he came to set Zinovieff's scheme, Birtwistle initially separated the Dream portion, including the fantasy, from the final distortion (i.e. the Nightmare minus the fantasy). He then prepared his own graph for the Dream section, which he labelled 'continuum of dream'. This is shown on Plate 3.1. The graph has a total duration of 24′15, and is written to scale (3 cm = 1 minute, and 1 mm = 2 seconds). The seventeen durations of the Dream section appear along the middle line; clearly legible, they were most likely written first:

2′20, 2′15, 2′08, 2′00, 1′54, **1′45** [1′46], 1′39, **1′32** [1′30], 1′22, 1′12, 1′03, **0′52** [0′53], 0′41, 0′25, 0′07, 1′29, 1′38

Three of the durations, marked in bold, differ marginally from the durations in the libretto (the correct sums are given in square brackets). The fact and fantasy portions are marked on the line above these numbers, marked 'A'

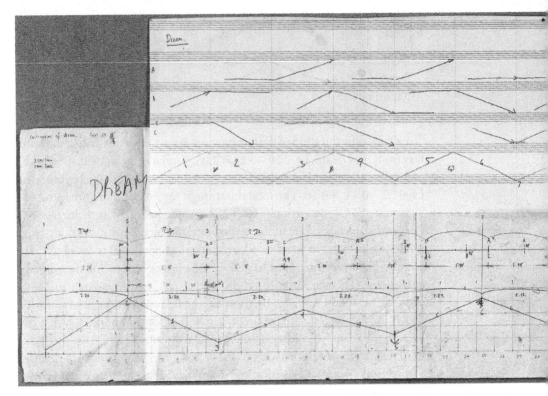

Plate 3.1 Graph for the Dream section, labelled 'continuum of dream', *The Mask of Orpheus*, Act II. PSS, Sammlung Harrison Birtwistle, *The Mask of Orpheus*, folder 18, skizzen H

and 'B', respectively; 'C' presumably refers to the distortion sections, which were sketched separately. Beneath this line, a different series of durations is written, as follows:

2′20, 2′30, 2′22, 2′28, 2′27, 2′12, 2′06, 2′16, 1′30, 2′28, 1′36

These eleven durations, which are generally longer than Zinovieff's (most are over 2 minutes; none fall below 1′30), clearly correspond to the diagonal lines marked '1' to '11', plotted on the grid in the lowest part of the graph. Evidently devised to contravene Zinovieff's plan, Birtwistle's durations relate to a separate rhythmic scheme that will be discussed later.[93] A similar principle is applied to the distortion sections. The important point to note at this stage is Birtwistle's allegiance to the libretto, on the one hand, but his

[93] Silas Birtwistle's collection reveals that a different version of this scheme was also sketched, as follows: 2′00, 2′17, 2′09, 1′58, 1′28, 1′54, 1′55, 3′18, 3′09, 1′57, 1′26.

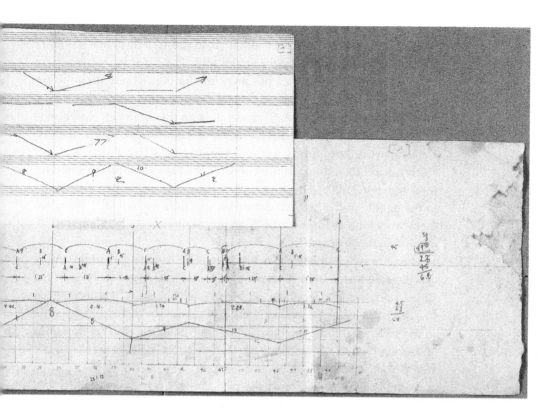

desire to overlay it, on the other.[94] Birtwistle clearly adds his own dimension
to the 'invented substructure', the 'completely artificial' musical design,
referred to earlier. As such, *Orpheus* represents a transitional stage between
Birtwistle's practice in the sectional works of the 1960s – when he felt his
duty was 'to stick to the initial idea. Within that mould I made my jelly' –
and his later belief in the sanctity of the context.[95]

Taylor states that the sketch for the distortion section 'for all seventeen
arches was planned as a single sequence, then cut into seventeen parts. A
similar process was used for the fact/fantasy sections.'[96] There is more to
add to this description. The Dream sections (i.e. fact and fantasy) were
indeed written out continuously.[97] The second number scheme was then

---

[94] This interest in layered durational schemes was explored further by Birtwistle in *Carmen
Arcadiae Mechanicae Perpetuum* (1977) and . . . *agm* . . . (1978–9). See Beard, '"From the
mechanical to the magical": Birtwistle's pre-compositional plan for *Carmen Arcadiae
Mechanicae Perpetuum*', *Mitteilungen der Paul Sacher Stiftung*, 14 (April 2001), 29–33.

[95] Birtwistle, cited in Hall, *HB*, 145.   [96] Taylor, 'Narrative and musical structures', 179.

[97] Birtwistle's A2-size sketches are divided into twelve equal columns. In the sketches for the
arches there are four crotchet beats in each column, therefore a maximum 48 crotchet beats
per page.

counted continuously from the beginning of Arch 1, resulting in additional divisions within certain arches – although, in practice, Birtwistle was more faithful to Zinovieff's scheme than to his own. The distortion sections were conceived as Taylor describes, but Birtwistle introduced seventeen further divisions. For example, in the middle of the distortion section in Arch 3, Birtwistle writes the number '2' in a circle, with the comment 'New Beginning' (i.e., this marks the start of the second duration in Birtwistle's scheme). Here, Birtwistle introduces a tempo change to crotchet=120. This is appreciably quicker than the previous tempo of crotchet=90, although a smooth transition is guaranteed by the ratio 4:3. The same tempo alteration occurs in the middle of the Arch 10 distortion, this time marked '8'.[98] There are even two tempo changes in the distortion section of Arch 12, marked '9' and '10' in the sketches.[99]

The various durational schemes relate to other parameters besides tempo, as will be discussed later. What should be established first, however, is the degree of correspondence between plan, sketch and score. This is revealed by Table 3.2, which lists Zinovieff's timings followed by Birtwistle's response in the sketches and the final score. The table notes the crotchet durations and tempi used to 'fill' the timings; when the score matches the sketch it is recorded as 'score = sketch'.

In his realisation of Zinovieff's plan and his own scheme, Birtwistle introduced further subdivisions, usually marked by changes of tempo. These culminate in a total of seven tempo changes in the score for the distortion in Arch 15. However, the overall timings of the fact, fantasy and distortion sections are remarkably faithful to Zinovieff's scheme. The few deviations are most likely errors, either of a copyist, or of Birtwistle himself. One alteration, noted by Taylor, occurs in the fantasy portion of Arch 1. Here the durations are tripled from nine crotchets in the sketch to 27 crotchets in the score. Evidence in the unpublished first draft, however, suggests that Birtwistle had intended to introduce a compensating change in tempo to crotchet=120, which would have resulted in the required timing of fourteen seconds, yet this indication is missing from the final score.[100]

Similarly, in Arch 8, evidence indicates that the tempo markings in the score are incorrect: to realise the required timings in the fact and fantasy portions, the tempo in the sketches is crotchet=60, not 120 as given in the score, which reduces these sections to half their intended length.

---

[98] PSS 0531-0619 and -0647, which relate to pages 155 and 196 of the final score respectively.
[99] PSS 0531-0654–5.
[100] Next to the 'crotchet = 120' indication above Charon's part is an arrow that points upwards to the main ensemble. PSS 0532-0461.

Table 3.2 *Zinovieff's scheme for the arches*

All beats are crotchets; decimals of 0.5 and above are rounded up to 1.

Act II, scene 1

Arch 1 [PSS 0531-0580–81]
Fact
libretto **2′06**; sketch 84 @ 40 = **2′06**; score = sketch
Fantasy
lib. **0′14**; sketch 9 @ 40 = **0′14**; score 26 @ 40 = 0′39 [or 26 @ 120 = 0′13] plus 2 @
90 = 0′01 = **0′40** [result of probable copyist error]
Distortion
lib. **0′16**; sketch 24 @ 90 = **0′16**; score = sketch

Arch 2 [0531-0584–87]
Fact
lib. **1′54**; sketch 76 @ 40 = **1′54**; score 75 @ 40 = **1′53**
Fantasy
lib. **0′21**; sketch 14 @ 40 = **0′21**; score 28 @ 80 = **0′21**
Distortion
lib. **0′18**; sketch 27 @ 90 = **0′18**; score = sketch

Arch 3 [0531-0588–90]
Fact
lib. **1′42**; sketch 10 @ 90 + 70 @ 45 = **1′40** + **pause**; score = sketch
Fantasy
lib. **0′26**; sketch 15 @ 45 = **0′20**; score 30 @ 90 = **0′20** + **pause**
Distortion
lib. **0′22**; sketch 53 @ 120 = **0′27**; score 16 @ 90 + 23 @ 120 = **0′23**

Arch 4 [0531-0592–6]
Fact
lib. **1′30**; sketch 67 @ 45 = **1′30**; score 64.5 @ 45 = **1′26** + **pause**
Fantasy
lib. **0′30**; sketch 22.5 @ 45 = **0′30**; score = sketch
Distortion
lib. **0′27**; sketch 39 @ 90 = **0′26**; 53 @ 120 = **0′27**

Arch 5 [0531-0597–99]
Fact
lib. **1′20**; sketch 43 @ 45 + 23 @ 60 = **1′20**; score = sketch
Fantasy
lib. **0′34**; sketch 34 @ 60 = **0′34**; score = sketch
Distortion
lib. **0′30**; sketch 20 @ 120 + 30 @ 90 = total **of 0′30**; score = sketch

(*cont.*)

Table 3.2 (*cont.*)

Arch 6 [0531-0601–02]

Fact
lib. **1′10**; sketch 70 @ 60 = **1′10**; score 72 @ 60 = **1′12**

Fantasy
lib. **0′36**; sketch 36 @ 60 = **0′36**; score 32 @ 60 = **0′32**

Distortion
lib. **0′35**; sketch 36 @ 90 + 22 @ 120 = **0′35**; score = sketch

Arch 7 [0531-0605–07]

Fact
lib. **1′00**; sketch 45 @ 60 = **0′45** [45 @ 45 = **1′00**, so likely to be a mistake]; score
44 @ 60 = **0′44**

Fantasy
lib. **0′39**; sketch 39 @ 60 = **0′39**; score 40 @ 60 = **0′40**

Distortion
lib. **0′39**; sketch 77 @ 120 = **0′39**; score 80 @ 120 = **0′40**

Arch 8 [0531-0609]

Fact
lib. **0′50**; sketch 48 @ 60 = **0′48**; score 48 @ ? [unclear as no tempo marking; the
prevailing tempo is 120 = 0′24]

Fantasy
lib. **0′40**; sketch 40 @ 60 = **0′40**; score 40 @ ? [as above; the prevailing tempo is
120 = 0′20]

Distortion
lib. **0′45**; sketch 68 @ 90 = **0′46**; score = sketch

Arch 9 [0153-0613]

Fact
lib. **0′41**; sketch 41 @ 60 = **0′41**; score = sketch

Fantasy
lib. **0′42**; sketch 39 @ 60 = **0′39**; score *c.* 40 @ 60 = **0′40 + pause**

Distortion
lib. **0′50**; sketch 74 @ 120 + 20 @ 90 = **0′50**; score = sketch

Act II, scene 2

Arch 10 [0153-0643]

Fact
lib. **0′08**; sketch 6 @ 45 = **0′08**; score = sketch

Fantasy
lib. **0′33**; sketch 15 @ 45 + 14 @ 60 = **0′34**; score = sketch

Distortion
lib. **1′19**; sketch [page missing] extant 12 @ 45 + 14 @ 60 + 9 @ 90 + 54 @ 90 =
1′12; score 88 @ 120 + 54 @ 90 + 3 @ 60 = **1′23**

Table 3.2 (*cont.*)

Arch 11 [0153-0649]
Fact
lib. **0′18**; sketch 13 @ 45 = **0′17**; score = sketch
Fantasy
lib. **0′45**; sketch 34 @ 45 = **0′45**; score = sketch
Distortion
lib. **0′63**; sketch 32 @ 120 + 57 @ 90 + 15 @ 120 = **0′62**; score 32 @ 120 +
57 @ 90 + 18 @ 120 = **0′63**

Arch 12 [0153-0657]
Fact
lib. **0′13**; sketch 10 @ 45 = **0′13**; score = sketch
Fantasy
lib. **0′40**; sketch 29 @ 45 = **0′39**; score = sketch
Distortion
lib. **1′10**; sketch 68 @ 120 + 53 @ 90 = **1′10**; score = sketch

Arch 13 [0153-0665]
Fact
lib. **0′24**; sketch 18 @ 45 = **0′24**; score = sketch
Fantasy
lib. **0′48**; sketch 36 @ 45 = **0′48**; score = sketch
Distortion
lib. **0′57**; sketch extant 40 @ 90 + 54; @ 120 = **0′54**; score 40 @ 90 + 56 @ 120 =
0′55 + pause

Arch 14 [0153-0673]
Fact
lib. **0′04**; sketch 4 @ 60 = **0′04**; score = sketch [except quaver = 120]
Fantasy
lib. **0′21**; sketch 21 @ 60 = **0′21**; score = sketch [except quaver = 120]
Distortion
lib. **1′32**; sketch [page missing] extant 97 @ 90 = **1′05**; score 29 @ 90 + 70 @ 120
+ 56 @ 90 = **1′32**

Arch 15 [0153-0679]
Fact
lib. **0′01**; sketch 1 @ 60 = **0′01**; score = sketch
Fantasy
lib. **0′06**; sketch 6 @ 60 = **0′06** [cut off and taped onto the start of the distortion
section]; score = sketch
Distortion
lib. **1′47**; sketch 45.5 @ 90 + 120 @ 120 + 18 @ 90 = **1′43**; score 47 @ 90 + 12 @
120 + 5 @ 90 + 9 @ 120 + 5 @ 90 + 76 @ 120 + 33 @ 90 = **1′48 + 0′04 pause**

(*cont.*)

Table 3.2 (*cont.*)

Act II, scene 3

Arch 16 [0531-0711]
Fact
lib. **0′21**; sketch 21 @ 60 = **0′21**; score = sketch
Fantasy
lib. **1′08**; sketch 68 @ 60 = **1′08**; score = sketch
Distortion
lib. **0′22**; sketch 33 @ 90 = **0′22** [numerous alterations, e.g 'end arch 15' in two locations and 'start arch 16', suggest that Birtwistle picked up here after the break in composition]; score 38 @ 90 = **0′25**

Arch 17 [0531-0715]
Fact
lib **0′19**; sketch 19 @ 60 = **0′19**; score 13 @ 40 = **0′20**
Fantasy
lib **1′19**; sketch 21 @ 60 = 0′21 + 20 @ 45 = 0′27 + 17 @ 40 = 0′26 = **1′14**; score 55 @ 40 = 1′23 + 26 @ 63 = 0′25 + *c*. 3 @ 72 = 0′02 + *c*. 6 @ 40 = 0′09 = *c*. **1′59**
Distortion
lib **0′10**; sketch 28 @ 90 = 0′19 + 15 @ 90 = 0′11 = **0′30**; score 22 @ 60 = 0′22 + 8 @ 40 = 0′12 = **0′34**

However, an alteration to the fact portion in Arch 7 is clearly attributable to Birtwistle. The timing required is 1 minute, which is possible with 45 crotchets at crotchet=45, but in the sketch Birtwistle chooses crotchet=60 instead. Birtwistle's only other substantial alteration is to the fantasy and distortion sections in Arch 17. The former is almost doubled and the latter is tripled in length, both in the sketches and the score, which was most likely Birtwistle's response to the need for an extended cadential gesture at this moment. The sketches from the start of Act II scene 3 reveal a number of less characteristic alterations, as Birtwistle changes his mind about where Arch 15 should end and 16 begin. The implication is that he restarted work on the opera around this point, after the break in composition.

The ramifications of the durational schemes in Act II will be considered in more detail later in the chapter. This discussion will conclude, however, with an examination of the structure of Act III.

Act III

Act III returns to the principle of cyclic return, or varied repetition, encountered in Act I. This is summarised in Table 3.3. According to Zinovieff, Act III is underpinned by a series of rising and falling tides:

Table 3.3 *Formal layout of Act III*

Scene 1, Oracle

Responses

3rd Time-shift
3rd Whisper of
Change (copied
from Acts I & II)

Oc. 1   FISHING NET

Scene 2, Lesson

		Sequence 1:	**Sequence 2:**	**Sequence 3:**	**Sequence 4:**	**Sequence 5:** The journey and metamorphosis of Orpheus's head	**Sequence 6:** Orpheus's head is silenced by Apollo	**Transitions:** Orpheus's 3rd Song of Magic
		Eurydice's death	Orpheus's death by suicide	Orpheus's death by thunderbolt	Orpheus's death by sacrifice			
				1st Recitative of Teaching / Aria of Prophecy/ Sentence of Religion / 3rd Terrible Death by Thunderbolt				
					3rd Ceremony, 1st Exchange / 3rd Immortal Dance (*) (recalls Act I Ceremonies)			
					3rd Allegorical Flower of Reason			
2	(*) recalls the 3rd Time-shift BIRD SKULL							

(*cont.*)

Scene 1, Oracle

	Responses					
3	BIRD SKULL				3rd Ceremony, 2nd Exchange (*) (repeat)	
4	FISHING NET			2nd Recitative of Teaching, etc. (repeat)		
5	OAR		3rd Dream of Fulfilment (recalls the cantus/continuum texture in Act II, Arch 17)			
6	FOSSIL SHELL	1st Cry of Memory 'The Yawn' (copied from Act I)				3rd Song of Magic 3 lines (incl. verse 4, line 1)

Scene 3, Sacrifice

7	FOSSIL SHELL	1st Cry of Memory (repeat)				3rd Song of Magic 6 lines (incl. verse 3, lines 1–2)
8	OAR		3rd Spoken Argument (a variant of the 3rd Dream of Fulfilment)			3rd Song of Magic 9 lines (incl. verse 2, lines 1–3)
9	FISHING NET			3rd Sentence of Teaching / Aria of Prophecy, etc. (repeat)		3rd Song of Magic 12 lines (incl. verse 1, lines 1–4)

10	BIRD SKULL	3rd Ceremony/ 3rd Exchange (repeat) (*)		3rd Song of Magic 15 lines (incl. verse 4, lines 1–5)
11	FOOTPRINT		3rd Dangerous Murmur / 3rd Metamorphosis / 3rd Love Duet / 3rd Song of Magic, verse 5	3rd Song of Magic 18 lines (incl. verse 1, lines 1–2 & verse 3, 3–6)
12	ROCKFALL			Oracle / 3rd Song of Magic verse 6 (*)
13				Extension of Oracle but no sung text (*) / Passing Cloud
14	ROCKFALL		Repeated fragment of 3rd Love Duet	
15	FOSSIL SHELL	3rd Ceremony/ 4th Exchange (repeat) (*)		

Exodos, Bees

ROCKFALL
FOOTPRINT
FOSSIL SHELL
OAR
BIRD SKULL
NET

> The concept of Tides is simple. A number of objects lie on a beach. The tide
> covers them as it rises and uncovers them as it falls. Each successive high tide
> is higher than the last (as the moon is becoming fuller) and so some of the
> objects are not covered by one tide but are by the next. The objects themselves
> are not important . . . but represent sequences of actions within the opera;
> . . . as the tide rises and falls, so are some of the same objects covered and
> uncovered and so the same dramatic sequences take place.[101]

Zinovieff claims that the structure of the tides 'is analogous to that of the
Arches' in Act II, and that 'it dominates all aspects of the music, words
and theatre' of the final act.[102] However, he admits that much of the act's
form and structure 'will remain hidden'.[103] In reality, the tides represent an
abstract idea that was not effectively conveyed in the original production,
as several critics noted.[104]

As Table 3.3 indicates, the act as a whole should be considered from
two perspectives: on the one hand, according to events as they occur in
chronological order, which form what Zinovieff refers to as 'occurrences'
(i.e. by moving from left to right along each row); on the other hand,
according to six so-called 'sequences' related to the deaths of Orpheus and
Eurydice (represented in the table by the vertical columns). Taking both
perspectives into consideration, it can be seen that each sequence is triggered
by one of the short musical ideas that represent the objects on the beach: a
fishing net, bird skull, oar, fossil shell, footprint and rockfall. A summary of
the relationship between the objects and the sequences, as it is described in
the libretto, is given in Figure 3.5. Orpheus's death by sacrifice (sequence 4)
is the dominant sequence, heard four times in total. This reflects Zinovieff's
idea that Act III is primarily concerned with ritual sacrifice, as a symbol
of Orpheus's death and the rituals practised by the Dionysian religion that
Orpheus opposed.[105]

Table 3.3 reveals that Birtwistle deviated from Zinovieff's scheme in three
instances: occurrence 13 is not signalled by the Rockfall object, nor by any
other means; 14 is signalled by the Rockfall, rather than the Footprint; 15 is
announced by the Fossil Shell, not the Bird Skull. The table also highlights
the structural importance of literal and varied repetition. This is mainly a
reflection of the act's concern with memory, but it strengthens the sense

[101] Zinovieff, 'Explanatory document', PSS 0533-0079.
[102] Zinovieff, *The Mask of Orpheus*, 52.   [103] PSS 0533-0084.
[104] Peter Heyworth commented, 'I entirely fail to sense the movement of the tides that is said to
        underline the music of this act' ('Circles turning on different orbits', *Observer*, 25 May 1986),
        while Andrew Clements remarked that 'the "tides" were only intermittently audible, and the
        overall sense of ebb and flow was all but lost' ('The Mask of Orpheus', *Opera* 37/7 (1986),
        854). However, both noted that the dramatic design was severely hampered by cuts made to
        the third act. For more on these cuts, see Cross, *The Mask of Orpheus*, Appendix B.
[105] For details of the mime actions in this act see Zinovieff, *The Mask of Orpheus*, 53.

Figure 3.5 The relationship between the objects and the sequences

The six sequences of death (the numbers relate to the objects on the beach):

6	Orpheus's head is silenced by Apollo
5	The journey and metamorphosis of Orpheus's head
4	Orpheus's death by sacrifice
3	Orpheus's death by thunderbolt
2	Orpheus's death by suicide
1	Eurydice's death

The fifteen occurrences of the objects on the beach:

Occurrences:	1	2	3	4	5	6	7	8	9	10	11	12	13	14	15
Objects:															
6 ROCKFALL												6	6		
5 FOOTPRINT											5		5		
4 BIRD SKULL		4	4						4						4
3 FISHING NET	3			3				3							
2 OAR					2			2							
1 FOSSIL SHELL						1	1								

of a one-to-one relationship between the libretto and the music. Half of the sequences recall or repeat music heard earlier in the opera: sequence 1 is a literal repeat from The Yawn in Act I scene 2; sequence 2 is modelled closely on Arch 17, from Act II; sequence 4 recycles material from the Act I ceremonies. Besides the repetition of these sequences, there is literal repetition of the music (but not the text) in sequence 3, and in the verses of the 3rd Song of Magic.

The 3rd Song of Magic has a pivotal role that marks the transition between each occurrence and the movement of the tides. Each of these gentle verses is announced by the perfect fifth G–D, played by a small ensemble of brass and woodwind. Birtwistle ignored Zinovieff's suggestion that the phrases should encompass declamatory, recitative and aria styles, instead opting for a clipped, declamatory style for the entire text. Birtwistle also omitted the 3rd Song of Failure – that is, an English translation of the 3rd Song of Magic.[106] However, Birtwistle did sketch settings of this text, with the same harp and xylophone continuum used in the first Oracle sequence (sequence 6, occurrence 12).[107]

The 3rd Ceremony, or Exchange, is the most complex sequence and comprises thirteen elements: Shout, Question, Love Duet, Demand, Invocation, Statement, Murmur, Reply, Dance, Chorus, Silence, Scream, and

[106] Ibid., 63.
[107] Another notable deviation from Zinovieff's plan is the use of verse 5 from the 3rd Song of Magic in sequence 5, occurrence 11.

Song. As indicated in the libretto, the Murmur and Chorus are simultaneous with the Statement and the Dance, respectively;[108] the cyclical nature
of the exchange is illustrated in the libretto by a circular diagram.[109] There
are four such exchanges in total. A full cycle is always completed, but each
exchange begins with a different event. Here, presumably for musical and
dramatic reasons, Birtwistle altered Zinovieff's scheme in the final exchange,
electing to begin and end with the Stravinskyan 'Sacrificial Dance' rather
than the Reply. Birtwistle prepared his own plan of the ceremony, based
on Zinovieff's; written immediately beneath his plan (but pasted over),
Birtwistle referred to the music at this moment as a 'HUGE MACHINE',
and instructed himself to 'Formalise the WHOLE of the TIDES'.[110] The
instrumental parts for all four ceremonies were conceived as a continuous
whole, plotted on a regular semiquaver grid (with a varied ostinato harmonic
background), after which the sections of the ceremonies were marked in red
pencil.[111]

To conclude, there is a dialectical tension in Act III between violent, disruptive interjections that symbolise Orpheus's dismemberment, and more
lyrical sections that evoke Orpheus's eternal, mythical song. Additional
punctuation is provided by electronic cadences, of two, three or seven
notes, which recall similar structuring devices in Birtwistle's *Oresteia* setting (1981).[112] As Adlington observes, while Orpheus is elevated to the
status of mythic God, the music in Act III 'assumes an appropriate tone
of meditative reflectiveness – its short, clearly distinguishable formal elements almost icon-like in their imperviousness to change and context'.[113]
Zinovieff's sectional schemes are now 'directly perceivable' in Birtwistle's
music,[114] which 'gains in eloquence and compassion'.[115]

The next section of this chapter examines Birtwistle's compositional
techniques in more detail, with particular focus on the arch structure in Act
II. The discussion is divided into three parts, which provide examples of
rhythmic, pitch and vocal techniques respectively.

Rhythm

Hall was the first to discuss Birtwistle's compositional techniques and his use
of random numbers in any detail. He concluded that 'no true mathematical,
analytic or logical thinking is actually involved', only the manipulation of

---

[108] Zinovieff, *The Mask of Orpheus*, 57 (table at the bottom of the page).   [109] Ibid., 46.
[110] PSS 0531-0957.   [111] PSS 0532-0003–39.   [112] See Beard, "'Batter the doom drum'".
[113] Adlington, *MHB*, 20.   [114] Adlington, 'Summary justice', 31.
[115] Whittall, 'Orpheus – and after', 55.

numerical patterns.[116] It is not wholly accurate to suggest that there is no analytic or logical thinking in Birtwistle's use of numbers, but true to say that for the most part they provide a means to manipulate material, to randomise or reorder ideas. This is illustrated by Birtwistle's translation of numbers into durations. Series of numbers were drawn from computer-generated charts stored in a 'Magic Book of Numbers' or generated by throwing dice.[117] The numbers were then plotted onto rhythmic grids, in which each row is defined by a single rhythmic unit.[118] Birtwistle's approach to these grids is characteristic of what Hall describes as the composer's central organising principle: 'start with an absolutely regular and uniform pattern... then superimpose upon it a pattern which is its extreme opposite – something capricious and unpredictable'.[119] This is illustrated by Example 3.1, which shows the sketch for a passage of heterophony during the funeral ceremony in Act I scene 3, from Fig. 105. The three basic elements and the order in which they were assembled is as follows:

- A regular pitch ostinato – *bb*, *a*, *b♮*, *f♯* – shared by the second clarinet, second bassoon, and second horn.
- A rhythmic grid with a regular unit on each line – from the clarinet down: demisemiquavers (every fourth tied); semiquavers; quintuplet semiquavers (every fifth tied).
- An irregular number series in each line: 7 11 9; 5 7 3; 4 8 6. Rhythms are produced by marking an attack and sustained duration according to the number series, counting from the first note in each group.

The result is similar to medieval isorhythm in which a repeated rhythmic pattern (the *talea*) overlaps with a pitch ostinato of a different length (the *color*). However, this technique is applied in three different ways, simultaneously. Moreover, in the score, three further parts are added to each rhythmic line respectively, resulting in twelve independently moving parts (this exemplifies Birtwistle's desire for as many layers as possible in *Orpheus*). Consequently, the underlying rhythmic grid is imperceptible to the listener, although it does ensure a general distinction between the individual parts.

---

[116] Hall, *HB*, 119.

[117] Birtwistle uses a range of dice with different numbers of faces. The 'Magic Book' comprises *c*.30 sides of sketches and number charts written by hand, and five sides of typescript numbers pasted into the book, presumably from the computer-generated tables given to Birtwistle by his schoolfriend Peter Lee, which he has used since *c*.1960. The book is currently in the possession of Birtwistle's son, Silas.

[118] Birtwistle had been using this technique since at least 1967, as revealed by sketches for the instrumental Interstices in *Monodrama* (1967); PSS, Sammlung Harrison Birtwistle. See Beard, 'The endless parade', 91–5.

[119] Hall, *HB*, 13.

Example 3.1 Sketch for heterophony in Act I scene 3, *The Mask of Orpheus*
(full score), p. 109, Fig. 105. PSS 0531-0520

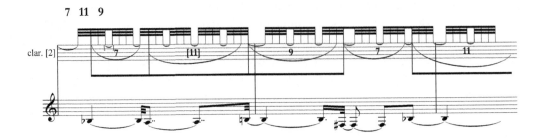

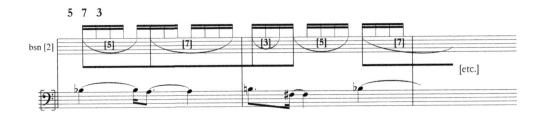

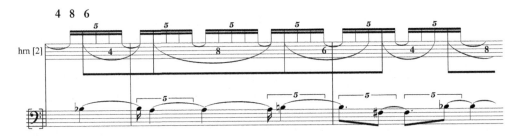

By far the most complex example of this procedure relates to the sketches
for the Whisper of Change (first heard on p. 83, Fig. 78); see Plate 3.2.
This 'part' reappears throughout the opera literally unchanged, and is a
harbinger of bad tidings: in Act I it precedes Eurydice's funeral ceremony;
in Act II it announces the beginning of the arches, which turn from dream to
nightmare, and accompanies Orpheus's suicide; in Act III it signals the start
of the third sequence, which concerns Orpheus's death by thunderbolt.[120]

[120] Zinovieff, however, lists only three Whispers of Change (one in each act), which are to
symbolise birth, death and eternity, respectively.

Each recurrence, with the exception of the third, marks the end of a Time Shift. This is one of the very few sections that is dated, which suggests that Birtwistle attached some importance to it; Plate 3.2 is marked 'Sunday. 14. 4. No. 29'.[121] Other pages for this section suggest it was sketched in April 1974.[122] Each of the twelve parts (three each of soprano, alto, tenor and bass) has a different rhythmic unit, for example: regular quavers in the 1st soprano; a dotted quintuplet quaver plus quintuplet quaver in the 3rd alto; demisemi-quavers with every third note tied in the 1st tenor; quintuplet semiquavers with every third then fourth note tied in the 3rd bass. There is approximate heterophony in each of the four vocal groups, while the rhythmic scheme ensures that all twelve parts move through their pitch material at a different rate.

The same technique is applied to the arches – the rhythmic grids were the next step after the 'continuum of dream' – during which there are usually three or more rhythmic strands.[123] For example, at the start of Act II scene 2, in the grid for Arch 10, there are three strands: triplet quavers (with the last quaver in each group tied to the first quaver in the subsequent group); quavers; and sextuplet semiquavers. Regular and irregular number schemes are often combined to determine when the attacks will occur. For example, at the start of the fantasy section of Arch 11 there is a staccato, triplet semiquaver texture in the trumpets and horns (p. 199). Initially, the attacks are determined by the following bipartite scheme (read from left to right):

$$
\begin{array}{lll}
4 & 6 & [\times 2] \\
4 & 7 & \\
3 & 8 & \\
2 & 9 & \\
1 & &
\end{array}
$$

However, Birtwistle did not always remain faithful to these grids: from Arch 11 onwards there is little evidence of Birtwistle proceeding to the next stage, in which pitches are applied to the grids, which suggests that around this point he began to depart from the scheme (and as Taylor notes, there are differences even at the start). The sketches for Arch 10 reveal that although part of the original rhythmic skeleton was retained (the electric bass guitar rhythm at the start is based on the line of quavers), the other layers and their related number schemes were either ignored or significantly

---

[121] PSS 0531-0502. 'No. 29' refers to the number of this part in Zinovieff's libretto.
[122] PSS 0530-0763 and -0764.
[123] By contrast, the sections of the Ceremony in Act III are mapped onto a single rhythmic strand of regular semiquavers. PSS 0531-0941–53.

Plate 3.2 Sketch for the Whisper of Change, first heard in Act I scene 3, p. 83, Fig. 78. PSS, Sammlung Harrison Birtwistle, *The Mask of Orpheus*, folder 16, skizzen F

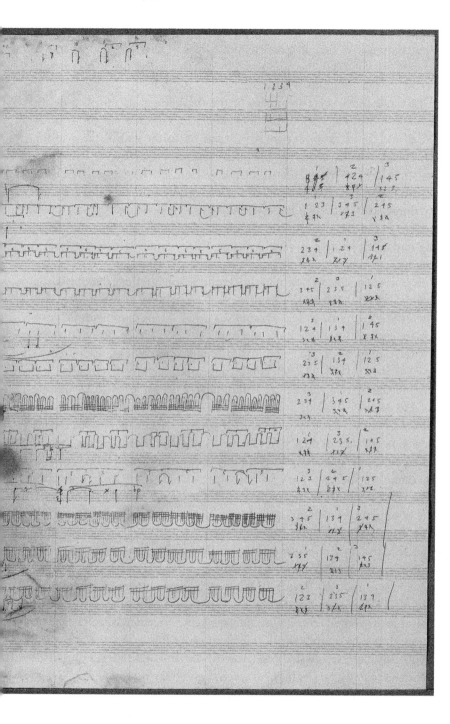

modified. It should also be noted that an instrumental part may be formed by a composite of two or more rhythmic lines,[124] and that even when the scheme was followed, the numbers only dictated where the attacks would occur, not the durations of notes.

At times, Birtwistle's treatment of the rhythmic grids reveals a desire to smooth over the sections in Zinovieff's plan. For example, the grid for the distortion section of Arch 10 is taped on to the end of the grid for the Dream portion. However, the pitch material – a seven-note ostinato – was first worked out in the distortion section. Birtwistle then returned to the Dream portion and added the seven-note ostinato on a separate rhythmic layer. Although the rhythm of the ostinato shifts from sextuplet quavers in the Dream portion to triplet quavers in the distortion, the phrasing and pitch content provide a degree of continuity across the formal divide.

It is now possible to return to the second set of durations that Birtwistle devised for the arches. These correspond to changes in tempo, but also alterations in the rhythmic schemes deployed. Along the rhythmic grids for the arches, Birtwistle plots the position of his eleven durations with the relevant number and an approximate indication of a change in tempo (e.g.: '3 accel'; '4 rall'; '5 accel', etc.). It appears, therefore, that the diagonal lines in the bottom part of the 'continuum of dream' (Plate 3.1) indicate relative increases and decreases in tempo. This was intended to produce what Birtwistle refers to as a 'terraced' rhythm, to ensure the tempo remains in a constant state of flux.[125] Yet Birtwistle often ignored these suggestions and retained the prevailing tempo. What does often change, however, is the rhythmic scheme.

Arch 1 has a constant triplet quaver pulse, arranged in crotchet units, with the last quaver in each group tied to the first in the subsequent group.[126] The first duration in Birtwistle's scheme is identical to Zinovieff's (2'20), therefore the rhythmic scheme alters at the beginning of Arch 2; here the triplet quaver pulse remains, but the tie is removed, and a new counting scheme is introduced. The third duration begins on the eleventh crotchet beat of Arch 3. Here the rhythmic scheme shifts to regular semiquavers, and attacks are marked every seven then seventeen semiquavers. The fourth duration begins on the twenty-third beat of Arch 4, where the grid alters to regular quavers. And so on. Yet, towards the end of the arches, Birtwistle appears to grow weary of his own scheme, and there is no change of tempo or rhythmic scheme in the last three durations – even though they are

[124] This technique was not new: in *Monodrama*, Birtwistle formed single lines from composites of three different rhythmic strata. PSS 0534-0361; *Monodrama*.

[125] PSS 0530-0727.   [126] See Taylor, 'Narrative and musical structures', Plate 1, 184–5.

Example 3.2 Sketch for extended woodwind melody in Act III scene 3, 3rd Spoken
Argument, occurrence 8, sequence 2, p. 322. PSS 0532-0213

	[A]			[B]		
[Rows:]	♩.	♩	♩·	♪	♪	♪·
[1]	3	2	1	3	1	2
[2]	1	3	2	1	2	3
[3]	2	3	1	2	1	3
[4]	1	2	3	2	3	1
[5]	3	1	2	3	2	1
[6]	2	1	3	2	3	1
[7]	3	1	2	1	2	3
[8]	1	3	2	3	2	1

[* = slight alteration to scheme]

marked in the sketches, as follows: '9' on the fortieth crotchet beat of
Arch 11; '10' on the twenty-second beat of Arch 13; '11' on the thirteenth beat
of Arch 17.

Elsewhere in the opera, Birtwistle generates rhythms differently, which
is consistent with his intention both to retain certain procedures and to
invent new ones for specific sections. At times, he writes out a series of
durations in conventional notation, then applies numerical schemes to
determine their order and distribution.[127] This method was used to produce
the extended melody in the main ensemble that accompanies Orpheus's
3rd Spoken Argument in Act III (from p. 322, Fig. 61^{+2}), as shown in
Example 3.2. Elsewhere, durations are plotted as numerical values (e.g.
where a semiquaver = 1, a dotted crotchet = 6, a breve = 16, etc.).[128]

---

[127] Some of the earliest sketches include rhythmic tables that are equivalent to pitch matrices.
One such table includes five rows and five columns; the durations progressively decrease in
each row (e.g. the first row consists of durations 7, 5, 3, 2, 1, where 1 is a crotchet). Number
schemes were then generated to select and reorder the durations (PSS 0530-0554).
[128] For example, on PSS 0530-0747.

Throughout the opera, numbers have a bearing on almost every aspect of the score, including the distribution of dynamics, pitches, intervals, contours, and chords. They determine the lengths of phrases, gaps between phrases, even which instruments will play and when. During Arch 3, for example, numbers determine the order and rapid succession of different ensembles (high, medium, low) and ornaments (trills, tremolos, etc.), in response to Zinovieff's text ('There is the smell of sweat and feasting...I can hear the cheering / I can hear the laughter').[129] Restrictions on space do not permit a full investigation of this topic, but the next section will concentrate on pitch and voice.

Pitch schemes

This section considers aspects of pitch in the broadest sense – that is, modes, contours, instrumental melodic lines, and harmony.

Modes and contours

Throughout the opera, various ensembles form continuous strands, or instrumental continuums, that often continue across Zinovieff's sections.[130] As source material for these continuums, Birtwistle compiled tables of scales, or 'modes' as he sometimes referred to them, from which he selected notes. The earliest continuum extends through the wedding ceremony, in Act I scene 1, and comprises three harps, three bassoons and unpitched percussion. This ensemble was sketched first and the vocal lines were adapted to it later (the vocal parts are more roughly notated on strips that are attached along the bottom of the relevant pages).[131] The continuum is based on a series of five modes. The changes in mode do not always adhere to Zinovieff's scheme. When the harps and bassoons move to mode II the shift coincides with the resumption of the 1st Complicated Question, after the 2nd Extension of the Love Duet (p. 37, Fig. 36). However, the moves to modes III, IV and V occur in the middle of Zinovieff's sections (Figs. 40^{-1}, 44^{-5} and 44^{+10}).

---

[129] PSS 0530-0631.
[130] The term *continuum* appears at the start of Act II (p. 132), where it relates to the so-called 'harp of Orpheus' ensemble of harp, Noh harp and amplified electric mandolin, guitar and bass guitar, directed by conductor II. The same ensemble (minus the Noh harp) forms a related continuum through Act II scene 2. This is first introduced (minus the harps) at the end of Arch 4, p. 159, Fig. 23. The other important continuum is the so-called 'Ensemble of Hell' for unpitched percussion, also directed by the second conductor. This is first heard, briefly, at the beginning of Arch 10 (the start of Act II scene 2) then reintroduced in the distortion section of Arch 11, p. 202.
[131] PSS 0531-0127-46.

Example 3.3 Analysis of Modes I–IV in bassoons 1–3, Act I scene 1, Wedding
Ceremony continuum, pp. 22–49

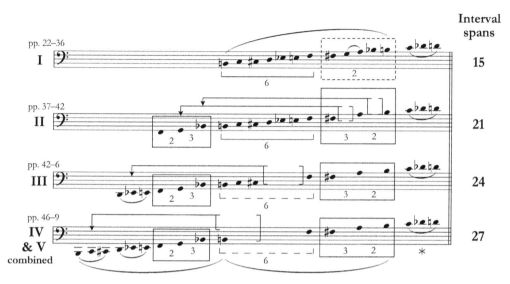

* doubled two octaves higher in the harps

The modes may be parsed three ways, between the bassoons, and the
left- and right-hands of the harps. In each successive mode, the bandwidth
expands. Mode I includes the smallest span of interval 11 in the left-hand
of the harps (*e* to *d♯′*); Mode V has the largest span of interval 32, also
in the left-hand of the harps (*F♭* to *e″*). Mode I is predominantly chromatic, but as the modes expand they incorporate larger intervals. This is
illustrated by Example 3.3, which examines the bassoons; modes IV and
V are combined here, as they do not differ significantly. Each mode is a
varied transposition of an unordered eleven-note series, which omits A♭;
the example shows the pitches (i.e. the registral position of the notes) as
they are fixed in the score. In each successive mode, notes are transposed
down an octave. What emerges is an approximately symmetrical scheme
that spans a little over two octaves, within which a central unit of interval 6
(a tritone) is framed by two units of interval 5 (a perfect fourth). By the
end of this process, a four-octave space has been created by the bassoons
and harps combined, with the bassoons' highest three notes doubled two
octaves above by the harps' highest notes.

Birtwistle employs a further scheme to distribute the pitches. Summarised
in Figure 3.6, this involves the use of contours, which are arranged into

Figure 3.6 Contour classes in the wedding ceremony continuum (where 1 is the lowest position and 5 the highest)

3A = <2, 1, 3>   4A = <2, 1, 3, 4>   5A = <1, 3, 2, 5, 4>
3B = <1, 2, 3>   4B = <2, 3, 1, 4>   5B = <1, 4, 2, 3, 5>
3C = <1, 3, 2>

three different classes, labelled A to C.[132] Birtwistle selected contours from tables that were compiled separately. One such table comprises 34, 27 and 34 variants of 3A, 3B and 3C respectively.[133] This high number was possible because the variants consist of seven contour positions (i.e. <1, 2, 3, 4, 5, 6, 7>). Forms of 3A include: <4, 3, 5>, <2, 1, 6> and <5, 3, 7>; in other words, the selections conform to the generic contour class <2, 1, 3>.

Birtwistle's earliest attempts to systematise contour are documented in a sketchbook titled 'Modual Book, The Triumph of Time', dated 2 April 1970, which, given its declared interest in time, it would be reasonable to describe as preparatory for *Orpheus*.[134] This book contains ideas that relate to *An Imaginary Landscape* (1971), *Prologue* (1971) and a first abandoned version of *The Triumph of Time*. Here, Birtwistle made similar attempts to those in his 'Goat-Song' system, that is, he drew up circular tables in which contour classes are related in terms of prime, retrograde, inversion, and retrograde inversion.[135] Another sketchbook from the same period reveals that Birtwistle used these contours to form the soprano line in *Nenia: the Death of Orpheus*. He began with an expanding chromatic wedge on C, from which he made various pitch selections. Each selection was then reordered to fit three-, four- and five-note contours, arranged in an overlapping scheme.[136]

Based on this evidence, it is possible to deduce that the wedding ceremony continuum comprises selections from the five modes, which were then reordered to 'fit' a contour class that was itself most likely predetermined

---

[132] These and other forms are listed on PSS 0531-0362.

[133] PSS 0540-0370; Nicht identifizierte Manuskripte.

[134] It should be noted, however, that contour is also a vital compositional component of *Linoi* (1968), *Cantata* (1969) and *Eight Lessons for Keyboards* (1969–70).

[135] These attempts to systematise contour anitcipate recent music theory. See Ian Quinn, 'The combinatorial model of pitch contour', *Music Perception* 16 (1999), 439–56. For more on contour theory in general see: Robert D. Morris, *Composition with Pitch-Classes* (New Haven: Yale University Press, 1987); Morris, 'New directions in the theory and analysis of musical contour', *Music Theory Spectrum*, 15/2 (1993), 205–28; and Elizabeth West Marvin, 'Generalization of contour theory to diverse musical spaces: analytical applications to the music of Dallapiccola and Stockhausen', in Elizabeth West Marvin and Richard Hermann, eds., *Concert Music, Rock, and Jazz since 1945: Essays and Analytical Studies* (Rochester, NY: University of Rochester Press, 1995), 135–71.

[136] For a more detailed discussion see Beard, 'An analysis and sketch study', Chapter 4.

Example 3.4 Sketch with contour scheme for distribution of Mode II in Wedding Ceremony continuum, Act I scene 1, 1st Complicated Question (cont.), p. 36, Fig. 36. PSS 0531-0134

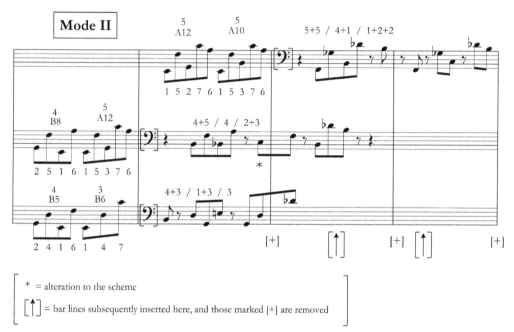

by a separate ordering scheme. In this particular context, the sevenfold contour divisions are redundant (a maximum of five is all that is necessary), which indicates that the source table was devised with the intention of making seven-note pitch selections elsewhere in the opera. Each contour was subdivided by an additional scheme to produce gaps within the phrases. This is shown in Example 3.4. (Here the notation to the left of the clefs is information about contour, not pitch). The scheme to determine the gaps between phrases consists of two stages: first the size of the contours is written (e.g. 5+5 = two five-note contours); then the subdivisions of those contours (e.g. 4+1 / 1+2+2). The numbers and letters written above the contours (to the left of the clefs) relate to the source tables listed in Figure 3.6 (e.g. 3B6 = version 6 (from 27) of contour 3B).[137]

The most important tables of modes in the sketches relate to the body of Act II, that is, to the arches sequence. Birtwistle drew up ten A2-size pages, each with twelve ten-note collections.[138] Within these tables,

---

[137] Elsewhere, Birtwistle employs nesting contours, whereby pitch movement is governed at macro and micro levels. PSS 0531-0062 reveals this in the woodwind accompaniment during Love Duet Extension 4.

[138] PSS 0531-0697–706.

Example 3.5a Source modes for the Arches in Act II. Extracts from the first two columns. PSS 0531-0697–0706

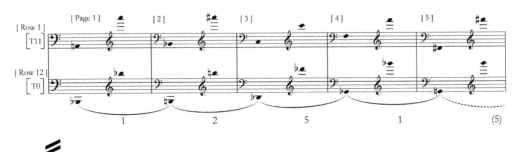

Example 3.5b Summary of mode tables for the Arches. PSS 0531-0697–0706

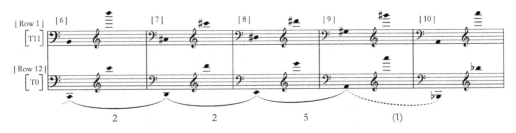

four-octave spaces are divided into two-octave spans. There are 120 permutations of an unordered mode that comprises intervals 1, 2 and 5 (semitone, tone and perfect fourth), a total of three times each, which fills a single octave. On each page there are twelve columns and twelve rows (therefore 120 columns and rows in total). Each column contains a different version of the generic mode (e.g. 12521552); mistakes in the upper rows suggest that the lowest was written first. The rows begin and end on the same pitch class in alternate columns (these six pairs of columns are labelled A to F on the first page), and each row is a transposition by a semitone (up from the bottom of the table, or down from the top). Example 3.5a shows the lowest and highest modes from the first and second columns on the first page (labelled A and B); Example 3.5b is a summary of all ten pages

showing the first and last notes of the highest and lowest rows on each
page, which reveals that the series as a whole outlines a version of the
generic mode (125152251). This mode was actually hinted at earlier: in
Act I scene 1 the piccolo solo that runs through Orpheus's 1st Song of
Magic is based on intervals 1521; in Act I scene 3 the flutes and clarinets in
the 1st Time Shift form chords that comprise permutations of 11225.[139] The
rotational aspect of the table recalls Stravinsky's serial practice, in particular
his treatment of a series as a loop of interval classes, and it is conceivable
that Birtwistle learned of this technique during his time in America.[140]

It is possible to match the table precisely to specific moments in the
arches sequence, although the task is not an easy one.[141] In general, the
modes determine the intervals between instrumental parts. Annotations
on the table and indications in the sketches and score suggest that more
than one row was often used simultaneously, and that Birtwistle migrated
randomly between different rows and even different pages in the table.[142]
At the opening of Arch 1, for example, a six-octave span (that is, four
octaves extended to six by the piccolo and double bassoon) is based on F♯
in the lower half and G♯ in the upper half, which suggests that Birtwistle
drew on two rows a tone apart. During the fact portion, the instruments
focus on these outer boundaries. The clarinets and bass clarinets then begin
to fill the mid- and low-register octaves with chords based primarily on
intervals 1, 2 and 5 (p. 143). At the end of the fact portion, on p. 144,
the parts fan out from e'' (in the fourth oboe) to a chord that comprises
intervals <251251152215> (from the lowest note up). This is shown in
Example 3.6. The source of these pitches and intervallic patterns is page 3
of the table, where they are clearly marked '1'. The notes in the score are
an octave higher than in the table; the source pitches are the last four
notes in column five, row four, and the entire mode in column six, row
four.

The resultant chords provide a bright, clipped rhythmic counterpoint to
the wailing saxophones ('becoming vulgar and coarse'), Charon's stammering intervention ('K- K- K-issed, killed killed killed'), and an additional layer
of chords in the lower woodwind and horns. These parts were grafted on
to the chord scheme drawn from the mode tables. Although initially these
modal chords are less audible than the other layers – particularly the horns,
which climax on a perfect fourth (F♯–C♯) – the final chord in the scheme

[139] PSS 0531-0175 and -0372 respectively.
[140] See Arnold Whittall, *Serialism* (Cambridge University Press, 2008), 137–41, and Joseph
       N. Straus, *Stravinsky's Late Music* (Cambridge University Press, 2001).
[141] A reference to the 'bass oboe' on the ninth page suggests that modes from this section were
       used on pp. 210–11 or (less likely) pp. 234–5. PSS 0531-0705.
[142] Annotations on the tables also suggest that, at times, Birtwistle selected segments from the
       modes, as seen in *Punch*.

Example 3.6 Analysis of mode in woodwind and trumpets, Arch 1, fantasy and start of distortion, pp. 144–5, Figs. 11 to 12

Mode table, page 3 (PSS 0531-0699), columns 5 and 6, row 4

is taken up and repeated by the upper woodwind and brass throughout the distortion section in a vigorous, jerking motion reminiscent of sections from *The Rite*.[143] Therefore a process that began relatively inaudibly in the fact portion culminates in the distortion.

A similar 'link' between fantasy and distortion sections occurs in Arch 4 (p. 159, Fig. 23). In other words, the modes form a consistent element that extends across Zinovieff's structural divisions.[144] However, the modes were often distorted, by either errors, methods of selection or other processes,

---

[143] These movements may have been plotted across six A4-size sheets. Taped together, these pages consist of grids with seven rows and seventy-five columns (four to five columns per arch). Diagonal lines (two dotted, two full) indicate rising and falling patterns. PSS 0530-0749–51 and PSS 0530-0703–5. Elsewhere, there is evidence of the modes being parsed into four-note subsets, which are then reordered (e.g. PSS 0531-0922).

[144] To this effect, Birtwistle clearly used the ten-note modes in the 'harp of Orpheus' continuum (PSS 0531-0889), and sometimes selected smaller sets from the modes (PSS 0531-0888). Yet

Figure 3.7 Intervallic structure of chord sequence in trombones 1–6: Arch 6, distortion section, pp. 172–3, Figs. 32^{+1}–33^{-1}

	5	5	1	5	1	5	1
1	1	1	1	2	1	2	1
2	2	2	5	1	5	1	5
5	5	2	2	1	2	5	2
1	1	1	1	1	1	1	1

Figure 3.8 Trombones 1–6: Arch 8, distortion section, pp. 183–5, Figs. 38^{+3}–39^{-2}

1	7	3	1	7	7	5	2	2	5	1	1	1	1	7	2	1	1
1	1	7	1	2	1	2	5	5	2	2	5	2	2	1	1	1	1
7	1	2	2	1	1	1	1	2	1	5	1	5	1	2	1	1	1
2	6	1	1	5	1	1	1	1	6	1	4	1	5	2	1	1	2
7	2	4	1	1	2	6	6	1	5	5	1	5	2	1	4	1	5

rendering them harder to locate in the table. An indication of this is provided by Figures 3.7 and 3.8. These figures summarise a series of chords which occurs in the trombones during the distortion section of Arches 6 and 8, but which is absent from Arch 7. Part of the first series of chords is shown in Example 3.7.

The sketches reveal that layers in the low woodwind, tubas and chorus that appear alongside the trombones are based on similar modes.[145] In such instances, however, Birtwistle did not necessarily use the tables at all. Rather, at times, he simply reordered intervals 1, 2 and 5, as and when required: for example, quaver triplet figures in the flute, lower woodwind and fourth trumpet on p. 166 (the distortion section of Arch 5) are derived from vertical permutations of these intervals (see Example 3.8).[146] Elsewhere, Birtwistle introduced variants that included intervals 6 and 7.[147]

elsewhere this continuum is formed from reordered chromatic wedges (as detailed for the bass guitar on PSS 0531-0570, which relates to p. 206, Fig. 52^{+3}).
[145] PSS 0531-0917 and -0919 respectively.　　[146] PSS 0531-0900; also PSS 0531-0573 and -0916.
[147] For example on PSS 0531-0893–4 and 0532-0092.

Example 3.7 Trombone chords in Arch 6, distortion, pp. 172–3, Fig. 32^{+2} to 32^{+6}

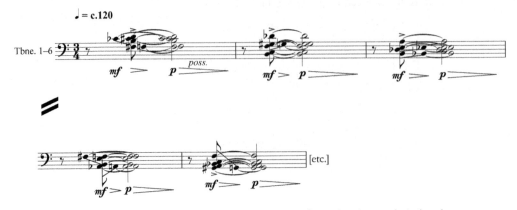

Example 3.8 Continuous triplet quaver figuration in woodwind and trumpet, Arch 5, distortion, p. 166, Fig. 27

Returning to the tables, a closer examination of the sketches reveals more about ways in which the source modes were utilised, adapted or distorted. At the start of Arch 2, the sketches indicate that the brass and bass clarinet chords comprise nine-note sets selected alternately from pages 6 and 7 of the table.[148] Subsequently, in the distortion section (Fig. 16), the woodwind and brass parts began initially with four chords selected from different parts of page 7, as shown in Example 3.9 (stages 1 and 2). The first chord is derived from the last three notes in row 12, column 3, and the same row, column 4; the second chord is based on the last three notes of row 7, column 11, and the same row in column 12. The next step was to generate a scheme in which the thirteen parts do not all move to the next chord at the same

---

[148] PSS 0531-0926.

Example 3.9 Use of modes from page 7 of mode tables in Arch 2, distortion, p. 149, Fig. 16⁺² onwards. PSS 0531-0703 (stage 1) and PSS 0531-0929 (stages 2 and 3)

Stage 1 Selections from Mode table (PSS 0531-0703)

Stage 2 (PSS 0531-0929)

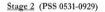

picc. 1, fls 2–4, obs 1–3,
cls 1+2, bass cl.,
tpts 1–4 and hns 1–4

Stage 3 (extract) (PSS 0531-0929)

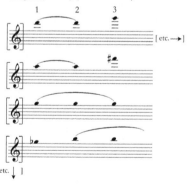

[etc. ↓]

Final score, p. 149, Fig. 16⁺²

alternative chord scheme interpolated

time (stage 3 in Example 3.9). The chord sequence is repeated four times. However, another set of chords, also based on the table, was interpolated between the chords derived from the initial scheme, and this new pattern was varied with each repetition of the four-chord sequence (see 'final score' in Example 3.9).[149]

The table was also used at times to generate pitch material for the harp, mandolin and electric guitar continuum; the source mode in the sketch for the continuum at Fig. 28, for example, relates to row 2, columns 3 and 4, on page 9 of the table. However, certain mistakes crept in during the transition from sketch to score: the harp's opening G in the score was actually F♯ in the sketch.[150] The sketches also reveal that Birtwistle sometimes used randomly generated octave displacements when adapting the source modes.[151] All of this renders the task of tracing the source modes particularly difficult.

Evidence for use of the modes is strong as far as the end of Arch 13. From Arch 14 onwards, however, intervals 1, 2 and 5 are less evident. Rather, the parts begin to coalesce around unisons and pitch centres related by interval 7 (the perfect fifth) – for example, Arch 14 opens with a unison g' in the altos and horns, and d'' in the sopranos and soprano saxophones (p. 219). The implication is that Birtwistle resumed composition on *Orpheus* at this stage, which is earlier than previously assumed.[152]

Instrumental lines

Hall has observed that the first Orpheus-related piece Birtwistle composed, *Nenia: the Death of Orpheus*, signalled a change of style, a shift away from the bold juxtapositions of *Punch* and *Verses for Ensembles* (1969) towards a 'primarily melodic, non-dynamic, processional style'.[153] In fact, this shift can be traced back slightly earlier to *Nomos* (1969) – composed the year *Orpheus* was commissioned – in which an extended melody is performed by amplified quartet. Nyman compared the melody in *Nomos* to 'a procession across a landscape ... a broad, slowly-progressing continuum'.[154] Similarly, in Act II of *Orpheus*, the orchestra begins to assert its independence from the drama through extended lines, particularly in the woodwind and soprano saxophones. These culminate in the languorous, melancholic woodwind

[149] PSS 0531-0929.   [150] PSS 0531-0889.   [151] PSS 0531-0922.
[152] Further support for this theory is provided by Birtwistle's fair copy in which the start of Arch 14 is taped on to the previous passage, which is unusual in the context of the preceding pages (PSS 0532-0581). On this page (and throughout Arch 14) there are words for Apollo (for example: 'PAN O A NO TOU TO KA TO'). Clearly, therefore, the fair copy was prepared before it was realised that it would not be possible to set Apollo's words – in other words, before the end of 1983. The electronic signals are marked in this copy, but not in the more detailed form present in the final score.
[153] Hall, *HB*, 73.   [154] Nyman, cited in Hall, *HB*, 73.

melody that accompanies Orpheus's death by hanging, at the conclusion of the second act.

The sketches reveal that an extended melody, described as a 'cantus', was planned to run from Arch 10 to 17. A further piece of evidence, the date 'Winter 80/81' on the reverse side of the drafts for the cantus, suggests that it may have been conceived after the break in composition.[155] The sketch for the cantus comprises two independent lines: flute, oboe and clarinet in the upper line; bassoon, cor anglais and horn in the lower – a duality that recalls the Love Duet in Act I. The first page is shown in Plate 3.3. The cantus was sketched across four A2-size pages. Each line comprises reorderings of three-note sets that occupy narrow registral bands (usually major thirds), which are arranged to produce approximately parallel movement at an average distance of a perfect fourth plus an octave.[156] In the top system, the vertical line through three staffs after the circled number two indicates the start of the fantasy section. The distortion begins in the second system at the vertical line with arrowheads; Arch 11 is indicated by the reverse double brackets near the start of the third system, and the fantasy section is marked by the next vertical line with arrowheads. Birtwistle also noted his own durations: on the bottom system, the first vertical line with arrowheads corresponds to the ninth duration in his scheme (the next line indicates the start of the distortion section). Clearly, these marks were added after the sequence of pitches and the rhythm had been written (the rhythm is notated above the upper line).[157] Paradoxically, therefore, although the intention was to extend a melody across the arches, the arches are imposed retrospectively onto the cantus.

Birtwistle did not remain faithful to his plan: during the fantasy portion of Arch 10, the rhythmic values are doubled; at the end of the distortion in Arch 11, the notes in the upper line overlap and the durations are considerably extended; in the distortion of Arch 12, the upper line continues in the soprano saxophones (pp. 207–18), but the lower line is only briefly resumed by the horns (pp. 209–11). When Birtwistle returns to the cantus plan he does so at the moment marked Arch 13, but by this time he has actually reached the beginning of Arch 14 (p. 219). This is the arch in which Orpheus awakes from his dream, and Eurydice is lost to him a second time. Here, the sketch explains the provenance of the G–D dyad mentioned earlier: the lines of the cantus cross over; the lower line (beginning on D) passes to

---

[155] The cantus draft is on PSS 0532-0111–22.

[156] The source sets for the cantus lines are most likely those on PSS 0531-0553–0558, which comprise two series of chromatic, five-note sets (each outlining interval 4 (or a major third)); series 'A' begins on d', a perfect fourth plus an octave above series 'B', which begins on a. Numerous three-note sets, like the ones in the cantus plan, are selected from the five-note cells.

[157] PSS 0531-0720–3. The word 'CANTUS' is written on the reverse side of the first page.

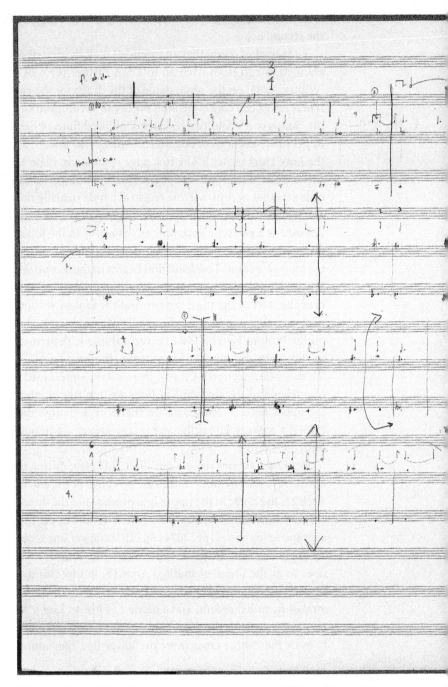

Plate 3.3 First of four sketch pages for an instrumental 'Cantus' in Act II scenes
2–3. PSS, Sammlung Harrison Birtwistle, *The Mask of Orpheus*, folder 19, skizzen I

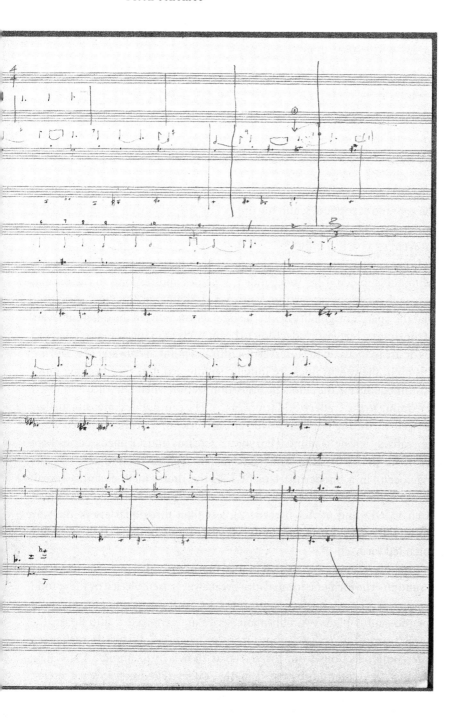

Example 3.10a Scheme to determine the cantus melody in Arch 16, Act II scene 3, pp. 239–42. PSS 0531-0746

the soprano saxophones, and the upper line (beginning on G) moves to the horns, with the result that the perfect fourth relation between the parts is inverted to a perfect fifth.[158]

What is significant about this alteration is that it illustrates Birtwistle's willingness to adapt his independent schemes and respond to the drama, here with a symbolic inversion. Moreover, it highlights Zinovieff's principle that the opera's originality lies in the interaction *between* the different layers of the drama. Birtwistle's decision to begin Arch 14 in this way also relates to his desire to focus on the interval of a fifth as a point of convergence. During this arch, the cantus lines are initially submerged, but they become more prominent during the climactic distortion section when Eurydice is dragged screaming to the Underworld (pp. 224–5). The cantus lines intensify further in Arch 15, during Orpheus's 'wild animal' cries of 'Euridice', uttered when he realises that he is alone. (Eurydice's screams and Orpheus's cries here recall the 'points of extravagant sonic metamorphosis' that Metzer suggests may occur in a 'modernist lament'.) As the drafts for the cantus reveal, however, Birtwistle abandons the cantus altogether at the conclusion of Arch 15 (the end of Act II scene 2), less than three-quarters of the way through the cantus plan, and at the very beginning of the section originally intended for Arch 15.

Separate schemes were then designed for the extended melodies in Arches 16 and 17. The former is located in a 'breakaway' ensemble, led by the second conductor. The pitch selection process is an exact inversion of the one used for the cantus plan: two chromatic series are arranged a fifth apart, the lower from *d'* to *f♯'*, the upper from *a'* to *c♯''*.[159] Birtwistle makes ten three-note selections from these sets, as shown in Example 3.10a. These are then reordered and rotated in two cycles (30 dyads in each cycle), the second of which is given in Example 3.10b. The order numbers in

---

[158] This moment is marked with three vertical strokes on PSS 0531-0721 (the notes in the lower line are also circled here). See also the draft on 0532-0111.

[159] PSS 0531-0746.

Example 3.10b Reordering of the three-note selections (second rotation cycle)

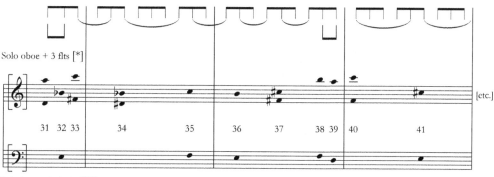

Example 3.10c Distribution of pitches from the second rotation (31–60)

[In the score [*] = 3 flutes and 3 unison oboes; [**] = 3 bassoons and 3 unison clarinets]

Example 3.10a relate to the second cycle only; the new set of numbers in Example 3.10b determines the placement of notes: in the first line, even numbers = an octave higher; in the second line, odd numbers = an octave lower. The distribution of the pitches is shown in Example 3.10c.[160] From this it can be concluded that Birtwistle based his scheme on the D–A dyad, around which the music coalesces, to dramatic effect, at the end of Arch 16 and throughout Arch 17, where this sustained dyad recalls the use of a drone in traditional laments (it is possible to speculate that this was one of the 'musical ideas' listed in Figure 3.2). His scheme also ensures a high percentage of other perfect fifth dyads. Yet the conclusion of Arch 16 is a mixture of coincidence and contrivance, as although the possibility that the second rotation might end on pitches D and A is built into the system, the fact that it does end there appears to be entirely fortuitous.[161]

[160] This begins in the middle of the penultimate bar of the conductor II ensemble, p. 240.
[161] On Birtwistle's fixation with D as a gravitational centre, and correspondences with the music of Peter Maxwell Davies, see Arnold Whittall, 'Comparatively complex: Birtwistle, Maxwell Davies and modernist analysis', *Music Analysis*, 13, 2/3 (October 1994), 139–59.

Harmony

In his earliest sketches, Birtwistle refers to his intention to employ 'varied harmonic growths' and 'harmonic ostinato', the latter defined by regular or varied rhythmic patterns, or by the sequence of chords.[162] The idea of varied harmonic growths most likely relates to the kind of incremental change witnessed in the harp and bassoon continuum in Act I scene 1. Similar gradual change characterises Orpheus and Eurydice Singers' parts in the Love Duet.[163] The clearest harmonic example occurs during the fact and fantasy sections of Arch 16, at the opening of Act II scene 3.

The sketches for this moment reveal a harmonic scheme in the wood-wind and brass. This soft, sustained texture is constructed from three-note chromatic sets based on the perfect-fifth-related pitch classes A, E and B.[164] A scheme is devised whereby each of these pitch classes is associated with a particular ensemble; the harmony is formed from tight clusters around each pitch class in each of the three different octaves below middle C. Slurs are written between the various three-note chords, linking identical pitches, which suggests Birtwistle was particularly interested in the fixed, or static, dimension of his process. Changes of chord are determined by a rhythm, mapped on a grid of regular quavers, alongside another scheme that determines shifts in the dynamics (between *p*, *pp* and *ppp*). The principle here is one of slight variation and very gradual change; initially, the clusters are distinct from one another, but they eventually overlap, while above them a high cantus unfolds in the piccolos. Although the pitch centres are blurred, the sketches nevertheless reveal a conceptual move towards coherence.

The wind ensemble cantus in Arch 17, directed by the second conductor, is described in the sketches as 'A monody from the Harmony of the World'.[165] It is unclear whether this was an allusion to Johannes Kepler's *Harmonices Mundi* (1619) – this includes Kepler's theory of a music of the spheres, in which the relative distances between the planets are considered to be equivalent to harmonic proportions in sound. Kepler's concern for geometry and mathematical proportions certainly resonates with Birtwistle's interests, and Kepler's suggestion that at one time in history, perhaps at their

[162] PSS 0530-0727.
[163] PSS 0531-0028–32. This approach was developed in *An Imaginary Landscape*, for example, in the double basses, Figs. 32–4, where the harmony alters by one note every three bars.
[164] Birtwistle's first step was to plot the distribution of chords on a table divided into 50 columns – one column per chord – and five rows, which relate to the instrumental groupings (PSS 0531-0724). The ensembles and chords were then worked out and distributed (PSS 0531-0726–31), although the rhythms and dynamics were formulated separately (most likely on PSS 0530-0804–11).
[165] PSS 0530-0823.

inception, the planets 'sang' together in perfect concord tallies with the idea that the musical strands 'come together' at this moment in the opera. Another relevant sketch is an analysis of the Amen to the Gloria in Machaut's Mass.[166] This sketch most likely dates from Birtwistle's time at the University of Colorado, Boulder (1967–8) where, according to Hall, Birtwistle studied Schenkerian analysis.[167] Birtwistle treats the Amen to a quasi-Schenkerian analysis in which he presents two middleground unfoldings from D to A.

Voices

> On the face of nature, 'history' is written in the signs of transience.[168]

> Like Orpheus's dismembered body, these signs are scattered across the landscape as allegorical fragments, with all the pain and unrequited desires of the past still written in its clots and bruises.[169]

Orpheus Singer's part at the beginning of Act I scene 1 is based on a refrain from the opening text: 'the King stands highest'. The text concerns the expedition of Jason and the Argonauts for the Golden Fleece, which Orpheus is reputed to have joined. As Zinovieff explains:

> The spoken poem is an allegory on two aspects of Orpheus' life. (The Argonautic expedition and the later teachings or mysteries). The 'King' refers to both Jason and his father, Aeson. The 'fifty' are the Argonauts . . . The sung recitative poem is also about the same expedition. It shows first how the exhausted Argonauts were given a vision of Apollo at the break of day and other memories which Orpheus has of the Argonautic expedition. This expedition probably was the fabled immigration of the Aeolians from Atlantis. These people used a very primitive alphabet (Pelasgic) and pre-hellenic language. Orpheus uses this fifteen consonant and seven vowel formula in his songs of magic.[170]

[166] PSS 0540-0463; Studien.

[167] Hall, *HB*, 49. This theory is supported by the fact that the paper on which the analysis is written – marked 'G. Schirmer, Inc., New York No. 4', with six staffs – was a type that Birtwistle began to use when he composed *Nomos* (1967–8), and the analysis is located amid sketches for *Nomos* (for example, PSS 0540-0461; Studien). However, Birtwistle later used many G. Schirmer sheets (with twelve staffs) when he began sketching *Orpheus*.

[168] Walter Benjamin, cited in Hent de Vries, *Minimal Theologies: Critiques of Secular Reason in Adorno and Levinas*, trans. Geoffrey Hale (Baltimore: Johns Hopkins University Press, 2005), 269. Cited in Chua, 'Untimely reflections', 578.

[169] Chua, 'Untimely reflections', 578.

[170] Zinovieff, 'Explanatory document', PSS 0533-0177. The original text is italicised. Zinovieff later expanded this description: 'The [sung] recitative refers to Orpheus' memories of the Argonautic expedition. (A vision of Apollo at dawn after shipwreck; the Symplegades; the Sirens; the Golden Fleece; singing the Argos into [the] sea when it was cast on the shore). The spoken words are an allegory on the same journey. They describe a slow transition from night

Although Birtwistle initially restricts Orpheus Singer and the accompanying tenors and basses to the vowels from the line 'the King stands highest', the sketches reveal that he originally divided the vowels into fourteen types, including 'a' as in 'above', 'father', 'pack' and 'saw'.[171] Some of these additional variants are sung by Eurydice Singer in The Yawn (recalled in Arches 4 and 5), and by the chorus in The Whisper of Change. The phonemes are notated in the score using symbols that are broadly consistent with the International Phonetic Alphabet. While Orpheus Singer – in his agonised search for language – enunciates and half-sings a randomised selection of phonemes, Orpheus Puppet interjects with spoken fragments of text that recall episodes and names from the mythical expedition. Here Birtwistle fragments and reorders the first twenty lines of Orpheus Puppet's text, after which Zinovieff's order is retained.

Orpheus Singer has five verses in this opening section. The first of these is spoken as a mixture of natural speech inflection and sustained phonemes, which ignores Zinovieff's request for sung text. The sketches reveal that one of Birtwistle's earliest tasks was to reorder the text, splitting up single words and separating their component syllables; the sketch for verse 3 is given in Figure 3.9. Birtwistle therefore made steps to interpret the text on his own terms. These reordered segments were then inserted into Orpheus Singer's line. Ultimately, Orpheus Singer's verses II to V are presented from two perspectives: the original order is retained, spoken with natural inflection, while the reordered words – preserved whole rather than broken into syllables – are inserted at random intervals and performed as prolonged half-song (this division of text and performance style very clearly recalls *Nenia: the Death of Orpheus*). Also interspersed within this scheme are sung references to Eurydice, which anticipate the Love Duet to come.

A number of key points emerge from the opening. Birtwistle was evidently concerned with breaking up the narrative and exploring the text purely in terms of its phonetic content. The result is a microcosm of Birtwistle's interest in the contrast between reflective aria and narrative-driven recitative. There is also a distinction between text that is in focus and out of focus so that gradually, as Orpheus Singer learns to speak, certain words are set in relief, such as 'king'.[172] As will be discussed in more detail in Chapter 7,

---

to day . . . by using the metaphor of changes in the body profile, hands and eyes of Jason.' Zinovieff, *The Mask of Orpheus*, libretto reproduced with NMC Recording (NMC D050), 1997, 18.

[171] PSS 0530-0726, which also lists various types of speech-song notation.

[172] The pathos of Orpheus Singer's attempts to form words was very subtly conveyed by Philip Langridge in the original production. This was broadcast by the BBC in June 1986. A copy is available at the National Sound Archive in the British Library, London: 1CDR0017730–1CDR0017732 D1-D4 NSA.

Figure 3.9 Sketch for Orpheus Singer, 1st Poem of Reminiscence, verse 3, Act I scene 1

III

			1	2	3	4 - 5			
1	1	The	king	stands	a-lone				
			3	1	5	2 4			

			1	2	3			
2	2	The	most	still				
			3	2	1			

			1	2	3	4 - 5	6	7
4	3	Reach	–ing	back	in – to	the	night,	
			6	4	1 7	3	8	

			1 2	3	4 - 5	6	
3	4	Two hands	stretched	be – hind	him,		
			4 5	3	2 6	1	

			1 2	3	4	5 6	
6	5	Los – ing	the	cold	wea – ther,		
			6 1	4	3	2 5	

			1	2	3	4	5	6	– 7	8	9
5	6	Grin	–ning	his	blue	eyes	In	– to	the	sun.
			9	2	1	8	6	4	3	5	7

King / still most / him be stretched hind / back night the ing / his ing to In the

this approach dominated Birtwistle's workshops on *Agamemnon* at London's National Theatre, held in January 1977.[173] Yet these experiments were superseded by a pulse-based mode of delivery in the *Oresteia* production in 1981, and this is reflected in the more focused approach in the newly composed sections of Act III. Nevertheless, as Adlington remarks, *Orpheus*, 'pre-eminently, sees a literal and very deliberate exploration of the transitional spaces between sound and word'. Orpheus's painstaking attempts to find words and the Oracle's 'wrenching spoken utterances and shrieking

[173] Birtwistle refers to the importance of the concept of ideas being 'in focus and out of focus' in what appears to be the sketch for a talk on his music, most likely presented while he was in America composing *Orpheus*. PSS 0530-0583.

vocalise' demonstrate that 'non-verbal utterance need not necessarily sig-nal . . . a retreat from expressivity in favour of a purely formalist approach to sound'.[174]

There are numerous instances of formalist experiment shading into lyri-cal, expressive device. Eurydice Singer's 'Ha-Ha-nds Hands Orpheus, give hands, Hearts much later' (p. 89) – a more stuttering, fragmented version of a line heard earlier (p. 17) – effectively conveys the new, more tense dramatic context caused by the threatening presence of Aristaeus. Similarly, the topic of lost childhood innocence is related to *Punch* by the setting of 'Visions from frightened childhood / Calling. / Dumbed by death' (p. 89), in which the final three words (highly reminiscent of Pruslin's libretto) are strictly punctuated.[175] Contour is also deployed to dramatic effect, most obviously in the Priests' 2nd Complicated Question (pp. 95, 101 and 110), where the line is passed rapidly between three voices, and the Oracle's unpitched <3, 1, 2, 4> contour scream at the end of Act I, recalled by Hecate in Act II, Arches 7 and 12.[176]

Conversely, although The Yawn, in Acts I and III, portrays Eurydice's boredom with Orpheus's song ('Euridice did not want magic. She wanted a son'),[177] Birtwistle exploits the opportunity for experiment, employing sustained vocal glissandi that move through a wide range of vowel sounds. A sample of the expressive instructions in the score gives further insight into the range of vocal delivery in the opera:

> inwardly, as if searching for words – not projected; projected; hold mouth shape; very exaggeratedly mouthed; mouthed in slow motion; the inflection of 'I remember' must remain the same throughout the poem; with natural speech inflection; with a degree of pitch, low in the voice sotto voce: closed lips; with tenderness and tension; with very clear enunciation; thin tone, no vibrato; with whole voice; extremely tenderly; spoken on monotone; *cant. espressiv.*; always very clipped; with force and intensity; low in voice with tight throat; with anguish; like a despairing invocation; dejected and sadly; becoming ecstatic; explosive, as if on the edge of convulsion; nervously, with equal accents on all syllables; as if peering into the dark; flowing but still with a degree of hesitancy; weighted and intense; very intense (savage); like a

---

[174] Adlington, *MHB*, 79.
[175] References to childhood and lost innocence include: 'I remember my singing "EURIDICE". / Dragging soft memories from children's children' (final score, p. 14); 'Into curved corners / where mirrors reflect infancy. / While the rocks dance in quiet sympathy' (p. 52); 'A doll lies by the riverside' (p. 73); 'Screaming into magic / childhood burns hottest / Soaring into magic' (p. 122); 'I can see mirrors in the water' (p. 135); 'I remember the children's tears' (p. 148); in Arch 4, children play in the sun.
[176] For the 2nd Complicated Question, pitches are applied to a series of contours, although this design is effectively hidden by octave displacements. PSS 0530-0780.
[177] Zinovieff, *The Mask of Orpheus*, 72.

frozen scream; scream!; shouted; exhale; inhale; undulate pitch; slowly
undulate tone; hysterical pitched speech; like a wild animal cry of terror;
measured but breathless; spoken formally, but with a degree of freedom.

One possible influence in this regard, which has not been noted previously,
is Milton Babbitt's *Philomel* (1964), a work that combines live performance
with tape, written with the poet John Hollander for the soprano Bethany
Beardslee. Birtwistle acquired a programme note from a performance of
Philomel in America in the 1960s,[178] which he passed to his son, Silas, and the
work was subsequently performed at the Wardour Castle Summer School
on 15 August 1965. As Elaine Barkin and Martin Brody have commented,

> [*Philomel*] is based on Ovid's interpretation of the Greek legend of Philomela,
> the ravished, speechless maiden who is transformed into a nightingale. New
> ways of combining musical and verbal expressiveness were devised by
> composer and poet: music is as articulate as language; language (Philomela's
> thoughts) is transformed into music (the nightingale's song). The work
> is an almost inexhaustible repertory of speech-song similitudes and
> differentiations, and resonant word-music puns (unrealizable without the
> resources of the synthesizer).[179]

Birtwistle's interest in the sounds of words, rather than their meaning,
certainly evokes the Babbitt example, and evidence that electronic music
had a bearing on vocal technique in the opera is revealed by an early draft,
in which Orpheus Singer is instructed to perform 'like a slow tape but not
lower'.[180] Something of the transitional property of Babbitt's approach to
the voice is also caught in Zinovieff's suggestion that 'if the music and words
and action are separate at times [in *Orpheus*], then the vocal line is the device
most used as a <u>bridge</u> rather than a definition of the structures'.[181] In other
words, voices in *Orpheus* are sites of intersection between semantics, sound
and drama.

Unsurprisingly, therefore, the vocal lines epitomise Birtwistle's guiding
concept of lyrical formalism. As noted earlier, the Duet of Love was generated
from three- to seven-note cells. Elsewhere, the vocal lines are often based on
chromatic wedges and other symmetrical patterns, as in *Punch*. One such
example is Aristaeus Puppet's line at the opening of Act I scene 3. This is

---

[178] The programme, in Silas Birtwistle's possession, is for a performance at Grinnell College,
Iowa, on 17 April 1964; the first half of the concert consisted of a song recital by Bethany
Beardslee, accompanied at the piano by Stephen Pruslin.

[179] Elaine Barkin and Martin Brody, 'Babbitt, Milton', in Stanley Sadie and John Tyrrell, eds., *The
New Grove Dictionary of Music and Musicians*, 2nd edn., vol. II (London: Macmillan, 2001),
287.

[180] PSS 0530-0868. This relates to the line 'The king's hands press forward' (final score, p. 10); the
performance instruction is altered in the score to 'like slow motion'.

[181] Zinovieff, 'Explanatory document', PSS 0533-0027.

Example 3.11a Source set in scheme for Aristaeus's vocal line during the 1st Time Shift, Act I, scene 3, p. 80. PSS 0531-0375

Example 3.11b Source set rearranged as a mode

Example 3.11c Distribution of pitch sets a, b and c in Aristaeus's line

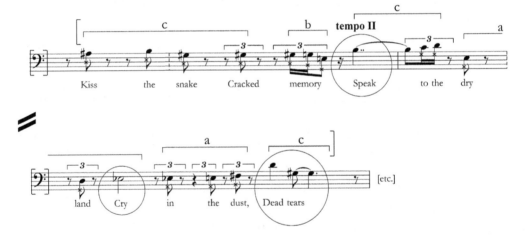

based on an expanding wedge on G, which unfolds according to the interval series 12112 in the upper and lower halves, as presented in Example 3.11a.[182] Having already written out the text and rhythm, Birtwistle arranged the pitches as a mode, rising from C to D an octave above, and bracketed three overlapping 2112 collections (Example 3.11b). He initially began the vocal line using the central collection (labelled b), but deleted this and started instead with the highest (labelled c), as shown in Example 3.11c. The line unfolded as a series of three-note selections from each bracketed set.

[182] PSS 0531-0375.

Example 3.12 Transposition and alterations to Orpheus's line in Arch 4, Act II scene 1, p. 156. PSS 0531-0884

Sketch

Full score, p. 156

As discussed earlier, at some point prior to the first performance, Birtwistle overhauled the Orpheus and Aristaeus vocal parts, transposing and at times recomposing the lines. Usually, Orpheus Singer's part was transposed up a minor third, but there are numerous exceptions and inconsistencies. For example, the 1st Song of Failure in Act I scene 3 was transposed up an augmented fourth, while 'Taste. Remember. Speak' in Act III scene 2 (p. 281, Fig. 26) was transposed up a perfect fourth.[183] Elsewhere, the clef was simply altered from bass to treble. This occurs in Act II, Arch 4, at Orpheus Singer's 'The arch is split' (p. 156), although here slight alterations were made to the pitch and rhythm, as illustrated by Example 3.12.[184] The effect of the changes here is profound, since the original consisted of a unison between voice and piccolo, with three further woodwind lines generated from the piccolo. In the revised version, the unison is replaced by a form of organum at an octave plus a minor third. The alterations to the

[183] PSS 0532-0679.   [184] PSS 0531-0884.

rhythm and pitches, however, disguise the original relationship, covering over the tracks of the original pairing between voice and piccolo.

This is a rare example of a one-to-one relationship between voice and instruments in the first half of the opera; generally speaking, Birtwistle fitted the vocal parts to the accompaniment in Acts I and II, whereas in the newly composed sections of Acts II and III, the instrumental parts were generated from the voices.[185] It is possible to speculate that this was a consequence of Birtwistle's tenure as Director of Music at London's National Theatre, which began in 1975, when he suspended work on the opera. His first project was *Hamlet* (1975), which required several conventional song settings; the practicalities of working with actors, and the overwhelming centrality of the text in theatre productions, may also have led to the shift of emphasis. The new approach is particularly evident in the sketches for the setting of the sixth verse of Orpheus's 3rd Song of Magic in Act III (sequence 6, occurrence 12). Here, the vocal part is written out neatly, above which the distribution of the accompanying parts is plotted on a grid of regular semiquavers that is consistent with the voice, marked with coloured brackets and number series.[186]

Finally, in light of the alterations to the vocal parts, it is necessary to reconsider the closing stages of Act II when the music and drama begin to coalesce. A significant amount of rewriting of the vocal lines occurred from the beginning of Act II scene 3, which suggests that this moment was of special significance to Birtwistle. Orpheus Singer's part was initially transposed up a perfect fifth but also altered from a rather lifeless line into a more lively and compressed form that mixes *Sprechgesang* with song, as shown in Example 3.13. In the score, soon after this moment, Orpheus Singer introduces the perfect fifth dyad C–G on 'can see' of the line 'I can see you' (p. 236), which is highlighted by a sustained C–G dyad in the soprano saxophones and oboes (this is revisited on p. 238). The sketches and Birtwistle's fair copy reveal that the dyad in the vocal line was originally conceived a perfect fifth lower, on G–D,[187] yet the saxophone and oboe parts were originally C–G, therefore, the transposition of the vocal line (brought about by altering the bass clef to treble) resulted in a purely fortuitous unison between voice and accompaniment. This suggests that it is the interval that is important, rather than the pitch classes. Also in the fair copy, Orpheus Puppet's line near the conclusion of the second act ends with E♭–C on 'Tide-moan',

---

[185]   For example, on PSS 0531-0129 the vocal line is 'fitted' to the harp and bassoon (mode I) and percussion (Act I scene 1, p. 32). The new approach is evident from Arch 16 onwards; PSS 0531-0750.

[186]   An exception is the 1st Recitative of Teaching, Act III scene 2, from p. 269. Here, the accompaniment is based on a single line that was conceived first; in an early draft the vocal part is attached to the bottom of the paper and is not as far developed as the instrumental line.

[187]   PSS 0530-0817.

Example 3.13 Transposition and alterations to Orpheus's line in Arch 16, Act II
scene 3, pp. 235–6

Example 3.14 Transposition and alterations to Orpheus's line at the end of
Arch 15, Act II scene 2. PSS 0532-0604 (first fair copy)

rather than C–A, although the D–A dyads in the orchestra were present
in the earlier version. Similarly, but more remarkably, the close of Act II
scene 2 was reworked, as shown in Example 3.14. The final version certainly
possesses a more satisfying arch-like shape, but it also introduces the falling,
minor third dyad G–E on 'highest'. This counterbalances a rising E–G dyad
in the brass, which was already present in Birtwistle's fair copy. But this alteration has greater implications, for it was extended back to Orpheus's cries
of 'Euridice', sung earlier in Arch 15 (pp. 227–32). In the score, these cries
comprise sustained notes on E and G, followed by more frantic outbursts
characterised as a 'wild animal cry of terror'. The frantic outbursts, however,

were originally sketched at a lower register, without any indication of the sustained notes.[188] Moreover, in Birtwistle's fair copy the sustained notes are on B and D;[189] pitch class E was to have been provided by Apollo's voice on the tape. Birtwistle's alterations therefore brought his original conception into greater focus, sometimes by chance, elsewhere by design.[190]

Narrative, time and space

Following an examination of the sketches, Adlington's claim that Birtwistle 'adheres only fitfully to the formal niceties of his libretto' requires clarification.[191] Birtwistle and Zinovieff were agreed, from the start, that the relationship between music and libretto would be asynchronous, yet in practice this amounted to a remarkably close adherence to Zinovieff's schemes at one level, and a reinterpretation of them at another. What emerges most clearly from this – as from the generative concept of lyrical formalism and the associated dialectic between expressive impulse and formal control – is a productive tension between various kinds of continuity and discontinuity. This is particularly well illustrated in Act III by the repetition of music from earlier in the opera, which effectively demonstrates the role of memory in the construction of narrative.

Jann Pasler has suggested that *Orpheus* is representative of 'a new kind of narrative', which she argues arose in operas and music theatre works in the 1980s:

> These narratives borrow the most important attributes of traditional
> narratives – the use of signifieds, well-defined structures, configuration,
> unifying reference points, transformation, and memory. But they continue to
> respond to the modern desire for expressing the multiplicity of existence,
> fragmentary and seemingly irrational orders, and meanings that go beyond
> those that are known.[192]

Pasler's comments are supported by Cross's suggestion that *Orpheus* refashions the myth of Orpheus from a late twentieth-century perspective.

---

[188] PSS 0530-0837.   [189] PSS 0532-0595–6.

[190] Birtwistle's introduction of the E–G dyad near the end of Act II is mirrored by the emergence of D–F in the 3rd Time Shift, at the start of Act III. Pitches D and F and the minor third interval in general were introduced as a unifying device in the drones and sung choruses of Birtwistle's music for the *Oresteia*, and they assume importance in a number of works through the 1980s, notably *Secret Theatre* (1984), *Earth Dances* (1985–6), *Endless Parade* (1987), *Salford Toccata* (1989), *Ritual Fragment* (1990) and *Gawain* (1989–91). The origins of this interest may, however, be traced back to the Machaut analysis, in which Birtwistle noted an 'attention to f', following the opening D. PSS 0540-0463; *Studien*.

[191] Adlington, *MHB*, 19.

[192] Jann Pasler, 'Narrative and narrativity in music', in her *Writing through Music: Essays on Music, Culture, and Politics* (Oxford University Press, 2008), 46.

Following a host of artists who responded to the Orpheus myth in light of the First World War and subsequent human tragedies (notably Auden, Anouilh, Camus, Casella, Cocteau, Dessau, Kokoschka, Krenek, Milhaud, Müller, Rilke and Stravinsky), Cross notes that leading late twentieth-century composers, such as Andriessen, Foss, Furrer, Glass, Henze, Neuwirth, Schaeffer and Tippett, also turned to the Orpheus myth in order 'to articulate something of what it means to live in the late-modern era'.[193] As such, the opera may be understood to express the fracturing of identity and violence to the individual represented in modernist art. This, in turn, recalls Zinovieff's remark that 'At the highest level it is with the evolution and degradation of civilized man that "Orpheus" is concerned.'[194]

By contrast, a Utopian dimension is apparent in Birtwistle's monumentalist desire to create a kind of 'total theatre' and 'a formal world that was utterly new'. Disunity, flashbacks and montage are often associated with the opera's more dynamic, innovative structures, such as the arches, and there is a modernist nostalgia for a lost sense of unity (for the Argonautic expedition and Orpheus's union with Eurydice), even if the opera 'concludes' that time cannot be reversed. All of which suggests Jürgen Habermas's notion that modernism is an unfinished project.[195] In this sense, *Orpheus* demonstrates a *new* modernist urge to innovate, following the 'postmodernist pastiche' in *Punch*.

Yet Pasler refers to *Orpheus*'s 'return to using narrative concepts' as postmodern.[196] Similarly, as noted earlier, Cross suggests that '*Orpheus* articulates the anxieties of a newly emerging post-industrial, post-imperial, post-modern age'. Arguably, *Orpheus* is representative of a continuing modernism that in certain respects articulates the concerns of its postmodern context. There is insufficient space here to explore this proposal fully. However, I will conclude with some brief observations on this issue in so far as it relates to the opera's concern with narrative, time and space.

Orpheus is an opera about time.[197] Orpheus attempts to turn back time; Hall even argues he has 'already made his choice' to look back 'before the

---

[193] Cross, *Harrison Birtwistle: The Mask of Orpheus*, 12. Cross comments that *Orpheus* is a lament for the horrors and the losses 'both personal and collective' of the twentieth century, while Orpheus's death stands for 'the collapse of civilized man'. 'The darkness of the underworld, it might be said, echoed the terrible chambers of Stalin's gulags and Hitler's death camps: abandon every hope, all you who enter'; 142, 9 and 143.

[194] Zinovieff, 'Explanatory document', PSS 0533-0008.

[195] Jürgen Habermas, 'Modernity – an incomplete project', in Hal Foster, ed., *Postmodern Culture* (London: Pluto Press, 1985), 3–15.

[196] Pasler, 'Narrative and narrativity', 48.

[197] For an excellent survey of the relationship between time and post-tonal music, see Robert Adlington's unpublished D.Phil. thesis 'Temporality in post-tonal music', University of Sussex, 1997.

action begins'.[198] Moreover, Orpheus's refrain, 'I remember', encourages a sense that the opera's fragmentary form is a reflection of Orpheus's attempts to recall the events of his past: the prior events to be narrated (the story or plot) are reorganised according to the vagaries of memory (the narrative).[199] Underpinning the opera, therefore, is a dialectic between time and narrative, and between lost time and time regained: each scene that includes Eurydice represents time lost and regained. *Orpheus* is a re-presentation of Orpheus's attempts to narrativise his situation, which result in a type of 'cognitive mapping', to use Fredric Jameson's term, whereby experience and memory shape form.[200]

The correlation between time and narrative – or, more specifically, between the activity of narrating a story and the temporal character of human experience – was famously proposed by the pre-eminent theorist on time and narrative Paul Ricoeur in a monumental three-volume study first published between 1983 and 1985, which grew from a project on metaphor published in 1975 – in other words, in a study that is almost exactly contemporary with *Orpheus*. Narrative, Ricoeur argues, is a reconfiguration of temporal experience: 'time becomes human time to the extent that it is organized after the manner of a narrative; narrative, in turn, is meaningful to the extent that it portrays the features of temporal experience'.[201]

At the root of Ricoeur's study are two concepts. The first is the non-congruence between two culturally constructed perspectives on time: cosmological (objective/clock time) and phenomenological (subjective/internal time). These may be characterised in terms of the views of Aristotle and Augustine respectively. Aristotle argued that we exist 'in' time, that 'things are in time as they are in number'. This implies that time exists as a material substance that may be strictly observed, measured and counted, and that time is a series of 'nows', or point-like instants. Aristotle's quantitative perspective recalls the prescribed durations of Zinovieff's libretto, as well as the metrical precision of the electronic music for the mime interludes. Ricoeur argues, however, that Aristotle was also guided by more ancient assumptions, such as the idea that we are contained by 'the cyclic organization of the cosmos, which harmoniously includes the passing of

[198] Hall, *HB*, 117.

[199] My distinction follows Vladimir Propp's notion of *fibula* and *sjuzhet* in *The Morphology of the Folktale*, trans. L. Scott (Austin: University of Texas Press, 1994); see also Gérard Genette's categories of story and narrative in his *Narrative Discourse: An Essay in Method*, trans. Jane E. Lewin (Ithaca, NY: Cornell University Press, 1983), and Seymour Chatman, *Story and Discourse* (Ithaca, NY: Cornell University Press, 1978).

[200] Fredric Jameson, *Postmodernism, or The Cultural Logic of Late Capitalism* (Durham, NC: Duke University Press, 1991), 52 and 416–17.

[201] Paul Ricoeur, *Time and Narrative*, vol. I, trans. Kathleen McLaughlin and David Pellauer (London: University of Chicago Press, 1984), 3.

the seasons, the succession of generations, and the periodic return of festivals', an idea that is reflected in *Orpheus*'s cyclic repetitions, and Birtwistle's reference to the harmony of the spheres.[202]

Augustine, on the other hand, argued that 'time is merely an extension . . . of the mind itself'; 'it is in my own mind . . . that I measure time. I must not allow my mind to insist that time is something objective.'[203] This qualitative position – later modified by Kant, Hegel, Heidegger and Adorno, among others – clearly resonates with the notion of cognitive mapping discussed above, and with Zinovieff's statement that *Orpheus* is concerned 'over and over again with the state of mind of Orpheus'. This perspective calls into question the obsession in *Orpheus* with durations, since the limits of a listener's real-time perceptions and the manner in which memory functions suggest that a listener is unlikely to perceive the opera's long-range proportional schemes.[204] As Adlington observes, '[t]he *distance* of precise temporal quantification from ordinary human existence is thereby emphasized, a move in keeping with the strikingly malleable treatment of time in the opera's story-telling as a whole'.[205]

The cosmological and phenomenological perspectives of time evoke the tension between reason and intuition discussed throughout this chapter. Currie observes that 'The philosophy of time from Zeno to Derrida can be read as a failure to escape the tensions involved in these aporias, or to banish the dualism from which they derive.'[206] Yet the crucial point, I believe, is that one perspective continually reintroduces the other, as in the expression 'the hour passed slowly'. We might trace this relationship in Birtwistle's rhythmic schemes, in which the underlying metrical scaffolds are concealed, yet they exercise enough control over the individual parts to ensure they remain distinct from one another. The carefully plotted cantus melody in Act II is gradually abandoned, yet Birtwistle felt the desire to replace it with new, more faithfully rendered schemes in Arches 16 and 17.

---

[202] Paul Ricoeur, *Time and Narrative*, vol. III, trans. Kathleen Blamey and David Pellauer (London: University of Chicago Press, 1988), 264.

[203] Saint Augustine, *Confessions*, trans. R. S. Pine-Coffin (London: Penguin Books, 1961), 274 and 276.

[204] Daniel Dennett's 'multiple drafts' theory of cognition suggests that, following a very short sensory memory, the mind assembles disconnected snapshots of ongoing events, which are fed into a working memory in which earlier snapshot reports are erased, are revised or decay. Narrative 'time-lines' may be formed, but no single narrative counts as the canonical version. Working memory, which is generally thought to have a capacity of twenty to thirty seconds, is then passed to a long-term memory, but selectively and in abstract form. See Daniel Dennett, *Consciousness Explained* (London: Penguin Books, 1993).

[205] Adlington, *MHB*, 105.

[206] Mark Currie, *About Time: Narrative, Fiction and the Philosophy of Time* (Edinburgh University Press, 2007), 92.

Ricoeur's second concept is enlisted in an attempt to solve the aporias of time. This is Aristotle's notion, articulated in his *Poetics*, that plot imitates action. Ricoeur develops this idea into what he terms emplotment, by which narrative structures time. Emplotment is a threefold process of mimesis in which the multiple events of a plot (mimesis$_1$) are gathered together and arranged into significant wholes (mimesis$_2$) that are then delivered to the receiver (mimesis$_3$): 'We are following therefore the destiny of a prefigured time that becomes a refigured time through the mediation of a configured time.'[207] Before the objection is made that Ricoeur's formula relates to language and not music, it should be considered that Aristotle's theory of plot concerned oral poetry, and that Ricoeur explicitly states that the third stage 'marks the intersection of the world of the text and the world of *the hearer* or reader; the intersection, therefore, of the world configured by the poem and the world wherein *real action* occurs and unfolds its specific temporality'.[208]

Ricoeur's adage might therefore serve to describe the relationship between the Orpheus myth arranged into the multiple events of a plot by Zinovi-eff (prefigured time) and our perception of that plot when attending a performance of *Orpheus* (refigured time). The mediating stage of mimesis (configured time) is formed by Birtwistle's interpretation of Zinovieff's libretto. However, this overlooks Birtwistle's input into the initial stage (e.g. the idea of the arches structure) and the extent to which Zinovieff configured the plot. Also, Ricoeur suggests that during configuration the significant wholes are related by causal-explanatory links, whereas in *Orpheus* such links are asserted and undermined by the libretto, by the music's promise and denial of continuous textures in Acts I and II, and by the concept of lyrical formalism. Rather than presume to 'solve' the problem, as Ricoeur appears determined to do, *Orpheus* restores a sense that the dialectics of time are irresolvable: the repetitions of music and drama in Act III could continue *ad infinitum*; meaning is deferred, even at the end of the opera.

Ricoeur argues that the aporias of time may be reinterpreted 'in terms of a dilemma between the assembled unity of time and its bursting apart as a function of memory, anticipation, and attention'.[209] This statement draws on Augustine's notion of the threefold present, that is, the idea that the past, present and future are all contained in the present. This concept corresponds well to music, in which there are no past or future tenses, only past-, present- and future-present tenses. Ricoeur concludes that 'the problem of time cannot be attacked from a single side only'; 'Our narrative

---

[207] Ricoeur, *Time and Narrative*, vol. I, 54. The original text is italicised.
[208] Ibid., 71, italics added.   [209] Ricoeur, *Time and Narrative*, vol. III, 250.

poetics needs the complicity as well as the contrast between internal time-consciousness and objective succession, making all the more urgent the search for narrative mediations between the discordant concordance of phenomenological time and the simple succession of physical time.'[210] He then advocates that '[I]t is in the way that narrativity is carried toward its limits that the secret of its reply to the inscrutability of time lies.'[211]

Relating these ideas to opera is not straightforward. However, Pasler has proposed a parallel based on the manner in which change is organised and experienced in narrative. Following Jean Piaget, she refers to the concept of 'narrative transformation'. This is the system of causal tension in a novel, which effects all kinds of change, from simple alterations, such as the status of a character (e.g. from positive to negative), to more complex changes, for example regarding knowledge (e.g. from a problem to a solution).[212] Pasler compares these ideas to thematic transformations in music, and to more 'complex states of being', such as the transformation from tension into resolution. Here, Pasler cites the threefold present, arguing that transformation involves expectation, memory, and attention in interaction with one another. This brings to mind the suitably named Whisper of Change parts in *Orpheus*, which signal transformation with an associated sense of foreboding. However, in the 'new kind of narrative', transformation 'does not depend on immediate connections from one section to the next but rather on some overall connectivity. The goal . . . is to make a cumulative impact.' Such '[p]ostmodern narratives', Pasler observes, 'do create an order – what Lyotard calls an "internal equilibrium" – but at the same time, unlike their predecessors, they "tolerate the incommensurable"'.[213]

Here Pasler risks contradiction. To 'create an order' may simply refer to the sequential progression of events in time, that is, to the Newtonian idea that '[a]ll things are placed in time as to order of succession'.[214] There is nothing 'new' about this perspective; as Currie remarks, 'The one-directionality of time is part of the physical fact of an expanding universe. And none of us is getting any younger. How feeble the interventions of the postmodern novelist, the poststructuralist philosopher and the cultural theorist appear in the face of these brute realities.'[215] By contrast, 'some overall connectivity'

---

[210] Ibid., 21 and 22.   [211] Ibid., 270.

[212] This is based on Tzvetan Todorov, *Poetics of Prose*, trans. Richard Howard (Oxford: Blackwell, 1977).

[213] Pasler, 'Narrative and narrativity in music', 47; Jean-François Lyotard, *The Postmodern Condition*, trans. Geoff Bennington and Brian Massumi (Manchester University Press, 1997), xxv and 7.

[214] I. Newton, *Sir Isaac Newton's Mathematical Principles of Natural Philosophy and His System of the World*, trans. F. Cajori (Berkeley and Los Angeles: University of California Press, 1962), 8.

[215] Currie, *About Time*, 76.

(Pasler also refers to 'a certain kind of whole') suggests something more integrated.[216] It is indeed possible to argue this case for *Orpheus*, as illustrated by Tables 3.1 and 3.3. These tables refer back to Aristotle's notion of 'mythemes', that is, the repetition of certain narrative themes in myth (such as murder in the Oedipus myth), which gave rise to Lévi-Strauss's notion of homologies of structure in myths. Lévi-Strauss represented such repetitions (usually phrases, set motifs or formulaic expressions intended to aid the memory of the orator) with tables that resemble Tables 3.1 and 3.3, in which the themes are symbolised by number. Yet such integrative interpretations amount to the kind of structuralist metanarrative that *Orpheus* simultaneously inscribes and resists.

There are several problems with Pasler's account. Firstly, the comparison of linguistic modes to musical ones is the subject of considerable scepticism. Representative of this viewpoint is Carolyn Abbate's position that music is an essentially mimetic, rather than diegetic, mode: music may assume the appearance of narrative, but it does not narrate.[217] (I will have more to say about this topic in relation to *Gawain* in Chapter 5). However, the idea of mimesis is clearly relevant in the context of Ricoeur's model of emplotment. Secondly, the language/music aporia arises because Pasler loses sight of opera, focusing on music as an autonomous entity. This question needs to be considered carefully in relation to *Orpheus*, however, since the sketches suggest that Birtwistle's music is part of a relational system: as Zinovieff remarked, it is in 'the struggles, transformations and transitions *between* the levels [of the drama] that the originality of the Opera lies'. Thirdly, Pasler is not specific about what might constitute her notion of 'overall connectivity'. She seems to suggest that the causal logic behind narrative events is somehow loosened in the new narratives. In *Orpheus*, this is illustrated by the Love Duet extensions, which do not function as plot devices. Similarly, the extended instrumental Time Shift at the opening of Act III, and the repeated sacrifices of Orpheus in Act III are excuses for purely musical expansion: they are robust statements that fill the auditorium, examples of Gumbrecht's production of presence extended outward from the drama into purely musical form. Such sections move beyond the causal logic of the drama, that is, they 'think and feel beyond' the structure of the plot, carrying narrativity, as Ricoeur suggests, 'toward its limits'.

Post-structuralism has taught that binaries, such as time and narrative, are actually hierarchies, in which one domain – in this instance time – is more important than the other. To counteract this tendency, cultural

---

[216] Pasler, 'Narrative and narrativity in music', 47.
[217] Carolyn Abbate, *Unsung Voices* (Princeton University Press, 1991), xi–xii.

theorists such as Edward Soja and Lawrence Grossberg have called for a compensatory emphasis on space in relation to time and narrative, leading to the development of a *topochronic* perspective on narrative.[218] Space here relates to the strictly bordered physical or imagined places in which events unfold. The repetitions in Act III, for example, evoke and are enacted within particular places: the pastoral banks of the river Enipeus, where Eurydice dies (lower stage front); the communal site of the ceremonies (upper stage left); the neutral location of Orpheus's 3rd Song of Magic (movements towards upper stage right). Zinovieff's notes often stress the importance of space in his conception, and he even spoke of his desire to divide the stage horizontally to depict 'over' and 'under' worlds.

Suggestive in this regard is Susan Friedman's reading of Arundhati Roy's *The God of Small Things* (1997), in which 'different spaces [such as a cinema, a factory or a room] in the novel contain history. The novel moves associationally in and out of these spaces, rather than sequentially in linear time, with each location stimulating different fragments of events, often lyrically rendered through motif, metonym, or image.'[219] According to this formulation, space/place generates narrative. However, unlike *The God of Small Things*, when we re-enter particular places in *Orpheus* it is not necessarily in order to move the narrative on. Rather, it is to resume a set of feelings and emotional associations that are essentially static. This relates back to Zinovieff's suggestion, mentioned earlier, that Orpheus 'tries to preserve as a memory the static situation of loving Euridice'. In such moments, memory, attention and expectation are replaced by the desire to preserve: the Love Duets preserve a sense of temporality as desire and incompletion; the repeated sacrifices of Orpheus preserve a sense of violent unrest. This approach began with the focus on topics in Act I. In Act II, however, the situation was different. There, each arch framed a 'little narrative', in which Orpheus described a specific location in some detail, supported, at times, by the music (as in Arch 4: 'I can see men cheering. / I can hear the laughter'). Conceptually, those spaces were distinct from one another. Yet a set of musical objects, including the two-octave modes and the cantus melody, moved through the arches, bringing a sense of association and causal connection.

---

[218] See for example E. Soja, *Postmodern Geographies: The Reassertion of Space in Critical Theory* (London: Verso, 1989), and L. Grossberg, 'The space of culture, the power of space', in Iain Chambers and Lidia Curti, eds., *The Post-Colonial Question: Common Skies, Divided Horizons* (London: Routledge, 1996), 169–88.

[219] Susan Stanford Friedman, 'Spatial poetics and Arundhati Roy's *The God of Small Things*', in James Phelan and Peter J. Rabinowitz, eds., *A Companion to Narrative Theory* (Malden, MA, and Oxford: Blackwell Publishing, 2005), 199. Friedman's observations are based on Bakhtin's notion of chronotope, or 'time-space', although she fails to point out that Bakhtin describes time as 'the dominant principle in the chronotope'. See Bakhtin, *The Dialogic Imagination: Four Essays*, trans. Caryl Emerson and Michael Holquist (Austin: University of Texas Press, 2000), 86.

In Act III, elements of the plot are freed so that, as in Stockhausen's concept of moment form, each moment 'equals a "cut" through the linearity of time, eschewing any causal connections with what preceded and what follows'.[220]

The clearest parallel to Friedman's *topochronic* model is Act I scene 3, in which the stage action is divided between three spaces. Here Orpheus's voice, which is carried by his movements from one part of the stage to another, represents what Zinovieff describes as an associational 'bridge' between the site-specific actions. The metaphor of a bridge is, of course, writ largest in the arches construction, which is the dominant spatial metaphor in the opera. In this context, Zinovieff's and Birtwistle's durational schemes represent the 'timing of space' and the 'spacing of time'.[221] As the sketches reveal, Birtwistle enters and moves through architectural schemes of some complexity, and although temporal factors are important, his attention is guided equally towards matters of space, such as the unfolding of modes, harmonic growth, and contour. Moreover, following his concept of lyrical formalism, Birtwistle 'maps out' his movements through the piece, often selecting different routes to the ones suggested by Zinovieff. This is highly redolent of another spatial metaphor, one that forms the subject of the next chapter: namely, the concept of the labyrinth.

[220] David Clarke, *The Music and Thought of Michael Tippett: Modern Times and Metaphysics* (Cambridge University Press, 2001), 115.
[221] Grossberg, 'The space of culture', 180.

4 *Yan Tan Tethera*: pastoral labyrinths and the scene–agent ratio

[T]he shepherd-poet of pastoral convention is obviously a persona and has long been accepted as one.[1]

One of the tasks of, shall we say, lyric poets of our period, might be just to sustain the pastoral metaphor, in its deep sense, against the ephemeralities of town fashions.[2]

Birtwistle talks a lot about landscapes . . . Where a composer like Vaughan Williams was concerned primarily with 'the skin of the landscape', Birtwistle wants to go deeper – all the way through to the geology where it makes sense to talk in terms of strata, faults and plates. He likes the thought that 'certain music will inhabit certain ranges, so there are corridors of activity which only certain forms of music can inhabit'.[3]

The more we are invited to empathize with maze-walkers, to share a subjective perspective, the more labyrinthine confusion dominates and art recedes.[4]

Commissioned by Robert Ponsonby in 1979 and composed in 1983–4, *Yan Tan Tethera*, subtitled 'a mechanical pastoral,' is a ninety-minute, one-act chamber opera for eight solo singers, small chorus, and sixteen-part ensemble – a very intimate scale by comparison to *Orpheus*. Though it was originally billed to receive a combined BBC radio and television premiere, the head of music and arts at BBC television eventually pronounced the work too expensive to produce. Ultimately the opera was premiered by Opera Factory and the London Sinfonietta at the Queen Elizabeth Hall on 7 August 1986. A studio production directed by Derek Bailey, with the same performers, was broadcast by Channel 4 in 1987, alongside productions of *Down by the Greenwood Side* and *Punch and Judy*, and a documentary on the composer titled 'Behind the mask'.[5] The opera's premiere therefore

---

[1] Edward T. Cone, *The Composer's Voice* (Berkeley and Los Angeles: University of California Press, 1974), 2.

[2] Michael Tippett, composer's note on *Songs for Dov* published with the recording on Argo ZRG 703, 1973; cited in Arnold Whittall, *The Music of Britten and Tippett: Studies in Themes and Techniques* (Cambridge University Press, 1990), 247.

[3] Wright, 'The mystery of the kiosk composer'.

[4] Penelope Reed Doob, *The Idea of the Labyrinth: From Classical Antiquity through the Middle Ages* (Ithaca, NY and London: Cornell University Press, 1990), 37.

[5] The documentary was produced by Anthony Snell, *Down by the Greenwood Side* was an Aquarius production, *Punch* was performed by Opera Factory.

coincided with a decade in which Birtwistle received widespread exposure
and acclaim, and in which he reached a form of stylistic maturity, most
notably in *Secret Theatre* (1984) and *Earth Dances* (1986). These instrumental works develop ideas explored in *Still Movement* (1984), for string
ensemble, which grew directly from new compositional preoccupations first
developed in *Yan Yan Tethera*. The opera is arguably a key work, therefore,
and it receives more attention here than in any other Birtwistle study.

It has been claimed, however, that 'the whole idea and original conception' of *Yan Tan Tethera* came from the librettist – the poet and playwright
Tony Harrison.[6] Certainly, Birtwistle's suggestion that *Yan Tan Tethera* is
based on a story he found in K. M. Briggs's *British Folk Tales* is question-
able, since none of the stories in Briggs's substantial four-volume collection
resemble the opera scenario in title or content.[7] One might argue, however,
that a librettist's input is of less significance than a composer's interpretation of a libretto or scenario. Indeed, the characteristic features of *Yan Tan
Tethera* – its focus on ritual, formal repetition and archetypal characters –
are entirely consistent with Birtwistle's prevailing concerns, and its ancient
folk setting recalls *Down by the Greenwood Side* and *Bow Down* (discussed
in Chapters 1 and 7, respectively). Moreover, while he composed the opera
in 1983, Birtwistle remarked that the work

> has things I've never done before and I'm really quite excited about it. Did
> you know that it was Stravinsky who divided Auden's text for *The Rake's
> Progress* into recitatives and arias? Auden wrote his libretto without the
> divisions. Well, I'm imposing something on Tony Harrison's libretto. Had I
> asked Tony to provide it for me, it wouldn't have worked; the result would be
> too formal in the wrong sense, too predictable.[8]

Birtwistle's desire to exercise more control over the dramatic and narrative
elements is clearly stated, and his claim to have imposed 'something' on
Harrison's libretto will be explored in the second half of this chapter.

Birtwistle's reference to *The Rake's Progress* is revealing for several reasons. W. H. Auden's libretto – ostensibly an interpretation of a series of eight
engravings produced by William Hogarth in the 1730s – includes various
pastoral allusions: the first scene, for example, was described by Auden as
a 'pastoral à la Theocritus'.[9] Geoffrey Chew has argued that only through

---

[6] Neil Astley, 'The Wizard of [Uz]', in Astley, ed., *Tony Harrison* (Newcastle-upon-Tyne: Bloodaxe
    Books, 1991), 10–11. This claim is also made for *Bow Down*, discussed in Chapter 7. A first
    draft of Harrison's libretto was completed in 1980, well before work began on the music.
[7] Hall, *HB*, 143. A more systematic study than the one undertaken for this chapter may, of course,
    reveal that aspects of different stories in Briggs's collection were combined in Birtwistle's mind.
[8] Birtwistle in Hall, *HB*, 144.
[9] Hogarth's engravings had been inspired by John Gay's pastoral opera *The Beggar's Opera*
    (1728).

an appreciation of the *Rake* as a pastoral fable, and its central character Tom Rakewell as a profoundly ambiguous pastoral hero, is it possible to fully comprehend the opera's unusual ending, its overall themes, and the workings of Stravinsky's neoclassical style. For this reason Chew elected to explore the *Rake* from Auden's perspective first before turning to the music.[10] A similar approach will be adopted here, since Harrison's perspective offers revealing insights into the music. Birtwistle's characterisation of the Stravinsky–Auden collaboration is therefore rather one-sided. It is true that Auden claimed it was 'the librettist's job to satisfy the composer, not the other way around'.[11] Yet Auden and his fellow librettist Chester Kallman clearly understood their ability to shape a composer's vision dramatically and musically: as Roger Savage notes, the *Rake*'s set pieces 'call upon an impressively broad spectrum of verse-forms, metres and poetic idioms' which 'vary the song',[12] and there are musical suggestions in the libretto (for example, that a duet should be sung 'prestissimo' with 'voices in canon').[13] As will be seen, Tony Harrison also had his own ideas about the musical setting.

In fact a consideration of *Yan Tan Tethera* benefits considerably from a sense of Harrison's perspective, in particular a comprehension of his version of literary pastoral conventions. Harrison evokes two of the earliest and most influential versions of pastoral: the first Idyll of Theocritus (*c*.316–260 BC), and the first Eclogue of Virgil (70–19 BC). As will be seen, Harrison's libretto is a rewriting of the representative pastoral situation pioneered by Theocritus and reconceived by Virgil. This is highlighted by Harrison's focus on two contrasting shepherds: Alan, a Northern shepherd, and Caleb Raven, a shepherd from the South.

---

[10] After considering Auden's debt to Christian imagery and Kierkegaard's aesthetics, Chew defines *The Rake's Progress* as a Christian pastoral fable; his description of Tom as a pastoral hero follows from Tom's ambiguous status: he is either comically foolish or naïvely saintly. Tom's progress 'becomes one from the Garden of Eden, scene of the fall, to the Garden of Gethsemane, scene of redemption'. Geoffrey Chew, 'Pastoral and neoclassicism: a reinterpretation of Auden's and Stravinsky's "Rake's Progress"', *Cambridge Opera Journal*, 5/3 (November 1993), 248 and 261.

[11] Cited in Stephen Walsh, *Stravinsky: The Second Exile. France and America 1934–1971* (London: Jonathan Cape, 2006), 211. See also Auden, 'Notes on music and opera', in his *The Dyer's Hand* (New York: Random House, 1962), 464–74.

[12] Roger Savage, 'Making a libretto: three collaborations over "The Rake's Progress"', in Nicholas John (ed.), *Stravinsky: Oedipus Rex, The Rake's Progress*, English National Opera Guide 43 (London: John Calder, 1991), 58.

[13] Despite an amicable collaboration with Stravinsky, Auden later acquired a reputation for being more interventionist: Humphrey Carpenter reports that in 1968 Tippett was 'uneasy at the prospect of working with such a domineering librettist', and in the same year Birtwistle declined Auden's invitation to work together, possibly because Auden lectured Birtwistle on the subject of opera and libretti. Carpenter, *W. H. Auden: A Biography* (London: George Allen & Unwin, 1981), 428.

Synopsis

Alan has left his home in the North of England and travelled south to the Wiltshire Downs, in which the opera is set. Caleb is a native of the Wiltshire Downs. The opera begins by foregrounding these two shepherds and their relationship: Alan waves to Caleb, but Caleb does not wave back. Caleb's white-faced sheep have bells forged from the church bell, stolen with the help of the Bad'Un; Alan's black-faced Cheviots have no bells.[14] This scenario establishes a dramatic framework or 'dialectical mode of perception' that is central to the earliest forms of pastoral.[15] Moreover the protagonists are distinguished from one another by the way in which they relate to their surroundings. Or rather, they are distinguished from each other by what Kenneth Burke refers to as the 'scene–agent' ratio, as will be discussed later.[16]

Central to the fate of the two shepherds is Caleb's jealousy of Alan's expanding flock and his desire for Alan's wife Hannah. Caleb enlists the help of the Bad'Un who, disguised as a Piper, lures Alan into the hill for seven years. Hannah meanwhile gives birth to twins who are immediately hidden away in the hill by the Bad'Un. Caleb then courts Hannah offering her gold and a new set of twins (she takes in the latter for their protection). Hannah resists Caleb's advances by using a spell Alan taught her, based on an ancient Northern counting system: 'Yan, Tan, Tethera / 1–2–3 / Sweet Trinity / Keep / Us and our sheep.' Eventually the twins and Alan are released, and Caleb is interned inside the hill. The opera ends with the 'eternally repeated pain / of [Caleb's] eternally repeated refrain ... Tethera Dik [thirteen]!'[17]

Although Harrison provides a basic linear narrative, which culminates in the release of Alan and the internment of Caleb, he nonetheless includes numerous textual refrains, for example: 'yan, tan, tethera'; the Piper's tune; Alan's spell; Alan's 'I think of the North, and don't want to stay, / though my flock's growing bigger each day'. One of Alan's stock responses to the Piper's tune is his line 'I know there's a piper but don't know where, / the tune always comes from behind me,' at which point he spins around, but the Piper has vanished. Birtwistle is very flexible in his approach to these

---

[14] Harrison's black–white dichotomy, which reflects the breeds of sheep native to the North and South respectively, was actually reversed in the original production, presumably in light of stereotypical yet racially insensitive associations of good with white and bad with black.

[15] Leo Marx, 'Pastoralism in America', in Sacvan Bercovitch and Myra Jehlen, eds., *Ideology and Classic American Literature* (Cambridge University Press, 1986), 44.

[16] Kenneth Burke, *A Grammar of Motives* (Berkeley and Los Angeles: University of California Press, 1969), 7.

[17] Tony Harrison, *Theatre Works: 1973–85* (Harmondsworth: Penguin, 1985), 319.

repetitions, most of which receive varied musical settings. Only one textual refrain is set to identical music, namely Alan's other response to the Piper's tune: 'Stuff my ears with earth and clay / so I can't hear the piper play.'

A visual representation of the opera's form is given in Table 4.1. In this table the basic elements of the drama are separated into four paradigmatic categories:

A 'scene–agent' mechanisms: instrumental pastorals heard when the hill rotates; the interdependent perspectives of Alan and Caleb; counting contests between the two shepherds (referred to by Birtwistle as a 'sheep counting toccata');[18] the passing of time; Hannah's lament when Alan is shut inside the hill (described by Birtwistle as a 'fugue').
B The landscape as sound: the Piper's melody; Caleb's sheep chorus ('These are the bells folk hear in the valley'); sections in which the hill opens or closes.
C Alan's spell to protect his family and flock.
D Dancing and spinning duets: Caleb and the Bad'Un; Caleb and Hannah.

The second half of this chapter will focus primarily on the first two of these categories, in particular the instrumental pastorals, in order to examine Birtwistle's version of the pastoral from the perspective of the score and musical sketches. The first half of the chapter, however, is concerned with Harrison's version of the pastoral, as revealed by reading the libretto through pastoral theory and the related topic of subjectivity.

Subjectivity

Both Birtwistle and Harrison stressed the importance of ritual and mechanism in *Yan Tan Tethera*. Birtwistle was clearly interested in the libretto's foregrounding of number and counting, which he described as 'a peg on which to hang a very interesting theatrical device'.[19] That device emphasises the mechanics of the drama, as Harrison's directions in the libretto illustrate:

> When SHEPHERD ALAN is in the foreground we see CALEB RAVEN in the distance. When CALEB RAVEN is in the foreground, we see SHEPHERD ALAN in the distance. The distant figures should suggest silhouettes, or wooden figures. The effect of the two hills revolving with the figures of the

---

[18] Written in Birtwistle's hand on the libretto typescript p. 11 (PSS 0539-0963).
[19] Birtwistle in Hall, *HB*, 144.

Table 4.1 *A thematic and formal outline of* Yan Tan Tethera

A	B	C	D
1st instrumental pastoral			
	Alan		
2nd inst. pastoral			
	Caleb		
		Caleb's sheep chorus ('This is the sound of the bells folk hear in the valley')	
			Caleb dances
3rd inst. pastoral			
		The Piper (×5) Alan: 'I know there's a piper' (×3)	
	Alan counts	The spell (×2) Alan teaches Hannah the spell	
	Counting contest		
4th inst. pastoral (the passing of a year)			
	Counting contest (cont.)	The Piper (×2) Alan: 'I know there's a piper' (×2)	
5th inst. pastoral		Caleb's sheep chorus	Caleb & the Bad'Un duet & dance
		The Piper (Alan is led into the hill) The spell	The Piper spins
6th inst. pastoral (varied rep. of 1st)		Variants of the Piper's tune	Hannah's labour pains, the spell & the birth of her twins

Table 4.1 (*cont.*)

A	B	C	D
	The Piper Caleb's sheep chorus		
	Hannah 'He waves'		
Hannah's lament / 7th inst. pastoral (& the passing of seven years)			Caleb spins
		Hannah sings the spell	The twins Jack & Dick dance
8th inst. pastoral ('The sun rises')	Hannah's twins are released from the hill		
9th inst. pastoral ('The sun begins to rise')	Alan is released from the hill		
	Caleb enters the hill		
	Alan, with his family & flock		

shepherds and their distinctive sheep should be that of 'weather men' figures in a peopled barometer, or like figures in an intricate clockpiece or those carved wooden figures from those moving German tableaux driven by small windmills and candle heat.[20]

Given Harrison's reductive description of the opera's two most important characters, one might wonder what happens to subjectivity in *Yan Tan Tethera* and in pastoral convention in general. Are the characters agents that enact a set of rituals, mere cogs in a machine? It is perhaps no accident that the term 'mechanical pastoral' recalls 'The Mechanicals' in Shakespeare's pastoral comedy *A Midsummer Night's Dream* – that is to say, a troupe of actors whose dramatic skills are notably wooden. The term 'mechanical' also recalls the highly stylised, artificial music theatre of Stravinsky, as typified

---

[20] Harrison, *Theatre Works*, 295 (the original is italicised). Birtwistle uses a similar metaphor in his interview with Hall: 'The whole thing is like a big clock mechanism, like one of those intricate clocks you get in Bavaria.' Birtwistle in Hall, *HB*, 144.

by *Oedipus Rex* (1926–7). Adorno, of course, has argued that the objective mask of Stravinsky's music hid not a human face but the worn-out stub of a tailor's dummy.[21] Several commentators have similarly asserted that in pastoral convention and in Birtwistle's music alike subjectivity is disregarded. Alastair Williams has argued that the mechanisms in Birtwistle's music 'downplay subjectivity', which he finds especially odd in an age 'fascinated by identity'.[22] Similarly Cross has compared Birtwistle's approach to Stravinsky's interest in 'ritualized anti-narrative', in which the focus is 'more on objective form than subjective content'.[23]

Cross argues that Birtwistle's interest in the pastoral focuses on what William Empson describes as the pastoral process of 'putting the complex into the simple'.[24] Viewed in this way pastoral is a mode of expression rather than a style or genre, in which the main interest occurs 'in the situation not the characters . . . The situation is made something valuable in itself.'[25] As Cross observes, this description is equally applicable to Birtwistle's musical processes:

> Music speaking or singing in the pastoral mode invites examination in terms
> of situation rather than character; the idea of the pastoral would thus appear
> to be appropriate more to a music concerned with exploring ritual than to
> that interested in developing a narrative argument. One kind of music can
> coexist with another, can share the same situation, can even come within the
> sphere of influence of the other, without its identity, its difference, being
> subsumed by the other . . . To privilege – as does pastoral theory – situation
> over character is to enable a more appropriate balancing of continuity and
> discontinuity in this music without giving primacy to either.[26]

Yet, one might reason, if situation is 'privileged' over character then situation is given 'primacy'. Accordingly character and subjectivity are downplayed. Empson remarks, however, that pastoral characters may seem unreal, 'but

---

[21] 'The shell of the objective . . . is now offered as truth, as super-subjective objectivity, all for the sake of such externalization . . . His [Stravinsky's] work plays the fool, thus offering its own grimace for practical purposes. It bows mischievously before the audience, removes the mask, and shows that there is no face under it, but only an amorphous knob. The conceited dandy of aestheticism from the good old days, who now had his fill of emotions, turns out to be a tailor's dummy: the pathological outsider as the model of innumerable normal men, all of whom resemble each other. The challenging shock of dehumanization by its own will and effort becomes the original phenomenon of standardization.' Theodor W. Adorno, *Philosophy of Modern Music*, trans. Anne G. Mitchell and Wesley V. Blomster (London: Sheed & Ward: 1994), 172.

[22] Williams, 'Ageing of the new: the museum of musical modernism', in Nicholas Cook and Anthony Pople, eds., *Cambridge History of Twentieth Century Music* (Cambridge University Press, 2004), 526.

[23] Cross, *HB: MMM*, 148.   [24] Empson, *Some Versions*, 1995, 25.

[25] Ibid., 50.   [26] Cross, *HB: MMM*, 148.

not the feelings expressed or even the situations described'.[27] This relates back to Friedrich Schiller's interpretation of pastoral poetry as a mode of feeling or perception (*Empfindungsweise*), one characterised by the sentimental desire for an unattained ideal.[28] While Cross's observations about Birtwistle's musical processes are instructive, his account of pastoral convention and the role of subjectivity in Birtwistle's operas should be examined further. Arguably Cross's binary, in which there is a hierarchy of situation over character, encourages a focus on the music's more objective aspects, but leads away from questions of subjectivity.

Yan Tan Tethera is arguably the most personal of Birtwistle's stage works as it comes closest in subject matter to his own life experiences. In the early 1960s Birtwistle moved from the North to the South of England (from Accrington near Manchester to Wiltshire, Dorset and Twickenham), and *Yan Tan Tethera* was completed in a remote part of southern France.[29] The opera also reflects Birtwistle's particularly acute relationship with and attitude towards landscape and nature. When reviewing the 'Behind the mask' documentary, broadcast the same year as the opera, Andrew Clements noted that:

> Some of [Birtwistle's] personal revelations seemed almost too honest: he looked back on his early life as a kind of Arcadia, surrounded by wild woods and fields in which he wandered and absorbed the natural world. Then a gigantic power station was built beyond his father's land, dwarfing the house, violating the landscape. It clearly had a traumatic effect; his teenage music . . . became an attempt to express the savagery of that intrusion.[30]

The obvious 'soft' and 'hard' pastoral associations in this description and the opposition between town and country are stark.[31] It is perhaps for this reason that the term *pastoral* appears in Birtwistle's music: *Down by*

---

[27] Empson, *Some Versions*, 17.

[28] Friedrich Schiller, 'On Naive and Sentimental Poetry (1795–6)', in H. B. Nisbet, ed., *German Aesthetic and Literary Criticism: Winckelmann, Lessing, Hamann, Herder, Schiller, Goethe* (Cambridge University Press, 1985), 180–232.

[29] The opera is personal to Harrison too: born and educated in Leeds to university level, Harrison has lived in many different places, yet his work often reflects a strong attachment to his home city and its role in shaping his sense of (Northern) identity.

[30] Clements, *Financial Times*, March 1987. Birtwistle made similar if not more heartfelt expressions in the 1971 BBC documentary 'A couple of things about Harry', in which he referred to the town 'encroaching' on the country, the imposition of two gigantic 'God's boots' (power station chimneys) near his parents' land, and the 'rape of the landscape' by industry and housing.

[31] Examples of these terms in music include the soft pastoral of Ravel's *Daphnis et Chloé* (1912) as opposed to the hard pastoral primitivism of Stravinsky's *The Rite of Spring* (1913). These designations also correspond roughly to what Marx refers to as 'sentimental' and 'complex' pastoral types; see Leo Marx, *The Machine in the Garden: Technology and the Pastoral Ideal in America* (New York: Oxford University Press, 1964), especially 3–32.

the Greenwood Side is subtitled 'a dramatic pastoral'; Birtwistle's sketches for *Nomos* reveal that his original title for that work had been *Arcadia*;[32] movements in the flute piece *Duets for Storab* (1983) include 'Stark Pastoral' and 'White Pastoral'; the sketches for *Deowa* (1983) for soprano and clarinet refer to 'seamless pastoral' and 'cold pastoral'.[33] Pastoral convention is also clearly evoked in the Orpheus myth (the lovers walking through the Elysian fields; Orpheus taming the wild animals), and by the Love Duets in *Orpheus*, in which, as Chew notes with regard to pastoral in general, 'the idealized surroundings... only heighten the sense of loss'.[34]

Unlike *Orpheus*, the relatively straightforward narrative in *Yan Tan Tethera* anticipates Birtwistle's move towards greater 'realism' in his operas from *Gawain* onwards. This raises the question whether *Yan Tan Tethera* also anticipates the development of more rounded characters witnessed in *Gawain*.[35] While composing the opera, Birtwistle spoke to Hall of his interest in Piero della Francesca's *Flagellation* (as discussed in Chapter 3). Notably he observed that 'In the foreground on the right are the figures of three men standing as if lost in their own worlds. But they're not puppets, they're genuinely human, and as far as information is concerned, they constitute the most important element in the picture.'[36] A few years later, in an interview regarding his co-production with Graham Devlin of *Punch* for the 1991 Aldeburgh Festival, Birtwistle contrasted the sanitised violence of the puppet show, which has had 'the humanity taken out of it', with his opera production in which 'we're actually putting it [the humanity] back'.[37]

If *Yan Tan Tethera* does mark a transition, then how is that manifested in an opera in which archetypal characters and formal repetition are so prominent? Where, if at all, does an awareness of subjectivity edge its way into Birtwistle's consciousness? As will be seen in the second part of the chapter, answers to these questions are provided by the music and by Birtwistle's musical sketches. However, it is first necessary to consider Harrison's perspective on the opera since he undoubtedly influenced Birtwistle in certain respects.

---

[32] PSS 0534-0661.   [33] PSS 0528-0036 and -0039, respectively.

[34] Geoffrey Chew and Owen Jander, 'Pastoral', in Stanley Sadie and John Tyrrell, eds., *The New Grove Dictionary of Music and Musicians*, 2nd edn., vol. XIX (London: Macmillan, 2001), 217.

[35] See for example Andrew Clements, '*Gawain* – an opera about people', *Opera*, 42/8 (1991), 11–16.

[36] Birtwistle in Hall, *HB*, 148.

[37] Birtwistle in Andrew Ford, 'The reticence of intuition: Sir Harrison Birtwistle', in Ford, *Composer to Composer: Conversations about Contemporary Music* (London: Quartet Books, 1993), 57.

Tony Harrison's version of the pastoral

A glance at the opening of Virgil's first Eclogue reveals that Alan and Caleb are Harrison's versions of the shepherds Meliboeus and Tityrus, who are versions of the herdsmen Corydon and Battus in Theocritus's *Idylls*. Through a mixture of parodic reference and palimpsest Harrison's libretto builds on Theocritus from whom the basic components of pastoral are derived, namely: an idyllic landscape; landscape as a setting for song; herdsmen as singers and pipe players. Such associations are explicitly stated at the start of Harrison's libretto where he explains: 'the scene is slowly revealed as the traditional "Arcadian" pastoral, green hill, bright blue sky, yellow sun.'[38] Positioned front of stage beside a hill or ancient burial mound, Alan sits surrounded by his sheep; in the distance, Caleb sits by another hill – actually the same hill seen from a different perspective. (In the stage and television productions, however, there were no hills; rather, the action centred on a cluster of sarsen stones).[39] This scenario's reductive retreat to a simpler, mythical past is a clear marker of the pastoral, and Harrison was also clearly attracted by Theocritus's use of strophic songs with refrains and singing contests as a match for Birtwistle's formal concerns.

Numerous commentators have attempted to define the pastoral. This discussion, however, will focus principally on the ideas of the literary theorist Paul Alpers whose definitions shed most light on *Yan Tan Tethera*. Alpers has observed that for many critics Theocritus's Idyll represents a landscape, while for others it represents 'two herdsmen in a characteristic situation'.[40] He suggests, however, that 'we will have a far truer idea of pastoral if we take its representative anecdote to be herdsmen and their lives, rather than landscape or idealized nature'.[41] Alpers then relates the representative anecdote of herdsmen and their lives to landscape via Burke's scene–agent ratio, that is 'the synecdochic relation . . . between person and place'.[42] According to Alpers, 'it is the representative anecdote of shepherds' lives that makes certain landscapes pastoral', such that 'we may say that landscapes are pastoral when they are conceived as fit habitations for herdsmen or their equivalents'.[43] By defining pastoral as the relationship between shepherds and landscape,

---

[38] Harrison, *Theatre Works*, 294. 'Arcadia' was a term introduced by Virgil.

[39] Andrew Clements was particularly critical of this omission and of David Freeman's direction in general in which 'there was an uneasy fusion between elements of stylisation and naturalism': Clements remarks that there was not enough deliberate alienation or mechanical formalism, and that the sheep chorus was too naturalistic. Review of *Yan Tan Tethera*, *Opera* 37/10 (1986), 1,201.

[40] Paul Alpers, *What Is Pastoral?* (London: Chicago University Press, 1996), 22.   [41] Ibid.

[42] Burke, *A Grammar of Motives*, 7.   [43] Alpers, *What Is Pastoral?* 28.

Alpers provides an interpretation of pastoral that is compatible with Cross's account of a more equal coexistence of ideas in Birtwistle's music. Alpers is also particularly instructive because he draws attention to the role of forced migration in key pastoral texts. In Shakespeare's *As You Like It*, for example, Orlando and Rosalind, among others, are driven from their homes into the Forest of Arden by what Wordsworth described as an 'adverse fate'.

In this sense, Harrison's libretto is closer to Virgil's first Eclogue, in which ideas that are merely implied by Theocritus are made explicit. Virgil focuses on two contrasting attitudes towards the landscape, or two versions of pastoral: on the one hand the 'pragmatic and concretely rural' attitude of the local shepherd Tityrus, who is secure in a known world, and on the other hand the 'idyllic' vision – because coloured by a sense of separation – of the émigré shepherd Meliboeus, who has been exiled from his home in the wake of a civil war.[44] In *Yan Tan Tethera*, Caleb, the local shepherd, prods the Wiltshire chalk mounds in search of buried gold. He values his native landscape in practical terms – that is, for what it offers to him, his desire fuelled by his knowledge of local Saxon burial mounds. By contrast, Alan pines for his homeland, the Northern fells. We are not told why Alan has had to leave the North, but his dislike of his new surroundings ('I don't care much for this place where I am'), and his sense of loss ('I long to go back / along the old drovers' track / back on the Pennine Way'), strongly suggest that he was driven from his home by some 'adverse fate'.[45]

Unlike Meliboeus, however, Alan describes a homeland that sounds far from idyllic: he refers to 'the rough crags and the Northern fells / where the rocks are steep and the moor winds moan / and the sheep don't go round waving bells'. The fact that Alan longs to return to a harsh landscape reinforces a sense of *Yan Tan Tethera* as a form of hard pastoral – a particularly English form of pastoral epitomised by the 1805 version of Wordsworth's *Prelude*:

[44] Ibid., 25. According to Alpers: 'Later passages reveal that Meliboeus's land has fallen victim to the land expropriations (40–39 BC) with which Octavian and Antony rewarded their veterans after the battle of Philippi [against Brutus and Cassius]', 162. In other words, Virgil's poem marks a transition from the old Roman Republic to Caesarian centrism. See Annabel Patterson, *Pastoral and Ideology: Virgil to Valéry* (Oxford: Clarendon Press, 1988), 3.

[45] Arguably, Alan's longing to return home and the Christian undertones to his spell (its reference to the 'Sweet Trinity') represent aspects of idealisation and divinity that rule out the possibility of labelling the opera 'anti-pastoral'. Gifford defines anti-pastoral as an expression that 'the natural world can no longer be constructed as "a land of dreams", but is in fact a bleak battle for survival without divine purpose'. Terry Gifford, *Pastoral* (London and New York: Routledge, 1999), 120.

> [...] the rural ways
> And manners which it was my chance to see
> In childhood were severe and unadorned,
> The unluxuriant produce of a life
> Intent on little but substantial needs.[46]

This version of pastoral may be traced back to Virgil's *Georgics*, in which the landscape is a harsh and unpredictable home to farmers. Ultimately Wordsworth objectifies his shepherd as '*A solitary object and sublime...* / Ennobled *outwardly* before mine eyes'.[47] Alan certainly shares Wordsworth's awe for the natural world and his 'recognition of a creative–destructive universe'[48] (as reflected by Alan's remarks that bread and cider 'won't seem so tasty when we're dead' and 'can't refresh a corpse's decomposing flesh'). Moreover, Wordsworth's idea that the shepherd is ennobled by harsh weather – the only real antagonist in the poem – and his sense that the shepherd's reward for his suffering is a freedom to roam are comparable to Alan's heroic longing to return to his Northern home where the 'moor winds moan'.[49]

Yet Harrison's moaning winds are another likely reference to Virgil's *Eclogues*. Virgil's local shepherd, Tityrus, plays a rustic pipe (*calamus agrestis*). To Meliboeus's ears, however, Tityrus's melodies reflect the landscape's 'woodland musings' (*musa silvestris*). What is important here is not only the idea that Tityrus's melody echoes nature, but that it echoes the sounds of the landscape. The melody is therefore representative of the shepherd Tityrus at his leisure, but also the landscape itself. Both scene and agent are represented by the melody played on a rustic pipe. In Harrison's libretto, Caleb (the equivalent of Tityrus) forms a pact with the Bad'Un, who performs the role of the Piper.[50] Alan (the equivalent of Meliboeus) hears the Piper's tune, which he identifies as 'a Northern air'. This melody eventually leads Alan into the hill.

Until the moment that he is released from the hill, near the end of the opera, Harrison portrays Alan, the 'good' protagonist, as a pastoral hero:

---

[46] William Wordsworth, *The Prelude: 1799, 1805, 1850*, ed. Jonathan Wordsworth, M. H. Abrams and Stephen Gill (New York: Norton, 1979), 8 (lines 205–9).

[47] As cited in Patterson, *Pastoral and Ideology*, 282. Another important and more polemical version of hard pastoral is Wordsworth's *The Ruined Cottage* (1797–8).

[48] Gifford, *Pastoral*, 153. Gifford describes such sentiment as 'post-pastoral'.

[49] This comparison is potentially problematic when it is considered that Wordsworth's hard pastorals have been criticised for failing to confront the power structures of land ownership and exploitation of rural workers, and therefore for having 'served to evade the actual and bitter contradictions of the time'. Raymond Williams, *The Country and the City* (London: Chatto and Windus, 1975), 60.

[50] The fact that the Piper is later revealed as the Bad'Un reflects the idea that 'Arcadia is a borderland in which not only shape-changing is possible, but also status, role and... gender changing too.' Gifford, *Pastoral*, 28.

he is a mythical archetype (an everyman, or simple man of nature), who is neither especially strong nor brave, but who attempts to resist the claims of the Bad'Un. (The distinction between a 'good' and 'bad' shepherd has an obvious historical precedent in the biblical tale of Cain and Abel: Cain, the sinful crop farmer, and Abel, the victim shepherd.[51]) Alan's defence is his magic spell. Yet he is vulnerable: marked as a victim by his status as immigrant, Alan is in constant fear of losing his flock and pregnant wife to the Bad'Un. To protect his family, Alan teaches Hannah the spell.

Observing that every protagonist has 'a given strength relative to his world', Angus Fletcher has argued that each character 'is a *modular* for verbal architectonics; man is the measure, the *modus* of myth'.[52] These remarks have prompted Alpers to suggest that:

> The figure of the shepherd is felt to be representative precisely in figuring every or any man's strength relative to the world. A great many citizens of late Republican Rome could read their situation in that of the two herdsmen of Virgil's first Eclogue – one victimized by the aftermath of civil war, the other dependent on the protector [a landowning or political benefactor] he has been fortunate to find. Such representative vulnerability goes naturally with the figure of the literary shepherd.[53]

A measure of each shepherd's vulnerability is the extent to which their comprehension of the world is bounded or limited in some way by what Alpers describes as the characters' consciousness of boundaries. Tityrus's horizons are the most limited: his awareness of Rome 'revolves around its difference and distance from the world he knows'. Meliboeus's nostalgia, however, is characterised by 'a desire for protective boundaries and a fear of their violation'.[54] Similarly, Caleb's horizons are limited whereas Alan fears the incursions of sound from the Piper and seeks to enforce a protective boundary around his flock and family with frequent repetitions of the spell. This question of the consciousness of boundaries is an important one to which I shall return since Birtwistle's sketches reveal that he was also particularly concerned with the concept of bordered space, specifically with the precise registral placement of ideas, and with layers and corridors of activity.

---

[51] Cain and Abel were the sons of Adam and Eve, and the Garden of Eden is an early representation of Arcadia. Even the idea that death exists in Arcadia – as suggested by a tombstone engraved 'Et in Arcadio Ego' ('Even in Arcadia, I [death] am here') in Guercino's and Poussin's paintings *The Arcadian Shepherds* (c. 1624 and 1629–30 respectively) – may be traced back to the presence of the serpent and apple in Eden. Christ is the ultimate representative of the good shepherd searching for lost sheep.

[52] Angus Fletcher, 'Utopian history and the *Anatomy of Criticism*,' in Murray Krieger, ed., *Northrop Frye in Modern Criticism* (New York: Columbia University Press, 1966), 34–5.

[53] Alpers, *What Is Pastoral?* 50.   [54] Ibid., 163 and 165.

By attending to its human figures, Alpers argues, pastoral's identifying features are revealed 'in elements of voice, style, and representation'.[55] Clearly, Alan mirrors Virgil's victimised citizen, Meliboeus. By contrast, Caleb, like Tityrus, has a benefactor – the Bad'Un – who has already helped him steal the church bell, and who assists with Caleb's plan to steal Hannah and discover the landscape's hidden gold.[56] Nevertheless Alan is forthright: his expression is rather plain and matter-of-fact, yet direct and assertive. Empson has observed that forthright speech is a characteristic of pastoral characters in general. However, in contrast to Schiller's psychological explanation that such directness is the expression of a naïve temperament, Empson argues that it is representative of particular rhetorical and social concerns. Indeed, Harrison's preference for plain speech in a Northern dialect reflects his interest in language as social critique, an idea that had been fine-honed in his version of Aeschylus's *Oresteia* for Peter Hall's 1981 production at the National Theatre (discussed in Chapter 7).

Since Virgil voiced social and rhetorical concerns more directly than Theocritus, Alpers suggests that Virgil turned Theocritus's exchange into 'something that looks like a drama', for which reason the first Eclogue is sometimes described as a rustic mime. Yet,

> the 'dramatic' effect comes less from depicted conflict or confrontation, of which there is hardly any, than from the separateness of the two speakers in a responsive exchange... Instead of speaking from and of a shared situation, Meliboeus and Tityrus each speaks, with considerable urgency, from his own situation. The felt difference gives a dramatic effect, but the means are pastoral.[57]

This description applies directly to Alan and Caleb in the opera: they are clearly independent, yet they never come into direct conflict (Harrison remarks of the shepherds that 'neither one addresses the other').[58] This is immediately clear at the opening of the opera when Alan complains 'I wave; he never waves back'.[59] It is also tangible during the sheep-counting toccatas in which each shepherd holds firmly to his own counting system (an idea that evokes the singing contests in Virgil's seventh and eighth Eclogues;

---

[55] Ibid., 37.

[56] Caleb's intentions towards Hannah are no different from his attitude towards the landscape that surrounds him (his search for gold). This illustrates the ecofeminist perspective that 'exploitation of the planet is of the same mindset as the exploitation of women and minorities.' Gifford, *Pastoral*, 165.

[57] Alpers, *What Is Pastoral?* 162 and 163.   [58] Harrison, *Theatre Works*, 304.

[59] This situation also mirrors Virgil's *Eclogues* in which, as Patterson observes, Tityrus is so oblivious 'of the responsibilities of the fortunate toward the unfortunate' that he 'fails to attend to the obvious, if indirect, appeals for his sympathy and concern', even going so far as to declare to Meliboeus that '"a god gives *us* this leisure"'. Patterson, *Pastoral and Ideology*, 3.

serial listing is also a rhetorical device associated with comic pastorals, or bucolics).

Clearly, Alan and Caleb differ in their relationship to the landscape. Following Meliboeus, Alan experiences the pain of a lover's separation from what he desires (his abandoned homeland). Alpers even suggests that Meliboeus 'imagines something close to erotic pleasure in the auditory plenum of the echoing woods'.[60] This point is important because it highlights the role of the landscape in and as sound. As will be seen in the next section, this relates directly to a key concept in Harrison's libretto – namely, 'the MUSIC of the hill', which is listed as one of the characters in the drama.[61]

Birtwistle's version of the pastoral

The central critical questions at the heart of Alpers's project may be summarised as follows: how does reality enter the pastoral work; how is its presence felt; and how are we made to feel 'the representative character of its two speakers'?[62] These questions are important because they suggest that the 'situation' that Cross argues is privileged by the pastoral mode is actually representative of human emotions and experiences. Alpers suggests that 'each shepherd speaks out of the heart of his experience, the shepherd's situation as he understands it. Each in a sense thinks his version of pastoral is *the* version of pastoral.'[63] As such, the topic of subjectivity begins to edge its way on to the stage.

To explore Alpers's central questions with regard to *Yan Tan Tethera* it is necessary to consider certain instrumental sections within the opera that Birtwistle describes as 'pastorals'.[64] These instrumental interludes provide windows on to the drama. They also represent Birtwistle's response to Harrison's concept of 'the MUSIC of the hill'. Harrison defines this concept in his directions for the opening of the opera:

> Total darkness. We hear the MUSIC of the hill, which is composed of voices (12 female, 1 male) . . . When the seasons change, and the hill (or hills) turn the only constant should be the MUSIC of the hill, which is the same voices as

60 Alpers, *What Is Pastoral?* 163.   61 Harrison, *Theatre Works*, 294.
62 Alpers, *What Is Pastoral?* 162.
63 Ibid., 166, although as Alpers notes, 'separation and loss are the conditions of their utterance' (171).
64 Birtwistle in Hall, *HB*, 152. The notion of an instrumental pastoral dates back to the instrumental episodes in Angelo Poliziano's *Favola d'Orfeo* (1471), from which grew sixteenth-century Italian dramatic pastorals, such as Guarini's *Il pastor fido* (1589), and the earliest operas, notably Monteverdi's *Orfeo*.

Example 4.1a The Piper's tune, *Yan Tan Tethera*, (full score, UE 17684), p. 30

the two choruses of sheep . . . The MUSIC of the hill should suggest its ancientness and mystery as a place of burial for the men who raised the enormous sarsen stones.[65]

In 1983, Birtwistle revealed that he had 'utterly contradicted' what he understood by Harrison's concept: namely, a musical idea that would be repeated literally, 'something ethereal, something simplistic to which you can return when an action has been repeated'. Instead Birtwistle composed music that is 'always different' and 'always concerned with the context in which it's placed . . . The context of the moment is unique and must exert an influence, a strong influence.'[66] He observed that these sections (the instrumental pastorals) occur either when the hills revolve or when there is a passing of time.[67] Collectively, therefore, one might say that Birtwistle's pastorals are a representative anecdote of Alan's and Caleb's experience of 'living in the cycles of a landscape'.[68] As such, they offer clues to Alpers's questions regarding the way in which the realities of the shepherds' lived experiences enter into the opera.

Pastoral labyrinths and the 'consciousness of boundaries'

It is commonly held that pastorals project a philosophical opposition between art and nature or between country and city, an opposition that in music 'is usually reinforced by the use of distinctive styles, with the "natural" style falling appreciably short of the complexity of the conventional style of the day'.[69] Despite the lack of a clearly defined philosophical opposition in Harrison's libretto, Birtwistle does make a distinction between a simple, modal-sounding Piper's melody (Tityrus's *calamus agrestis*) and a more complex musical language. The melody, which is shown in Example 4.1a, consists of four pitch-classes (G, A, B, C♯) that form a

---

[65] Harrison, *Theatre Works*, 295–6 (the original is italicised).
[66] Birtwistle in Hall, *HB*, 146.
[67] Hall, *HB*, 152. The pastorals are not named in the score, but they usually correspond with Harrison's direction that 'the hill moves'.
[68] Gifford, *Pastoral*, 156, apropos Fraser Harrison, *The Living Landscape* (London: Pluto, 1986).
[69] Chew and Jander, 'Pastoral', 217.

Example 4.1b Alan, p. 31

of how I'm not   happy and how my heart's not   very con- tent   in these   foreign parts

continuous whole-tone segment. All subsequent variations played by the
Piper are restricted to this whole-tone set.[70] It is noticeable that the vocal
parts of the two shepherds are also relatively simple (they are generally confined to a narrow register with stepwise motion), and that Alan even echoes
the Piper's melody when he sings of his unhappiness and discontent 'in these
foreign parts', extending the Piper's collection to a five-note whole-tone segment (F, G, A, B, C♯); see Example 4.1b.[71] Birtwistle therefore highlights the
scene–agent ratio: by echoing the Piper's 'Northern air' Alan expresses the
idea of landscape through and as sound. The distinction between simple and
complex musical languages in the opera, however, is more fluid than fixed.
The Piper's melody is actually the most frequently recurring musical idea
and exists in numerous extended whole-tone or chromatic variants, which
appear nearly continuously throughout the opera. Example 4.1c shows the
spinning variant heard at the opera's moment of *anagnorisis* and *peripeteia*,
when Alan finally sees the Piper and is led into the hill.

These variants and other related melodic lines that occur in several of the
instrumental pastorals form part of more complex, labyrinthine textures.
The association between *Yan Tan Tethera* and the idea of a labyrinth was
actually suggested by Birtwistle when he remarked:

> At one level I'm doing what I always do. An analogy would be wandering
> through a town with squares, various squares, some more important than
> others, a town with roads on which you go round and round, in through one
> square out through another.[72]

It is interesting that the metaphor Birtwistle chose to describe his approach
to the opera is an urban maze. Through this urban metaphor, Birtwistle re-
admits the country–city opposition that Harrison apparently downplayed.
Moreover, as Penelope Reed Doob has observed, a further opposition exists
in 'the inherent paradox of the labyrinth: its ability to signify both complex
artistic order and chaotic confusion, depending on whether it is viewed

[70] Even the Piper's 'different air' uses this pitch collection (p. 88). All score references are to
     Harrison Birtwistle, *Yan Tan Tethera*, full score (London: Universal Edition, 1984), UE 17684.
[71] Alan's later line 'When I hear that Piper play / I think of the North, and I don't want to stay'
     uses the same five-note whole-tone set (pp. 41–2).
[72] Birtwistle in Hall, *HB*, 144.

Example 4.1c Spinning variant of the Piper's tune when Alan sees the Piper, pp. 104–5

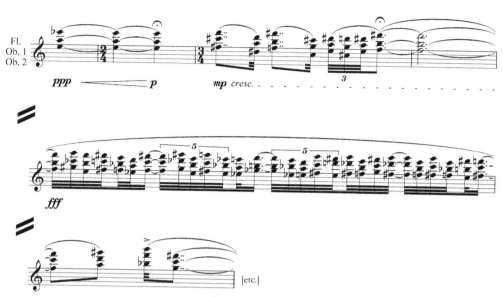

from without as a static artefact, a magnificent product of human inge-nuity, or experienced from within as a bewildering process, a dynamic prison'.[73]

With this description in mind the sketches are highly revealing, for they offer insight into both the objective 'static artefact' on the one hand and the subjective 'dynamic prison' on the other.[74] The artefact is illustrated by Example 4.2, which is a transcription of a plan that was probably one of the first things to be sketched. The plan presents an ordered division of registral space. Earlier sketches indicate Birtwistle experimenting with cycles of fourths, fifths and tritones, and one of the sets on the bottom staff of the plan (labelled set II) was also sketched independently.[75] It seems likely, therefore, that Birtwistle began with the three pitch cycles written on the lowest staff, principally two five-note cycles of fourths a tritone apart (this is supported by the fact that Birtwistle decided to 'omit' certain pitches). I have labelled these 'set I' (C, F, Bb, Eb, Ab) and 'set II' (F♯, B, E, A, D), respectively. (The third 'symmetrical set with tritone' does not appear to have assumed any importance in the scheme written above.) The next step

---

[73] Doob, *The Idea of the Labyrinth*, 38.

[74] There are 237 sides of sketches and drafts, 185 sides of fair copy, and 53 sides of text for *Yan Tan Tethera* in the Paul Sacher Stiftung.

[75] Experiments with cycles of intervals 5, 6 and 7 appear on PSS 0539-0605, and 'set II' on PSS 0539-0542 and -0487.

Example 4.2 Registral plan, in *Yan Tan Tethera* sketch folder 2/7, and on PSS 0539-0606

was to redistribute sets I and II. This was determined in the central part of the page by the two lines of bracketed numbers with arrowheads above the pitches. The top bracketed line relates to set II, the lower bracketed line to set I. The numbers refer to the order of pitches in the five-note sets, from the lowest note up (for example, in set II: 1 = F♯, 2 = B, 3 = E, 4 = A, 5 = D). In the top bracketed line, therefore, every third number from the first (1, 2, 3 circled, 4 and 5) relates to a 'straight' version of set II. This line, which I will refer to later as set IIa, was then labelled 'A' to 'E'. The intervening numbers ([ ] 2, 1, [ ] 3, 2, [ ] 4, 3, [ ] 5, 4, [ ]) determine a reordered version of set II labelled 'F' to 'M', which I will later designate set IIb. The numbers in the lower bracketed line present a straight version of set I extended by single repetitions of numbers 2, 3 and 4. This line was labelled 'N' to 'U'. The result is a palindromic sequence of twenty-one pitches arranged roughly three octaves above and three octaves below the central eleventh pitch, e'. Because the two principal source sets (I and II) are a tritone apart it was possible to devise the ascending line so that it comprises steps of intervals 5 and 1 (perfect fourths and semitones) only. In fact, the same palindromic five-interval cycle is applied above each of the notes labelled 'A' to 'E': namely, 51515. Strung together, this produces a palindrome centred on letter 'C', as follows: (A) 51515 (B) 51515 (C) 51515 (D) 51515 (E). Across this pattern, set I is also palindromic, as follows: 5, 12, 5, 12, 5, 12, 5. It is likely that Birtwistle decided intuitively that e' would be at the centre of this scheme.

Birtwistle then proceeded to the three staffs at the top of the page. Here each pitch 'blossoms' into a symmetrical five-note cluster, with the original pitch at the centre of each chromatic cell. (This effectively fills in the spaces within each cycle of fourths, although note the minor third gaps between the pairs of cells in line F to M, which I will return to later). The top staff comprises set IIa; the second staff consists of set IIb; the third staff presents the extended version of set I. Overall the plan has resulted in a multiplication of the two principal sets: mirroring the opera's subtitle, the plan is a kind of 'mechanical organism' that prescribes a harmonic field (or scene), within which the musical sets and cells (or agents) will unfold. Birtwistle then drew the series of diagonal lines and square brackets between the pitches to highlight octave and perfect fifth relations; dotted lines indicate octaves between the added notes. Two other markings suggest ways in which Birtwistle intended to use this plan: 'chorus range' implies its use in the sheep choruses; 'ob. 1' (written beneath cell 'T') suggests that it was intended for the orchestra as well. In fact, the plan can be traced clearly in the opening section in all parts, and at least as far as the first counting contest (p. 65), after which it appears to have been replaced by other similar schemes.[76]

What is so revealing about this 'static artefact' is the possibility it offers of experiencing Birtwistle's music from the opposite perspective, that is, in terms of subjective agents entering into and passing through a musical labyrinth. The opening bars of the opera now appear as an 'entrance' to the pastoral labyrinth, since they represent a musical mobile derived entirely from permutations of cell 'C' – the chromatic cluster around the central *e'* in Birtwistle's plan.[77] This is shown in Example 4.3. Marked in the score as 'NIGHT/SPRING', these are the opening bars of the opera and the start of the first instrumental pastoral.[78] Of significance here are the bells and the bell-like tones of the horn, gongs and harp. Are these the bells on Caleb's sheep forged from the stolen church bell, therefore an evocation of the opposition between town and country? This question raises another ambiguity that is central to the opera: are the bell sounds associated with the sheep and therefore agents in the opera; or do they evoke the landscape and therefore the scene in which the opera is set (the sounds of the sheep bells echoing through the valley)? The fact that the gongs and bells sound a total of thirteen times suggests that the opening mobile is in fact Birtwistle's response to Harrison's concept of 'the MUSIC of the hill, which is composed of voices (12 female, 1 male)' – that is, the same thirteen voices that form Caleb's sheep chorus (Harrison also points out that 13 is the 'unlucky number').

The music continues by introducing set IIb in the woodwind (alto flute, oboe and cor anglais) and set IIa in the strings. In the woodwind the cor anglais is confined to notes from cell I, the oboe to cell J, while the alto flute draws on both I and J; see Example 4.4a. The resulting octave displacements in the flute, however, form a disjunct composite line in which a characteristic 'gap', or bordered space, is maintained in the centre of the line (as heard in the pastoral-sounding flute solo at the opening of *Secret Theatre*). As will be seen, this concept assumes more importance later in the opera. Immediately after the woodwind entry the strings also enter with tremolo

---

[76] For example, the first bassoon in the fifth instrumental pastoral (pp. 81–3) is based on two adjacent five-note sets that do not appear in the original plan; the second bassoon shadows the first at randomly alternating intervals of 5, 6 and 7 (PSS 0539-0608). At times non-adjacent or overlapping five-note sets that do not appear in the original plan are also used, for example for the cello and double bass during the duet between Caleb and the Bad'Un (pp. 91–2 and 93–4; PSS 0539-0617 and -0620). This suggests that in later stages Birtwistle may have 'improvised' on the original plan.

[77] An earlier version of the opening, scored for bell, harp, cello and double bass, reveals that Birtwistle at one point intended to begin on a B-centred texture, using an equivalent to cell I. PSS 0539-0543.

[78] This is referred to in the sketches as a 'nocturnal pastoral'; PSS 0539-0493.

Example 4.3 First instrumental pastoral, introductory mobile based on cell C, p. 1, bb. 1–4 (numbers added to show the distribution of notes from cell C)

Example 4.4a First instrumental pastoral, woodwind, p. 1, bb. 4–8

Example 4.4b First instrumental pastoral, strings, p. 1, b. 5

glissandi based on set IIa (from the double bass up: cells A, B, C, D, E); see Example 4.4b. Punctuating the texture are intermittent bell sounds in the gongs, harp and bells that simultaneously evoke the sheep and the opera's Arcadian landscape setting. When 'DAWN BEGINS', the woodwind shifts to set I (here the oboe draws on cells S and T, as marked in the plan, while the bassoon and double bassoon utilise O and P; the strings continue with cells A to E). At the moment that we begin to see the 'real' sunrise from behind the hill (at the ruled bar line on page 4), the strings move to set I (cells O to T arranged upwards from the double bass), which mirrors the arrangement in the woodwind (O and P in the bassoon, Q and R in the cor anglais, S and T in the flute).[79] Finally, when the sun is 'FULL UP' the music shifts to set II fixing on high unison B naturals (the highest note in cell M), with a low F sharp in the double bass (the central note in cell A).

The use of string glissandi is an important feature here, in other instrumental pastorals, and throughout the opera. These sliding gestures recall two earlier pastoral operas, namely Britten's *A Midsummer Night's Dream* (1959–60) and Tippett's *The Knot Garden* (1966–70). As Meirion Bowen notes, the opening glissando storm-motif of Tippett's opera 'is at its most tense' during the second act, which is subtitled 'Labyrinth'. Here the motif appears 'in the rhythmically contracted versions that introduce the whirling of the characters within the maze'.[80] During this act characters are thrown together as pairs, yet ultimately they repel one another. By contrast, Philip Brett has argued that the otherworldly glissandi heard at the start of Britten's *Midsummer Night's Dream* are suggestive of that opera's eerie, primeval woodland setting, but also of sleep and breathing.[81]

Birtwistle's string glissandi share some of these concerns. Those at the opening mimic Alan's waving motion to Caleb, which Caleb ignores. They therefore embody both Alan's subjective expression and the representative pastoral anecdote of two opposing viewpoints: the strings wave; the woodwind's sustained lines continue impassively. Birtwistle's glissandi later evoke various kinds of repetitive yet static mechanical motions, such as spinning, twisting or burrowing. Such motions even attach themselves to the more complex versions of the Piper's melody, as an embellishment of that tune's pastoral arabesques. Despite the association of such actions with human agency, Birtwistle was probably more interested in these gestures as examples of stasis in progress, or 'still movement' (which became the title of the work he composed immediately after the opera, in March–April 1984).[82] Harrison expresses this idea slightly differently in his directions for the first

---

[79] The cells used in the woodwind are revealed in the sketches: PSS 0539-0489.

[80] Bowen, 'A Tempest of our time', in Nicholas John, ed., *The Operas of Michael Tippett* (London: John Calder, 1985), 95.

[81] Brett, 'Britten's Dream', in Ruth Solie, ed., *Musicology and Difference: Gender and Sexuality in Music Scholarship* (Berkeley and Los Angeles: University of California Press, 1995), 268–9.

[82] The words 'STILL MOVEMENT' actually appear in sketches for earlier works: first, beneath a copy of the final bars of *Melencolia I*, titled 'Melencolia model' (PSS 0539-0729), and second, beneath a sketch for a viola line during Hannah's duet with Caleb (PSS 0539-0679; FS, pp. 138–9). In the duet Hannah sings the spell, which causes Caleb to spin. The viola line and other aspects of the section are reworked at the opening of *Still Movement*. The fact that *Still Movement* is scored 'for thirteen solo strings' reflects Caleb's words at this moment: 'Thirteen! Thirteen! / 13 and none, / take this ring from the grave. / Your husband has gone'.

Example 4.5 Alan's first entry and accompanying strings (viola 2 and cello omitted), p. 6

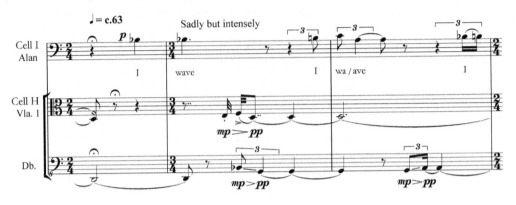

counting contest, where he refers to 'the movement and immobility of a mechanical device'.[83]

Further light is shed on this idea by Alan's initial vocal entry, as shown in Example 4.5. Alan's entire vocal part in the first section is based on cells H and I, from set IIb.[84] Exceptions to this occur on the word 'back', which moves into cell C from set IIa, and later when Alan mentions his homeland ('the Northern fells'), where his line leaps up a seventh from H to cell C.[85] (A comparison of Example 4.1a with Example 4.2 reveals

---

[83] Harrison, *Theatre Works*, 304.

[84] The sketches reveal that Alan's line was worked out continuously and independently; PSS 0539-0500.

[85] Caleb's response (the section beginning 'He waves, I never wave back') is also largely restricted to cell I, yet there are excursions into cells B, C and P.

that the Piper's whole-tone collection also moves 'as if' in a labyrinth, from cell P to Q, then up via the dotted line into Alan's cell I). Alan's restriction to cells determined by the plan is important for several reasons: it illustrates the scene–agent ratio – that is, Alan's inextricable link to the musical environment (or landscape) around him; it explains his narrow, somewhat flat and featureless expression; it highlights – as Alpers would say – his 'consciousness of boundaries', and his desire to return home. It is also noticeable that the strings and woodwind that accompany Alan sit just on top of or just below his vocal line, and that they too are confined to narrow lines determined by the plan. As shown in Example 4.5, Alan enters in cell I. Beneath his part, the glissando idea continues in the double bass, while a new melodic process begins in the first viola based on cell H, a perfect fifth below the voice. In other words, scene (viola) and agent (voice) are associated by set IIb, but they express different 'versions' of that set (cell I in the voice; cell H in the viola). There are even moments of symmetrical equivalence between the voice and viola, for example when Alan moves into cell C, which is identical to cell H but an octave higher. Similarly, towards the end of its line the viola creeps into cell B, which is identical to cell I but an octave lower (see Example 4.2). The viola's line is characterised by pauses interrupted by spinning embellishments that anticipate the Piper's tune and its associated variants. These 'still movements' spread throughout the orchestra as the section develops, culminating at Alan's line 'and sheep don't go round wearing bells' where the texture is filled with spinning arabesques (p. 12). In effect, the musical landscape is saturated by more or less distorted variants of the Piper's melody.[86]

As Birtwistle suggested, Harrison's idea that 'the MUSIC of the hill' would be identical each time it appeared is 'utterly contradicted' by the instrumental pastorals. The second pastoral comprises three different strands: sustained high woodwind lines (a variant of the impassive woodwind at the opening); spiky staccato figures in the low woodwind and low strings (these anticipate similar figures in the counting contests where they evoke the 'wobble' of moving sheep); dense tremolo chords in rhythmic unison in the middle and upper strings (the moaning moor winds of Alan's home, perhaps). Despite the obvious textural contrast, however, both first and second instrumental pastorals are based on Birtwistle's registral plan: the upper woodwind is restricted to cells L and T; the staccato figures draw on N, P and Q. However, a new technique is deployed for the strings. As shown

---

[86] At one moment a chromatic variant in the flute and two oboes (in unison) is heard simultaneously with another variant in the horn, and the original Piper's melody (p. 45). Alan sometimes even hears the ensemble variant before the Piper's actual melody (for example, p. 71).

Example 4.6 Second instrumental pastoral, string section, p. 13. Analysis derived from the sketches. PSS 0539-0506–7

in Example 4.6, the string texture is built from three-chord slices in which every part is based on notes selected from a different cell. The sketches reveal that the scheme used was based on randomised vertical selections from twelve different cells (C–D, H–L and P–T).[87]

The third instrumental pastoral is uncharacteristically 'simple', in that it comprises two almost identical, narrow strands of material – one in the flute, oboe and cor anglais, the other in the bassoons and horn – lightly supported by tubular bells and harp (pp. 28–9). What does relate this section to other

87 PSS 0539-0506–7.

Example 4.7 Sketch for Caleb's sheep chorus and supporting violins and violas, pp. 17–23, 26–8, 84–5 and 118–19. PSS 0539-0518

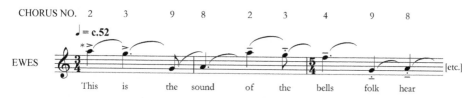

* each with bell-like attack and long delay

parts of the opera, however, is the fact that the two strands are separated by a registral gap: the cor anglais does not fall below *d″* and the horn does not rise above *f♯′*. It is as if two agents, similar yet slightly out of step with one other, pass through the same scene, but are held apart by an invisible force. (Eventually the two agents merge with the scene as they pause and are absorbed into a series of interrupting bell sounds.) A related idea can be observed in the chorus of Caleb's sheep ('This is the sound'), another important refrain. As shown in Example 4.7, the sketches reveal that the chorus is based on an independent system that rotates pitches from two pairs of three-note sets: the first pair is separated by interval 5, the second by interval 6. This forms an inner line (the chorus line, marked with an asterisk) that generates the outer string parts by approximately parallel

Example 4.8 Sketch for the first oboe, from the 'transition' to the fourth instrumental pastoral, p. 68. PSS 0539-0591

motion at intervals 5, 6 and 7 (perfect fourth, tritone and fifth). Acoustical variety (a more realistic bell sound) is created by assigning each note of the chorus's unison line to a different singer, which is sung with a 'bell-like attack' and held across the next note (see the 'Chorus No.' series (2, 3, 9, 8 etc.) at the bottom of Example 4.7).

As noted earlier in relation to the opening alto flute line, the effect is a disjunct motion that maintains a 'corridor' of space at its centre. Another example is illustrated by an oboe part in the second counting contest, just before the fourth instrumental pastoral (p. 68). Here a gap of interval 4 separates a simple grace-note figure and the principal line, the former based on a three-note cell, the latter on a six-note cell (see Example 4.8).

At times, the existence of such registral spaces assumes a more literal meaning. Hannah's entrance is one such example. Originally, Harrison intended Hannah to sing an extended soliloquy in which she berates Alan for neglecting her and caring more for his sheep than his wife. However, most likely for musical and dramatic reasons, Birtwistle elected to cut Hannah's soliloquy by 41 lines, focusing instead on its opening refrain 'I feared, O I feared, that you had fled' (which is actually a revision of Harrison's original text, brought forward in the opera to suit the musical design). As shown in Example 4.9, Birtwistle first sketched the oboe and flute accompaniment to Hannah's part, which produces a disjunct line (derived from a five-note chromatic cell) within which the voice is mostly contained, or perhaps trapped: it is noticeable that Hannah's voice pushes at the lower boundary (for example at 'cider and bread') and symbolically crosses it at 'I feared, O I feared'.

There are other ways in which some of the opera's themes enter into the compositional processes. Harrison explains that in addition to the 'unlucky' number thirteen, numbers three (tethera) and seven (lethera) are 'lucky' or 'magic' numbers.[88] Various charts suggest that Birtwistle worked consciously with these numbers at a structural level, although it has not been

---

[88] Harrison, *Theatre Works*, 297.

Example 4.9 Sketch for Hannah's first entrance and flute and oboe accompaniment, pp. 48–9. PSS 0539-0560

possible to uncover ways in which they were applied.[89] However, when Alan first counts his sheep, the accompanying cello and double bass lines from the pizzicato continuum are restricted to thirteen pitches. As shown in Example 4.10, these are selected from two five-note cells (one is cell G, the other a mixture of I and C), and one three-note cell (possibly drawn from cell H). The selection process is determined by randomised number series of 1 to 0 (where 0 = 10), drawn from the composer's 'Magic Book of Numbers' (initially numbers 1–6 = the middle cell; 7–8 = the lower cell; 9–0 = the upper cell).[90] This results in a doubly disjunct composite line, with spaces either side of the central three notes.

A similar process of filtering determines the pitch material for the string accompaniment to the first counting contest, where three- and four-note selections are made from overlapping chromatic six-note sets.[91] The texture here is remarkable for its dense mechanistic layers distinguished by different phrase lengths (each with three-, four- or five-note onsets) and contours. Yet more remarkable is the otherworldly fourth instrumental pastoral, which interrupts the counting contest to depict the passing of a year (pp. 69–71). Here the concepts of scene–agent ratio and still movement converge to dramatic effect.

In one sense the fourth pastoral is a variant of the woodwind–string dichotomy and punctuating bell refrains heard at the very opening. However, this time there are three waving – or rather 'burrowing' – variants of the original glissando gesture in the second bassoon, third violin and first viola.

---

[89] PSS 0539-0653–4 comprise rhythmic skeletons similar to those discussed in Chapter 3, with events marked up to 13, and semiquaver pulses counted in units of 23 (which is the combined total of 3, 7 and 13.).

[90] This book is currently in the possession of Silas Birtwistle.   [91] PSS 0539-0589.

Example 4.10 Sketch for the double bass pizzicato accompaniment to Alan's counting, pp. 34–6 and 37–9. PSS 0539-0538

The other parts have narrow or disjunct melodic lines based on cells in the plan (the string section is shown in Example 4.11a). The sketches reveal that the melodic lines were conceived in three registral tiers, each comprising a pair of eight-note sets separated by a gap of interval 8. Birtwistle referred to the gaps as 'free' areas and spaces, and these are filled by the burrowing glissandi (the sketch for the second bassoon and its boundary parts is shown in Example 4.11b). The sketches therefore evoke the scene–agent ratio. Moreover the glissandi parts exhibit a degree of autonomy since they may choose the direction in which they glide. In exercising their free choice (agency) they push at the boundaries (scene) imposed by the melodic lines (see Example 4.11c). Following Abbate, it is possible to hear in these striking gestures 'numinous intruders' or narrating voices that 'create their own dissonant moments, interrupting the spaces surrounding them', ideas that 'assuage their characters' deafness, by breaching the separation of noumenal and phenomenal and bringing "unheard" sound into the human world on stage'.[92]

By contrast, the fifth pastoral is a variant of the second: it retains the tremolo strings of the second pastoral, but the wobbling sheep pizzicati

[92] Abbate, *Unsung Voices*, 152 and 155.

Example 4.11a Fourth instrumental pastoral ('the passing of a year'), strings only, p. 69

* Vln. 3 all harmonics (○).
Arrows indicate choice of notes by performer.

Example 4.11b Sketch for the fourth instrumental pastoral, pp. 69–71.
PSS 0539-0593

Example 4.11c Fourth instrumental pastoral, viola, cello and bassoon, pp. 69–70

are replaced by a bell refrain; the formerly impassive melodic lines now 'spin' with variants of the Piper's arabesques; the horn component of the opening mobile is also introduced, still based on cell C (pp. 81–3). The sixth pastoral, which follows Alan's internment and immediately precedes Hannah's return, is a reworking of the opening; an annotation in Birtwistle's hand on his typescript of the libretto reveals that he plotted the reprise at an early stage. This version comprises variants of the opening horn line, string glissandi, impassive woodwind, and a bell refrain. Later Hannah sings a variant of Alan's opening line that marks a reversal of the opening situation: Caleb waves to Hannah; she does not respond.

Birtwistle's cycle of instrumental pastorals culminates in Hannah's seven-year lament, which is effectively a 'magical' seventh pastoral with the addition of the chorus of Alan's sheep. Birtwistle described this section as 'an organic fugue-like texture'. As he explained:

the text is strophic . . . On one level the music repeats, but on another there's a long . . . organic fugue-like texture in the orchestra which goes right through the section then blossoms in the final chorale when the counting reaches the magic number seven. So I have a strophic superstructure as foreground and an organic substructure as background which are independent . . . of each other.[93]

Although this recalls the music–text distinctions in *Orpheus*, here the disjunction reflects the scene–agent ratio, which in some respects is brought into greater clarity than before. As Taylor has outlined elsewhere, there are three voices in Birtwistle's 'fugue', each marked 'seamlessly flowing':[94]

Voice I: first bassoon and first viola
Voice II: second bassoon and cello
Voice III: flute and first violin.

Birtwistle's use of the term 'Voice' in a series of tables used to determine the pitch material for each part is of course consistent with the language of a fugue. Yet it is noticeable that the instrumental voices mirror the registers of the opera's three principal characters, Alan, Caleb and Hannah. In addition there are stylistic similarities between Hannah's vocal part and Voice III in terms of rhythm and contour. Taylor suggests that the strophic elements (skirling woodwinds, bell refrain, pizzicato continuum) fit between the 'fugal' voices, which are each restricted to an octave range; see Example 4.12. This may have been Birtwistle's original concept, but in the score the boundaries are decidedly porous. It is true that Hannah's vocal line, the vibraphone and gongs fit precisely within the two-octave space prescribed by Voices I and III; Alan's sheep chorus fills this space almost exactly too, and the skirling figures in the oboes almost always remain below Voice III. However, the harp repeatedly crosses Voices I and III, and although the double bass fits between Voices I and II in the sketch, in reality its notes sound an octave lower.

Ultimately Hannah's lament is irreducibly ambiguous. On the one hand, the situation may be interpreted as a metaphor for the experience of living 'in the cycles of the landscape' in which the instrumental voices shadow (or substitute for) the opera's central characters (agents) whose existence is punctuated by the cyclic strophic elements (scene). On the other hand, the situation may be compared to a labyrinth, in which the instrumental voices act as boundaries (scene) to the strophic elements (agents), which move through the corridors of space allotted to them. Such ambiguity effectively

---

[93] Birtwistle in Hall, *HB*, 144–5.   [94] Taylor, 'Narrative and musical structures', 180.

194

Yan Tan Tethera

Example 4.12 Source sets and ranges for the 'Voices' and refrain elements during Hannah's lament, pp. 122–37. Based on PSS 0539-0661-3

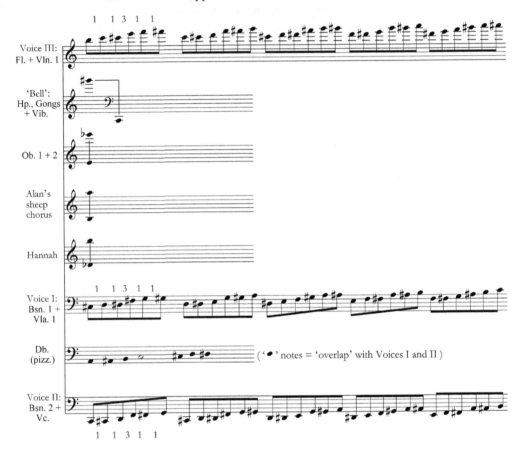

highlights 'the synecdochic relation . . . between person and place',[95] that is to say, the sense within the pastoral mode that scene and agent are reflected in each other. This is highlighted by the fact that the 'fugal' voices form porous boundaries. The sketches also reveal that the six-note sets these parts are based on (shown in Example 4.12) each have the same interval sequence of 1–1–3–1–1. In other words, a gap exists even within these boundaries, one that relates back to the minor third between each pair of cells in Set IIb in the registral plan (between the last note in cell F and the first note in G, etc.).

At which point we should return to Alpers's central questions: how does reality enter the pastoral work; how is its presence felt; and how are we made

---

[95] Burke, *A Grammar of Motives*, 7.

to feel 'the representative character of its two speakers'? A consideration of Birtwistle's musical sketches and score suggests that there are numerous ways in which the composer both complements and enriches Harrison's perspective on the pastoral, even when he intended to contradict Harrison. Reality for all the characters in *Yan Tan Tethera* involves prescribed borders and felt limitations; Alan in particular – like his Virgilian opposite Meliboeus – has an almost obsessive consciousness of boundaries. Like Odysseus, Alan experiences the Piper's Siren song with a mixture of fear that the sound will penetrate his defences (which causes him to stuff his ears 'with earth and clay'), pleasure when the sound breaks his defensive borders (which draws him into the hill), and pain (he screams with discomfort when he hears the Piper and when he enters the hill). Alan the opera character remains an archetype, but his situation and expressions are real. His experience as an immigrant not only brings questions of subjectivity to the fore, it also illustrates that identity is a fluid, relational process that requires the construction of boundaries (expressed by repetitions of the spell) but may be subject to change. The instrumental pastorals serve as representative anecdotes, contrasting versions of the pastoral that express in musical terms key pastoral dichotomies, such as Caleb's indifference to Alan, and Hannah's lament, which develops an ambiguously reflexive relationship between scene and agent. Moreover Birtwistle's compositional processes suggest that certain boundaries are porous, and that Alan's ability to recognise a specific landscape in the sounds that resonate around him – his aural responsiveness to his environment – has somehow assisted him and his fate: he returns to an expanded family, flock, and pasture, while Caleb is locked away for eternity.

5 The shadow of opera: dramatic narrative and musical discourse in *Gawain*

> Here is a voice
> baffled by endless echoes.
>
> . . .
>
> you carry it
> closer than your shadow.[1]

'*Gawain* is about story-telling and, in some respects, it's quite naïve.'[2] Despite this remark by Birtwistle, the ideological implications of storytelling are inescapable, since, according to Ricoeur, 'emplotment is the operation that draws a configuration out of a simple succession'.[3] In other words, storytelling is a subjective process that involves the selection, ordering and arrangement of events, or actions, through time. These subjective decisions, no matter how trivial, reveal the narrator's perspective.[4] The nature of an operatic project in particular requires that a configuration be drawn from more than one perspective, generating multiple, often conflicting, interpretations. However, in *Gawain* (1989–91; revised 1994 and 1999), the topic of narrative becomes even more absorbing when the innately theatrical nature of Birtwistle's purely instrumental music is taken into account. Much attention has already been given to this aspect of the composer's instrumental works, especially with regard to the influence of Aristotle's analysis of formal archetypes in Greek tragedy, the physical movements of players, and the implication that soloists and groups of instruments have either clearly defined roles or enter into an exchange or negotiation of identities.[5] One

---

[1] David Harsent, *Gawain* (London: Universal Edition, 1991), 74 and 71.

[2] Birtwistle, in an interview with Mark Pappenheim, *Independent*, 8 April 1994, 21.

[3] Ricoeur, *Time and Narrative*, vol. I, 65.

[4] For some scholars, notably Carolyn Abbate, a narrator's subject position is revealed by unusual or bizarre effects. Yet as Christan Metz has observed in relation to cinema, there is no reason why 'uncommon angles should express the viewpoint of the film-maker any more than perfectly ordinary angles, closer to the horizontal'; Christian Metz, 'The imaginary signifier', *Screen*, 16/2 (1975), 56.

[5] For a more detailed discussion of these topics see Cross, *HB: MMM* and Adlington, *MHB*. An indication of the currency of these ideas is reflected in the title of the London Southbank Centre's 1996 concert series 'Secret Theatres: The Harrison Birtwistle Retrospective' and its 2004 series 'Birtwistle Games'. In addition, Jürg Stenzl has commented that 'Birtwistle's music is always dramatic, a theatre of sculptural sound'; 'A "More Secret World"', in F. B. Humer, M. Haefliger, K. Jacobs, and G. Hanson, eds., *Roche Commissions: Sir Harrison Birtwistle* (Lucerne: Roche, 2004), 35.

implication is that hidden rules determine the events, as in a game or ceremony. But what happens to Birtwistle's concept of instrumental theatre when he composes an opera? In particular, how are the 'real world' concerns of a narrative and dramatic framework in *Gawain* reconciled with Birtwistle's interest in a more 'abstract' instrumental theatre?

It is widely held that *Gawain*, the first stage work Birtwistle described unambiguously as an opera, denotes a shift away from the artifices of *Punch* and *Orpheus* and a move towards more literal storytelling, although elements of time reversal and cyclical verse structures remain. *Gawain* brought Birtwistle together with the poet David Harsent in a reworking of the late fourteenth-century anonymous narrative poem *Sir Gawain and the Green Knight*. That Birtwistle asked Harsent to make a large number of alterations to his original libretto has already been documented.[6] This chapter, which draws on the sketching processes of both librettist and composer, reveals the nature and ramifications of those changes, in particular the contradictions and multiple narrative layers that resulted from the Harsent–Birtwistle collaboration. A consideration of Birtwistle's sketches reveals a preoccupation with line, in particular with finding different ways of shadowing vocal and instrumental parts, and ambiguously shrouding originary lines in layers of varied reflection. These musical devices represent Birtwistle's response to Harsent's interest in divided subjectivity, and to the idea that Gawain should develop a sense of his own identity.

At the time of the first performances it transpired that Birtwistle wished to 'make a separate drama for the orchestra, so the instruments are like voices, but you can't hear what they're singing; there's another drama which is "secret".'[7] This is a variation of his earlier remark that in *Orpheus* the orchestra contains a through-composed, organic substructure of its own, independent of more strophic music that supports the action on the stage.[8] Yet in *Gawain*, Birtwistle suggests, an alternative plot is encoded in purely musical terms. His reference to 'voices', however, implies a form of discourse or rhetorical process. This chapter explores the implication of the composer's remarks by focusing on modes of musical narration, drama and plot. What follows begins with an outline of the opera's synopsis and principal themes, and an examination of numerous unpublished manuscripts that shed light on the evolution of Harsent's libretto. This provides a context for

---

[6] Rhian Samuel, 'Birtwistle's *Gawain*: an essay and a diary', *Cambridge Opera Journal*, 4/2 (1992), 163–78.

[7] Andrew Porter, 'Knight's progress', *New Yorker*, 7 January 1991 [n.p.].

[8] Cited in Adlington, *MHB*, 19. However, Birtwistle drew a distinction between this artificial, pre-composed device and a more intuitive substructure in *Yan Tan Tethera*, in which 'situations occur when the music creates a counterpoint to the drama in ways I have not predicted'; cited in Hall, *HB*, 145.

the chapter's second half, which examines the music from the perspective of Birtwistle's musical sketches in relation to theories on music, narrative, and drama, in particular Gregory Karl's theory of musical plot.

Synopsis and narrative themes

Harsent was invited to write the libretto for *Gawain* after publishing his series of poems entitled *Mr Punch* (1984), a work that is remarkably close in conception to Birtwistle's *Punch*, despite the fact that Harsent was unaware of the opera.[9] Harsent wrote a first version of Act I while *Orpheus* was being rehearsed, in 1986, and he completed Act II the following year.[10] Birtwistle began composing in 1989 and from this time onwards the libretto underwent a series of substantial revisions. Key ideas from the libretto are present in Harsent's poem 'The Windhound', published in 1989. The poem explores two subjects, an anonymous woman and a windhound, as contrasting expressions of the same idea, personified by the pronoun 'she'. This double-voiced subject is placed in a shifting landscape of outer and inner worlds – by the sea, in a bar-room, on a hillside, in city back streets – where the separate, instinctive desires of the woman and hound collapse into one.[11]

Similar themes of divided identity, shape shifting, self-interest, and the conflict between inner and outer worlds pervade the opera.[12] Act I opens in the ordered but sullen world of Arthur's court. Morgan le Fay, the opera's magical conspirator, who is invisible and inaudible to the members of the court, plots Arthur's downfall. The mood changes when the Green Knight enters, goading the court, defying its customs, and challenging Arthur's knights to cut off his head. To the court's amazement, after his beheading by Gawain, the Green Knight picks up his head and reminds Gawain that he awaits the same fate one year later. A year passes (depicted at the end of Act I) and Gawain's journey to meet the Green Knight a second time begins (at the opening of Act II). On his way he rests at a castle, where he is tested once again, this time by the castle's keeper Sir Bertilak de Hautdesert. The

---

[9] Harsent's collaborations with Birtwistle have extended beyond *Gawain* to include *The Woman and the Hare* (1999), *Ring Dance of the Nazarene* (2003), *The Minotaur* (2005–7), and *The Corridor* (2008).

[10] Harsent in conversation with Beard, 21 January 2008.

[11] The danger is that this device, which neatly expresses the slippery nature of identity, 'teeters on the brink of confirming the deep but also careless misogyny of our culture'; Deryn Rees-Jones, 'The politics of seeing' [review of David Harsent's poetry collection *Marriage*], *Poetry Review*, 92/2 (2002).

[12] Two characters in the opera, Sir Bertilak de Hautdesert and the Green Knight, are incarnations of the same person and for this reason are performed by the same singer (in the original production these roles were created by John Tomlinson, who later created the Minotaur).

two agree to an unusual game: Bertilak will hunt while Gawain rests, after which they will exchange whatever they 'might have gained'.[13] Naturally, Gawain believes he has nothing to lose and everything to gain. Acting under the influence of Morgan le Fay, Lady de Hautdesert attempts to seduce Gawain while her husband is away. Twice Gawain resists, but on the third occasion he accepts from her a life-preserving sash, which he fails to declare to Bertilak. Gawain rides out to meet the Green Knight and receives three axe blows. The worst of these results in a nick to the neck, which is punishment for his failure to admit possessing the sash. This leads to a sense of shame and self-doubt when Gawain returns to Arthur's court. His self-interest not only upsets the balance of values in Arthur's court but also exposes the dual nature of the Green Knight, who, having played the role of Sir Bertilak, admonishes Gawain for his failure.

Despite the Green Knight's association with the Green Man of folklore, and thus with nature and concepts of rebirth and renewal, and his apparent embodiment of the wild, untamed outdoors (Birtwistle describes his entrance into Arthur's court as positively anarchic),[14] he also upholds the court's moral values. When he is beheaded, the forceful articulation of his amplified offstage voice by his severed onstage head has clear parallels with other operatic voices of paternal and civic authority, such as Mozart's Commendatore and Wagner's Titurel.[15] In this sense the Green Knight portrays a form of the dualities evoked by the 'Windhound' poem and employs the kind of modernist trope of an 'unresolved tension between difference and similarity, with which Birtwistle is very much at home'.[16]

Birtwistle was also attracted to the Gawain story because of its resonances with the music dramas of Wagner, in particular *Götterdämmerung* and *Parsifal*.[17] Hall has even noted that to help solve the problem of 'how to keep music moving forward', particularly in an opera that involves cyclic return, Birtwistle studied *The Ring* in 1988.[18] At the time of *Gawain*'s premiere many critics noted similarities to Wagner's operas in terms of the (sparing) use of leitmotif, in particular what Rhian Samuel described as the 'axe motif', and the scale of the orchestral music, which situates the work squarely in the realm of Grand Opera.[19] Another similarity is Birtwistle's preoccupation with extended line. This interest may be traced back to the early 1980s when

[13] Harsent, *Gawain*, 53.
[14] This comment was made during an interview for the BBC's televised broadcast of *Gawain* in April 1992.
[15] The amplified voice is marked in the score as 'menacing, awesome and mysterious.'
[16] Arnold Whittall, 'The mechanisms of lament: Harrison Birtwistle's "Pulse Shadows"', *Music & Letters*, 80/1 (1999), 97.
[17] See Hall, *HBIRY*, 78, 80, and 89.   [18] Hall, *HBIRY*, 78.
[19] For example, Michael Kennedy reported: 'It is not only Arthur's court, its knights, magic, transformation scenes and journey of self-discovery that make the comparison [to *Parsifal*]

Gawain, then untitled, was originally commissioned.[20] In *Deowa*, composed
early in 1983, the soprano and clarinet weave extended counterpoint in an
attempt to capture what Birtwistle refers to in the sketches as 'seamless
pastoral' and 'seamless song'. Moreover, as discussed in Chapter 4, the
voices of the 'fugue' in *Yan Tan Tethera* are marked 'seamlessly flowing'.
These concepts are reminiscent of Wagner's 'endless' or 'infinite melody'
('unendliche Melodie'), discussed in his 'Music of the Future' essay, which
Birtwistle seems to have alluded to in *An Interrupted Endless Melody* (1991),
for oboe and piano, completed shortly after *Gawain*.

Other links to Wagner exist in terms of subject matter and narrative
sources. Both *Parsifal* and *Gawain* depict isolated, closed communities,
bound by unwritten social codes that compel Gawain to ask Arthur to
'release me from my place' when he wishes to take up the Green Knight's
challenge. Yet Harsent has little respect for Arthur's court, describing its
members as ignorant and pompous boys – 'beardless boys', in the words of
the Green Knight. Harsent's substantial unpublished early sketches for the
libretto contain a more detailed illustration of his views:

> There are two strains that seem particularly important in terms of the
> libretto's burden. First, the contrast (largely a metaphorical one) drawn
> between the 'life indoors' and the 'life outdoors'. Secondly, the putting on of
> knowledge.
>   Arthur's court, and Arthur himself, are content with (almost dependent
> on) their rituals and lore: as a means of Proscribing [*sic*] the vagaries of the
> 'life outside'. The poet hints – I shall more than hint – at a notion of the
> emotional defensiveness that derives from ritual courtliness and (by the same
> token) the pressures opposing that ritual – a raw, unstructured 'life outside':
> not just a life bereft of the comfort of rules, but one delineated by risk and the
> pain of self-discovery. In a Jungian sense, Arthur and the court represent a
> blindness of the psyche. Of Arthur, the poet says[:]
>
>> He was so joly of his joyfnes and sumwhat childgered;
>> His lif liked him lyght, he lovied the lasse
>> Auther to longe lye or to longe sitte,
>> So busied him his yong blode and his brayn wylde.[21]
>
> This callowness appears almost smug and self-congratulatory to a modern
> ear: a boorish unworldliness which again emerges when Gawain returns

feasible, but also the music's Wagnerian scale'; 'Birtwistle rides into King Arthur's court',
Independent on Sunday, 2 June 1991.

20 *Gawain* was commissioned on 8 June 1983.

21 This translates as: 'He was charming and cheerful, child-like and gay / And loving active life,
little did he favour / Lying down for long or lolling on a seat, / So robust his young blood and
his beating brain'; *Sir Gawain and the Green Knight*, trans. Brian Stone (Harmondsworth:
Penguin, 1974), 24.

wearing the symbol of his sin, only to have members of the court adopt it – lightly, unthinkingly – as an emblem which they immediately trivialise.[22]

These thoughts are expanded in some of Harsent's more recent comments on the opera:

> [One aspect] that particularly interested me was what I saw as the extended metaphor of the indoors/outdoors division between culture and nature, between society's rules and a self-governing wilderness, between the trappings of a spurious decency and unignorable appetites, between the mendacity inherent in 'civilised' behaviour and the unfakeable bare bones of landscape and weather.[23]

Harsent's project is therefore revisionist in nature, standing in critical opposition to Wagner's nostalgic, nineteenth-century longing for *Gemeinschaft*, a society based on notions of kinship, shared mythological language, belief in the supernatural, and the resistance of internal threats to 'the utopian order... from the potentially disruptive force of human passion and sexuality'.[24] However, it reinforces a set of culturally specific mythic associations that would have appealed to Birtwistle, who was particularly attracted to the Gawain story because of its setting in the north of England and its use of local dialect.

One of Harsent's alterations to the original narrative was the transformation of Morgan le Fay from relatively marginal status in the poem to the 'principal driving-force' of the opera.[25] He describes Morgan as 'the winner', since, owing to her actions, Gawain begins to question the values of Arthur's court.[26] Contrary to the original *Gawain* poet, who 'viewed Morgan's motive as evil', Harsent sees Morgan's role as 'essentially virtuous, no matter what her motive',[27] and he depicts the two onstage narrators,

---

[22] PSS, Birtwistle Sammlung, *Gawain* libretto (henceforth *Gaw*/Lib) 1, typescript, 9. There are 2,108 sides of Harsent's sketches and drafts stored in box files at the Paul Sacher Stiftung. Birtwistle's manuscripts amount to 670 sides of sketches and drafts, and 451 sides of fair copy; Silas Birtwistle owns additional material. The Basle manuscripts are now on microfilm. However, this was not the case when I originally researched this work, and therefore all references here are to the original documents.

[23] Harsent, in the interview with Lydia Vianu, 'Poetry is a way of life', *Desperado Literature*, www.lidiavianu.go.ro (accessed 16 August 2011).

[24] John Bokina, *Opera and Politics: From Monteverdi to Henze* (New Haven: Yale University Press, 1997), 93. However, Wagner's *Parsifal* is not as straightforward as Bokina implies. See Barry Emslie, 'Woman as image and narrative in Wagner's *Parsifal*: a case study', *Cambridge Opera Journal*, 3/2 (1991), 109–24, and Slavoj Žižek, 'The everlasting irony of the community', in Slavoj Žižek and Mladen Dolar, *Opera's Second Death* (New York and London: Routledge, 2002), 151–80.

[25] Harsent, 'Morgan le Fay', essay in the programme booklet for the Royal Opera House, Covent Garden, production of *Gawain* in January 2000, 38.

[26] See Peter Porter, 'Inner and outer worlds', interview with David Harsent in the programme booklet for *Gawain*, January 2000, 36.

[27] Ibid., 35.

Morgan and Lady de Hautdesert, as 'invisible manipulators'. However, he conceives Guinevere as the only person in the opera to see Arthur's court for what it really is:

> Guinevere, as she sings the lines [to Gawain: 'Now you are more yourself, / let's speak again'], is taken aback by her own sudden apprehension of the falsity of Arthur's and the court's fiercely defended idea of chivalry. She understands that it's Arthur's blindness – his refusal to admit a real world in which sin is committed – that forces him to deny Gawain's true experience and to make a heroic token of the sash.[28]

This qualifies Rhian Samuel's impression of the opera as wholly lacking in sympathy towards women.[29] She directly criticises Birtwistle in this regard, citing his quip that he would like to see the misogyny of the original poem fully exposed, a view that could be seen to be illustrated by the fact that Guinevere's lines are not musically distinct from those around her.[30] But while Samuel's observation may justly apply to Birtwistle's vision of the opera, it does not adequately reflect Harsent's perspective.

Further differences of intention between composer and librettist are high-lighted by Harsent's unpublished sketches and early drafts, and an early draft of the libretto which bears annotations Birtwistle made before he began composition. These documents will be considered now in some detail since they throw revealing light on the opera's narrative themes as well as issues relevant to Birtwistle's musical perspective on the drama.

Libretto and dramatic structure

Two published versions of Harsent's libretto for *Gawain* exist. The first, used in the 1991 performances, contains an extended scene at the end of Act I titled 'Turning of the Seasons', during which Gawain is stripped, washed and armed. At the same time, the passing seasons are depicted by a procession of mime artists, who present a series of five tableaux (from Winter to Winter), and a monks' chorus sings Marian antiphons and sections of the Dies Irae.[31] A shorter and revised version of the opera, prepared for Covent Garden in

---

28 *Gaw*/Lib 14a, 74. An early version of the end of Act II also contains the following instructions: 'Guinevere senses the malevolence [of Morgan le Fay] and registers a feeling of deep unease. She's fearful for Gawain, and scornful of the pact of chivalry that forces him to go in search of the Green Knight' (*Gaw*/Lib 9, 21). For the 1994 revision some of Guinevere's important lines were cut, although Harsent, in an undated letter to Birtwistle (*Gaw*/Lib 2nd version, 2–8), claimed to have made some attempt to retain a sense of her 'prescience' in the revised version of the 'Turning of the Seasons' scene.

29 In the interview with Vianu ('Poetry is a way of life'), Harsent even states that 'The women in the piece – Morgan, Bertilak's wife, Guinevere – interested me much more than the self-regarding, callow boys of the Arthurian court.'

30 Samuel, 'Birtwistle's *Gawain*', 176.   31 Harsent, *Gawain*.

1994, was subsequently the basis for a recording released in 1996.[32] The principal alteration in the revised version was the reduction of the Turning of the Seasons section from forty minutes to a little over ten.[33]

Harsent's libretto is written in a stylised form of poetic verse that occasionally incorporates more naturalistic dialogue. It therefore keeps faith with the spirit of the original poem while incorporating contemporary idioms in a manner comparable to T. S. Eliot's *Murder in the Cathedral* (1935). Stylised features include the frequent repetition of phrases, leading Adlington to comment that throughout *Gawain* 'the music flirts moodily with both libretto and drama, at times haughtily indifferent, elsewhere responsive, even pictorial'.[34] An example of this occurs when Gawain arrives at Castle Hautdesert. There are four repetitions of the phrase 'help us to learn' in Lady de Hautdesert's words to Gawain. Although Birtwistle employs a similar downward contour in the voice with each repetition, recurring woodwind and brass chords run counter to the text's scheme. It is all the more surprising, therefore, to discover that the composer requested the textual repetitions himself (see Figure 5.1).[35] According to Samuel, Birtwistle claimed that his own role in structuring the libretto had been a crucial one:

> I had asked Harry about the role he played in creating the structure of the libretto. (He had told me several times before that the original libretto lacked many of the repetitive sequences of the final version and that he had instructed David Harsent as to its form.) ... Harry admitted that he'd distributed the text amongst the seasons and that the significant organisation of the libretto was an aspect more fundamental to *Gawain* than to many operas. It was vital therefore that critics and writers should realise the extent to which this was part of the *musical* creation.[36]

Adlington sees the music's tendency to 'flirt moodily' with the repetitions in the text as indicative of a 'tug and pull' between the opera's ritualistic and narrative tendencies, as well as Birtwistle's more general desire to respond to a libretto as a series of dramatic situations rather than words.[37] This conflict may additionally be seen as an extension of the purely instrumental works, in

---

[32] This was a live recording of the Royal Opera House production, conducted by Elgar Howarth, made for BBC Radio 3 on 20 April 1994 and released in 1996 on CD, Collins Classics, COLL70412.

[33] Revisions started at least as early as December 1992. The revised text comprised a composite of elements from the original version, the whole bound together by a new female chorus; seasonal texts for Morgan le Fay and Lady de Hautdesert were cut entirely. A large section from the end of the opera, where the knights approach Gawain in succession, was also cut in 1994 and is therefore not in the commercial recording. However, this section was restored in 1999 (see Figs. 150–73).

[34] Adlington, *MHB*, 87.

[35] *Gaw*/Lib 13: 1, 32–3. Here the phrase is actually worded 'help us learn'.

[36] Samuel, 'Birtwistle's *Gawain*', 175.   [37] Adlington, *MHB*, 29 and 36.

Figure 5.1 Revision, at the composer's request, of Lady de Hautdesert's lines, Act II scene 2

Early draft (dated 1989)

Lady de Hautdesert: Now we shall learn…
                             Everyone knows
                             Of Gawain's skills in love:
                             His gentleness, his honour, his soft speech.
                             You must be our teacher – **help us learn**
                             The proper place of passion, how to step
                             Lightly between objection and desire;
                             How to take love's scent,
                             How to draw the quarry, how to guess
                             Its line of flight, how to run it down
                             And then…bring it to hand.

Published libretto (1991), p. 50

Lady de Hatudesert: **Help us to learn**
                             The proper place of passion,
                             Help us to learn
                             The distance between objection and desire;
                             Help us to learn
                             How to take love's scent,
                             How to draw the quarry, how to guess
                             Its line of flight; **help us to learn**

which repetitive schemes such as verse and refrain forms counterpoint more linear devices, as well as reflecting the composer's belief in the 'sanctity of the context', which ensures that the music's progress cannot be overdetermined in advance.[38] Yet when it is realised that Birtwistle requested many of the repetitions in the text, the libretto may be understood as a form of pre-compositional design that the composer was at liberty to contravene, much in the way that he had superseded predetermined schemes in the past.[39] Such inconsistencies might then be interpreted in a more positive light, leading to a fruitful tension rather than a 'damaging rift of compositional intention'.[40] Moreover, as Adlington has acknowledged, a clearly structured

---

[38] Hall, 'The sanctity of the context', 14–16.
[39] Besides the examples in this book, see David Beard, '"From the mechanical to the magical": Birtwistle's pre-compositional plan for *Carmen Arcadiae Mechanicae Perpetuum*', *Mitteilungen der Paul Sacher Stiftung*, 14 (April 2001), 29–33.
[40] Adlington, *MHB*, 30. Adlington does, however, offer the explanation that 'This apparent disregard for the structure of the text could conceivably be explained in terms of one of the opera's principal themes: the unreined natural world that Harsent depicts as a persistent threat to human certainties is symbolised by a "wild" music that fails to respect the text's cosy repetitiousness' (29).

libretto, 'far from demanding a correspondingly coherent musical response, largely *relieves* music of precisely that responsibility'.[41]

If there is a compositional challenge in this work, however, it lies in balancing the needs of the libretto with the desire for a purely instrumental theatre. That said, it would be misleading to suggest that the music is insensitive to the drama. Besides a general sense of ebb and flow that matches the action on stage, there are many moments of clear identification between the orchestra and characters, reflected in the pairing of strident horns with Arthur and gruff bassoons with the Green Knight, while Cross has noted the presence of 'conventionally expressive' vocal lines, a strong musical characterisation for Gawain, and a moment of recognition and reversal in Gawain's final aria.[42] Nonetheless, signs of character development are extremely restricted in the libretto.[43] True emotions are often disguised through formulaic utterances, while detailed notes concerning character relations, sketched by Harsent, are absent from the published libretto and score.[44]

Yet Harsent's detailed notes and stage directions informed Birtwistle's music in clearly tangible ways. This is a crucial point because it challenges the assumption of some commentators that Birtwistle was unresponsive to Harsent's ideas, and that their visions were mismatched.[45] An especially revealing document in this regard is a working copy of the libretto, dated 15 March 1989, in which Birtwistle's detailed annotations reveal a keen sense of theatrical suspense and timing combined with a visual and spatial awareness, which recalls Gumbrecht's remarks about presence (see Chapter 1).[46] Morgan's consistently high register and somewhat constricted, at times hurried delivery, in association with Lady de Hautdesert, is clearly a response to Harsent's direction that the pair are gleeful, excited and apprehensive. At the Green Knight's first entrance, Birtwistle noted that the pair should sing in a 'very fast patter' as a way of heightening the tension, yet he conceived of this moment as a 'tableaux' [*sic*]. Empty boxes indicate Birtwistle's intention to insert musical refrains between each verse of Morgan's opening text, where Birtwistle eventually introduced literal repetition.

[41] Adlington, *MHB*, 36.

[42] Cross, *HB: MMM*, 218, 139 and 77 respectively.

[43] Adlington comments that something of the original poem's 'psychological two-dimensionality', stemming from its evocation of 'an idealised world, in which Gawain is a stylised representation of chivalric gallantry and courtesy, rather than a character in the modern sense . . . is carried through into the opera'; *MHB*, 28.

[44] In his sketches for the first draft of the libretto Harsent refers to Bertilak 'masking [his] aggression [towards Gawain] by using the terms of their bargain'. *Gaw/Lib* 9, 34.

[45] See, for example, Irene Morra, *Twentieth-Century British Authors and the Rise of Opera in Britain* (Aldershot: Ashgate, 2007), 47–53.

[46] At the time of writing this document is in the possession of Silas Birtwistle.

Figure 5.2 Outline of the dramatic structure in the opera's definitive version

Act I

Arthur's court

Door knocks (×3)
Green Knight enters after 2nd and 3rd door knocks
Gawain beheads Green Knight

Green Knight issues challenge

Gawain's arming
Turning of the Seasons

Act II

Gawain's journey

Castle de Hautdesert

Seduction & hunt scenes (x3)

Green Chapel
Green Knight admonishes Gawain

Arthur's court – Gawain's return

When Baldwin, Agravain and Arthur first respond to the Green Knight, Birtwistle writes: 'really thick low chord with movement in it'; additional responses from the other knights were also inserted to intensify the dialogue in this scene. In particular, Birtwistle's annotations reveal his attraction to those moments of 'pure' theatre, such as the door knocks, entrances and exits, and the opening/closing door.

An outline of the principal dramatic elements as they appear in the final version of the opera is presented in Figure 5.2. Some of the most palpable contrasts between Harsent's first completed draft and the final version can be identified at the opening of the work.[47] The dramatis personae originally included warriors, dwarves and grotesques, to serve as Gawain's opponents during his journey to the castle. Harsent had initially envisaged a chorus of servants performing the opening lines (later given to Morgan), and intervening refrains of 'Noel' sung by a chorus of knights (subsequently removed). Originally, the riddles were to be sung by Arthur, and there was no Fool, or the Morgan and Lady de Hautdesert pairing at the very opening. Additionally, Birtwistle had requested that Harsent alter or introduce many of the opera's most important musico-dramatic elements, notably the three door knocks delaying the entrance of the Green Knight.

Other changes included: the insertion of the Fool's 'Who is it?' refrains; development of the Green Knight's monologue after his beheading (from

---

[47] Hall suggests the first draft was complete in 1986 following its commission in 1984 (*HBIRY*, 50 and 52).

eight to thirty lines); additional text for Gawain before he raises the axe; the introduction and expansion of Morgan's lullaby; the addition of three door knocks to announce Bertilak's return from hunting, and Gawain's response 'Who's there?'; additional text as Gawain prepares to leave the castle; expansion of the Green Chapel scene, to dramatise the moment when Gawain meets the Green Knight; increased ritual repetition when Gawain is disarmed; the insertion of Gawain's final soliloquy; removal of text in which the Green Knight reveals his true identity to Gawain, and the latter's responses; and a significant alteration to the concluding text, originally sung by Morgan le Fay rather than the Fool. An aria that Harsent conceived for Arthur near the end of the opera, expressing his empathy for Gawain, was completely removed. The Turning of the Seasons scene, originally conceived as the opening of the second act, is not an important feature of the first draft,[48] and neither is the text for the journey very extensive, whereas Harsent's notes and text relating to the scenes in Bertilak's castle are easily the most substantial.[49] This led to significant cuts, including the reduction of a soliloquy for Gawain on his arrival, and the removal of an erotic mime scene and several pages of text for Morgan le Fay and Lady de Hautdesert, whose lines were then largely reconceived.

These observations would suggest that what mattered most to Harsent often mattered least to Birtwistle. Even Harsent's final word on the narrative was eventually excised. His original libretto ended with a riddle from the Fool: 'I'm an answer without a question. I'm the colour of water, a gift from an empty hand. I'm blind, I'm blameless, I'm bliss. What am I?' The answer, indicated elsewhere in Harsent's sketches, is 'ignorance', and the final sound was to have been the Fool's laughter, ending Harsent's version with a jibe at Arthur's court.[50] Ultimately, Birtwistle preferred a circular ending that recycles Morgan's line 'Now, with a single step' from the end of Act I and the beginning of Act II.

There are, however, certain indications of Harsent's influence on Birtwistle. The idea of intercutting music and mime in the hunt scenes, and the notion of 'recitative' during the journey, to which Gawain contributes a 'counterpoint', are present in Harsent's first sketches.[51] His idea

---

[48] The text representing the Turning of the Seasons was later distributed among the verses detailing Gawain's arming, as well as additional texts and Latin verses relating to the Christian calendar.

[49] Harsent has commented that 'What happens at Castle Hautdesert interested me more than anything else in the poem'; P. Porter, 'Inner and outer worlds', 36.

[50] *Gaw*/Lib 3, Act III, scene 1, 14 contains the following sketch for this passage: 'fool – Arthur riddle: ends: I'm bliss. (ignorance) I'm –, I'm blind, I'm bliss'. Another sketch for this riddle has the word 'Ignorance' circled and written at the top of the page.

[51] *Gaw*/Lib 2, 2 and 2, 8, which states: 'Chanted lines from Morgan and Lady de H. to progress [the] narrative'.

that the journey represents a 'journey of the mind' can be distinguished clearly in the highly fragmented musical structure of this section, with its premonitions of the hunt scenes and the harrowing images of the beheading still to come.[52] It is also worth considering the extent to which Birtwistle was influenced by Harsent's frequent references in the early sketches to 'leit-motifs', by which he means recurring ideas in the text that will relate the various episodes. For example, Harsent's sketches bring to light a series of jealousies between Gawain and Arthur, Bertilak and Gawain, and Morgan and Arthur. At one point he considers:

> Bertilak poss. to echo Lady de Hs remarks about chivalry&good manners etc., but with menace underlying the notion.
> NB Some leit-motif [*sic*] that can be used for beheading moment to underline fact that motive has to do with earlier jealousy . . .[53]

Harsent's ideas concerning this moment appear to have a direct musical representation. Bertilak's statement to Gawain 'Now we shall learn something of courtly love' is followed by an ostinato dance rhythm that is later recast in more menacing form in the cimbalom and marimba during the beheading scene, when Bertilak, transformed into the Green Knight, raises the axe a second time (Fig. 122).[54]

Both Harsent's division between inner and outer worlds and the concept of a double for Gawain were of significance to Birtwistle's vision of the opera. The latter underwent a series of adaptations and greatly preoccupied Harsent, although the eventual representations of Gawain's double in the first production were restricted to mime artists at the back of the stage during the journeys to and from the castle in Act II. This severely compromised Harsent's original desire for an interactive relationship between Gawain and his double that would culminate in a confrontation between the two. Gawain was to remove his double's tunic and mask, revealing physical wounds in order that 'we see (Dorian Gray-like) the effect that Gawain's adventures have had on him spiritually. I still like the idea of the double having a mask of the Gawain singer/actor's own face.'[55] A musical response to this dramatic gesture can be found through a sketch study of Birtwistle's concern with developing various means of shadowing a musical line (the central focus of the next part of this discussion).[56] More broadly, this compositional

---

[52] This idea is noted in the stage directions of the first draft; *Gaw/*Lib 9, 22.

[53] *Gaw/*Lib 3, 24r. After the second axe blow Harsent considers the Green Knight saying 'Surely you know love's rules', but this is altered to 'Remember the rules we made when I stood in Arthur's court', uttered after the first axe blow.

[54] 'Fig.' references are to Harrison Birtwistle, *Gawain* full score (London: Universal Edition, 1999), UE 21014.

[55] Taken from a letter from Harsent to Birtwistle dated 2 June 1989.

[56] Birtwistle's sketches for Act I are dated Spring/Summer and Autumn 1989. Act II was completed in Winter 1990–91.

preoccupation suggests a possible musical analogy for Harsent's interest in divided identity as expressed in his poem 'The Windhound' as well as the *Gawain* libretto. As we shall see, in certain instances varied replication (shadowing) of a vocal line may saturate the orchestral texture, a process that results in the subject (the vocal line) being literally reflected in and dispersed throughout the musical fabric.[57]

Line

Birtwistle has suggested that *Gawain* is based on a single line.[58] This offers a musical analogy for Harsent's interest in identity and subjectivity and also suggests the presence of a secret drama – a musical agent whose continuous movement is a metaphor for Gawain's journey, his *Bildungsroman*-like pressing forward – or a narrating 'voice'. This latter idea is indirectly suggested by Hall when he notes the presence of a line whose 'somewhat sad character . . . is totally at odds with the words and music Birtwistle gives the singers. In it we get the first glimpse of a world lying behind the action'.[59] The contrasting forthright or withdrawn character of such lines, which results from shifts in register, dynamics, instrumentation and tempo, is comparable to differing narrative points of view. Yet at times the lines are so forceful that they assume a presence within the drama itself, for example during Gawain's journey. Following Edward T. Cone, such lines might be interpreted as aspects of the composer's controlling voice.[60] Yet often they conjure up the notion that it is 'as if' a voice speaks – or rather 'sings' – from within the orchestra in an attempt to communicate 'while knowing the inadequacy of speech'.[61]

There are numerous examples of slower-moving lines in the orchestral texture (for instance in the first violins, piccolo trumpet and first oboe from Fig. 33 to Fig. 35, then in the first violins between Figs. 38 and 40, in Act I), but the profusion of orchestral lines makes identifying a 'source' problematic.

---

[57] Alastair Williams has observed a similar dispersal in the musical treatment of Montezuma's subjectivity in Wolfgang Rihm's music drama *Die Eroberung von Mexico*; 'Voices of the Other: Wolfgang Rihm's music drama *Die Eroberung von Mexico*', *Journal of the Royal Musical Association*, 192/2 (2004), 240–71.

[58] Samuel, 'Birtwistle's *Gawain*', 167 and 173. To illustrate this idea, Birtwistle drew for Samuel 'a line on a brown paper envelope – it spiralled around a circle. . . . [a]nd he drew the repeated sections as rectangles on the circle' (173). However, in a BBC television broadcast of the opera in April 1992 Elgar Howarth reported the composer saying that *Gawain* is based on a single chord.

[59] Hall, *HBIRY*, 91.   [60] Cone, *The Composer's Voice*.

[61] Julian Johnson, *Mahler's Voices: Expression and Irony in the Songs and Symphonies* (Oxford University Press, 2009), 288; see also Lawrence Kramer, '"As if a voice were in them": music, narrative, and deconstruction', in his *Music as Cultural Practice, 1800–1900* (Berkeley and Los Angeles: University of California Press, 1990), 176–213.

The sketches neither confirm nor deny the existence of a fundamental line. Both the 'wildly' disjunctive linear motion of brass and violas at the Green Knight's entrance (Figs. 41–3) and the fragments of a line for instrumental parts around Figs. 18 and 23 are written out independently, but there is no information to explain how these were generated.[62] More detailed evidence does exist in relation to *Mrs Kong* and the Celan setting 'Todtnauberg' (1995), which suggests that the vocal lines were composed first and derived from small groups of pitches, most probably drawn from tables that are not extant.[63]

Equally problematic is Birtwistle's remark that the orchestra at times 'may relate more closely than the voice part to the fundamental line'.[64] Vocal melodies are initially sketched without accompaniment (usually rhythm first, with a tempo marking, then with pitches) before they appear clearly legible with more roughly assembled orchestral parts that embellish, simplify, or directly mirror the progress of the voice.[65] If simultaneous vocal melodies are required, either a single line is distributed among the parts, or a line is composed first and counterpoint is generated from it, as in Morgan's part at the opening of Act I, which was clearly conceived before that of Lady de Hautdesert.[66]

A more detailed consideration of the instrumental counterpoint against Lady de Hautdesert's vocal line near the start of the first act (Fig. 3^{+4}) will further elucidate these working methods (see Example 5.1). The first violins and flutes provide a counter-melody that often moves in contrary motion to the voice and only occasionally intersects with its pitch material, while a much simpler line – in the clarinets, violas and cello – filters the voice's pitch material, reducing it to a rocking line beginning D–C–D–E–Eb. The sketches indicate that this simpler line was conceived afterwards but in relation to the vocal melody.[67] Despite its degree of independence, the higher melody

---

[62] These fragments exist on sketches 1/10, 49 and 60, and 2/10, 36.

[63] The practice of beginning with the vocal lines was established when Birtwistle resumed work on *Orpheus*, before which the voices had been grafted on to pre-composed instrumental textures (see Chapter 3, and Taylor, 'Narrative and musical structures'). An indication of a collection being used to determine a vocal line in Act I of *Gawain* is Baldwin's chant-like intervention at Fig. 54, based on a six-note set also in the percussion. There are also signs of five-note collections being used for Lady de Hautdesert's line at Fig. 41^{+4}, Act II, on 5/10, 24.

[64] Samuel, 'Birtwistle's *Gawain*', 167.

[65] A series of ring-bound sketchpads owned at the time of writing by Silas Birtwistle comprises the earliest sketches for the opera.

[66] Hall comments that in the opening duet 'the vocal lines for Morgan le Fay and her companion [on 1/10, 9] are written out neatly as if they had been composed previously and simply copied' (Hall, *HBIRY*, 52). However, this is not the case: the orchestral parts contain very few alterations, whereas Lady de Hautdesert's part is roughly written, with numerous corrections.

[67] Sketch 1/10, 14. This page also contains workings for a supporting ostinato texture in the strings and marimba. Overall, the scenario resembles the cantus/continuum distinction

Example 5.1 Lady de Hautdesert's line shadowed by winds and strings, *Gawain* (full score, UE 21014), Act I, Fig. 3⁺⁴ to Fig. 4⁻¹

Example 5.2 Sketch for flute and vocal parts, Act II, Fig. 146^{+1} to 146^{+4}. PSS *Gawain* folder 9/10, 34

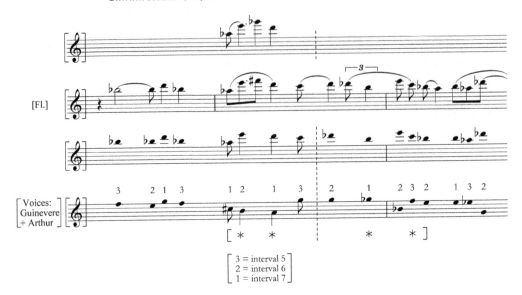

embellishes both the voice and the slower-moving counter-line. Although the instrumental lines are two different manifestations of the same idea (the vocal part), the simpler line is redolent of a 'source': it shadows the voice closely, emphasising a rocking contour and narrow register.[68] Observing a similar effect in Birtwistle's song 'White and Light' (1989), Whittall has remarked that 'there is the most essential and productive ambiguity between lines which were conceived as a consequence of vocal melody and yet which sound as if they are prior, creating a context for that melody'.[69] Harsent's dramatic concern for the slippage of identity, which is central to both 'The Windhound' and the *Gawain* libretto, is mirrored in this musical process that proliferates a single idea throughout the orchestral fabric.

A number of techniques are used to produce such textures. To create instrumental counter-lines, numbers are often associated with specific vertical intervals and applied randomly. In some instances this leads to approximately parallel movement. Example 5.2 illustrates this in relation to the flute and the vocal parts of Guinevere and Arthur in Act II (Fig. 146^{+1}). Characteristically, there are slips or deliberate alterations in Birtwistle's application of his system (the asterisks mark where the 'wrong' interval has

familiar from *Secret Theatre*, although the melodic (cantus) element is more complex in this instance. For more on cantus and continuum see Hall, *HBIRY*, 26–35.

[68] This pitch area later gives rise to the four-note 'axe motif' (D–F–D♭–E), first heard in Act I (Fig. 81).

[69] Whittall, 'The mechanisms of lament', 89.

Figure 5.3 Random number scheme to replicate flute line in approximately parallel motion

5	6	6	5	6	6
1	1	1	2	2	2
6	5	6	6	5	6
2	2	2	1	1	1
6	6	5	6	6	5
---	---	---	---	---	---
1	3	5	6	4	2
	7				8

been applied) as well as further embellishments (see the added F♯/G♭ in the flute). Another method involves the application of a generic chord above or below an instrumental line. For example, in Act II (Fig. 112[-2]) intervals 1, 2, 5, 6, 6 applied beneath the notes of a flute line are randomised to produce an ascending woodwind texture. The scheme generates six different lines, with two instruments on each line. As the difference between the intervals in each row is no more than a semitone, the result is an approximately parallel movement; the order of the columns is determined by the numbers under the dotted line (see Figure 5.3).[70] A third approach is illustrated by Morgan le Fay's vocal line at Figs. 6–7. The vocal line was originally sketched alongside workings for string chords that are entirely unrelated to the voice. At a later stage, however, Birtwistle devised an extended heterophonic line that embellishes the vocal line in such a way that it appears as if the voice is shadowing the woodwind (see Example 5.3). A fourth method is to elaborate a simpler, filtered version of a vocal melody or instrumental part. This occurs alongside Arthur's melody in Act I (Fig. 14), where a number system is used to determine which instruments are assigned particular notes from the counter-line, leading to a dense web of heterophonic sound (see Plate 5.1); this is the 'somewhat sad' line referred to by Hall.[71]

What is ambiguous in this last example is, once again, the question of which line came first. The sketches suggest it was the vocal line, which was drafted independently and then copied out neatly and continuously before the orchestral music was added. However, it remains unclear how the orchestral line was formed. The fact that it shadows the voice closely

[70] This is presented on sketch 7/10, 41. A similar scheme is used to produce the approximately parallel-moving woodwind parts at Figs. 173–4 in Act II, although here the intervals are applied above the B♭ clarinet (further workings exist on sketch 10/10, 59).

[71] Sketch 1/10, 37. The counter-line appears in the horns, clarinets, bassoons, violins and violas. When the voice is silent, additional notes are inserted in the counter-line. This technique is also used to generate the instrumental lines at Fig. 92, when Arthur's earlier text is reworked at 'now I can eat' (sketch 3/10, 54).

Example 5.3 Upper woodwind line and Morgan le Fay, Act I, Fig. 6^{+3} to 6^{+8}

suggests an intuitive method, but this contradicts evidence elsewhere of Birtwistle using number schemes in the orchestra. If the vocal lines were generated by predetermined schemes then the same fund of pitches could be used for the instrumental lines. Yet the evidence for this is inconclusive. For example, when vocal lines are rewritten in the sketches there is enough difference between the versions to suggest the pitches were intuitive, but enough similarity to leave open the possibility that Birtwistle was either elaborating a smaller series of pitches or selecting pitches from a larger set (see Example 5.4). An example from 'Todtnauberg' provides evidence of the use of pitch sets for a vocal line (see Example 5.5). However, this example does not reveal whether a scheme was employed to determine the selection and reordering of notes from the ten-note set. If selections from such sets are made intuitively then there is scope for considerable variation when a line is rewritten, for example if a different ordering is chosen, or certain notes are

Example 5.4 Alterations to Lady de Hautdesert's vocal line, Act II, Fig. 95

Sketch, _Gawain_, 7/10, 9

Sketch and score, Act II, Fig. 95 – 95⁺³

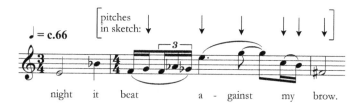

Example 5.5 Use of pitch set in sketch for 'Todtnauberg', _Pulse Shadows_, p. 72

[* E♭ in score]
[+ B♮ in score]

omitted and others repeated. (Some errors, or deliberate alterations, also crept in between this sketch and the published score.)

As a consequence of techniques like those shown in Example 5.2 and Figure 5.3, orchestral lines frequently appear to shadow the vocal melody but avoid its pitch content altogether: in Act I (Figs. 20–1) various melodic ideas appear in the woodwind that are essentially independent of Arthur's line but reflect its timbre and register;[72] either side of Fig. 71 the bassoons and tubas shadow the movement of Gawain's melody but their pitch content

---

[72] Sketch 1/10, 52 shows these fragments were first conceived as a single counter-line to Arthur's part and subsequently partitioned out.

Plate 5.1 Sketch for the instrumentation at Arthur's line 'Some fable of bravery, then', Act I, Fig. 14. Sammlung Harrison Birtwistle, PSS, *Gawain*, folder 1/10, 37

is different.[73] Occasionally, counter-lines were determined separately from vocal lines and simply grafted on to them, as with the flute line at Fig. 23^{+2}.[74] Additionally, the violin part at Fig. 84^{+3} is an elaboration of the brass and lower woodwind material, derived from a seven-note set that is entirely independent of the voice.[75] As the Green Knight exits for the world outside, this sense of detachment flourishes in numerous instrumental lines derived from six-note sets that are totally independent of the voice (Figs. 88–90).[76] Self-governing contrapuntal writing has even greater freedom in the original Turning of the Seasons section (exemplified by Figs. 139–41). At other times, shadowing movement exhibits a more rhythmic nature and approximately mirrors the speech patterns of characters, for example in the horns and trombones when the Green Knight states his challenge (Act I, Fig. 50^{+1}), and in the bassoons when he admonishes Gawain (Act II, Fig. 127). This declamatory device – a more literal example of the notion of a speaking voice within the orchestra – recalls the fact that the opera's ultimate source text, the poem *Sir Gawain and the Green Knight*, would originally have been read aloud.[77]

Music, narrative and drama

The sketches have provided evidence of remarkably varied approaches to the formation of instrumental lines throughout *Gawain*. One clue to a possible 'plot' for the line (in a purely abstract sense) is its tendency to jump to or reappear in different registral bands, each confined to roughly an octave. For example, between Figs. 16^{+6} and 24^{-6} in Act I, the 'somewhat sad' line that Hall refers to follows a contour pattern of <2, 4, 3, 1, 3>, where 1 is the lowest octave, and 4 the highest. Each shift of register is prompted by a varied refrain that comprises a number of short, fragmentary ideas. What role do these varied refrains have in the abstract musical drama?

A conceptual framework that offers both a useful vocabulary and a means of exploring such refrains is provided by Gregory Karl's attempt to adapt plot analysis techniques from linguistics and narratology to music. Karl's ideas

---

[73] This may reflect the fact that at this moment Gawain is squaring up to the Green Knight, the split between the lines implying a metaphor for Gawain's inflated ego.

[74] Evidence for this is contained on sketch 1/10, 60, where the flute pitches are written out along the bottom of the page prior to their insertion above the vocal line.

[75] Sketch 3/10, 24. The subsequent violin line that accompanies the Green Knight at Fig. 85^{+4} is also derived independently, from five-note sets that are mistranscribed from treble clef, to bass clef, and back to treble.

[76] Sketch 3/10, 35. These sets are [0,1,2,6,7,8] hexachords.

[77] For more on the idea that rhythmic patterns in *Gawain* are analogous to the metric schemes of the original poem see Robert Adlington, '"Good lodging": Harrison Birtwistle's reception of *Sir Gawain and the Green Knight*', in Richard Barber, ed., *King Arthur in Music* (Cambridge: D. S. Brewer, 2002), 127–44.

require some modification, however, since his approach was devised for 'instrumental music composed in the framework of Romantic-expressive aesthetics' and focused on the first movement of Beethoven's Piano Sonata in F minor, op. 57 (the *Appassionata*).[78] Before turning to Karl's ideas, some of the more salient points from recent debates about music, narrative and drama will be outlined.

Narrativity in music?

Clearly, music lacks the grammatical nuances that would permit the kinds of distinction between verbs, tenses, and narrative points of view that are fundamental to literary narrative. However, a significant body of narrative-based music analysis exists. Motivated by what Jean-Jacques Nattiez describes as a 'narrative impulse' among listeners, such studies have interpreted musical gestures, shifts in musical style, texture and tempo, and thematic repetitions and incursions – usually in relation to tonal genres – as suggestive of differing narrative positions, tenses, plots, narrative archetypes, voices, and agency. Adorno, however, has argued that although music is sometimes made to 'act' as if someone is narrating, neither content nor meaning is apparent: music 'narrates without narrative'.[79] For others, notably Nattiez and Carolyn Abbate, musical narrative is 'at best, a metaphorical and limited concept, at worst, a product of wishful thinking'.[80] Yet opera inevitably encourages one to think of music's relation to text and drama, however the narrative dimension is theorised.[81]

Within recent narrative-based studies a consensus has emerged on two points. Firstly, music is not directly equivalent to literary or other kinds of narrative, nor does it narrate in any conventional sense. Rather, music narrates in its own way, which is temporal and therefore potentially *analogous* to the 'actions, tensions and dynamisms' of literary works or drama.[82] Secondly, certain kinds of music are more suggestive of narrativity or drama

---

[78] Gregory Karl, 'Structuralism and musical plot', *Music Theory Spectrum*, 19/1 (Spring 1997), 13–34.

[79] Theodor Adorno, *Mahler: A Musical Physiognomy*, trans. E. Jephcott (London: University of Chicago Press, 1992), 76.

[80] Byron Almén, 'Narrative archetypes: a critique, theory, and method of narrative analysis', *Journal of Music Theory*, 47/1 (2003), 1.

[81] Abbate herself is not immune from this tendency: on a single page of *Unsung Voices*, for example, she refers to 'a narrating *voice*', 'narrating gestures of many kinds', 'Wagnerian narration', 'modes of narrative speaking', 'instrumental narration', the '*narrating voice*', 'musical narration'; *Unsung Voices*, 19 [italics in original].

[82] Anthony Newcomb, '"Once more between absolute and program music": Schumann's second symphony', *Nineteenth-Century Music*, 7/3 (1983–4), 248. Almén describes music as a 'sibling' rather than a 'descendant' of literary narrative; 'Narrative archetypes', 2–3.

than others.[83] Particularly amenable to narrative interpretation is music that is combined with text, a programme, or explicit drama: therefore opera and music theatre are likely to encourage such readings. To these points it may be added that some composers have openly declared an interest in what they perceive to be music's narrative potential, as illustrated by Birtwistle's suggestion of a secret musical drama in *Gawain*.

In one of the most useful discussions of music and narrative, Byron Almén has listed five problems with the idea that music can narrate.[84] Almén's strategy is to neutralise such objections by critiquing them. In particular, he re-examines the way that literary narratives function, and he highlights the arbitrary nature of all narratives, which rely on the perceiver to infer connections. One important point Almén draws attention to is what Genette has described as the scene/summary distinction: the former refers to the action as it unfolds, the latter to the narrator summing up events. Birtwistle's music in *Gawain* complicates this distinction. On the one hand, certain musical ideas are analogous to agents in a drama (represented action). On the other hand, these musical agents often respond to the action on stage. These responses may be interpreted simply as further actions, or they may suggest forms of commentary (reported action), in a manner that is comparable to what Genette terms 'simultaneous' narrative.[85] A similar blurring of the scene/summary binary is achieved by the libretto in which the Fool's repeated riddles ('There was … Who is it?') and Morgan and Lady de Hautdesert's refrains ('Soon you will see / Soon you will hear') function as narrative points of view that continually interject, yet in doing so themselves become part of the action. *Gawain* revels in its own 'narrative impulse' and emphasises the point that narrating is itself an act.[86]

Where music is deemed more likely to suggest narrative or drama, a set of plot-led analytical questions may result in a different kind of musical analysis to one based on purely musical considerations. This is illustrated by Nicholas Reyland's investigation into Lutosławski's concept of 'akcja' (literally 'action' or plot), which valuably highlights the possibility of following up a composer's remarks about intended narrative affects.[87] Lutosławski's reference to dramatic 'events' in his instrumental music is comparable to

[83] See Vera Micznik, 'Music and narrative revisited: degrees of narrativity in Beethoven and Mahler', *Journal of the Royal Musical Association*, 126 (2001), 193–49; Micznik advocates 'a graduated spectrum within which certain texts present various degrees of narrativity' (245).
[84] Almén, 'Narrative archetypes'.
[85] Genette, *Narrative Discourse*, 217.
[86] See Jean-Jacques Nattiez, 'Can one speak of narrativity in music?', *Journal of the Royal Musical Association*, 115/2 (1990), 243.
[87] Nicholas Reyland, '*Livre* or symphony? Lutosławski's *Livre pour Orchestre* and the enigma of musical narrativity', *Music Analysis*, 27/2–3 (2008), 253–94.

forms of musical agency that I will explore in a moment, in what I refer to as 'constellations'.[88] Such considerations lead Reyland inwards, to identify the transformation of ideas defined by particular intervals, and outwards, to a listener's experience of 'change', shifts in 'discourse level', and 'plot threads'.[89] Similar considerations will be examined in Gawain's journey, through what I term a 'pitch agent plot'. The difference, of course, is that the context of the present discussion is post-tonal opera, and – to the best of my knowledge – there has been no comparable attempt to map narrative theory in this domain.

Debate about narrativity in music has also raised the question of whether music is not more analogous to drama than to narrative. The following discussion will consider Birtwistle's music from both perspectives, although in many ways it is more closely analogous to drama: that is, a temporal sequence or succession of 'dramatic *actions*' that 'forms a *plot* that holds the actions together'.[90] In *Gawain*, it is particular dramatic situations, initially at least, that hold such actions together. With this in mind, we can return to the model developed by Karl.

Musical plot

Drawing on Cone, Karl proposes a model that includes musical equivalents to literary foils, roles, and functions.[91] In literature a character may be understood as the foil of another if '*parallels* in life circumstances, personal history, or appearance' exist that mark them as similar, but essentially they must retain contrasting outlooks (*differentia*) that provide insights into their actions.[92] In tonal music this amounts to 'relations between different versions of the same theme or motive'.[93] An analysis of *Gawain*'s music in Karl's terms necessitates distinguishing two types of musico-dramatic 'agents': first, short musical figures, which are metaphors for events on stage at specific moments, often repeated without variation or development; and, second, musical lines that are more extended and rhetorical in

---

[88] Reyland notes that Lutosławski's concept of 'akcja' is a symptom of his resistance to 'high modernist structures which he deemed catastrophic for music's communicative power'; '*Livre* or symphony?', 279.

[89] Ibid., 262, 278, and 179 respectively.

[90] Fred E. Maus, 'Music as drama', *Music Theory Spectrum*, 10 (1988), 65 and 71. See also Maus, 'Narrative, drama and emotion in instrumental music', *Journal of Aesthetics and Art Criticism*, 55/3 (1997), 293–303.

[91] Cone, *The Composer's Voice*.

[92] Karl, 'Structuralism and musical plot', 17. Foil is meant in the sense of 'a person or thing that enhances the qualities of another by contrast'; *Concise Oxford Dictionary* (Oxford: Clarendon Press, 1995).

[93] Karl, 'Structuralism and musical plot', 18.

character, which 'speak' from the orchestra and form a network of distinct but syntactically related motifs.[94]

In response to Vladimir Propp, Karl defines roles as 'idealized character types, recurring from tale to tale, that may be assumed by a number of more or less interchangeable beings. The role of villain, for example, may be played equally well by a giant, a bandit, a witch, a stepmother, or some other unsavoury entity.'[95] In *Gawain* it may not be necessary, or indeed appropriate, to define musical objects in terms of their character type, although it is possible to make a broad distinction between musical ideas that are forthright and those that are more reticent. The latter are linked to the world of the court, while the former are frequently associated with the world outdoors. Karl maintains that functions such as villainy may assume dissimilar forms (murder, abduction, etc.), but they motivate other characters to intervene and attempt to counteract such actions. He suggests that in music these events constitute actions such as disruption, subversion, interruption, integration, divergence, and withdrawal; this, though, as Maus has observed, requires the collapse of agents and actions into one another.[96] In *Gawain*, such actions are triggered either by specific dramatic gestures, like the door knocks and Guinevere's repeated request that Arthur take his seat, or by specific ideas in the text, such as bravery, conveyed in Arthur's repeated question 'Who's brave?'

The interruptive function of Arthur's question is expressed by a steady yet incisive rhythmic figure in the woodwind, as shown in Example 5.6a. Yet such associations are subject to change. At Fig. 12^{+4}, for example, the rhythmic figure appears in the trumpets and fourth horn, with a *crescendo* from *mezzo piano* to *forte*. Yet at Fig. 13^{+4} the rhythmic figure is muted (it is marked *piano, con sordino* in the trumpets and horns). This alteration reflects an annotation Birtwistle made to his copy of the libretto, in which he remarked that Arthur 'goes into himself' at this point. The figure withdraws further, at Fig. 50^{-3}, when the question 'Who's brave?' is uttered by the Green Knight: it appears after the question, lower in register, in the harp and cimbalom. The discursive register shifts yet again when the Green Knight issues his challenge: here a disrupted, declamatory version

---

[94] I adopt the more neutral term 'agent' in preference to Karl's use of 'protagonist' and 'antagonist', in order to avoid the anthropomorphic and culturally loaded connotations of such terminology; in this more relativistic context there is no reason why a descending scale should be considered the antagonist of an ascending scale.

[95] Karl, 'Structuralism and musical plot', 19. See Vladimir Propp, *The Morphology of the Folktale*, trans. Laurence Scott, in *International Journal of Linguistics* 24 (1958); reproduced as V. Propp. *The Morphology of the Folktale*, trans. L. Scott (Austin: University of Texas, 1994). Propp's structural analyses were limited to Russian fairy tales selected from Afanás'ev's folktale collection.

[96] Maus, 'Music as drama', 70.

Example 5.6a Interruptive function of the woodwind rhythmic agent associated with Arthur's 'Who's brave?' Act I, Fig. 20^{-2}

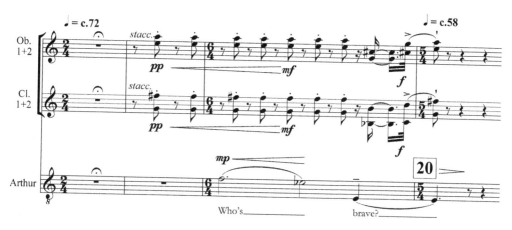

appears in the brass, as if a narrating voice recites a shadow version of the Green Knight's lines (Example 5.6b). However, when the question returns at Fig. 54 the rhythmic agent is absent, despite the fact that Birtwistle instigated the textual refrain at this point. At Fig. 95, shortly after the Green Knight leaves the stage, it returns in the harp and marimba, this time much slower and without the textual refrain. Later, in Act II, Fig. 138^{+3}, the agent is transmuted into a series of door knocks, shadowed by the orchestra (Example 5.6c). Here the otherworldly effect simultaneously evokes and calls into question the narrative distinction between represented and reported action, or scene and summary.

Karl's theory will be used to identify agents such as this, which appear in direct relation to specific dramatic gestures, both to examine the schemes in which they are presented and to reveal ways in which they are released from their original contexts. What is important about Karl's theory is its structuralist perspective, which treats agents' actions as the basic units of plot. The theory is therefore relevant to this book's focus on the relationship between abstract musical schemes (Birtwistle's subplot) and the practical and real world concerns of drama (the *Gawain* libretto). The notion of a foil is also instructive since it draws attention to Birtwistle's pairing of musical ideas, and to their position, alteration and re-voicing. What emerges is a variation on the idea that stories do not exist in a single version but are varied through retelling. As in *Orpheus*, narrative is articulated through abstract compositional schemes: the units of plot, or narrative 'events', are treated like compositional blocks that are subjected to selection, permutation and reordering. Moreover, the musical agents often react to or anticipate actions on stage in a manner that both contributes to and reports on the drama.

Example 5.6b Withdrawal of the rhythmic agent after the Green Knight's 'Who's brave?' Act I, Fig. 50⁻³ (harp and cimbalom), followed (in the brass) by a disrupted, declamatory version of the same agent while the challenge is issued

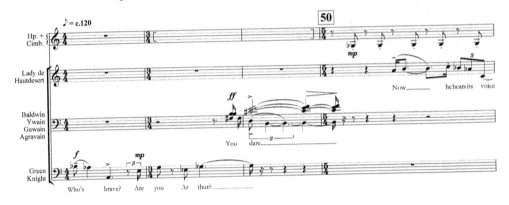

Constellations

A review of *Gawain*'s opening reveals a number of key agents that are directly associated with the stage action, acquiring refrain-like functions in relation to the libretto's strophic forms (see Example 5.7). The first two agents, a rapid ascending scale ending on E and a series of slower, descending

Example 5.6c Integration of the rhythmic agent with door knocks, echoed by the orchestra, Act II, Fig. 138^{+3}

scales, constitute two different versions of the same idea (see a1 and a2 in Example 5.7). The two are related through their inclusion of pitches specifically associated with Gawain (G and B♭) and the Green Knight (A♭ and A♮). Their focal pitches E and A♭ outline interval class 4, which assumes importance as the outline of the axe motif (D♭–F) and appears at the beginning of Act II in the form of the focal pitches D and G♭. However, as Karl's theory demands, the two have contrasting outlooks. While the former agent has

Example 5.7 Musical agents a1 and a2 at the opening of Act I

Example 5.8 Musical agents b and c, Act I, bb. 5–9

an active role, heightening dramatic expectation and initiating new, more urgent passages, the descending scales are more acquiescent, bringing dramatic gestures and sections to a close. These two agents therefore provide a foil for one another and carry a vital role in structuring the drama.

The first page of the score establishes two further agents: a chord (agent b) and a tuba motif characterised by iambic rhythms (agent c), as shown in Example 5.8. As it appears here, the chord is strident, suggesting a link to the world outdoors. During the lullaby scenes in Act II the chord becomes integrated with the iambic motif. However, the warmer register and new context considerably soften its effect (Example 5.9a). Here Karl's theory draws attention to the chord's contrasting outlooks. Similarly, the iambic tuba motif (agent c) has an active role associated with hunting and the world outdoors. Its foil is a cadential figure in the tubas, first heard at Fig. 1^{+5}. This achieves its definitive form (F♯–B–C) at Fig. 23 (Example 5.9b), followed by frequent reiterations (for example, Figs. 24, 25 and 31^{+7}). At Fig. 25 the tuba foil acquires an association with the door closing. Elsewhere it anticipates the music immediately following the beheading

Example 5.9a The foil of agent b, Act II, Fig. 50

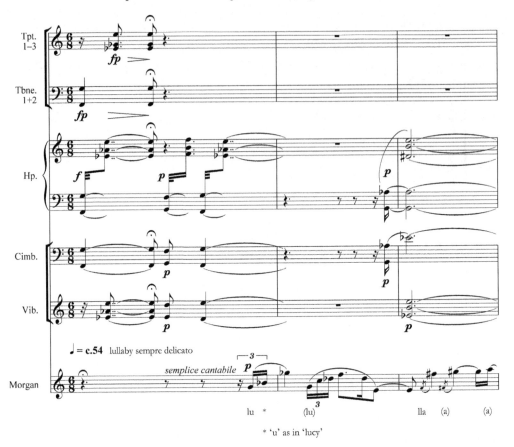

* 'u' as in 'lucy'

Example 5.9b The foil of agent c, Act I, Fig. 23

scenes. By contrast, the ascending scale (agent a1) predicts the lifting of the
axe and builds suspense before each of the door knocks.[97] Although agents

---

[97] Although these agents are gesturally distinct from one another, there are signs of relations that
undermine such categorical distinctions. The cadential tuba figure relates to the tuba descent
in bar 2 (agent a2), while the lower three pitches of agent b (G–Ab–Bb) reproduce the first

al and a2 are sometimes deployed independently, they frequently appear in immediate succession, as in the Turning of the Seasons section at the end of Act I, and as an accompaniment to the killings at the end of each hunt scene in Act II.[98] However, when the door opens for the first time in Act I without revealing the Green Knight (Fig. 31), musical as well as dramatic expectations are frustrated because the descending agent fails to appear, replaced instead by ghostly representations of the chord and iambic motif in the horns. When the Green Knight does finally enter, after the second door knock, all of the agents from the opening are utilised, although the placement of agents in the orchestra and their relative lengths and ordering are significantly changed. Through such alterations the portrayal of the Green Knight's other-worldliness becomes a persuasive feature of the music drama.

At Fig. 12^{-1} a rocking idea, first heard in the orchestra during the opening duet of Morgan and Lady de Hautdesert, reaches its definitive form of C–B♭–A♭–B♮–C (marked d in Example 5.10). This is the first agent in a new series of motivic associations that supersede those of the opening. This new framework is associated with the rather mundane world of the court, and it reappears as the Green Knight departs (Fig. 91), and when the action returns to Arthur's court in Act II (Fig. 136). The sketches indicate that Birtwistle requested that Arthur's lines in these sections be extended, suggesting that the composer saw potential at this point for further musical invention.[99] As befits their association with Arthur's court, the new agents share a listless, directionless quality (they are labelled d–f in Example 5.10). This situation is repeated at Fig. 13 but without agent d, whereas at Fig. 19 each agent is restored to its original location with the addition of short lyrical ideas in the flugelhorn and cor anglais related to agent c (the iambic brass motif).

Such an approach to composition, in which quasi-dramatic situations are frequently revisited, is a hallmark of Birtwistle's style, dating back to *Tragoedia* and *Verses for Ensembles*. In *Gawain* a number of different musical constellations relate to the drama on stage. When these recur, the original order of the constituent elements is not necessarily retained: some may be left out, others added. At a certain point, elements may become detached from their constellations, cropping up in ostensibly random places. These ideas may retain their original dramatic meaning or become musical objects

three notes of agent al, along with a slight variant (G–A–B♭) contained in agent c (third tuba). This pattern of intersecting three-note sets anticipates the Gawain signature motif (G–B♭–G♭), first linked to Gawain at Fig. 63 as he reveals his name to the Green Knight.

[98] Their function during the Turning of the Seasons is similar to the 'bob and wheel' pattern of the original poem, by which a series of verses with irregular metrical schemes is rounded off by a verse in regular metre with end-rhymes.

[99] Details of this are noted in Harsent's hand on *Gaw*/Lib 10, 3 and 5.

Example 5.10 Musical agents d, e, and f, Act I, Fig. 12⁻¹ to 12⁺⁶

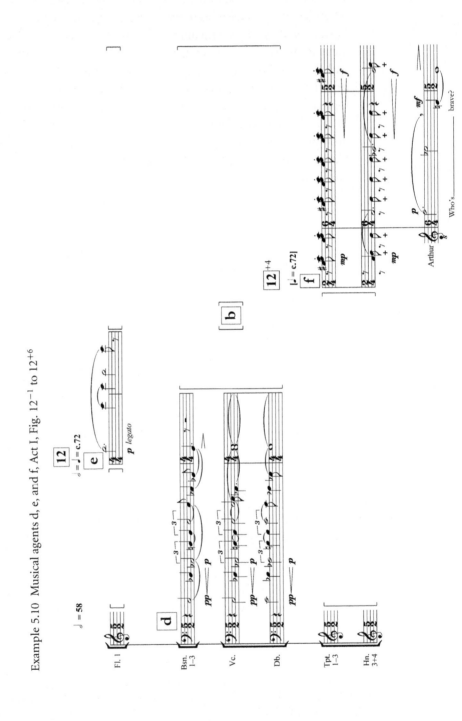

in their own right, freeing themselves from their original context. This mirrors a process that Christopher Morris (following Dahlhaus and Abbate) has observed in Wagner's *Ring*. Morris notes how the leitmotif forges a 'forced alliance between music and stage, an alliance that music gradually relinquishes once set free to "be" music . . . [M]usic drama sets up an imaginary process of increasing musical independence that has as its conclusion an absolute Music.'[100] However, far from representing a reactionary step in the direction of Wagner's musical procedures, Birtwistle's use of motifs corresponds to his own well-established compositional practices.

From Fig. 26 the various agents outlined so far are emancipated from their ritualistic functions, so that when the Green Knight adopts Arthur's 'Who's brave?' refrain (Fig. 54), the expected elements are absent, replaced by an angular ostinato. An example of agents being partially freed from their original contexts but still allied to the drama on stage occurs shortly before Fig. 61, when the Green Knight asserts that war cries leave him cold. Subsequently, the rhythmic agent associated with the idea of bravery (agent f) undergoes a shadowy transformation as it is merged with earlier agents – rising and falling glissando scales (agents a1 and a2) and high woodwind chords, echoed by low brass chords (agent c). In contrast, a variant of the cadential brass motif in the middle of the Green Knight's vocal line (Fig. 86) appears out of place. Similarly, in sections designed to heighten suspense in anticipation of the Green Knight's arrival (Figs. 26–7), a variant of the rocking figure (agent d) appears, despite its association with the mundane world of the court, while the descending scale assumes a new form in the brass freed from its cadential function (Fig. 28^{+5}). Although initially these constellations enact their own drama or choreography and also provide a counterpoint to specific events on stage, eventually they are liberated from the demands of the libretto and achieve an independent form of instrumental theatre.

Pitch agent plot

An indication that plot theory may be applied to particular pitch centres in Birtwistle's music is suggested by the instrumental pieces *Secret Theatre* and *Earth Dances* (1986), in which the recurrent dyad D–F might be considered a dramatic agent that assumes a number of varied roles and functions. In *Gawain* the moment of the Green Knight's beheading is marked by

---

[100] Christopher Morris, *Reading Opera between the Lines: Orchestral Interludes and Cultural Meaning from Wagner to Berg* (Cambridge University Press, 2002), 174. Of related interest is Debussy's belief 'that *Parsifal*'s music simply has not much to do with what is happening on stage'; see Carolyn Abbate, 'Metempsychotic Wagner', in her *In Search of Opera*, 114.

Example 5.11 Summary of pitch agent plot

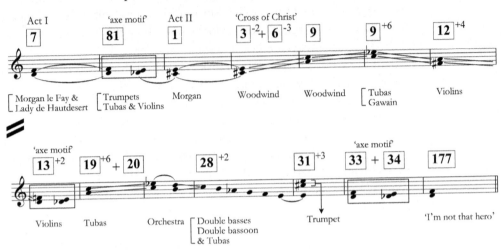

these same pitches, where they appear within the context of the four-note 'axe-motif': D–F–Db–E. The pairing of D and F first emerged at Fig. 7, during the opening duet of Morgan and Lady de Hautdesert, while the axe motif may be traced from Fig. 50 when the Green Knight issues his challenge. What follows is suggestive of a hidden narrative that shadows Gawain's expedition and which takes the form of a spiral quest; a graphic summary is presented in Example 5.11.[101] During the orchestral interpretation of Gawain's journey at the beginning of Act II, a foil to the D–F agent emerges in the form of C♯ and E. These two pitches have been 'prepared' in the context of the axe motif and appear as a significant motif for the first time at the start of Morgan's line (Fig. 1). Subsequently, they pass to the woodwind ('*fff*' in the highest register at Fig. 3^{-2}), alongside Gawain's anguished exclamation 'Cross of Christ, save me', expressing fear both of his destiny and of the wilderness through which he passes (repetitions of this refrain were introduced at Birtwistle's request).

The identity of the C♯–E foil becomes more slippery as the musical representation of Gawain's journey advances, its outline preserved in a chain of interval-3-related transpositions; this process is initiated at the fourth and fifth of Gawain's 'Cross of Christ' refrains, when the foil is transposed to A–C and C–Eb (Figs. 9 and 9^{+6} respectively). The association with Gawain's refrains is then temporarily relinquished as the agent moves fully into the orchestra (presented as F♯–A harmonics in the violins, from Fig. 12^{+4} onwards), leading to a variant of the axe motif (Fig. 13) and

---

[101] Some of the registral placements in Example 5.11 have been altered: the woodwind A (clarinet 2) and C at Fig. 9, for example, is shown an octave lower in the table.

two short bursts of A–C in the tubas (Figs. 19^{+6} and 20).[102] Appearances then oscillate between C–E♭ and B–D (the latter employed in a cadential function) prior to a stepwise descent in the double basses, contrabassoon and third tuba from Fig. 28: C–B–A♭ . . . G–F–E. Subsequently, E establishes a pedal that underpins a flowering trumpet motif based around C♯–E at Fig. 31^{+3}, which accompanies the ninth 'Cross of Christ' refrain and re-establishes its association with Gawain's anguish. The journey concludes with a variant of the axe motif at Figs. 33 and 34, as the action turns to the relative safety of Castle Hautdesert, and the music settles around D, F and A.[103] However, the D–F agent is transformed in the closing stages of the opera, where it too is associated with Gawain's inner conflict (his final soliloquy ends 'I'm not that hero', with D–F on the first two words).

The pitch agent plot outlined here is by no means fully audible every step of the way. On the contrary, its presence is sometimes restricted to visual clues in the score, such as dynamic markings and performance directions. Such evidence bears the familiar hallmarks of an abstract plan that is somewhat obscured in the act of composition, not least since it is submerged in a rich orchestral fabric. Yet such plots remain valid in the composer's mind because they are part of what he terms a 'linear complexity', rather than density. 'That doesn't mean that there's no density in what I do', he has commented, 'but there is also the opposite of it.'[104]

It may be concluded from the pitch agent plot and constellations that musical agents in *Gawain* develop a subplot that at times suggests a direct link between events on stage and associated musical gestures, but at other times either loosens such associations or abandons them.

Unheard voices

As noted earlier, Birtwistle has suggested that there is a more rhetorical category of agents that arise from the desire for instruments to be 'like voices, but you can't hear what they're singing'. In one sense these words resonate with what Naomi Cumming, following Jerrold Levinson, terms 'virtual agency':

> The effect of virtual agency is certainly not absent, but it is not of an agency that is obviously 'personal' or 'expressive' of an emotional state. Rather, it

---

[102] Some of these moments are not clearly audible. However, certain clues in the score, such as the '*ffff*' marking for the repeated string harmonics at Fig. 12^{+4}, and the direction 'in relief' for the tubas' C–E♭ at Fig. 21^{+6}, suggest their importance in Birtwistle's mind.

[103] An F pedal first heard at Fig. 36, as Gawain enters the castle, returns at Fig. 43 when Bertilak encourages Gawain to make himself at home.

[104] Birtwistle during the composition of *Gawain*, cited in Ford, *Composer to Composer*, 54.

serves the purpose of questioning an aesthetic where human subjectivity dominates . . . It is as if there are other 'voices' in the world that should be heard.[105]

In contrast to those instrumental lines in *Gawain* that shadow or extend human (vocal) presence, Cumming draws attention to the alternative perspectives that 'other', more detached instrumental voices may provide. This is to some extent comparable to Carolyn Abbate's concept of 'unsung voices'. In contrast to Cone's 'monologic and controlling "composer's voice"', Abbate proffers 'an aural vision of music animated by multiple, decentered voices localized in several invisible bodies'.[106] For Abbate, music is not narrative, but 'it possesses moments of narration, moments that can be identified by their bizarre and disruptive effect. Such moments seem like voices from elsewhere, speaking (singing) in a fashion we recognize precisely because it is idiosyncratic'; these voices have 'a characteristic way of speaking' and are 'marked by multiple disjunctions' with the surrounding music.[107] Throughout *Gawain*, there are numerous isolated instrumental solos that are marked by 'multiple disjunctions' for one or more of the following reasons: they are not part of the process of shadowing a vocal line; they do not relate directly to the action on stage or to the sung text; they are not explicitly leitmotivic; they are prominent in the score but not clearly audible in performance. They are, however, associated in terms of rhythm, tempo, or contour and as such imply collective points of view. These motifs are far more prevalent in the second act, and they can be divided into two paradigmatic types.

One type appears in brass instruments and serves the function of interrupting or intercutting unrelated material, recalling montage procedures in earlier works such as *Punch*. Throughout the depiction of Gawain's journey short trumpet motifs appear during two of the brief blackouts that punctuate the early stages of the journey (Figs. 18 and 31), and a related motif is used near the end of the opera, either side of Fig. 179, in a series of intercutting sections that recall Gawain's journey. Similar, fragmented motifs in the contrabass trombone (Fig. 33^{+6}) are inserted between Morgan's lines 'Mile after mile / day after day / week after week'.

The second type (see Example 5.12a–f) is related to a six-note motif in the flute at Fig. 64 (Example 5.12a), when Gawain reveals his name, and

[105] Naomi Cumming, *The Sonic Self: Musical Subjectivity and Signification* (Bloomington and Indianapolis: Indiana University Press, 2000), 205. See also Jerrold Levinson, *Music, Art, and Metaphysics* (Ithaca, NY: Cornell University Press, 1990).

[106] Abbate, *Unsung Voices*, 13.

[107] Abbate, *Unsung Voices*, 29, 48, and 19. Similarly, in Kramer's view 'instrumental music seeks narrative as a strategy of deconstruction', while Johnson refers to material that is 'framed as "other" by its episodic or parenthetic separation from the main narrative'; Kramer, '"As if a voice"', 188, and Johnson, *Mahler's Voices*, 223.

an extended variant of that motif joined by oboes and clarinets as Gawain raises the axe (from Fig. 72^{+3}). It is possible that this theme is Birtwistle's response to Harsent's first draft of the libretto in which a figure stands and watches Gawain raise the axe.[108] During the three lullaby scenes in Act II there are three woodwind melodies that relate back to the shadow motif in terms of tempo and contour (see Example 5.12b–d); these accompany Morgan's attempts to calm Gawain during his nightmares to the words 'sleep without fear of the dream'. Besides a shared tempo, there are a number of syntactical relations between these motifs; these are indicated by square and dotted brackets in Example 5.12. For instance, the initial dyad (G♯–D) in Example 5.12a appears in the middle of Example 5.12b (written A♭–D), and the rising figure in the second half of the melody (beginning C♯–D♯) is reintroduced both at the opening (altered to D♭–E♭) and at the end of the same extract (where C♯–F♯–E is altered to C–G–D).

Another related melody appears in the clarinet as the Fool asks: 'Something stranger than charity / something greener than grief / something colder than justice / more secret, more than belief. / What is it?' (Fig. 138^{-7}; Example 5.12e).[109] This clarinet melody, which was written after the voice and supporting violins, embellishes the violins and replaces the accompaniment that previously supported the Fool when he delivered the same riddle in Act I (Figs. 33–5).[110] Through its allusion to Gawain's nightmares the melody has 'put on knowledge', a concept that, as noted above, Harsent claims was central to his version of the narrative. The implication is that the answer to the Fool's question is 'fear'. Retrospectively, this adds a layer of uncertainty to the seemingly bold musical subject position adopted during Gawain's acceptance of the challenge and his execution of the Green Knight (Example 5.12a). Unlike the fearless Gawain of the original poem and Harsent's libretto, Birtwistle's Gawain doubted himself even as he took up the challenge.[111]

---

[108] *Gaw/Lib* 10, 16.

[109] The first sketch for this melody is on 9/10, 15.

[110] In Act I the Fool's question was followed by the third door knock, which revealed the Green Knight, whereas the reworking, in Act II, is followed by ghostly echoes of the door knock in the orchestra and Morgan's invisible entrance.

[111] This dimension of the opera, especially the concept of a doppelgänger, contrasts strongly with the original poem, in which the inner Gawain is identical to the outer one. As Stone comments, 'Gawain is an undivided man'; *Sir Gawain and the Green Knight*, 20. These thoughts are amplified by Derek Pearsall, who remarks that 'There is no suggestion that [Gawain] has any fears or qualms or inner debate about the quest he has undertaken . . . [W]e never imagine him . . . saying to himself, What am I doing here? Why am I doing this? Who am I? . . . which bespeaks a mind at ease with itself. His outer life is his inner life'; Pearsall, 'Courtesy and chivalry', in Derek Brewer and Jonathan Gibson, eds., *A Companion to the Gawain Poet* (Cambridge: D. S. Brewer, 1999), 359.

Example 5.12a Flute 1, when Gawain has told the Green Knight his name. Act I, Fig. 64

Example 5.12b Flute 1, during Morgan's lullaby to calm Gawain while he rests at Castle Hautdesert. Act II, Figs. 50^{+6}, 71^{+6}, 85^{+6}

Example 5.12c Bassoon 1, in Morgan's lullaby. Act II, Figs. 51^{+4}, 73^{-4}, 87^{+4}

Example 5.12d Oboe 1, in Morgan's lullaby. Act II, Figs. 52^{-1}, 73^{-4}, 88^{-1}

Example 5.12e Clarinet 1, at the Fool's riddle, 'Something stranger than charity'. Act II, Fig. 138^{-7}

Example 5.12f Violins (plus flutes, oboes, and clarinets from Fig. 116^{+3} to 116^{+5}), immediately after Gawain's 'fear of death like a voice beating my brow'. Act II, Fig. 116

Example 5.13a Flugelhorn, following Arthur's request that Gawain tell the court his tales of bravery. Act II, Fig. 164⁻²

Example 5.13b Summaries of (i) flugelhorn, Act II, Fig. 164⁻²; (ii) horns and violins, at Gawain's 'Not greed and love? I'm guilty of both', Act II, Fig. 128; (iii) horns, at Gawain's 'We expected nothing but innocence', Act II, Fig. 174⁺⁹

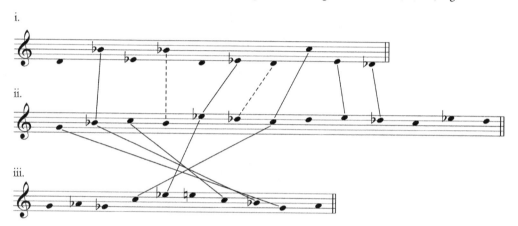

An apparently disconnected melodic idea of a similar type appears in the flugelhorn in Act II (Fig. 164⁻²) in conjunction with a statement of the Gawain signature in the woodwind and brass (Example 5.13a).[112] This follows Arthur's request that Gawain tell everyone his tales of bravery. Gawain does not reply, but the melody is suggestive of his thoughts – it is a slight variation of an earlier horn and violin line that shadowed the vocal part at the moment of Gawain's self-discovery (Fig. 128; see Example 5.13b). A similar horn line reappears at Fig. 174⁺⁹ as a shadow of Gawain's soliloquy, delivered at Arthur's court, in which he openly declares his doubts about himself. As evident in Example 5.13b, the second horn line is an approximate retrograde of the first.[113] It has already been noted that Harsent originally intended that Gawain would confront his double on stage during his

[112] This appears in a section of the second act that was cut for the 1994 performance but retained in the score for the 1999 performance.

[113] The sketches reveal that Birtwistle conceived both horn lines while working on the vocal parts. Sketch 8/10, 35 contains instructions to 'start slow horns', and the first three notes (G–B♭–C) are written (although the B♭ is misspelt as D♭). On 8/10, 38, the horn part, written directly above the voice, filters the voice's notes.

soliloquy, undressing him to uncover wounds symbolic of his spiritual injuries. Although this idea was abandoned, something of its significance is retained in the retrograde musical gesture, implying a distorted mirror image.[114]

The invisibility of Morgan and Lady de Hautdesert is seen by Harsent as symbolic of 'aspects of the world that the court won't admit to (sin, dishonour)'. Harsent describes the inability of the other, predominantly male characters to see them – resulting from Morgan's magic – as 'more a denial – wilful blindness'.[115] If characters on stage are unable to see certain things, could it not also be that they are unable to *hear* the kind of enigmatic 'voices' described above, which may constitute further representations of the 'blindness' of the collective psyche in the court? Notably, when Gawain begins to develop self-awareness, fear reaches him 'like a voice beating my brow'.[116] In the orchestra this is followed by a ten-note melody emerging from a unison E played in the upper strings and woodwind (Example 5.12f). This line bears an uncanny resemblance to the eleven-note clarinet melody at the end of the Fool's riddle later associated with the idea of fear (Fig. 138[−7]; Example 5.12e). Here, then, both Harsent's metaphor for Gawain's fear and Birtwistle's interest in the 'vocality' of his instruments find appropriate expression in the music's intricate network of rhetorical melodic lines – lines that are predominantly associated with dramatic ideas rather than actions.

'There is nothing here to own, except the mechanics of immersion'

'The example of my own work that I held in mind when I was starting *Gawain*', Harsent explains, 'was a short sequence called 'The Windhound', which only appears in my *Selected Poems*. It dealt, to some extent, with the loss of instinct, as does *Gawain*.'[117] The emergence of Gawain's sense of identity – his realisation that he is not the hero of the opera – is a dialectical expression of his understanding that by following his instinct (the desire to preserve his life) he has broken the codes of Arthur's court, which demand the suppression of such primal responses.[118] This moment

---

[114] This reflects text used in the first draft of the libretto at Gawain's moment of self-discovery: 'Not greed and love? It was! As a mirror-image is loved and lusted for'; *Gaw*/Lib 9, 46.
[115] *Gaw*/Lib 4, 1.
[116] Harsent, *Gawain*, 68.
[117] Harsent, in 'Poetry is a way of life'. The title of the present section is a quotation from 'The Windhound'; Harsent, *Selected Poems* (Oxford University Press, 1989), 95.
[118] In the section of Act II that was cut in 1994 but restored in 1999, Gawain declares: 'I wanted fame / I loved myself too much / I'm guilty of cowardice too.'

of personal discovery also marks a universal statement about integrity and honesty. In this sense Harsent's libretto is a variant of a well-established cultural question, which Rose Rosengard Subotnik locates in various post-Enlightenment legacies, including late Beethoven, Romanticism, and the critical theory of Adorno, namely: 'Can an individual who stands in every sense for abstract universal values, and avoids the concreteness of an explicitly cultural definition, be thought of as acting in self-interest?'[119] Similarly, the prevalence of extended melodic lines in *Gawain* – a musical metaphor for subjective expression – is continually undermined by the dispersal of those linear elements throughout the orchestra. This results in a dissolution of the subject that follows instantly from its appearance. Ultimately, although it gestures towards more clearly defined narrative and musical subjects than Birtwistle's earlier music theatre works, *Gawain* offers a return of the subject while simultaneously withdrawing it – rather like the cut-out figures that Jackson Pollock, towards the end of his life, inserted into his paintings. While the opera and its characters are not quite simulacra, the poetic and musical preoccupations of the work continually bring the concepts of identity and subjectivity into question, expressed musically through the use of line and shadow. Although Birtwistle's music has always been concerned with line, *Gawain* emerges as a key work in terms of its continual blurring of distinctions between source and shadow.[120]

In summary, two types of musical agency have been identified in *Gawain*; these are summarised in Figure 5.4. Following extensive collaborative changes to the libretto, principally generated by the composer, a sequence of dramatic situations was finalised. One musical response to these situations was the creation of schematic constellations that, at least initially, directly relate to actions on stage, although their subsequent rearrangement and separation from their original dramatic function promulgates a purely instrumental theatre. A second response was located in a series of syntactically related motifs that may be seen as analogous to the 'voices' referred to by Birtwistle in his comments about a secret drama. Positioned outside the opera's schemes of repetition, the free association of these motifs suggests that they reflect concepts and ideas rather than actions or agents. Inevitably,

[119] Rose Rosengard Subotnik, 'Whose *Magic Flute*? Intimations of reality at the gates of the Enlightenment', in her *Deconstructive Variations: Music and Reason in Western Society* (Minneapolis: University of Minnesota Press, 1996), 29–30.

[120] The association of dispersed lines and Gawain's loss of identity is perhaps another reflection of Birtwistle's interest in Wagner, in particular a sense that 'vulnerability, introspection and melancholy are innate attributes of most if not all of Wagner's major characters, attributes deeply etched into the musical substance'. Arnold Whittall, 'A public–private partnership: Wagner's voices in *Die Meistersinger*', *Wagner Journal*, 2/3 (2008), 56.

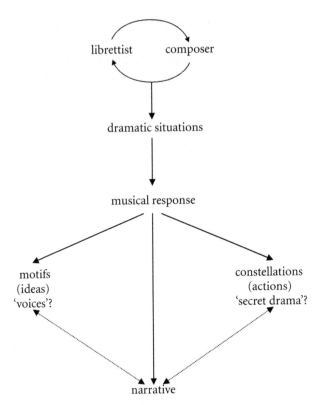

Figure 5.4 Summary of the genesis of narrative processes in *Gawain*

these two parallel schemes have a reflexive relationship with the opera's central narrative themes and structure.

Despite Gawain's psychological concerns, Birtwistle informs listeners about his character's emotions, as well as his own empathy for their emotional states, in very different ways from, for example, Berg or Britten. As Colin Matthews has noted, central to the dramatic schemes of these earlier composers was a place for their own narrative voice: 'the Act II passacaglia [in *Peter Grimes*] is where Britten pours out his sympathy for his characters, and, as in the great D minor interlude of *Wozzeck*, the composer occupies centre stage. Here there is no need of interpretation, for the message of anguish and compassion is unequivocal.'[121] In *Gawain*, by comparison, Birtwistle offers a more equivocal portrait of a male character trapped by social conventions, a figure manipulated and misunderstood by those around him. It is true that Birtwistle provides Gawain with a final expressive aria with richly dark tones (prominent are cellos, tubas, bassoons

---

[121] Colin Matthews, liner notes to Benjamin Britten, *Peter Grimes*, conducted by Bernard Haitink, EMI CD CB 7548322 (1993).

and three clarinets at the lowest end of their register), and that this text was not in Harsent's original libretto. Yet Gawain's return to D–F on the words 'I'm not that [hero]' brings the pitch agent plot back to its starting point, as if to confirm that attitudes in Arthur's court are unaltered (see Example 5.11). Nevertheless, when aspects of the music's secret drama are taken into account, the composer's narrative position, which elucidates our sense of Gawain's psychological plight, is more clearly revealed.

6 'A face like music': shaping images into sound in *The Second Mrs Kong*

Birtwistle's interest in visual images is well documented, from his fascination with the visual arts and cinema to his frequent recourse to visual metaphor to describe his compositional processes, as discussed in Chapter 1. It therefore seems appropriate that his opera *The Second Mrs Kong* (1994) is, ostensibly at least, about the world of ocular perception. Yet this topic is as diverse as the word *image* itself: the opera includes images presented on a surface or screen, those evoked in the libretto by the American writer Russell Hoban, and others held in the memories of the characters. The concept of *image* also extends to Birtwistle's perennial concern with sketching plans or schemes that are as much to do with how they appear on the page as how they are transformed into sound. With these issues in mind, this chapter examines the significance of images in *Mrs Kong* and asks what relevance they had for the librettist and composer.

In a short essay in the published libretto, Hoban describes one of the defining scenes in the 1933 RKO film *King Kong*, a scene that is projected on stage at an important moment in the opera:

> When, bleeding from his many wounds, he [Kong] holds in his hand the woman he can never possess, then puts her gently down on the ledge as he once more faces the aeroplanes, what looks out of his eyes is what lives in all of us – the wild and wordless, lost and lonely child of all the world. That is the idea of Kong in THE SECOND MRS KONG. Our Kong is not an ape but an idea.[1]

Any attempt to read meaning from an image will reflect not only the image's point of view, what Heidegger terms its 'look' (*Anblick*), but also the perceiver's sense of self.[2] That Hoban saw something of himself in this scene from the film is revealed by an unpublished letter that he sent to the director of Glyndebourne Opera, where *Mrs Kong* was premiered in 1994. In

---

[1] Russell Hoban, 'Kong and the Vermeer girl', in *The Second Mrs Kong: An Original Opera Text* (London: Universal Edition, 1994), n.p. [i–ii].

[2] Martin Heidegger, *Kant and the Problem of Metaphysics*, trans. Richard Taft (Bloomington: Indiana University Press, 1997), 66. As Jean-Luc Nancy observes: 'There is no image without my too being in its image'; *The Ground of the Image*, trans. Jeff Fort (New York: Fordham University Press, 2005), 7. This was literally so during the original Glyndebourne production of *Mrs Kong* when Birtwistle appeared in a sequence of 'television clips' in Act I scene 3.

his letter, Hoban states that 'Kong is Jewish' and, moreover, that there 'is something of the lost and lonely, wild (but not wordless) child of all the world in my people'.[3]

The reciprocal process between self and image illustrated by Hoban's interpretation will be explored thoroughly in this chapter as it has particular ramifications for an understanding of the opera's themes and the relationship between text and music. A guiding critical framework in this regard is provided by Jacques Lacan's psychoanalytical theory. The role of reflected images and image identification in identity formation are key concerns for Lacan whose ideas have been applied to film by theorists such as Christian Metz and Slavoj Žižek. Lacan's theories invoke voice as well as image, for which reason they have proved popular in opera studies, in particular his notions of desire (following Freud), vocal lack and excess.[4] In addition to an underlying Lacanian perspective, what follows has also been informed by critical thought on image, particularly that of Walter Benjamin, Jean-Luc Nancy and Jean Baudrillard.

As will be seen, Hoban had a deep interest in cinematic and pictorial images and ways in which viewers identify with them. My contention in this chapter is that the abstract processes in Birtwistle's music, as revealed by the sketches, are in some ways similar to the ideas in Hoban's text. Yet those abstract concerns must be considered in relation to the composer's growing commitment in the 1990s to opera's 'real world' representational demands, which leads to similar tensions between music and libretto as those seen in *Gawain*. However, whereas a focus on line was paramount in *Gawain*, Birtwistle develops a different strategy in *Mrs Kong* based on the abstract manipulation of intervallic sets, or musical shapes. The relevance of these procedures becomes apparent in music composed to accompany the film scene described above, which will be analysed later in some detail. Before this, the chapter sets out Hoban's and Birtwistle's interests in images, respectively, followed by a consideration of image identification through different media by the opera's central characters. It then considers ways in which text and music interact.

[3] Hoban in a letter to Anthony Whitworth-Jones dated 5 November, 1994; Glyndebourne Opera Archive.

[4] Relevant opera studies that draw on Lacan include: Lawrence Kramer, *Opera and Modern Culture: Wagner and Strauss* (Berkeley and Los Angeles: University of California Press, 2004); Slavoj Žižek and Mladen Dolar, *Opera's Second Death*; and Paul Harper-Scott, 'Being-With Grimes: the problem of Others in Britten's first opera', in Rachel Cowgill, David Cooper and Clive Brown, eds., *Art and Ideology in European Opera* (Woodbridge: Boydell & Brewer, 2010), 362–81.

Synopsis

In several novels that predate his libretto for *Mrs Kong*, Hoban showed a vivid interest in iconic images and in the ways such images inspire identification from viewers. Such concerns were evidently uppermost in his mind when, in 1993, he began work on the text of the opera. This interest is clearly illustrated by the work's focus on 'Pearl', the subject of Vermeer's painting *Girl with a Pearl Earring*, and Kong, the protagonist of the RKO *King Kong*. The appeal of such iconic subjects resided not only in their representation of the 'beauty and the beast' dichotomy central to the film, but also in their potential to illustrate how visual images function, and the ways consumers of culture respond to them.[5] Pearl is now a postcard image, reproduced innumerable times and available in gift shops around the world and on the internet. Similarly, Kong's image continues to be replicated, most recently in Peter Jackson's 2006 remake of the original film. But Kong differs from Pearl by virtue both of his filmic, and therefore narrative, presence and in the almost mythical status he has acquired since 1933. The two images are therefore likely to elicit different responses from viewers. While Pearl may prompt personal thoughts and intimate feelings not specifically connected to a narrative, Kong will evoke an epic story of unrequited love, loneliness and death.[6]

The Second Mrs Kong opens in the World of Shadows where an eclectic array of imaginary people (fictional and mythical figures from different media and times) is assembled: they are all dead. Ferrying the dead to this world is Anubus, the jackal-headed god from Egyptian mythology, who indulges each of the occupants of his world by allowing them to relive certain moments from their past (three unrelated groups, including Orpheus and Eurydice, revive their relationships in a sequence that is repeated four times). The central scene in Act I re-enacts the moment when Vermeer painted Pearl: in this scene Pearl first becomes aware of Kong's existence when she hears his voice emerging from the Mirror that Vermeer asks her to use. We are then introduced to Kong, who appears as a rather forlorn and anxious character, searching for the meaning of his existence and denying his own death. He has heard Pearl through the Mirror and his desire is aroused. Meanwhile, now living in 'a stockbroker's high-tech penthouse', Pearl surfs television and video selections.[7] Encountering an excerpt from the 1933 *King Kong*

---

[5] 'It was beauty killed the beast' are the last words uttered in the original *King Kong*; this formulation, also used in the original advertising for the film, returns in various forms throughout the opera.

[6] Since the appearance of Tracy Chevalier's novel *Girl with a Pearl Earring* (London: HarperCollins, 2003) and the eponymous film directed by Peter Webber (2004), it is possible that Pearl's image may also evoke a narrative for certain viewers.

[7] The score stipulates where the television and film sequences occur; the latter are specified (the original *King Kong* and *Brief Encounter*), but the former are not.

film, she is inspired to reach Kong via the internet and their relationship unfolds. Assisted by Orpheus, Kong decides to return to the World of the Living to find Pearl.

Act II begins with Kong and Orpheus leaving the World of Shadows. During their journey they are distracted by four female temptations, one of whom tears off Orpheus's head. When Kong and the Head of Orpheus arrive at the entrance to the World of the Living, Kong is tested once more, this time by the Sphinx, Madam Lena, in one of the opera's more comic scenes. Surviving these trials, Kong and Orpheus arrive in 'a bad part of town' via a manhole cover. While telephoning Pearl to ask for her address, Kong and the Head of Orpheus are set upon by Kong's nemesis, Death of Kong (played by Anubis). Kong wins the fight and rushes to meet Pearl, who awaits his arrival nervously. Despite their declarations of love, however, the couple are unable to touch, the Mirror informing them that theirs is a love 'that cannot be fulfilled'.[8] The opera dissolves into a stream of voices and echoes, joined by Orpheus and Eurydice, as well as other characters for whom love has proved illusory.

Hoban's images

The libretto for *Mrs Kong* is shaped by Hoban's personal, intense and ongoing response to both the original *King Kong* film and the Orpheus myth, evident in his novels *Turtle Diary* (1975) and *The Medusa Frequency* (1987), as well as his collection of essays and fiction *The Moment under the Moment* (1993). As Hoban comments in *Turtle Diary*, the original *King Kong* film teems with reflected images of heads, faces and physiognomic responses to dramatic events, most arrestingly the representation of Fay Wray's scream, first rehearsed on a boat sailing to Skull Island and then seen 'for real' when she is taken away by Kong. In the opera Orpheus's head is severed from his body and carried by Kong from the World of Shadows into the World of the Living, while Kong and the audience view selected moments from the film: the first of these screenings focuses on Kong's face as it confronts an approaching train, a sight that terrifies the train's driver. Hoban was also often concerned with the difficulty of fixing a visual image in the mind. In *The Medusa Frequency*, for example, Hoban construes the Orpheus myth in terms of the human mind's inability to preserve an event or mental image (such as the loss of Eurydice); he terms the resulting gap 'the indeterminacy of being', a discontinuity in which an idea or person reappears while progressively becoming more vague. In this novel, for example, the central character, a frustrated author, associates spherical

---

[8] Hoban, *The Second Mrs Kong*, 34.

objects with recurring but unstable impressions of Orpheus's talking head.[9] Vermeer's girl also enters the author's mind, along with episodes from Greek mythology.

Similarly, in *Mrs Kong* images originate in voice and imagination. Faces begin as imagined rather than seen. Despite their larger-than-life visual manifestations, Kong and Pearl are initially introduced to one another through word alone. Unable to see one another, they communicate at first through the mind of Vermeer, who has temporarily brought Pearl into the World of Shadows where Kong resides. This distance is maintained in the internet dating scene (Act I scene 3), during which Kong mouths the familiar operatic trope of the voice as love object, whereby the characters fall in love with one another's voices: 'In these words I hear the voice of Beauty and I am afraid.'[10] Kong's singing voice, which breathes life back into the Kong that we saw die at the end of the film, also allows the development of love requited (in the original film Kong's love remained unrequited).

Hoban's tendency to circle back to recurring themes such as the head of Orpheus echoes Birtwistle's habit of presenting the same musical objects from different perspectives. For Birtwistle this repetition often takes the form of verse–refrain schemes: string quartet movements and songs that function as ritornello to each other; or a chorus that is also a refrain.[11] Like Hoban's faces, recognisable objects appear in Birtwistle's music unexpectedly, 'like digging things out of the ground'.[12] He has described the fugue at the end of *Pulse Shadows*, for example, as 'a bit like a found object...I don't know whether it's a fugue or not.'[13] In other words, Hoban's concern with ideas and images in flux resonates with Birtwistle's compositional techniques. Highlighting this very point, Adlington has suggested that 'Hoban's obsession with remembering and forgetting, and the "indeterminacy of being" that is endured by all ideas due to the vagaries of memory, surely finds a parallel in Birtwistle's sectional musical form'. According to Adlington, it is the music's 'structural

---

[9] In Hoban's novel the head of Orpheus comments: 'From the very first moment that beauty appears to us it is passing, passing, not to be held'; *The Medusa Frequency* (London: Bloomsbury, 2002), 68. Hoban's association of image with idea is even parodied in the novel when its subject, a novelist, encounters an unusual man in an art gallery who comments: 'I speak only in pictures. With me the image is everything, carrying within it as it does the proto-image, the after-image, and the anti-image. This is why here I have come [*sic*] to speak to the Vermeer girl and to hear what she will say to me' (86).

[10] Hoban, *The Second Mrs Kong*, 18.

[11] For example, the string quartets and songs in *Pulse Shadows*, according to Birtwistle, 'are both functioning as the ritornello to the other'; quoted in Lorraine, 'Territorial Rites 1', 8.

[12] Birtwistle on his settings of Celan's poetry, in 'A conversation with Harrison Birtwistle', interview with Robert Adlington, in Peter O'Hagan, ed., *Aspects of British Music of the 1990s* (Aldershot: Ashgate, 2003), 115.

[13] Ibid., 115–16. Arnold Whittall describes it as 'an imaginary fugue' in his 'The mechanisms of lament', 97.

ephemerality – the focus on moment-to-moment fantasy – that makes it so much in tune with post-modern scepticism about organic logic and forms, and correspondingly undemanding (in terms of specific obligations or expectations) on listeners'. He concludes that 'Birtwistle's music in *Mrs Kong* thus gives a very particular resonance to Vermeer's observation that Pearl's face is "like music, partly now and partly remembered"'.[14]

Birtwistle's images

There are several reasons why a libretto about the emotive power of images would have appealed to Birtwistle. Visual metaphors have long been his favoured medium for describing his music: at various moments Birtwistle has invoked landscapes and processions in relation to orchestral pieces, and he has made extensive use of instrumental choreography and other spatial devices in his ensemble works.[15] The composer's penchant for imagery is further reflected in his interest in the visual arts: witness his illustrated talk on Paul Klee's influence on his music, and interviews detailing his views on artists such as Piero della Francesca, Brueghel, Vermeer, Cézanne, Picasso, Klein, Bacon, Rothko, Barnett Newman and Pollock.[16] These artists attract Birtwistle both for their use of subject matter 'to express paint and painting, rather than the other way around', and for what he describes as their 'formality'.[17] Although visual analogies may offer valuable insights into Birtwistle's musical processes, and possibly into his music's meanings, the two media remain separated by a wide gap. Most conscious of this rift is Birtwistle himself: fully aware of the differences between the creative

---

[14] Robert Adlington, 'Harrison Birtwistle's recent music', *Tempo* 196 (1996), 5.

[15] Choreography and spatial distribution of performers are used in *Verses for Ensembles*, *Secret Theatre*, *Ritual Fragment* (1990), *Panic* (1995) and *Theseus Game* (2003). The presentation of musical motifs in *The Triumph of Time* is compared by Birtwistle to Brueghel's etching of a procession of disconnected objects (see Hall, *HB*, 175–6). Ideas stemming from studies by Erwin Panofsky and Günther Grass of Albrecht Dürer's engraving *Melencolia I* inform the composer's programme note to his eponymously titled orchestral work. In the programme note to *Silbury Air* (1976), Silbury Hill in Avebury, Wiltshire, is offered as a metaphor for musical processes (see Hall, *HB*, 177). Geological strata are evoked in comparison to the musical layers in *Earth Dances*. *Exody '23: 59: 59'* (1997) is said to consist of 'gateways' and 'windows', 'which are framed and self-contained glimpses, like a curtain opening for a moment and then closing again'; quoted in Lorraine, 'Territorial rites 2', 16. More recently, *String Quartet: The Tree of Strings* (2007) derives inspiration from a poetic image in the eponymous poem by Sorley Maclean.

[16] Birtwistle originally delivered his illustrated Klee lecture 'Ears & eyes', together with members of the London Sinfonietta, at the Hayward Gallery, London, on 7 and 8 March 2002. The talk, which was advertised as addressing the question 'Can there be a direct connection between painting and music?', was later repeated at the Lucerne Festival in 2003 under the new title 'Eyes to Hear, Ears to See'. Birtwistle's interest in Klee (discussed in Hall, *HB*) is most directly expressed in *Carmen Arcadiae Mechanicae Perpetuum* (1977), which is a response to Klee's *Twittering Machine*. For his thoughts on Klee and other painters, see Lorraine, 'Territorial rites 1' and 'Territorial rites 2'.

[17] Lorraine, 'Territorial rites 1', 8.

processes in the two media, he has declared his envy of the immediate connection painters have with their final image.[18]

This awareness may stem from the fact that in the late 1960s Birtwistle began experimenting with treating a musical line or contour in ways somehow comparable to Klee's concepts of 'taking a line for a walk' and guiding a viewer through the details of a picture (Birtwistle's equivalent concept is '*listening* to a painting').[19] Around the same time Birtwistle sought to develop a musical analogy for organic processes visible in the natural world, influenced by the graphic models of plant and animal mutations in D'Arcy Thompson's *On Growth and Form*, one of the composer's favourite books.[20] As mentioned in Chapter 3, Birtwistle attempted to systematise his use of related contours in two sketchbooks, one of which, dated 2 April 1970, is titled 'Modual Book. The Triumph of Time'. Contour tables in this sketchbook were used to generate melodic lines for at least one piece that he began sketching that year.[21]

An early attempt at directing musical line through the agency of contour is *Nomos*, composed in 1967–8. In this work an expanding seven-note shape is played by an amplified wind quartet, repeated fourteen times, leading to the climax of the piece when the most expansive form of the shape is reached (Example 6.1).[22] However, as Adlington has observed, this compositional idea results in a problematic musical image, since the twofold possibility of conceptualising such a melody – either as an abstract phenomenon that may, potentially, be visualised, or as a dramatic agent – creates a perceptual tension as each vies for supremacy, one option most plausible at one moment, the other at the next, 'depending on the form that the melody takes'.[23]

In the light of these compositional dilemmas and of an examination of Birtwistle's sketches for the opera, *Mrs Kong* emerges both as a retrospective of the composer's earlier preoccupations and as a dramatisation of his desire to translate visual images into musical ideas. Closely related to this interest is the mechanism of identification, for it is through identifying with images

---

[18] 'I'm more envious of that than anything.' He has also commented: 'There's no equivalent of throwing paint in music, is there?' Ibid., 7 and 4.

[19] Ibid., 4.

[20] D'Arcy Wentworth Thompson, *On Growth and Form*, abridged and ed. John Tyler Bonner (Cambridge University Press, 1997). Hall discusses the relevance of D'Arcy Thompson's book to Birtwistle's instrumental piece *Medusa* (1969); Hall, *HB*, 50–1.

[21] Three-, four- and five-note contours were extracted from the 'Modual Book' for use in *Nenia: The Death of Orpheus*. These contours indicate degrees of rise and fall rather than specific interval sizes or pitches. Ideas for *Prologue* and *An Imaginary Landscape* also appear in the two sketchbooks.

[22] For a more comprehensive account of this process and a discussion of the sketchbooks, see David Beard, 'An analysis and sketch study'. See also Beard, 'The endless parade'.

[23] Adlington, *MHB*, 158.

Example 6.1 Extracts from an expanding seven-note shape played by amplified flute, clarinet, horn and bassoon, in *Nomos* (1967–8) (full score, UE 14671), bb. 35–96 (phrasing added)

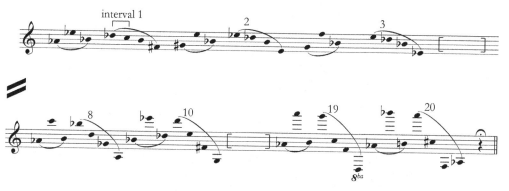

of themselves, and of one another, that Pearl and Kong hope to attain true selfhood. The question is how this desire for identification manifests itself in the opera, and whether Birtwistle develops an identification of his own with Hoban's text. To explore these questions in more detail it is necessary to turn to Lacan and responses to his theories.

Primary identification

Central to Lacan's concept of primary identification is the mirror stage, the moment when a child first catches sight of its reflection, which initiates an early phase of ego construction. As Bruce Fink explains, Lacan conceives the ego as 'an imaginary production, a crystallization or sedimentation of images of an individual's own body and of self-images reflected back to him or her by others'.[24] For Lacan, the importance of identification lay in the subject's recognition of itself in its mirror image.[25] Yet this is actually a misrecognition since the child views its reflection as an Ideal, something more perfect than itself. This relationship between the ego and its specular image forms the basis of Lacan's concept of the 'imaginary' (the order of images and appearances), in contrast to the 'symbolic' (the linguistic and communicative order, expressed by languages, laws and customs)

[24] Bruce Fink, *The Lacanian Subject: Between Language and Jouissance* (Princeton University Press, 1997), 84. See also Jacques Lacan, 'The mirror stage', in *Ecrits: A Selection*, trans. Alan Sheridan (New York: W. W. Norton & Co., 1977).
[25] The specular image may appear in any reflective surface, but Lacan also includes the Mother's face.

and the 'real' (a more elusive order that comprises that which resists symbolisation: the ineffable, the organic and material, traumatic dreams and hallucinations).[26]

A defining feature of the imaginary is a sense of detachment and alienation from the reflected image and a corresponding desire to be whole with the reflection. This manifests itself in a desire to be recognised (the desire of the Other's desire).[27] A subject is also likely to be attracted to what other people desire. (For example, Vermeer's attraction to Pearl leads to her painting, which in turn leads others to desire her, notably Kong.) Desire is set in motion by an object-cause of desire – symbolised in the opera by Pearl – which Lacan terms the 'object *a*'. This is an aspect of the object rather than the object itself, a quality that the subject identifies with. The subject fixates upon objects in which they perceive the 'object *a*' in a futile attempt to fill the void, to restore a sense of oneness. Such wholeness is illusory, however, since the actual object of desire (unity with the specular image) is unattainable, an idea that has particular relevance to the opera's concluding scene.

According to Hoban, Kong's desire for what cannot be is conveyed in his 'lost and lonely' look. This interpretation reflects Hoban's personal identification with Kong as an embodiment of the collective alienation felt by Jews during the 1930s, when the original *King Kong* film was made. The association occurred to Hoban when he saw a documentary on the film 'in which Josef Goebbels, his face lit by the dancing flames of burning books, looked towards a millennium of racial purity'.[28] He even attempted to include Goebbels in the opera.[29] Ultimately, for Hoban, Kong's look is the expression of a sense of human (not only Jewish) alienation, isolation, and vulnerability in the face of hostile forces.[30] This is the 'idea' behind Kong's image, and the lack that generates his desire. Yet Kong's lines are given particular resonance in light of Hoban's allusion to the Holocaust (see Example 6.2).

Kong's quest for Pearl, like the Lacanian subject's for the object *a*, will not reach fulfilment, however, because desire is continually reproduced: in

---

[26] For more detailed definitions see Dylan Evans, *An Introductory Dictionary of Lacanian Psychoanalysis* (London and New York: Routledge, 2007), and http://web.uvic.ca/~saross/lacan.html# (accessed 21 August 2011).

[27] In Lacanian theory the original big Other is the Mother. However, the Other applies primarily to the symbolic order and secondarily to a subject that embodies the symbolic order for another subject.

[28] Hoban, *The Second Mrs Kong*, n.p. [i].

[29] Hoban in a letter to Anthony Whitworth-Jones dated 5 November 1994; Glyndebourne Opera Archive. Hoban's letter reveals that in his early drafts he toyed with a relationship between Kong and Goebbels, but 'never really got that duo to work right'.

[30] These anxieties are actually characterised in the opera as four 'temptations': doubt, fear, despair, and terror (Act II scene 1).

Example 6.2 Kong, *The Second Mrs Kong* (full score, UE 16549), Act II scene 3, Fig. 72^{-4} to 72^{+3}

Hoban's formulation, it is 'the longing for what cannot be' that 'moves the world from / night to morning'.[31] Moreover, in his quest to discover the idea behind his image Kong becomes somewhat fixated upon surface appearances. As such, he fails to fully symbolise his identifications, which 'is the only way to dislodge the disabling fixations of the imaginary'.[32] As will be seen, however, a symbolic interpretation of Kong's imaginary realm is suggested by Birtwistle's music.

Secondary identification

Extending the idea of a mirror stage, Christian Metz has articulated a distinction between 'primary' and 'secondary cinematic identification'. Primary identification describes the experience of spectators who adopt the camera's viewpoint as their own. Secondary identification occurs when a viewer identifies with the subject position of a character.[33] This requires a level of fantasy in order to think 'behind' a character. As such, secondary identification involves an exchange between self (what the viewer brings to the film) and other. Yet, as Mary Ann Doane has observed, 'Cinematic identification can operate "properly" only on condition that a limit is acknowledged and a distance maintained. Rather than effecting a complete collapse of spectator onto character (or film), identification presupposes the security of the modality "as if".'[34]

Metz is actually more alert to this reality than Doane suggests, as his description of the 'play of identification' that occurs when viewing a film reveals: 'At every moment I am in the film by my look's caress. This presence

[31] Hoban, *The Second Mrs Kong*, 34.   [32] Evans, *An Introductory Dictionary*, 83.
[33] Christian Metz, 'The imaginary signifier', 58.
[34] Mary Ann Doane, 'Misrecognition and identity: the concept of identification in film theory,' *Cine-Tracts: A Journal of Film and Cultural Studies*, 3/3 (1980), 25.

often remains diffuse, geographically undifferentiated, evenly distributed over the whole surface of the screen; or more precisely hovering . . . ready to catch on preferentially to some motif in the film, according to the force of that motif and according to my own fantasies as a spectator.'[35] It is in Metz's notion of 'hovering' and Doane's concept of a 'distance maintained' that Birtwistle is to be found. As Hoban's narrative unfolds, Birtwistle's music hovers somewhere behind the characters and plot, ready to 'catch on' when it suits his imagination.

Throughout *Mrs Kong*, Hoban and Birtwistle show their principal characters identifying with various pictorial and cinematic images in order to dramatise the distinction between these images and the often abstract ideas associated with them. Identification is both channelled and challenged through various media, including a mirror, the internet, video, film, television and telephone.[36] Crucially, Kong's preoccupation with searching for the idea behind his image, and the attendant oscillation between self and other, mirrors the relationship between text and music in the opera, which has been described as 'intermittent' rather than 'coherent'.[37] Yet what for some critics seemed to be a lack of fit between music and stage action could instead be seen in terms of Metz's 'play of identification'. Where a traditional correspondence between music and drama might be considered as equivalent to Lacan's primary narcissism, Birtwistle forges a relationship between music and libretto that is more akin to secondary identification.

Interpreting Pearl

In the *King Kong* film the fictional film-maker Carl Denham's implicitly colonialist ambition is to teach Kong to fear. He achieves this goal by presenting Kong with an image of perfect beauty, the face of Ann Darrow, a sight that both sparks Kong's desire and leads to his terrifying downfall. In the opera Pearl replaces Darrow, a choice influenced by the fact that Hoban saw in her eyes 'the terror of Creation'.[38] Such beauty is terrifying, Hoban

---

[35] Metz, 'The imaginary signifier', 56.

[36] During the internet scenes in the original Glyndebourne production the text appeared on a large screen; the typing rhythm is notated in the score.

[37] Adlington, *MHB*, 36. Adlington's criticisms are directed specifically at the use of 'dramatic crescendo' or 'apprehensive pause' to mark 'watershed moments in the plot', while 'between these moments the music goes its separate way, repeatedly ignoring the slapstick paciness of the action on stage in favour of an intense, brooding lyricism'. The orchestra is certainly reluctant to engage with Hoban's humour, especially in Act II scene 1. However, Adlington concludes that 'the consistent complication of representation in Birtwistle's theatres may have the effect not of a retreat from reality but of enforcing a renewed engagement with it' (37).

[38] Hoban, 'Kong and the Vermeer girl', n.p. [v].

believed, because it cannot be captured (for example, in painting) or fully comprehended.[39]

Lacan's notion of the mirror stage is particularly useful in understanding the character of Pearl, especially in the context of Kaja Silverman's re-reading of Julia Kristeva's thoughts on the mother–child relationship. Silverman observes that 'not only is her [the mother's] face the visual mirror in which the child first sees itself, but her voice is the acoustic mirror in which it first hears itself'.[40] In Act I scene 2, when Pearl models in Vermeer's studio, Vermeer instructs Pearl to look into a mirror in order to retain her pose. The Mirror informs Pearl that she will meet Kong in the future. Her message is conveyed with two voices, an onstage soprano and an offstage, pre-recorded tape of the same singer (its Echo). This acoustical device (most likely Birtwistle's idea) realises musically and theatrically the fragmentation of Pearl's identity, dispersed among the seventeenth century, the present moment, and the future – what Hoban refers to as the 'discontinuity of image'.[41]

The moment when Pearl views her own image in the Mirror bears some of the features of both Lacan's and Metz's primary identification. But, crucially, it is through the Mirror that Pearl and Kong first hear each other's voices; once Kong has 'heard Pearl's voice he can think of no one else'.[42] This invokes Kristeva's suggestion that the 'ideal identification with the symbolic upheld by the Other . . . activates speech more than image. Doesn't the signifying voice, in the final analysis, shape the visible, hence fantasy?'[43] Later, in Act I scene 2, the iconic image of Pearl from Vermeer's painting is made visible to the audience. In the original production, directed by Tom Cairns, replicating images of Pearl's face were projected on a large screen at the rear of the stage as a 'Chorus of Viewers' sang 'Pearl, Pearl, the Vermeer girl, hundreds of thousands of beautiful Pearls', accompanied by densely layered textures in the orchestra. This moment not only exposed the commodification and reification of Vermeer's painting, it also resonated with Jean Baudrillard's description of television images occupying 'gigantic spaces of circulation,

---

[39] Of Vermeer's *Girl with a Pearl Earring*, Hoban remarked: 'How easy it is to look at this famous picture and how difficult to see it! If we could grasp that image, any image, in its entirety we might perhaps grasp everything but it can't be done – the mind won't reach all the way to the full terror'; ibid. In his elision of beauty and the destructive aspect of the sublime, and his sense that beauty, like memory, is always passing, Hoban recalls Rilke's *Duino Elegies*.

[40] Kaja Silverman, *The Acoustic Mirror: The Female Voice in Psychoanalysis and Cinema* (Bloomington and Indianapolis: Indiana University Press, 1988), 150.

[41] Hoban, *The Second Mrs Kong*, n.p. [v].

[42] From an unpublished synopsis by Hoban dated 18 January, 1994; Glyndebourne Opera Archive.

[43] Julia Kristeva, 'Freud and love: treatment and its discontents', *The Kristeva Reader*, ed. Toril Moi (New York: Columbia University Press, 1986), 253, cited in Silverman, *The Acoustic Mirror*, 119.

ventilation and ephemeral connections' – a point underlined by Birtwistle's uncharacteristic instruction to repeat the section.[44] The visual information overload at this moment in the opera resembled Baudrillard's obscene and negative 'ecstasy of communication'; but, more important, it illustrated his predicted loss of the image, in which 'the total instantaneity of things' precludes reflection and metaphor.[45]

Interpreting Kong

If the preclusion of reflection and metaphor is symbolised in the opera at this moment by Pearl, elsewhere it is the character of Kong who is linked with the inert media image and the neutralisation of self. Such, at least, is the implication of Kong's nemesis, 'D.O.K.' (Death of Kong), when he sings: 'The idea of Kong is that he's dead.'[46] However, the operatic Kong, by virtue of his singing voice and operatic status, resists these negative forces, in particular the sense that his cinematic form, like Baudrillard's contemporary subject, 'can no longer produce himself as a mirror . . . is . . . only a pure screen, a switching center for all the networks of influence'.[47] Unlike his cinematic ape counterpart, the operatic Kong is a modern, Western subject, troubled with existential questions.[48] At times, however, an audible, primitive Other emerges in the form of Kong's notated, pre-linguistic cries: 'Ah-nah-ee-ay-ou-ay-ou-ay-ou-ay-ou'. These are initially heard when Kong first appears, storming round the stage, banging on doors. His operatic quest to realise his desires for love and selfhood mirrors the one in the film and occasionally demands the suspension of his rationalising tendencies ('I will not listen' he sings at the start of Act II when he meets the Four Temptations). Although the original film's colonialist perspective is not altogether lost, the modern operatic Kong does detect the lie in his former manifestation when, in Act I, he sings: 'Sometimes I dream . . . a jungle painted all on glass.'[49] Furthermore, Kong's opening dialogue with Inanna (a failed beauty queen) reveals a certain resignation to his destiny as nothing more than 'an idea'. In order to comprehend what that idea is, Kong must engage

---

44 Jean Baudrillard, 'The ecstasy of communication', trans. John Johnston, in Hal Foster, ed., *The Anti-Aesthetic: Essays on Postmodern Culture* (New York: New Press, 1998), 150.

45 Ibid., 150 and 149, respectively, where Baudrillard also remarks: 'What used to be lived out on earth as metaphor, as mental or metaphorical scene, is henceforth projected into reality, without any metaphor at all . . . [T]he instantaneity of communication has miniaturized our exchanges into a succession of instants' (147–8, 149).

46 Hoban, *The Second Mrs Kong*, 30.   47 Baudrillard, 'The ecstasy of communication', 153.

48 In the original production, Kong was sung by the tenor Philip Langridge in a white T-shirt and the lower half of a gorilla costume.

49 Hoban, *The Second Mrs Kong*, 14.

with his character in the film, hence those moments in the opera when he views himself on-screen.[50]

On the first such occasion (Act I scene 2) Kong fails to recognise anything of himself in the image on-screen. As he sits in the corner of the stage viewing a projection of the 1933 film that has just been delivered to him, he comments: 'I'm not the giant head, the giant hand, the little puppet moving on the screen – there never *was* a giant ape!'[51] This echoes Jean-Luc Nancy's belief that an image is detached, distant and withdrawn and therefore 'implies not so much reproduction as competition... The image disputes the presence of the thing.'[52] In Lacanian terms, Kong's failure to 'assume' or appropriate his image is symptomatic of narcissism, which introduces a degree of aggressivity between the ego and its counterpart – an idea that is symbolised by Kong's confrontation with Death of Kong. As Joan Copjec observes, narcissism 'seeks the self beyond the self-image, with which the subject constantly finds fault and in which it constantly fails to recognize itself... At war both with its world and with itself, the subject becomes guilty of the very deceit it suspects.'[53]

This particular version of image reception resonates with Martin Scorsese's film *Taxi Driver* (1976). Birtwistle has alluded to Bernard Hermann's soundtrack as a source for the melancholic, bluesy saxophone that recurs throughout *Mrs Kong* where it is associated with the yearning for what cannot be, but the film's narrative, and especially its central character, Travis Bickle, may also have influenced the opera's conception.[54] In one of *Taxi Driver*'s most iconic scenes, Bickle (Robert De Niro) stares into a mirror where he is faced by an imagined Other who demands: 'You talkin' to me?' This defining image again illustrates Metz's secondary identification in which a sense of disruption exists because a subject will inevitably flick back and forth between self and other. In *Taxi Driver* this effect is further enhanced by the New York setting, since New York is often constructed as 'the ultimate city of alienation and disconnection, the definitive nighttown [*sic*], a place that, however much a dark reflection of the real city, is even

---

[50] Similarly, concerning the function of the film interlude in Berg's *Lulu*, in which Lulu is shown in prison, Silvio José Dos Santos has observed that 'Lulu *has to see* her reflected image to regain her identity'; 'Ascription of identity: the *Bild* motif and the character of Lulu', *Journal of Musicology*, 21 (2004), 295.

[51] Hoban, *The Second Mrs Kong*, 14.   [52] Nancy, *The Ground of the Image*, 2 and 21.

[53] Joan Copjec, *Read My Desire: Lacan against the Historicists* (Cambridge, MA and London: MIT Press, 1995), 36–7.

[54] Birtwistle discussed his interest in Hermann's soundtrack for *Taxi Driver* during a BBC Study Day on *The Second Mrs Kong* held in the Voice Box, Royal Festival Hall, London, November 2004. A bluesy style is also required of the saxophone that accompanies Madame Lena's attempted seduction of Kong in Act II scene 2, while in scene 3 the same instruction applies to Inanna's vocal line.

more the external projection of one man's interior struggles'.[55] Something similar is echoed in Act II scene 3 of the opera, when Kong arrives in a hybrid city, part London, part New York. Here he is forced by Death of Kong to view his death scene once again, then fight his aggressive counterpart 'to the death', another Lacanian concept. However, Kong's cinematic image is not something he desires to be: he rejects the image but, in a Platonic sense, seeks the idea behind it.[56]

Kong's identification with Pearl

Hoban and Birtwistle depict Kong and Pearl not only through identifications with their own media images; the two principals also aspire to selfhood by identifying with one another. One of the ways Kong attempts to forge a self is through his relationship with Pearl's portrait. When Kong first sees her face, it is in the form of a photographic image of Vermeer's painting sent to him over the internet (at Fig. 136 in the score); in the first production this appeared to the audience on a giant computer screen.[57] Hoban's stage directions suggest that the music 'registers the impact of the photo on Kong', but the music creates a more general sense of suspense and perhaps arousal, signalled by densely saturated textures in the upper register.[58] Appropriately, although somewhat disturbingly, this musical gesture can be interpreted as pointing to both Kong's and the audience's engagement in an act of fetishistic scopophilia. When the picture fades, the music suggests Kong's feelings: a languid alto saxophone solo with baroque-like sighing figures unfolds across sustained accordion chords while Kong asks: 'What am I, that you should think of me? What can I be to you?'[59]

While the music presents Kong's subject position and encourages our identification with him using conventional operatic and cinematic techniques, it also suggests that Kong's doubts about his identity are associated with his efforts to identify with Pearl. In his working copy of the libretto, Birtwistle annotated Kong's question with the words 'and starts', suggesting that he intended to initiate a musical process of some kind at this moment.[60] What 'starts' in the music is a fast-moving demi-semiquaver

[55] James Sanders, *Celluloid Skyline* (London and New York: Bloomsbury, 2001), 395.

[56] The parallels with the character of Kong further extend to Travis's description of himself as 'God's lonely man' (compare Kong's 'lost and lonely child of all the world'); cited in David I. Grossvogel, *Scenes in the City: Film Visions of Manhattan before 9/11* (New York: Peter Lang, 2003), 81.

[57] All score references are to Harrison Birtwistle, *The Second Mrs Kong*, full score (London: Universal Edition, 1994), UE 16549.

[58] Hoban, *The Second Mrs Kong*, 18.   [59] Ibid.

[60] PSS microfilm 0537-0338, dated 14 May 1993. There are 475 sides of sketches and drafts for *Mrs Kong* in the Paul Sacher Stiftung (some sections of Act I are missing), in addition to 268

pulse, first established in the violas at Figs. 143–4, where the declarations of love begin. Although it is unclear precisely what this new musical texture is intended to signify, it functions as musical underscore to the image of Pearl that must be lingering in Kong's mind. As a kind of signifier without a signified, the underscore may be connected to Kong's memory of Pearl's portrait, seemingly implying that the meaning of her image for Kong is, in Barthes's terms, obtuse rather than obvious.[61]

While aspects of Kong's struggle I have outlined so far reflect relatively conventional modes of musical representation, including bluesy saxophone and musical underscore, elsewhere the opera develops more complex representational models. Such frameworks emerge when Birtwistle seems to engage directly with Hoban's ideas. In order to examine in some detail these models and their links with the librettist's aesthetics, I will focus on three specific moments in the opera. The first is set in what Hoban terms a 'place of memory', and it amounts to what can be called a 'synchronic image'. Here Birtwistle responds to Hoban's idea, discussed earlier, that Pearl's image is 'partly now and partly remembered'.

The synchronic image: 'the place of memory'

VERMEER: In her face I see time's ancient shadow reaching forward, reaching back.[62]

It is not that what is past casts its light on what is present, or what is present its light on what is past; rather, image is that wherein what has been [*das Gewesene*] comes together in a flash with the now [*das Jetzt*] to form a constellation. In other words: image is dialectics at a standstill. For while the relation of the present to the past is purely temporal, the relation of what-has-been to the now is dialectical: not temporal in nature but figural [*bildlich*].[63]

The musical, choreographic, cinematographic, or kinetic image is no less immobile . . . : it is the distension of a present of intensity, in which succession is also a simultaneity.[64]

---

sides of fair copy, and 32 sides of libretto typescript, some of which have been annotated by Birtwistle.

[61] The concepts of 'obvious' and 'obtuse' images ('obtuse' being defined by the presence of a supplement that has no clear meaning), are derived from Roland Barthes, 'The third meaning', in his *The Responsibility of Forms: Critical Essays on Music, Art and Representation*, trans. Richard Howard (Berkeley and Los Angeles: University of California Press, 1985), 41–62.

[62] Hoban, *The Second Mrs Kong*, 10.

[63] Walter Benjamin, *The Arcades Project*, trans. Howard Eiland and Kevin McLaughlin (Cambridge, MA: Belknap Press of Harvard University Press, 1999), 463.

[64] Nancy, *The Ground of the Image*, 10.

The scene in *Mrs Kong* that most obviously suggests an image that is 'partly now and partly remembered' is Act I scene 2, in which the 'place of memory' is constructed. This is a private, inner space, represented onstage by a transparent cube, where Vermeer relives the moment when he painted Pearl. Vermeer's interiority is constructed by these visual cues, and also by the music, which is a subtle handling of the concept of image production (here painting) as a process of identification.

One of the ways in which Birtwistle translates into sound Hoban's idea of an image floating between temporal moments is by engaging with conventional operatic means of expressing the inner self, specifically a lamenting gesture voiced by instruments with human-sounding timbres, a device favoured by Verdi. Referring to it as a form of 'weeping interior voice', Melina Esse has observed that in Verdi's operas 'these "voices" are typically not granted extended lyrical melodies; rather, they obsessively harp on a falling semitone, imitating the sound of a body racked with sobs'.[65] In *Mrs Kong* the sighing gesture is melancholic and gently resigned, and it appears as a rising motif, C–Db, first heard in Vermeer's line 'Pearl. Such a simple name' (Example 6.3). Following a unison *c'* in the violins, when Vermeer describes his new model as 'a pearl' (Fig. 67), the motif re-emerges as a series of drawn-out gestures, in suitable low- to middle-register instruments, passing from bassoon to tenor saxophone, clarinet and, finally, the cellos.[66] In the sketches the motif can be traced back to the moments when Pearl first appears (Fig. 60) – the first violins move from a *c'''–d'''* dyad to *db'''–eb'''* (these dyads are circled and 'Pearl Vermeer' written above them)[67] – and when Vermeer declares his name to Pearl (Fig. 63), his vocal part emphasising *db* and *d'*. Further suggestions of the motif's significance and possible meaning are given by its reappearance when the Mirror informs Pearl and Kong that they must remain apart forever (Act II, Fig. 98). At this moment, a *C* pedal in the accordion, double basses and contrabassoon underpins piccolo and first violin parts that continually return to *d'''* and *db'''*, while the Echo's sustained notes on the second syllable of 'ever' hover *in medias res*, implying the longed-for identification that the sighing idea represents (Example 6.4).[68]

---

65 Melina Esse, '"Chi piange, qual forza m'arretra?" Verdi's interior voices', *Cambridge Opera Journal*, 14/1–2 (2002), 60.

66 The motif also appears later in Vermeer's vocal part, from Fig. 77⁻⁶, when he addresses Pearl: 'Look into the mirror [*c'*] it will help [*db*] you hold the pose [*c'*]'.

67 PSS 0536-0576.

68 These pitch relations are explored further in the opera's companion instrumental piece, *The Cry of Anubis* (1994), where the pairing of pitches D and E is given an assertive role (see the timpani and tuba solos in bar 214; these pitches are also the last in the piece), while the darker, more melancholy quality of the chromatic C–Db motif is elaborated in *The Shadow of Night*

Example 6.3 Inverted sighing gesture (C–Db), Act I scene 1, Fig. 66 to 67[+7]

In her reading of Verdi's representation of interiority, Esse also examines the physical gestures that singers have used to communicate the inner states of female characters, concluding that 'the surface gestures of

(2001), where it is transposed to Bb–Bh–Bb, which invokes the sighing formula at the opening of Dowland's 'In darkness let me dwell'.

Example 6.4 Mirror: 'See in my silver-shadowed waters yourselves together and apart for ever', Act II scene 4, Fig. 98^{-3} to 98^{+3}

melodrama lie at the core of the Verdian interior'.[69] Hoban's libretto instead uses Vermeer's hesitant speech as a means of suggesting an appropriate

69 Esse, 'Verdi's interior voices', 76. Esse's reading focuses on the character of Amelia in *Un ballo in maschera*, and specifically on the staging of her Act II aria.

mode of performance (for example: 'I forgot what I was going to say. (*pause*) Pearl?'). Both Vermeer's identification with Pearl's image and his idea of her as 'partly now, partly remembered' are characterised by mental and physical hesitancy – such hesitancy has also traditionally been read in Vermeer's painting, especially in Pearl's smile. This ambiguous aspect of Pearl's image proves troubling both to the operatic Vermeer, who sings 'On her face, I see a question', and to the fictional author in Hoban's *The Medusa Frequency*, who continually probes the images of Pearl in his study for meaning, finding her face 'full of questioning and uncertainty'.[70]

Hoban's ideas clearly influenced Birtwistle in his setting of the scene, not least in his deployment of the sighing motif, which composes out the hesitation of Hoban's dialogue. The use of gongs (from Figs. 67–8) may also symbolise the instability of memory, via the acoustical impermanence of the timbre.[71] While both the sighing motif and the gongs reflect Vermeer's thoughts and physical condition, a series of descending woodwind scales (Fig. 72) depart from the scene depicted onstage, anticipating instead Kong's fall as it will appear to Pearl when she views it on-screen (Fig. 117) (Example 6.5), while the scene as a whole is punctuated by anguished alto and tenor saxophone gestures that anticipate the alto saxophone's evocation of Kong's yearnings on seeing Pearl's face (from Fig. 138).[72] In response to Hoban's idea, therefore, Birtwistle's music consciously mixes elements that symbolise past, present and future.

A closer look at these musical ideas as they first appear in the sketches, however, suggests that they are in fact different facets of an underlying compositional principle, namely the continual permutation of a small number of related shapes. Sketches for the horns, tubas, lower strings and accordion during this scene indicate that their chords are based on two primary types: either <[2–][2–][3+]> or <[2–][2–][2–]>.[73] The resulting pitch sets often include C and D, suggesting a link to the sighing motif. In fact, the cellos and double basses that accompany Vermeer's line 'In her

[70] Hoban's fictional author finds it 'impossible to know what her look might have been a response to . . . her face full of questioning and uncertainty. Was there also fear? Fear of what? What had she to fear from him?' Hoban, *The Medusa Frequency*, 14.

[71] Gongs are associated with the idea of impermanence at other moments in the opera, most notably when Kong kills Death of Kong (Act II, Fig. 71^{+1}).

[72] The association of the falling scales both with the past and with the idea of things 'that cannot be' is first established when, in Act I scene 1, Anubis sings to the dead: 'Have I not fed upon the carrion of your longings and your crazy dreams of love that cannot be?' Hoban, *The Second Mrs Kong*, 1.

[73] PSS 0536-0587. The pitches are arranged in linear order across two staffs, seven sets on each staff. The numbers refer to intervals: 2– indicates an interval of 2 or less, whereas 3+ refers to an interval of 3 or more. Within the opening < and closing > signs, intervals are listed in the order they appear in the sketches, read from top to bottom in vertical collections and from left to right in linear configurations.

Example 6.5 Falling scales anticipating Kong's fall as it eventually appears to Pearl, Act I scene 1, Fig. 72^{+2} to 72^{+10}

face I see time's ancient shadow' stem from reorderings of two chromatic four-note sets, which are closely associated with the sighing motif: C–C♯–D–D♯, and C♯–D–D♯–E (both <[2–][2–][2–]> therefore). The falling scales linked to Kong's death (in the strings, accordion, vibraphone and cimbalom, from Fig. 72) unfold eight-note modes, each comprising two four-note sets separated by interval class 5 (the perfect fourth or its inversional equivalent the perfect fifth).[74] Commonly occurring shapes here are <[2–][2–][2–]> and <[2–][3+][2–]>. This suggests a possible intertextual reference to Max Steiner's soundtrack for the original 1933 film, in which the principal leitmotif consists of three descending chromatic notes. (Although used in varied ways throughout the film, the motif is ultimately associated with Kong's fall and death, at which point it is extended to seven descending notes.) While it is possible to imagine an association between the related shapes and Vermeer's desire for Pearl (since they invoke Steiner's musical interpretation of Kong's desire for Ann Darrow), the scene is more important for the way it conveys the idea of impermanence. This notion, triggered by Pearl's image, finds an apposite metaphor in Birtwistle's transformation of abstract musical ideas (the use of musical shapes) into the representational needs of the scene, expressed by the sighing motif, falling scales, saxophones and gongs.

The diachronic image: Birtwistle's film music

While the scene in the 'place of memory' explores synchronicity, conveyed by the layering of ideas representative of past, present and future, elsewhere images are represented as unfolding in real time. Given the suggestion of more literal temporal unfolding, I have defined this model as a 'diachronic image'. The origin for this idea is what Hoban described as 'the moment under the moment', which is connected to a separation between the artificially continuous experience of 'reality' and the discontinuous thoughts and memories that come and go beneath this experience. Hoban used film as a metaphor to illustrate this idea:

> The flickering of a film interrupts the intolerable continuity of apparent world; subliminally it gives us those in-between spaces of black that we crave. The eye is hungry for this; eagerly it collaborates with the unwinding strip of celluloid that shows it twenty-four pictures per second, making real by an act of retinal retention the here-and-gone, the continual disappearing in which the lovers kiss, the shots are fired, the horses gallop . . . [75]

Birtwistle responds to Hoban's ideas during a short passage of film music composed to accompany the climactic scene from the film: Kong on top of

[74] PSS 0536-0592.
[75] Hoban, *The Medusa Frequency*, 87. By extension, in 'The work of art in the age of mechanical reproduction' Walter Benjamin observed that, although the cinematic image 'cannot be arrested', 'the spectator's process of association in view of these images is indeed interrupted by their constant, sudden change'. For Benjamin, this constituted 'the shock effect of the film', an effect that would both overturn habitual modes of viewing and reveal the alienating conditions of modernity to the masses; *Illuminations*, ed. Hannah Arendt, trans. Harry Zohn (London: Fontana, 1992), 231.

the Empire State Building being shot at by airplanes, laying Ann Darrow to rest on a ledge before falling to his death. This scene is screened in Act II scene 2, as Death of Kong seeks to reinforce Kong's demise. As late as January 1994 (the libretto was finalised in February) the intention was not to have music accompany the film. In a working copy of the libretto we read: 'We see, by rear projection, silent footage from the 1933 film while Death of Kong does the roar of the airplanes and the chatter of the machine guns.'[76] By February this had become: 'We see Kong defying the airplanes, being shot down, and falling. All music and sfx [sound effects] will be in score. Footage possibly in slow motion for dramatic emphasis.'[77] The idea of showing the film in slow motion was ultimately abandoned, but both the decision to place all sound effects in the orchestral score and the idea of transforming the original clip into an example of silent film remained.[78]

Having decided to compose his own 'soundtrack', Birtwistle somewhat uncharacteristically, within the context of this opera and his practice at this time, sketched a scenario for the entire section (see Plate 6.1). Twenty-eight pitch events are written along two staffs. Usually each event comprises a single four-note shape in one of the staffs, but at times two shapes coincide (this is indicated by vertical lines). Along the upper staff the pitch material is placed in a high register, always above the top line, while pitches in the lower staff are written an octave below.[79] The pitch material in the sketch does not relate closely to the version in the final score, suggesting that several undisclosed compositional stages significantly altered the sketch. The first four-note set, on the top line of the sketch (Ab–Db–D–G) is replaced by a five-note set (C♯–D–D♯–F–G) at Fig. 58. The first set on the lower line of the sketch is marked 'Trp-hrns'. Although the boundary pitches here roughly correspond to those of the trumpets at Figs. 59–60 (g′ to g″), they do not relate to the pitch material or range of the horns. The comment at event 24, 'could be played by vla vlc', suggests that some pitches were realised in different octaves to those notated in the sketch. Judging by the location of this remark, it is likely that Birtwistle chose to end his 'film score' at this moment, with the boxed material cascading through lower-register instruments as a representation of Kong's fall.

[76] Working libretto, PSS 0537-0367, dated 13 January 1994.

[77] Working libretto, PSS 0537-0369, dated 4 February 1994.

[78] In the original 1933 film Steiner did not provide music from the arrival of the planes until the moment when it is obvious that Kong is seriously wounded, at which point the music accompanies his farewell to Ann Darrow. Otherwise, the scene is characterised by the eerie sound of the planes, the drone of their engines and the crackle of machine-gun fire.

[79] In the lead-up to the arrival of the planes in the 1933 movie, Steiner's music is densely scored and contains perhaps the greatest concentration of ideas in the film as a whole, with prominent brass dissonances whose clustered shapes may well have inspired Birtwistle's original conception for his own soundtrack.

Birtwistle's 'film music' is characterised by a dense body of straining orchestral sound, as if attempting to hold an object high, keeping it in suspension. With the exception of the machine-gun imitations on woodblock (cued to synchronise with gunfire in the film), it displays only subtle shades of contrast; the dip and rise in the lower staff at events 10 and 11 of the sketch may relate to scales in the oboes and saxophones at Fig. 59^{+5} of the completed score. Overall, the sense of diverging and coalescing shapes evident in the embryonic sketch is almost completely lost in its realisation, submerged under a dense orchestral fabric, rather like Hoban's image of twenty-four pictures per second merging into one. Birtwistle's interpretation of this film scene combines both literal and expressionistic elements, reflecting Kong's own description offered in Act I scene 2: 'The airplanes buzzed and stung, his blood ran out, his strength was gone.'[80] A sense of straining to resist an inevitable fall is powerfully evoked.

On a different, less dramatically specific level, the music also seems to be reaching for something unattainable, as if the film and the opera were trying to come together as one. Kong's cries of defiance on the tower are a reminder of what Michal Grover-Friedlander has called 'the attraction of cinema to opera': it is as if Kong is breaking into song.[81] Perhaps paradoxically, the obviously representational elements in the orchestra are merged with a sense of the music pursuing its own direction, a disposition that more than hints at the view of Adorno and Eisler that the relationship of music and image should not be organised around similarity but should instead embody 'question and answer, affirmation and negation, appearance and essence', a dialectic 'dictated by the divergence of the media in question and the specific nature of each'.[82] The paradoxical quality of Birtwistle's music is also indicative of the persistence of an imaginary Kong (in the Lacanian sense) beyond his symbolic depiction on the screen. Lawrence Kramer has observed a similar divergence in mixed media in general:

> The process of mixture involves an attempt by one medium, usually the imagetext, to think its other, and a response in which, however indirectly or implicitly, the other, usually music, thinks for itself. The musical remainder is often obscure or marginal, forgotten in the mutual reinforcement of each medium by the other, but it is always there, always capable of emerging as the most compelling, most revealing, most chastening or animating force in the mixture.[83]

[80] Hoban, *The Second Mrs Kong*, 18.
[81] Michal Grover-Friedlander, *Vocal Apparitions: The Attraction of Cinema to Opera* (Princeton University Press, 2005).
[82] Theodor W. Adorno and Hanns Eisler, *Composing for the Films* (London and New York: Continuum, 1994), 70.
[83] Lawrence Kramer, 'The voice of Persephone: musical meaning and mixed media', in his *Musical Meaning: Toward a Critical History* (Berkeley and Los Angeles: University of California Press, 2002), 187.

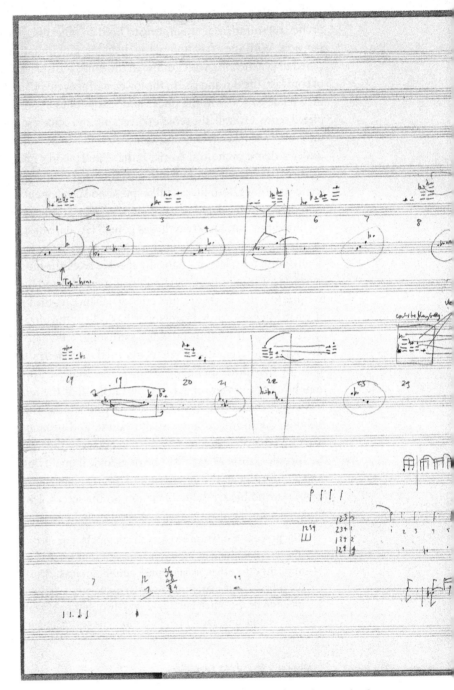

Plate 6.1 Sketch for the 'film sequence' of Kong's fall from the Empire State Building, Act II scene 2. PSS, Sammlung Harrison Birtwistle, *The Second Mrs Kong*, folder 6/12, 43

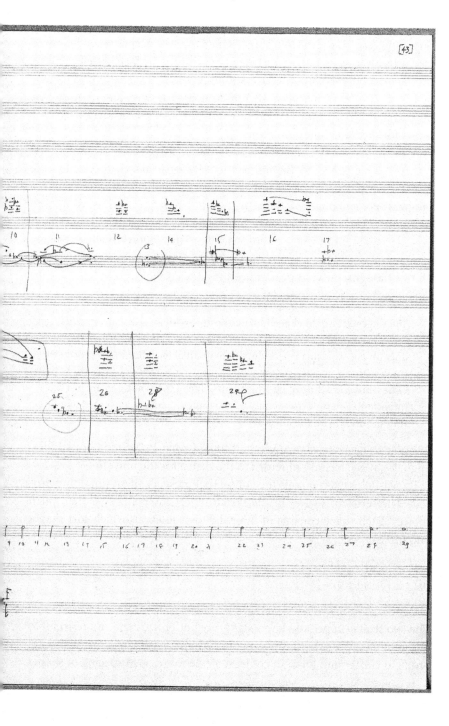

I would argue that something like what Kramer is describing characterises Birtwistle's sketch for the film scene, which can be interpreted in two ways. One possible interpretative path takes us away from the sketch itself, concentrating on its significant transformation into the score. The second focuses on its existence as an autonomous, self-contained gesture. These two opposing possibilities constitute a dialectic through which to consider Birtwistle's music for the film scene as a whole.

A likely explanation for Birtwistle's desire to go beyond his original precepts is suggested by his interest in Klee's *Notebooks*, specifically the transformations from sketch to final artwork, in which intuitive ideas are progressively systematised (what Birtwistle has referred to as 'composed intuition').[84] From the mid 1980s on, Birtwistle has also often reflected on how 'decisions about where to go derive from the context of where you are at any moment'.[85] In an interview with Hall in 1983 Birtwistle elaborated on this thought, providing an indication of what the concept 'idea' means to him and how to go beyond it:

> You can create a formal position before the event, an elaborate schemata, and that you can call your idea. That's what you're trying to express. You have a duty to that schemata [*sic*], a duty to that initial idea. But in the process of composition you make contexts which are not necessarily concerned with it. Other things are thrown up which have a life of their own and are just as important. You now have a duty to two things . . . one is concerned with the text, the other with the music.[86]

In order to have a clearer understanding of what Birtwistle's 'initial idea' might be, it is necessary to return to the sketch for the film clip.

Birtwistle's sketch reveals the conceptual presence of an unfolding process. The series of shapes in the sketch reflect interval rather than pitch choices. Each shape consists of three different intervals which sort shapes into three types:

(a)   <[4+][3−][4+]>
(b)   <[3−][4+][3−]>
(c)   <[3−][3−][3−]>

The two strata (upper and lower staffs) are both proximate and resistant to one another. Type (c) only appears on the lower staff, where the material is prone to cluster and knot, in contrast to the more open spacing of shapes

---

84   Birtwistle in Lorraine, 'Territorial rites 1', 7.
85   Birtwistle in Lorraine, 'Territorial rites 2', 16.
86   Birtwistle in Hall, *HB*, 145; the context is a discussion of *Yan Tan Tethera*. Hall later used the phrase 'the sanctity of the context' to describe this new approach; see Hall, 'The sanctity of the context'.

Example 6.6 Sketch with type (a) shapes for the xylophone and cimbalom, Act II scene 3, Fig. 61^{+2} to 65^{-3}. PSS 0536-0867

9	7	6	7	5	6	6	7	5	8	6
1	2	1	1	2	1	2	1	1	1	2
4	4	6	6	6	7	5	5	7	5	5

Example 6.7 Sketch with type (a) shapes for the first violins and number scheme determining the order of their use, Act II scene 3, Fig. 73^{-1} to 74. PSS 0536-0883

8	7	6	5	7	6	5	4
1	1	1	1	1	1	1	1
5	6	7	8	5	6	7	8

7	3	1	5	2	6	4	8
5	7	3	1	6	2	8	6 [4]
1	7	5	3	4	8	2	6
5	1	7	3	2	6	4	8
1	7	3	5	4	8	6	2
7	1	5	3	6	2	8	4

on the upper staff. However, this distinction is undermined at various moments when two contrasting shapes are brought together, as distorted mirror reflections (see events 1, 5 and 15), while at 22 and 26–8 type (b) shapes coincide, with an exact mirroring of <2, 5, 2> at 27, and a near-exact pairing of <1, 7, 1> with <1, 6, 1> at 28.

This passage is unique, as a comparison with Birtwistle's obsessive use of four-note sets throughout the opera proves. Conceivably there are practical reasons for the employment of four-note shapes; this number of pitches fits conveniently into each hand of the accordion part (a part that lends a distinctive timbre to the opera's sound world, especially through its role as a kind of continuo instrument), and it may potentially be related to subgroupings of the woodwind, brass and string sections. Nevertheless, an intriguing relationship can be established between the three notes of Max Steiner's primary leitmotif, which permeates his entire score for the 1933 *King Kong*, and the three intervals common to Birtwistle's shapes. Usually, one type of four-note shape is employed rather than two or three, as in the film sequence. For example, the xylophone and cimbalom chords from Fig. 61^{+3} to 64, prior to the film music, are based on variations of the (a) shape (Example 6.6). Following the film sequence, the violin chords from Fig. 73^{-1} to 74 are also based on the (a) type (see Example 6.7; the lower six lines constitute the numbering system that governs the order in which the

Example 6.8 Sketch with type (a) shapes in two layers used to generate woodwind, crotales, glockenspiel and marimba counterpoint, Act I scene 1, Fig. 99 to 101[+3]

Reordered to form:

eight chords are eventually used).[87] An example of simultaneous variants of type (a) is given in Example 6.8, in which pitches are reordered and transposed into different octaves, here used to form a contrapuntal cantabile woodwind texture accompanying Kong's line 'Sometimes I dream the misty mountains of an island that I've never seen, sometimes a jungle painted all on glass.'[88]

In general, the application of these shapes across the work is characterised by a certain static quality resulting from the desire to explore varied divisions of a particular interval space. While aspects of this practice may be traced back to the late 1970s, notably to *Silbury Air* (1977), the tendency earlier had been either to vary a generic chord or to apply interval series (such as 5, 6, 7) above or below a particular line of predetermined pitches. In *Mrs Kong*, however, interval shapes generally do not revolve around such pivots, but are detached; where pivotal lines are used, they will invariably also have been generated by the permutation of four-note sets. Examples 6.9a and 6.9b illustrate this permutation in relation to the rather Berg-like string melody that accompanies Pearl's line 'A Kong who never was, waiting in the shadow of the future' (Act I, Figs. 84–5). Furthermore, the evidence of the film sketch, as well as a similar outline for the fight

---

[87] Elsewhere in the opera, four-note sets formed from three large intervals are commonly used, for example to generate the xylophone, vibraphone, marimba and cimbalom material from Fig. 122 to Fig. 126.

[88] In the score, this texture is doubled by crotales, glockenspiel, vibraphone and cimbalom.

Example 6.9a Sketch with type (b) shapes used to form a melodic line in the cellos and violas, Act I scene 1, Fig. 84^{-1} to 85^{+4}. PSS 0536-0605

Reordered to form:

Example 6.9b Cellos, Act I scene 1, Fig. 84^{-1} to 85^{+4} (adapted from the reordering in Ex. 6.9a)

between Swami Zumzum and Mr Dollorama (two incidental characters) in Act I, suggests a consciousness of shapes unfolding both within prescribed time frames and across a broader temporal span, in contrast to the more disconnected application of similar devices in *Silbury Air*. The sketch for the film scene might even be regarded as a mimetic part to the opera's whole, since it seeks, within a limited time frame determined by the length of the film clip, to establish a relationship among the many varying shapes that have evolved throughout the opera. And I would suggest that it is highly relevant that these processes seem to intensify in response to the film extract.

While it is certainly possible to speculate about these processes as metaphors for the various conflicts and 'desiring resolutions' integral to both the film clip and the opera as a whole (Kong and Pearl; Kong as idea; image and idea), or to interpret them as Birtwistle's response to Hoban's concept of the instability of images, it is equally important to acknowledge that these ideas were conceived in a non-verbal musical domain, and that a vital and determining characteristic of Birtwistle's aesthetic is a compositional concern to manipulate contour across the work, almost in spite of the drama unfolding on stage. Moreover, it is the transformation of shapes through unknown compositional stages and their voicing in extreme registers and straining timbres that evinces metaphorical interpretations, rather than their 'archetypal' status in the sketch plan. Nevertheless, descriptions of the sketch's content do invite description in terms such as 'mirroring' or 'distorted mirror image'. It is through the study of the sketch, then, that the musical manifestations of the primary and secondary identification processes fundamental to the opera's meaning are rendered perceptible. In this sense, the sketch stages a narrative central to the opera's dramatic trajectory, traced through a series of misrecognitions (events 1, 5, 10 and 15) and resulting conflicts (9–11 and 24) leading to recognition (27) and an acceptance of difference (28).

As in secondary identification, 'a complete collapse of spectator onto character (or film)' is averted.[89] The divergent elements in Birtwistle's music further support this interpretation: while certain aspects of the music suggest complicity with the notion of disinterested spectacle by underlining Kong's plight (the machine-gun fire, straining timbres and extremes of register), a feeling that the music ultimately 'goes its own way' implies a resistance to the cinematic image. Moreover, the music's overall effect evokes what Nancy describes as the 'force' – the 'energy, pressure, or intensity' – that distinguishes an image from the 'thing' that it represents.[90]

Images of infinitude

The drive towards the union of Kong and Pearl is essential to the opera, since these two, more than anyone else on stage, embody the opera's aesthetic desire to unify image, voice and idea. Although this union is ultimately impossible, both libretto and music offer an endpoint (not a true resolution) via a musical image of infinitude: a vision of endless song and, by association, of enduring love. Hoban's answers to Pearl and Kong's existential questions, which merely reiterate ideas that they had already sensed but were unwilling to accept, buttress this image of infinitude because they are ineffectual: the Mirror's words to Kong that he is 'the lost and lonely child of all the world',

[89] Doane, 'Misrecognition', 25.   [90] Nancy, *The Ground of the Image*, 2.

which echo his own admission of this fate after killing the Death of Kong, do not weaken Kong's desire to be with Pearl.[91] This accurately reflects the Lacanian notion that 'desire can never be satisfied: it is constant in its pressure, and eternal'.[92]

The image of infinitude delineated in the opera's final scene is therefore paradoxical: the same yearnings will endure, but they must be construed differently. While certain musical devices connote increased synthesis (for example, from Fig. 52^{-1} the chords in the woodwind mirror the unfolding string texture),[93] this multiplication of vocal lines and orchestral layers suggests plurality and yearning rather than unity and closure. Following Inanna's short aria, from Fig. 79, descending lines unfurl in the orchestra, each generated from four-note shapes using intervals larger than interval 3. While the falling contours imply an allusion to Kong's death (one made more explicit in the opera's closing bars), the prevalence of a commonly shared musical shape echoes the equilibrium established at the end of the film music sketch. There is even a sense that the orchestra finally recognises Pearl when it shadows her line 'Why do I feel so nowhere and so not at all?'[94] Although this points to a greater sense of subjective presence within the orchestra and an apparent recognition of Pearl and her fate, such melodic elements are soon associated with a more abstract process, namely repetition.

A watershed moment in this process occurs when Pearl, awaiting Kong's arrival, finally begins to interrogate her own image (Fig. 84), asking the Mirror, 'How do I look? Let me see myself.' Birtwistle's sketches reveal that his original intention had been to introduce a 'very fast under current [*sic*] which gets slower+slower to end of opera'.[95] Ultimately, he initiated a series of unchanging ostinato patterns, beginning with a four-note motif in the flute ($b'–c'''–f'''–e\flat''$) that is restated three times and shadowed by the lower woodwind.[96] Pearl's moment of critical engagement is also marked by an increase in tempo, the introduction of 'stabbing' semiquavers in the strings, and a noticeable agitation in her voice. She approaches the Mirror but it turns away, informing Pearl that her appearance is the way it has always been, 'unchanged through all the years'.[97]

When Kong begins knocking on the door of Pearl's apartment, asking to be let in, she delays him while trying to make sense of her reflection in the

[91] In the same passage Pearl is informed she is 'the face that Vermeer painted, forever partly now and partly remembered'.
[92] Evans, *An Introductory Dictionary*, 37.
[93] The sketch for this section (PSS 0536-0851) shows the woodwind chords at the top and the string texture immediately below.
[94] Hoban, *The Second Mrs Kong*, 31–2.   [95] PSS 0537-0346.
[96] PSS 0537-0010.   [97] Hoban, *The Second Mrs Kong*, 32.

mirror: 'I don't know what I'm seeing . . . I'm afraid of what I saw' (Fig. 86). Pearl's distrust of her reflection brings her closer to Kong, who of course rejects his own cinematic image, and this is marked by the continual return of their parts to pitches Db and Gb: musically, this is the closest Kong and Pearl have come to one another.[98] Contrary to Pearl's earlier acceptance of her reflected image in Act I, during the scene with Vermeer, this critical response signals a separation between the operatic Pearl and her reflected image, an idea that in the closing stages of the opera is embodied musically by elements that are both fixed and free. For example, the duets between Kong and Pearl, like those for Orpheus and Eurydice, are set in a free tempo, independent of the conductor, but they are underpinned by a low E pedal (a reference to the opening of *The Mask of Orpheus*, where Orpheus recalls fragments of his past over E and F pedals). And the orchestra's multiple melodic lines allude to a distinction Birtwistle had earlier established, in *Secret Theatre*, between an extended melodic texture (or cantus) and a repetitive rhythmic ensemble (or continuum).[99] Such musical distinctions, or separations, are cast in revealing light by Slavoj Žižek's account that the object *a* 'is not a positive entity existing in space [but] ultimately nothing but a certain *curvature of the space itself* which causes us to make a bend precisely when we want to get directly to the object'.[100] It is therefore possible, as Martin Scherzinger has suggested, to extrapolate from this the idea of a certain curvature of musical space by which the object *a*'s presence 'is experienced only in the negative form of its consequences' – namely, here, in the non-alignment of textures.[101]

At the moment when Mirror informs Pearl and Kong that they cannot be together, a six-note ostinato begins (see Example 6.10). This comprises a six-note melodic cell (F–A–Bb–Gb–G♮–Ab) and seven durations (4, 3, 5, 3, 3, 8, 6), which begin on the second note. The melodic cell appears seven times, while variation is introduced by the ostinato's irregular migration from horn to cello to cor anglais to alto saxophone, determined by the use of random numbers.[102] A further ostinato in the horns and trumpets follows, a five-note cell beginning on D, a pitch associated throughout the opera with the idea of memory. This ostinato becomes progressively slower

[98] There seems to be no obvious significance in this choice of pitches.

[99] For a more detailed explanation of the terms 'cantus' and 'continuum' and their use in *Secret Theatre*, see Hall, *HBIRY*, 26–35.

[100] Slavoj Žižek, *Enjoy Your Symptom: Jacques Lacan in Hollywood and Out* (New York and Routledge: 2001), 48–9.

[101] Martin Scherzinger, 'The return of the aesthetic: musical formalism and its place in political critique', in Andrew Dell'Antonio, ed., *Beyond Structural Listening? Postmodern Modes of Hearing* (Berkeley and Los Angeles: University of California Press, 2004), 270.

[102] Numbers also determine the order of the five different durations used (1 unit = 1 semiquaver).

Example 6.10 Sketch for ostinato, Act II scene 4, Fig. 102^{-1} to 105^{-4}. PSS 0537-0038

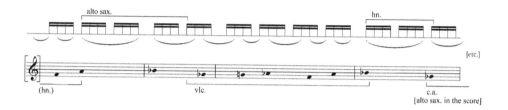

Example 6.11 Kong and Pearl, Act II scene 4, c. Fig. 109^{+6} to close of opera

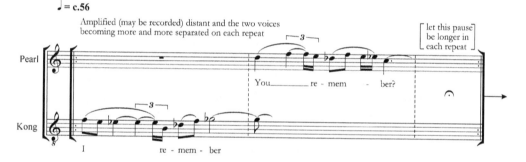

and eventually terminates on E, only to be followed by a nine-note cell in the horns, which rises chromatically from E to G♯ and returns to E. Although this extended sighing motion reintroduces a more overtly representational and vocal character into the orchestra, in general Birtwistle's ostinatos establish a more indirect identification with Hoban's repetitive answers to Pearl and Kong and, in conjunction with the multiplication of lines, connote some sort of equilibrium, almost a 'steady state'. The opera ends movingly with the floating voices of Kong, Pearl, Orpheus and Eurydice singing of their memories of love and desire for union (see Example 6.11). A Lacanian perspective suggests it is the imaginary order that is being recalled, and the abiding image is of the lovers' separation, illustrated by the increased duration between each vocal repeat. In this we are again reminded that desire is not related to an object but to a lack. As Lacan and *Mrs Kong* would have it:

> There is no (sexual) *relation* of one person to another, no pregiven unity, no forgiveness clause for human imperfection (or lack), only the masquerade that seeks to deny loss and cancel the pain of anxiety produced by the void. Life plays between the voice and the gaze, yielding deception, frustration... the disembodied voices droning on and on[.][103]

And yet the importance given throughout the opera to remembering, from Anubis's observation in the opening scene that the dead 'live' on their memories, suggests that, paradoxically, memories feed desire.

An 'arm's length' approach?

It should be clear by now that the concern with images in *Mrs Kong* runs deeper than merely an interest in multimedia or the 'focus on moment-to-moment fantasy' that Adlington has connected with 'post-modern scepticism about organic logic and forms'. The importance of the concept of identification for Birtwistle is reflected in the different musical processes associated with Kong and Pearl, which structure the opera in highly distinctive terms. The result is not so much an 'imagetext', in Kramer's terms, in which music would appear to retain the upper hand, but a dialectic of two different media and minds, related by shared intent.

Given the extent to which Birtwistle's music responds to Hoban's libretto, it may seem surprising that the music–text relationship in the opera has been viewed with a degree of criticism. Birtwistle has been accused of an 'arm's length approach', resulting in music that flirts moodily with both drama and words, 'occasionally responsive and even pictorial', according to Adlington, 'but more often haughtily indifferent'.[104] Adlington is uneasy about the 'very subtle relation' between voices and orchestra, while 'text articulation and sensitivity to the libretto's focal moments' appear to be low on the composer's priority list.[105] I hope to have shown how music responds to key dramatic moments in the action and to the symbolic layers of the libretto.

The fact that the music's surface features are related at a deeper level, however, may jar with the libretto's eclectic styles and images. This need be a problem only if the relationship between words and music is expected to

---

[103] The reference to 'no (sexual) *relation*' here refers to Lacan's idea that there is no immediate relation between the sexes (i.e. men and women), since relations are mediated by language. Ellie Ragland, 'The relation between the voice and the gaze', in Richard Feldstein, Bruce Fink and Maire Jaanus, eds., *Reading Seminar XI: Lacan's Four Fundamental Concepts of Psychoanalysis* (Albany: State University of New York Press, 1995), 202.

[104] Adlington, *MHB*, 36. See also Tom Sutcliffe, review of the Glyndebourne production of *The Second Mrs Kong*, *Musical Times*, 136 (July 1995), 373–5; and Ivan Hewett, 'The second coming', *Musical Times*, 136 (January 1995), 46–7.

[105] Adlington, 'Harrison Birtwistle's recent music', 4.

be immediate and self-evident, on the level of Lacan's primary narcissism. Once we open up the possibility that Birtwistle's responses to the libretto's ideas have more in common with 'secondary identification', then the charge of an 'arm's length approach' evaporates. Any sense that the vocal parts are not clearly related to the orchestra (at least until the end of the work), for example, may acquire meaning as an underlying metaphor for Kong's quest to locate the idea behind his image – a point that is thrown into especially revealing light when compared to the very close relationship between voices and orchestra in *Gawain*, discussed in Chapter 5.

The Second Mrs Kong is also revealing in terms of its revision of Birtwistle's earlier working methods. In particular, his interest in marshalling contour and shape, evident in works from the late 1960s and early 1970s, can be seen to retreat from the middleground to the background, and therefore to a more abstract, conceptual level. It is the location of these abstract forms in the context of an opera that dramatises the relationship between images and ideas, however, that illuminates the reasons behind Birtwistle's practice. The focus of the concept of identification in *Mrs Kong* does not deny the gulf between visual and aural media: on the contrary, it explores and perhaps even widens it. What is more, it promotes the opera house as a space particularly suited to exploring the relationship between these media, while reaffirming opera's penchant for presenting old stories and especially old images from new and unusual perspectives.

7   Corporeal music: *Bow Down, The Io Passion* and *The Corridor*

Anterior to its status as a sign, music is an action on and of the body.[1]

Birtwistle has made what Harry Partch called 'corporeal music': sounds – such as we've long forgotten, to our bitter cost – that involve bodily action along with words so that . . . one lives, moves and has one's being in them, while they last.[2]

the most subtle and central quality of those actions we tend to call ritual is the primacy of the body moving about within a specially constructed space . . . the body movements of ritually knowledgeable agents actually define the special qualities of the environment, yet the agents understand themselves as reacting or responding to this environment.[3]

the ritual mode of performance is characterised by deliberate, disciplined use of the body.[4]

This chapter examines the intersection of music, action and conceptions of the body in selected stage works and incidental music by Birtwistle. During his time at London's National Theatre, where he was Director of Music from 1975 to 1983, Birtwistle cultivated new approaches that in certain instances are comparable to what Wilfrid Mellers, following Harry Partch, terms 'corporeal music'. Clearly, most music is corporeal in the sense that it is performed, and music may be interpreted from this perspective.[5] Also, given the metaphorical nature of language and our reliance on 'experiential gestalts' – that is to say, our tendency to understand and experience one kind of thing in terms of another – it is possible to comprehend all music

---

[1]   David Lidov, 'Mind and body in music', *Semiotica*, 66–1/3 (1987), 69. A slightly revised version of this article appears in David Lidov, *Is Language a Music? Writings on Musical Form and Signification* (Bloomington and Indianapolis: Indiana University Press, 2005), 145–64.

[2]   Wilfrid Mellers, 'Body music' [a review of *The Mask Of Orpheus*], *Times Literary Supplement*, 6 June 1986; see also his *The Masks of Orpheus: Seven Stages in the Story of European Music* (Manchester University Press, 1987), 168.

[3]   Catherine Bell, *Ritual: Perspectives and Dimensions* (New York: Oxford University Press, 1997), 82.

[4]   Tom F. Driver, *Liberating Rites: Understanding the Transformative Power of Ritual* (Boulder, CO and Oxford: Westview Press, 1998), 83.

[5]   Examples of such an approach include Roger Graybill, 'Toward a Pedagogy of Gestural Rhythm', *Journal of Music Theory Pedagogy*, 4/1 (1990), 1–50, Elisabeth Le Guin, *Boccherini's Body: An Essay in Carnal Musicology* (Berkeley and Los Angeles: University of California Press, 2006), and Alexandra Pierce, *Deepening Musical Performance through Movement: The Theory and Practice of Embodied Interpretation* (Bloomington: Indiana University Press, 2007).

as being in some way representative of bodily movement.[6] What is meant in this context, however, is forms of music theatre that reflect what Daniel Albright refers to as 'the modernist urge to restore corporeality to art', or what Harold B. Segel terms 'the modernist physical imperative'.[7] Partch's concept of corporeal music comprised a vision of total theatre in which music, voice and action are intimately linked through ritualised performance techniques.[8] This chapter will examine similar evidence. However, we will see that Birtwistle's approach varied from the use of signals to instruct action in his incidental music, to what one might term total ritualistic theatre in *Bow Down* (1977), which posits 'the common basis of all acts of performance in the human body',[9] to more or less symbolic musical representations of action in *The Io Passion* (2004) and *The Corridor* (2009), which reflect the influence of Wagner considered in Chapter 5.

The principal works discussed in this chapter have many aspects in common: all evolved directly from Birtwistle's association with actors and theatre directors, all involve small ensembles, several explore the relationship between mime and music, all involve tensions between artificial and natural styles, all employ role doubling, ritualised action and cyclic recurrence, all experiment with the use of space (some place musicians onstage), and all are concerned with relations between the sexes. Crucially, the stage works discussed here illustrate the development of Birtwistle's music theatre after he left the Pierrot Players and represent the fruit of workshops and rehearsals held at the National Theatre, both during and after Birtwistle's time there as Director of Music.

Consistent with this book's focus on source reading in a cultural-theoretical context, this chapter examines various 'texts' – published and unpublished scores, audio recordings of workshops, libretti, prompt scripts, Birtwistle's musical sketches – in relation to the following critical question: how is Birtwistle's concept of musical representation shaped by his concern for the body and physical action, and by the dramatic themes of the works concerned? This question will be considered in relation to theoretical

---

[6] George Lakoff and Mark Johnson, *Metaphors We Live By* (London: Chicago University Press, 2003), 5.

[7] Daniel Albright, *Untwisting the Serpent: Modernism in Music, Literature, and Other Arts* (London: University of Chicago Press, 2000), 102, and Harold B. Segel, *Body Ascendant: Modernism and the Physical Imperative* (London and Baltimore: Johns Hopkins University Press, 1998), 11. See also Tim Armstrong, *Modernism, Technology, and the Body: A Cultural Study* (Cambridge University Press, 1998). Armstrong argues that modernism is characterised by 'the desire to *intervene* in the body; to render it part of modernity by techniques which may be biological, mechanical, or behavioural' (6).

[8] See W. Anthony Sheppard, *Revealing Masks: Exotic Influences and Ritualized Performance in Modernist Music Theater* (Berkeley and Los Angeles: University of California Press, 2001), 180–3.

[9] Adlington, 'Music theatre', 240.

perspectives on representation, ritual and the body suggested by Antonin Artaud, Catherine Bell, Jacques Derrida and David Lidov, among others.

Artaud's 'true' theatre

Birtwistle's interest in anti-naturalistic, avant-garde theatre is clearly illustrated by his use of masks, mime, stylised gesture, non-linear narrative, framing devices, distancing effects and ritual. As has been seen, such characteristics reflect Birtwistle's (mis)readings of Greek tragedy, popular and folk traditions, the mummers' play, Japanese Noh drama, Schoenberg's *Pierrot lunaire* and Stravinsky's stage works, the latter influenced by the experimental theatre director Vsevolod Meyerhold. Also important, to the earlier works especially, is Bertolt Brecht's desire to resist realism or illusion and to stress the artificiality of theatre (although Birtwistle seems less concerned with Brecht's notion that audiences should retain an objective, critical distance). Moreover, Britten's Church Parables – *Curlew River* (1964), *The Burning Fiery Furnace* (1966), *The Prodigal Son* (1968) – and Goehr's *Triptych* – *Naboth's Vineyard* (1968), *Shadowplay* (1970), *Sonata about Jerusalem* (1971) – furnished Birtwistle with contemporaneous examples of pared-down, ritualistic music theatre, influenced by Brecht, Noh and medieval drama.

Many of Birtwistle's abiding theatrical concerns may also be traced back to early twentieth-century theatre writers and directors such as Edward Gordon Craig, Jean Cocteau, W. B. Yeats and Alfred Jarry. Meyerhold's focus on the mechanics of theatre (his fragmentation of plays into discrete episodes, rearranged and sometimes expanded) is also clearly relevant to Birtwistle. However, the name most commonly mentioned in relation to Birtwistle, and which looms large in accounts of avant-garde theatre, is that of Antonin Artaud. Adlington compares Birtwistle's mysterious, exotic rituals to those imagined by Artaud, while Hall cites Artaud's Theatre of Cruelty manifestos (originally published in 1938) in relation to the 'abrupt juxtapositions . . . rapid cutting and freezing' in *Punch*, the 'yards high' effigies and spectacular *mise-en-scène* in *Orpheus*, and the 'sometimes bizarre manipulations of time' in *Gawain*.[10] More intriguingly, Cross refers to Artaud's advocacy of 'a theatre concerned with myth, ritual and magic, with something metaphysical, which rediscovered "the idea of a unique language somewhere between gesture and thought"' – a concept that I shall return to throughout this chapter.[11]

---

[10] Adlington, *MHB*, 31; Hall, *HB*, 72 and 122; Hall, *HBIRY*, 95.
[11] Cross, *HB: MMM*, 67, which cites Antonin Artaud, *The Theater and Its Double*, trans. Victor Corti (London: Calder, 1993), 74.

Yet it remains unclear how, indeed whether, Artaud is relevant to Birtwistle in a deeper sense. Although there is some evidence that Birtwistle was aware of Artaud, any comparisons must acknowledge real differences between the two.[12] Unlike Artaud, Birtwistle is not explicitly interested in attacking repressive, mechanical attitudes in society, or in liberating the primitive side of the psyche through an exploration of madness, irrational spontaneity or delirium.[13] Whereas Meyerhold approached theatre from the outside – as, one could argue, does Birtwistle – Artaud worked from a concept of the inner being, or from what Jacques Derrida has termed the 'metaphysics of presence'. Moreover, Susan Sontag has argued that 'One can be inspired by Artaud . . . But there is no way of applying Artaud.'[14] And yet, Artaud's concept of the theatre does raise issues that are pertinent to the works discussed in this chapter and it is worth exploring these, even if they prove to be points of divergence. The body is central to Artaud's theatrical vision, and it is useful to keep in mind Julia A. Walker's definition of Artaud's concept of 'cruelty' as 'the state in which one is stripped of everything except the awareness of being in a body, the state in which one is reduced to the quivering nerve, jagged and exposed to the raw yet invigorating winds of life'.[15]

In addition to a shared concern to invent novel or 'rediscovered' forms of ritualistic theatre, there are three potentially fruitful points of comparison between Birtwistle and Artaud. One point is highlighted by Artaud's belief that everyday life is an imperfect copy of a higher form of reality that a 'true' theatre may express symbolically. Here ritual theory helps to explain Artaud's association of 'true' theatre with ritual. Artaud's idea is founded on a 'thought–action' dichotomy that Catherine Bell has identified

[12] When discussing *Orpheus* in 1975, Birtwistle appropriated Artaud's sentiment, if not his actual words, when he commented that he wanted the puppets to reach 'as high as the proscenium arch' (Higgins, 'Harrison Birtwistle'). It is unlikely, however, that Birtwistle's knowledge of Artaud rivals that of Boulez or Rihm. See Martin Zenck, 'Antonin Artaud – Pierre Boulez – Wolfgang Rihm: Zur Re- und Transritualität im europäischen Musiktheater', in Hermann Danuser and Matthias Kassel, eds., *Musiktheater heute*, 235–61, and Seth Brodsky, 'Write the moment: two ways of dealing with Wolfgang Rihm 1', *Musical Times*, 145 (2004), 57–72. Here Brodsky describes Rihm's *Tutuguri* (1980–2) as 'arguably as "Artaud-inspired" a work as exists in written music' (62).

[13] See John D. Lyons, 'Artaud: intoxication and its double', *Yale French Studies*, 50 (1974), 120–9; and Christopher Innes, *Avant Garde Theatre, 1892–1992* (London and New York: 1993), 59–94.

[14] Susan Sontag, *Antonin Artaud: Selected Writings* (New York: Farrar, Strauss and Giroux, 1976), lvii.

[15] Julia A. Walker, 'Why performance? Why now? Textuality and the rearticulation of human presence', *Yale Journal of Criticism* 16/2 (2003), 149–75. It was in direct response to this idea that Deleuze, in the context of a book on the painter Francis Bacon, extrapolated from Artaud's notion of a body without organs. Deleuze argues that Bacon paints 'the fact of the body', that is, the body as 'flesh and nerve': 'Presence, presence . . . this is the first word that comes to mind in front of one of Bacon's paintings.' Gilles Deleuze, *Francis Bacon: The Logic of Sensation*, trans. Daniel W. Smith (London and New York: Continuum, 2003), 45 and 50.

as a Hegelian/Marxian structuring principle in much ritual theory.[16] Bell presents the work of American anthropologist Clifford Geertz as exemplar. Geertz argues that at an initial stage in ritual theory, myth is distinguished from ritual, as the thought world is from the lived world, or as cultural conceptions are from social dispositions. Yet in a second stage the thought–action categories become integrated in ritual performance, in which cultural knowledge is both stored and enacted. In a third stage, further 'homologized oppositions' are proposed by and between participants and observers.[17] A circular, mutually reinforcing relationship between ritual and everyday life results in a symbolic act whose participants Bell refers to as 'ritualized agents' who, according to anthropologist Victor Turner, exist in a state of liminality. As Bell remarks, following Louis Althusser: 'through an orchestration in time of loosely and effectively homologized oppositions in which some gradually come to dominate others, the social body reproduces itself in the image of the symbolically schematized environment that has been simultaneously established'.[18] Christopher Innes implies something similar when he remarks that Artaud's theories 'presuppose a dialectical relationship between the stage and the world'.[19] This dialectic, which relates back to Cross's point about a language somewhere between gesture and thought, should be unpacked a little further, for it relates directly to the central theme of this book.

Artaud argued that the theatre 'must become a sort of experimental demonstration of the profound unity of the concrete and the abstract'.[20] Theatre is most effective, he believed, when it captures emotions as they pass into gestures, rather than into words, and he referred evocatively to this process as the 'cartilaginous transformation of ideas'.[21] However, while ritual theory invariably subordinates action to thought, Artaud wished to bypass the mechanics of signification that he felt characterised traditional theatre.[22] For in his view theatre remains 'the most active and efficient *site of passage* for those immense analogical disturbances in which ideas are arrested in flight at some point in their transmutation into the abstract'.[23] In this regard, Artaud was representative of a broader modernist desire for a 'shift of

---

[16] Ultimately, of course, this discourse is indebted to Descartes's separation of the body from the soul or the mind.

[17] See Catherine Bell, *Ritual Theory, Ritual Practice* (Oxford University Press, 2009), 25–9, and Clifford Geertz, *The Interpretation of Cultures* (New York: Basic Books, 1973).

[18] Bell, *Ritual Theory*, 110. See Louis Althusser and Etienne Balibar, *Reading Capital*, trans. Ben Brewster (London: Verso, 1979), especially 25ff.

[19] Innes, *Avant Garde Theatre*, 62.   [20] Artaud, *The Theater* (trans. Richards), 108.

[21] Ibid., 109.

[22] Alastair Williams, 'Voices of the Other', 264. Jacques Derrida has remarked: 'Artaud wanted the machinery of the prompter [*souffleur*] spirited away [*soufflé*]'; Derrida, 'La Parole soufflé', in his *Writing and Difference*, trans. Alan Bass (London and Henley: Routledge and Kegan Paul, 1978), 176.

[23] Artaud, *The Theater*, 109.

emphasis from the spoken word to the physical gesture'.[24] However, Jacques Derrida, who was otherwise sympathetic to Artaud's manifesto, argued that it is impossible to separate human emotions from their means of representation: Derrida rejected the possibility of the unmediated expression of emotion.[25] Indeed, in direct response to Artaud's theories, Derrida famously argued that in all expression – written, spoken or gestural – meaning is always different, always deferred.[26] In seeking to bypass signification, Artaud had in fact drawn attention to the persistent and 'cruel' – that is to say, necessary – presence of signification.[27] Derrida even suggests that Artaud understood it was impossible to escape representation: 'He knew this better than any other.'[28] Nevertheless, Derrida acknowledged that Artaud 'presses against the limits' of representation, which is to say, Artaud aspired to reach beyond such limits into a region of unmediated expression that would address the senses, rather than the intellect, a region that Derrida associated with madness, and Deleuze with hysteria.[29]

Birtwistle does not share Artaud's utopian strain. Arguably, however, he does perceive the conflict between representational action and avant-garde claims to musical autonomy.[30] The main proposition in this chapter is that in *Bow Down, Io* and *Corridor*, Birtwistle's response to the problems highlighted by Artaud is to focus attention on the 'act' of representation itself. Derrida has argued that all action is enacted representation that necessarily involves repetition: the actor interprets (repeats) a preconceived text or gesture. Yet one might contrast this with Jane Ellen Harrison's idea that in ritual 'the acts performed are meaningful mimetic acts which are intended to re-present and not to represent something'.[31] Birtwistle's stage works combine these two perspectives: his use of 'varied' repetition generates

---

[24] Segel, *Modernism*, 15.

[25] Derrida, 'La parole soufflé' and 'The Theater of Cruelty and the Closure of Representation' in his *Writing and Difference*, 169–95 and 232–50.

[26] Derrida comments: 'As soon as I speak, the words I have found (as soon as they are words) no longer belong to me, are originally *repeated* [. . . and yet] Artaud desires a theater in which repetition is impossible'; 'La Parole soufflé', 177.

[27] 'But through another twist of his text, the most difficult one', Derrida argues, 'Artaud affirms the *cruel* (that is to say, in the sense in which he takes this word, necessary) law of difference; a law that this time is raised to the level of consciousness and is no longer experienced with metaphysical naïveté'. Ibid., 194. However, Artaud's focus on immediate audible or sensuous experience is supported by recent interest in 'presence'. See Jean-Luc Nancy, *The Birth to Presence*, trans. Brian Homes et al. (Stanford University Press, 1993); Gumbrecht, *Production of Presence*; Carolyn Abbate, 'Music – drastic or gnostic?' *Critical Inquiry*, 30 (2004), 505–36; and Michelle Duncan, 'The operatic scandal of the singing body: voice, presence, performativity', *Cambridge Opera Journal*, 16/3 (2004), 283–306.

[28] Derrida, 'The Theater of Cruelty', 248.

[29] Williams, 'Voices of the Other', 266. See also Deleuze, *Francis Bacon*, especially 44–55.

[30] Adlington, 'Music theatre', 233.

[31] Erika Fische-Lichte, *Theatre, Sacrifice, Ritual: Exploring Forms of Political Theatre* (London and New York: Routledge, 2005), 41. Jane Ellen Harrison (1850–1928) was one of the so-called 'Cambridge ritualists'.

musical and gestural schemes that are simultaneously fixed (or implied) and free. Consequently, Birtwistle unwittingly highlights Derrida's argument that 'What is tragic is not the impossibility but the necessity of repetition.'[32] One question that arises from this, however, is whether Birtwistle assigns any weight to the act of performance itself as a means to modify, accentuate or reverse textual meaning. Whether, that is, to paraphrase Karol Berger, the present (sensation) is permitted to intrude upon the absent (image, concept) – an idea that will be considered at the end of this chapter in relation to *The Corridor*.[33]

A second point of comparison is Artaud's desire to develop a ritual language based on precise, 'concrete', signs or gestures. In this regard, it has been argued that Artaud's theatre was what might loosely be called 'a *phenomenological theatre* (as opposed to semiological) in that it seeks to retrieve a naïve perception of the thing – its "objective aspect" – before it was defined out of sight by language'.[34] Moreover, Ann Demaitre has noted that Artaud advocated theatre as a form of 'poetry in space' whereby theatre's discursive aspects (text, dialogue, verbal narrative) should be fully subordinate to its 'material' elements ('music, dance, plasticity, pantomime, mimics, gestures, intonation, architecture, light-effects, scenery, and so on').[35] As Innes remarks:

> Metaphysics are to be imprinted in the mind through the skin. The dynamics of consciousness are embodied in scenic rhythms. The linear harmonies of a picture affect the brain directly. Theatre therefore had to develop a ritual language by rediscovering universal physical signs, or 'hieroglyphs', while verbal expression became incantation.[36]

One might add more generally that Artaud advocated the invention of a language that is unique to the theatrical medium and not bound by the written word. Yet arguably Artaud had limited success in realising his own ambitions: as a director he resorted to traditional conventions and even drew on the stock formulas of expressionist silent film, resulting in a form of gothic melodrama. As Innes describes:

---

[32] Derrida, 'The Theater of Cruelty', 248.
[33] Karol Berger, 'Musicology according to Don Giovanni, or: Should we get drastic?' *Journal of Musicology*, 22/3 (2005), 490–501, 499.
[34] Bert O. States, *Great Reckonings in Little Rooms* (Berkeley and Los Angeles: University of California Press, 1987), 109; cited in Robert Leach, *Makers of Modern Theatre: An Introduction* (London and New York: Routledge, 2004), 175.
[35] Ann Demaitre, 'The Theater of Cruelty and alchemy: Artaud and le grand oeuvre', *Journal of the History of Ideas*, 33/2 (April–June 1972), 243.
[36] Innes, *Avant Garde Theatre*, 60.

A brief glance though [Artaud's film scenarios . . .] gives us 'a gesture of cursing'; a man with 'his head in his hands, as if he held the terrestrial mass' being 'sunk in thought'; a man who opens a door by striking it with his fist 'like one exalted', and . . . is shaken by 'a paroxysm', and gestures 'with intensity, frenzy, passion', his face in a 'hideous grimace'.[37]

As noted above, therefore, in seeking to move beyond the mechanics of signification, Artaud drew attention to the tendency of the 'material' to cleave to the 'discursive'. The mismatch between Artaud's theoretical ambition and his pragmatic solutions is directly relevant to Birtwistle's own experience, as will be discussed in the next section. That said, Artaud's tendency to fall back on conventional gestures resonates with ideas forwarded by metaphor theorists that there are certain nonpropositional schemata on which people commonly agree – that there are 'distinct motor movements of the body' with which 'people appear to experience the maximum sense of "fit" between their inherited folk categories and the world as they experience it'. At this middle level of classification people experience gestures 'as real, verifiable by experience, and sufficiently socially stable to be the building blocks of shared knowledge systems'.[38] As George Lakoff and Mark Johnson state: 'There appear to be *both* universal metaphors *and* cultural variation.' As will be seen, such arguments are relevant to the physical movements in *Bow Down* and *Io*.[39]

A third point of comparison is Artaud's emphasis on training actors and developing a vocabulary of 'scenic rhythms' that is subsequently notated. Birtwistle's time at the National Theatre coincided with a rise in experimental theatre in the 1970s (in 1976 there were as many as eighteen state-funded alternative theatre groups in Britain),[40] set against a broader backdrop of innovations by avant-garde theatre directors such as Jean-Louis Barrault, Peter Brook and Jerzy Grotowski. Brook's 'Theatre of Cruelty' workshop with the Royal Shakespeare Company in 1964 was the first systematic attempt to test Artaud's theories in practice, and the 1960s and 1970s saw the establishment of various theatre laboratories in Europe and the USA, including Barrault's Théâtre des Nations, Brook's Centre for International Theatre Research, Grotowski's Living Theatre, and Richard Schechner's Performance Group. The 1950s, 1960s and 1970s also, of course, saw the rise of music theatre in works by Cage, Nono, Berio, Stockhausen, Kagel, Pousseur,

[37] Ibid., 84.
[38] Bell, *Ritual Theory*, 157, n. 184. See also George Lakoff, *Women, Fire and Other Dangerous Things* (Chicago University Press, 1987), 32–7, 46 and 200.
[39] Lakoff and Johnson, 'Afterword, 2003', in *Metaphors We Live By*, 274.
[40] Andrew Davies, *Other Theatres: The Development of Alternative and Experimental Theatre in Britain* (Houndmills and Basingstoke: Macmillan Education, 1987), 168.

Schnebel and Aperghis, among others. Indeed, the 'strenuous course of movement instruction and physical education' that producer Colin Graham set for the original cast of *Curlew River* was comparable to the bodily discipline demanded by Stockhausen in works such as *Plus-Minus* (1963) and *Stimmung* (1968).[41] Birtwistle was surely encouraged by this climate of experimentation, but when he began work at London's National Theatre he stated that his first job was 'to examine, and explain, the relationship between music, movement and the spoken word'.[42]

'Incidental' music at London's National Theatre

Upon taking up his new role at the National Theatre in 1975, Birtwistle outlined his task in the following terms:

> Normally I sit in a room alone and compose and make the decisions; here at the National I am with a group of musicians and we have to work it out together. There is no question of having a layer of music reflecting the action, rather it is a matter of forcing the musicians to watch what is happening on stage, to be part of it and indeed on occasions to motivate the drama . . . The basic reason for coming to the National is that my responsibilities here seem to me one way of breaking the present impasse between the composer and the theatre. There are virtually no outlets nowadays. The opera houses are all geared to the grand statement and they are never willing to allow a failure.[43]

Asked whether he would be reaching back to his work with the Pierrot Players, he replied:

> Yes, naturally. But there is one important difference. What we wrote was rarely done in the theatre: we were all working in the context of music, we hardly ever had a 'production'. Here of course I am writing in the context of the stage. But I think one has to be very careful of the present vogue for music/theatre ensembles [*sic*] or the 'let's get it all together boys', as I call them. The first job is to examine, and explain, the relationship between music, movement and the spoken word.

Birtwistle's incidental music is often functional, that is, he provides music as and when it is required by the drama. Vocal lines, for example those for Ophelia and the Clown in *Hamlet* – Birtwistle's first assignment in 1975 – are mostly simple, stepwise tunes designed to be sung by actors.[44] This approach was retained in later productions such as *The Country Wife*

[41] Arnold Whittall, *The Music of Britten and Tippett*, 210–11.
[42] Birtwistle in Higgins, 'Harrison Birtwistle'.   [43] Ibid.
[44] The National Theatre Archive (henceforth NTA) files reveal that for this production Birtwistle consulted, but did not copy, song settings recommended in Horace Howard Furness, ed., *A*

and *Volpone*, both performed in 1977, and even the 1981 production of the *Oresteia*.[45] Yet Birtwistle remarked that when, for example, a fanfare is requested at a specific moment 'I have to find a way of doing it. That word "find" is rather alien to me.'[46] Indeed, in some instances the music Birtwistle 'found' was not his own: the music compiled in 1977 for William Wycherley's *The Country Wife* (1675) drew heavily on Lully's 'tragédie en musique' *Amadis* (1684), the original 1979 production of *Amadeus* plundered Mozart and Salieri, while Paul Mills's *Herod* (1978) – prepared with Birtwistle's assistant Dominic Muldowney – incorporated plainsong, polyphonic conductus and Machaut's rondeau 'Tant doulcement'.

Herod, however, was an interesting attempt to break with convention. This one-hour production for three saxophones (soprano and baritone; one doubling piccolo), two percussionists, two sopranos, countertenor and six actors (with role doubling), was described as a 'ritualistic evocation of the Nativity', based on 'images associated with Christian art: the sleeping shepherds, the holy star, the winter landscape, the kneeling Magi'.[47] The musicians, dressed in cassocks, processed on and off the stage where they were raised on a dais; the actors performed downstage and in the gangway that divided the audience. There was only one action scene, in which a child was symbolically killed by two soldiers in front of its mother and Herod. Music was intrinsic to the dialogue, leading one critic to remark that the band 'are too often prone to steal the attention that should be concentrated on the actors'.[48] Another critic, however, noted that the juxtaposition of abrasive percussion and skirling wind against the calm liturgical chant mirrored Mills's desire to show that 'what has become formalised and stable was, at the time, volatile and frightening'. In other words, the distinction between myth as stable thought and ritual as volatile action was represented by the contrast between vocal chant and instrumental refrain.

Clearly, as Cross has observed, this period presented Birtwistle with an important opportunity to focus on 'the basics of rhythm, melody and gesture'.[49] Muldowney subsequently remarked that what he learned from Birtwistle was 'not the sound of his music but a much more abstract and simple thing: how gestural it is, and how simple those gestures are'.[50] This is nowhere clearer than in Birtwistle's music for the 1976 production of

---

New Variorum Edition of Shakespeare, Vol. 3, Part I: Hamlet, 6th edn (Philadelphia and London: J. B. Lippincott Company, 1877), 330, 333, 349 and 350.

[45] In *Volpone*, the voices were supported by conventional harmonies played by guitar.

[46] Higgins, 'Harrison Birtwistle'.

[47] John Barber, 'Reinstating meaning of Christmas [*sic*]', *Daily Telegraph*, 12 December 1978.

[48] B. A. Young, 'Herod', *Financial Times*, 12 December 1978.   [49] Cross, *HB: MMM*, 116.

[50] Muldowney in conversation with Paul Griffiths, in Griffiths, *New Sounds, New Personalities: British Composers of the 1980s* (London: Faber, 1985), 161–2.

Marlowe's *Tamburlaine the Great*, directed by Peter Hall with the Lancastrian Albert Finney as Tamburlaine, a Scythian shepherd turned ruthless, world-conquering warlord.[51] Two ensembles were positioned on either side of the stage, each comprising the composer's characteristic combination of wind and percussion, including piccolo, flute, oboe, cor anglais, bass clarinet, pairs of trombones and saxophones, bells, glockenspiel, bongos and side drum. This antiphonal arrangement was often highlighted by contrasts in dynamics – *fortissimo* in one group answered by *piano* in the other, for example – and was intended to create a sense of conflict during the battle scenes. Battles were represented by the percussion who played to an empty stage that was spotlighted in 'blood' red; the light then gradually spread to bathe the stage entirely.

Elsewhere the music consisted of short bursts during entrances and exits, with heightened punctuation at the ends of scenes. Heightened, that is, because in Artaud's terms the music is both concrete and hieroglyphic. A case in point is a recurring four-bar cadence shown in Example 7.1. The combination of 'chirping' piccolo and 'grotesque' trombones with plunge mutes here is both ominous and intriguing. This music is first heard when King Sigismond of Hungary enters with other Christian rulers to form a pact with their adversaries, the Turks, against Tamberlaine (Part II, Act I scene 1). Sigismond's second entry occurs immediately after the most poignant moment in the entire play, at the end of Act II scene 4 (Part II), when Tamburlaine is told that his wife Zenocrate has died. Tamburlaine's response is to declare that he will burn the city and 'march about it with my mourning camp, / drooping and pining for Zenocrate'.[52] A slow pulse is then heard in the percussion, as shown in Example 7.1. However, Sigismond's music, which follows immediately, captures the dual aspect of Tamburlaine's grief more effectively. It also anticipates Tamburlaine's own physical decline: although he does not lose a single battle, Tamburlaine contracts a fatal malady as a consequence of burning Islamic holy texts. According to his physician, Tamberlaine's urine becomes thick and obscure, but his veins are 'parched and void of spirit'.[53]

---

[51] This was the first performance on the Olivier stage, the main auditorium at the newly opened National Theatre. Albert Finney had previously acted the title role in the 1975 production of *Hamlet*, also directed by Hall; this opened at the Old Vic then transferred to the National's Lyttleton stage in 1976. Other plays that Birtwistle worked on during his time as Music Director include: *Julius Caesar* (1977; with Muldowney), *Brand* (1978; with Jonty Harrison), *The Cherry Orchard* and *The Double Dealer* (both 1978; with Muldowney), *As You Like It* (1979; with Muldowney), two one-act dramas by Yeats (*c*.1981), and *The Trojan War Will Not Take Place* (1983). Electronic soundtracks for *Brand* and *Amadeus* were realised by Jonty Harrison.

[52] Christopher Marlowe, *Doctor Faustus and Other Plays*, eds. David Bevington and Eric Ramussen (Oxford University Press, 2008), 93.

[53] Ibid., 132.

Example 7.1 Extract from incidental music for *Tamburlaine the Great*, Part II, Act II scene 4 (unpublished score stored at the National Theatre Archive, London)

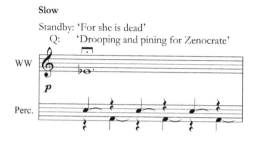

* Tbnes – use of mutes (plungers) on *crescendi* should be grotesque

Crucially, in *Tamburlaine* the percussion is used to introduce pulses and signals to which the actors must often respond. An instance is shown in Example 7.2, in which the soldier chorus responds to the percussion, and from which an incisive, rhythmic counterpoint develops between the actors and musicians. The two main parts of *Tamburlaine* were introduced with a regular pulse. Yet, as Example 7.2 reveals, in his attempt to 'examine, and explain, the relationship between music, movement and the spoken word' Birtwistle was not naturally drawn to regular pulsation. Rather, he wanted to explore a pulse that was 'always reassessing itself',[54] the kinds of pulse developed in *Silbury Air* (1977), *Carmen Arcadiae Mechanicae Perpetuum* (1977–8), and *Pulse Sampler* (1981). Fascinating evidence for this is revealed by a series of previously undocumented audio recordings of workshops held

---

[54] Birtwistle, cited in Adlington, '"Good lodging"', 138.

Example 7.2 Extract from *Tamburlaine*, Part II, Act III scene 3

Techelles: 'How say you soldiers, shall we not?'

in rehearsal room 2 of the National Theatre from 10 to 14 January 1977, the so-called '*Agamemnon* Experiments'.[55]

The '*Agamemnon* Experiments'

we want to do something that's never happened in an English theatre before.[56]

By far the most ambitious project Birtwistle was involved in during his time at the National was Peter Hall's production of Aeschylus's *Oresteia* trilogy, translated and adapted by Tony Harrison. Hall originally intended to stage *Agamemnon* in 1976, followed by the remainder of the trilogy, but a series of delays and strike action prevented this until November 1981. The 1977 workshops were initiated by Hall, who wanted to bring together Birtwistle, Harrison and a group of sixteen actors (male and female), to approach the text 'with every sort of experiment' with the idea that Birtwistle would 'help to define what the rhythms and shape of the text might be'.[57] The resulting workshops are only distantly related to the final production, and the seventeen male and female actors who were involved in them formed an entirely different group to the all-male actors cast in 1981.

It is evident from the recordings of the workshops that, independent of one another, Birtwistle and his assistant Muldowney had prepared a series of experiments based on an early version of the text by Harrison, which they took it in turns to direct. Their focus was to work out ways of

---

[55] These workshops were some of the first to be held in the newly opened National Theatre, which officially opened on 25 October 1976.

[56] Dominic Muldowney, from audiocassette recordings made by Tony Harrison of the '*Agamemnon* Experiments', stored at the Archive of Performances of Greek and Roman Drama, Faculty of Classics, University of Oxford.

[57] A memo from Hall to Birtwistle and others involved, dated 15 November 1975. '*Agamemnon* Experiments' file, the NTA. Memos and other correspondence in the NTA suggest a first set of workshops was held in January 1976.

delivering the chorus sections. On hand to provide music when needed was Jonty Harrison, now an established composer, and two other musicians.[58] From the outset, Birtwistle broke the text down into fragments. He tried out different ideas, using the experience as a kind of aural sketch. This recalls Peter Brook's remarks from 1968, regarding his notion of 'Immediate Theatre':

> The purpose of an exercise is to reduce and return: to narrow the area down and down until the birth of a lie is revealed and caught. If the actor can find and see this moment he can perhaps open himself to a deeper, more creative impulse.[59]

Replace the word 'actor' with 'composer' and this gives a clue to Birtwistle's approach to the workshops.[60] At times this caused tension between the actors and musicians: the actors were encouraged to respond and comment, but they were also reminded that they were there to facilitate the musicians. Much time was devoted to instructing the actors in certain basic concepts to do with register, dynamics and pulse, conveyed through simplified notation and exercises. The musicians' patience was tested, however, and it becomes clear why rigid pulse schemes were eventually incorporated in the 1981 production as a scaffold for the actors. However, the principal sticking point was the actors' desire to read through the text first, to become acquainted with its rhythm. Harrison argued this was unnecessary since he had adopted a 'blatant metre': a regular scheme with four stresses in each line, based on the trochaic tetrameter typified by Longfellow's *The Song of Hiawatha* (1855), or the twelve-syllable '*Beowulf* line'. Although not fully developed into the craggy, Anglo-Saxon style he desired, Harrison's 1977 text already included the stylistic features that characterised his final translation: percussive consonantal alliteration; compound words (such as 'bloodclan' and 'she-God'); terse single-line interchange (known as stichomythia); refrains in the lyrical sung sections.[61] In the workshops, Harrison pointed out that he had attempted to strip away as much connective syntax – subordinate clauses and other discursive links – as possible, since it 'clogs what is being said'.

---

[58] One of the other musicians, probably John Wesley Barker, played saxophone and flute during the sessions.

[59] Peter Brook, *The Empty Space* (London: Penguin Books, 2008), 126.

[60] Birtwistle's approach followed Artaud who expressly did not wish his new theatre to be left 'to the caprice of the wild and thoughtless inspiration of the actor . . . I would not care to leave the fate of my plays . . . to that kind of chance. No.' Moreover, Artaud was determined that his 'gropings, researches, and shocks' would culminate 'in a work *written down*, fixed in its least details, and recorded by means of notation'. Artaud, *The Theater*, 110 and 111.

[61] By comparison to the final version, Harrison's text for the workshops had fewer compound words and was generally less stylised or 'craggy' in character.

Harrison entered the workshops in the hope that Birtwistle would find ways to liberate his text from conventional forms of delivery. In Harrison's mind the *Oresteia* is about the discovery of debate (represented most vividly by the chorus sections) and the establishment of a new order, in which men seized social and legal responsibility from women. He therefore hoped Birtwistle would find ways to convey the disputations, clamour and moral complexities of a moment of seismic political change. At times, Harrison sounds remarkably similar to Birtwistle, especially when he states that he seeks a form of harshness, but without excluding lyricism. The actors, however, were reluctant to let go of the discursive meaning of words: they found it difficult to relinquish their natural desire to interpret the text. In response, the actors were told that the mechanics had to be in place first before they could begin to introduce expression into their performance. Moreover, Birtwistle suggested that the mechanics they developed in the workshop would become 'the text on which you can produce something'.[62] Yet certain actors remained unconvinced and argued that the mechanics should come from the meaning of the text.

Lacking an instrumental ensemble, the workshops placed an emphasis on vocal experiment that was almost entirely absent from the 1981 production. The latter is known for its rather strict approach to pulse, which was varied but not layered, and for its striking instrumental timbres: piercing baroque clarinets and amplified harp on one side of the stage, a percussion barrage on the other. In the final production, music motivated and structured the action: short three-note bursts, more economical even than those in *Tamburlaine*, framed the stichomythia, and pulse mobiles in the percussion literally galvanized the actors into verbal and physical response. Some of these principles were applied in 1977, but in general in the workshops Birtwistle was more concerned with forming complex, layered textures. He spoke to the actors of his desire for sounds that are in and out of focus, and many of the effects he worked on recall the opening of *Orpheus*. This is especially evident in his treatment of the Parodos, in which the chorus – the old men of Athens, who have been waiting ten years for news from the war in Argos – march on stage for the first time.

In 1981, this entrance was announced by a steady pulse and repetitions of an incisive, four-note motif, which becomes associated with the House of Atreus (Agamamnon's blood line which includes Orestes). In the score

---

[62] There are some similarities here to Birtwistle's approach later the same year when he prepared *Pulse Field* (1977) with the dance director Jaap Flier. Flier reported that Birtwistle 'felt that he must discover how dancers think before he could start writing the score', but this led to tensions because 'dancers are very intuitive, and think with their bodies, so . . . they resented being asked to do simple movements over and over so he could analyse the mechanics.' Cited in Hall, *HB*, 110–11.

Example 7.3 The 'Macro Pulse' in the *Oresteia* (transcribed aurally)

this idea is misleadingly referred to as the 'macropulse'; the basic form of this idea, which is often decorated, is shown in Example 7.3.[63] Yet in the workshops in 1977 Birtwistle had taken a very different approach to the entrance. He began his workshop on the Parodos by compiling a texture from three basic layers:

- a continuum produced by sustained humming sounds. The durations of exhalations were determined by each individual's physical capacities. Each exhalation was followed by a factual statement of the words 'ten years'.
- Six interjections of 'ten years' spoken at random. These triggered responses in the spoken text.
- The text, spoken above and across the humming continuum. Drum strokes and the six interjections of 'ten years' signalled when to begin sections of spoken text, or when to single out particular words or phrases that were declaimed in a stylised manner and repeated as refrains usually by individual chorus members but sometimes in unison.

Birtwistle's emphasis on breathing mirrored Artaud's own exercises with actors, and Artaud's belief that theatrical time 'is based upon breath'.[64] That Birtwistle was conscious he might reassert human presence in this way is suggested by his comment to the actors that 'your breathing is your tempo, and that's what makes you different from the others'. Moreover, Birtwistle's layering technique resonates with Artaud's remark that the secret of theatre in space 'is dissonance, dispersion of timbres, and the dialectic discontinuity of expression'.[65] Artaud's words epitomise the run-through of *Agamemnon* on the last day of the workshops, in which the embellishments had extended to overlapping speech and pulses, tapping, shouts, whistles, laughter and other randomly inserted noises, and a hierarchy whereby certain words and names shone out like beacons at times, but were mumbled or muttered at others.[66]

---

[63] For a detailed discussion of the music for the 1981 production see Beard, '"Batter the doom drum"'.

[64] Artaud, *The Theater*, 112.   [65] Ibid., 113.

[66] The final run-through also included soprano solos in a modal style reminiscent of Ophelia's songs in Birtwistle's *Hamlet*. In 1981, the sung sections in the *Oresteia* were limited to the few lyrical choruses and were sung by the entire chorus in unison.

In complete contrast to this slightly chaotic, spontaneous-sounding performance, the final production was characterised by a rigid clarity of purpose
and expression.[67]

As noted above, in the workshops Birtwistle was interested in stylised
delivery, and particular names or words were isolated and broken down
into their constituent syllables. The name Agamemnon, for example, was
divided into two forms ('Aga-mem-non' and 'Agam-em-non') that were
declaimed in hard, clear tones, but with inflection.[68] Various ways of presenting these versions were tested, including two groups speaking the two
forms simultaneously, and exaggeration of the gaps between syllables. In
some instances, Birtwistle dismissed the results, leading the actors to believe
they had done something wrong. Further tensions arose whenever the actors
reverted to conventional practice, since the idea was to discover new techniques. Several of the challenges would have required many rehearsals to
perfect, but it is above all apparent that Birtwistle strove for a situation in
which the actors would be absolutely alert to sound as a stimulus to action.
In one instance, different timbres were associated with words of symbolic
significance – a high woodblock with 'night', a medium woodblock with
'net', and a pan lid with 'Zeus'. These three sounds were played randomly,
and the actors were to respond immediately, in unison, with the correct
word and a forward step on each interjection. Birtwistle imagined that this
'vocabulary' could be introduced at any time, requiring actors to break away
from the main text. Harrison then commented that one of his goals was to
develop 'expectation and randomness', which he associated with the play's
development of a democratic society.

When, for the first time, the workshop passed to Muldowney, he introduced a method that could not have been more different from Birtwistle's.
Muldowney commented that he had prepared his exercise over the weekend
and that it was modelled on the call-and-response technique in African

---

[67] As Hall rightly argues, as well as pacing the action and timing the climaxes, the use of regular
pulsation in the 1981 production 'gave the affair a powerful sense of something primeval lying
beneath the surface of events, something only a phenomenon as elemental as pulse could
suggest'. Hall, *HB*, 105.

[68] Birtwistle was keen to avoid what he termed the 'Dalek' effect, in which inflection was lost. He
therefore demonstrated the effects he desired, often adeptly, for example when he wanted an
elongated vowel on 'blood'. His treatment of words as sound objects mirrors similar concerns
explored in avant-garde theatre. Clare Finburgh has argued that Paul Claudel and Artaud
prompted Jean-Louis Barrault, Antoine Votez, Ariane Mnouchkine, Peter Brook and other
theatre directors to explore what she refers to as 'the musicality of the human voice', or 'oral
sonority': 'The actor's voice is appreciated for its immediate concrete materiality, not just for
its ability to communicate semantic signification and teleological diegesis.' This, she argues,
led to forms of 'poetically acoustic theatre'. Clare Finburgh, '"Voix/voie/vie": the voice in
contemporary French theater', *Yale French Studies*, 112 (2007), 105–7.

song.[69] Against a constant pulse lasting eight beats, he requested two claps followed by 'ten years' (all on the beat), then two claps followed by 'ten years of waiting' spoken quickly and regularly, 'really machine-like' within the space of the remaining two beats. The result, which was applied to the remaining text, is instantly recognisable not only as the opening of the 1981 production but also as the template for the entire final production. Yet this idea did not become an important part of the workshops and was not used in the final run-through.

Rather, when Birtwistle resumed the workshop, he instructed Jonty Harrison to introduce a drum stroke 'instinctively' at the end of predetermined phrases as a form of full stop (for example: 'Mewing warcries' [drum] 'preybirds shrilling' [drum], and so on), which recalls the effect shown in Example 7.2. The actors had to pause briefly after each stroke before speaking the next line or phrase. Inevitably, the actors sped up. This led Birtwistle to comment: 'What we should get is a very strange pulse in the drums. It's very difficult . . . It produces a very interesting rhythm, very hesitant.' A blackboard was used to explain that although the lengths of the phrases varied, the actors should keep the gap between the drum and the start of the next phrase constant. This worked. The actors were then advised to make their speech 'bounce off the drum' and to vary the length of the gaps between drum and phrase. In this way, Birtwistle added, the actors might begin to feel that they were driving the pulse. This resonates entirely with Whittall's remark, in relation to Birtwistle's later, suggestively titled *Pulse Shadows* (1989–96), that 'If pulse (present, implied) is . . . an "objective standard", its shadow is altogether more personal, more human, more troubling.'[70]

Birtwistle has since expressed reservations about the adoption of regular pulsation in the 1981 production, arguing that 'it's not to do with pulse, it's to do with stress. The idea of the variable pulse; it's where the stress comes. You can put everything into a regular pulse, but that's not the point.'[71] Those aspects of the 'Agamemnon Experiments' that did not make it into the 1981 production, however, did lead directly to a new series of workshops and rehearsals later in 1977. These sessions, which ran for ten weeks with Birtwistle, Harrison and several of the same actors and musicians, resulted in *Bow Down*, an hour-long work of experimental music theatre, premiered in July 1977.

[69] It is unclear whether Muldowney consulted Birtwistle on this exercise beforehand, although the likelihood is that it was prepared independently.

[70] Arnold Whittall, 'The mechanisms of lament', 86.

[71] Birtwistle in conversation with Beard, 18 November 2008.

Bow Down

> [*Bow Down*] proposes a conception of performance that is about the
> exploration of the body's physical potential and constraints.[72]

Following Peter Brook's notion of the 'empty space', which was indebted
to Artaud and to Barrault's concept of the 'barren stage', *Bow Down* was
conceived and originally performed on an empty stage upon which the
performers created their own environment.[73] A chorus that comprises five
actors and four musicians is seated, facing the audience, in a semicircle
that defines the space in which the action will take place. This arrangement was influenced by knowledge that earlier versions of the ballad were
'danced as a chorus circle'.[74] It was also clearly indebted to Japanese Noh
theatre in which four musicians and the actors share the stage, their stylised
gestures integrated into a sparse, ceremonial drama. Another predecessor
is *Down by the Greenwood* Side, in which most of the action takes place
within a ceremonial circle, and which draws on a dark, ancient ballad (see
Chapter 1). Similarly, *Bow Down* is structured around a series of narrative
sequences of the Ballad of the Two Sisters, each based on a different North
British, American or Scandinavian version. This results in a series of varied repetitions that arguably serve to establish what is peripheral and what
is core to the narrative.[75] Two sibling princesses are visited at their castle
by a Suitor. The Suitor courts the elder Dark Sister, but falls in love with
the younger Fair Sister.[76] Jealous and spiteful, the Dark Sister pushes her
sibling into a river, in some versions into the sea, where she drowns. The
girl washes downstream to a mill where the Miller steals her jewels (literally
and metaphorically) then throws her back in the water to drown. Eventually, washed to shore, the Fair Sister's body is discovered by a Blind Harper
who fashions the bones into a harp frame and her hair into strings. When

---

[72] Adlington, *MHB*, 25.

[73] *Bow Down* was first performed at the Cottesloe Theatre, in London's National Theatre. The
programme also included René Clair's film *Entr'acte*, from the ballet *Relache* (1924), with
music by Satie, and Kagel's *Repertoire*, a mimed section from *Staatstheater* (1967–70). *Bow
Down* has enjoyed a number of touring productions, including a Big Bird production in
Bradford in 1982, repeated at Battersea Arts Centre in 1984, a performance directed by Peter
Gill, John Burgess and Graham Devlin at the Southbank Summerscope Festival in 1987, and a
Major Road Theatre Company production directed by Graham Devlin, which toured the UK
in November 1992 (with performances at the Huddersfield Contemporary Music Festival and
the Queen Elizabeth Hall, London), for which Birtwistle composed additional music.

[74] From an anonymous note in the programme booklet to the first performance, July 1977.

[75] Jeremy Kingston, 'Bow Down', *Financial Times*, 6 July 1977. Similarly, Birtwistle and Harrison
claim that they are concerned with 'essentially the "same" story'. Prefatory 'Note' in the
published score, dated 21 February 1980.

[76] Birtwistle's interest in dark/light, good/evil dualities here predates *Yan Tan Tethera*, but was
anticipated by an untitled piece of music theatre he composed for children in the mid 1960s.
See Chapter 1.

the harpist subsequently performs at the Dark Sister's wedding, the harp sings of the Fair Sister's fate. The Dark Sister is tortured into confession and buried alive; in some versions the Miller, too, is hung.

Tony Harrison's authorial presence becomes more noticeable as the work progresses and is particularly evident in a Chaucerian style of characterisation, for example when the Miller's Daughter implies that she has slept with nobility, or when the Miller's Servant expresses his lust for the Fair Sister: 'Though battered by the boisterous brine, / this lady's body is the most fine'. Here, the consonantal alliteration, rhyming couplet and metrical scheme (four stresses per line) clearly reflect Harrison's work on the *Oresteia*. More disturbing evidence of his presence is the depiction of necrophilia and genital mutilation in the Miller's scene, to which certain critics have taken particular exception.[77] There are possible echoes here of Brook's Artaud-inspired production of Peter Weiss's *Marat/Sade*, from 1964, in which a scene of disembowelment was introduced for shock effect. Leach suggests that Artaud's theatre 'undoubtedly plays out common fantasies of rape and murder'. However, his remark that Artaud's emphasis is always 'on the path *through* physicality to spirituality' also holds true for *Bow Down*,[78] which, in contrast to the emphatic *Oresteia*, has a slow, 'Kabuki-like intensity'.[79] During the Miller's scene, violence is enacted upon an imaginary body: the Fair Sister, representing the girl's ghost, stands beside the Miller, her soft sung refrains accompanied by gentle crotales. Ultimately, the Miller's scene functions as a moment of ritual sacrifice – an idea revisited in *The Io Passion*.

Despite its fragmented structure, *Bow Down* presents a linear narrative that comprises seven episodes, or dramatic sequences, ordered chronologically: these are labelled A to G in Table 7.1. However, a non-linear aspect is formed by the return of the first sequence, the depiction of the Fair Sister drowning (see sequences A, C and A^1 in Table 7.1). Through the work, Ballads and action scenes are presented either in succession or conjunction. However, whereas some Ballads outline the entire story, others focus on particular aspects of the narrative: these are labelled 'comp.' and 'part.', respectively, in Table 7.1. The 'partial' Ballads occur at appropriate moments and therefore contribute to the narrative development, although even the 'complete' Ballads reveal insights that add to the unfolding plot (this is indicated by text citations in Table 7.1). Another structuring device is the

---

[77] For example, Harold Atkins referred to the work's 'grisly and tasteless overtones' ('Bow Down', *Telegraph*, 6 July 1977), while William Mann described the Miller's scene as 'comic but stylistically excrescent' ('Bow Down', *The Times*, 6 July 1977). See also Janet Wolff, *Resident Alien: Feminist Cultural Criticism* (Cambridge: Polity Press, 1995), which refers to *Bow Down*'s 'horrendous fantasies of male violence', 32.

[78] Leach, *Makers of Modern Theatre*, 170.

[79] Bayan Northcott, 'Out of the concert hall', *Sunday Telegraph*, 17 July 1977.

Table 7.1 *The formal and dramatic themes of* Bow Down

Thematic sequences	Mimed action	Breathing, pulse, speech and chant	Ballad	Song & instrumental mobiles	Spoken drama with dialogue
A	Fair Sister drowns	'O sister'			
	Blind Harper journeys along the coast (inside choral circle) Sisters: the rack & cat's cradle		1. part. (whole & in fragments) Blind Harper (Danish)	Sisters: 'I'll be true to my true love / If my love will be true to me'	
B	Suitor rides horse (outside circle)		2. part. 'There were two sisters in a bower . . . There came a Knight to be their wooer'	Sisters: 'I'll be true to my true love . . .' / Percussion mobiles	
	Sisters & Suitor dance		3. part. 'He courted the eldest with glove and ring . . .'	Wind & percussion mobiles	
		Chorus refrain: 'Bow down, bow down, bow down'	4. comp. '. . . The miller he took the gay gold chain, / And pushed her in the water again . . .'		
C	Blind Harper journeys; Sisters play in the bower	'bow down'	1.	Sisters: 'I'll be true to my true love . . .'; 'Down by the waters rolling'	
		Chorus refrain: 'With a hie downe, downe-a downe-a'	5. part. * '. . . O sister, sister, come play by the sea . . .'	'Wash your hair in the salt-sea brine, / It will never be as fair as mine'; oboes: sustained semitone dyads	*

Table 7.1 (*cont.*)

Thematic sequences	Mimed action	Breathing, pulse, speech and chant	Ballad	Song & instrumental mobiles	Spoken drama with dialogue
		Chorus refrain: 'With a hie down . . .'	6. comp. '. . . And when they came unto the sea-brym, / The elder did push the younger in . . .'		
A¹	Blind Harper journeys Fair Sister drowns	'O sister'	1.	Fair Sister: Drowning Song 'I'll be true to . . .'/ flute mobile	
D				Oboes: sustained perfect 5th dyads 'Prove true, my love, prove true to me'; 'Down by the waters rolling'; 'I'll be true to my true love'; 'Sing I die, sing I day'; 'I'll be true . . .'	Miller's daughter Miller & his Servant
E	Blind Harper ×3 journeys Blind Harper turns Fair Sister into harp		1.	Bamboo flute improvisation Chorus: sustained notes/pulse on bamboo pipes	
		Chorus refrain: 'Binnorie, o Binnorie' & 'By the bonnie mill-dams o'Binnorie'	7. comp. '. . . My luve, my dear, how can ye sleip, / Whan your Isabel lyes in the deip! . . .'		

(cont.)

Table 7.1 (*cont.*)

Thematic sequences	Mimed action	Breathing, pulse, speech and chant	Ballad	Song & instrumental mobiles	Spoken drama with dialogue
F	Dark Sister's wedding in the King's Court			Bodhrans & oboes: sustained dyads & duets (parallel 4ths and 5ths)	
				Harp's Song (O true love...') echoed by Suitor, King and Chorus	
	Dark Sister on the rack		8. part. (2 lines) 'There were two sisters in a bower / There came a knight to be their wooer'	bodhrans & oboes (perfect 4th dyads) Dark Sister: 'Sing I die...' / percussion mobiles	
			9. comp. '... My sister Jane, she tumbled me in'	Dark Sister: [b]o[w] [d]ow[n]	
G	Dark Sister buried alive Sisters embrace	Chorus: [b]o[w] [d]ow[n]		Dark Sister's Song	
	Blind Harper ×3 stamp on grave; Fair Sister walks the circle	'Drag her down to where I drowned...'			Dark Sister pleads for her life
	Sisters come face to face				Dark Sister: '... My sister's hand out of the sea...'

Example 7.4 The refrain in Ballad 4, *Bow Down* (performing score, UE 16180),
p. 6

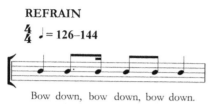

REFRAIN

Bow down, bow down, bow down.

recurrence of the Blind Harper who mimes a journey along the coast. In
language that echoes Zinovieff's libretto for *Orpheus*, Harrison writes:

> He is walking the sea-shore. He seems to have one foot in the water and one
> foot on the sand. As he feels the water deepen he evades it with a dexterity
> which has come from centuries of doing the same thing. His wavering 'dance'
> follows the ebb and flow of the tides. He has been following the Northern
> coasts, searching, listening.[80]

In sequences A, C and A[1] the Blind Harper is represented by an actor who
walks clockwise along the inside of the chorus circle. However, in sequences
E and G, he is depicted in triplicate. In E, each actor presents a different stage
of the Harper's journey: one walks around the outside of the circle, another
along the inside, and the third circles the body of the drowned sister, then
fashions her body into a harp. In sequence G, the three Harpers stamp upon
the Dark Sister's grave.

The work's title appears to be derived from Ballad 4 in which 'Bow
down, bow down, bow down' forms a refrain (see Example 7.4). Harrison
would certainly have been attracted by the refrain's consonantal and vocalic
alliteration, and its chant-like quality, which would have also appealed to
Artaud.[81] 'Bow down' also generates the image of a particular physical
movement associated with social ritual: the Suitor bowing to the princess
sisters, perhaps? Harrison may even have been drawn to this verbal/gestural
topic as a marker of social hierarchy, which is inverted when the Fair Sister's
dead body ('this grand lady') is violated by the Miller and his 'lackey' in
sequence D. It is a doubly ironic title, moreover, since the Fair Sister herself
ultimately 'bows down' to the bottom of the sea, and a modified form

---

[80] From the published performing score: Harrison Birtwistle, *Bow Down* (London: Universal
Editon, 1983), UE 16180, 2; also reproduced in Harrison, *Theatre Works*, 127. There is only
one side of sketch for this work in the Paul Sacher Stiftung.
[81] In Artaud's theatre, 'words will be construed in an incantational, truly magical sense – for their
shape and their sensuous emanations, not only for their meaning'; Artaud, *The Theater*, 125.

of bowing assumes importance in the drowning sister's forward rolls that initiate sequences A, C and A¹.

It has been suggested that the actors in *Bow Down* 'are just as much musicians as the musicians are actors', and that there is only 'a relatively slight difference in emphasis' between the two.[82] It is worth exploring this further, for the roles are in fact distinct – although there is a more general point here to which I will return. The actors (numbered 2, 3, 5, 7, 8) and musicians (1, 4, 6, 9) are arranged symmetrically on the stage. Each performs from a selection of fourteen instruments; the musicians play between six and nine instruments each, the actors between two and five (including end-blown bamboo pipe and penny whistle). The transverse bamboo flute, oboes, woodblocks, afuches,[83] crotales, Chinese drum and bodhran are exclusive to the musicians. No instruments are exclusive to the actors, but all nine players have a set of claves and a set of sand blocks.[84] The actors are responsible for all actions and sometimes exchange places, whereas the musicians do not leave their seated positions. Actors 3 and 7 normally assume the roles of the Fair and Dark Sister respectively, and 8 the Blind Harper, whereas the musicians, besides their chants and song, are only once given the opportunity to speak: during Ballad 4, lines are distributed evenly throughout the chorus.[85]

Birtwistle's rhythmic and melodic writing is relatively simple, even for the musicians who could, conceivably, have been given more complex music. The music anticipates devices used in the 1981 *Oresteia* production: regularly varied instrumental mobiles (short musical units based on internal repetition) that underpin speech and song; the punctuation of recitation with irregular percussion beats; cadential punctuation marks at the ends of lines (for example sustained dyads during the fifth Ballad when the Fair Sister is pushed into the sea); basic 2:1 rhythmic patterns combined into composite patterns; cellular, modal-sounding melodic lines; additive processes; the emergence of solo voices from the chorus. Hall cites Birtwistle's claim that 'Everything stems from a simple pulse and three basic intervals.'[86] However, there are only two interval types in sequence A (minor thirds and whole tones), and numerous intervals from sequence B onwards. The notation in the score, which was reconstructed by Jonty Harrison after the performance, is adapted to suit the unusual nature of the piece: where there are

---

[82] Adlington, 'Music theatre', 238.

[83] An afuche is a type of cabaca that consists of metal beads strung around a hand-held shaker, or rattle.

[84] The table at the front of the score incorrectly records that eight players have sand blocks.

[85] The numbers used here in relation to actors and musicians are drawn from the published score, which differs from the published libretto (Harrison, *Theatre Works*, 125–48).

[86] Hall, *HB*, 111.

no bar lines, 'up' and 'down' beats are marked with vertical arrows; simple whole-tone movements are represented on a single line; pitched notation is primarily used for pairs of instruments or voices, mostly in parallel motion, instrumental mobiles, and monodic vocal lines.

Most of the singing is performed by actors 3 and 7. Nevertheless, the musicians are given more complex music to play and a distinction is therefore retained between the actors and musicians. What is called into question, however, is the distinction between 'music' and 'action'. Adlington observes that *Bow Down* 'posits a wider, inclusive category that emphasises the common basis of all acts of performance in the human body'.[87] One might also say that, at times, music itself becomes a kind of 'act' – that is, music performs the same function as the actors' physical movements and is equivalent to their gestures.[88] There is no clearer illustration of this than the role assigned to individual breath cycles as a means to structure the drama. The score introduces the notion of 'a choral pulse based on breathing', initiated by a drum stroke, which relates back to the *Agamemnon* workshops. As the unpublished prompt script, or 'bible' as it is known at the National Theatre, records, 'each end of breath is marked by a rub on the sand blocks': an 'event' may be considered completed only when the last person has signalled the end of their breath cycle with a tap of the sand blocks.

As mentioned above, sequences A, C and A^1 begin with a representation of the Fair Sister breaking the water's surface to gasp for breath. A note on the bodhran directs the chorus to begin its intake of breath. A second beat signals that the chorus should begin to exhale – musicians 4 and 6 to the unvoiced phoneme 'S', from 'sister', the others normally – and that actor 3 should 'unravel and move upward'.[89] Each performer arrives independently at a 'peak' in their exhalation, presumably a moment shortly before they run out of breath. At which point the chorus shifts to the unvoiced phoneme 'a', as in 'father', while actor 3 breaks the water's surface, utters 'o', as in 'boat', then sinks. This sequence is repeated three more times, with the only difference that actor 3's statements are varied fragments of the phrase 'O sister'. What is important here is that the moment of 'peak' exhalation will be different for each performer, therefore a random pattern of changes in phoneme will occur within a relatively fixed window of time. This is more audible in sequence A^1, where the chorus chant 'sister' when their exhalations end. The

---

[87] Adlington, *MHB*, 25.
[88] Although, as Adlington notes, this highlights 'the constraints of the distinct categories – music, speech, dance and so on – that we traditionally impose upon acts of performance.' Ibid.
[89] An unvoiced sound is achieved when a vocal sound is emitted without vibration in the throat. In the score, speech is voiced, half-voiced or unvoiced. As in *Orpheus*, phonetic sounds are drawn from words in the libretto.

effect, which recalls Birtwistle's use of random numbers, produces varied repetition within a prescribed field.

Such passages clearly represent a culmination of Birtwistle's desire to 'examine, and explain, the relationship between music, movement and the spoken word'. Within the context of his oeuvre, *Bow Down* is perhaps Birtwistle's most unusual work, especially from the perspective that the performers' bodies and movements are central. Each sequence is initiated when one or more players stand and move along the inside or outside of the choral circle, eventually returning to their starting point. Sometimes the actors are requested to 'roam the circle freely', elsewhere the choreographed movements coincide with the start or completion of a musical process. In sequence A, for example, actor 8 walks round the inside of the semicircle. As that actor reaches each performer they, in turn, move either from breath to song, or from one musical mobile to another. Moreover, the use of masks encourages the actors to make more use of their entire bodies, since they cannot rely on facial expressions. Masks also permit the actors to freely exchange roles. At the end of the fifth Ballad, for example, the Dark Sister tears the mask from the Fair Sister to reveal the male actor beneath, who then narrates the sixth Ballad.[90]

Mime is especially important. One particular mimetic act, referred to in the bible as 'the rack', is used to frame the work. In sequence A, the Dark Sister moves behind the Fair Sister and places her arms around the latter's arms and waist; the Fair Sister tries to lift her arms but is restrained. This is seen again in sequence G when the King and Suitor take hold of the Dark Sister, moving forward with each drumbeat played between words in the text. The irregular pulse and movement that result are clearly derived from the '*Agamemnon* Experiments'. Yet the most arresting moment in the work, which embodies its central concerns, occurs in sequence E. It is described in the bible as follows:

Harper Makes Harp

Fred [Warder] as the blind harper makes a harp out of morag, first bends her arms[,] elbows out hands by sides. Lifts knees up one at a time leaving her feet on the floor, puts her knees on the floor sliding feet out to the side. Moves behind her[,] lifts her onto her knees from behind, brings her feet in behind her, turns the body facing stage right, brings her arms down to place them on her ankles. Removes the harp mask from the bucket[,] put[s] it on her, bring[s] the head forward. He kneels behind her[,] lifts[,] moves down stage

---

90   Harrison's libretto refers to actors taking up the 'narrative position' at such moments, from which they 'address different sections of the audience', but there is no such direction in the score, which simply states that the Ballads are addressed to the audience. See Harrison, *Theatre Works*, 129.

holding her as high as possible[,] places her down center stage[,] slowly
strokes the body from the knees[. W]hen he gets to the head REMOVES <u>THE</u>
<u>MASK</u>.[91]

Here the central idea of the performing body is revealed as integral to the Ballad itself. Moreover, this moment is suggestive of the kind of naïve, 'concrete'
image Artaud had in mind when he stated his intention that 'movements,
poses, bodies of characters will form or dissolve like hieroglyphs'.[92] According to one critic at the original production, the resultant image 'existed as
a strange, true transformation' that drew him in to what had otherwise
seemed a private ritual.[93] This recalls Meyerhold's concept of the 'raccoursi'
or 'silhouette', a brief pause in the action in which 'the actor halts and
we, the audience, note the gesture, the bodily posture, the stage grouping,
before us; for an instant we receive an overall picture, which is yet charged
with the dynamic of the scene, and our understanding is illuminated'.[94] Yet
this moment is also symbolic because a genuine sense of equality is struck
between the remaining actors and the musicians who together play very
soft sustained notes on bamboo pipes. These give way to a slow, *mezzo forte*
pulse, which doubles when the harp is completed, followed by very loud
overblown notes to a slow pulse as the harp is lifted.

1982–2002

Peter Hall's production of the *Oresteia*, performed at the National Theatre
in 1981–2, and subsequently in Greece, at Epidaurus, achieved something
of a cult status. This owed much to its use of masks, stylised choreography, and Harrison's distinctive version of the original Greek text. However,
while these aspects often divided opinion among critics, Birtwistle's music
received more general approval and it was widely understood that, rather
than being a detachable adornment, the music became 'an inseparable part
of the event'.[95] The *Oresteia* marked a watershed for Birtwistle in terms of
his association with the National and his profile in general. With the performances of *Secret Theatre*, *Orpheus* and *Earth Dances* later that decade
his reputation was secured. Birtwistle's musical style, however, shifted during the 1980s towards an interest in continuity, melody and structural

---

[91] *Bow Down* bible, 10, NTA.
[92] Artaud in a letter to André Gide, cited in Claude Schumacher and Brian Singleton, eds., *Artaud
on Theatre* (London: Methuen, 2001), 78.
[93] Jeremy Kingston, 'Bow Down'. William Mann, in his review for *The Times*, was also moved to
remark that the harp scene was 'grandly and movingly staged'.
[94] Leach, *Makers of Modern Theatre*, 75.
[95] Michael Billington, 'Masks that obscure a tragedy', *Guardian*, 30 November 1981.

clarity – the latter more indebted to the 1981 production of the *Oresteia* than to the '*Agamemnon* Workshops'. Further shifts in style emerged in the 1990s. With *Gawain*, as seen in Chapter 5, Wagner's influence surfaced in terms of narrative and linear unfolding. Yet in *Pulse Shadows* (1989–1996) and *Mrs Kong* (discussed in Chapter 6), Birtwistle explored the idea that music 'gives you time for reflection' and 'can illuminate the image'.[96]

These comments were made when Birtwistle was working on *The Bacchai*, directed by Hall at the National in 2002. Having prepared more conventional incidental music for Shakespeare productions directed by Hall in 1984 and 1988,[97] Birtwistle was presented, in *The Bacchai*, with an opportunity to return to Greek theatre from a new perspective. Euripides' play offered many opportunities to illustrate the text, with its earthquake scene, exotic colour and Dionysian abandon. A wider array of instruments was employed than in the *Oresteia* and the focus was on differentiating the four main chorus sections. Birtwistle matched his music to the mood of each scene and provided the choruses with danceable rhythms that fitted the need for a more lively choreography than was required in the *Oresteia*.[98] In other words, Birtwistle's music made greater concessions to the demands of the drama, and was less concerned with governing the action than that in the *Oresteia*.[99] The music's vigour and dynamism instead reflected the visceral worlds of *Earth Dances* and *Panic* (1995) and paved the way for *The Minotaur* (2005–7), discussed in Chapter 8. However, from 2000 to 2004, Birtwistle developed a scenario that had occurred to him for a chamber opera in which many of his preoccupations from the 1970s would be viewed in fresh light. This new project, *The Io Passion*, developed from workshops held in the National Theatre Studio.[100]

Three week-long workshops were held between December 2000 and February 2003. The first was attended by the composer, six actors, the librettist Stephen Plaice, the director Stephen Langridge and the designer Alison Chitty. In the second workshop, held in November 2001, two of the actors were replaced by singers (one male, one female). Birtwistle did not begin composing until Spring 2003 and did not introduce the actors

---

[96] Birtwistle cited in Jonathan Croall, *Peter Hall's Bacchai* (London: National Theatre, 2002), 31.

[97] These were *Coriolanus* (1984) and the 'late' plays *Cymbeline*, *The Tempest*, and *The Winter's Tale* (1988).

[98] However, Birtwistle's dance music for the Furies in the *Oresteia* provided a model for *The Bacchai*.

[99] For more on the music for *The Bacchai* see Beard, '"Batter the doom drum"', 395–6, and Croall, *Peter Hall's Bacchai*.

[100] *The Io Passion* was commissioned by Almeida Opera and the Bregenzer Festspiele. It was first performed at the Aldeburgh Festival on 11 June 2004, then subsequently in London, Bregenz and various UK venues in July and November 2004. New productions have since been staged in Berlin and Vienna.

or musicians to his score until the first music rehearsal in April 2004, just two months before the premiere in June that year. Prior to this, the singers had been involved in learning complicated movement sequences. Plaice began writing his libretto during the first workshop. He corresponded with Birtwistle between the workshops but was asked for many additions when composing began, which led to fourteen revisions. Plaice, who had been recommended by Langridge, was already an established playwright and librettist who had run his own theatre groups since the 1980s and written libretti for projects commissioned by Glyndebourne. Yet, still to this day, the process that led to *The Io Passion* is 'by far the most radical' he has experienced.[101]

The Io Passion

> what is distinctive about ritual is not what it says or symbolizes, but that first and foremost it *does things*: ritual is always a matter of 'the performance of gestures and the manipulation of objects'.[102]

> I don't want to write any more theatre pieces where somebody gives me a text and I just fill out the narrative, like film music.[103]

What immediately distinguishes *The Io Passion* from Birtwistle's other stage works is its origin as a non-verbal conception that was developed from a workshop with no musicians. To begin from a visual scenario rather than a script and to extrapolate from that scenario in workshops was an approach strongly advocated by Artaud. Yet this raises the question of the music's relationship to the action. The drama evolved from Birtwistle's conception of the set, rather than from a pre-existing narrative or libretto. The purpose of the workshops was to develop a series of actions equivalent to a silent film, although this idea grew from Birtwistle's interest in the dumb show in *Hamlet* (Act III scene 2: 'Enter a King and Queen, very lovingly').[104] Music was then 'fitted' to the drama after it had been finalised in the workshops. If taken at his word, Birtwistle sought an alternative kind of relationship between music and drama, the precise nature of which will be explored in this discussion.

---

[101] Stephen Plaice in conversation with Beard, 13 September 2011.

[102] Bell, *Ritual Theory*, 111; the quotation at the end is from Claude Lévi-Strauss, *The Naked Man: Introduction to a Science of Mythology*, vol. IV, trans. John Weightman and Doreen Weightman (New York: Harper and Row, 1981), 671.

[103] Birtwistle in interview with John Woolrich cited in Andrew Clements, 'Strange fits of passion', *Opera*, 55/8 (2004), 908–10.

[104] This famous mime scene prompts Ophelia's response, 'Belike this show imports the argument of the play'. *The Alexander Text of the Complete Works of William Shakespeare*, ed. Peter Alexander (London and Glasgow: Collins, 1987), 1,050.

Figure 7.1 *The Io Passion*: final stage layout

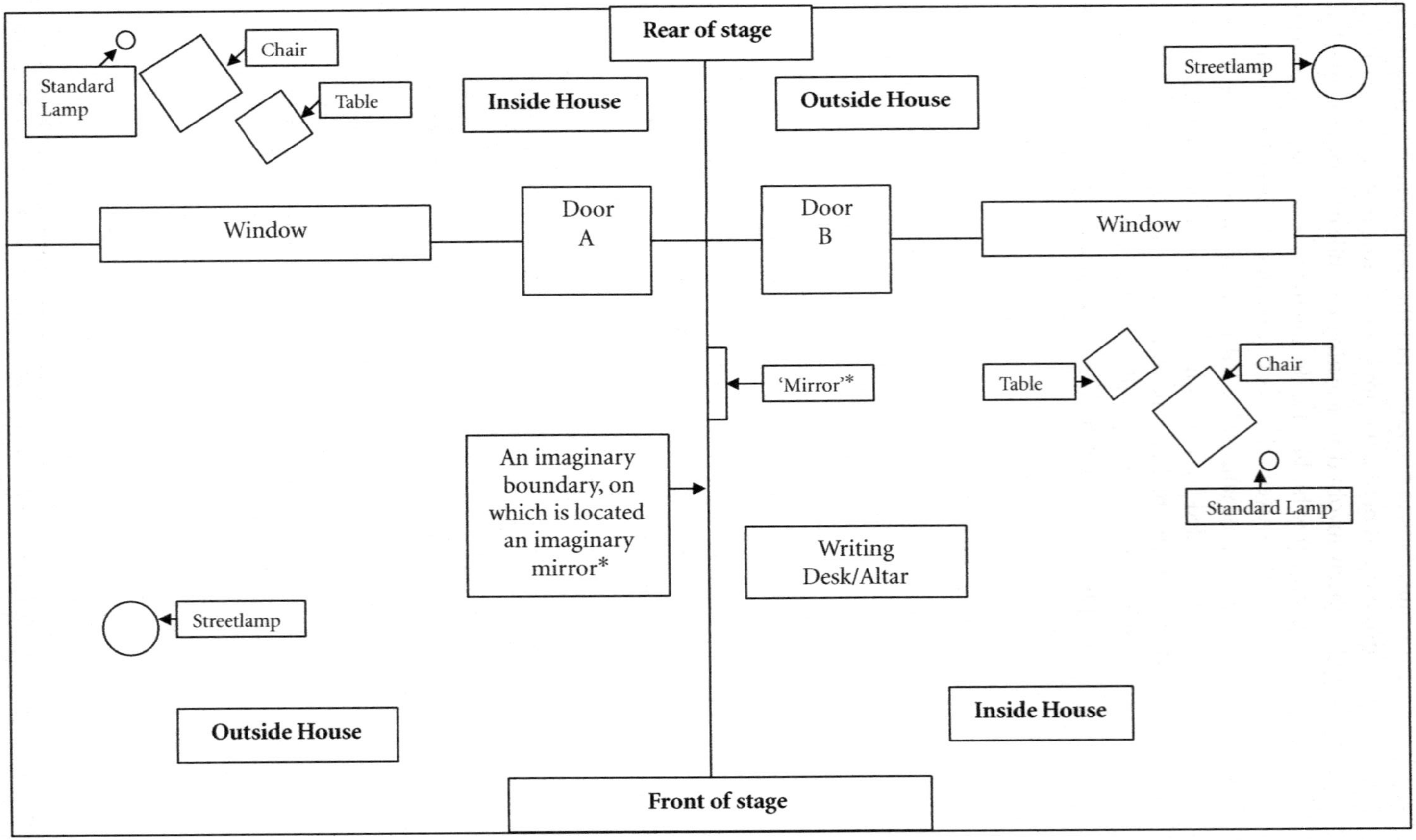

Rear of stage

Inside House

Outside House

Streetlamp

Standard Lamp

Chair

Table

Window

Door A

Door B

Window

'Mirror'*

Chair

Table

Standard Lamp

An imaginary boundary, on which is located an imaginary mirror*

Writing Desk/Altar

Streetlamp

Outside House

Inside House

Front of stage

According to Plaice, Birtwistle's initial idea, drawn on the back of a napkin in a café, was a stage divided into four compartments:

- stage left: the inside and outside of a house
- stage right: the outside and inside of the same house.

The final layout is given in Figure 7.1. The principle here is that actions performed on one side of the stage are mirrored diagonally in the other. From this idea Birtwistle developed the scenario of a woman alone inside the house and a man waiting outside in the street. They are estranged lovers, separated since a mysterious incident that occurred while they holidayed in Greece. The man seeks reconciliation; the woman does not. Birtwistle decided that communication would be possible only by letter or through their dreams; Plaice therefore began with the letters and some of the verse sections. By the third workshop it was decided that each character would be represented on stage by two singers and an actor (there are therefore six performers in total: two baritones, two sopranos, a male and a female actor). The woman is seen at her daily routines but is disturbed by the arrival of a letter posted by the man. As the letter is posted from the street through door A, stage left, we see it emerge through door B, stage right. The letter balances, then falls onto the mat. This forms the nucleus of a sequence of sixteen actions performed by Woman 1 (actor) and Man 1 (baritone).[105]

Initially the sequence is mimed in silence on a darkened stage. It is then repeated in an 'antefit' followed by seven 'fits', each accompanied by the work's ensemble of basset clarinet and string quartet, and each punctuated by a version of the Woman's dream.[106] The word 'fit' is appropriate in this context: derived from the Old English *fitt*, an archaic term for the section of a poem (such as the four Fitts of *Sir Gawain and the Green Knight*), in modern usage the word may describe someone who is ready to act, but also the sudden occurrence of a physical activity or emotional mood. The sixteen actions in each sequence are as follows.

(1) The streetlamp goes off – the stage is lit instead by the moon whose various stages mark the passing of time throughout the drama; (2) the man enters and waits under the streetlamp, his eyes on the window; (3) the woman enters from inside the house, walks to the window and opens the blind; (4) she checks herself in the mirror, flicks away a hair, or imaginary

---

[105] Harsent had previously suggested the idea of presenting two sides of the same door in an early version of his libretto for *Gawain*: the two doors would be symbolic of the outside and inside worlds so central to that opera.

[106] Plaice comments that 'We may be seeing the events of the same day repeated seven times, or it may be that the events are repeating themselves a day, a week, a month later.' Stephen Plaice, 'The Io Passion', *Aldeburgh Soundings: The Newsletter of the Friends of the Aldeburgh Foundation* (Spring 2004), 4.

fly, and exits; (5) the man walks to the window, peers inside; the woman
re-enters the room and the man retreats back to the streetlamp; (6) the
woman, who entered in the previous action, carries a tea tray, then sits in
an armchair, pours and drinks a cup of tea; (7) she clears the table and
exits with the tray; (8) the man exits; (9) the streetlamp comes on; (10) the
woman re-enters the room, switches on the lamp, draws down the blind
and takes a book to a chair; she begins to read and gradually falls asleep;
(11) she sits bolt upright, then slumps back; again she sits upright in her
sleep and brushes away a fly; (12) the man re-enters and crosses to the door
where he delivers a letter then leaves; (13) the letter lands on the mat and
wakes the woman; after reading more of her book, the woman picks up,
opens and reads the letter; (14) the woman angrily stuffs the letter back
in its envelope, opens a drawer, takes out a pen and paper, and begins to
write; (15) she finishes writing, places the letter in an envelope, looks in the
mirror and applies lipstick, brushes away a hair, or an imaginary fly, puts on
a scarf, switches off the lamp and leaves; (16) the man re-enters, waits under
the streetlamp, walks towards the door, is about to knock but hesitates and
returns to wait under the streetlamp.

The events are set in the early decades of the twentieth century: the libretto
refers to the exterior of an 'early twentieth-century house' and a 'Magritte
style streetlamp'. Birtwistle compared the psychological restraint of inter-
actions between the Man and Woman to the psychodramas of Strindberg
and Janáček,[107] and Langridge, the director, spoke of his desire to capture
the refined Edwardian world of the painter Gwen John (1876–1939), many
of whose works feature a seated woman holding or reading a book.[108] It
also seems relevant that the period in which *Io*'s action sequences are set
witnessed a resurgence of interest in pantomime, illustrated by Max Rein-
hardt's *The Miracle* (1911) and works by Frank Wedekind, Hugo von Hofmannsthal and Wassily Kandinsky. Moreover, in 1910, the Viennese dancer
Grete Wiesenthal referred to a 'new pantomime' that would communicate
through 'the large mass movements of the individual figures – their lying
or sitting, standing or walking – [as] narrated by the action'.[109]

When the woman in *Io* takes up her book she reads about the myth of
Io. Sent out on the slopes of Lerna to pasture her father Inachus's sheep,
Io is raped by Zeus, who had disguised himself as one of her flock. Zeus's
wife Hera is suspicious and comes to investigate. Zeus turns Io into a white

107 Clements, 'Strange fits', 909.
108 From an interview featured in a video recording of the original production held by Boosey &
      Hawkes.
109 Grete Wiesenthal, 'Tanz und Pantomime', *Hofmannsthal Blätter*, 34 (1986), 37; cited in Segel,
      Modernism, 37.

heifer (hence references to her in some sources as the White Goddess), which he then gifts to Hera. Still suspicious, Hera sends a Gadfly to torment Io with its constant stings. Having settled on this myth, Plaice explains that the workshops became concerned with the question: 'How did the ancient myth fit together with the modern image of the two estranged lovers?'

> The myth is at first an unseen, essential structure, like a muscle controlling a limb, but it eventually bursts up through the routine surface and presents itself in its raw power, emerging and submerging as the lovers struggle to contain their feelings about their failed relationship. The interplay between the cyclical surface gestures of the lovers and the latent force of the original myth, between the modern and the ancient aspects of the drama, created a third possibility – a heightened emotional exchange that had to be sung. So the piece found a starting-point for opera in the dynamic tension between ritual and veristic drama. Delving deeper into the myth, it was then discovered that there had been Mysteries at Lerna, religious rites, the content of which have not come down to us. Had we, in the myth-sections of the workshops, inadvertently rediscovered the essence of these rites around the figure of Io, and her initiation into sex and divine punishment? By extension, had we exposed the roots of the modern couple's sexual psychodynamics in ancient ritualistic worship? The relationship between the myth and the image suddenly appeared transparent.[110]

At a general level, the work has an over-arching sense of transition from mime through speech to song. Moreover, various musical and mimetic sections are interpolated into the action scheme, including two confrontations between the Man and Woman, three representations of the Myth of Io, four Aubades, five Ariettas, and seven Nocturnes. This is summarised in Table 7.2. The masked mythical characters – the messenger Hermes, Io, Inachus, Zeus, Hera and the Gadfly – are introduced in fit III, titled 'Mysteries'. Although their first and third enactments involve mime with speech and song, the second, in fit IV, is pure mime. During the myth enactments, the writing desk becomes a sacrificial altar on which Zeus's sexual conquest of Io is enacted. Actions 1–9 are omitted from fits IV and V; however, fit VI, titled 'Opera', is the longest sequence owing to the extended third representation of the myth. The work's climax occurs in the second Man/Woman confrontation near the end of fit VII, titled 'Sacrifice', which is combined with a variant of the third Io myth. In this scene the Man and Woman cross the invisible border that separates the inside from the outside of the house and they come to physical blows, although the action still belongs to

---

[110] Plaice, 'The Io Passion', 4. Following Birtwistle's interest in Robert Graves, Plaice's principal source texts were Graves's *The Greek Myths* and *The White Goddess*.

Table 7.2 *Formal layout of* The Io Passion

[untitled]	Actions 1 to 16: unaccompanied & in shadow				
Antefit: Before (*black moon*)	1 to 16: quintet				
Fit I: The House (*new moon*)	1 to 8: quintet	Nocturne 1: quintet	9 to 16: quintet		
Fit II: Letters (*half moon*)	Aubade 1; 1 to 3: quintet	Arietta 1: Woman 2 (song), cl. & vc.	4 to 9: quintet	Nocturne 2: quintet; repeated Gs in cl.	10 to 16: quintet, Woman 1 (speech) & Man 3 (*Sprechgesang*)
Fit III: Mysteries (*half moon*)	[Aubade 2?]; 1 to 9: quintet & Man 1 (*parlando*)	Nocturne 3: quintet	Arietta 2; 10: Woman 2 (song)	Myth of Io 1; 10 to 12: quintet, Woman 1, Hermes/Man 3 & Inachus (speech), Io (song), & Zeus, Gadfly & Hera (mime)	13 to 16: quintet
Fit IV: Rough Night (*full moon*)	1 to 9 omitted		Nocturne 4; from 10: quintet & Man 1 (song)	Myth of Io 2; 10 to 12: all characters (mime); frenetic action & music	13 to 16: quintet & Woman 3 (song fragments)

Fit					
Fit V: Quartet [*three-quarters moon waning?*]	(as above)	Nocturne 5 (as above)		13 to 16: quintet, Woman 3 & Man 3 (offstage pre-recorded speech)		12 to 16: quintet, Man 3 & Woman 3 (offstage speech)
Fit VI: Opera [*three-quarters moon waxing*]	Aubade 3; 1 to 8: quintet plus Woman 1, Man 1, Hera at window instead of Woman 2, & Zeus delivers letter (all mime)	Nocturne 6: quintet (Hera at window jerks her head); followed by 9	Arietta 3; 10: string quartet & Hera (song) with melodramatic gestures	Myth of Io 3; 10: quintet, Inachus, Io, Zeus, Hera (song, half-song, and speech)	Arietta 4 'quasi alla danza'; 10 cont. and 11: quintet & Hera (song)	Myth of Io 3 (cont.); during 11: quintet, Io & Gadfly (song; extends to very high register)
Fit VII: Sacrifice (*quarter moon waning*)	Aubade 4; 1 to 3: quintet	Arietta 5: string quartet & Woman 2 (song)	4 to 9: quintet	Nocturne 7; 10: quintet	Man/Woman confrontation 2; variants of 5, 4, 15, 14 & a variant of Myth of Io 3 with role reversal: Man 1, Woman 2, & Hera (song)	12 to 16 modified: quintet & Woman 3 (Arietta-style song)

the woman's dream. At the end of the work, the roles are reversed and the man is pushed by the woman onto the altar and symbolically murdered. One is reminded here of Artaud's statement that his new theatre 'will cause not only the recto but the verso of the mind to play its part; the reality of imagination and dreams will appear there on equal footing with life'.[111]

Io clearly returns to the kinds of dualities previously explored in *Gawain*. However, whereas in *Gawain* the opposition between naturalism and artifice was largely the unintended consequence of an interest in Wagner, in *Io* the opposition between real and mythical worlds, or between veristic and ritualistic theatre, is the intended subject of the work. The other important opposition is the duality of 'Inside' and 'Outside', hence 'Io'. While this applies in the most literal sense to the inner and outer perspectives of the house, it is modified in the title by the word 'Passion'.[112] Derived from the Greek verb *pascho*, to suffer, 'passion' has a dual nature: on the one hand, intense suffering, on the other, intense possibly sexual pleasure. Bach's Passions are also alluded to by the lyrical Ariettas, and in the second of these the cello is instructed to play 'sul tasto (viol-like)', which recalls the baroque parody in *Punch*.

From the modifier 'Passion' it is possible to infer that *Io*'s inner–outer dichotomy relates to an individual's actions and emotions – that is, the 'thought–action dichotomy' at the core of ritual theory, or what Plaice terms 'the relationship between the myth and the image'.[113] Clearly, whereas actions are visible, thoughts (generally speaking) are not, yet both are grounded in the body. Extrapolating from this point, the musicologist David Lidov has introduced the terms *exosomatic* and *endosomatic*:

> The endosomatic world is one we feel; the exosomatic world, one we see. The exosomatic realm, preeminently visual, is stabilized and articulated by the physiology of gestalt perception. Its objects commute without apparent distortion; that is, we can move ourselves and many other things around in it without altering them. The endosomatic realm is largely unarticulated. To be sure, it has its distinctive entities just as the other space has its fogs and clouds. Hunger is as definite a thing as a tea cup. But as a general rule the conditions of the body shade into each other and affect each other, and there is only [a] little room to maneuver when it comes to reordering them. The

---

[111] Artaud, *The Theater*, 123. An obvious representation of Artaud's concept occurs in fit II: as the woman writes her letter to the man she reads its measured content, but her double, who stands behind her, sings her real, more hostile thoughts.

[112] The title's allusion to Christ's Passion may well be a consequence of, or reaction to, Birtwistle's *The Last Supper*, composed a few years earlier; this work is discussed in Chapter 8. However, *Io* explores the topic of suffering in different ways: physical action is not central to *The Last Supper*, and there is no explicit Christian theme in *Io*.

[113] In the video interview, Langridge speaks of people in the Edwardian world trying to hold on to a certain mode of behaviour in contrast to their real emotions.

> endosomatic space is chiefly a realm of flux and influence. Its chief contents are changing states rather than fixed objects.[114]

Lidov argues that exosomatic entities – that is, visible objects – are primarily represented 'by the replication of their appearances'. However, an endosomatic entity is signified 'by its antecedent or consequent' – for example, a feeling of sadness may be consequent to loss, sadness antecedent to recrimination. Lidov concludes, therefore, that 'Representation of the inner world is first of all a matter of contact with its continuous transformations,' whereas the outer world is effectively static.[115] A dialectical exchange between these two perspectives is, I would propose, the underlying concept behind *Io*. However, in Birtwistle's hands, Lidov's assertions unravel: as will be seen, the music in *Io* questions both the fixity of the outer, visible world and the fluidity of the inner world.

An illustration that Lidov's ideas are relevant to the libretto is provided by Arietta I, the moment when words are first introduced into the drama. Here the four compartments of Birtwistle's visual scenario are realised in musico-poetic form. Sung by Woman 2, the Arietta comprises 4 four-line stanzas, with an overall form of ABA¹B¹. Each stanza is accompanied by an ostinato in the cello (varied slightly in each of the four sections) and rounded off by a four-note refrain in the clarinet (G♯–A–F–E). In stanza A, the woman sings of the seasons, but the outdoor setting is pale and barren. Stanza B refers to objects inside a house, their associated sounds and the woman's 'fear of the knock' at the door, represented by two *fortissimo* 'col legno' chords in the string quartet. Stanza A¹ depicts an exotic, imagined outdoor world, while in B¹ the woman imagines an exotic indoor world, in which she sits 'on sumptuous cushions / With Antioch's Queen'. Yet her description of this vision as a 'philandering dream' – with its suggestion of infidelity and betrayal – highlights the fact that objects, like the door to the woman's house, are inextricably linked to experiences and emotions.

Further confirmation of the endo-exosomatic concept behind *Io* – and a reminder that 'fit' may describe sudden seizures, epilepsy, hysteria, apoplexy, fainting and paralysis[116] – is provided by the fact that Plaice's narrative mirrors important aspects of Freud's 'Fragment of an Analysis of a Case of Hysteria' (1905).[117] According to Freud, the subject of his analysis, Dora, had suppressed the knowledge of an 'incident' while on vacation with a

[114] Lidov, 'Mind and body in music', in *Is Language a Music?*, 150.   [115] Ibid., 151.

[116] Della Thompson, ed., *The Concise Oxford Dictionary*, ninth edition (Oxford: Clarendon Press, 1995), 510.

[117] Sigmund Freud, *The Complete Psychological Works of Sigmund Freud*, vol. VII, 'A Case of Hysteria', 'Three Essays on Sexuality' and Other Works, ed. James Strachey (London: Vintage, 2001).

family friend, Herr K., and she had developed violent feelings of disgust following an earlier incident when she was unexpectedly kissed by Herr K. This, Freud believed, had led to various physical symptoms: she dragged her right foot, had a nervous cough, and suffered aphonia (loss of voice), but was a fluent letter writer. Dora's repeated actions were diagnosed as a form of neurosis, as were her sexual phantasies, which also focused on the body as a site of meaning.[118]

While it is clear that the endo- and exosomatic worlds were inextricably linked in the mind of the librettist, the question arises whether Birtwistle also perceived an association between these two worlds and, if so, what form that took? To address this question I turn now to the score, musical sketches and an early draft of the libretto.

Music / movement / word

At one level Birtwistle's music for *Io* is often languid, reflective, understated. Yet this character to some extent hides the intricate compositional processes that lie beneath. As in *Pulse Shadows*, the quartet's music is often based on what Hall terms 'rhythmic development' whereby short cellular patterns are layered and continuously varied.[119] At another level the music responds directly to the work's recurring actions and physical movements, in which respect it may be said to 'fit' the action, in the modern sense of that term. If the former level suggests the cerebral 'continuous transformations' of the endosomatic world, then the latter is more clearly associated with the relatively fixed replication of appearances in the exosomatic world. At the exosomatic level a series of recurring motifs (taken in the broadest sense) is associated with particular movements and objects. There are motifs for the street and standard lamps being switched on and off, the drawing down and raising of the blind, the flicking away of a hair or fly, the door knock, the posting of the letter, the Gadfly's sting, the woman's reading, writing, falling asleep and breathing, the man's walking, and Io's transformation into a cow. In an important sense, therefore, *Io* adopts Artaud's interest in 'a *phenomenological theatre*' that 'seeks to retrieve a naïve perception

---

[118] Freud controversially concluded that Dora had 'given in' to Herr K. during the incident and was therefore actually in love with him, although he believed it was Frau K. who was 'the ultimate object of love for everyone in the narrative'. Peter Brooks, *Body Work: Objects of Desire in Modern Narrative* (Cambridge, MA and London: Harvard University Press, 1993), 236.

[119] Hall, *HBIRY*, 115. These 'local verse structures', as Adlington refers to them, represent a development, on a smaller scale, of Birtwistle's verse-like repetitions from the 1960s and 1970s, and of the variant of this principle adopted in the 1980s and 1990s, in which ideas lasting several bars are subjected to localised variation. See Adlington, *MHB*, 151–2, and Robert Adlington, 'In the shadows of song: Birtwistle's nine Movements for String Quartet', in O'Hagan, ed., *Aspects of British Music*, 47–62.

of the thing – its "objective aspect'" – before it is 'defined out of sight by language'.[120]

Io's combination of clarinet and string quartet immediately recalls Birtwistle's Clarinet Quintet (1980), which like *Io* was conceived for the clarinettist Alan Hacker, although in *Io* the solo instrument is a basset clarinet. Adlington has suggested that the Clarinet Quintet marks an important moment when Birtwistle 'drifted away from an adherence to rigid formal schemata [. . . towards] an ardent belief in the importance of local continuity', even though the Quintet's starting point had been eight miniatures, each 'as long as the paper' Birtwistle was using.[121] Similarly, despite *Io*'s reliance upon a predetermined sequence of events, the music conveys a sense of continuity, although at a micro level that is comparable to the string quartet movements in *Pulse Shadows*, titled Fantasias and Friezes.[122] The difference in *Io* is that although the endosomatic level has its own compositional logic that is ostensibly independent from the drama, its processes are initiated, interrupted or cut short by events on stage. At times, numerous *tenuto* markings suspend the music's flow to allow actors space to perform designated gestures or to improvise. Consequently, the two contrasting levels in *Io* are characterised by a certain 'mobile staticity', which recalls the concept of a musical 'frieze' that Birtwistle began to speak of in the 1990s in relation to *Slow Frieze* (1995) and *Pulse Shadows*.[123]

An example of this approach occurs in fit I in the music that accompanies the mime actions on stage. Here the music is atomised, broken down into micro units. Each time a unit is repeated a tiny alteration or addition is made. The resultant microstructure realises on a smaller scale the verse–refrain principle found in Birwistle's earliest music. Example 7.5 shows the music leading to action 11. As in Frieze 4 from *Pulse Shadows*, fragmented units (in the viola and cello) are set against a more continuous layer (in the violins): the alternating pizzicato and arco elements were sketched independently; the arco units have accumulated steadily from single notes in each instrument at the start of fit I. The *rallentandos, tenuto* markings and B♭ pedal in the clarinet all relate to the stage action (the woman falling asleep). A different process, from fit IV, immediately after the second myth enactment, is revealed by a sketch shown in Example 7.6a. Based on a form of rhythmic shuffle, rather

---

[120] States, *Great Reckonings*, 109.
[121] Adlington, *MHB*, 145 and Birtwistle cited in *MHB*, 143.
[122] *Pulse Shadows* is another possible model for the *Io* ensemble since the quartet movements are interspersed with Paul Celan settings for soprano, two clarinets, viola, cello and double bass. Other precedents are the combination of string quartet and wind quintet in *Tragoedia*, and solo clarinet and strings in *Melencolia I*.
[123] For a discussion of Birtwistle's notion of 'frieze' in relation to modular Doric and continuous Ionic friezes see Adlington, 'In the shadows', 49–51.

Example 7.5 Fit I, actions 10–11, *The Io Passion* (full score, Boosey & Hawkes, 2004), p. 12

⑩ Gradually she falls asleep.

⑪ During her sleep, she sits bolt upright.

Example 7.6a Sketch for fit IV

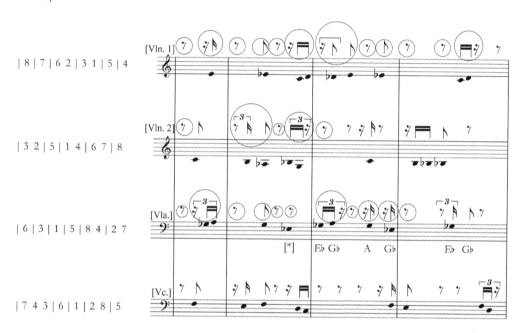

[* = mistake, corrected by the pitches
written as letters]

than development, the sketch began with eight different rhythmic cells, each
assigned a number; four permutations of the numbers were then written
with vertical red pen markings to denote additional quaver rests. Although
the sketch suggests a fragmented texture, Birtwistle tied notes across rests to
produce two-, three- and four-note phrases as shown in Example 7.6b.[124]

Before returning to examine other endosomatic processes, it is first necessary to look more closely at the exosomatic motifs referred to above.
Although many motifs suggest relatively concrete representations, the opening is more resistant to interpretation. *Io* begins with simple ascending and

[124] The sketches and drafts for *The Io Passion* had not been sent to Basle at the time they were
consulted for this study, therefore there are no folder or microfilm numbers. This material
was bundled together in rolls stored in Birtwistle's studio at the end of his garden. I am
especially grateful to the composer for allowing me access to this material, which amounts to
around 180 sides.

Example 7.6b Fit IV, p. 84, Fig. 79

⑫   The MAN 1 re-enters, crosses diagonally straight to the door.

The myth characters exit.

descending phrases, first in the clarinet then throughout the quartet. The rise-and-fall motion may suggest breathing, an association that is supported by the fact that each arching phrase in the strings is cued by a slow clarinet pulse on *bb*, an idea that is later used to lull the woman to sleep. Elsewhere, the ascending/descending motion recurs in different guises, principally when the window blind is opened or closed, or when the letter is posted at the door. Another related gesture, which will be discussed later, is a descending motion in the clarinet: always signalled by a sustained *c″* but each time varied, this motif becomes associated with the man's entrances, exits and movements across the stage. Yet the opening texture returns in something like its original form only once, namely during the third myth enactment when Io is transformed into a cow. One might therefore interpret the opening as a transformation of some kind, or as a representation of the act of falling asleep, which would place the entire drama in the context of a dream.

Example 7.7a Sketch for the opening

Sketches for the opening reveal several false starts. Common to all these versions, however, is the concept of a static harmonic field centred on the open strings of each instrument in the quartet. Example 7.7a shows one of Birtwistle's earliest sketches. Here (with some anomalies) open note heads symbolise open strings. The sketch works with the idea of approximate parallel movement, with the violins roughly a fifth above the viola and cello. Example 7.7b analyses the actual pitches used, using similar notation. The score begins with the clarinet's first seven notes, played softly and slowly. The clarinet then cues each string instrument in turn with a sustained B♭. The cello is first, followed by the viola, then violin 2 and violin 1, each part entering when the previous instrument has reached its highest note. This process is repeated several more times, the string lines becoming more elaborate, before the section is brought to a close by the clarinet's lamp motif, which coincides here with the streetlamp switching off.

The decision to begin with D in the cello followed by G, rather than C and G, is found in all the early sketches, which suggests that some degree of importance was attached to these two pitch classes. The sketch illustrates a conscious decision to mix open string notes with neighbour notes so that although Birtwistle introduces a sense of voice leading the harmonic field is essentially static. Hall traces this interest in open strings back to *Monody for Corpus Christi* (1959), inspired by Holst's Four Songs for Voice and Violin, Op. 35 (structured around the open strings of the violin) and *Four Songs of Autumn* (1987–8), and he has drawn attention to a sketch for the opening of Frieze 1 of *Pulse Shadows* in which open strings provide

Example 7.7b Analysis of the opening, final version

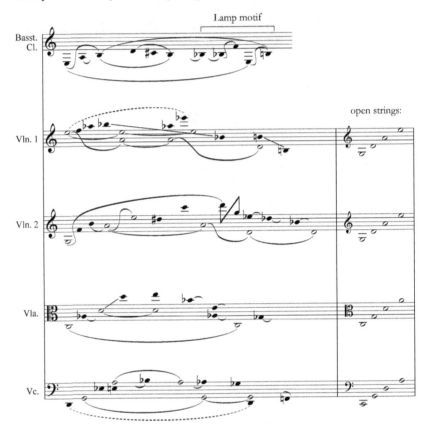

centres for oscillating ostinatos.[125] Extrapolating from Hall's observation, Adlington notes a moment of string crossing in the second half of Fantasia 4 that, not unlike the opening of *Io*, 'bears more than a passing resemblance to the process of tuning up'.[126] In other words, the initial sketches for *Io* are informed by the 'physicality of particular instruments'.[127] As Birtwistle has remarked: 'I can't write music which I don't understand physically – that vibrates here [hand on chest] ... you know, if I don't know what it's like to play'.[128] This is especially clear during the work's darkly comic representation of Zeus's copulation with Io in fit VI – an ironic version of the ascending/descending idea, shown in Example 7.8a.[129] Here the strings

---

[125] See Hall, *HB*, 20 and *HBIRY*, 76–7.   [126] Adlington, 'In the shadows', 56.
[127] Birtwistle in Adlington, 'A conversation', 111.   [128] Ibid., 115.
[129] Clements's description of this scene as 'a hilariously robust bout of sex' is accurate, but for that reason disturbing (Clements, 'Strange fits', 909). Although Plaice clearly invites humour in his text, with Zeus's lines 'Like a bubble / Popped for fun / Like a hundred sherberts / Under the tongue', he does not encourage a literal depiction: there are no grunts or groans in the

Example 7.8a Climax of the 'seduction', fit VI, p. 130 (viola and violin 2 omitted)

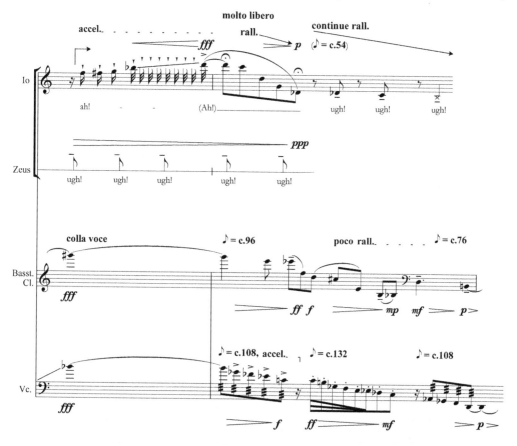

are divided between Zeus's on-beat thrusts in the cello and viola, and Io's off-beat gasps in the violins: G and D assume particular importance in the cello (see Example 7.8b); Io's climactic note is *d‴*, the clarinet's is *g♯‴*; the cello's final descent ends on *D* (see Example 7.8a).

By far the most pervasive motif that arises from the opening, with its fourth- and fifth-based intervallic structure, is the four-note phrase (B♭– F–E–B) usually played by the clarinet whenever a lamp is switched on or off. As shown in Example 7.9, the motif's four notes occupy the centre of the harmonic field defined by the open strings, and its last two notes echo the clarinet's opening ascent (see Example 7.7b). Although this motif

published libretto. Perhaps with this in mind, Io is given affirmative cries of 'yes' in the musical setting to suggest her consent. However, an audience member might still feel uncomfortable with the invitation to laugh at Zeus's actions and with the implications of this revision of the myth. For a consideration of similar issues see J. P. E. Harper-Scott, 'Britten's opera about rape', *Cambridge Opera Journal*, 21/2 (2010), 65–88.

Example 7.8b Sketch for viola and cello in Io's 'seduction', fit VI, Myth of Io, pp. 127–9

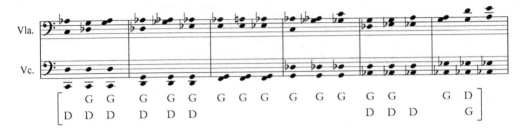

Example 7.9 Lamp motif, first version, p. 4, and its symmetrical relation to the quartet's open strings

① The Streetlamp goes off.

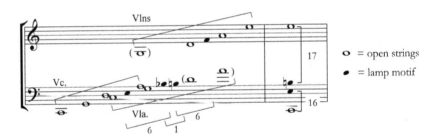

is sometimes repeated literally, it is often treated freely, its pitches placed in different registers, its content extended or truncated. Such variability undermines Lidov's claim that the exosomatic world is essentially fixed. In fact, the only motif that remains fixed is a two-note idea in the clarinet that mirrors (or mimics) the viola's G and A strings. This is first heard near the close of fit VI, immediately after the third myth enactment, when the woman is woken from her sleep by the falling letter. The motif is played twelve times while the woman reads and responds to the letter and again at the very end of the section, where it replaces the lamp motif. It is next

Example 7.10 A version of the man's 'walking' motif, p. 72

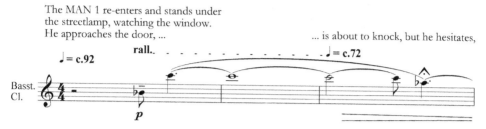

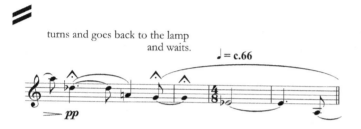

heard in fit VII when the woman enters with the tea tray, then when she awakens from her dream, and again as the clarinet's last two notes in the work. What this suggests is that the motif is associated with the process of role reversal that unfolds in fit VII, whereby the woman assumes control of the drama. Yet while the woman may ultimately assert herself over the man, her motif conforms to the static harmonic framework with which the work began.

More complex ideas mirror the stage action, such as the man's walking motif, which begins on a sustained c'' usually followed by a descending line that is varied on each occasion, and the tremolo fly motif. However, these motifs also infiltrate and begin to shape the endosomatic level. A version of the man's motif is given in Example 7.10. There is nothing conclusive in the sketches to prove the genesis of this idea, but circumstantial evidence suggests it may have been based on random selections from several variants. The motif usually occurs in conjunction with the man's actions (2, 5, 8, 12 and 16); however, it is not introduced until partway into fit II,[130] and is sometimes deployed in anticipation of his entrance, for example during the final moments of the first myth enactment in fit III. During the second and third myth enactments the motif is used to underscore a parallel between the man and Zeus: the frenetic second myth, for example, begins with c'' twice

---

[130] The motif initially appears in the first violin on page 15 of the score, then in the clarinet for the first time on page 20.

sustained in the clarinet, followed by a series of violent gestures and short descending scales initiated by this pitch.[131] Whether Birtwistle had specific actions in mind is unclear, however, since the few directions in the score do not correspond to the events in the original production (moreover, the actions in the original production sometimes matched but at other times ignored the music's implied gestural language).

Repetitions of c'' are also evident throughout the two Man/Woman confrontations, during which this pitch assumes a more general association with the man. Yet the motif does not always appear on cue: when the man re-enters at the end of fit IV, for example, it is absent (p. 87 of the score).[132] At other times, the man's exosomatic movements are shadowed at the endosomatic level, for example when the quartet forms slow-moving harmonies from pitches in the clarinet's descending line at the close of fit II. Ultimately, the man's motif is claimed by the woman. The penultimate version is accompanied by the woman's words 'Here am I, Io / Queen of Antioch' (p. 163), and its final form begins with the sustained c' but is cut short by the woman's G–A motif.[133]

A version of the fly motif is shown in Example 7.11. Variants of this tremolo, triplet quaver motif usually occur whenever the woman flicks away a hair or imaginary fly, the implication being that the mythical world has momentarily encroached upon the woman's quotidian existence. However, this idea never settles into something like a 'prime' form, which, in contrast to Lidov, suggests that the exosomatic level is inherently unstable. The first time a version of the motif is heard, near the start of fit I, it appears in the violins and is literally grafted on to the unfolding endosomatic layer in the viola and cello, at a faster tempo and in a different metre. The sketches confirm that this motif was often added later to the more continuous endosomatic layers. There are some omissions, however: near the end of fit II, for example, the woman flicks away a hair yet the motif is absent; whether this is an oversight is unclear.

As the work progresses the fly motif infiltrates the endosomatic level and is elaborated there. During fit II, as the woman responds to the man's letter, a continuous fifteen-bar variant of the tremolo motif appears in the viola at the lines 'We disturbed something we shouldn't have' (pp. 39–41).

---

[131]   Similar rapid descents occur in the third myth enactment when Io counts her sheep; these stop when Zeus reveals himself as the eleventh sheep. Later, when Hera sniffs Zeus's fingers suspiciously, the clarinet is instructed to play the descent from C with 'oily' glissandi.

[132]   All score references are to the published full score: Harrison Birtwistle, *The Io Passion* (London: Boosey & Hawkes, 2004).

[133]   The early draft reveals that Io's final lines are two stanzas that were originally part of a seven-stanza verse scheme in fit V. This text was written during the first workshop (Plaice in conversation with Beard).

Example 7.11 A version of the 'fly' motif, fit III, p. 47

④ She [...] flicks her hair and goes out.

This initiates a new process in which each string part has an independent rhythmic framework, reminiscent of the layering processes in *Orpheus*. The motif's increased influence on the endosomatic layer is evident near the close of fit III where it is associated with the woman's anger at the man's letter, and an extended variant is heard at the same point in fit IV. It even assumes importance in the Nocturnes: in Nocturne 3 an extended tremolo line is passed between the viola and second violin, and in Nocturne 4 the strings' tremolo lines are imitated by the clarinet. Violent tremolos dominate the first Man/Woman conflict, particularly when the woman refers to 'the ways you touched me' and at the man's declaration 'I'll leave on you an indelible stain.' When the four voices inside the woman's head begin to question who they are a regular pulse is generated by repeated c''s associated with the man set against irregularly spaced tremolo chords in the strings. Here the man's motif anticipates his arrival but combines with the fly motif in an attempt to bring the woman out of her traumatic dream.

This tension is dissipated somewhat by gentle, sextuplet demisemiquaver figures in Aubade 3. Yet the fly motif's association with the increased threat of physical violence is confirmed when it accompanies Hera's line 'why should I pick a fight?' in Arietta 3. Moreover, when Zeus 'grabs' Io during the third myth enactment the shuddering motif assumes a more explicit relation to Io's violation and, slightly later, her trembling and shaking. When finally the woman reaches across the invisible divide and begins to smear lipstick across the man's face the fly motif returns with a vengeance. This reaches a particular height of intensity when the woman begins to write on the man's body – an action that will be considered later. Notably there is no fly to disturb the woman at the end of the drama. While this suggests that she has somehow moved on with her life, her final verses revisit the Io myth and the woman's dream from Arietta 1. Moreover, the static accompaniment, underpinned by a repeated ostinato in the cello (*Bb–Eb*), which recalls the lamp motif introduced at the opening, suggests the 'mobile staticity' of a frieze in which linear progress is conditioned by statuesque permanence.

Having surveyed the exosomatic motifs it is now possible to examine the relationship between endo- and exosomatic levels in the music in more detail. In an early draft of the libretto, dated 5 December 2002, the terms Fit, Arietta, Aubade and Nocturne are absent.[134] It can be reasonably surmised, therefore, that these terms and sections were introduced by Birtwistle. The Aubades, Ariettas and Nocturnes function in a similar manner to the instrumental pastorals in *Yan Tan Tethera*: collectively they form verse-like sequences that alternate with the action scenes, yet each offers its own perspective on the drama. The Aubades are brief sections heard at the start

---

[134] This draft libretto, stored at the NTA, differs from the final version in numerous other ways. A running total of 58 minutes 22 seconds is recorded at the end, which is half an hour less than the final version. There are eighteen actions, rather than sixteen, and none are omitted from any of the sequences. The woman receives two letters, the first when she enters with the tea tray, the second when she is woken by the letter. The titles and positions of the moon are different in all but the first two cycles: sequence III is titled 'Myth, *full moon*'; IV is 'Stung, *half moon (waning)*'; V 'Recovery, *old moon*'; VI 'Forgetting, *no moon*'; VII 'New Moon, *new moon*'. Additional episodes and roles from the Io myth are included (for example, Io is held captive by Argus Panoptes), and the mythical characters are described as 'Dawn Raiders'. In an accompanying formal chart, prepared by the designer, Alison Chitty, the first myth, a brief scene in which Io is chased by the Gadfly, is titled 'Myth Play', the second 'Grunt/Noh play', and the third 'Neuro Myth'. Elements from these scenes were redistributed in the final version and the second myth was a prototype for the Man/Woman confrontation. The original form of fit IV comprised a dialogue between the man and woman only. It might be surmised therefore that Birtwistle influenced the decision to develop this cycle into a quartet and perhaps also its culmination in a scene in which the man and woman question their identities and conclude that they are merely voices in the female protagonist's mind. This transition from melodrama to existential conflict is far more effective than the static early draft.

of fits that begin in the early hours of the day.[135] Despite some obvious differences, each is related by the presence of demisemiquaver runs: sextuplets in 1 and 3; triplets in 2; quintuplets in 4. However, the Ariettas and Nocturnes exist outside the action: the former articulate the thoughts of the woman and her double Hera, the latter those of the man. Besides the persistent presence of the soprano, the cycle of Ariettas is not clearly unified. There are, however, certain associative threads, namely: the soprano tends to begin around $c''/c\sharp'-e\flat''/e''$ in all Ariettas; the cello is paired with the soprano in 1, 2 and at the start of 5; the clarinet is absent from 3 and 4; there are door-knock chords in 1, 2 and 4; short descending phrases recur throughout 1, 3 and 5.[136]

A similar approach characterises the Nocturnes, although these are closer to the instrumental pastorals in *Yan Tan Tethera* in the sense that they are intricate mechanistic timepieces. Associative threads here include: clarinet multiphonics in 1 and 6; cello ostinatos in 1, 3, 4 and 6; 'sul tasto' in 1, 2 and 5; harmonics in all except 3; allusions to the fly motif in 3, 4 and 7; the man's vocal part in 4 and 5; alternating arco and pizzicato in 5, 6 and 7; extended clarinet lines in 1, 4, 6 and 7. Various links are also established between the Nocturnes and the opening: in 1 the clarinet's multiphonics imitate the action of crossing over different strings, while the viola is restricted to notes between its G and D strings;[137] the clarinet is restricted to repeated G pedals in 2 and 3; there are natural harmonics in 5 and 6; D and G form the opening double-stopped chord in the cello ostinato in 6 (with C in the viola), while the clarinet alludes to its very first ascending phrase.

If the Nocturnes have an underlying principle it is varied ostinato, and this is most clearly evident in the cello. As illustrated in Example 7.12, the cello in Nocturne 1 has a five-note ostinato that suggests a modified form of the lamp motif. This idea is presented in slightly altered form in the cello in Nocturne 3: the sketches reveal that the ostinato here comprises a six-note *color* and a five-note *talea*, as shown in Example 7.13. In Nocturne 5 a three-note refrain in the clarinet alternates with a varied ostinato in the violins and viola (three 'sul tasto' chords followed by one, two or three pizzicato chords); however, the cello's line relates back to the rise and fall of the opening. As

[135] The Aubades may have been written together: when the sketches were consulted at the composer's home most of the Aubade sketches were grouped together whereas those for the Ariettas and Nocturnes were separated.
[136] In Arietta 1, the descending phrases in the soprano line culminate in a longer descent when the woman sings of her 'fear of the knock'.
[137] The viola's independence from the other parts here (it moves at a faster tempo with smaller note values) and elsewhere recalls similar 'breakaway' gestures in *Pulse Shadows*, for example in Frieze 1 and 'White and Light'. Moreover, the frantic scribble of Io's writing motif closely resembles the pulsating semiquaver counter-subject introduced in the viola in bar 6 of Fantasia 4.

Example 7.12 Cello ostinato in Nocturne 1, pp. 8–11

Summary of pitch associations between ostinato and lamp motif

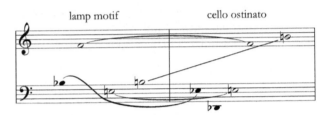

Example 7.13 Cello ostinato in Nocturne 3, pp. 50–2

talea: 3 5 5 5 12 (where 1 = ♪)

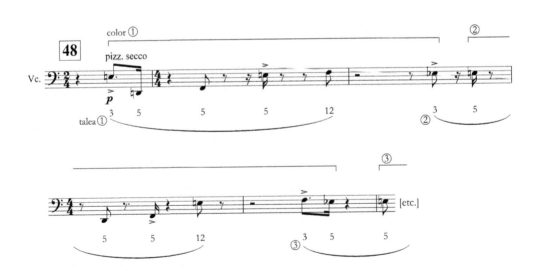

Example 7.14 Analysis of the continuous cello line in Nocturne 5, pp. 88–91 (phrasing added)

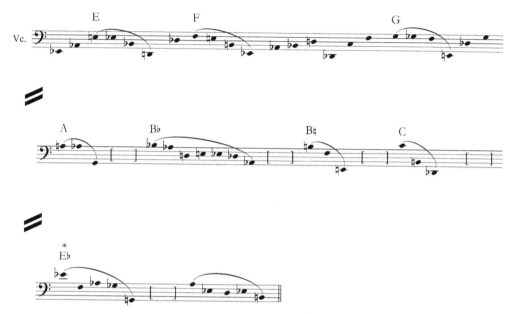

* 'The arrow's split from tip to feather'

summarised in Example 7.14, the peak of the cello's arching phrases rise stepwise from *e* to *eb'*, its apex timed to coincide with the climax of the man's lament. Nocturne 7 relates back to the static harmony of Nocturne 3, and its repeated string chords allude to the work's underlying emphasis on open strings, with chromatic inflections and brief, fly-motif-style tremolos. The clarinet, however, has numerous falling phrases that gradually expand until a version of the man's motif is presented, with an extended descent from *c''* for two and a half octaves, followed by the lamp motif.

Most complex of all is Nocturne 6. In the quartet there are two ostinatos, presented simultaneously at independent tempi, both of which comprise fixed and more freely varied elements. In the violins, the metrical scheme alternates regularly between 5/8 and 6/8. As shown in Example 7.15a, the 5/8 bars represent the fixed element: these comprise the same five chords, that is, four dyads and a trichord (the latter includes an open-string D and an artificial fourth harmonic on the A string).[138] The 6/8 bars are more freely varied: these comprise variants of a six-note model shared by the two violins. A number scheme was used to distribute the pitches, as shown in

---

[138] The trichord is always tied over to the first demisemiquaver in the subsequent 6/8 bar.

Example 7.15a Chord series in the violins' 5/8 bars in Nocturne 6, pp. 113–16

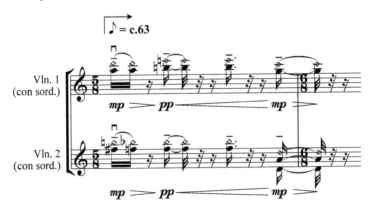

Example 7.15b Model and sketch for the violins' 6/8 bars

Sketch:

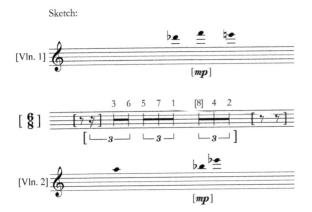

Example 7.15b. The results were then notated as pizzicato triplet semi-quavers (each 6/8 bar begins with a quaver duration tied over from the previous 5/8 bar and ends with two quaver rests). Within this scheme, B♭ and F – notes from the lamp motif – are singled out with an *mp* dynamic in contrast to *pp* for the other events. A similar principle was applied to the viola and cello. These have a fixed metrical scheme with regular 7/8 bars.

Example 7.15c Viola and cello, first two quavers in opening 7/8 bar, p. 113

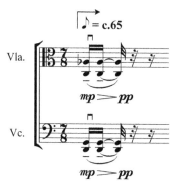

Example 7.15d Scheme to determine the viola and cello's first two quavers in each 7/8 bar, pp. 113–16

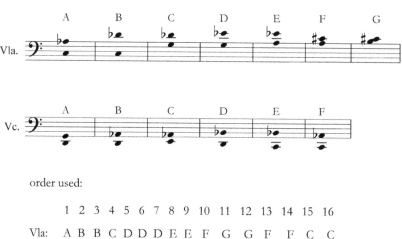

order used:

	1	2	3	4	5	6	7	8	9	10	11	12	13	14	15	16
Vla:	A	B	B	C	D	D	D	E	E	F	G	G	F	F	C	C
Vc.:	A	A	B	B	B	C	C	B	D	D	D	E	E	F	F	F

The first two quaver beats are filled by a four-note chord played twice (see Example 7.15c). This chord is the more freely varied element, formed from selections from seven dyads in the viola and six dyads in the cello (see Example 7.15d).

The remaining five quaver beats are determined by a fixed scheme in which selections are made from four groups, that is, two groups each for viola and cello, as shown in Example 7.15e. Once again, a link to the lamp motif is suggested through the greater emphasis given to pitch classes E and B flat, which occur in both instruments (see I and IV in Example 7.15e). The next step in the sketching process was to write out permutations of

Example 7.15e Model for the remainder of the viola and cello's 7/8 bars

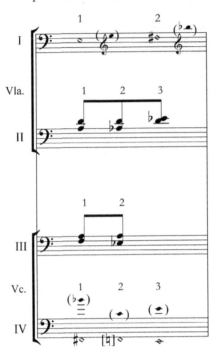

the numbers 1 to 8, each equivalent to a semiquaver (51376428, etc.): even numbers relate to the viola, odd ones to the cello. Next came a series of four-note filters (2368, 246[7], 1457, etc.), which determine the precise location of events. In the first eight-number series, for example, number 3 in the filter falls on 3 in the eight-note permutation (see Example 7.15f). This necessitates a selection for the viola, in this instance the first event from group I. Birtwistle then moved through groups I to IV in sequence. However, there are various adjustments or errors: in the first eight-number permutation 1 is given to the cello rather than viola, 6 in the first filter (2368) is shifted to 7, and 8 is given to the viola rather than the cello; the last number in the second filter (246[7]) is incorrectly written as 6; in the third filter (1457) 4 is moved to 8, and 5 is missing (in the score the correct pitch is included, but it is given to the viola and moved forward to the third semiquaver). At times such alterations were presumably made for musical reasons, but at other times additional schemes were brought into play.[139]

---

[139] For example, the alteration of event 6 to 7 is explained by the fact that in the first three eight-note groups Birtwistle wanted the cello's bowed harmonics to fall on number 2.

Example 7.15f Sketch for the viola and cello, pp. 113–14

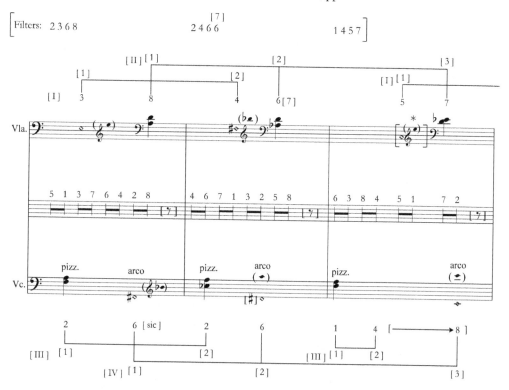

* Omitted from the sketch; in the score brought
forward to the third semiquaver (number 8 in the permutation).

A third independent tempo is given to the clarinet, whose contrasting part – linear and sustained rather than repetitive and fragmented – makes use of multiphonics. The sketches reveal that these originated in a series of eighteen dyads based on permutations of intervals 13, 14, 16, 17, 20, 21, 25 and 27 projected above an expanding wedge on *d'*. From this series, which was originally sketched in transposition, ten dyads were selected from a total of eighteen; these were then reordered as shown in Example 7.16 (the slurs indicate that the multiphonics are approached alternately from high and low notes).[140] The prominent appearance in these dyads of pitches from the lamp motif (Bb–F–E–B) reveals a conceptual link to the strings (albeit one that was removed when the part was transposed) and provides another example of the relationship between endo- and exosomatic levels in the

[140] In the sketch the clarinet dyads for this Nocturne are written a minor third higher than in the score. This is highly unusual: elsewhere Birtwistle always drafts in C. This suggests that he may have been working from a table of some kind written in transposition.

Example 7.16 Sketch for the clarinet in Nocturne 6, pp. 114–6 (a minor third higher than in the final score)

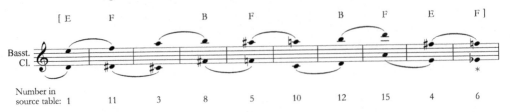

* = altered in the score to an octave.

music. However, the sketches reveal that, in contrast to Lidov's assertions, Birtwistle's endosomatic level is often essentially fixed through the use of ostinatos.

Writing on the body

As Adlington has observed, Birtwistle tends to respond to the string quartet as a 'neutral medium' for the exploration of the minutiae of compositional techniques, which may explain his choice of this ensemble for a drama concerned with dreams and inner thoughts.[141] Moreover, the tension in *Io* between abstract 'writing' processes and concrete 'action' is dramatised visually at the climax of the Man/Woman conflict when the woman writes on the man's body. This action echoes the man's intention to leave on the woman 'an indelible stain', and it recalls the fact that, for Freud, Dora's hysterical symptoms are a form of writing on the body.[142] It also highlights a desire to make the body signify, to transform it – like Io's body – into a site of representation and meaning. In this sense it symbolises what Peter Brooks refers to as 'the ever-renewed struggle of language to make the body mean, the struggle to bring it into writing', to 'make the body into a text'.[143] To some extent, Artaud was also guilty of this desire: his use of the word 'hieroglyph' to describe the concrete gestures he sought in theatre betrays the fact that his concept was something to be 'read', somehow contingent upon text and writing. Yet, as Brooks observes, the body is 'at once a cultural construct and its other, something outside of language that language struggles to mark and to be embodied in'.[144] In Plaice's *Io*, there is a suggestion that the man is killed by the woman's act of writing on his body, and one might say that her insistence on ascribing meaning to his body destroys it. However, in Birtwistle's music, the naïve representations of

141 Birtwistle in Adlington, 'A conversation', 111.
142 Peter Brooks, *Body Work*, 22.   143 Ibid., 22 and 7.   144 Ibid., xiii.

concrete objects and exosomatic actions feed into the endosomatic musical processes. Both worlds are enriched by this interaction.

The Corridor

As with *Io*, *The Corridor* began as a visual scenario that was developed in workshops at the National Theatre. The team for the original production included the librettist David Harsent, director Peter Gill,[145] designer Alison Chitty, soprano Elizabeth Atherton and tenor Mark Padmore.[146] Birtwistle wished to focus on the moment Orpheus turned to look back at Eurydice and lost her forever, although the two characters are simply named Man and Woman. In *Orpheus*, Birtwistle had downplayed the turn, but he now saw the opportunity to expand Orpheus's split-second loss across a forty-five-minute chamber opera in the manner of Schoenberg's *Erwartung*: he imagined the work as 'a single moment from the Orpheus story magnified, like a photographic blow-up'.[147] He also saw it as an opportunity to realise Eurydice's transformation into a puppet as described in the libretto to *Orpheus*, but which had not, he felt, been satisfactorily achieved in that opera.

Corridor was also conceived as a companion piece to *Semper Dowland, Semper Dolens: Theatre of Melancholy* (2009). In this work six Dowland lute songs, arranged for tenor and harp, are interspersed between instrumental settings of Dowland's *Seaven Teares Figured in Seaven Passionate Pavanes*.[148] A form of narrative is suggested by the songs, which deal with lost love, betrayal and infidelity, culminating in the final song 'In Darkness Let Me Dwell', while the instrumental arrangements are 'images, somehow, of love-like tableaux'.[149] Birtwistle described *Semper Dowland* as 'a concert piece

---

[145] Peter Gill established the National Theatre Studio in the 1980s, and in 1987 he used the Studio to develop new productions of *Bow Down* and *Down by the Greenwood Side*.

[146] Harsent joined after the first workshops had been held. Originally, perhaps in light of his intention that Eurydice would be the focus of the work, Birtwistle had approached two American female poets to write the libretto. Dissatisfied with the results, he turned to Harsent, with whom he had recently collaborated on *The Minotaur*, as discussed in Chapter 8. From conversation with Beard, 18 November 2008.

[147] Birtwistle in the programme note to the London premiere of *The Corridor*, Queen Elizabeth Hall, 6 July 2009.

[148] *Semper Dowland* extends Birtwistle's interest in Elizabethan society's fascination with the relationship between melancholy and creativity previously explored in *The Shadow of Night* (2001) and *Night's Black Bird* (2004), which allude to 'In darkness let me dwell'. When the author visited Birtwistle on 1 August 2008 there was a photocopy on his desk of pages from Ian Spink's *English Song: Dowland to Purcell* (London: Batsford, 1974). These pages included the opening bars of 'In Darkness' and the following description: 'It typifies Dowland at his best; the brooding melancholy and the conservative technique pushed as far as it will go to achieve an intensity of expression unequalled in England until Purcell' (23).

[149] Birtwistle in programme note to the London premiere.

plus action',[150] and in the original performance a slender narrative was suggested by the movements of two dancers (one male, one female) and the position of the tenor at a desk, recalling *Io*.

Corridor extrapolates on the themes of loss and sexual tension outlined in *Semper Dowland*. Located at the boundary or interface between life and death, Orpheus turns and Eurydice winds her way back to Hades across the stage in a slow, spiral motion before her body finally disintegrates. The 'corridor' extends between the lower, darkened side of the Underworld (stage left) and the upper, lightened 'mouth of the cave' (stage right), or 'the world outside' as Harsent describes it.[151] Divided into nine sections, the work is punctuated by Orpheus's aria-like lamentations accompanied by onstage harp.[152] Eurydice's journey leads her to a realisation about herself and her relationship to Orpheus. On her journey she interacts with Shades – humans who have died and passed to the Underworld – represented by a quintet of musicians seated onstage in a line: flute, clarinet, violin, viola and cello.[153] In the original production this line was extended by the harp, which only plays when the Man sings.[154] When downstage of the musicians, in sections 1, 2, 3, 5, 7 and 9, the Woman is in character as Eurydice. When upstage, in sections 4, 6 and 8, the Woman is out of character, as the performer herself – a point I will return to later in relation to the Man. In this narrator's role the Woman observes and comments on events, her knowledge of the myth conveyed through speech rather than song.

The formal layout and dramatic structure of *Corridor* are given in Table 7.3. As in *Io*, the principle of moving through the same series of actions from different perspectives is retained: although the turn is enacted at the end of section 1, each subsequent section revisits this moment. Formal divisions are emphasised by four contrasting vocal styles: sung dialogue between the Man and Woman; the Woman's sung monologue; spoken or declaimed

---

[150] Birtwistle in conversation with Beard, 18 November 2008.

[151] Harsent in conversation with Beard, 26 November 2008. In the original production the corridor was represented by a roll of red linoleum shadowed by a thin, horizontal line lit in red along the back wall; however, the idea of a sloping stage was abandoned. Chitty's use of red (Eurydice also wore a red dress) recalled her design for *The Last Supper* in which Christ wore a red sash over a white suit.

[152] Harsent has suggested that the sections were his idea, in the manner of his libretto for Huw Watkins's music theatre piece *Crime Fiction* (2009). However, he acknowledges that Birtwistle decided to break up Orpheus's song and distribute it throughout the work and that Birtwistle's more 'hands on' approach led to 'endless additions'. Harsent's freedom to invent followed only after he had established what was indispensable to Birtwistle. Harsent in conversation with Beard, 26 November 2008.

[153] Birtwistle has explained that he chose these instruments in preference to others because of their 'character' and visual appearance, but also because they relate to *Semper Dowland*, scored for alto flute and clarinet (doubling piccolo, bass flute and bass clarinet), violin, two violas and two cellos. Birtwistle in programme note to the London premiere.

[154] The libretto suggests that the harp and tenor might be placed offstage but both were onstage at the premiere.

Table 7.3 *Formal layout and thematic structure of* The Corridor

Section	Pages in score	Man & Woman; sung dialogue; downstage	Woman; sung monologue; downstage	Woman; spoken; upstage	Man; Orphic song; (offstage)
1	1–11	**Refrain:** 'No! Not yet!' i 'Step into the light' ii 'Can you still see me?' iii the Man turns			
2	11–27	i 'You looked back because...' ii 'I thought I saw you clear' iii 'Even now / You turned; so must I'			
3	28–48	**A** 'Look back: what can you see?... Can you hear me?'	**B** i 'The God drew me down' ii 'When he [Orpheus] brought me out... I knew he would turn to find me' iii 'Dust beneath my feet... Now the world falls away'		**C** 'His Song', lines 1–6 (verse 1 & beginning of verse 2)
4	49–66			**A** (addressed to the Shades): i 'Imagine it: her journey down to hell' ii 'Then she came to the gate' iii 'Sunlight on his back'	**B** lines 7–10 (verse 2 cont.)
5	67–78		**A** i 'I'm no one I used to be' ii 'Being dead was something I had to learn' iii 'Waterlights and an echo... calling me on'		**B** lines 11–13 (verse 3)

(cont.)

Table 7.3 (*cont.*)

Section	Pages in score	Man & Woman; sung dialogue; downstage	Woman; sung monologue; downstage	Woman; spoken; upstage	Man; Orphic song; (offstage)
6	79–90			**A** (addressed to the Shades): i 'Could anyone love anyone like that?' ii 'This perfect love' iii 'His lament'	**B** lines 17–20 (verse 4)
7	91–104		**A** i 'Suppose he'd brought me out' ii 'In life he loved me' iii 'What did he want from me?...his masterstroke'		**B** lines 21–26 (verse 5)
8	104–119			**A** (addressed to herself and the Shades): **Refrain**: 'Can you dance her down to hell?' **Verses**: (×5) on Orpheus's future	**B** lines 27–35 (verse 6)
9	119–132		**A** 'Bag of words'		**A** final word: 'Eurydice'

sections by the Woman; the Man's Orphic lament, entitled 'His Song'. In the first three sections, Eurydice and Orpheus enter into dialogue, after which their songs become independent. Meanwhile, the upstage Woman interacts with the musicians, asking them questions, to which they reply in music. The musicians assume a further dramatic function when the Woman asks them to guide Eurydice through the darkness back to the Underworld: 'Will you dance her down to hell?' she asks. Harsent has commented that Birtwistle's original idea involved a man in a corridor.[155] However, once he had settled on Eurydice as the focus he imagined her in a darkened cave, highly sensitive to the touch and sound of her surroundings, which he wanted described in detail. Birtwistle became 'very caught up with the physicality of what was happening to Eurydice' and especially concerned to 'think through the physical texture' of the piece.[156]

While Birtwistle's Artaudian 'awareness of being in a body' leads to some visceral gestures in the quintet, especially in section 7, it is particularly evident in a kind of urgent vocal delivery in the laments (the 'parlando' of the third verse is highly reminiscent of Britten's Parables), and by the fact that the instruments are often instructed to 'follow' the voices ('colla voce').[157] As Birtwistle remarks, 'The voice [Eurydice's] is, most of the time, rhythmically free and the conductor is following her, indicating that freedom to the rest of the players.'[158] In other words, the emphasis shifts to what J. L. Austin refers to as verbal utterance as action, 'in which to *say* something is to *do* something; or in which *by* saying or *in* saying something we are doing something'.[159] Voices in *Corridor* therefore have 'a tangible physical effect' both within the narrative and on the ensemble.[160]

It might be argued however that, as in *Gawain*, what interested Harsent most mattered less to Birtwistle. Harsent's energies were clearly focused on the Woman/Eurydice, on exploring her human responses to Orpheus's actions. Orpheus's loss was external – he expected Eurydice to be by his side, expected her love to equal his – whereas Eurydice was torn from within. As Harsent remarked, 'Orpheus wants Eurydice back, but does she want to go? How is it going to be for her? She's not certain that the land of the living is the place to be.'[161] This gives rise to a tension: Eurydice is annoyed with Orpheus, first for turning, then later for dragging her away from the Underworld. The implication is that Orpheus's actions were hubristic: that he wished to return Eurydice from the Underworld to fulfil his own needs.[162] If that is so, the

---

[155] When discussing *The Minotaur* with Birtwistle in 2002, Harsent suggested a modern version in which a man and woman occupy separate rooms of a house; the man tries to leave but there is no external door, only passages, corridors, windows and stationary people forming friezes in different rooms. The opera would be a 'tiny psychodrama' in which the man walks the corridors of the house becoming gradually more hysterical. It is highly likely that this idea informed Birtwistle's scenario for *Io*, which implies that in certain respects *Io* was a pilot for *Minotaur*. Harsent in conversation with Beard, 26 November 2008.

[156] Ibid.   [157] Walker, 'Why performance?' 157.

[158] Birtwistle in programme note to the London premiere.

[159] J. L. Austin, *How To Do Things with Words*, 2nd edn, ed. J. O. Urmson and Marina Sbisà (Oxford: Clarendon Press, 1975), 12.

[160] Duncan, 'The operatic scandal', 298.

[161] Harsent in conversation with Beard, 26 November 2008.

[162] This tension is revealed in the terse dialogues in sections 1 to 3, but also when the harp cuts off the Woman's monologue in section 3 with sharp chords that literally halt the quintet in order to make way for the Man's lament.

Woman suggests, then his violent fate was deserved. A corresponding shift in emphasis becomes apparent in section 7 when Eurydice reveals that she has come to terms with death and is comfortable in the Underworld.[163] The prospect of the physical world is unbearable to her. Spittle, a kiss, the sun, the ground under her feet, even the wind are painful to her. For the final disintegration, in section 9, Harsent provided Birtwistle with a 'bag of words' filled with fragments of text Eurydice had sung before. As she returns to the spirit world, Eurydice's words are enveloped in music and her separation from Orpheus is complete.

Workshops for *Corridor* were held in 2007 and 2008,[164] after which Peter Gill, the director, was given scope to realise the implications of the agreed scenario. A number of actors were used in the workshops, but not in the final production. Three musical sketches for the workshops, dated February 2008 and each labelled '1st sketch for Corridor', give some insight into Birtwistle's earliest conceptions.[165] The first page is a sketch for the soprano in which certain words and phrases from sections 5 and 7 are anticipated, notably 'the God calling me on'.[166] However, the opening text, in Greek, was not retained in subsequent drafts.[167] The second page comprises a continuous melodic line in the bass clef, separated into twelve distinct phrases labelled A to L. Each unit is divided from the next by a breath mark, and the range corresponds to the tenor's part, yet there is no obvious connection to the score (although phrases E and J resemble a disjunct motif that becomes associated with the Man's voice calling Eurydice on: see Examples 7.17a and 7.17b). It is unusual for Birtwistle to compose vocal music without a text, but the sketch is possibly an attempt to determine the Man's vocal style ahead of receiving the libretto. The third page is divided into two sections labelled A and B; written in the treble clef, it is unclear whether this is for voice or instrument but the likelihood is clarinet. The page comprises short units that are to be repeated, not unlike music in sections 1 and 4. The units are separated by *tenuto* markings that recall those used in *Io* to allow time

---

[163] In this regard, Harsent acknowledges the influence of Robert Lowell's poem 'Orpheus, Eurydice and Hermes' (1959), in which Eurydice is 'full of her decisive death': leaning 'on the God's arm' she 'didn't give the man in front of her a thought, nor the road climbing to life', 'Being dead fulfilled her beyond fulfillment'; *Hudson Review* 12/1 (1959), 54–6. Lowell's poem is adapted from Rilke's 'Orpheus, Eurydike, Hermes' (1904).

[164] Harsent's first draft dates from November 2007.

[165] As with *The Io Passion*, the musical manuscripts for *The Corridor* had not been sent to Basle at the time they were consulted for this study but were stored at the composer's home. This material amounts to approximately 70 sides of sketches and drafts, and just under 100 sides of libretto typescript, with annotations by Birtwistle.

[166] Other words and phrases in this sketch that appear in the final version include 'shadows', 'a face washed in sunlight', 'whispers' and 'fading'.

[167] The text appears to read: 'Na, Na, Na, giri so, na giri so, E-tho o na giri so, prep pi na, gi ri so E-E-THO'.

Example 7.17a Extracts from '1st sketch for Corridor', for workshops
on *The Corridor*

Example 7.17b Section 5, *The Corridor* (full score, Boosey & Hawkes, 2009), p. 74

for actions to be performed. One possibility is that Birtwistle's first sketch
was intended to provide music to match specific gestures or actions – the
steady tread, around one pulse per second, suggests a slow walking motion –
but that this later gave way to a more through-composed conception.

Birtwistle's handling of the work's formal design is revealing, especially
when the score is read against the musical sketches and revisions to the
libretto undertaken between early July and late August 2008. The opening
establishes a harmonic framework of overlapping fourths and fifths that
recalls *Io*: a chord of E, B, B♭ and F in the harp and quintet is supported by F
in the soprano, and D–F in the tenor. Birtwistle's desire to 'think through the
physical texture of the piece', and the distinctiveness of each member of the
quintet, is immediately evident when a 'breakaway' demisemiquaver figure
in the viola, which begins on repeated Es, is initiated by a second chord.
At a faster tempo than the main ensemble, this figure recalls the writing
motif in *Io* but is here associated with Eurydice's movement 'towards the
light'; variants in sections 4 and 7 occur at references to sunlight and the

'blaze of noon'. Following a third chord the Man sings of stone beneath Eurydice's feet and the violin breaks out with chiselled dyads whose lowest note forms a repeated pedal on the open G string; open strings later assume importance in sections 4 and 8. After a fourth chord the quintet splinters into four different tempi, a device that characterises the final part of sections 2, 4 – when the Woman addresses the Shades – and 7.

Section 1 continues in this fragmented manner: each tactile image elicits a different musical texture that is halted by the Woman's cries of 'Yes!' or 'No! No, not yet'; some of these cries were added by Birtwistle.[168] Sensations are transient, images constantly slip away, and at the end of section 1 the Man turns.[169] In section 2 the demisemiquaver viola figure is taken up immediately in the strings as underscore to the terse dialogue exchange, while the flute and clarinet form rhythmic counterpoint with the harp.[170] The strings generate a sense of propulsive movement that culminates in rapid ascending scales, yet these suddenly slow and fragment. A reverse motion is then suggested by the second and third parts, which are characterised by every kind of falling scale. Moreover, at the outset, sustained harmonies in the strings are formed from variants of a ten-note line that passes aimlessly between the instruments, as shown in Example 7.18. Early versions of the libretto reveal that the third part (pages 21–7) was added at Birtwistle's request, conceivably because he wished to intensify the sense of the god pulling at Eurydice 'like a voice at my back drawing me down', while on stage she is seen to move gradually away from Orpheus, step by step.[171]

The resulting tripartite scheme becomes a structural principle at various levels. For example, the dialogue at the start of section 3 was another addition requested by Birtwistle, presumably in order to link the first three sections. As a result the sections form a series of tripartite groups, as follows: 1, 2, 3 / 4, 6, 8 / 5, 7, 9. In fact, Birtwistle overhauled Harsent's original scheme considerably. The three opening sections were formed from what had originally been two sections, and the third part of B in section 3 evolved from cuts, additions and the transfer of text from section 6. Harsent's original commentary-based text for sections 4, 6 and 8 was replaced by additional questions, new text and repetitions of words and phrases, and

---

[168] This verse–refrain pattern is mirrored in section 8 by the Woman's frequent requests for the quintet to 'dance' her down to hell.

[169] Orpheus's turn is marked by a long pause followed by a cadential figure in the harp, which recalls similar gestures in *Tragoedia* and *Melencolia I*.

[170] The harp and woodwind at the start of section 2 were conceived together. Permutations of numbers 1 to 7 were applied independently to preconceived rhythmic patterns to determine whether notes would be played by the left, right or both hands in the case of the harp and by the flute, clarinet or both instruments in the woodwind.

[171] All such page references are to the full score: Harrison Birtwistle, *The Corridor* (London: Boosey & Hawkes, 2009).

Example 7.18 Wandering line in the strings, section 2, ii, pp. 18–19 (the annotated lines and numbers are derived from the sketches)

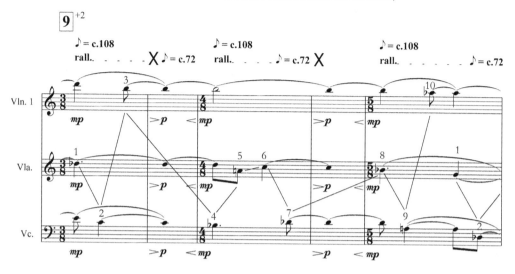

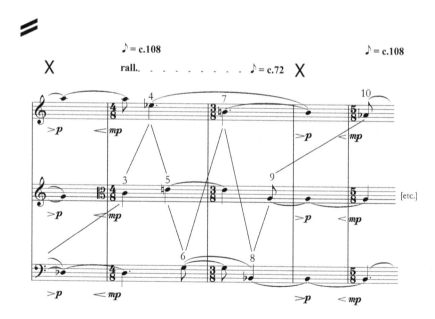

Harsent was particularly concerned to know whether the tone, location and number of questions seemed right.[172] Birtwistle's request for additional

---

[172] From an email sent by Harsent to Birtwistle, via a third party, on 8 July 2008, printed out and annotated by Birtwistle.

Example 7.19 Section 6, ii, p. 83

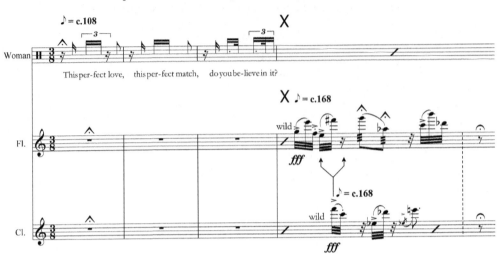

questions was motivated by his desire for 'a genuine integration between
speech and instrumental music'.[173] This resulted in a form of instrumental
speech, or mime, as illustrated by the flute and clarinet's 'wild' response
to the question 'This perfect love, this perfect match, do you believe in it?'
(see Example 7.19). While the attempt to communicate is clearly conveyed,
it is impossible to 'read' such answers with any certainty. Yet this recalls
Artaud's interest in the pre-symbolic origins of human utterance, that is,
in acts of communication that begin as physical gestures before thought is
transformed into word.

   A lack of musical repetition at the larger, structural level is consistent with
the idea of passing through a corridor. Orpheus's song verses, for example,
bear little resemblance to each other, and in section 7 a principle of pairing
instruments is applied for the first time, clearly in response to the line 'a
tangle of voices'. There is a linear element also in the Man's song, which
progresses from factual statement ('She was dead and gone' in verse 1),
through explanatory narrative (descriptions of Eurydice's steps towards the
light in verse 2 and the turn in verse 3), through commentary (an expression of regret in verse 4, followed by pain in verse 5), to myth (verse 6
is a dark eulogy to the 'cruel', 'bleak' and 'blighted' status of Eurydice's
name).[174] Musically, 'His Song' culminates in section 8 with deeply expressive melismas on Eurydice's name. By contrast, Eurydice's sung monologues

---

[173] Birtwistle in programme note to the London premiere.
[174] The sketches reveal that Birtwistle originally intended to set verses from 'His Song' alternately
       as aria and *Sprechgesang*.

(3, 5, 7, 9) all end with forms of musical fragmentation. Even after Eurydice's declaration at the end of section 7A that her second death is 'mine and
mine alone', supported by chords in rhythmic unison and pitch doublings
between voice and flute, the texture splinters completely: all instrumental
parts move at independent tempi and bar lines are removed.

Of Eurydice's journey Birtwistle has remarked that:

> as she travels, she's deteriorating, transforming, disintegrating as she goes
> deeper. The music also disintegrates as she goes down. To do this, I create
> music for her that repeats, and as it repeats, it fractures and slows down, like a
> clock winding down.[175]

The association of physical deterioration with a mechanical 'winding down'
is evident in a series of literally repeated ostinatos at the close of the Woman's
monologue in section 3 (pages 44–5). Section 8 consists almost entirely of
such mechanical ostinatos; as in section 1, each line of text generates a
different instrumental pattern. Yet section 8 merely prepares the way for
a 'masterstroke' of compositional process in the final section, which is
a musical representation of Eurydice's 'dance to death'.[176] This complex,
multiple-layered mechanism comprises a stretto-like texture in which five
ostinatos are layered on top of one another, one for each player in the
quintet. The ostinatos are shown in Example 7.20a.[177]

The sketches reveal that Birtwistle began by assembling his five ostinatos
on the same page, at the top of which he wrote a 22-quaver-long rhythm
for the cello ostinato. A six-note descending ostinato is also included on
the page (see F in Example 7.20b). Shared between flute and clarinet, this
sustained-note figure mirrors the Man's final utterances of the name 'Eurydice' and gradually casts its shadow across the other ostinatos. This is
appropriate because it relates back to similar descending phrases in the
voice on the lines 'casting our shadows back' and 'turned and gave her back
to the dark' at the end of the laments in sections 4 and 5 respectively (see
Example 7.20b). The cello ostinato is heard nine times in total, but, like the
others, it is never repeated identically (see A in Example 7.20a). Its 'prime'
form comprises 28 notes, but over time it is gradually shortened as follows:
28, 20, 20, 20, 13, 16, 15, 10, 5. Other alterations include changes to pitch,
rhythm and the durations between statements, some of which are mistakes.

[175] Birtwistle in programme note to the London premiere.
[176] The Woman makes several ironic references to Orpheus's 'masterstroke', that is, his failed
scheme to bring her back.
[177] Versions of the string ostinatos occur earlier in the work: the violin and viola dyads are heard
in section 8 at Fig. 76, marked 'quasi una sarabanda'; the cello ostinato is foreshadowed in
sections 3 (third part), 6 (first part) and 8.

Example 7.20a Ostinatos in section 9, pp. 119–32

Nine

Example 7.20b Descending 'shadow motif' in section 9, and antecedents

F

Section 9, sketch for descending 'shadow' motif

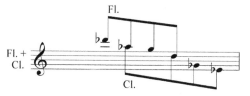

Section 4, 'His Song', p. 66

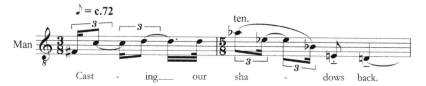

Section 5, 'His Song', p. 78

Section 9, p. 122

Table 7.4. *Permutational table for Eurydice's 'dance to death'*

	1	2	3	4	5	6	7	8	9
7512380649	3	1	5	2	4	1	1	4	3
6751832904	4	5	1	3	2	4	2	2	1
5086193247	1	4	2	1	5	5	3	5	4
0479216358	5	2	3	4	1	3	4	1	2
9620784135	2	3	4	5	3	2	5	3	5

However, the contour is rarely altered, therefore the basic identity of the ostinato is retained.

A closer examination of the sketches reveals further insights into Birtwistle's abstract representation. Across a sequence of four pages Birtwistle wrote a continuous series of quavers, which correspond to semi-quavers in the score. Beneath this line of durations 41 permutations of numbers 1 to 0 are written, where 0 = 10. In fact, only five permutations are used, as shown in Table 7.4.

As the table reveals, Birtwistle drew up a series of possible orderings for these permutations, determined by the columns marked 1 to 9. However, he did not follow this table precisely. Rather, he reordered the columns and even incorporated internal repetitions, omissions, and different orders. The columns from Table 7.4 that appear to have been selected and adapted are as follows (in the order they appear): 1; 3; 4 (with a repetition of 1); a different ordering of all five permutations; 2 (1–3); 7 (1–4); 7 (with 4 omitted); 9 (1–2); 9 (2 omitted but 5 repeated); a different ordering of three permutations.

Each number in the resultant line corresponds to a semiquaver in the score. A different rhythmic skeleton was then mapped out on five separate lines, one for each instrument in the quintet, and the entire sequence was divided into seven twelve-bar sections (the metre is a constant 3/8).[178] The twelve-bar divisions control a filtering process that determines where rests will fall within each layer of the rhythmic skeleton. The ostinatos are distributed across the skeleton and, in principle, the notes are written only when they are permitted by the number scheme. For example, the sketches indicate that in the second, third and fourth twelve-bar sections the following numbers are filtered in each part:

---

[178] There are additional bars in the score at the end of the piece that are missing from the sketches.

flute	12	123	1234
clarinet	34	345	3456
violin	56	567	5678
viola	78	789	7890
cello	90	901	9012

In practice, however, Birtwistle overrides his scheme on occasions, either deliberately or by mistake, both in the sketch and subsequently in the drafts. Towards the end of the dance, in the section that corresponds to the fourth page in the sketches sequence, the filtering process has increased to such an extent that the music is thinned out almost entirely, leading to a ghostly effect at the words 'his masterstroke'. The numbers filtered out in the fifth and sixth twelve-bar sections are as follows:

flute	1234567	23456789
clarinet	5678901	45678901
violin	9012345	78901234
viola	3456789	01234567
cello	7890123	34567890

Example 7.21a illustrates how this scheme was applied in the sketch. Along the bottom of the sketch are numbers that correspond to the twelve-bar sections, which determine a change in the filtering scheme; note also the 22 quavers and original rhythm of the cello ostinato. Circled notes indicate *fortissimo* dynamics. The version in the final score is given in Example 7.21b. A comparison reveals slight differences in the vocal line and octave transpositions in the flute. More significantly, Birtwistle alters the placement of notes in the cello in bars 11 and 4 of the sketch, and adds the woodwind's sustained descending phrase and string harmonics. In the final twelve-bar section the ostinatos effectively give way to the wispy harmonics and descending 'shadow' motif.

Theatre of cruelty

Harsent has commented that 'there is a sort of colossal emotional violence' about the moment when Orpheus turns.[179] Although this is not apparent in the music in section 8 when the Woman refers to Orpheus's death, it is conveyed by the urgency of the Man's final lament that follows – by his stuttering 'Eu-Eu-Eu-Eu-Eu', but particularly by his final strained *b'*, which

[179] Harsent in the programme note to the London premiere.

Example 7.21a Sketch for section 9, pp. 128–9

Example 7.21b Section 9, pp. 128–9

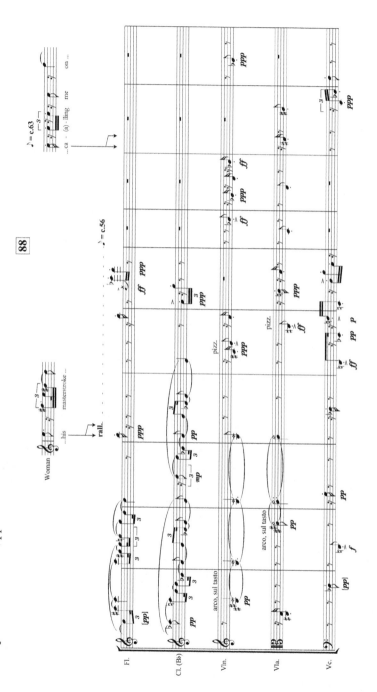

Example 7.22 'His Song' (verse 6), section 8, p. 119

was clearly intended to push the tenor out of his comfort zone and draw attention to the 'presence' of the moment (see Example 7.22). Harsent's imagery, too, is positively Artaudian in its references to 'rot', 'ruin', 'poison' and the 'cruel' breaking of bones. As Abbate has remarked:

> A terrible physical reality is precondition for the miracle [of song...] To be complacent about the head, to say it is just a metaphor, thus may reflect willed blindness to the awful aspects of Orpheus's fate, and to a symbolic force that is allied with horror, and not with poetry alone.[180]

Birtwistle's compositional processes are to some extent equivalent to this concept: when he remains faithful to the scheme for Eurydice's dance he destroys his own ostinatos, yet when he disregards those number schemes he does violence to his own carefully constructed plans.

In terms of physical movement on stage, *Corridor* is a largely static work that eschews the kind of visible violence witnessed towards the end of *Io*. Rather, conflict is expressed through the terse vocal exchanges, the quintet's clearly etched responses to Eurydice, and the intensity of the Man's lament. In a sense, this is a logical extension of the increasingly operatic nature of *Io*, in which song comes to the fore in the closing stages. Yet this situation also speaks to the irony of the Orpheus myth that although Eurydice passes away, the magnetic pull of Orpheus's voice – what Abbate terms his 'voice object' – increases as it grows in emotional strength. Yet when the tenor strains to sing the last note of his final lament he draws attention to himself as performer rather than character. Birtwistle therefore assigns a certain weight to the act of performance itself as a means to accentuate textual meaning, at which moment drama and real life merge into a form that Artaud would have described as 'true' theatre.

---

[180] Abbate, 'Orpheus. One last performance', in *In Search of Opera*, 1.

8 *The Last Supper* and *The Minotaur*: eyes 'half filled and half deserted'

Birtwistle's decision to base a dramatic work on the Last Supper reflects a wider artistic trend for Christian and spiritual themes at the approach to the millenium.[1] Yet arguably, as with *Punch* and *Orpheus*, the details of the story mattered less to Birtwistle than the story's existence in popular mythology and its forms of ritual and revelation. Similarly, the decision to base an opera on the subject of the Minotaur sat comfortably with Birtwistle's perennial concern for myth, ritual and – the focus of this chapter – duality. By this reckoning the two operas might be considered interchangeable. Yet Birtwistle's librettists – the North American poet Robin Blaser and David Harsent respectively – could not be more different. As in earlier chapters, the question is: how did these librettists inform their respective dramas and did Birtwistle respond to or depart from their ideas? Given the divergent nature of the two libretti, this chapter is less fully integrated than its predecessors. However, the very question of the possible or impossible relationship between two seemingly contradictory objects is central to both works: how is the division between the human and the divine in Christ, or the man and the beast in the Minotaur, to be represented in opera?

In his review of the Berlin premiere of *The Last Supper*, Paul Griffiths felt there was a 'separateness of libretto and score' and that for the most part the libretto resembled 'a heavy curtain, painted with images of sanctity, behind which the music is throbbing and punching with its own ideas of what gods are'.[2] Moreover, Whittall remarked that 'Blaser's text is an exegete's paradise, or nightmare, simply because both theological and dramatic certainties are so difficult to distil from it.'[3] Birtwistle's music necessarily 'grapples' with

---

[1] Other examples include Louis Andriessen's *Trilogy of the Last Day* (1993–7), John Adams's *El Niño* (2000), Gérard Grisey's *Quatre chants pour franchir le seuil* (1996–8), Jonathan Harvey's *Death of Light/Light of Death* (1998), and John Tavener's *Total Eclipse* (1999); for more on this topic see Arnold Whittall, 'Birtwistle's *Last Supper* and Adams's *El Niño*: echoes of old beliefs', *Musical Times* 143 (Winter 2002), 16–26.

[2] Paul Griffiths, review of *The Last Supper*, *Tempo*, 213 (2000), 42. *The Last Supper* was co-commissioned by the Deutsche Staatsoper, Glyndebourne Opera and the Royal Festival Hall, London. It was premiered in Berlin at the Deutsche Staatsoper on 18 April 2000, conducted by Daniel Barenboim; Ghost, Christ and Judas were sung by Susan Bickley, William Dazeley and Thomas Randle respectively. This production received further performances in Berlin in June 2000 before its UK premiere in Glyndebourne on 21 October 2000. The opera toured the UK in November and December 2000, then received a concert performance at the Queen Elizabeth Hall, London, on 26 January 2001. Glyndebourne ran a second production in August 2001, since when the opera has been performed in Milan, Turin, Vienna and Zwolle.

[3] Whittall, 'Birtwistle's *Last Supper*', 24.

Blaser's 'semantic complexities' in a work that lasts an hour and forty-five minutes, with no interval.[4] Yet Whittall also speaks valuably about Blaser and Birtwistle exploring 'the void beyond human experience' as a shadow that is brought 'centre-stage'.[5] Libretto and music, he argues, represent a quest for answers to questions that cannot be answered, yet together they face such questions with stoic liberal humanism. One question Blaser draws particular attention to is how to reconcile Christ's teachings and the notion of community with humanity's history of war, genocide, inequality and racism. Birtwistle's anxiety when setting Blaser's text led to a number of erasures and palimpsests in his sketches and drafts. By themselves, these represent an apposite metaphor for humanity's desire to rewrite history or erase horrific crimes. Birtwistle's erasures, however, also draw attention to particular scenes and specific contrapuntal and harmonic processes that reveal his own, more abstract response to the philosophical and theological questions raised in Blaser's text.

By contrast, *The Minotaur* explores the inextricable duality of animal and human in Everyman.[6] Despite the likelihood that they are half-siblings, and despite being locked into a cycle that draws them together, the opera's three protagonists – Ariadne, Theseus and the Minotaur – wish only to break the ties that bond them. The labyrinth has been constructed to hide human shame at past indiscretions – the unnatural union of Queen Pasiphae and a bull – its walls and passageways erected to enforce order in the world. Yet here there is no sense of community, just individuals safeguarding their interests or lamenting their sense of isolation and detachment. These themes are familiar from *Gawain* and *Mrs Kong*, yet here we are brought closer to the anti-hero than in any of Birtwistle's previous operas. All roads lead to the Minotaur's death, but his series of dreams and his final dying song reveal precisely the kind of potentiality in humans that Blaser explores. If the Minotaur's potentiality is to be fully realised, however, then the beast must die.

Blaser's *Last Supper*

Blaser's libretto is arguably the most complex and ambiguous that Birtwistle has set. The central premise is that 'the Western mind' has summoned up the disciples and Christ to re-enact the Last Supper in order to view

---

[4] Ibid., 25.   [5] Ibid., 26.

[6] *The Minotaur* is also concerned with the duality between the divine and the animal in man, as reflected in the Minotaur's link to the gods: his father is Poseidon and his name, Asterios, means 'starry'. Ruth Padel, 'Around the Minotaur', in the programme booklet for the Royal Opera House production of *The Minotaur*, April 2008, 12.

the millennium through the eyes of the year 2000.[7] The single-movement drama comprises four actions: assembling the disciples (in the original production these entered and exited via a brightly lit tunnel); building the table; Christ washing the disciples' feet; the Last Supper itself. Two key moments within this scheme, however, are the arrivals of the twelfth disciple, Judas, and, shortly after, Christ. The dramatic impact of Judas's appearance is equivalent to the Green Knight's entrance in *Gawain* in that it radically disturbs the status quo. Also inserted into the drama are three Visions based on sacred Latin texts associated with Christ.[8] These are sung by a pre-recorded chorus while mimed tableaux of stages from Christ's final days are enacted; in the original production these were acted out in a raised area above the main action. The Visions present events in reverse order: the crucifixion; the stations of the cross; Christ in the garden of Gethsemane. A summary of the work's overall structure is given in Table 8.1. The work falls roughly into halves, the second of which begins after Christ's entrance and the first Vision. However, a structural parallel between the table-building and footwashing scenes situates Judas's entrance at the centre of the drama.

In talks and interviews given in 2000, Blaser was at pains to explain that his libretto was not a theological argument in support or denial of faith. Rather, he was concerned that the text would set up a tension 'between the ritual that belongs to the way we think of the disciples and of Christ, and the realism of them, as men who make a living [and] who come out of an absolutely terrible historical period'.[9] In researching the text, Blaser became fascinated with the discovery that Judas was the only disciple from a city and he determined to salvage Judas from anti-Semitic persecution.[10] The opera's 'fundamental question', Blaser stated, is 'set by Christ: who is the

[7] The Ghost initially indicates that only eleven disciples have been invited ('Tonight, you and I / invite the eleven disciples'; Robin Blaser, *The Last Supper: Dramatic Tableaux* (London: Boosey and Hawkes, 2000), 7). However, when the final pieces of the table are assembled there are '13 places and 13 chairs', and when Judas arrives the Ghost informs the audience that 'You and I invited him'; Blaser, *The Last Supper*, 16 and 18.

[8] Vision I, 'O bone Jesu, exaudi me', is based on two lines from the anonymous prayer 'Anima Christi', the oldest surviving version of which dates back to *c.*1310 – 'O good Jesus, hear me / and do not allow me to be separated from You'; Vision II is the first verse of the 'Pange lingua', a thirteenth-century hymn for the Solemnity of Corpus Christi attributed to Saint Thomas Aquinas – 'Sing, my tongue, / the mystery of the Body glorified, / and the blood of boundless worth, / shed as ransom for the world [. . .]'; Vision III is the third verse of the 'Pange lingua' 'On the night of the last supper, / Reclining with His brothers [. . .]'; translations in Blaser, *Last Supper*, 23, 33 and 39.

[9] Blaser, in an interview for the BBC Radio 3 broadcast of the Glyndebourne premiere, 21 October 2000. He has also commented of the libretto: 'It is a major paradigm of western thought that you're dealing with. And it should be dealt with with respect and care – and *I* Miriam Nichols, 'Interview with Robin Blaser', in Nichols, ed., *Even on Sunday: Essays, Readings, and Archival Materials on the Poetry and Poetics of Robin Blaser* (Orono, ME: National Poetry Foundation, 2002), 378.

[10] From a conversation between Beard and Patrick Wright, 3 November 2010.

Table 8.1 The Last Supper: *formal outline*

1	Chorus: QUIS SIT DEUS?
	Entrance of Ghost
2	**Entrance of the Disciples**
	Peter
	Andrew
	dance
	James & John
	Bartholomew & Philip
	Thomas & Matthew
	Little James, Simon & Thaddeus
	dance
3	**The table is assembled**
	The *Pater Noster* & Isaiah 6.1–13
4	**Entrance of Judas**
	Questions to Judas
	Judas's aria
	Judas's riddle
	Christ's answer & entrance
	VISION I: The crucifixion
5	**Christ addresses the disciples**
	Footwashing: Christ washes the feet of all twelve disciples
	Christ: 'The Holocaust shattered my heart'
6	**The Last Supper**
	Judas lays a red cloth over the table & then leads Christ to his place
	dance
	VISION II: The stations of the cross
	Tableau: Leonardo's *The Last Supper* / Ghost cites A. M. Klein
	Ghost joins the table
	The disciples depart
	VISION III: The betrayal
7	**Christ in the Garden of Gethsemane**
	Christ: 'Whom do you seek?'
	A cock crows.

betrayer and what has been betrayed?' In one sense this relates to Judas: Blaser's Judas suggests he was doing Christ's bidding and had assumed God would intervene. Was Judas therefore the betrayed? Yet Blaser also implies that it is Christ's message, his 'religion of love', that has been betrayed by the Church's hubris and complicity in wars and other crimes.[11]

---

[11] Blaser, *The Last Supper*, 30.

Throughout the libretto, questions are raised about the nature of God: at the opening, the female Chorus Mysticus sings 'Quis sit Deus? Quod est nomen eius?' (What is God? What is his name?)[12] Christ's onstage presence is charismatic yet distinctly human (no miracles are performed), and it is he who draws the disciples' attention to voices of scepticism, the 'shadows talking', who at one point sing that 'God isn't. God is never again.'[13] Yet the moment of dramatic revelation when Christ appears, followed by Birtwistle's moving first Vision, suggest that he is divine, while the sound of a cockcrow at the end hints at the possibility of another betrayal.

One of Blaser's models for his interrogative style is Dante, whose epic poems informed Blaser's notion of what 'poetry should be'.[14] Blaser studied Dante's work in the 1940s at Berkeley with the German Jewish historian Ernst Kantorowicz, and prior to starting his libretto he produced a poem titled 'Great Companion: Dante Alighiere' (1997). Here Blaser refers to a 'discoursing' in Dante's *Inferno* 'of myth, cosmology, philosophy, theology, history, economics, and current issues' and 'an ever changing polyphony of amorous thought': Dante, Blaser suggests, 'is our guide to a poetics of interrogation'.[15] Hence, in 1993, Blaser stated that Dante's *Comedy* 'is a primary document in our effort to imagine and measure a human community worthy of our words – and in which we hold only a "middle place"'.[16]

Dante has been described as 'the first creative writer of our millennium who abhorred the widespread materialism, religious cynicism and political opportunism that disfigured his world'.[17] In the libretto such sentiments surface most prominently during the footwashing scene when, in response to each disciple's question 'What's this?', Christ lists various prejudices and atrocities perpetuated through history, often in God's name. The libretto's principal agent of interrogation and mediator, however, is a soprano named

---

[12] These key theological questions relate back to Exodus 3:13, in which Moses asks God what he should say to the Israelites when they enquire what God's name is. The question 'What is God?' is also raised at the start of Jean-Luc Nancy's 'Of divine places', which informed Blaser's libretto; Nancy, *The Inoperative Community*, ed. Peter Connor, trans. Peter Connor, Lisa Garbus, Michael Holland and Simona Sawhney (Minneapolis and London: University of Minnesota Press, 2006), 110–50.

[13] Blaser, *The Last Supper*, 25. This text is a reference to Gérard de Nerval's 'Christ among the olives' from the sequence *Les Chimères* (1854), a version of which Blaser published in 1965. Nerval's poem refers back to the German romantic novelist Jean Paul's 'Speech of the dead Christ from the universe that there is no God' (1796), from his romantic novel *Siebenkäs*.

[14] Blaser, 'Poetry and positivisms: High-Muck-a-Muck or "Spiritual Ketchup"' in *The Fire: Collected Essays of Robin Blaser*, ed. Miriam Nichols (Berkeley and Los Angeles: University of California Press, 2006), 52.

[15] Blaser, 'A Note' [to 'Dante Alighiere'], 1997, revised 25 January 2006; in *The Holy Forest: Collected Poems of Robin Blaser*, ed. Miriam Nichols (Berkeley and Los Angeles: University of California Press, 2006), 457.

[16] Blaser, 'The recovery of the public world', in *The Fire*, 74.

[17] David H. Higgins, 'Introduction', in Dante, *The Divine Comedy*, trans. C. H. Sisson (London and Sydney: Pan Books, 1980), 11.

Ghost, a role suggested by Blaser in order to bring a female voice into the opera.[18] The Ghost's opening address is substantial. In seventy-five lines all of the opera's principal themes are outlined in powerfully evocative language with the kind of imagery that is remarkably well suited to Birtwistle's interests, for example its references to 'fragments', 'voices' speaking from the ground, and the 'subterranean stream' of history. The Ghost begins by announcing that she is the ghost of 'you' – that is, 'we', the audience.[19] The absence of 'Holy' from her name implies that she represents 'the spirit of the modern, secular age'.[20] Moreover, Whittall argues that:

> As far as Blaser's text is concerned, the Ghost might . . . represent the voice of the Western liberal as sceptical pessimist, acknowledging that 'God is the being we are not', appalled by the 'brutality and terror of our century', summoning up Jesus and his disciples in an effort to discover what role 'the mysteries of God' might have for us, and, near the end, apparently alarmed by the threat posed by a belligerent Messiah 'coming in his tank'.[21]

To this it should be added that it is the Ghost who declares that 'God isn't. God is no more', yet her text is also replete with biblical references.[22] Indeed, Birtwistle sensed that the Ghost is Blaser himself, to which the poet replied disingenuously, 'yes it is, and I'm going to audition for the part'.[23]

It has been argued that we gain from the Ghost an impression of our time as 'bare and reduced, both disillusioned and damaged by its own history'.[24] At the Berlin premiere Blaser explained that 'a sense of "breakage" seemed to be a defining characteristic of our times' and he counted 'the "great belief system" of Christianity as one of the things that have broken';[25] our task now, he argued, is to come to terms with living in the 'shatters of that in which we trust'.[26] There are philosophical reasons why Blaser introduced the metaphor of 'breakage', as will be discussed later. However, one might equally argue that Christianity has simply receded in modern times. As

---

[18] Although the Ghost is consistent with mediators in other Birtwistle operas (Choregos, Morgan le Fay, Mirror, Ariadne), she was integral to Blaser's original conception of the libretto. See Nichols, 'Interview with Robin Blaser', 377.

[19] Stan Persky notes that use of the second-person singular, the pronominal 'you', often placed in quotation marks, is characteristic of Blaser's work and was first used in his poem 'Moth' (1962). This device, Persky argues, reveals in Blaser's work the sense of 'a god or spirit of otherness' that is in sympathy with contemporary concern for the Other. See 'About Robin Blaser', www.dooneyscafe.com/archives/241 (accessed 22 December 2010).

[20] Whittall, 'Birtwistle's *Last Supper*', 16.   [21] Ibid., 18.

[22] Ghost's introduction alone paraphrases or quotes from the following: Psalm 102:7; Revelation 1:12; 1 Corinthians 15:52; Luke 11:34; Matthew 25:13 and Isaiah 29:4.

[23] Nichols, 'Interview with Robin Blaser', 377.

[24] Patrick Wright, 'Facing up to the subterranean stream: the challenge of Robin Blaser's libretto', in the programme booklet to the Glyndebourne premiere of *The Last Supper*, October 2000, 41–2.

[25] Ibid., 42.   [26] Blaser, *The Last Supper*, 27; the line is sung by Christ.

Whittall remarks, 'Any present-day dramatic treatment of a Christian story exists in an ambiguous context of conflicting ideals and realities – on the one hand, acknowledging the survival of the Christian religion, and, on the other, observing its failure to win universal acceptance and to transform human behaviour.'[27] In the latter part of the libretto Christ addresses the Ghost directly and invites her to join the disciples at the table. When Christ and his party leave, however, she does not depart with them. In other words, there is no message of conversion in Blaser's libretto and no resurrection.

Agamben and Nancy: the 'irreparable' and the 'broken'

Birtwistle was introduced to Blaser by Patrick Wright, a freelance journalist and author who studied with Birtwistle in the 1960s and with Blaser in the 1980s.[28] In 1997 Wright interviewed Blaser for BBC Radio 3's *Night Waves*.[29] After hearing the programme and reading some of Blaser's work Birtwistle adopted the title of Blaser's poem *Exody* (1990–3) for his orchestral score *Exody '23: 59: 59'* (1996–7).[30] Subsequently, at the Chicago premiere of Birtwistle's work in February 1998, poet, composer and broadcaster met to discuss a possible collaboration on the subject of the Last Supper. Birtwistle was instantly impressed by Blaser. Opposed to the notion of the poet as creative intelligence, Blaser was an assembler of texts, his poems shot through with quotations and allusions to earlier writers, for he fully subscribed to the Adornian view that, following the Holocaust, poetry can no longer continue in the lyrical mode. Rather, he argued, poets should relocate 'the high lyric voice' by 'convening' cultures and traditions – by which Blaser appears to mean bringing different cultures and traditions together in a spirit of reciprocity.[31]

During the 1940s and 1950s Blaser was associated with the so-called San Francisco Renaissance and the Black Mountain School. Along with Robert Duncan, Jack Spicer and Charles Olson, Blaser rejected the imposition of narrative in favour of avant-garde experimentalism: he worked with Cage-inspired aleatoricism, open forms and 'serial poems'. The latter concept is

[27] Whittall, 'Birtwistle's *Last Supper*', 18.

[28] Wright studied with Birtwistle as a boy at Port Regis preparatory school, Dorset, then with Blaser as a Master's student at Simon Fraser University, Canada.

[29] The programme, titled 'Relocating the high lyric voice', was broadcast on 22 January 1997; it is available online at http://writing.upenn.edu/pennsound/x/Blaser.php (accessed 1 November 2010).

[30] Hall, *HBIRY*, 142. According to Wright, Blaser intended the word 'exody' as a metaphor for traditions being drawn through time, as a cork is pulled from a bottle; from conversation between Beard and Wright, 3 November 2010. Birtwistle's subtitle is a reference to the last second of the day as a 'moment of leaving'; cited in Adlington, *MHB*, 120.

[31] Blaser, 'Relocating the high lyric voice'.

defined in remarkably Birtwistlian terms in Blaser's essay 'The fire' (1967) in which the form is compared to a processional or Ovidian *carmen perpetuum*, 'a continuous song in which the fragmented subject matter is only apparently disconnected'.[32] Indeed, Whittall has suggested that Birtwistle's vocal writing in the opera is predominantly 'what we might term the processional arioso' in which vocal lines unfold 'without obvious melodic processes'.[33] Blaser's concept of serial poems culminated in *The Holy Forest* (1993; revised 2006), a collected edition that comprises over twenty poetic cycles, written between 1956 and 2004, through which is threaded a series of twenty-six poems titled 'Image-Nation'.

In Blaser's poetry and libretto alike, research and quotation are assimilated and transformed by a distinctive and imaginative voice. His language is both dialogical, in the sense of having many voices, and dialectical, as the title 'Image-Nation' implies, via the pun on 'imagination'. Blaser's favourite imagery, like Birtwistle's, comes from the myth of Orpheus: 'It is precisely in the image of the scattered body and mind of Orpheus that I place whatever I know about the poetic process – that scattering is a living reflection of the world.'[34] Accordingly, Blaser's libretto draws on numerous authors, some of whom are acknowledged in the libretto, such as Edmund Spenser, Richard Crashaw, Thomas Traherne, Charles Olson and A. M. Klein, while others, such as Avital Ronell, Gérard de Nerval and George Steiner, are not. Yet Blaser records a 'special indebtedness' to Jean-Luc Nancy's *The Inoperative Community* and Giorgio Agamben's *The Coming Community* when 'thinking through' his libretto.[35]

What was it about these two cultural philosophers that attracted Blaser, and what did he draw from their essays? Nancy and Agamben are concerned with individual and social ontology in the context of a philosophy of the Left. Broadly speaking, Blaser is sympathetic to this context; in 1967 he spoke of 'the importance of community' and added, 'I am demonstrably bad at the kind of communism one dreams of, yet I have repeatedly worked in and added to a community of that sort.'[36] As will be seen, the concept of community is central to *The Last Supper* and it is arguably in response to this idea that Birtwistle developed the work's distinctive musical style. Agamben and Nancy reflect a recent affiliation between post-structuralist

---

[32] Robin Blaser, 'The fire', in *The Fire*, 5. Blaser's musical interests – Bach, Boulez, Cage and Carter – are also more or less Birtwistlian.

[33] Whittall, 'Birtwistle's *Last Supper*', 25. Another possible analogy is to Birtwistle's *Exody* in which a processional journey is fragmented by sideways glances through 'windows' in the structure. See Adlington, *MHB*, 119–20 and Hall, *HBIRY*, 145–6.

[34] Blaser, 'The fire', 9.   [35] Blaser, *The Last Supper*, 2.

[36] Blaser, 'The fire', 12. See also Scott Pound, 'Writing/repeating community: Robin Blaser's *Image-Nation* series', in Nichols, ed., *Even on Sunday*, 167–77.

interest in otherness and the metaphysics of religion, and both warn that attempts to design society will result in forms of totalitarianism. This latter point resonates with work by Hannah Arendt, the German Jewish political theorist who Wright suggests was an important presence throughout Blaser's oeuvre.[37] In the libretto Blaser refers to Arendt's concept of the 'subterranean stream of history', which she discusses in her preface to *The Origins of Totalitarianism* (1951).[38] This is the catalogue of human atrocities that generations have attempted to cover over or forget, but which, according to Christ, 'bursts / out of the cracks and crevices of belief'.[39] Arendt argues it is necessary to bear consciously 'the burden which our century has placed on us – neither denying its existence nor submitting meekly to its weight'.[40] This idea is highlighted by Christ's list of crimes against humanity in the footwashing scene and symbolised by the dust (*de pulvere*) Christ washes from the disciples' feet.[41]

By one of the twentieth century's uncanny twists of fate Arendt was tutored by – and romantically attracted to – Martin Heidegger, the hugely important philosopher who at one time supported Hitler's cause.[42] It is therefore doubly significant (or ironic) that the two texts by Agamben and Nancy are also indebted to Heidegger, in particular to his concept of *Dasein*, that is, the notion of existence as 'Being-in the world': a being is engaged with the world and comprehends its existence in terms of this engagement.[43] *Dasein* is, therefore, not only 'mine', as Blaser's poetry is not only 'his'. As Nancy summarises, 'the *Dasein* is right away a world "that I share with others", or "a world-with"'. Being then becomes a matter of 'being-with' and 'being-according-to-sharing'.[44] It is clearly with this in mind that the Ghost, in the final lines of the opera, sings 'Here we are – you and I – / sharing our lives' – an idea represented literally in the music by a line passed between the Ghost and a solo flute (see Example 8.1).[45] Not only is the Ghost a mediator – between us, Christ and the disciples – but she is also our (the

---

[37] Arendt's work was the subject of Blaser's Charles Olson lectures, given at Buffalo in 1987; available at http://writing.upenn.edu/pennsound/x/Blaser.php (accessed 22 December 2010).

[38] Hannah Arendt, *The Origins of Totalitarianism* (San Diego, New York and London: Harcourt Brace Jovanovich, 1973), ix.

[39] Blaser, *The Last Supper*, 29.   [40] Arendt, *The Origins*, viii.

[41] Christ's list draws heavily on Nancy who refers to religion's 'political and moral despotism, its hatred of reason as much as of the body'; *The Inoperative Community*, 141. These words are also paraphrased by the Ghost; Blaser, *The Last Supper*, 5.

[42] It is worth noting in this context that the subject of Arendt's doctoral thesis was the concept of love in the writings of Saint Augustine.

[43] Peter Sedgwick, *From Descartes to Derrida: An Introduction to European Philosophy* (Oxford and Malden, MA: Blackwell, 2001), 122.

[44] Nancy, *The Inoperative Community*, 103.

[45] All musical references are to the published full score: Harrison Birtwistle, *The Last Supper* (London: Boosey & Hawkes, 2008).

Example 8.1 Shared line between Ghost and solo flute, *The Last Supper* (full score, Boosey & Hawkes, 2008), bb. 1,915–8

audience's) shadow, and she closes the opera by informing us that neither death nor love, where we find ourselves 'beyond ourselves', are our own. A similar idea is expressed in Blaser's poetry, by his use of other authors' texts and his belief that language 'is not our own – no more than our life or death is in our ownership'.[46]

According to Heidegger, however, an important aspect of existence is the condition of being 'abandoned' or 'set free' in the world. Agamben refers to this state as 'the irreparable': all worldly entities are 'thrown' irreparably into the world; Beings are 'consigned irreparably to their being-thus'.[47] Both Heidegger and Agamben stress, however, that Beings are not essences but potentialities: *Dasein* is the potential for being and for not being – one may choose to do something or not. Moreover, Agamben envisions a 'coming community' in which individuals simply are what they are, and do what they do, without common identities or causes: they develop the potential for 'not not-being'.[48] They are neither general nor particular but are what Agamben refers to as 'whatever' beings, or 'whatever' singularities. In the

[46] Blaser, 'The irreparable' [2003], in *The Fire*, 98.
[47] Giorgio Agamben, *The Coming Community*, trans. Michael Hardt (Minneapolis and London: University of Minnesota Press, 2005), 39.
[48] Ibid., 40.

coming community, people share nothing more than their singularity, and community exists only in as much as people are not alone. To what extent Blaser endorsed this vision is unclear. However, Agamben's notion that people are neither general nor particular provides a link to Nancy and Blaser. For Nancy declares, in a line that is paraphrased by the Ghost, 'man and the god are together in an identical region of being'.[49] In other words, God is a form of 'whatever being' that is not tied to a group or specificity but is with all beings.

A different but related theme in the libretto is the act of watching or seeing: the Ghost has the refrain 'I watch'; she sees herself 'in your eyes'; and she asks us to 'Be watchful.'[50] Such imagery relates to Blaser's critical response, elsewhere, to society's media-led obsession with spectacle. Visual identification is also one of the means by which entities enter into language. However, the profane objectification of existence through language, which 'names' things and people according to their appearance, actually exposes the transcendent, since a name is only a substitute for 'the thing being-called'. Blaser likewise argues that the poet's role is one of 'searching the presences / that weren't there – before the words carved them'.[51] In the opera this is symbolised by a riddle that Judas presents to the disciples. Thomas asks Judas who he thinks Jesus is, to which Judas responds that Christ is the answer to a riddle: 'What can go in the face of the sun / yet leave no shadow?' After three wrong answers and increasingly hostile demands that Judas 'answer' – a moment that recalls the ceremonies in *Orpheus* – the riddle is finally solved by Christ, who answers: 'The wind.' In the process of singing these words Christ reveals himself from among the disciples. The riddle therefore functions as a critique of the disciples' urge to pin down the nature and meaning of God: He moves among them but casts no shadow.[52] Nancy, following Seneca, expresses a similar idea when he declares that our eyes are both 'filled and deserted by divinity', a seminal line that is given to the Ghost.[53] Similarly, as Agamben states, 'At the point you perceive the irreparability [the being-thus] of the world at that point it is transcendent.'[54] Evil, however, 'is the reduction of the taking-place of things to a fact like others, the forgetting of the transcendence inherent in the very taking-place of things'.[55]

---

[49] Nancy, *The Inoperative Community*, 124; Blaser, *The Last Supper*, 6.
[50] Blaser, *The Last Supper*, 5–7. Similarly, Christ's first instruction when he enters is to 'Watch' (24). This imagery is often derived from biblical sources, for example Psalm 102:7: 'I watch, and am as a sparrow alone upon the house top'.
[51] Blaser, 'Image-Nation 26 (being-thus' [1 October 2000], in *The Holy Forest*, 432.
[52] Hence Agamben's remark that 'What is properly divine is that the world does not reveal God'; Agamben, *The Coming Community*, 90.
[53] Ibid., 126.   [54] Ibid., 106.   [55] Ibid., 15.

As Agamben suggests here, there is a potential darker side to the irreparable.[56] In *Exody* and in Christ's lines during the footwashing scene, Blaser refers to 'the existential given', by which he most likely means the gift of human life.[57] Yet this gift has been violated by the exclusion and alienation of blacks, women, Jews, homosexuals and others.[58] The potential for exclusion arises when language is used to name, identify and essentialise. This is exemplified in the opera by the treatment of Judas: labelled a 'Betrayer', he is violently rejected by the disciples through aggressive words and, in the original production, physical threats. What makes this rejection more shocking is that it follows on from the Lord's Prayer/'Pater Noster', sung in English and Latin. Moreover, this is alternated with declamations from the Hebrew testament (Isaiah 6:1–13) in an interplay that challenges 'history's segregation of Christianity and Judaism'.[59] The boldest attack on this schism, however, comes at the climax of the footwashing scene when Christ declares: 'The Holocaust shattered my heart.' Blaser had originally used the word 'broken' rather than 'shattered'.[60] This was altered because several people who read the libretto before the first performance felt the phrase was too clichéd. Yet there is a notable musical precedent for this choice: Handel's 'Thy rebuke hath broken his heart', in *Messiah*, Part II scene 1 (Christ's Passion).[61] Blaser claims that he derived the word from Nancy for whom the concept of 'the broken' refers both to society's loss of faith and to the idea that acts of faith or love involve a break or fracture: 'As soon as there is love, the slightest act of love, the slightest spark, there is this ontological fissure that cuts across and that disconnects the elements of the subject-proper – the fibers of its heart.'[62] The other 'cuts across' the heart, which is broken; yet 'the heart is not broken, in the sense that it does not exist before the break. But it is the break itself that makes the heart.'[63]

Birtwistle's *Last Supper*

During the writing process Birtwistle requested that certain words be replaced by simpler alternatives, for example 'subterranean' with

---

[56] It is this darker aspect that Blaser focuses on in his essay 'The irreparable', as does Wright in 'Facing up'.

[57] See Miriam Nichols, 'Spilling the names of God: Robin Blaser's *The Last Supper*', *Mosaic*, 36/2 (2003), 168–9.

[58] Blaser's use of the term 'existential given' is adapted from Hans Mayer, *Outsiders: A Study in Life and Letters*, trans. Denis M. Sweet (Cambridge, MA: MIT Press, 1984). Originally published in 1975, this is a study of the alienation of women, Jews and homosexuals in literature from Marlowe to the late twentieth century.

[59] Wright, 'Facing up', 44.   [60] Wright in conversation with Beard, 3 November 2010.

[61] The text in this section is derived from Psalm 69:20: 'Reproach hath broken my heart; and I am full of heaviness: and I looked *for some* to take pity, but *there was* none; and for comforters, but I found none'.

[62] Nancy, *The Inoperative Community*, 96.   [63] Ibid., 98 and 99.

'underground', 'antisemitism' with 'hatred of Jews'. Not all such requests were accepted: 'subterranean' was not replaced. The intention, however, was to make the lines easier to sing or to convey meaning more directly. A case in point in the footwashing scene was a proposed alteration to Christ's line from 'Pre-emptions of God's judgment' to 'Judging as if they were God.'[64] Although the latter is perhaps easier to grasp in the opera house, the former conveys the deeper hubris of a claim to have greater power than God. It also has the virtue of an internal rhyme ('empt' and 'ment'). Correspondence between Wright and Blaser's assistant Peter Quartermain reveals that Blaser was resistant to such changes and at times successfully defended his choice of words: ultimately, 'Pre-emptions of God's judgment' was retained. Nevertheless, early versions of the libretto and score reveal that Christ's list during the footwashing scene was rewritten several times in the six months between the Berlin premiere and the Glyndebourne performances and this resulted in a certain amount of musical re-composition. The original list in this scene was cryptic at times and it seems that Blaser was prompted to expand his text, even doubling Christ's lines at one stage, in an attempt to clarify his meaning.[65]

Although Birtwistle questioned aspects of Blaser's text his response to the libretto is remarkably vivid and imaginative.[66] To avoid smothering the words, a medium-sized orchestra of thirty-five players is used with no violins. The opera's vocal dimension is as varied as anything Birtwistle has written: the score comprises thirteen male soloists, solo soprano, Chorus Mysticus (a nine-part female choir that sings mainly biblical references in Latin), a pre-recorded nine-part female Chorus Resonus (often used to provide transformed echoes of the Chorus Mysticus), and an eighteen-part mixed choir for the pre-recorded Visions.[67] Generally, darker tones predominate, particularly through doublings of mid- and low-register

[64] Revealed in a letter from Peter Quartermain to Wright dated 27 July 2000, kindly forwarded to Beard by Quartermain.

[65] For example, 'Genetic definitions of worthless life', which was performed in Berlin, became 'The deeming of lives as worthless – demonic thought'; Blaser, *The Last Supper*, 28. In one unused revision Christ converses twice with each disciple in turn, rather than the single exchanges in the published version.

[66] A number of critics remarked on the range of musical expression: Rodney Milnes referred to 'the extraordinary range of musical colour – extraordinary even by Birtwistle's standards – that comes at you from all sides' ('Another place at the table', *The Times*, 6 August 2001), and Anna Picard to an 'urgent score' that 'thrusts out chunks of beauty; colours from the souk to the symphony hall and textures from the antiphonal rigidity of the Lutheran mass to the lush harmonic swamp of Schoenberg' ('The agony and the ecstasy of a Last Supper reunion', *Independent*, 29 October 2000).

[67] In the original production the Chorus Mysticus was positioned at the rear of the stage, but only partially visible; at the start they appeared as masked faces above a wall, which anticipated a similar idea in *The Minotaur*. In a production by Neue Oper Wien in April 2008, however, the chorus was onstage, costumed and integrated with the main action. This innovative production was first staged at the Atelierhaus der Akademie der bildenden Künste Wien, Semperdepot, and performed later in Holland.

Example 8.2　Voices 'speaking out of the ground': Ghost and brass, bb. 204–10

instruments that simultaneously imply the 'shadow presences' and 'sub-terranean stream' referred to by the Ghost in her opening address. Here in particular the brass's slow declarative chords evoke the sound of voices 'speaking out of the ground' (see Example 8.2).[68] Blaser's theme of spectacle

68　Blaser, *The Last Supper*, 6–7. The text here is a reference to Isaiah 29:4 in which God threatens that if the inhabitants of Jerusalem worship false gods they will be reduced to ghostly voices in the ground. Such moments are especially reminiscent of *Gawain*; see Chapter 5 and Adlington, "'Good lodging'".

is also highlighted musically, for example by luminous unison doublings of the Ghost's line 'alight in one another's eyes' (bars 146–50).

Another concept in the libretto given particular musical importance is Christ's association with 'the wind' and John's comparison of Christ to 'a wind, like a breath'.[69] This image, which invokes Blaser's notion of the existential given (the gift of life) and the potentiality inherent in the *Dasein*, informs the opera's opening in which a low heartbeat pulse on D♭ is combined with short rising glissandi in the cellos. The impression of sharp intakes of breath is confirmed by amplified exhaling gestures in the accordion marked 'air only'. Eerie breath-like sounds are also heard when the Ghost summons up the spirits of the disciples from the past: open vowels and sibilants are sung glissando by the two choruses with swelling sounds in the accordion (see Example 8.3). This effect is further enhanced by *sul ponticelli* tremolandi in the strings and soft bent pitches in the horns and trombones, punctuated by piercing fragments of birdsong in the highest woodwind. Later, Christ's answer to Judas's riddle is amplified throughout the theatre. This triggers amplified tam-tam strokes (a sharp metallic resonance) and breathing sounds in the instruments and chorus who gently enunciate the fragmented syllables of 'Alleluia'. In such moments the sense of an ineffable, transcendent realm beyond the everyday world is powerfully evoked.

The association of unearthly effects with Christ is turned on its head, however, immediately after the second Vision when the mood becomes troubled following Christ's questions: 'Who is the betrayer? What has been betrayed?' Here music and text invoke the darker side of the irreparable and the human desire to essentialise. Unvoiced sibilants and voiceless vowels in the Chorus Mysticus, quarter tones in the strings, amplified wind sounds from the accordion, idiosyncratic figures in the woodwind and nervous, amplified whispers and declamations from the disciples bring a distinct chill to the air. Shortly after this, Christ assumes an uncharacteristically bellicose voice when declaring 'God said: "Tell them I AM / I AM sent you to them', in a retelling of the story of Moses and the burning bush (Example 8.4).[70] When the disciples and Christ then freeze in the position of Leonardo da Vinci's *Last Supper* (1495–8), 'bathed in the harshest possible bright light',[71] the Ghost quotes from A. M. Klein's 'Ballad of the Days of the Messiah' (1941), written during the Nazi invasion of Russia.[72] Militaristic drum rhythms and piping woodwind underscore the poem's image of the

[69] Blaser, *The Last Supper*, 9.
[70] Blaser, *The Last Supper*, 35; the reference is to Exodus 3:13–15.
[71] Harrison Birtwistle, *The Last Supper*, full score (London: Boosey & Hawkes, 2008), p. 317. In the original production, however, the scene was lit in vertical rainbow strips (blue, red, orange, purple, yellow) as a parody of Andy Warhol's *The Last Supper* (1986).
[72] Klein was born in Ukraine but moved to Canada at an early age.

Example 8.3 Accordion, Ghost, Chorus Resonus and Chorus Mysticus, bb. 261–4

*) Breath only: 'o' as in *stone*, 'a' as in *apple*. Raise basic pitch only by the indicated intervals.

Example 8.4 Christ and Chorus Mysticus, bb. 1,695–1,700

Messiah approaching in a tank. However, these darker visions give way abruptly to the ritual of the Last Supper itself and a return to the softer, lyrical Christ whose line culminates on a falsetto E♮ on the word 'love' (this initiates an extended line that will be discussed later). As well as echoing Simon's earlier reference to 'love', this moment recalls the entrance of Judas, whose 'Amen' at the close of the 'Pater Noster' ended on the same note (see Example 8.5).[73] A musical association is therefore implied between Judas and two kinds of love: Simon's love, shadowed by anger, and Christ's love, which is 'a human skill' like justice. When Christ invites the disciples to leave with him to the garden of Gethsemane, in the lead into the final Vision, 'Air only' sounds in the accordion and whispered vowels in the chorus return. Finally, the accordion's gesture of released air is the last instrumental sound before the cockcrow.

---

[73] Birtwistle's sketches reveal he originally intended an E♮ centre at the opening, rather than D♭; PSS 0525-0539 and -0651.

Example 8.5 Association of love and Judas through pitch class E

Bars 601–3   Simon

[I'm no longer Simon the Assassin, but rage seems to sha- dow__] all I   love._____

Bar 782   Judas

A   -   men.__

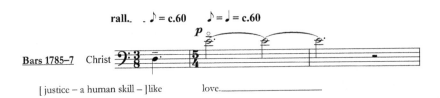

Bars 1785–7   Christ

[justice – a human skill –] like   love._____

To gain a more fine-grained appreciation of Birtwistle's perspective on the libretto, we may turn to the musical sketches and drafts stored in Basle.[74] Although this material reveals a great degree of consistency with *Gawain* and, especially, with *Mrs Kong*, there are important differences. The most obvious of these is the extent to which Birtwistle agonised over certain sections, revising and sometimes completely overturning his original intentions. This is most evident in the sketches for the table-building scene, which raises the question of why this section mattered so much to the composer. In summary: Birtwistle's sketches reflect a desire to do justice to Blaser's poetic imagery; they flag up sections for closer attention, notably the opening, the table-building scene, the entrance of Thomas and Matthew, and the Last Supper ritual; and they reveal a score filled with the 'shadow presences' of the composer's original intentions.[75]

74 There are 694 sides of sketches, drafts, fair copy and libretto for *The Last Supper* in the Sammlung Harrison Birtwistle of the Paul Sacher Stiftung; the fair copy is incomplete, and there are just 2 sides of draft libretto.
75 Blaser, *The Last Supper*, 6–7. This suggests a parallel to the Ghost's three-times-repeated refrain 'of what we meant'.

'Quis sit Deus?'

In the lead-up to the Chorus Mysticus's opening theological question 'What is God?', one might reasonably expect to find some kind of abstract musical context for the drama to follow. Sketches for the opening do indeed indicate this. Moreover, they reveal Birtwistle picking up from his orchestral work *Exody* in which he had explored a harmonic tension 'between symmetrically based procedures and those based on modes'.[76] Early versions of the opening of *The Last Supper* employ six-note sets with intervallic steps of 2–2–2–1–1 or 1–1–2–2–2 sometimes joined together to form a symmetrical twelve-note set. These sets were used to generate a series of descending bass-line scales that lead to the chorus's opening question. In the final score, however, the original symmetries are 'broken' by the addition of interval 3 steps. In other words, the opening is 'half filled and half deserted' by Birtwistle's initial modal design.

When the Ghost later answers the chorus's question by stating that 'God is the being we are not', the entire string and lower woodwind accompaniment throughout her verse is formed from permutations of symmetrical 1–2–2–1 sets.[77] Indeed, Birtwistle seems to have consciously associated questions of God's identity with musical symmetries. This is powerfully illustrated by the strings' fifty-times-repeated *fortissimo* chord that accompanies Judas's statement that his betrayal of Christ resulted from a 'terrifying misapprehension of the presence and absence of God'. As shown in Example 8.6, the chord spans two octaves from D to d'. With the exception of the double bass, each part plays a perfect fifth grouped into two or four staccato semiquavers.[78] Moreover, the same symmetrical shape is present in both octaves: D–F♯–A–C♯, or the intervallic set 4–3–4. In total there are twelve notes, six in each octave. Yet the inclusion of three neighbour notes (E♭, A♭ and G) breaks the symmetry. A similar effect is achieved at the close of the opera by a softly ascending tremolo scale, each note of which is held to form a chord. The scale passes four times through the cello and viola sections while the Ghost sings that love and death are not our own (see Example 8.7). Although internal segments of this scale are symmetrical, collectively they amount to an asymmetrical whole: to paraphrase Nancy, one might say that symmetry is both present and absent. The inclusion of interval 3 also recalls Birtwistle's decision to break the symmetries in his descending scales at the opening.

---

[76] Birtwistle, cited in Hall, *HBIRY*, 147–8.   [77] PSS 0525-0614.
[78] The four-note groups mimic the four syllables in 'terrifying' and 'misapprehen[sion]', which are also sung to semiquavers.

Example 8.6 Analysis of repeated tutti string chord that accompanies Judas's line: 'a terrifying – misapprehension – of the presence and absence of God', bars 898–905

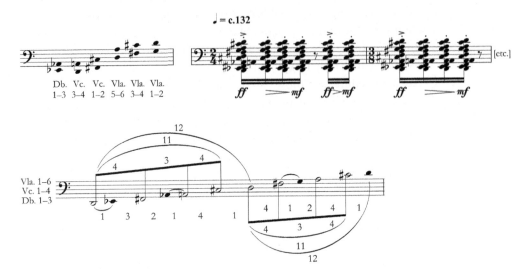

Example 8.7 Analysis of repeated chord in cellos and violas (heard as an ascending scale), bars 1,915–28. This accompanies Ghost's final lines, shown in Example 8.1

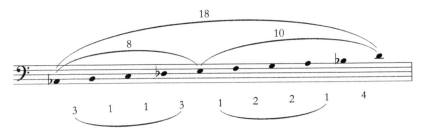

To return to the six-note sets sketched for the opera's introduction, these also provided pitches for a woodwind refrain whose rocking triplet motion punctuates the opening D♭ heartbeat pedal.[79] Although each refrain is varied slightly in terms of pitch and rhythm, pitch classes D and D♭ are always present. Clearly, D♭ is an important pitch centre at the opening and it later provides a gesture of closure when it returns in a four-octave unison in the accordion at the end of the table-building scene (bars 742–51). The 'Pater Noster', which follows on immediately, then begins with a sustained low A♭ and high A♮ pedal separated by five octaves in the accordion

---

[79] This refrain is reminiscent of the floating, tritone-centred motion at the start of Schoenberg's Variations for Orchestra, Op. 31, although it is unlikely this is a deliberate allusion.

Example 8.8 'Watch' / Judas motif, b. 321

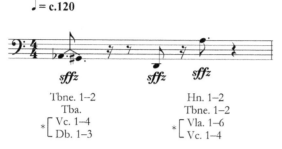

* Strings play down bows
  on each note

(bars 751–5) and it concludes with a six-octave unison on F (bars 779–82).[80] The presence of such pitch centres recalls the use of 'gateways' in *Exody*, in which octave doublings mark strategic points along the music's journey.[81] Such moments highlight the disciples' re-entry into the real or 'temporal' world. Moreover, the D/Db–A/Ab pitch axis also implies a window through which we 'watch', as suggested by a *sforzando* unison motif in the low brass and strings (Ab/G♯–D–A) following Andrew's remark 'They want us to look with them / through the three zeros of the year two thousand'; see Example 8.8.[82]

The table-building scene

> In the Eucharistic meals of the early Church . . . the words were of little significance. The emphasis within those rites was on the doing of certain actions, specifically those thought to have been done before by Christ himself.[83]

One of the main attractions of the Last Supper story for Birtwistle was that, like the Orpheus myth, it charts the transition of an historical event into a ritualised religious act from which the story becomes mythologised.[84]

[80] In this context it is worth noting that the choral refrain 'Out of the dust / de pulvere', which occurs when Christ washes the feet of every disciple in the footwashing scene, begins on Ab (sung by Matthew and Thaddeus), climaxes on Ab–A♮, then closes on D (in the three highest and four lowest voices of the Chorus Mysticus, respectively). However, although the choral refrain is nearly always unaltered, the instrumental accompaniment is different on each occasion.

[81] See Hall, *HBIRY*, 147–8.

[82] Blaser, *The Last Supper*, 8. This somewhat abrupt motif also anticipates the next line in which Peter wonders if Judas has been invited.

[83] Bell, *Ritual Theory*, 112.

[84] Jonathan Cross, 'Introduction to the story and music' from '*The Last Supper*' Guide, a promotional compact disc by Glyndebourne Productions, 2000.

This is reflected in the first half of the opera by a focus on the disciples as real people. The use of vocal characterisation is one obvious means of evoking reality: Peter (the 'rock') is a bass and the lowest voice; John is a hesitant, stammering baritone; Thomas (the 'doubter') is a querulous yet strident tenor; Philip is a bass-baritone; James and Little James are boyish countertenors. Such characterisation is occasionally reinforced by particular instrumental pairings: bass clarinet and bassoon with Peter; pairs of oboes and bassoons with Andrew; two oboes with James and Little James (such duets have a deeper significance, which will be discussed below). At other times the music is more illustrative: John's stammering in bars 542–4, for example, is mirrored by fragmented rhythms and irregular bow strokes in the strings; the sketches reveal that the accompaniment here comprises varied yet static four-note chords that rotate around a fixed c'''.[85] A sense of the disciples' identities is both further developed and lessened, however, during the table-building scene (bars 649–751).

There are obvious narrative, dramatic and musical reasons for the table-building scene: it informs us further about the lives of each disciple, it structures the drama, and it provides Birtwistle with an additive scheme. Yet there is also a conceptual purpose: to explore the opera's underlying theme of community as 'a matter of repeatedly exposing relations rather than substance'.[86] In particular, the table-building scene reflects Nancy's concept that community is 'the exposure of all and of each, in his solitude, to not being alone'.[87] During the scene, each disciple (excluding the absent Judas) collects a part of the table under construction and sings, in turn, of his profession or vocation (fisherman, carpenter, student, politician, and so on). As such, each disciple is representative of a different community. Yet Blaser also draws attention to the disciples' shared task by describing their hands, which are rough, gnarled, scarred, stained, soft, or calloused. A community is therefore exposed through a shared physical action (building a table), rather than by identification with a particular ideology or identity. This is an example of what Nancy, in response to Agamben, refers to as 'not a community of essence, [but rather] a being together of existences; that is to say: precisely what political as well as religious identities can no longer grasp. Nothing less.'[88]

---

[85] PSS 0525-0721.   [86] Pound, 'Writing/repeating community', 168.

[87] Nancy, *The Inoperative Community*, 143.

[88] Nancy, cited on the back cover of Agamben, *The Coming Community*. Nancy argues that totalitarianism results when community is 'presupposed', which is the inversion of his idea that it 'is only exposed' (xxxix). By extension, Agamben is interested in the radical potential of communities that resist a common identity: 'What the State cannot tolerate in any way ... is that the singularities form a community without affirming an identity, that humans co-belong without any representable condition of belonging (even in the form of a simple

Musically the scene is set to a lively and fragmented stretto- or fugue-like texture, which is later recalled in the setting of the Klein quotation (the Messiah in his tank). The gradual accumulation of voices is punctuated by ensemble refrains and eventually culminates in a choral 'Alleluia'. The sketches, however, reveal that there were at least eleven stages before the definitive version was finalised, and that at least one complete draft and several rough drafts were abandoned entirely. A provisional summary of the compositional stages is presented in Table 8.2.

Stage 1 reveals that the rhythms of the vocal lines came first, written out more or less precisely as they appear in the score. The idea of bass instruments at the start was also already in place, presumably as a reflection of the fact that Peter is the first to sing. Stage 2, shown in Plate 8.1, confirms that the pitches in the vocal lines were also settled almost immediately, although there is no indication of their genesis (evidence elsewhere suggests that, in general, vocal lines were either freely selected from source sets or strictly determined by sets then rewritten more intuitively).[89] Here, too, is the first indication that Birtwistle intended to build a fugue-like texture. However, the entry pitches of each line (C, B♭ and D♭) differ from those in the final version (A, D♭, E♭) and the first pitch is repeated. Moreover, the long held notes create a continuous steady tread that is completely at odds with the disjointed, quaver-pulsed vibrancy of the final version (see Example 8.9). It seems that Birtwistle then decided to rationalise his intended fugue by sketching a plan, shown in Plate 8.2. In this third stage the entry pitches differ yet again, both from stage 2 and from the final version (see Table 8.2, Stage 3). As is typical of Birtwistle's plans, this one exceeds the actual number of entries used in the score: ten lines were planned, with ten notes in each line. The whole is divided into two low to high ascents, rising through three octaves. Ultimately, Birtwistle utilised only the first half of this scheme: in the score, the imitative texture continues until the entry of Little James, at which point the music becomes more homophonic and the quaver-pulsed imitation is transferred to alternating harmonic blocks.

Stage 4 reveals that Birtwistle's first attempt to realise his pitch scheme was still based on the notion of sustained, slow-moving parts, which led to a more neatly written draft in stage 5. Yet this approach was abandoned

---

presupposition)'; Agamben, *The Coming Community*, 86. A recent example is the online community Anonymous: http://en.wikipedia.org/wiki/Anonymous_%28group%29 (accessed 6 February 2011).

[89] For example, there are chromatic sets, or modes, with occasional whole-tone steps in the margins of the sketch for the Ghost's line 'I watch with you the fragment of totalities of what we meant', but these are not followed strictly. Moreover, the version in the score occupies a slightly narrower registral span and comprises substantive differences of pitch and contour (PSS 0525-0597). Evidence elsewhere suggests that at times Birtwistle wrote out an entire chromatic scale then selected the pitches he would use, possibly by using a number scheme.

Table 8.2 *Compositional stages prior to the definitive table-building scene*

Stage	PSS MF no.	Description
1	0525-0710	Text and rhythms for all vocal parts in the scene and modes for the accompaniment (indicated by the annotation 'contra bass [&] trbn'), with replications of intervallic sets 3–5–2–1 and 2–5–2–2.
2	0525-0711 See Plate 8.1	All vocal lines, with rhythms and pitches, and a sketch with accompaniment that begins on low, sustained C pedals, followed by a second entry on B♭ and a third on D♭; the instrumentation is 'conta bsn; cb clar; tuba'.
3	0525-0712 See Plate 8.2	A fugue-like pitch scheme for the accompaniment structured by the entries of each disciple. There are ten instrumental lines in total with ten beamed pitches in each line (although the last two lines are truncated); the implication is that there is gradually increasing rhythmic diminution in each line. The entry pitches of the first five lines (F, E♭, A, B and F, respectively) chart a rise of three octaves (interval 36): the second five lines (G, D, D♭, A and G♭) rise almost three octaves (interval 35).
4	0525-0907, -0910, -0896, -0904, -0909, -0903	A rough draft based on the stage 3 pitch scheme with three low, sustained 'sfffz' F pedals at the opening, scored for 'tuba, cbsn, cbas clr [&] 3cb', and a second entry on E♭. All lines are continuous, with long held notes. Although Birtwistle embellishes the lines and deviates in other ways, the skeletal outline of the pitch scheme is discernible.
5	0525-0698, -0713..., -0861?...	A new rough draft: still with continuous sustained lines but a reinterpretation of the stage 3 pitch scheme and initially more neatly written than stage 4.
6	0525-0865 See Exx. 8.10 and 8.11	A sketch for a new, more dynamic and fragmented accompaniment with disjointed iambic figures and a quaver pulse. At the top of the page Birtwistle sketches a complementary scheme with two interlocking three-note sets, one descending through intervals 1 and 3 (E♭, D, C), the other ascending through intervals 1 and 3 (C, D♭, E). The upper-stemmed, descending set is then notated with filled note heads. The lower-stemmed, ascending set is notated with open note heads. This concatenated cell is the basis of a subsequent table (stage 7). Eight versions of the lower-stemmed set are then written along two staffs in the middle of the page, with internal permutations of intervals 1 and 3 (these variants relate to stage 7, rows 1 and 5). This is followed by a series of eight interlocking contours, which is a first version of stage 7, row 1. Variants of the sets are then written out with octave displacements and iambic rhythms, which links this sketch to stage 8 (0525-0905).

Table 8.2 (*cont.*)

Stage	PSS MF no.	Description
7	0525-0911 See Exx. 8.12 and 8.13	A table that comprises eight columns and twelve rows; each cell contains a six-note set formed from two interlocking three-note sets (see main text for a full description). Besides various possible relations between the table and subsequent stages (see main text), a fragmentary sketch in the bottom right-hand corner of the page suggests a link to stage 11 (0525-0897).
8	0525-0905	An early rough draft of the opening derived from column I, row 1 of the table: the use of octave displacements and iambic rhythms links this directly to stage 6. It seems likely that the original idea was to move up through the table from the lowest line. However, the pitches (E–E♭–D–C–D♭–D, etc.) and rhythm (up- and down-bow markings emphasise disjointed quaver–dotted crotchet patterns) differ from the opening in the final version.
9	0525-0914	Another two rough drafts of the opening. The first line is possibly derived from column III, row 9 (marked '1' in the table) while the second entry in the second draft suggests column III, row 2. The first line (A♭–G–E–G♭–A♭–A♮, etc.) is close to the final version. There is also a return to a sustained texture: the first three notes in the first draft are dotted minims. However, these values are halved in the second draft, and a more active quaver motion begins at Peter's 'gain my bread'.
10	0125-0912, -0913	A neater draft of stage 9 but with differences: the opening dotted minims are shortened by a quaver rest; each note is strongly accented; the line fragments into staccato quavers with rests at 'gain my bread'. Where the second line (marked 'vlc, bass cl., bs[n]') is joined by the third line (marked 'vlas') the texture is especially syncopated with a clear quaver pulse. Here Birtwistle writes: 'More counterpoint like this.' This version continues for another half page only. A sketch for the fourth line written along the bottom of the page, in filled and empty note heads, suggests that this, too, is derived from the table although it is unclear precisely how.
11	0525-0897, -0877, -0901, -0902, -0895, -0898, -0894, -0893, -0892, -0867, -0868, -0869, -0853, -0854, -0900, -0848	Sketches and rough drafts for the final version (bb. 649–717) but excluding the ensemble sections, which were clearly added later. The definitive form of the eleven-note opening, divided into three short phrases, may be derived from row 7, columns I–IV, and the continuation of the first line and the start of the second line combined suggest rows 1–3, columns I–II. Sketches for the viola and cello from bar 665 reveal alternative methods of generating the counterpoint based on permutations of intervals 1, 2 and 3. There are also sketches for four-note chords deployed in the strings, woodwind and brass from bar 696 onwards (the entrance of Little James).

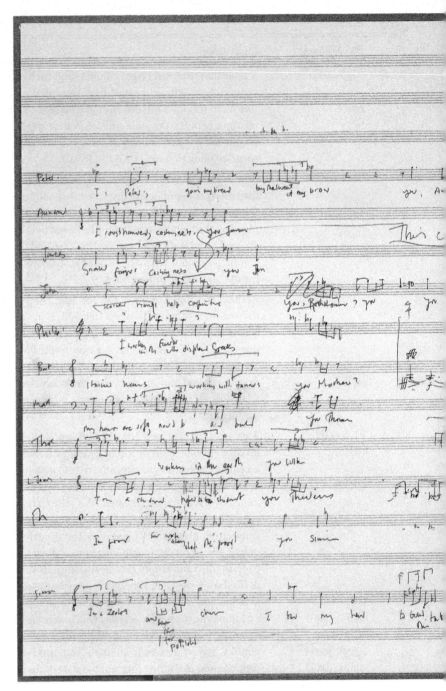

Plate 8.1 Sketch for the disciples' parts and an early version of the opening 'fugue' for the table-building scene in *The Last Supper*. PSS, Sammlung Harrison Birtwistle, *The Last Supper*, folder 2/9, 32

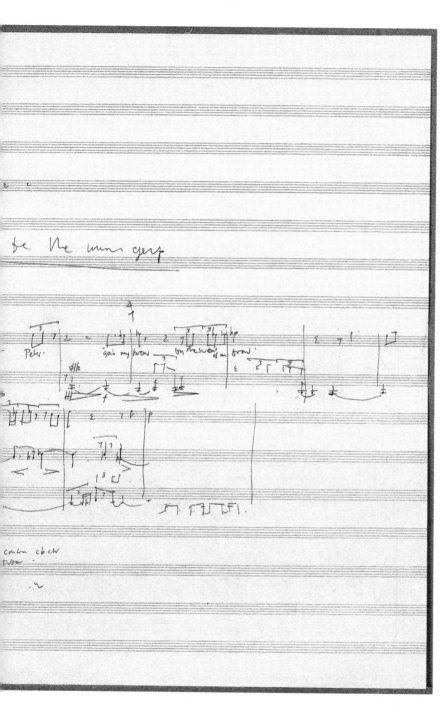

Example 8.9 The table-building 'fugue', bars 649–62 (excluding timpani)

and a more abstract process was begun in stage 6. Here the essence of Birtwistle's perspective on the drama is revealed in a six-note set, or gestalt, that comprises two concatenated three-note sets. An upper-stemmed set, written in filled note heads, descends through intervals 1 and 3 from Eb. A lower-stemmed set, written in open note heads, ascends through

Example 8.9 (*cont.*)

intervals 1 and 3 from C (see Example 8.10). On the same sketch page, Birtwistle writes out variants of the three-note shapes beginning on C and, this time, on E. There are at least five ways in which Birtwistle distributes the resultant pitches. His first idea is to stagger the three-note sets (Example 8.11a). He then writes a series of variants of the lower-stemmed cell and applies octave displacements (Ex. 8.11b). Next a new series of three-note

Plate 8.2 Fugue-like pitch scheme for the table-building scene, structured by the entries of each disciple. PSS, Sammlung Harrison Birtwistle, *The Last Supper*, folder 2/9, 33

Example 8.10 First sketch for the table-building 'gestalt'. PSS 0525-0865

Example 8.11 Sketches for distribution of the gestalt. PSS 0525-0865
Example 8.11a

Example 8.11b

shapes is devised: these are distributed through octave displacement, given
iambic rhythms and reordered internally (Ex. 8.11c). Birtwistle then returns
to the original pitch cell and writes out a series of variants of the downward-
and upward-stemmed shapes, which forms the basis of a table that follows.
The sketch reveals two ways of distributing these shapes with reorderings
both inside and between the cells (see Examples 8.11d and 8.11e). There are
two possible readings of Example 8.11d. Either (1) the first three upward-
stemmed notes (along the top staff) are selected from the first six-note cell
and the downward-stemmed notes from another cell (possibly the third),
or, more likely, (2) four notes are selected from the first six-note cell (1, 4,
5, 6), and then reordered (5, 6, 4, 1). A similar process is then applied to the
third cell. Example 8.11e is less clear, but it suggests an attempt to overlap or
integrate selections from different cells. The basic six-note gestalt therefore
combines two seemingly contradictory principles, namely the symbiosis
and bifurcation of two interdependent three-note cells.

   The next step, stage 7, was to compile a table of 96 variants of the six-
note gestalt. There are eight columns (divided into two groups of four)

Example 8.11c

Example 8.11d

Example 8.11e

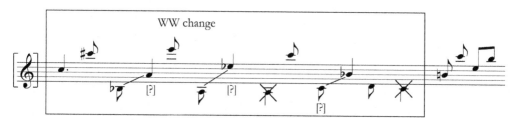

and twelve rows; extracts are shown in Example 8.12. It seems likely that Birtwistle began at the bottom of the table since the first six-note set (column I, row 1) is the one he sketched at the start of stage 6. Moreover, row 1 is a slightly altered version of a row sketched in stage 6, the first half of which is shown in Ex. 8.11d.[90] The shapes in the table are formed from permutations of intervals 1–3, intervals that are utilised in this opera to a greater extent

[90] The order of the empty note heads in column II, row 1 differs from the earlier sketch and the second filled note head in column IV, row 1 is A rather then B.

Example 8.12 Extracts from the gestalt source table for the table-building scene

Figure 8.1 Summary of intervals used in the stage 7 pitch table (PSS 0525-0911)

Columns	I	II	III	IV		V	VI	VII	VIII
[open]	+1+3	−1+3	+1−3	−1−3		+3+1	−3+1	+3−1	−3−1
[filled]	−1−3	+2+1	−2−1	−1−2		−1−3	−1−2	−2−1	+1+1*

* The lowest three rows in this column are +1+2. This suggests that Birtwistle made an error in row 4, which was replicated in rows 5–12.

Figure 8.2 Summary of the first open and filled notes in row 12 of the pitch table

[open]	B		B		B		B			B		B		B		B	
[filled]	D		C		B♭		A			F		D♭		C		A	
		−2		−2		−1		(+8)			−4		−1		−3		

than in previous stage works.[91] A summary of the intervals and the upward
(+) and downward (−) steps is given in Figure 8.1. From this figure it can
be observed that the filled note heads follow an irregular pattern whereas
the open note heads follow interval steps 1–3 in columns I–IV, and 3–1 in
columns V–VIII.

Ascending through the figure from the lowest 'source' row, each subsequent row is transposed up a semitone: in column I, for example, the first
open-head notes ascend from *c'* to *b'* and the first filled-head notes ascend
from *e♭* to *d''*. However, in each row the first open-head notes remain
constant: for example, *c'* is the first pitch in every column along row 1. Yet
the first filled note in each column is different. For example, the pitches
and intervals for the first open and filled notes along row 12 (at the top of
the table) are shown in Figure 8.2. It is unclear what rationale determined
these intervals but the aim is clearly to provide a degree of contrast within
a limited interval span (interval 8). As will be discussed later, the intervals
used here (1–4) assume importance at the end of the opera.

In the table as a whole we can observe Birtwistle's familiar principle of
varied repetition designed to produce a series of objects that are different yet
related. The present context, however, recalls Agamben's notion of 'whatever' being, which is 'neither particular nor general': that is, each six-note set
is neither fully individual nor entirely generic.[92] The sketches do not confirm
categorically that the final version is based directly on the table. However,
the various ways in which Birtwistle distributed the sets in stage 6 strongly
suggest that if he did use the table he would have exercised systematic
or intuitive selection when doing so. In the final version the opening pitches

---

[91] For example, permutations of intervals 1–3 are used to generate the trombone duet in the first
dance, bars 343–57 (PSS 0525-0578), and intervals 1–4 to generate the accompaniment to the
Ghost's Klein quotation (the Messiah coming in his tank), bars 1,708–48 (PSS 0526-0129).

[92] Agamben, *The Coming Community*, translator's notes, 107.

Example 8.13 Possible ways in which the pitches at the start of the table-building scene were derived from the gestalt table; bb. 649–55

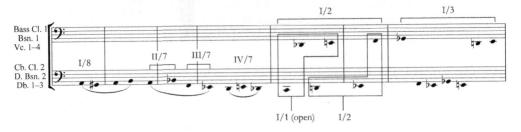

are consistent with rows 7 and 8 (see Example 8.13). The idea that Birtwistle began here is supported by annotations of '1 2 3 4' between rows 7 and 8 in the first four columns and an 'X' at the start of these rows, but also by the fact that row 7 is at the symmetrical centre of the table, a tritone higher than row 1.[93] When the second line begins it seems likely that the two parts were formed either from whole cells, such as I/2 and I/3, or that segments were combined, possibly derived from I/1–3, as shown in Example 8.13.

Stages 8–10 chart three aborted attempts at proceeding from the table. Initially the iambic rhythms were deployed at the very opening (in the score they begin at the entry of the second line), and in stage 9 Birtwistle reverted to the slow, sustained texture. Evidence suggests that pitches were drawn from rows 1 and 9 of the table, and that the stage 3 pitch scheme (shown in Plate 8.2) had been abandoned altogether. Moreover, these sketches reveal that the kind of syncopated, quaver-pulsed rhythmic counterpoint used in the final version was 'discovered' in stage 10 (at the third entry Birtwistle writes: 'More counterpoint like this'). It is only in stage 11 that the first sketches and rough draft of the definitive form appear. Here the first eleven notes are written out in their final rhythm but without bar lines, Peter's vocal line coincides with the second entry (it is a bar later in the final version), and the ensemble refrains are not present. In the final version the fugue texture ends with the first choral refrain (bars 678–82, after Bartholomew has sung), after which the parts bounce off one another in a lively quaver pulse. However, sketches in stage 11 draw attention to a form of harmonic imitation which takes over from the entrance of Little James onwards: blocks of four-note chords are passed around the orchestra. Similar four-note shapes assume importance elsewhere in the opera, as will be discussed in the following section.

---

[93] The only other numerical annotation on the table appears between rows 9 and 10, where the order '4312' is written in columns I–IV respectively.

Example 8.14 'Where gods and mortals abide', b. 487

The important point about the table-building scene is that the fugue derives its energy from a tensile, imitative counterpoint in which one voice responds immediately to the other. This recalls Heidegger's notion of *Dasein* in which a dynamic potentiality arises from the condition of 'being-with' or 'being-according-to-sharing'. Certainly, one might question the extent to which the six-note gestalts determine the final texture since the shapes are so thoroughly altered by internal reordering and octave displacement. However, the principle of 'symbiotic bifurcation' is audible in the interdependent character of the rhythmic imitation. Moreover, the emerging fugue texture resonates with Nancy's idea that communities are not essences but are 'exposed' through a series of relationships and by 'the *event* of being-in-common', and with his remark that community is 'a bond that forms without attachments, or even less fusion, . . . a bond that unbinds by binding, that reunites through the infinite exposition of an irreducible finitude'.[94] It is unlikely that Birtwistle had this direct association with Blaser's sources in mind. Yet Blaser certainly shared his ideas with the composer, both in conversation and through the content of his libretto. More plausible is the idea that Birtwistle distributed his six-note gestalts with a general concept in mind, such as the simultaneous presence and absence of God. Moreover, it is intriguing that varied six-note figures, reminiscent of the gestalts, punctuate the disciples' discussion of the Greek Kosmos, 'Where gods and mortals abide' (see Example 8.14).[95]

---

[94] Nancy, *The Inoperative Community*, xl.

[95] Another association between the table and Blaser's concept of the 'existential given' is suggested by a sketch for three-note ascending and descending shapes (PSS 0526-0082). Grace-note figures were generated from these shapes for the flutes and oboes to accompany Christ's list of 'discriminations' during the footwashing scene. When the score was revised in light of an alteration to the libretto ('Discriminations' was replaced by 'What has been done against'), these figures were removed; the revised version is a sparser texture perhaps intended to detract less from the text.

'Shadow presences... in an identical region of being'

> Something miraculous happens when you build a household or a community
> around the uninvited and the broken. That's how a community avoids
> becoming conceited or middle-class or just up itself.[96]

As the sketches for the table-building scene reveal, the opening fugue-
like texture is formed from pairs of concatenated three-note sets that are
fractured, displaced and redistributed between two or more parts. At the root
of this texture is an abstract musical concept that I have termed 'symbiotic
bifurcation'. Yet this abstract concept also receives more concrete, outward
expression in the arrival of the disciples in pairs and in the numerous
instrumental duets, which Cross has compared to the obbligato duets in
Bach's Passions.[97] In addition to ceremonial trumpet fanfares in the opening
and closing sections, the most memorable duets include: a pair of alto flutes
that hover, halo-like, over Christ's voice when he gives thanks for 'the Being
thou givest' (bars 1,161–1,197);[98] a jagged clarinet and cello duet throughout
the Ghost's Nerval quotation ('God isn't. God is never again'); a plangent cor
anglais duet in Judas's moving aria. Such moments are usually highlighted
by an instruction that the players move to solo platforms on either side of
the orchestra.

   Yet, as the table-building sketches illustrate, more covert 'duets' also
operate beneath the music's surface. One such example occurs in the introduction when the Ghost sings an adapted quotation from a poem by Charles
Olson: 'The fragrance of violets / has the smell of life.'[99] The imagery here
relates to Blaser's association of Christ with the wind, an idea reinforced after
Christ's entrance with lines from the Song of Songs that call upon the north
and south winds to 'Blow upon my garden that the spices thereof / may flow
out.'[100] Blaser's imagery therefore develops the belief of seventeenth-century
metaphysical poets, such as Traherne and Crashaw, that divinity exists in
the human world. Birtwistle's sketches for his setting of Olson's text begin
with a series of three-note chromatic sets. These are initially arranged into a
symmetrical pattern comprising four three-note sets: the lowest (D♭–D–E♭)
is transposed up through intervals 3 and 6 (the former is displaced by two

---

[96] Tobias Jones, 'A life less ordinary', *Observer*, Magazine section, 31 October 2010, 78.
[97] Cross, *HB: MMM*, 240–1.
[98] This is an extended quotation from Thomas Traherne's 'Thanksgivings for the body', in his
      Poems, Centuries and Three Thanksgivings, ed. Anne Ridler (London: Oxford University Press,
      1966), 375–81.
[99] Charles Olson, 'The story of an Olson, and bad thing' (1950), in *The Collected Poems of
      Charles Olson: Excluding the Maximus Poems*, ed. George F. Butterick (Berkeley and Los
      Angeles: University of California Press, 1997), 175–82. The relevant lines in Olson's poem
      actually read 'The sweetest kind of essence, violets / is the smell of life' (178).
[100] Blaser, *The Last Supper*, 24.

Example 8.15 Sketch for instrumental lines at Ghost's 'The fragrance of violets / has the smell of life', bb. 228–41. PSS 0525-0637

Reordered to produce two six-part lines (here given in the original barring)

octaves). The result is two parallel lines each with intervals 11411. This basic unit is then transposed up three times, each time by a semitone, to form three other variants (see Example 8.15). A number system is employed to reorder the pitches (see numbers 1–6 along the bottom of the set table). When the pitches are reordered some are moved to different registers. The two resultant lines are then distributed between six parts each: the upper line passes between two flutes, oboe and three pairs of violas; the lower line moves between the bass clarinet, bassoon and four independent cellos (see the lower half of Example 8.15). The two lines are further disguised, however, by the fact that the woodwind all play short two-, three- and four-note phrases 'cantabile' whereas the strings have single, detached harmonics or 'sul tasto' notes that are sustained across each line. A melodic duality is hidden by a timbral duality. The notes of the two original lines are therefore distributed throughout the texture in an obscure yet pervasive manner that evokes the divine aromas the Ghost refers to.

A similar principle is applied to the distribution of numerous four-note harmonies, which recalls the importance of such shapes in *Mrs Kong* (see Chapter 6). At times the use of four-note chords is straightforward, for example when Thomas and Matthew first enter and converse with one another out of earshot of the other disciples. To create a sense of parenthesis the music becomes suddenly soft with floating woodwinds (flutes, oboes, bass clarinets and bassoons) punctuated by short chords in the accordion.

Figure 8.3 Rotations of intervals 5, 6 and 7 to form a four-note harmonic background at the entrance of Thomas and Matthew, bars 509–16; PSS 0525-0687

5	7	6	7	6	7	5
6	5	7	6	5	6	5
7	6	5	5	7	5	6

Figure 8.4 Permutation table for interval set 1–2–4; PSS 0525-0727

4	1	3	4	5	6
1	1	2	2	4	4
2	4	4	1	1	2
4	2	1	4	2	1
4	2	3	1	5	6

All the instrumental parts are derived from four-note chords based on permutations of intervals 5, 6 and 7, as shown in Figure 8.3. Following this parenthetical aside, Matthew and Thomas are greeted by Peter: 'Glad you're here wandering history with us.' From this moment, through Thomas's description of his travels to India and the time when he put his hand into Christ's 'wound of immortality', the harmony becomes considerably denser, yet the underlying principle remains the same.

As with the table-building scene, there were several false starts and abandoned versions before the form was finalised. Birtwistle began with the idea of rotating four intervallic sets: 1–2–4, 1–2–5, 1–2–6 and 1–2–7. Number tables were then written to provide a fund of permutations, such as the one shown in Figure 8.4. Here permutations of the 1–2–4 set are reordered by numbers along the top and bottom of the table.[101] Next a plan was drawn up involving rotations of contours (for example, where 1 = low, 2 = middle and 3 = high: <1, 3, 1, 2>, <1, 2, 1, 3>, <3, 1, 2, 1>, <2, 1, 3, 1>). Three groups of four such contours were sketched out, re-ordered, then used to determine the placement of the chords. Each of the three 'bands' (high, middle and low) determined register and instrumentation (for example, band I = high woodwind, violas 1–4 and accordion). It seems likely that the intervallic sets were applied either above or below a predetermined series of narrowly circling pitches in each band (for example, beneath a''', bb''', b''' or c''' in band I). A fragment of this plan is audible in bars 527–9, as shown in Examples 8.16a and 8.16b (the chords sketched in Example 8.16a are indicated by annotated numbers ([1], [2], etc.) in Example 8.16b).

---

[101] PSS 0525-0727.

Example 8.16a Sketch for harmony at James's 'What did our doubting Thomas know?', bb. 527–9. PSS 0525-0689

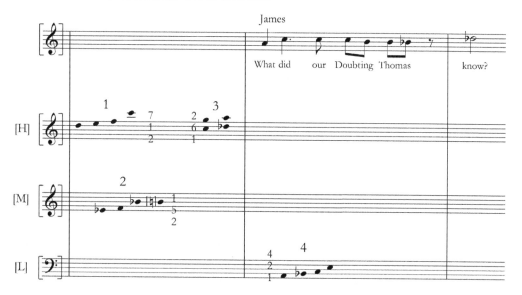

Example 8.16b Realisation of sketch, bb. 527–9

However, this plan was superseded by a more complex scheme in which each band was divided into two strands, with four parts in each strand:[102]

Ia   violas 1–4
Ib   flutes 1–2 & oboes 1–2
IIa   violas 5–6 & cellos 1–2
IIb   trumpets 1–2 & horns 1–2
IIIa   cellos 1–2 & divided double basses (1–2 & 3)
IIIb   bass clarinets 1–2 & bassoons 1–2

Here variants of the original intervallic sets are introduced, labelled a, b and c. Yet this version was superseded by a further stage in which each band was developed separately and in more detail. An extant sketch reveals that the original intervallic sets were reordered again and each band was subdivided according to a new series of durations.[103] These ensured that the strands within each band would not coincide (for example, the strings, woodwind and accordion in the highest band).

In Birtwistle's final version, some of the original plan is audible but there are numerous alterations, including more sustained chords in the brass and octave doublings in the lower strings. The result is a complex web of sound. Dynamic swells on each four-note chord and frequent contrasts of timbre produce music that moves swiftly in and out of focus in a manner that recalls similar-sounding harmonic instability in Stockhausen's *Gruppen*. Throughout the arrival of the disciples Birtwistle's music is restless, shifting continually in a moment-to-moment response to the text, through pauses, tempo changes and occasional word painting. Yet Birtwistle's complex harmonic design is a deeper response to Blaser's imagery of 'shadow presences' and 'regions of being' in which the profane and the divine are coexistent.[104] It is possible that Birtwistle's distribution of four-note chords discussed here was prompted by Peter's reference to the disciples 'wandering history'. Moreover, the compositional strategy and disorienting effect

---

[102]   In this version the accordion forms a fourth independent band, although it is later subsumed back into the three-band scheme. PSS 0525-0728.

[103]   PSS 0525-0695.

[104]   The harmony here arguably resonates with Cees Nooteboom's description of paintings by Francisco de Zurbarán (1598–1664), which prompted Birtwistle's interest in the artist and inspired his conception of the Visions. Nooteboom refers to Zurbarán's skill at evoking the play of light and colour in material, which he likens to Cézanne. Intense, mystical passion is created not by the pious scenes represented in Zurbarán's paintings, but by patches of exquisite detail that the eye might easily miss, for example in the fabric of a monk's tunic. Birtwistle's harmonies evoke a similar quality of the fleeting or sublime. See Cees Nooteboom, *Roads to Santiago: Detours and Riddles in the Lands and History of Spain*, trans. Ina Rilke (London: Harvill Press, 1998), 84–5.

are germane to the broader themes of the opera and do not, to my mind, represent a 'separateness of libretto and score'.[105]

One place where score and libretto are literally related, of course, is in the vocal writing. Yet it is precisely in song that, to paraphrase Blaser, the characters find themselves 'beyond' themselves.[106] This idea has particular relevance to *The Minotaur*, as will be discussed shortly. Both *The Last Supper* and *The Minotaur* are closely related to *Gawain* through a shared interest in divided identity (see Chapter 5), and all three operas raise questions about human potentiality and presence in the world. Before turning to *The Minotaur*, therefore, we should first briefly consider questions of identity that arise from the vocal and instrumental 'voices' in *The Last Supper*.

'Who do you think I am?'

> narrative identity continues to make and unmake itself, and the question of trust that Jesus posed to his disciples – Who do you say that I am? – is one that each of us can pose concerning ourself, with the same perplexity that the disciples questioned by Jesus felt. Narrative identity thus becomes the name of a problem at least as much as it is that of a solution. A systematic investigation of autobiography and self-portraiture would no doubt verify this instability in principle of narrative identity.[107]

The use of voice in *The Last Supper* is remarkably varied. The Visions, for example, 'transcend' the surrounding music not only because they evoke Renaissance polyphony – Palestrina, Carver or Fayrfax, perhaps – but because they reveal a new level of sensitivity to the meaning of words, particularly in the first Vision. This begins with an especially delicate texture: a short, lament-like chromatic descent (A–Ab–G), sung in unison, is followed by a series of rising fourths (G–C, Bb–Eb, Eb–A) and a near octave leap in the sopranos (Eb–E) on the 'O' of 'O bone Jesu'. These rising intervals are like gestures, reaching out; echoed throughout Vision I they powerfully convey the text's entreaties to Jesus to 'hear me' ('exaudi me'). Numerous critics singled the Visions out for special mention, with one noting that they are 'of such special beauty as to mark some kind of acme for Birtwistle'.[108] Yet, at the same time, the Visions are glacially detached from the 'reality' of the main opera, from the physical presence of the disciples (their line

---

[105] Paul Griffiths, review of *The Last Supper*, 42.

[106] For example, it may be argued that music 'participates in the construction of subjectivity by allowing us to inhabit with our bodies and to experience something beyond the confines of ourselves.' Alastair Williams, 'Swaying with Schumann: subjectivity and tradition in Wolfgang Rihm's "Fremde Szenen" I–III and related scores', *Music & Letters*, 87/2 (August 2006), 396.

[107] Ricoeur, *Time and Narrative*, III, 249.

[108] Edward Seckerson, 'Jesus Christ, supper star', *Independent*, 25 October 2001.

Example 8.17 Thomas, bb. 565–9

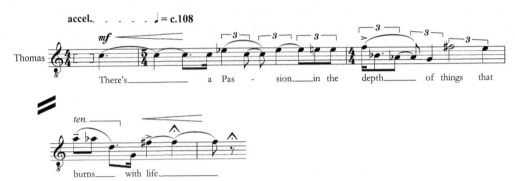

dances, hand claps and foot stamping – all clearly choreographed in the original production) and the turbulent streams of history that swirl around them.[109] In this context, Thomas's line 'There's a Passion in the depth of things that burns with life' is especially striking, an effect compounded by an ascent in his line from C through E♭, E♮, F and F♯ to A and A♭ on 'burns' (see Example 8.17). It has even been suggested, rightly perhaps, that the work's most operatic character is Judas: his responses to the disciples are eloquent and his heartfelt aria implies that he is torn and conflicted – an effect that was heightened in the original production by the fact that the disciples remained still, their heads turned down as if in shame.[110] Yet the cor anglais duet that accompanies Judas actually forms a single line with his voice. Is Birtwistle's Judas less conflicted than he would have us believe?

An overview of Christ's vocal lines suggests that they were most likely drawn from small chromatic collections: movement is often restricted to intervals 1–4. Frequent octave displacements, however, lend a sense of character in a manner that is not dissimilar to the treatment of the sets in the table-building scene. A case in point is the opening of the Traherne prayer, shown in Example 8.18. The predominance of small intervals becomes especially apparent in the opera's closing section, from 'Let us welcome life' in the lead-up to the second Vision (bars 1,891–1,909). Here Christ's unleavened line is mirrored by string chords restricted to intervals 1–4 (Example 8.19).[111] While questions about Christ's identity

[109] Tom Service similarly noted that 'Birtwistle's amazingly sensuous music' for the Visions is 'utterly lucid and yet deeply ambiguous'; 'The Last Supper', *Guardian*, 7 August 2001. The few extant sketches for the Visions indicate that in the second half of Vision I ('and do not allow me to be separated from you'), Birtwistle began with the sustained first soprano line, then devised a bass ostinato (B–G♭–F–A); the inner parts are determined by rotations of intervals 4–7 above B.

[110] Tom Sutcliffe has remarked that 'in a similar exercise to Bulgakov's *Master and Margarita* [Birtwistle] makes Tom Randle's fascinating Judas the most sympathetic of all his characters'; review of the second Glyndebourne production of *The Last Supper*, *Evening Standard*, 9 August 2001.

[111] PSS 0526-0207 reveals that four-note sets based on rotations of 1, 2, 3 and 1, 2, 4 were used.

Example 8.18 Christ, bb. 1,162–5

Example 8.19 Christ and string accompaniment, bb. 1,891–4 (number annotations added to indicate intervals)

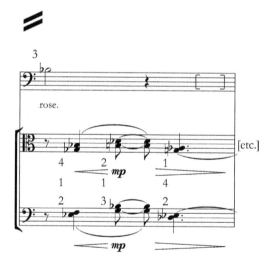

certainly remain at the end, his vocal presence is given additional grav-itas by an extended instrumental line that begins on a unison E at the start of the Holy Communion, from Christ's 'This is my body'. First heard in the violas, the line spreads to the cellos, horns and trombones (bars 1,786–1,859).[112] Significantly, the line extends beyond the section when Christ sings alone and embraces the moment when the Ghost joins the disciples. An early sketch charts a recurring 'bells' refrain on the line, which relates back to the ritualistic repetitions of 'de pulvere' in the foot-washing scene. A scurrying flute duo and tremolo string refrain are also mapped on the sketch. Evidently, however, there were alterations to this scheme: few of the recurring ideas appear where they were sketched, and the line was rewritten less than halfway into the plan (from bar 1,819). The new line ascends gradually, reaching a steady state roughly an octave and a half above the original. Yet in the closing bars even this line was rewritten. This was to enable a sudden ascent through another octave in a gesture that reaches out to – and echoes – the Ghost's climactic A♭ on 'life' when she asks: 'Of the unknown? / I'd sing of life.'

The Minotaur

> The Minotaur, under a beam of heavenly light, comes from the open sea; half-man, half-animal, he is a man in harmony with his animal needs, or a creative animal – good and evil, beautiful and ugly at one and the same time.[113]

In many respects *The Last Supper* and *The Minotaur* could not be more strongly contrasted.[114] Aside from the suggestion of a warlike Messiah, there is no violence or eroticism in the former work. By contrast, *The Minotaur* drips blood and lust. Yet, as will be seen, the Minotaur is the archetypal example of a Being thrust into the world and immediately abandoned: in Agamben's terms, he is consigned irreparably to his 'being-thus' – that is, half-man, half-animal. The animal murders and rapes innocently and without compunction, but the human quests for self-knowledge and potentiality. Finally, when the human breaks through, the Minotaur comes only to realise that 'Between man and beast, [there is] next to nothing.'[115] What man and beast share is the same 'gift of life' that Blaser celebrates in *The Last Supper*. Yet in the darkened musical landscape of *The Minotaur* it is the visceral rather than the transcendent notion of existence that dominates.

---

[112] The sketches suggest this was generated from five-note sets; PSS 0525-0760 and -0759.

[113] Sebastian Goeppert and Herma C. Goeppert-Frank, *Minotauromachy by Pablo Picasso*, trans. Gail Mangold-Vine (Geneva: Patrick Cramer, 1987), 103. I am extremely grateful to Birtwistle for loaning me his own copy of this book.

[114] *The Minotaur* received its world premiere at the Royal Opera House, Covent Garden, on 19 April 2008. The roles of Ariadne, Theseus and the Minotaur were taken by Christine Rice, Johan Reuter and John Tomlinson respectively, and the orchestra was conducted by Antonio Pappano.

[115] David Harsent, *The Minotaur* (London: Boosey and Hawkes, 2008), 45; see also 65.

Rhian Samuel has remarked that even when the Minotaur expresses himself in human terms he does not identify with his victims. Rather, he wallows in self-pity.[116] While this is undeniable, the Minotaur's condition is not far from Blaser's irreparable world in which contemporary human existence becomes a perpetual lament for societies' ancient ruptures, tragedies and failures.[117] When Theseus delivers the fatal blow to the Minotaur, the Crowd of onlookers emits a sudden and startling release of breath that instantly recalls *The Last Supper*. What follows is not so much a final aria, as in *Mrs Kong*, but rather a fragmented lament that is explicitly associated with death. The orchestra splits into two independent strands, the music thins, and we are drawn in to face the beast. Yet, for the first time in Birtwistle's stage works, we witness and confront death not as ritual or high tragedy but rather as a moment of intimacy and shared presence. The powerful sense of 'being-with' the Minotaur in the opera's closing moments realises the Ghost's sentiment of 'sharing our lives', yet in a manner that complements moments in *The Last Supper*, in particular Christ's entrance.[118]

Myth and synopsis

The Minotaur is an archetypal figure from Greek mythology associated with the Minoan civilisation of the Bronze Age (1900–1400 BC), located on the island of Crete. Evidence exists of a labyrinth at Knossos on Crete, but more extensive networks of underground tunnels are to be found in Merassa in the southern mountains, which comprise around 2.5 kilometres of chambers and corridors. It is likely that these originated as natural caves that were extended by Roman quarrying and later modifications.[119]

The essential details of the myth are as follows. Pasiphae's husband King Minos requests a sign that his right to rule Crete has the approval of the gods. Neptune sends a white bull from the sea. This is intended as a sacrifice, but Minos chooses to keep the bull. As punishment, Pasiphae is made to love the bull. She asks the inventor Daedalus to build a fake cow in which she hides; this lures the bull and, as a result of their union, Pasiphae gives

---

[116] Samuel, 'Birtwistle's *The Minotaur*', 220.

[117] As Whittall remarks: 'the world of *The Minotaur* seems, ultimately, to be a world in which the animal, the inhuman, threatens to (re)gain the upper hand'. Whittall, 'First perfomances. London, Royal Opera, Covent Garden: Birtwistle's *The Minotaur*', *Tempo*, 246 (2008), 51.

[118] As one review of *The Minotaur* observed: 'When we hear [John] Tomlinson's chunky but vulnerable bass sing of beautiful things, we understand the Minotaur's suffering, his longing and his bitterness – and recognise part of ourselves.' Andrew Clark, 'The Minotaur, Royal Opera House, London', *Financial Times*, 21 April 2008. Another critic noted that 'the misery' Birtwistle communicates 'through the Minotaur's verbal and non-verbal sounds is profound.' Anna Picard, 'The Minotaur, Royal Opera House, London', *Independent*, 20 April 2008.

[119] For more on this see www.zestcambridge.co.uk/labyrinthlost/ and www.labyrinthos.ch/Labyrinth-Hoehle.english.html (both accessed 3 May 2011).

birth to the Minotaur, a monster with the head of a bull and the body of a man. Shamed by the visible evidence of his wife's infidelity, Minos orders Daedalus to devise the labyrinth as a prison in which to shut the Minotaur away. In retribution for the death of his son, Androgeos, killed in Athens, Minos demands that lots be drawn every year (or every nine years in some versions) to select seven young men and seven young women (these are the Innocents in David Harsent's libretto). These youths are sent to Crete as a sacrifice to the Minotaur. That is, until Theseus, son of the Athenian king Aegeus – although in Harsent's version possibly the son of Poseidon – travels with the youths to Crete with the intention of killing the Minotaur and breaking the cycle of retribution. On his arrival, Theseus meets Ariadne, Minos's daughter. She falls in love with Theseus and assists him in his quest by giving him a dagger (the Minotaur has not seen a weapon before) and a ball of twine to unwind as he enters, which enables him to retrace his steps. Theseus flees with Ariadne to Naxos where he abandons her.

Harsent pares the myth down to its essentials. He begins on the Cretan shoreline where Ariadne awaits the arrival of the ship bearing the annual cargo of sacrificial youths. The opera ends with the Minotaur's death at the hands of Theseus. There is no King Minos, Pasiphae, or Daedalus. Instead the plot centres on the interrelated triangle of Ariadne (daughter of Pasiphae), Theseus (possibly the son of Poseidon) and the Minotaur (son of Poseidon and Pasiphae). For Ariadne, Crete is a cage that she is desperate to escape. Theseus is potentially her means to flee, but to ensure this Ariadne must exert guile. Harsent's principal interest was Ariadne, yet ultimately she and Theseus are instruments of a plot that focuses on the Minotaur. As shown in Table 8.3, the formal layout is teleological, although a familiar verse–refrain pattern introduces the possibility of viewing the same situations from different perspectives. The two sides of the Minotaur are explored by separating out the animal from the man: the former grunts, rapes and kills inside the labyrinth, while the latter emerges when the beast sleeps; in his dreams, Asterios, as Ariadne calls him, communicates through language and is confronted by his double.

There are thirteen scenes in total that divide into four themes: Ariadne is the principal voice in scenes 1, 4 and 10; Ariadne and Theseus have extended dialogue in scenes 2, 8 and 11; the action enters into or is located inside the labyrinth in scenes 3, 5, 7 and 12;[120] the Minotaur sings in English when he sleeps in scenes 6 and 9 and when he confronts and recognises Theseus in

---

[120] Events in the labyrinth scenes are as follows: the Innocents enter in scene 3; a young female Innocent is killed in scene 5; the remaining Innocents enter and are killed in scene 7; Theseus enters in scene 12.

Table 8.3 *Formal layout of* The Minotaur

Ariadne	Ariadne and Theseus	Labyrinth	Minotaur
1. arrival [*]	2. the choice	3. the labyrinth	
4. Ariadne		5. the labyrinth the chase / the death [*] 7. the labyrinth pass / kill ($\times$4)	6. the Minotaur dreams
	8. a proposition [*]		9. the Minotaur dreams
10. the Oracle at Psychro	11. a blind bargain	12. the labyrinth	13. the death of the Minotaur

[*] = instrumental toccata

scene 13. Interspersed between these scenes are three instrumental toccatas, and, at the end of scenes 5, 7 and 12, female, vulture-like creatures named the Keres enter to devour the victims. During the dream scenes the Minotaur's double appears in a mirror; he also sees there a dark figure, which he later realises is Theseus. Another innovation is scene 10 in which Ariadne travels to Psychro, on Crete, to consult the Oracle. There she meets the Snake Priestess, a towering, bare-breasted baroque-like figure, sung by a countertenor, who sings a mixture of Latin, Hebrew and Klingon. Before being permitted to ask a question via Hiereus, a translator, Ariadne must say truthfully what has motivated her trip to the Oracle. She initially answers 'pity' but we subsequently learn it is actually because of 'fear'.

Sources

In a documentary compiled for the commercial DVD recording of the original production, the director Stephen Langridge explains that, several years prior to any music being written, Birtwistle met with Harsent, designer Alison Chitty and Langridge to discuss the project.[121] Intended to establish Birtwistle's conception of the drama, these meetings involved looking 'at different references from artists, and so on, to find a visual language'.[122]

---

[121] Chitty had previously worked with Birtwistle as set and costume designer on productions at the National Theatre in addition to *Gawain*, *The Last Supper* and, with Langridge, the 1996 production of *The Mask of Orpheus* and *The Io Passion*; she also subsequently worked on *The Corridor* and *Semper Dowland*. In 1987, Chitty even worked with Peter Gill on productions of *Down by the Greenwood Side* and *Bow Down*.

[122] Stephen Langridge in 'Myth is universal', on the commercial DVD recording of the original production of *The Minotaur*, Royal Opera House/Opus Arte 2008, OA 1000 D.

Evidence in the sketches suggests that Birtwistle later visualised aspects of the production while composing, perhaps for the first time: one sketch includes a drawing of the Snake Priestess.[123] It seems that the production team meetings preceded Harsent's work on the libretto, and Birtwistle certainly discussed ideas with Harsent before any text had been written. Indeed, Harsent believes that his first job is 'to work out what Harry wants'.[124] Yet, in the DVD documentary, Birtwistle states:

> The music is *always* a comment on the text; it can only be that. Because it cannot be the other way around. . . . It's [in] a permanent relationship with the text. The text is the motivator. But once you have something, you might need more text, you might need less text. Sometimes I say to David 'go darker', or 'push that idea and make it more like itself'. But, nevertheless, it is from a very specific point in the text that he's provided.

These remarks appear to suggest a shift in attitude from earlier stage works in which Birtwistle was eager to stress the primacy of his musical concerns. As noted in Chapter 7, since the early 1990s Birtwistle has demonstrated a greater willingness to respond to texts and their images, albeit on his own terms. Yet, one may ask, what shapes Birtwistle's vision before he even sees a libretto? And to what extent was Harsent's text influenced by Birtwistle?

Hall has revealed that the earliest model for Birtwistle was a ballet scenario titled *The Minotaur: A Ballad* by the Swiss author Friedrich Dürrenmatt.[125] The relevance of this text is immediately apparent. Dürrenmatt's Minotaur knows only 'a violent happiness and a violent pleasure' after which he sleeps and dreams of a girl and, later, that he is a man.[126] The walls of Dürrenmatt's labyrinth are mirrored glass, through which shines the sun and moon and in which the Minotaur sees other beings, as Harsent's Minotaur sees his double. He also sees there a premonition of Theseus, as in Harsent's dream scenes, and he dances with the reflections of a young girl, just as Harsent's Minotaur rapes and kills a young girl in scene 5. Knowing nothing of life or death, Dürrenmatt's Minotaur does not realise that he kills the girl, nor does he comprehend why dark birds fly off with her body, as Harsent's Keres devour the Innocents' remains. Angered by Theseus's knife thrust, the Minotaur launches a wild killing spree, 'tearing limbs, guzzling blood, breaking bones,

---

123 This tendency actually extends back to *Punch*, as illustrated by a sketch from around 1960 that depicts Birtwistle's idea for a suspended cradle for the baby, which would swing like a pendulum (the sketch is currently owned by Silas Birtwistle).

124 Harsent in conversation with Beard, 21 January 2008.

125 Birtwistle states in an interview with Hall that he was handed the script by Dürrenmatt's widow when he visited Basle sometime before November 1997. Hall, *HBIRY*, 151.

126 Friedrich Dürrenmatt, *The Minotaur: A Ballad*, in Dürrenmatt, *Selected Writings*, Vol. II: *Fictions*, trans. Joel Agee (London: University of Chicago Press, 2006), 306.

rummaging in bellies and wombs'.[127] Eventually, the Minotaur recognises himself in the reflections and realises that he is alone, but also that he transcends borders put there by the gods to retain order in the world, to prevent it from 'falling back into the chaos from which it sprang'.[128] From this it is evident that many ideas passed from Dürrenmatt to Harsent, either directly or via Birtwistle. Comments made to Hall in 1997 reveal that Birtwistle originally intended to use dancers and that his earliest reference point was *Orpheus*. In the intervening years, however, Birtwistle's ideas evolved in ways that suggest the influence of at least three other sources: a poem, an etching and a study.

Immediately prior to *The Minotaur*, Birtwistle composed *Neruda Madrigales* (2004–5), which is a setting of Neruda's 'Ode to the Double Autumn'. The obvious attractions here are references to a bull and to music, but there is other imagery in the poem that anticipates the opera. The poem's focus is the sea, which immediately relates to the Minotaur myth (the bull from the sea), the opera's opening scene, and – in the original production – a slow-motion film of deep-sea waves projected during the opening and throughout the instrumental toccatas. Langridge has spoken of the importance of the idea of 'muscular movement in the sea', of a 'deep sea swell' that might represent a 'nameless dread'.[129] Such imagery may well have been inspired by the idea in Neruda's poem that, while the Autumn landscape is still, the sea is a living organism. Neruda likens the sea's energy to the thrust of desire, howling machines, and a bull's innards. Comparisons between Birtwistle's Minotaur and the sea in the poem are striking, in particular the sense that at night both cry like abandoned infants but are roused by the day, which in Neruda's poem is signalled by a drumbeat.[130] Knowledge of Birtwistle's interest in Neruda's poem arguably deepens the symbolism of certain key moments in the opera, in particular a series of instrumental waves throughout scene 1 and the instrumental toccatas, piercing woodwind shrieks when the Innocents enter the labyrinth, the Minotaur's arousal by two onstage timpanists, the throbbing orchestral sounds when he is awake, and the tormented self-pitying of his dreams and final song.

---

[127] Ibid., 310.   [128] Ibid., 311.   [129] Langridge, 'Myth is universal'.

[130] In *Neruda Madrigales*, for chorus and ensemble, which is a setting of the original Spanish text, Birtwistle passes over the reference to a drumbeat and focuses instead on an earlier reference to an axe cutting a tree. This is an extremely arresting moment with sharp chords followed by vocal exhalations that recall *The Last Supper*. Neruda's polarised images of autumn stillness and forceful movement are reflected in static chords at the opening, the confinement of each choral part to narrow registral bands determined by a meticulous pre-compositional table, and chiaroscuro contrasts in the unusual ensemble of low and high woodwind, marimba, cimbalom and harp. Towards the end, a fast moving, Ligeti-like continuum of high flutes and bass clarinets mirrors the poem's image of the sea as a living organism, while the sea's cries are suggested by piercing, isolated notes in the clarinet.

The two other sources mentioned above are Picasso's 1935 etching *Minotauromachy* and a study of this artwork by Sebastian Goeppert and Herma C. Goeppert-Frank, which Birtwistle had at his desk while composing.[131] Picasso's etching depicts his lover Marie-Thérèse Walter dressed as a rejoneadora (a horse-mounted female bullfighter) strewn across her dying horse, which has been gored by the Minotaur. The man-bull, possibly a symbol for Picasso himself, approaches the woman.[132] Evidently disturbed by the light of a candle held towards him by a young girl, the Minotaur stumbles forward, his oversized, heavily shaded head tilted downwards in a melancholy pose. The Minotaur's right arm and hand are outstretched towards the girl's candle apparently trying to block out the light. He is being shown something, a truth, perhaps, that he does not want to know. The truth in Picasso's life was that Marie-Thérèse was pregnant and his marriage to his first wife, Olga Koklova, broke down when she found this out.

Within this relatively small etching (49.5cm × 69.3cm) a number of objects, or symbols, jostle for space. A summary of Picasso's visual symbols and their relation to the opera is given in Table 8.4.

It is possible that the Minotaur's oversized head in *Minotauromachy* informed the wire mesh mask that Chitty designed for John Tomlinson in the original production. Lit from within during the darkened dream scenes, this permitted a view through the cage-like construction to Tomlinson's face. The Minotaur's broken demeanour, powerfully conveyed in Tomlinson's performance, and many of the symbols in *Minotauromachy* (ladder, candle, cubic building and open sea) relate back to Dürer's copperplate engraving *Melencolia I* (1514), which in 1976 inspired Birtwistle's eponymous orchestral piece. Yet the one aspect of Picasso's etching that is missing from the opera is the young girl. Birtwistle wanted her to be included, but Harsent argued against this on the grounds that she is too obviously a part of Picasso's 'specific psycho-drama' rather than 'a universal figure or aspect of the myth'.[133] The symbolism of the girl relates to other drawings by Picasso in which she leads a blind Minotaur while he reaches out to touch her head.

Goeppert and Goeppert-Frank relate the Minotaur's outstretched arm to twelfth-century depictions of Christ whose oversized arm reaches out while

[131] A booklet inside the copy of this book loaned to the author by Birtwistle suggests that he travelled to see the etching and its early versions at an exhibition entitled 'Picasso's greatest print: the *Minotauromachy* in all its states', at Los Angeles County Museum of Art, sometime between 16 November 2006 and 25 February 2007.

[132] Picasso's Minotaur imagery evolved gradually from the mid 1920s through the 1930s. Its first definitive appearance, however, can be dated from the Surrealist-influenced journal *Minotaure*, edited by Efstratios Eleftheriadis and Albert Skira, first published in May 1933: Picasso devised a Minotaur-with-dagger collage that was reproduced on the magazine's front cover.

[133] Harsent in email to Beard, 29 January 2008.

Table 8.4 *Thematic correspondences between Picasso's* Minotauromachy *and* The Minotaur

Minotauromachy	The Minotaur
Minotaur	Minotaur
Defeated rejoneadora with a sword	Theseus takes a dagger into the labyrinth
Bullfighter's horse, gored and shrieking[a]	The Innocents are chased around a bullring and gored to death by the Minotaur; their cries are notated in the music
Girl with a bunch of flowers in one hand and a candle in the other	
Christ-like man on a ladder, his head turned to face the Minotaur	Ladders lead down into the labyrinth: we see the Innocents and Theseus descend by this means
Two women look down from an elevated window in a cubic building	A crowd of onlookers peers over the perimeter wall of a bullring
Two doves perched in front of the women	Ariadne carries a dove to the Oracle at Psychro
A sailboat on the sea	A sailboat brings the Innocents to Crete; we see the boat between the beach on the stage and the sea in the background
Storm clouds and rain	The instrumental toccatas are accompanied by moving images of waves

[a] Symbolically, the rejoneadora is pregnant and lies over the dying horse, suggesting the twinned themes of birth and death.

Thomas inspects his wound.[134] Christian iconography is also reflected in the young girl whose arm gestures and hat (like a halo) are comparable to depictions of the Archangel Gabriel announcing the birth of Christ to Mary – although even though the girl's bunch of flowers may symbolise birth, her candlelight reveals to the Minotaur the full horror of his actions.[135] The rain pouring from what appears to be a slit in the cloud is remarkably similar to a cloud break in Dürer's *The Annunciation* (*c.*1510), for which

---

[134] Picasso is reported to have admired such Romanesque images when he visited the Museum of Catalan Art in Barcelona in the summer of 1934.

[135] Goeppert and Goeppert-Frank, *Minotauromachy*, 70.

there are earlier precedents. In Picasso's etching the light beams shine on the Minotaur. This leads the Goepperts to suggest that Picasso's image 'is an astonishing, wilful, but clearly legible symbol for divine, i.e. God-given, fertility. The beam of light on the nape of the Minotaur's neck demonstrates his creative force.'[136] Ladders, however, are often associated in Picasso's work with the Crucifixion, as in Christian iconography. The man on the ladder is slender, bearded, dressed in a loincloth and has a scar under his left arm. In other words, Picasso's etching contains multiple references to Christ. Yet the man appears to be ascending, fleeing the scene – his lighter portion on the left side of the etching is pushed away by the heavily shaded region of the Minotaur approaching from the right.[137]

Various elements in the opera's plot could also be ascribed to Picasso's numerous Minotaur etchings from the early 1930s, which explore their subject from different perspectives. Notable among these versions is the 'dying Minotaur', who is clearly in great pain, his hand held to his wound while members of the crowd reach forward to touch him. There are sleeping Minotaurs with contemplative women, reminiscent of Ariadne in the dream scenes, and beside the more brutal depictions of rape are ones in which the Minotaur caresses sleeping girls.[138] The Minotaur's gait in *Minotauromachy* recalls Picasso's various blind Minotaurs, although he stares ahead and tries to ward off the candlelight. The Goepperts relate this to images in Michelangelo's fresco of the Last Judgement on the altar wall of the Sistine Chapel: here the bright light comes 'from the figure of Christ, preparing himself for the gesture of damnation, which simultaneously blinds and terrifies'.[139] Langridge's production during the Minotaur's dying moments conveyed something similar to this sense of warding off a vision. There are even images in *Minotauromachy* that may have suggested ways to present the ravaging Keres: around 1936 Picasso cast his new lover Dora as a claw-footed 'bird-beast', and even the Minotaur was transformed into a winged bull (*c.*1934–40) – although these examples do not match Harsent's vision of winged female creatures that resemble 'blood-and-crud-encrusted sprung umbrellas'.[140] *Minotauromachy* also includes illustrations in which a woman

---

[136] Ibid., 76.
[137] The Goepperts argue, persuasively, that the bearded figure resembles Leo Stein, brother to Gertrude, who 'discovered' Picasso and Matisse in 1905; Stein was initially an important supporter of Picasso's work but he gave away his collection when Picasso turned to cubism.
[138] Goeppert and Goeppert-Frank observe that in Picasso's Minotaur etchings from 1933 the Minotaur 'appears in a variety of situations: sometimes, he is a drinking, high-spirited fellow, then tender and importunate and, finally, lulled and sleeping'. Goeppert and Goeppert-Frank, *Minotauromachy*, 32.
[139] Ibid., 48.
[140] Harsent, from an early draft of the libretto dated 30 April 2007. For Picasso's bird-like images, see Goeppert and Geoppert-Frank, *Minotauromachy*, 53.

or Naiad holds a mirror to the dying Minotaur's face, as if to suggest a moment of self-recognition or self-knowledge.

Shaping the libretto

Harsent began writing his libretto in 2005, although conversations with Birtwistle began in 2002.[141] Harsent's initial idea was to develop a modern version set inside a room in a house with many doors, but Birtwistle wished to remain more faithful to the myth. Birtwistle had three key concerns: to express the man/beast duality; to present the labyrinth as a bullring; to include a divided chorus of onlookers to witness the Innocents' deaths and to goad them like a football crowd. Yet there were features that Harsent claims he included either because Birtwistle would respond to them, such as the 'pass' and 'kill' sections in scene 7, or because they reflected his own interests, such as the importance given to Ariadne who is present in every scene except the final two. If Harsent had had his way, the opera would have included a long history of the myth sung by Theseus before entering the labyrinth, and ended with Theseus emerging triumphantly from the labyrinth then raping Ariadne as a sign that the 'hero' is no different from the Minotaur.[142] The two would have sailed away and put in at Naxos where Ariadne would be abandoned. Yet in Birtwistle's mind the opera had to end with the Minotaur's death: 'it seems to me the flow is to that point . . . If you've got this long death, you can't suddenly lay off and come back to it, I mean, you're down the slippery slope to the end, and that's it.'[143]

Comparisons between two drafts of the libretto, dated 15 December 2005 and 30 April 2007, give some indication of Birtwistle's involvement in shaping the libretto.[144] In the earlier draft there are seventeen scenes; these differ in content and order from the 2007 version in significant respects. In scene 2, Ariadne and Theseus dream themselves into the labyrinth. In the early draft this was conveyed by two independent soliloqies that were later

[141] Harsent in conversation with Beard, 21 January 2008.

[142] In some senses Harsent thinks of Theseus as worse than the Minotaur: 'I'm very suspicious of heroism, or what heroism masks. I think that nobody in *The Minotaur* is heroic except, perhaps, in a sort of way, the Minotaur himself.' Fiona Sampson, 'The myth kitty [interview with Harsent]', in the programme booklet to the Royal Opera House production of *The Minotaur*, April 2008, 48.

[143] Birtwistle in Beard, 'Beauty and the beast', 15. Birtwistle's desire for the opera to culminate in a set piece for Tomlinson was influenced by the death scenes in Mussorgsky's *Boris Godunov* and Verdi's *Simon Boccanegra*, and he modelled the Minotaur's part on Hagen's tessitura in Wagner's *The Ring*. Whittall has also suggested that Fafner's death music from *The Ring* 'could be felt to have cast a long shadow over *The Minotaur*'. Arnold Whittall, 'First perfomances', 50.

[144] The 30 April 2007 draft is identical to the published version in terms of the structure and order of scenes; the principal differences relate to stage directions and some additional lines.

spliced, initially line by line, then phrase by phrase. What became scene 3, when the Innocents enter the labyrinth, was not a distinct scene in the early draft. This was later instated, with additional text and stage directions, to develop the sense of animosity between Theseus and Ariadne, and to reveal Theseus's sympathy for the Innocents: Theseus 'stares after them, clearly moved by their plight', while Ariadne suggests he forget them since 'They're as good as dead.' Moreover, Birtwistle added a moving lament in which Theseus echoes the anxious calls of the Innocents, sung over a sustained whole-tone chord – an important point, to which I will return. In the 2005 draft, the Minotaur entered through a doorway led by a young girl, as in *Minotauromachy*; by April 2007 the girl had been removed (in the final libretto the Minotaur is onstage when the scene begins). In the earliest draft the Crowd is a single group, but in the later draft they are divided and their text, as well as that for the Minotaur and Ariadne, is expanded and reconceived. These changes clearly enhanced what is one of the opera's most dramatic moments. Substantial repetitions of words such as 'blood', 'death' and 'mine' were also added to the text for Ker 1 at the end of this scene.

There were no toccatas in the early version, although there were three dream scenes. In the dreams, however, there was no second Minotaur, nor any of the lengthy responses that this shadow figure prompts, which are again some of the most memorable features of the opera.[145] Considerable alterations were made to the two remaining labyrinth scenes, including the introduction of the Crowd's taunts. By 2007 the texts for the Keres had been completely rewritten and the largest labyrinth scene had grown into an elaborate series of four chase-and-kill sequences. Eventually, the larger labyrinth scene and the one remaining were swapped so that the longest occurred last. What became scenes 8 and 9 appeared in reverse order in 2005, and the Oracle scene was much shorter and more cryptic than the 2007 version, with different text for the Snake Priestess. Here, too, Theseus had a substantial, 29-line monologue that explained the background to the yearly sacrifice of Innocents, after which the child with a posy and candle led him into the labyrinth. Alterations to the final scenes included the introduction of the Minotaur's gradual breakthrough to coherence (in the earlier draft he spoke as soon as he recognised Theseus), and the removal of Theseus's rape of Ariadne, which, contrary to Harsent's remarks cited earlier, actually preceded the Minotaur's death. In the dying scene the Minotaur died sooner: the origin of what became his dying lament was sung by the

---

[145] The dream-scene exchanges between the Minotaur and Ariadne were also extended in subsequent revisions.

Crowd, and the imagery was less developed. The final scenes in the early draft reveal that Theseus distrusts Ariadne because she has betrayed her father; as they sail away, Theseus reveals his suspicion that he is a half-brother to the Minotaur – information that was ultimately moved to scene 8.

What this comparison reveals is that Birtwistle prompted numerous additions and structural changes, and that he inspired Harsent to write some of the opera's most distinctive lines, notably in the dream scenes. The result suggests a true collaboration in the sense of artists encouraging one another to produce something more inspired. Harsent himself seems to acknowledge this and has spoken of the effectiveness of additional text he wrote for the end of scene 8 when he was encouraged by Birtwistle to 'go dark'.[146] A crucial component in this moment was an intense blue light created for the original production by Paul Pyant. Harsent compares the quality of Pyant's lighting to D. H. Lawrence's poem 'Bavarian Gentians', in which Persephone carries these deep, dark blue flowers as a torch to light her way down to the Underworld. As a consequence of Lawrence's characteristically intense style and increased repetitions of the word 'blue', the flowers become darker but also warmer as she descends. During the rehearsals for *The Minotaur*, Birtwistle remarked that when you achieve this kind of light you can do anything in the theatre.[147]

Birtwistle's Minotaur

If *The Minotaur* has an obvious partner, it is *Gawain*. In light of their shared librettist, both operas have themes of duality and divided identity, and both adopt more traditional characterisation and linear narrative than Birtwistle's other stage works, although there is arguably a closer association between music and stage action in *The Minotaur*. The pass-and-kill sequences in scene 7 recall the lullaby–hunt sequences in *Gawain*: the passes are varied, but the first three kills involve literal repetition. Iambic rhythms in the Minotaur's dream scenes also recall the horn calls heard when Gawain is lulled to sleep by Lady de Hautdesert while her husband, Bertilak, is away hunting. The hunt trope is cast in a new perspective, however, since the Minotaur is both hunter and hunted. In *The Minotaur*, the iambic rhythms anticipate the word 'nothing' in the Minotaur's seminal line 'Between man and beast, next to nothing', sung in scenes 9 and 13. Yet this also recalls

---

[146] Harsent in conversation with Beard, 26 November 2008. The additional lines begin 'The Cretan sky is black, the sun burns black / a black sea', and end 'A black wind / strikes off the stones.'

[147] Harsent in conversation with Beard, 26 November 2008. The blue lighting is present throughout much of the opera but it becomes a particular focus as a thin horizontal line at the end of scene 8; see CD2 of the commercial DVD, at 11'04.

Arthur's refrain 'It's nothing, nothing, nothing', in response to the Green Knight's three 'entrances'. Elsewhere in *The Minotaur*, pairings between instruments and voices recall *Punch* and *The Last Supper* and the debt these works have to Bach's Passions.

Despite these affinities, *The Minotaur* has a dense yet fine-grained orchestral colour that suggests a new approach to harmony and timbre, the details of which will be explored in the remainder of this chapter.[148] Also, at times, *The Minotaur* generates a greater visceral presence than Birtwistle's other stage works. This is conveyed by the Innocents' cries and screams, the Minotaur's roars and half-speech, and the threatening presence of the Keres. These sinister creatures, who clear away the carnage after the Minotaur's killing sprees, produce perfect examples of what the psychologist Klaus Scherer has termed 'affect bursts': explosive, primal shrieks that evoke Darwin's theories about nature sounds and emotion communication.[149] The effect during the original production was terrifying, regardless of the dripping blood and torn-out hearts. Yet this owed more to Artaud than to *Affektenlehre*, and the notion of Grand Opera as refined entertainment was thoroughly challenged.

Given the opera's central theme of Theseus's ability to find his way in and out of the labyrinth by following Ariadne's thread, it is not surprising that Birtwistle has spoken of the presence of a single line throughout the opera.[150] Yet, as in *Gawain*, that line is often being alluded to but is not literally present at all times. There are numerous unison lines and heterophony in the upper woodwind and strings, and also a recurring bass line, referred to in one sketch as a 'moving bass', which provides short links or transitions between and within each scene (see Example 8.20). These winding, ponderous lines, which move by interval steps 1, 2 or 3, suggest the meandering movements of a subject in a labyrinth and are a vital component in the achievement of what has been described as Birtwistle's 'apotheosis of through-composition'.[151] They also recall similar moving basses in Wagner's *Die Meistersinger*, particularly during the scene in Hans Sachs's workshop, where they convey Sachs's sense of loss and loneliness.

---

[148] Numerous critics who reviewed the original production of *The Minotaur* remarked on its harmonic detail and orchestral colour: Andrew Clark referred to a 'mastery of colour, texture and pace' ('The Minotaur'), Andrew Clements to the 'great lucidity... delicacy and transparency' of the score ('The Minotaur', *Guardian*, 16 April 2008), John Allison felt the opera was 'altogether more refined' than *Gawain* ('Labyrinthine magic', *Sunday Telegraph*, 20 April 2008), Fiona Maddocks described the score as Birtwistle's 'most voluptuous yet' ('The Minotaur's monster performance', *Evening Standard*, 16 April 2008), and Rupert Christiansen, despite concluding that Birtwistle 'can't do real people or subtle feeling', commented on the 'finely calibrated harmony' of the toccatas ('Enthralling, hypnotising – and unloveable', *Daily Telegraph*, 17 April 2008).

[149] See Klaus R. Scherer, 'Expression of emotion in voice and music', *Journal of Voice*, 9/3 (1995), 235–48.

[150] Samuel, 'Birtwistle's *The Minotaur*', 218.   [151] Whittall, 'First performances', 50.

Example 8.20 'Moving bass' line, *The Minotaur* (full score, Boosey & Hawkes, 2008), scene 1, p. 6, bb. 37–42

In addition to drawing attention to the presence of a continuous line, however, Birtwistle has remarked that:

> The real control is over intervals in the piece. It's quite consonant. I go off on something melodically – it's technical – I have two simultaneous whole-tone scales, jumping from one to another at certain places – like changing gear. I only exit at certain points, by certain intervals. There's a permanent state of switching between the two.

In response, Samuel comments: 'This seems quite a challenge to a music analyst: two distinct whole-tone scales provide all the notes available! It's also another of Birtwistle's gleeful challenges to those who want to sift through his pitch materials and find a system.'[152] A gleeful challenge, indeed, and one that might be designed to throw analysts off the track. In fact, there is clear evidence in the sketches of Birtwistle using whole-tone dyads, or selections from the two whole-tone scales, at certain moments in the opera. Essentially, Birtwistle employs three different compositional strategies, which often overlap: (1) the use of whole-tone dyads or other segments from whole-tone scales; (2) the application of specific intervals, sometimes resulting in consistent 'intervallic fields'; (3) selections from twelve-note chromatic scales, almost invariably notated on C.[153]

The clearest evidence of strategic whole-tone structuring occurs in scenes 3–4, particularly towards the end of scene 4 in the lead-up to the Minotaur's first, dramatic entrance. In scene 3, as the Innocents enter the labyrinth, their anxious cries are joined by piercing '*sfffz*' chords in the upper woodwind (in the original production, clearly influenced by Picasso's imagery, the Innocents climbed down ladders high above the stage).[154] These woodwind chords (D–E–Gb–Ab) are drawn from the whole-tone scale that includes C, which I shall refer to as W-T 1 (see Example 8.21a).[155] As scene 3 draws

---

[152] Samuel, 'Birtwistle's *The Minotaur*', 218.

[153] The sketches and drafts for *The Minotaur* amount to approximately 950 sides. Since these had not been deposited in Basle at the time of writing but were still in the composer's possession when I consulted them, there are no microfilm or folder numbers. I am extremely grateful to Birtwistle for granting me access to this material.

[154] It is worth noting that ladders were also used in the original production of *Orpheus* during Act II, in scenes depicting the Underworld.

[155] There are two six-note whole-tone scales: 'W-T 1' includes C, whereas 'W-T 2' includes C♯.

Example 8.21a Instrumental cries as the Innocents enter the labyrinth, scene 3, p. 126, bb. 46–7

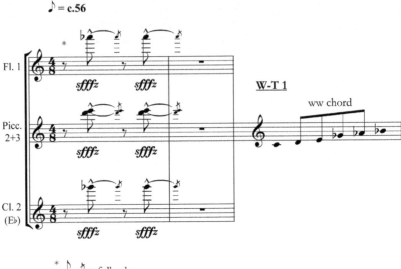

to a close, Ariadne and Theseus lament for the Innocents. Theseus's 'Olola' laments – sung, according to the score, 'more in sympathy [with] than in response' to the Innocents – are heard above a sustained chord in the strings (F–G–A–Db–Eb), which is drawn from the other whole-tone scale, W-T 2 (Example 8.21b).

Towards the end of scene 4, Ariadne describes the Minotaur 'with disdain'. During this description, Ariadne's line is supported by sustained chords in the strings that comprise whole-tone segments. These are deployed in such a way that they clearly suggest an association between the two whole-tone scales and the divided nature of the Minotaur. As Example 8.22 reveals, a series of six sustained chords, each comprising a varied combination of segments from W-T 1 and W-T 2, leads to a G–Ab unison gesture in the upper woodwind and alto saxophone, followed by a descent in the saxophone to a low D. Whole-tone dyads in the harps punctuate the moment that Ariadne refers to her half-brother by his name, Asterios. Her final syllable is sung to Bb. This note is echoed an octave higher by a series of bright Bbs in the strings, which alternate with darker unison middle Cs in the violas and cellos. From this relative oasis of clarity – a chiaroscuro whole-tone dyad (Bb–C) – the music gradually intensifies in anticipation of the moment when the Minotaur is revealed to the audience.

The transitional section that follows is one of the most delicately handled in Birtwistle's oeuvre. Moreover, it conveys a vital tension between

Example 8.21b Theseus's lament and cries from the Innocents over W-T 2, scene 3, p. 129, b. 58

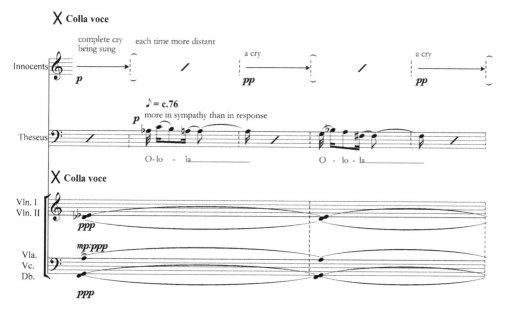

whole-tone and chromatic modes. Above unison Cs in the lower strings, the violins' initial focus is the whole-tone dyad A♭–B♭. As the string texture becomes more dense, and the brass introduces soft but darker-hued chords, which combine semitone and whole-tone dyads, the upper woodwind unfold a series of sustained whole-tone dyads, approached by

Example 8.22 Whole-tone-based harmonies near the close of scene 4, in anticipation of the Minotaur's dramatic entrance, pp. 145–7, bb. 98–111

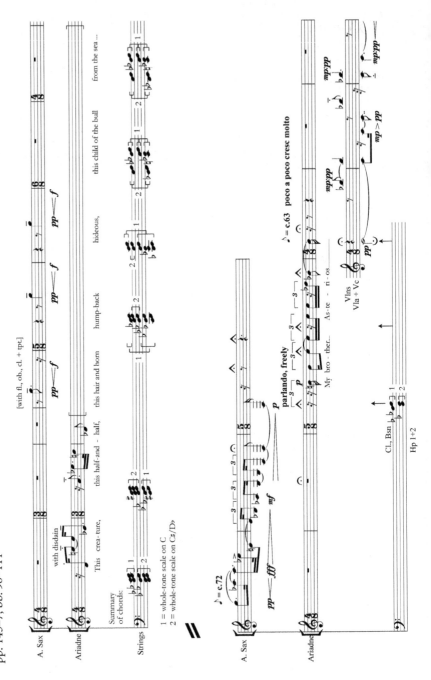

Example 8.23a Whole-tone dyads in the upper woodwind, scene 4, p. 148

* The small notes should always be an even speed: 4 notes = c.192

slow-moving rising scales (see Example 8.23a).[156] The effect is to transpose up and disperse out the Ab–Bb dyad heard previously in the strings.
However, a fascinating harmonic sketch reveals that both the woodwind
and string chords were determined by two six-note modes selected from
a fully chromatic scale, located after the fifth bar line in the sketch (see
Example 8.23b). The upper staff in the sketch, which relates to the upper
woodwind and strings, is drawn from the lower-stemmed set; the lower staff,
realised in the lower strings and woodwind, is based on the upper-stemmed
set. To some extent the regular partition of the upper half of the scale (from
G onwards) and the decision to begin at opposite ends of the stemmed sets
(at C and A♯) create the possibility that Birtwistle exploits whereby whole-
tones are emphasised.[157] More densely chromatic layers were added later in
the brass towards the end of this scheme. With the stage in darkness, scene 4
culminates in a triple *forte*, 43-part chord, with a low, forceful trichord in the
trombone and tubas: F–C–F♯, derived from the upper-stemmed set. Scene
5 is then launched by a D unison in the lower brass, woodwind and strings,

---

[156] The darker-hued brass texture reappears in scene 9 each time the Minotaur sings the refrain
'all too human' after each of the following: 'this lust', 'this rage', 'this hard heart', 'this life in
darkness', 'this deal with death', 'this inescapable sorrow'. The sketches reveal that these
brass refrains were formed from regular alternations of intervals 1 and 2 above and below
intervals 5–7.

[157] Sketches for the whole-tone string chords in scene 4 at Ariadne's disdainful description of
the Minotaur as 'this half and half' reveal that these intervals were also selected from full
chromatic scales on C.

Example 8.23b Sketch for transition to first appearance of the Minotaur, scene 4, pp. 147–9, bb. 109–19

[see Ex. 8.23a]

Example 8.24 Sketch with eight-note mode

Suddenly in a place where had not been before

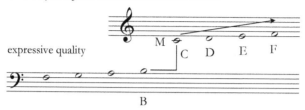

expressive quality

which, in the original production, triggered the lights to illuminate the Minotaur centre stage, the curved wall of a bullring, and the masked heads of the chorus staring over the wall at the monster. As one critic remarked: 'the moment when the beast stands revealed is a brilliant coup de théâtre.'[158]

An indication that Birtwistle consciously prepared this kind of pitch-centricity is revealed in a sketch for Ariadne's and Theseus's vocal parts in scene 3. Along the top of this page Birtwistle sketches out various modes and pitch constellations around middle C, and along the top writes: 'Suddenly in a place where had not been before' and 'expressive quality'. Immediately beneath this is an eight-note mode that comprises two segments from W-T 1 and W-T 2: F–G–A–B–C–D–E–F, as shown in Example 8.24.[159] This gives some indication of what Birtwistle may have meant when he referred to switching between whole-tone scales at certain points: pitch class B, in this instance, represents an exit point, and C an entrance, or *vice versa*. There is a direct link between this sketch and the delicately handled transitional section in which a segment of the mode (F–G–A–B–C) is used to form chords in the viola, cello and trombone parts, which spread from the initial unison Cs.[160] The sketch may also relate to a duet in scene 2 when Theseus asks 'Who are you?' and Ariadne sings 'You are Theseus,' since both parts centre on or around B, C, D, E, which may be intended to reflect the likely familial relationship between these two characters; see Example 8.25. Later, in scene 11, when Theseus and Ariadne duet again, C occupies a gravitational centre in their vocal lines. There is an even more explicit association between C and the notion of an entrance or exit point when low pedal Cs in the contrabass clarinet and double basses accompany the moment when

---

[158] Michael Church, 'First night: the Minotaur, Royal Opera House, London', *Independent*, 16 April 2008.

[159] It is unclear what the letter 'M' represents (possibilities include: Minor 2nd, Middle C, Minotaur). There are also C, G, F and D major scales written out on this sketch page, but it is unclear how these relate to the score.

[160] The F–G–A–B, W-T 2 segment is a subset of the upper-stemmed segment in Ex. 8.23b. It is later deployed in the final chord of scene 7, that is, at the close of the opera's first half. The sketches reveal that this segment was selected for the violas from a fully chromatic scale; the entire chord comprises nine pitch classes, five of which belong to W-T 2.

Example 8.25 Ariadne and Theseus duet, scene 2, p. 66, bb. 37–42

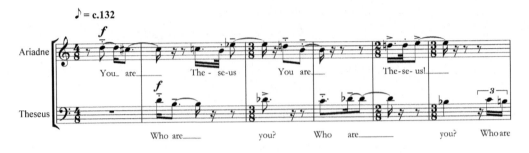

Example 8.26 Pitch class C centricity in Ariadne's and Theseus's parts, scene 11, pp. 375–6, bb. 49–53

Ariadne reveals her plan to lead Theseus to the Minotaur then back again, and Theseus's angry acceptance that they will both 'set sail for Athens' (see Example 8.26).[161] Middle C is the note Ariadne sings in scene 1 on 'want' in her line 'I know what they [the pebbles on the shore] want': they want, like Ariadne, to be 'washed clean', but also to escape Crete.[162] C is also the

161 This occurs in scene 11, bars 17–22, from Ariadne's line: 'Then go into the labyrinth'. Earlier a prominent unison line began on C in the violins when Ariadne referred to 'A ship on the horizon'; scene 1, bar 84.

162 Ariadne's C on 'want' in scene 1 is echoed by the violins in bars 124 and 128, and again by the violins and woodwind in bars 131–3.

only pitch in the orchestra when the Minotaur dies, played by the cimbalom and cellos. These associations recall the opera's two closest forebears: *Earth Dances* and *Exody*; both begin and end on pitch class C.

The sketch may also relate to the first toccata, which precedes scene 2. The three instrumental toccatas clearly reflect the framing function of the toccatas in *Punch* and the alternative perspectives offered by the Passing Clouds in *Orpheus* and by motets in *The Last Supper*. Birtwistle has explained that these sections are 'a contradiction to the way that we think of toccata'.[163] This is presumably a reference to the toccatas' uncharacteristically slow tempi and darkly expressive, ruminative character, although their use of regular, mechanical repetition is more indicative of a toccata. The intention was that these sections would provide a pause in the action, like an engine ticking over. However, the toccatas are also instructive, in ways that recall the instrumental pastorals in *Yan Tan Tethera*. For example, an early version of the opera's only real leitmotif is heard in the brass in Toccata 1, as shown in Example 8.27a. This motif is a kind of war cry that is heard when Theseus first names the Minotaur, when the Minotaur is first seen, when the principal Ker refers to 'slaughter', and ultimately when Theseus confronts the Minotaur. In the toccata, a very soft, slow version of the motif is heard ten times, each statement separated by two crotchets. Later versions of the motif are louder and faster and consequently more intense, as shown in Example 8.27b.[164] The pitch content varies in each version, but a characteristic of its appearance in the toccata is the C–D whole-tone progression in trumpet 4 – in other words, a whole tone from the eight-note mode in the sketch. This is amplified by *fortissimo* C–D dyads in the violins and horns that punctuate each pause between the repeated war cry motifs (see Example 8.27a).[165] This dyad was first heard in the opera's opening bars, in the trombones, harps and cellos, as part of four wave-like gestures that are each initiated by a unison F – that is, the start and end pitch of the eight-note mode. It is also a focal point in the Minotaur's final lines – 'Between womb and tomb / between help and harm / between most and least / between man

---

[163] Birtwistle in Beard, 'Beauty and the beast', 13.

[164] Versions of this war cry motif are heard in the violins and upper woodwind in scene 1 (bars 69–72), trombones in scene 2 (bars 52–6), percussion in scene 3 (bars 45–54), horns and trumpets in scene 7 (b. 267), trumpets in scene 10 (bars 68–72), trumpets in scene 11 (bars 86–103), then, in scene 12, horns and percussion (bars 4–30), full brass (bars 34–7), and upper woodwind (bars 77–87).

[165] C and D are also the first notes in the rapid opening to scene 10. This scene begins with a rising 'moto perpetuum' line in the cimbalom and double basses that begins with repeated notes on C, then D, then E (W-T 1), after which it breaks from the whole-tone pattern; the intervals in the line are: 2–2–3–1–2–3–2–2–1–3–2–2–1. In bar 8, the line is repeated but shifts up a semitone on to Db, Eb, F (W-T 2). This idea returns at bar 138 when Ariadne asks her second question, 'Will I go with Theseus to Athens?' shortly after Hiereus sings 'Let him go hand over hand / To the centre and back again.'

Example 8.27a An early version of the war cry motif, in context; Toccata 1, p. 57, bb. 1–2

N.B. Certain parts have been omitted

Example 8.27b War cry motif when the Minotaur first appears, scene 5, p. 151, b. 7

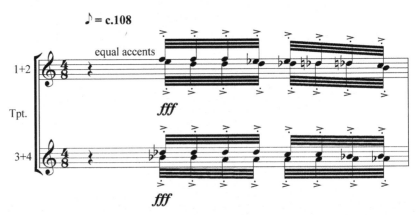

Example 8.27c C–D dyad in closing bars, scene 13, p. 427, *c.* bb. 70–4

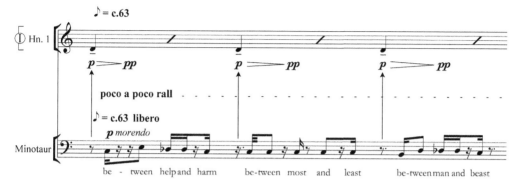

and beast / Next – to – nothing' – which is centred on C juxtaposed with
soft Ds in the horn (see Example 8.27c).[166] The importance of this dyad
and its association with the Minotaur also recalls the symbolic use of these
pitch classes in *Mrs Kong* (see Chapter 6).

At the top of the texture in Toccata 1, repeated at regular 22 triplet-
quaver durations, is a unison G–A♭ figure in the upper woodwind
(see Example 8.27a), which anticipates the later gesture on those pitches
shown in Example 8.22, heard in the alto saxophone shortly before the
Minotaur appears.[167] This figure lends a yearning, melancholy affect that
may relate to Birtwistle's reference to an 'expressive quality' in the sketch.
It also recalls the C–D♭ inverted sigh in *Mrs Kong* (see Example 6.3). The
overall effect of the first toccata is of a set of wheels turning slowly and
regularly, in which the woodwind figure recalls Ariadne's comment, in
the previous scene, that every night she hears the cries of the Innocents.
Similarly, the slow-motion war cry motif echoes words sung by Theseus
immediately before the toccata: 'his death cry or mine hanging in the air
/ Every night. I hear it in my sleep'.[168] In other words, the toccata is not
only a possible response to Neruda's description of sea waves, as discussed
above, but also a direct response to Harsent's text.

If both the transition leading to the Minotaur's first appearance and the
first toccata provide relatively clear evidence of Birtwistle's use of whole-
tone segments, elsewhere in the opera the situation is more complex. The

---

[166] Harsent, *The Minotaur*, 65.

[167] Apart from the common use of repetition, each toccata is different. In the second toccata the
G–A♭ figure is transposed to less frequent statements of E–F in the trumpet, while the upper
woodwind share an unfolding line based on A♭, A, B♭, B, C. This line becomes more
expansive in the third toccata, although the sigh figure is absent. Here also, semitone and
whole-tone dyads in the horns, trumpets and trombones recall the transition section at the
close of scene 4 that led to the Minotaur's first appearance.

[168] Harsent, *The Minotaur*, 7.

remaining sections of this chapter consider the evidence for: more abstract uses of whole tones; intervallic fields; selections from total chromatic scales; and Birtwistle's approach to line – the latter with particular reference to the Minotaur's dreams and dying scene.

'The moon's an eye'

Scene 1 comprises an extended soliloquy sung by Ariadne as she paces a moon-drenched beach in anticipation of the Innocents' arrival.[169] Ariadne is the opera's mediator: she addresses the audience and characters, and is the agent who brings Theseus and the Minotaur together. She is also a gatekeeper: she polices the labyrinth and prevents Theseus from entering before the others, thereby ensuring that the drama lasts longer than it might. Moreover, her position at the intersection of land and sea conveys both her sense of entrapment on the island and her desire to escape: the beach is the entrance point for the Innocents, but also a potential exit for Ariadne. The opening is therefore pervaded by a series of dualities that relate to the Minotaur's divided identity. As mentioned above, there is also a duality to the whole-tone system since it exists as two equal-tempered six-note modes, hence Messiaen's categorisation of it as his first mode of limited transposition. Any whole-tone dyad belongs to one or other of the two modes. Therefore randomised applications of whole-tone intervals, linearly or vertically, will result in alternations from one version of the mode to the other, or references to both simultaneously.

An indication that Birtwistle wished to employ whole tones in more abstract ways than those discussed above is highlighted by the orchestral music during scene 1. Following a series of orchestral wave-breaks and a passage of heterophony in the violins and upper woodwind, discussed below, the music thins to a single 'moving bass' line and, in the original production, Ariadne lets a handful of sand trickle through her fingers. At this moment, a process begins that originated in the sketches as a series of eighteen chords. The starting point is not revealed in the sketches, but it is likely that Birtwistle began with a five-note chromatic set: Ab–A–Bb–B–C. He then, most likely, made six three-note selections from this set to produce the top line of the series of chords; the first eight chords are given in Example 8.28. The top staff in the chord table comprises six rotations of intervals 5, 6 and 7 (the tritone, perfect fourth and fifth, respectively). The next step was to write out a series of whole-tone dyads: those on the second

Example 8.28 The first eight chords from a series of eighteen in a harmonic sketch that relates to scene 1, bb. 41–57

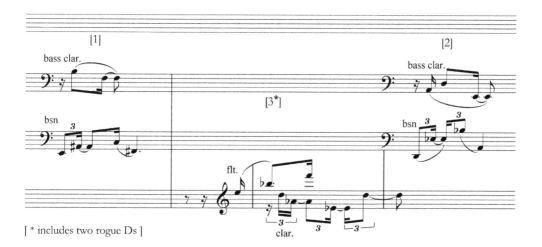

[* includes two rogue Ds]

staff fit symmetrically around the original series of pitches in the top staff (B–Bb–A, etc.); those on the third staff fit symmetrically around the second line of pitches in the top staff (F–Eb–E, etc.). In other words, the rotations of intervals 5–7 determine which whole-tone dyads are deployed.

The sketch reveals that Birtwistle then used these chords to generate a series of woodwind duets in the bass clarinet and bassoon, and in the flute and clarinet, as shown in the lower part of Example 8.28 (the numbers in square brackets indicate which chord each duet is based on). He then decided to introduce the chords in the tubas, trombones, harps and cimbalom, and to shadow these chords in the violas and cellos. The first three chords are separated by other material, but when Ariadne's vocal part begins – 'The moon's an eye that cannot blink or look away' – Birtwistle repeats chord 3 and moves through the sequence more swiftly up to chord 8, although

Example 8.29a Sketch for viola and cello chords at Ariadne's 'How perfect, to live in this moment', scene 1, bb. 68–72

Example 8.29b Rotation of intervals 5, 6 and 7 in clarinet duet, scene 1, p. 12, b. 69

this time the brass shadow the strings. Although this particular scheme is abandoned at this point, Birtwistle generates subsequent harmonies using the same principle. The trombones move in whole-tone dyads, and there is even a series of literally symmetrical chords when Ariadne sings 'How perfect, to live in this moment / with nothing at my back and nothing to face': a series of six chords comprise 2–6–5–6–2, 2–4–7–4–2 and 2–5–6–5–2.[170] Here the placement of whole tones is reversed: those determined by the upper note are transposed down an octave; those determined by the lower note are transposed up an octave (see Example 8.29a). Above the wave-like motion of these alternating chords a skirling clarinet duet, based on more rapid, demisemiquaver rotations of intervals 5–7, evokes a description in Neruda's poem of the tumultuous spray of a wave crest (see Example 8.29b) – although the second time this skirl appears it is joined by the first variant of the war cry motif, in the flutes, oboes and violins.[171]

This 'wheels within wheels' process culminates in a densely scored though very soft texture at the first varied refrain of Ariadne's opening line: 'The moon's a goddess, though her name's a secret...' (Harsent places these single-line refrains between each verse). Here the harmony comprises rotations of intervals 1, 2, 5, 6, 7 – a series that is utilised consistently throughout

---

[170] This occurs in the violas and cellos, scene 1, bars 67–72.   [171] Scene 1, bars 69–70.

Example 8.30 Sketch for string chord, scene 1, b. 74

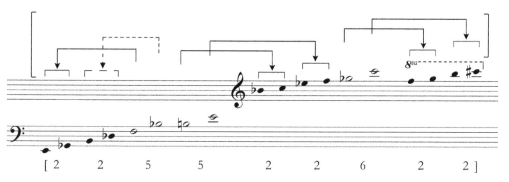

the opera. The first of these chords is shown in Example 8.30. Although the pitch classes of the whole-tone dyads are still determined by the rotations of 5–7, they are placed in different registers, usually an octave higher or lower than the determining pitches. At 'The sea is locks and chains' the string and trombone chords are predominantly whole-tone, but dyad refrains in the woodwind rotate intervals 5–7.[172] Elsewhere Birtwistle muddies the water, inventing pitch sets and modes with an equal mix of whole tones and semitones. For example, the sketches reveal that this approach was used to generate string and woodwind chords that accompany the Innocents in scene 1,[173] the war cry motif, and the instrumental harmony when Hiereus sings 'This clew is your clue' in scene 10.[174] Sometimes Birtwistle resorts to his familiar use of chromatic wedges. To produce a series of varied refrains in the cellos and double basses at the start of scene 3, for example, Birtwistle began with a chromatic wedge on E, although one that does not unfold regularly (see Example 8.31). He then produced a series of four-note sets by applying rotations of intervals 5, 6, 7 or 8 above each note in the wedge (stage 2 in Example 8.31). Next he produced a series of 'shadow' sets in which each note is intervals 1, 2, 3 or 4 above or below the original (stage 3). Each vertical dyad forms a pair, which is then distributed from the lowest part up (stage 4).

Often Birtwistle employs intervallic fields in which entire instrumental strands are characterised by a single set of intervals. In scene 3, for example – with the exception of the cellos and double basses discussed above – several strands have one set of intervals in common: 1, 2, 5, 6, 7. This, of course, provides a link to sections in scene 1, but it also recalls the use of a generic

---

[172] Scene 1, bars 161–71.

[173] Scene 1, bars 193–202; here, the chords comprise strict alternations of intervals 1 and 2.

[174] Scene 10, bars 127–36. To determine the linear intervals in the war cry motif, a series of randomised numbers was written from 0 to 9: 1–5 dictated interval 1; 6–0 indicated interval 2.

Example 8.31 Sketch for a cello and double bass refrain, scene 3, p. 118, bb. 1–41

[Stage 1]

[Stage 2]

[Stage 3]

[*]

[* see Stage 4]

[Stage 4: score realisation of 2 from Stage 3, Scene 3, p. 118, bars 2–3]

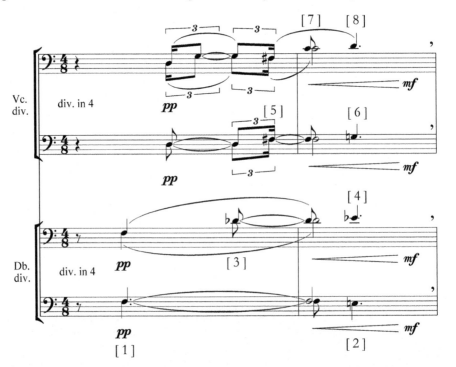

mode, based on permutations of intervals 1, 2, 5, in Act II of *Orpheus* (see Chapter 3). What is remarkable is the way in which an invariant harmonic field is disguised by textural contrast and varied invention. At times, such fields are directly linked to continuous lines, as in *Gawain* (see Chapter 5). The opening bars of scene 3, for example, comprise a cor anglais solo shadowed by slower-moving chords in the strings. Subsequently, the line passes to the first violins, which are shadowed by chords in the flutes and oboes. The sketches reveal that the woodwind chords are formed from vertical rotations of intervals 1, 2, 5, 6, 7 above the violin line, as follows: {1–7–1, 1–6–1, 1–5–1}, {2–7–1, 2–6–1, 2–5–1}, {2–7–2, 2–6–2, 2–5–2}, {1–7–2, 1–6–2, 1–5–2}. Here the principle of a central interval of 5–7 flanked by intervals 1 and 2 relates back to the harmony in scene 1.[175]

Harmonic consistency through the opera and within each scene continues with scene 4. Here intervals 1, 2, 5, 6, 7 determine every aspect except the voice. For example, when Ariadne describes the moment that the white bull, Poseidon, 'covered' her mother there are interval 6 dyads in the violins and violas and, in the upper woodwind, chords formed from vertical rotations of intervals 5–7, flanked above and below by a whole tone (for example 2–6–7–5–2). Such consistency is evident elsewhere in the opera and is apparent towards the end, for example in scene 12, when the Minotaur recognises Theseus.[176]

Accounting for Birtwistle's use of fully chromatic scales is a more complicated task: at least, the rationale for his selection processes is less clear. In most cases, all twelve pitches are utilised and the purpose of the selections is to allocate groups of pitches to specific instruments. However, a wide variety of segments are chosen. The most common selections are four groups of three notes or three groups of four, although there are more unusual examples, such as two groups of eight. In at least one instance, the segments relate to the intervallic field discussed above, since the three intervallic shapes, or 'filters', comprise intervals 1–5–2, 6–1–2 and 1–6–2; the selected pitches are then distributed vertically in the horns, trumpets and trombones respectively.[177] As mentioned above, there is at least one instance when the chromatic scales are used for whole-tone selections. In the majority of cases, however, the filters used to select pitches are restricted

[175] A similar process of stacking sets of three intervals, each one a permutation of intervals 1, 2, 5, 6, 7, is applied to the strings in scene 3, as the Innocents come into view (bars 32–7). For example, from the cellos up, the first chord in bar 32 comprises: 2–7–1, 6–2–5, 1–7–2, 5–1–7, 1–6–1. Originally, the intervals in each set were different but occasional alterations and mistakes made during the sketching process resulted in some sets being repeated.

[176] The sketches reveal that the demisemiquaver chords in the woodwind at this moment are formed from rotations of intervals 5–7 (scene 12, bars 112–22).

[177] This occurs in scene 12, bars 44–9. However, the final note in the first trombone is incorrectly written as F♮ rather than C♯.

Example 8.32 Use of filtered segments from fully chromatic scales to form chords

Example 8.32a Pitch selection from fully chromatic scales on C♯ and C. From an unidentified sketch

Example 8.32b Summary of relations between the two chromatic scales

Three-note filters

to intervals 1–3, and occasionally include 4 and 5. Two examples are revealing. On one page, which may have predated the others, Birtwistle refers to '5 small labyrinths each with [four?] characteristics'. To this is added: '3 on the [symbol?] lab[yrinth?] – [turn? round?]'.[178] Although it is difficult to ascertain precisely what these comments relate to, the sketch suggests that Birtwistle thought of the fully chromatic scales as small labyrinths, small in the sense of being localised to a particular section of the music. Beneath these comments is a series of chords, and below these two fully chromatic scales, as shown in Example 8.32a. The first scale comprises a symmetrical division with four three-note segments. To the right of this scale Birtwistle has written what could be a sharp sign, but might equally be a mixture of flat and sharp signs, to indicate his intention to transpose the filters from the first scale. As shown in Example 8.32b, three of the filters are transposed, but one is altered. The chords formed from this sketch are

[178] When the author visited Birtwistle in August 2007, this sheet had been separated from the main rolls of sketches, which suggests it had particular significance.

Example 8.32c Sketch for upper woodwind, scene 7, p. 232, bb. 95–7. (In addition to the information in editorial brackets, the boxes around chords have been added.)

distributed between the upper strings, cellos and bass clarinet; it is not clear where they are deployed but the sketch is clearly related to another for the upper woodwind in scene 7. This sketch features six different filtrations of fully chromatic scales. As shown in Example 8.32c, a series of four chords is formed from three apparently unrelated filtrations. Moreover, the fact that at times segments from two different scales are used to form one chord highlights the more esoteric nature of this process, in contrast to moments of relative clarity elsewhere in the opera.

'Between man and beast / Next – to – nothing'

The evidence in the sketches suggests that Birtwistle's remarks about alternations between whole-tone scales, which are entered and exited by certain intervals, is true in a general sense, but more complicated in practice. The

Example 8.33 Analysis of line and harmony in the violins, violas and horns, scene 1, pp. 28–30, bb. 166–75

short slur = held across the following note or notes

long slur = the unison note line

focus so far has been on harmony and moments of pitch-centricity, but the question remains whether Birtwistle's remarks apply to his treatment of line. In light of the opera's central themes – Theseus's journey to the centre of the labyrinth, Ariadne's desire to escape, the Minotaur's voyage of self-discovery – Birtwistle often generates, or alludes to, extended instrumental lines, and associates the three central characters with particular timbres: yearning alto saxophone with Ariadne; strident brass with Theseus; plaintive lower woodwind with the Minotaur. Before examining some of these pairings it will be useful to consider Birtwistle's approach to instrumental lines more generally.

One of the most impressive scenes in terms of its handling of line is scene 1. An example is Birtwistle's setting of Ariadne's fifth full stanza.[179] This comprises a series of cyclic elements: recurring dyads in the upper woodwind (rotations of intervals 5–7); separated phrases from Ariadne's stanza, each one cued by a chord in the percussion ([chord] 'I have walked here night after night' [chord] 'as if each dawn could be the start of something'); rising and falling phrases in the lower woodwind, cellos and double basses; unison notes in the horns, violins and violas. Initially the percussion chords and woodwind dyads occur simultaneously, but the other elements rotate independently from one another and from Ariadne's phrases. The upper string and horn unison notes unfold a line that comprises intervals 1–4 (C, E, Eb, D, E, F, Ab). Each note initiates a small-scale harmonic unfolding that comprises a four-note set based on a permutation of intervals 1, 5, 6, 7, as shown in Example 8.33.

Further evidence that Birtwistle's lines do not conform literally to his remarks is provided by sketches for an extended section of heterophony in the violins and flutes during the orchestral introduction in scene 1.[180] Here

[179] Scene 1, bars 166–83.   [180] Scene 1, bars 18–34.

the line is effectively contained within a single octave span from g'' to ab'''. This space is divided into eight five-note sets (labelled A to H), which are selected by the application of filters with intervals 1–5. The rationale behind these selections is unclear, but B♭ – the pitch heard in unison at the very start of the line – is present in all eight sets. The five-note selections are reordered into seven-note sets then strung into a continuous line in the first violin; another filtration system is then employed to determine which notes sound in the other parts. In other words, movement between the whole-tone scales has no relevance whatsoever to this prominent, extended line, heard during the opera's introduction. The sketches also indicate that the instrumental solos paired with particular voices were formed in numerous different ways that rarely relate to Birtwistle's comments.

Regarding the pairing of alto saxophone with Ariadne, Samuel has remarked that the saxophone is not Ariadne's alter ego but rather 'an extension of her voice'.[181] Yet, Samuel argues, the saxophone contradicts Ariadne by sounding 'assured' when she admits to feeling fear, and 'abandons' her when her ruthlessness 'becomes so blatant'.[182] It is perhaps tempting to overinterpret the saxophone's presence in this regard. Birtwistle has stated that the 'coupling' was not predicted, 'it just happened. I just thought we needed a saxophone; the orchestra needs a voice that's distinct.'[183] This seems plausible when it is considered that the saxophone first appears in scene 1 in association with the arrival of the Innocents, not with Ariadne.[184] The first explicit association between the two occurs in scene 3 when Ariadne's duplicitous side is revealed: Theseus must choose the hand in which Ariadne holds a stone to determine when he may enter the labyrinth, but her hands are both empty. The saxophone comes closest to Ariadne's line in the recitative-like scene 4, in which Ariadne narrates early episodes from the Minotaur myth.[185] Here the saxophone assists the narration, playing in a 'sleazy' style when Ariadne describes her mother's lust for the bull, then 'not sleazy' when the narrative turns to Poseidon's anger and Pasiphae's birth pangs. When the lines join at '[the white bull] covered her' the implication is that the saxophone represents the bull. In other words, the saxophone occupies different subject positions. This narrative function even extends to the orchestra when a unison woodwind refrain that accompanies the

---

[181] Samuel, 'Birtwistle's *The Minotaur*', 233.   [182] Ibid.

[183] Birtwistle in Beard, 'Beauty and the beast', 20.

[184] Scene 1, from bar 198, marked 'in clear relief'. The link to the Innocents continues in scene 3, as they descend into the labyrinth, and in the two other labyrinth scenes where the saxophone joins the woodwind in dense, fast-moving textures that convey a general sense of panic.

[185] For the first thirty-six bars of scene 4 Birtwistle employs varied ostinatos in the double bass and cello, plotted on a rhythmic skeleton. This operates in a similar way to ostinatos in *The Corridor*, as discussed in Chapter 7.

birth pangs takes its initial pitch from the saxophone.[186] The saxophone's structural role culminates near the end of this scene with the G–A♭ sighing gesture and descent to D, discussed above, which signals the transition to the Minotaur's first appearance. After this, far from abandoning her, the saxophone actively conspires with Ariadne: it joins her when she lulls the Minotaur to sleep and is intermittently present alongside her in the dream scenes; it underscores her attempt to woo Theseus in scenes 8 and 11; it expresses her joy at finding a way to assist Theseus in scene 10; and it dances her offstage in scene 11, after which Ariadne is not seen again. Ultimately, Ariadne facilitates the plot, and when Theseus and the Minotaur have been brought together both Ariadne and the saxophone are abandoned. Moreover, the saxophone's complicity in Ariadne's plot to escape highlights the Möbius-like nature of her character, in which human rationality and animal instincts are inextricable.

By contrast, the Minotaur, when he sings in English, is shadowed by a variety of instruments: bass clarinets, bassoons and cor anglais in the two dream scenes; the oboe and numerous other wind instruments in the final scene. In many respects, these three scenes – 6, 9 and 13 – represent the heart of *The Minotaur*, since they bring us closest to the man–beast dualism. Moreover, these are among the most intimate moments in Birtwistle's dramatic oeuvre, exploring the kind of small-scale detail typical of his music theatre works but in the context of a major opera. Yet Birtwistle is aided considerably in these scenes by the vividness and economy of Harsent's text. As such, they provide a fitting place to conclude this study.

A key feature of the dream scenes (6 and 9) is the presence of an offstage, pre-recorded voice, named Minotaur 2, described by Harsent as 'an interlocuter & interrogator';[187] in the original production a large, Minotaur-like figure was visible in an onstage mirror. This device recalls Birtwistle's earlier collaboration with Harsent, *The Woman and the Hare* (1999), in which a series of poems is shared between a female narrator and soprano, and it anticipates the division between speech and song in *The Corridor*. It also recalls Harsent's intention in *Gawain* that the eponymous hero should confront his shadow figure, 'Dorian Gray-like' (see Chapter 5).[188] Birtwistle rejected that idea, yet he felt that the Minotaur and his double should communicate 'because he has to talk to somebody ... you have to have him confront himself. I thought that was rather potent.'[189] In reality, the two Minotaurs speak at rather than to one another: this is *not* Dürrenmatt's

---

[186] Scene 4, bars 29–35 and 49–59.
[187] Harsent in conversation with Beard, 21 January 2008.
[188] In a letter from Harsent to Birtwistle dated 2 June 1989, *Gaw*/Lib, PSS.
[189] Birtwistle in Beard, 'Beauty and the beast', 11.

Example 8.34 Whole-tone symmetry in the violins, scene 6, p. 200, bb. 71–2

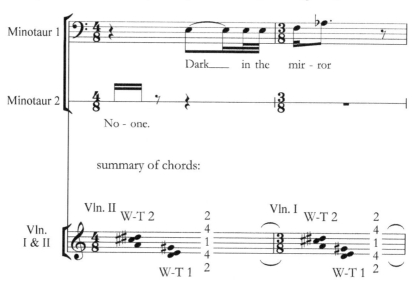

Minotaur who lets out 'a long-drawn bellowing, mooing howl of joy at no longer being the only one ... joy at there being a second Minotaur'.[190] The two dream scenes have a shared structure: alternate statements by Minotaurs 1 and 2; dialogue between Ariadne and the Minotaur; narration of an episode from the myth (by Ariadne in scene 6 and by the Minotaur in scene 9); appearance of Theseus in the mirror. The notion of doubling is extended to the use of pairs of instruments in scene 6, then trios when Theseus appears. A balance of the two whole-tone scales is also evident in this scene, for example in the violins when the Minotaur sees someone 'Dark in the mirror' beside his double (see Example 8.34).

Another key component of the dreams, which returns in the final scene, is the iambic figure mentioned earlier. This relates back to the 'hunt' motif in *Gawain*, where it is associated with the world outdoors. It is first heard in scene 6 in the bass clarinet and first bassoon when the Minotaur's double declares: 'The world outside is lost to you.' Yet later, when the Minotaur sings of 'these innocents', brought to him as gifts that he has to spoil, the motif is tightened into a Scotch-snap that evokes the 'Io' cries of the Innocents, as if their anguished sounds continue to haunt the Minotaur in his dreams. These figures appear in the upper woodwind where, with the upper strings and trumpets, they form a series of chordal refrains based on rotations of intervals 2–7 above an expanding wedge on E in the viola; see Example 8.35.[191]

---

[190] Dürrenmatt, *The Minotaur*, 312.   [191] Scene 6, bars 41–51.

Example 8.35 Echoes of the Innocents' cries in the Minotaur's dream, scene 6, p. 194, bb. 42–4

Numerous versions of the iambic motif spread throughout the orchestra in the first part of scene 9. An important characteristic here is Birtwistle's treatment of the refrain 'all too human', which appears at the end of every line in a six-line stanza. These repetitions underscore Harsent's idea that the Minotaur's human side is a burden to him: the scene expresses the tension he feels at being 'neither' animal 'nor' human (which interestingly echoes Agamben's 'neither particular nor general'). As mentioned earlier, each refrain prompts the return of whole-tone and semitone dyads in the brass – the same dark-hued harmony heard in the transition to the Minotaur's first appearance – although the specific pitches are varied each time. Yet the refrain informs this scene in other ways, too. The four syllables and falling contour of the Minotaur's refrain are anticipated in the previous stanza by a combination of the iambic motif with four-note descending phrases in violas and cellos.[192] Moreover, in the text that follows the six-line stanza – text that was added after 2005 – there is an extended series of four-note descending phrases in the violas, cellos and trombones, based on four-note selections from fully chromatic scales. The melancholy falling contours recall the Minotaur's drooping head in Picasso's *Minotauromachy*, and the resultant wave motion relates back to scene 1 and the first toccata. Moreover, middle C assumes the role of a boundary against which the singer continually strains, as if pushing at a door that remains permanently closed; the same is true of the falling figures, which are confined to a similar tessitura (see Example 8.36).

In the final scene the iambic motif returns, initially in the tubas at 'The beast is vile, so the man must go unloved,' then in a series of wind solos, including oboe, cor anglais, horn, trumpet and flute. These instruments separate from the conductor's beat to form a group that follows the Mino-taur's independent tempo. Clearly, this idea forms the seed of what would become *The Corridor*, in particular the notion that Eurydice is danced to death by onstage instruments. The logic of the repeated iambic motifs also

---

[192] Scene 9, bars 15–22.

Example 8.36 Middle C as a boundary, and melancholic, falling figures in scene 9, p. 315, bb. 56–9

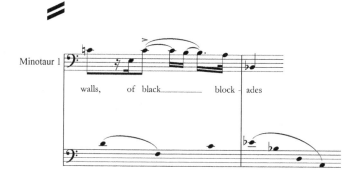

becomes apparent when the Minotaur himself takes up the Innocents' 'Io moi' cry of anguish, immediately before the penultimate stanza – a gesture that relates back to an extended 'Io moi' lament by Ariadne at the end of scene 8. Moreover, a discrete shadow in the form of a fully chromatic descent in the violins and violas passes behind the Minotaur at 'Death is the sound of wing beats and a voice chanting in darkness' (see Example 8.37). This chromatic line falls from c'' to c – the pitch class associated with exits and entrances – and ends at the point that 'sotto voce' tom-toms, woodblocks and other percussion begin a ghostly continuum beneath the final stanza.

'Then, before the sun came, there came the birds'[193]

There is a complementarity between *The Minotaur* and *The Last Supper* that although governed by their respective themes is indicative of more divergent trends in Birtwistle's prolific output since 2000. The Minotaur's suffering and eventual death, highlighted in particular by the plaintive oboe

---

[193] Dürrenmatt, *The Minotaur*, 313.

Example 8.37 Chromatic shadow passing behind the Minotaur, scene 13, pp. 425–6, bb. 62–7

solo at the opening of the final scene, may evoke a Christ-like sympathy for the man-beast, yet that opera's more violent scenes complement the absence of the Passion and crucifixion from *The Last Supper*. The two operas flank the day/night cycles of *The Io Passion*, and in themselves represent an antipode between dark/visceral and light/cerebral. A similar distinction exists between the introverted worlds of *The Shadow of Night*, *26 Orpheus Elegies* (2003–4), *Night's Black Bird*, *Cortège* (2007), and *Semper Dowland*, on the one hand, and more extrovert works such as *The Axe Manual* (2000), *Theseus Game* (2002), *Ring Dance of the Nazarene* (2003), *Cantus Iambeus* (2004), *Crowd* (2005) and the Violin Concerto (2009–10), on the other. Overall, Birtwistle has developed an increased concern for harmony and fugue, which in part reflects recent arrangements of Bach and Dowland. Vocal music, too, is increasingly important, and music for strings, as illustrated by *Bogenstrich* (2006–9), *String Quartet: The Tree of Strings* (2007), and the Violin Concerto. *Neruda Madrigales* and *Angel Fighter* (2010) are perhaps harder to categorise, yet where the former shares themes with *The Minotaur*, so the latter – with a text by the *Io Passion* librettist Stephen Plaice – develops ideas from *The Last Supper*.

What both operas reveal, however, is a remarkable willingness to take on texts written by strong personalities, and to engage actively with the concepts and images of those poets. It is not incorrect to stress Birtwistle's single-mindedness, but to exclude the many other dimensions that have informed, shaped and structured his vision would be misleading. Clearly, music often comes first in Birtwistle's approach to stage works, and his musical concerns shape the libretti that he sets. Yet his readiness to engage with a variety of dramatic topics, in ways that challenge or renew operatic conventions, and his ability to relate abstract compositional processes to real world concerns, open out his stage works to enquiry on a range of levels that should continue to foster debate on Birtwistle and his contribution to contemporary opera and music theatre for some time to come.

Bibliography

Abbate, Carolyn, *In Search of Opera* (Princeton University Press, 2001).
'Metempsychotic Wagner', in *In Search of Opera*, 107–44.
'Music – drastic or gnostic?' *Critical Inquiry*, 30 (2004), 505–36.
'Orpheus. One last performance', in *In Search of Opera*, 1–54.
Unsung Voices (Princeton University Press, 1991).
Adlington, Robert, 'A conversation with Harrison Birtwistle', in O'Hagan (ed.),
   Aspects of British Music, 111–18.
'"Good lodging": Harrison Birtwistle's reception of *Sir Gawain and the Green
   Knight*', in Richard Barber (ed.), *King Arthur in Music* (Cambridge: D. S.
   Brewer, 2002), 127–44.
'Harrison Birtwistle's recent music', *Tempo*, 196 (1996), 2–8.
'In the shadows of song: Birtwistle's Nine Movements for String Quartet', in
   O'Hagan (ed.), *Aspects of British Music*, 47–62.
'Moving beyond motion: metaphors for changing sound', *Journal of the Royal
   Musical Association*, 128/2 (2003), 297–318.
'Music theatre since the 1960s', in Mervyn Cooke (ed.), *The Cambridge Com-
   panion to Twentieth-Century Opera* (Cambridge University Press, 2005),
   225–43.
'Summary justice' [review of Harrison Birtwistle festival, Southbank Centre],
   Musical Times, 137 (July 1996), 31–4.
'Temporality in post-tonal music', D.Phil. thesis, University of Sussex, 1997.
The Music of Harrison Birtwistle (Cambridge University Press, 2000).
Adorno, Theodor, 'Bourgeois opera', in David J. Levin (ed.), *Opera through Other
   Eyes* (Stanford University Press, 1994), 25–44.
Mahler: A Musical Physiognomy, trans. E. Jephcott (London: University of Chicago
   Press, 1992).
Philosophy of Modern Music, trans. Anne G. Mitchell and Wesley V. Blomster
   (London: Sheed & Ward, 1994).
'Vers une musique informelle', in his *Quasi una Fantasia: Essays on Modern Music*,
   trans. Rodney Livingstone (London: Verso, 1992).
and Hanns Eisler, *Composing for the Films* (London and New York: Continuum,
   1994).
Agamben, Giorgio, *The Coming Community*, trans. Michael Hardt (Minneapolis
   and London: University of Minnesota Press, 2005).
Albright, Daniel, *Untwisting the Serpent: Modernism in Music, Literature, and Other
   Arts* (London: University of Chicago Press, 2000).
Allison, John, 'Labyrinthine magic', *Sunday Telegraph*, 20 April 2008.

Almén, Byron, 'Narrative archetypes: a critique, theory, and method of narrative analysis', *Journal of Music Theory*, 47/1 (2003), 1–39.

Althusser, Louis, and Etienne Balibar, *Reading Capital*, trans. Ben Brewster (London: Verso, 1979).

Alpers, Paul, *What Is Pastoral?* (London: Chicago University Press, 1996).

[Anon.], 'Petrarch's sonnets set to music', *Times Educational Supplement*, 19 June 1966.

[Anon.], *Sir Gawain and the Green Knight*, trans. Brian Stone (Harmondsworth: Penguin, 1974).

Arendt, Hannah, *The Origins of Totalitarianism* (San Diego and New York: Harcourt Brace Jovanovich, 1973).

Armstrong, Tim, *Modernism, Technology, and the Body: A Cultural Study* (Cambridge University Press, 1998).

Artaud, Antonin, *The Theater and Its Double*, trans. Mary Caroline Richards (New York: Grove Press, 1958).

Ashby, Arved, review of Daniel Albright, *Untwisting the Serpent*, *Journal of the American Musicological Society*, 56/3 (Fall 2003), 740–7.

(ed.), *The Pleasure of Modernist Music: Listening, Meaning, Intention, Ideology* (Rochester, NY: Rochester University Press, 2004).

Astley, Neil, 'The Wizard of [Uz]', in Astley (ed.), *Tony Harrison*, 10–13.

(ed.), *Tony Harrison* (Newcastle-upon-Tyne: Bloodaxe Books, 1991).

Atkins, Harold, 'Bow Down', *Telegraph*, 6 July 1977.

Attali, Jacques, *Noise: The Political Economy of Music* (Minneapolis and London: University of Minnesota Press, 2006).

Attinello, Paul, Christopher Fox and Martin Iddon (eds.), 'Other Darmstadts', *Contemporary Music Review*, 26/1 (2007).

Auden, W. H., 'Notes on music and opera', in his *The Dyer's Hand* (New York: Random House, 1962), 464–74.

Augustine, Saint, *Confessions*, trans. R. S. Pine-Coffin (London: Penguin Books, 1961).

Austin, J. L., *How to Do Things with Words*, 2nd edn, ed. J. O. Urmson and Marina Sbisà (Oxford: Clarendon Press, 1975).

Bakhtin, Mikhail, *Rabelais and His World* (Bloomington and Indianapolis: Indiana University Press, 1984).

The Dialogic Imagination: Four Essays, trans. Caryl Emerson and Michael Holquist (Austin: University of Texas Press, 2000).

Barber, John, 'Reinstating meaning of Christmas [sic]', *Daily Telegraph*, 12 December 1978.

Barkin, Elaine, and Martin Brody, 'Babbitt, Milton', in Stanley Sadie and John Tyrrell (eds.), *The New Grove Dictionary of Music and Musicians*, 2nd edn, vol. II (London: Macmillan, 2001), 283–7.

Barthes, Roland, 'The third meaning', in *The Responsibility of Forms: Critical Essays on Music, Art and Representation*, trans. Richard Howard (Berkeley and Los Angeles: University of California Press, 1985).

Bassetto, Luisa, 'Marginalia, ou *L'opéra-fantôme* de Pierre Boulez', in Jean-Louis Leleu and Pascal Decroupet (eds.), *Pierre Boulez: Techniques d'écriture et enjeux esthétiques* (Geneva: Contrechamps Éditions, 2006), 255–98.

Baudrillard, Jean, 'The ecstasy of communication', trans. John Johnston, in Hal Foster (ed.), *The Anti-Aesthetic: Essays on Postmodern Culture* (New York: New Press, 1998), 145–54.

Beard, David, 'An analysis and sketch study of the early instrumental music of Sir Harrison Birtwistle, *c.* 1957–77', D.Phil. dissertation, University of Oxford 2000.

   '"Batter the doom drum": the music for Peter Hall's *Oresteia* and other productions of Greek tragedy by Harrison Birtwistle and Judith Weir', in P. Brown and S. Ograjensek (eds.), *Ancient Drama in Music for the Modern Stage* (Oxford University Press, 2010), 369–97.

   'Beauty and the beast: a conversation with Sir Harrison Birtwistle', *Musical Times*, 149/1902 (Spring 2008), 9–25.

   'Birtwistle's labyrinth [a preview of *The Minotaur*]', *Opera*, 59/4 (2008), 372–81.

   '"From the mechanical to the magical": Birtwistle's pre-compositional plan for *Carmen Arcadiae Mechanicae Perpetuum*', *Mitteilungen der Paul Sacher Stiftung*, 14 (April 2001), 29–33.

   '*Taverner*: an interpretation', in Nicholas Jones and Kenneth Gloag (eds.), *Peter Maxwell Davies Studies* (Cambridge University Press, 2009), 79–105.

   'The endless parade: competing narratives in recent Birtwistle studies', *Music Analysis*, 23/1 (2004), 89–127.

Beinhorn, Gabriele, *Das Groteske in der Musik: Arnold Schönberg's 'Pierrot lunaire'* (Pfaffenweiler: Centaurus-Verlagsgesellschaft, 1989).

Bell, Catherine, *Ritual: Perspectives and Dimensions* (New York: Oxford University Press, 1997).

   Ritual Theory, Ritual Practice (Oxford University Press, 2009).

Benjamin, Walter, *Illuminations*, ed. Hannah Arendt, trans. Harry Zohn (London: Fontana, 1992).

   The Arcades Project, trans. Howard Eiland and Kevin McLaughlin (Cambridge, MA: Belknap Press of Harvard University Press, 1999).

Berger, Karol, 'Musicology according to Don Giovanni, or: Should we get drastic?', *Journal of Musicology*, 22/3 (2005), 490–501.

Bernstock, Judith E, *Under the Spell of Orpheus: The Persistence of a Myth in Twentieth-Century Art* (Carbondale and Edwardsville: Southern Illinois University Press, 1991).

Billington, Michael, 'Masks that obscure a tragedy', *Guardian*, 30 November 1981.

Blaser, Robin, *The Fire: Collected Essays of Robin Blaser*, ed. Miriam Nichols (Berkeley and Los Angeles: University of California Press, 2006). Including: 'The fire', 3–12; 'Poetry and positivisms: High-Muck-a-Muck or "Spiritual Ketchup"', 38–63; 'The recovery of the public world', 64–86; and 'The irreparable', 98–110.

The Holy Forest: Collected Poems of Robin Blaser, ed. Miriam Nichols (Berkeley and Los Angeles: University of California Press, 2006). Including:

'Image-Nation 26 (being-thus', in *The Holy Forest*, 432–4.

The Last Supper: Dramatic Tableaux (London: Boosey and Hawkes, 2000).

Bokina, John, *Opera and Politics: From Monteverdi to Henze* (New Haven: Yale University Press, 1997).

Boulez, Pierre, 'Opera houses? Blow them up!', *Opera*, 19/6 (1968), 440–50.

Bowen, Meirion, 'A Tempest of our time', in Nicholas John (ed.), *The Operas of Michael Tippett* (London: John Calder, 1985), 93–8.

'Harrison Birtwistle', in Lewis Foreman (ed.), *British Music Now: A Guide to the Work of Younger Composers* (London: Elek, 1975), 60–70.

Bradbury, Ernest, review of the York Music Festival, *Musical Times*, 107 (August 1966), 696.

Brecht, Bertolt, *Brecht on Theatre: The Development of an Aesthetic*, trans. John Willett (London: Eyre Methuen, 1974).

Brett, Philip, 'Britten's Dream', in Ruth Solie (ed.), *Musicology and Difference: Gender and Sexuality in Music Scholarship* (Berkeley and Los Angeles: University of California Press, 1995), 259–80.

Brodsky, Seth, 'Write the moment: two ways of dealing with Wolfgang Rihm 1', *Musical Times*, 145 (2004), 57–72.

Brody, Alan, *The English Mummers and Their Plays: Traces of Ancient Mystery* (London: Routledge and Kegan Paul, 1969).

Brook, Peter, *The Empty Space* (London: Penguin Books, 2008).

Brooks, Peter, *Body Work: Objects of Desire in Modern Narrative* (Cambridge, MA and London: Harvard University Press, 1993).

Brown, Julie, *Bartók and the Grotesque: Studies in Modernity, the Body and Contradiction in Music*, Royal Musical Association Monographs 16 (Aldershot: Ashgate, 2007).

Burke, Kenneth, *A Grammar of Motives* (Berkeley and Los Angeles: University of California Press, 1969).

Butler, Judith, *Excitable Speech: A Politics of the Performative* (London and New York: Routledge, 1997).

Calico, Joy H., *Brecht at the Opera* (Berkeley and Los Angeles: University of California Press, 2008).

Carlson, Marvin, *Performance: A Critical Introduction* (New York: Routledge, 2003).

Carnegy, Patrick, 'Mythopoeic decisions', *Times Educational Supplement*, 9 May 1986.

Carpenter, Humphrey, *W. H. Auden: A Biography* (London: George Allen & Unwin, 1981).

Chatman, Seymour, *Story and Discourse* (Ithaca, NY: Cornell University Press, 1978).

Chevalier, Tracy, *Girl with a Pearl Earring* (London: HarperCollins, 2003).

Chew, Geoffrey, 'Pastoral and neoclassicism: a reinterpretation of Auden's and Stravinsky's "Rake's Progress"', *Cambridge Opera Journal*, 5/3 (November 1993), 239–63.

and Owen Jander, 'Pastoral', in Stanley Sadie and John Tyrrell (eds.), *The New Grove Dictionary of Music and Musicians*, 2nd edn, vol. XIX (London: Macmillan, 2001), 217–25.

Christiansen, Rupert, 'Enthralling, hypnotising – and unloveable', *Daily Telegraph*, 17 April 2008.

Chua, Daniel K. L., 'Untimely reflections on operatic echoes: how sound travels in Monteverdi's *Orfeo* and Beethoven's *Fidelio* with a short instrumental interlude', *Opera Quarterly*, 21/4 (Autumn 2005), 573–96.

Church, Michael, 'First night: The Minotaur, Royal Opera House, London', *Independent*, 16 April 2008.

Clark, Andrew, 'The Minotaur, Royal Opera House, London', *Financial Times*, 21 April 2008.

Clarke, David, *The Music and Thought of Michael Tippett: Modern Times and Metaphysics* (Cambridge University Press, 2001).

Clements, Andrew, 'Birtwistle unmasked', *Financial Times*, 17 May 1986.

'*Gawain* – an opera about people', *Opera*, 42/8 (1991), 11–16.

review of 'Behind the mask' documentary, *Financial Times*, March 1987.

review of *Yan Tan Tethera*, *Opera*, 37/10 (1986), 1,199–1,202.

'Strange fits of passion', *Opera*, 55/8 (2004), 908–10.

'The Mask of Orpheus', *Opera*, 37/7 (1986), 851–7.

'The Minotaur', *Guardian*, 16 April 2008.

Collier, John Payne, *Punch and Judy, with Illustrations Drawn and Engraved by George Cruikshank*, 2nd edn (London: S. Prowett, 1828).

Collins, Douglas, 'Ritual sacrifice and the political economy of music', *Perspectives of New Music*, 24/1 (Autumn–Winter 1985), 14–23.

Cone, Edward T., *The Composer's Voice* (Berkeley and Los Angeles: University of California Press, 1974).

Copjec, Joan, *Read My Desire: Lacan against the Historicists* (Cambridge, MA and London: MIT Press, 1995).

Croall, Jonathan, *Peter Hall's Bacchai* (London: National Theatre, 2002).

Cross, Jonathan, *Harrison Birtwistle: Man, Mind, Music* (London: Faber and Faber, 2000).

Harrison Birtwistle: The Mask of Orpheus (Aldershot: Ashgate, 2009).

'Introduction to the story and music', from '*The Last Supper*' Guide, promotional compact disc by Glyndebourne Productions, 2000.

'Lines and circles: on Birtwistle's *Punch and Judy* and *Secret Theatre*', *Music Analysis*, 13/2–3 (July–October 1994), 203–25.

Crosse, Gordon, 'Birtwistle's *Punch and Judy*', *Tempo*, 85 (Summer 1968), 24–6.

Cumming, Naomi, *The Sonic Self: Musical Subjectivity and Signification* (Bloomington and Indianapolis: Indiana University Press, 2000).

Currie, Mark, *About Time: Narrative, Fiction and the Philosophy of Time* (Edinburgh University Press, 2007).

Danuser, Hermann and Matthias Kassel (eds.), *Musiktheater heute: Internationales Symposium der Paul Sacher Stiftung Basel 2001* (Mainz: Schott Musik International, 2003).

Davidson, Michael, review of Netherlands Opera Production of *Punch and Judy*, *Opera*, 44/4 (1993), 465–6.

Davies, Andrew, *Other Theatres: The Development of Alternative and Experimental Theatre in Britain* (Houndmills and Basingstoke: Macmillan Education, 1987).

de Vries, Hent, *Minimal Theologies: Critiques of Secular Reason in Adorno and Levinas*, trans. Geoffrey Hale (Baltimore: John Hopkins University Press, 2005).

Deleuze, Gilles, *Francis Bacon: The Logic of Sensation*, trans. Daniel W. Smith (London and New York: Continuum, 2003).

Dematire, Ann, 'The Theater of Cruelty and alchemy: Artaud and Le Grand Oeuvre', *Journal of the History of Ideas*, 33/2 (April–June 1972), 237–50.

Dennett, Daniel, *Consciousness Explained* (London: Penguin Books, 1993).

Derrida, Jacques, *Writing and Difference*, trans. Alan Bass (London and Henley: Routledge and Kegan Paul, 1978).

Detienne, Marcel, *The Writing of Orpheus: Greek Myth in Cultural Context*, trans. Janet Lloyd (Baltimore and London: Johns Hopkins University Press, 2003).

Doane, Mary Ann, 'Misrecognition and identity: the concept of identification in film theory', *Cine-Tracts: A Journal of Film and Cultural Studies*, 3/3 (1980), 25–32.

Doob, Penelope Reed, *The Idea of the Labyrinth: From Classical Antiquity through the Middle Ages* (Ithaca, NY and London: Cornell University Press, 1990).

Downes, Stephen, 'Hans Werner Henze as post-Mahlerian: anachronism, freedom, and the erotics of intertextuality', *twentieth-century music*, 1/2 (2004), 179–207.

Driver, Tom F., *Liberating Rites: Understanding the Transformative Power of Ritual* (Boulder, CO and Oxford: Westview Press, 1998).

Duncan, Michelle, 'The operatic scandal of the singing body: voice, presence, performativity', *Cambridge Opera Journal*, 16/3 (2004), 283–306.

Dunsby, Jonathan, *Schoenberg: Pierrot lunaire* (Cambridge University Press, 1992).

Dürrenmatt, Friedrich, *The Minotaur: A Ballad*, in *Selected Writings*, 3 vols., vol. II, *Fictions*, trans. Joel Agee (London: University of Chicago Press, 2006), 303–13.

Empson, William, *Some Versions of Pastoral* (London: Penguin, 1995).

Emslie, Barry, 'Woman as image and narrative in Wagner's Parsifal: a case study', *Cambridge Opera Journal*, 3/2 (1991), 109–24.

Esse, Melina, '"Chi piange, qual forza m'arretra?" Verdi's interior voices', *Cambridge Opera Journal*, 14/1–2 (2002), 59–78.

Evans, Dylan, *An Introductory Dictionary of Lacanian Psychoanalysis* (London and New York: Routledge, 2007).

Finburgh, Clare, '"Voix/voie/vie": the voice in contemporary French theater', *Yale French Studies*, 112 (2007), 99–115.

Fink, Bruce, *The Lacanian Subject: Between Language and Jouissance* (Princeton University Press, 1997).

Fische-Lichte, Erika, *Theatre, Sacrifice, Ritual: Exploring Forms of Political Theatre* (London and New York: Routledge, 2005).

Fletcher, Angus, 'Utopian history and the *Anatomy of Criticism*', in Murray Krieger (ed.), *Northrop Frye in Modern Criticism* (New York: Columbia University Press, 1966), 31–73.

Ford, Andrew, 'The reticence of intuition: Sir Harrison Birtwistle', in Ford, *Composer to Composer: Conversations about Contemporary Music* (London: Quartet Books, 1993), 52–9.

Franklin, Peter, *Seeing through Music: Gender and Modernism in Classic Hollywood Film Scores* (Oxford University Press, 2011).

Freeman, David, 'Composer and producer speak', in programme booklet for the English National Opera production of *Orpheus*, May–June 1986.

Freud, Sigmund, *The Standard Edition of the Complete Psychological Works of Sigmund Freud*, vol. VII (1901–1905), 'A Case of Hysteria', 'Three Essays on Sexuality' and Other Works, ed. James Strachey, Anna Freud, Alix Strachey and Alan Tyson (London: Vintage, 2001).

Friedman, Susan Stanford, 'Spatial poetics and Arundhati Roy's *The God of Small Things*', in James Phelan and Peter J. Rabinowitz (eds.), *A Companion to Narrative Theory* (Malden, MA, and Oxford: Blackwell Publishing, 2005), 192–205.

Geertz, Clifford, *The Interpretation of Cultures* (New York: Basic Books, 1973).

Genette, Gérard, *Narrative Discourse: An Essay in Method*, trans. Jane E. Lewin (Ithaca, NY: Cornell University Press, 1983).

Gifford, Terry, *Pastoral* (London and New York: Routledge, 1999).

Goeppert, Sebastian and Herma C. Goeppert-Frank, *Minotauromachy by Pablo Picasso*, trans. Gail Mangold-Vine (Geneva: Patrick Cramer, 1987).

Graybill, Roger, 'Toward a pedagogy of gestural rhythm', *Journal of Music Theory Pedagogy*, 4/1 (1990), 1–50.

Griffiths, Paul, 'Hans Werne Henze talks to Paul Griffiths', *Musical Times*, 115 (1974).
  Modern Music and After (Oxford University Press, 2010).
  New Sounds, New Personalities: British Composers of the 1980s (London: Faber, 1985).
  Peter Maxwell Davies (London: Robson Books, 1985).
  review of *The Last Supper*, *Tempo*, 213 (2000), 41–2.
  'The twentieth century: 1945 to the present day', in Roger Parker (ed.), *The Oxford History of Opera* (Oxford University Press, 1996).

Grossberg, L., 'The space of culture, the power of space', in Iain Chambers and Lidia Curti (eds.), *The Post-Colonial Question: Common Skies, Divided Horizons* (London: Routledge, 1996), 169–88.

Grossvogel, David I. *Scenes in the City: Film Visions of Manhattan before 9/11* (New York: Peter Lang, 2003).

Grover-Friedlander, Michal, *Vocal Apparitions: The Attraction of Cinema to Opera* (Princeton University Press, 2005).

Gumbrecht, Hans Ulrich, 'Production of presence, interspersed with absence: a modernist view on music, libretti, and staging', in Karol Berger and Anthony Newcomb (eds.), *Music and the Aesthetics of Modernity: Essays* (Cambridge, MA: Harvard University Press, 2005), 343–55.

   Production of Presence: What Meaning Cannot Convey (Stanford University Press, 2004).

Guthrie, M. A., *Orpheus and Greek Religion* (London: Methuen & Co. Ltd., 1935).

Habermas, Jürgen, 'Modernity – an incomplete project', in Hal Foster (ed.), *Post-modern Culture* (London: Pluto Press, 1985), 3–15.

Hall, Michael, 'Composer and producer speak', in the programme booklet for the English National Opera premiere of *The Mask of Orpheus*, May 1986.

   Harrison Birtwistle (London: Robson Books, 1984).

   Harrison Birtwistle in Recent Years (London: Robson Books, 1998).

   'The sanctity of the context: Birtwistle's recent music', *Musical Times*, 129 (January 1988), 14–16.

Harper-Scott, J. P. E., 'Being-With Grimes: the problem of Others in Britten's first opera', in Rachel Cowgill, David Cooper and Clive Brown (eds.), *Art and Ideology in European Opera* (Woodbridge: Boydell & Brewer, 2010), 362–81.

   'Britten's opera about rape', *Cambridge Opera Journal*, 21/2 (2010), 65–88.

Harpham, Geoffrey Galt, *On the Grotesque: Strategies of Contradiction in Art and Literature* (Princeton University Press, 1982).

Harrison, Tony, *Theatre Works: 1973–85* (Harmondsworth: Penguin, 1985).

Harsent, David, *Gawain* (London: Universal Edition, 1991).

   'Morgan le Fay', essay in the programme booklet for the Royal Opera House, Covent Garden, production of *Gawain*, January 2000, 38.

   Night (London: Faber and Faber, 2011).

   Selected Poems (Oxford University Press, 1989).

   The Corridor (London: Boosey and Hawkes, 2009).

   The Minotaur (London: Boosey and Hawkes, 2008).

Hayes, Malcolm, 'Pandas mate at last', *Sunday Telegraph*, 26 May 1991.

Heidegger, Martin, *Kant and the Problem of Metaphysics*, trans. Richard Taft (Bloomington: Indiana University Press, 1997).

Heile, Björn, 'Darmstadt as other: British and American responses to musical modernism', *twentieth-century music*, 1/2 (2004), 161–78.

   'Recent approaches to experimental music theatre and contemporary opera', *Music & Letters*, 87/1 (2006), 72–81.

Henderson, Robert, 'The Mask of Orpheus', *Daily Telegraph*, 23 May 1986.

Hewett, Ivan, 'The second coming', *Musical Times*, 136 (January 1995), 46–7.

Heyworth, Peter, 'Circles turning on different orbits', *Observer*, 25 May 1986.

Higgins, John, 'Harrison Birtwistle: the composer and the stage', *The Times*, 10 December 1975.

Hoban, Russell, *The Medusa Frequency* (London: Bloomsbury, 2002).

   The Moment under the Moment (London: Pan Books, 1993).

   The Second Mrs Kong: An Original Text (London: Universal Edition, 1994).

   Turtle Diary (London: Pan Books, 1980).

Holden, Amanda (ed.), *The New Penguin Opera Guide* (London: Penguin Books, 2001).

Howarth, Elgar, 'The Mask of Orpheus', *Opera*, 37/5 (1986), 492–5.

Hutcheon, Linda, *A Theory of Parody: The Teachings of Twentieth-Century Art Forms* (Urbana and Chicago: University of Illinois Press, 2000).

  Irony's Edge: The Theory and Politics of Irony (London: Routledge, 1995).

Iddon, Martin, 'Darmstadt schools: Darmstadt as a plural phenomenon', *Tempo*, 256 (2011), 2–8.

Innes, Christopher, *Avant Garde Theatre, 1892–1992* (London and New York: Routledge, 1993), 59–94.

Jameson, Fredric, *Postmodernism, or The Cultural Logic of Late Capitalism* (Durham, NC: Duke University Press, 1991).

Johnson, Julian, *Mahler's Voices: Expression and Irony in the Songs and Symphonies* (Oxford University Press, 2009).

Johnson, Mark, *The Body in the Mind: The Bodily Basis of Meaning, Imagination, and Reason* (London: University of Chicago Press, 1987).

  The Meaning of the Body: Aesthetics of Human Understanding (Chicago University Press, 2007).

Jones, Tobias, 'A life less ordinary', *Observer*, Magazine section, 31 October 2010.

Karl, Gregory, 'Structuralism and musical plot', *Music Theory Spectrum*, 19/1 (Spring 1997), 13–34.

Kay, George, ed., *The Penguin Book of Italian Verse* (London: Penguin, 1958).

Kennedy, Michael, 'Birtwistle rides into King Arthur's court', *Independent on Sunday*, 2 June 1991.

Kildea, Paul (ed.), *Britten on Britten* (Oxford University Press, 2003).

Kingston, Jeremy, 'Bow down', *Financial Times*, 6 July 1977.

Kramer, Lawrence, '"As if a voice were in them": music, narrative, and deconstruction', in his *Music as Cultural Practice, 1800–1900* (Berkeley and Los Angeles: University of California Press, 1990), 176–213.

  Opera and Modern Culture: Wagner and Strauss (Berkeley and Los Angeles: University of California Press, 2004).

  'The voice of Persephone: musical meaning and mixed media', in his *Musical Meaning: Toward a Critical History* (Berkeley and Los Angeles: University of California Press, 2002), 173–93.

Lacan, Jacques, *Ecrits: A Selection*, trans. Alan Sheridan (New York: W. W. Norton & Co., 1977).

Lakoff, George, *Women, Fire and Other Dangerous Things* (Chicago University Press, 1987).

  and Mark Johnson, *Metaphors We Live By* (Chicago and London: Chicago University Press, 2003).

Langridge, Stephen, 'Myth is universal', on the commercial DVD recording of the original production of *The Minotaur*, Royal Opera House/Opus Arte 2008, OA 1000 D.

Lawrence, D. H., *Last Poems (1932)* in *The Complete Poems of D. H. Lawrence*, 2 vols., vol. II, ed. Vivian de Sola Pinto and Warren Roberts (London: Heinemann, 1964).

Le Guin, Elisabeth, *Boccherini's Body: An Essay in Carnal Musicology* (Berkeley and Los Angeles: University of California Press, 2006).

Leach, Robert, *Makers of Modern Theatre: An Introduction* (London and New York: Routledge, 2004).

 The Punch and Judy Show: History, Tradition and Meaning (London: Batsford Academic and Educational, 1985).

Lebrecht, Norman, 'Knights at the opera', *Independent*, Magazine section, 18 May 1991, 57–9.

Lefkowitz, Murray, 'Antimasque', in Stanley Sadie and John Tyrrell (eds.), *The New Grove Dictionary of Music and Musicians*, 2nd edn, vol. I (London: Macmillan, 2001), 734–5.

Lehmann, Hans-Thies, *Postdramatic Theatre*, trans. Karen Jürs-Munby (London and New York: Routledge, 2006).

Levinson, Jerrold, *Music, Art, and Metaphysics* (Ithaca: Cornell University Press, 1990).

Lidov, David, *Is Language a Music? Writings on Musical Form and Signification* (Bloomington and Indianapolis: Indiana University Press, 2005).

 'Mind and Body in Music', *Semiotica*, 66–1/3 (1987), 69–97.

Lorraine, Ross, 'Territorial rites 1', *Musical Times*, 138 (October 1997), 4–8.

 'Territorial rites 2', *Musical Times*, 138 (November 1997), 12–16.

Lyons, John D., 'Artaud: intoxication and its double', *Yale French Studies*, 50 (1974), 120–9.

Lyotard, Jean-François, *The Postmodern Condition*, trans. Geoff Bennington and Brian Massumi (Manchester University Press, 1997).

Maddocks, Fiona, 'The Minotaur's monster performance', *Evening Standard*, 16 April 2008.

Mann, William, 'Bow down', *The Times*, 6 July 1977.

 review of *The Mask of Orpheus*, *Opernwelt*, 27/8 (August 1986), 47.

Marlowe, Christopher, *Doctor Faustus and Other Plays*, ed. David Bevington and Eric Ramussen (Oxford University Press, 2008).

Marsh, Roger, '"A multicoloured alphabet": rediscovering Albert Giraud's *Pierrot Lunaire*', *twentieth-century music*, 4/1 (2007), 97–121.

Martin, Priscilla, 'Allegory and symbolism', in Derek Brewer and Jonathan Gibson (eds.), *A Companion to the Gawain Poet* (Cambridge: D. S. Brewer, 1999), 315–28.

Marx, Leo, 'Pastoralism in America', in Sacvan Bercovitch and Myra Jehlen (eds.), *Ideology and Classic American Literature* (Cambridge University Press, 1986), 36–69.

 The Machine in the Garden: Technology and the Pastoral Ideal in America (New York: Oxford University Press, 1964; repr. 2000).

Matthews, Colin, liner notes to Benjamin Britten, *Peter Grimes*, conducted by Bernard Haitink, EMI CD CB 7548322 (1993).

Maus, Fred Everett, 'Music as drama', *Music Theory Spectrum*, 10 (1988), 56–73.
'Narrative, drama and emotion in instrumental music', *Journal of Aesthetics and Art Criticism*, 55/3 (1997), 293–303.

McClary, Susan, *Feminine Endings: Music, Gender, and Sexuality* (Minneapolis and London: University of Minnesota Press, 1991).

McFerran, Ann, 'Knights to remember', *Weekend Telegraph*, [n.d.] January 1991.

Mellers, Wilfrid, 'Body music' [review of *The Mask Of Orpheus*], *Times Literary Supplement*, 6 June 1986
The Masks of Orpheus: Seven Stages in the Story of European Music (Manchester University Press, 1987).

Metz, Christian, 'The imaginary signifier', *Screen*, 16/2 (1975), 14–76.

Metzer, David, *Musical Modernism at the Turn of the Twenty-First Century* (Cambridge University Press, 2009), especially Chapter 4, 'Lament', 144–74.

Meyerhold, V. E., *Meyerhold on Theatre*, trans. Edward Braun (London: Eyre Methuen, 1981).

Micznik, Vera, 'Music and narrative revisited: degrees of narrativity in Beethoven and Mahler', *Journal of the Royal Musical Association*, 126 (2001), 193–49.

Milnes, Rodney, 'Another place at the table', *The Times*, 6 August 2001.

Morra, Irene, *Twentieth-Century British Authors and the Rise of Opera in Britain* (Aldershot: Ashgate, 2007).

Morris, Christopher, *Reading Opera between the Lines: Orchestral Interludes and Cultural Meaning from Wagner to Berg* (Cambridge University Press, 2002).

Morris, Robert D., *Composition with Pitch-Classes: A Theory of Compositional Design* (New Haven: Yale University Press, 1987).
'New directions in the theory and analysis of musical contour', *Music Theory Spectrum*, 15/2 (1993), 205–28.

Nancy, Jean-Luc, *The Birth to Presence*, trans. Brian Homes et al. (Stanford University Press, 1993).
The Ground of the Image, trans. Jeff Fort (New York: Fordham University Press, 2005).
The Inoperative Community, ed. Peter Connor, trans. Peter Connor, Lisa Garbus, Michael Holland and Simona Sawhney (Minneapolis and London: University of Minnesota Press, 2006).

Nattiez, Jean-Jacques, 'Can one speak of narrativity in music?', *Journal of the Royal Musical Association*, 115/2 (1990), 240–57.

Neruda, Pablo, *The Poetry of Pablo Neruda*, ed. Ilan Stavans, trans. Mark Eisner (New York: Farrar, Straus and Giroux, 2003).

Newcomb, Anthony, '"Once more between absolute and program music": Schumann's second symphony', *Nineteenth-Century Music*, 7/3 (1983–4), 233–50.

Newton, Isaac, *Sir Isaac Newton's Mathematical Principles of Natural Philosophy and His System of the World*, trans. F. Cajori (Berkeley and Los Angeles: University of California Press, 1962).

Nichols, Miriam, 'Interview with Robin Blaser', in Nichols (ed.), *Even on Sunday*, 349–92.

   'Spilling the names of God: Robin Blaser's *The Last Supper*', *Mosaic*, 36/2 (2003), 163–78.

   (ed.), *Even on Sunday: Essays, Readings, and Archival Materials on the Poetry and Poetics of Robin Blaser* (Orono, Maine: National Poetry Foundation, 2002).

Nooteboom, Cees, *Roads to Santiago: Detours and Riddles in the Lands and History of Spain*, trans. Ina Rilke (London: Harvill Press, 1998).

Northcott, Bayan, 'Out of the concert hall', *Sunday Telegraph*, 17 July 1977.

Nyman, Michael, 'Harrison Birtwistle's "Punch and Judy"', *Listener*, 10 October 1968, 481.

O'Hagan, Peter (ed.), *Aspects of British Music of the 1990s* (Aldershot: Ashgate, 2003).

   'Pierre Boulez and the project of "L'Orestie"', *Tempo*, 241 (2007), 34–52.

Olson, Charles, *The Collected Poems of Charles Olson: Excluding the Maximus Poems*, ed. George F. Butterick (Berkeley and Los Angeles: University of California Press, 1997), 175–82.

Osborne, Nigel, 'Orpheus in Paris', in the programme booklet for the English National Opera premiere of *The Mask of Orpheus*, May 1986.

Padel, Ruth, 'Around the Minotaur', in the programme booklet for the Royal Opera House, Covent Garden, premiere of *The Minotaur*, April 2008, 12–16.

Pappenheim, Mark, interview with Birtwistle, *Independent*, 8 April 1994, 21.

Pasler, Jann, 'Narrative and narrativity in music', in her *Writing through Music: Essays on Music, Culture, and Politics* (Oxford University Press, 2008), 25–48.

Patterson, Annabel, *Pastoral and Ideology: Virgil to Valéry* (Oxford: Clarendon Press, 1988).

Pearsall, Derek, 'Courtesy and chivalry', in Derek Brewer and Jonathan Gibson (eds.), *A Companion to the Gawain Poet* (Cambridge: D. S. Brewer, 1999), 351–64.

Picard, Anna, 'The agony and the ecstasy of a Last Supper reunion', *Independent*, 29 October 2000.

   'The Minotaur, Royal Opera House, London', *Independent*, 20 April 2008.

Pierce, Alexandra, *Deepening Musical Performance through Movement: The Theory and Practice of Embodied Interpretation* (Bloomington: Indiana University Press, 2007).

Plaice, Stephen, 'The Io Passion', *Aldeburgh Soundings: The Newsletter of the Friends of the Aldeburgh Foundation* (Spring 2004), 4.

   'They said they were looking for a gloomy poet. I got the job', *Guardian*, 11 June 2004.

Porter, Andrew, 'Another Orpheus sings', *New Yorker*, June 1986, 84–8.

   'Knight's progress', *New Yorker*, 7 January 1991.

Porter, Peter, 'Inner and outer worlds', interview with David Harsent in the programme booklet for the Royal Opera House, Covent Garden, production of *Gawain*, January 2000, 31–7.

Pound, Scott, 'Writing/repeating community: Robin Blaser's *Image-Nation* series', in Nichols (ed.), *Even on Sunday*, 167–77.

Propp, Vladimir, *The Morphology of the Folktale*, trans. L. Scott (Austin: University of Texas Press, 1994).

Pruslin, Stephen, programme note for performance of *Monodrama*, Queen Elizabeth Hall, London, 30 May 1967.

   programme note for performance of *The Visions of Francesco Petrarca*, York Festival, June 1966.

   'Punch and Judy', liner note to CD recording of *Punch and Judy*, Etcetera KTC 2014, 1989.

   Punch and Judy: A Tragical Comedy or a Comical Tragedy. Opera in One Act (London: Universal Edition, 1968).

Quinn, Ian, 'The combinatorial model of pitch contour', *Music Perception*, 16 (1999), 439–56.

Ragland, Ellie, 'The relation between the voice and the gaze', in Richard Feldstein, Bruce Fink and Maire Jaanus (eds.), *Reading Seminar XI: Lacan's Four Fundamental Concepts of Psychoanalysis* (Albany: State University of New York Press, 1995), 187–203.

Rees-Jones, Deryn, 'The politics of seeing' (review of David Harsent's poetry collection *Marriage*), *Poetry Review*, 92/2 (2002).

Reyland, Nicholas, '*Livre* or symphony? Lutosławski's *Livre pour Orchestre* and the enigma of musical narrativity', *Music Analysis*, 27/2–3 (2008), 253–94.

Ricoeur, Paul, *Time and Narrative*, 3 vols., vol. I, trans. Kathleen McLaughlin and David Pellauer (London: University of Chicago Press, 1984).

   Time and Narrative, 3 vols., vol. III, trans. Kathleen Blamey and David Pellauer (London: University of Chicago Press, 1988).

Rilke, Rainer Maria, *Sonnets to Orpheus*, trans. C. F. MacIntyre (Berkeley and Los Angeles: University of California Press, 1997).

Ross, Alex, review of *The Second Mrs Kong*. http://www.therestisnoise.com/2006/08/london_1995.html (accessed 22 August 2011).

Rupprecht, Philip, *Britten's Musical Language* (Cambridge University Press, 2001).

   review of Anthony Pople (ed.), *Theory, Analysis and Meaning in Music* (Cambridge University Press, 1994), *Journal of Music Theory*, 41/1 (1997), 157–75.

   '"Something slightly indecent": British composers, the European avant-garde, and national stereotypes in the 1950s', *Musical Quarterly*, 91/3–4 (2008), 278–325.

Said, Edward, *The World, the Text, and the Critic* (London: Vintage, 1991).

Salzman, Eric, and Thomas Desi, *The New Music Theater: Seeing the Voice, Hearing the Body* (New York: Oxford University Press, 2008).

Sampson, Fiona, 'The myth kitty [interview with Harsent]', in the programme book-
    let to the Royal Opera House, Covent Garden, production of *The Minotaur*,
    April 2008, 41–8.
Samuel, Rhian, 'Birtwistle's *Gawain*: an essay and a diary', *Cambridge Opera Journal*,
    4/2 (1992), 163–78.
    'Birtwistle's *The Minotaur*: the opera and a diary of its first production', *Cambridge
    Opera Journal*, 20/2 (2008), 215–36.
Samuels, Robert, 'The Mask of Orpheus', *Tempo*, 158 (1986), 41–4.
Sanders, James, *Celluloid Skyline* (London and New York: Bloomsbury, 2001).
Santos, Silvio José Dos, 'Ascription of identity: the *Bild* motif and the character of
    Lulu', *Journal of Musicology*, 21 (2004), 267–308.
Savage, Roger, 'Making a libretto: three collaborations over "The Rake's Progress"',
    in Nicholas John (ed.), *Stravinsky: Oedipus Rex, The Rake's Progress*, English
    National Opera Guide 43 (London: John Calder, 1991), 45–58.
Saylor, Eric. '"It's not lambkins frisking at all": English pastoral music and the Great
    War', *Musical Quarterly*, 91/1–2 (2008), 39–59.
Scherer, Klaus, R., 'Expression of emotion in voice and music', *Journal of Voice*, 9/3
    (1995), 235–48.
Scherzinger, Martin, 'The return of the aesthetic: musical formalism and its place
    in political critique', in Andrew Dell'Antonio (ed.), *Beyond Structural Listen-
    ing? Postmodern Modes of Hearing* (Berkeley and Los Angeles: University of
    California Press, 2004), 252–77.
Schiller, Friedrich, '*On Naive and Sentimental Poetry* (1795–6)', in H. B. Nisbet
    (ed.), *German Aesthetic and Literary Criticism: Winckelmann, Lessing, Hamann,
    Herder, Schiller, Goethe* (Cambridge University Press, 1985), 180–232.
Schumacher, Claude, and Brian Singleton (eds.), *Artaud on Theatre* (London:
    Methuen, 2001).
Seckerson, Edward, 'Jesus Christ, supper star', *Independent*, 25 October 2001.
Sedgwick, Peter, *From Descartes to Derrida: An Introduction to European Philosophy*
    (Oxford and Malden, MA: Blackwell, 2001).
Segel, Harold B., *Body Ascendant: Modernism and the Physical Imperative* (London
    and Baltimore: Johns Hopkins University Press, 1998).
Service, Tom, 'The Last Supper', *Guardian*, 7 August, 2001.
Shakespeare, William, *The Alexander Text of the Complete Works of William Shake-
    speare*, ed. Peter Alexander (London and Glasgow: Collins, 1987).
Sheppard, W. Anthony, *Revealing Masks: Exotic Influences and Ritualized Perfor-
    mance in Modernist Music Theater* (Berkeley and Los Angeles: University of
    California Press, 2001).
Silverman, Kaja, *The Acoustic Mirror: The Female Voice in Psychoanalysis and Cinema*
    (Bloomington and Indianapolis: Indiana University Press, 1988).
Snowman, Nicholas, 'Birtwistle the dramatist: some reflections', in the programme
    booklet for the first production of *Gawain*, Royal Opera House, Covent Garden,
    May–June 1991.

Soja, E., *Postmodern Geographies: The Reassertion of Space in Critical Theory* (London: Verso, 1989).

Sontag, Susan, *Antonin Artaud: Selected Writings* (New York: Farrar, Strauss and Giroux, 1976).

Spink, Ian, *English Song: Dowland to Purcell* (London: Batsford, 1974).

Spitzer, Michael, *Metaphor and Musical Thought* (London: University of Chicago Press, 2004).

States, Bert O., *Great Reckonings in Little Rooms* (Berkeley and Los Angeles: University of California Press, 1987).

Stenzl, Jürg, 'A "More Secret World"', in F. B. Humer, M. Haefliger, K. Jacobs and G. Hanson (eds.), *Roche Commissions: Sir Harrison Birtwistle* (Lucerne: Roche, 2004), 29–37.

Straus, Joseph N., *Stravinsky's Late Music* (Cambridge University Press, 2001).

Subotnik, Rose Rosengard, *Deconstructive Variations: Music and Reason in Western Society* (Minneapolis: University of Minnesota Press, 1996).

Sutcliffe, Tom, review of the Glyndebourne production of *The Second Mrs Kong*, *Musical Times*, 136 (1995), 373–5.

    review of the second Glyndebourne production of *The Last Supper*, *Evening Standard*, 9 August, 2001.

Taylor, Michael, 'Narrative and musical structures in *The Mask of Orpheus* and *Yan Tan Tethera*', in Danuser and Kassel (eds.), *Musiktheater heute*, 173–94.

Thompson, D'Arcy Wentworth, *On Growth and Form*, abridged and ed. John Tyler Bonner (Cambridge University Press, 1997).

Till, Nicholas, '"I don't mind if something's operatic, just as long as it's not opera." A critical practice for new opera and music theatre', *Contemporary Theatre Review*, 14/1 (February 2004), 15–24.

Todorov, Tzvetan, *Poetics of Prose*, trans. Richard Howard (Oxford: Blackwell, 1977).

Tooley, John, *In House: Covent Garden, 50 Years of Opera and Ballet* (London: Faber and Faber, 1999).

Traherne, Thomas, 'Thanksgivings for the Body', in his *Poems, Centuries and Three Thanksgivings*, ed. Anne Ridler (London: Oxford University Press, 1966), 375–81.

Turner, Victor, *From Ritual to Theatre: The Human Seriousness of Play* (New York: PAJ Publications, 1982).

Walker, Julia A., 'Why performance? Why now? Textuality and the rearticulation of human presence', *Yale Journal of Criticism*, 16/2 (2003), 149–75.

Walsh, Stephen, review of Hall, *Harrison Birtwistle*, *Soundings*, 12 (1985), 75–8.

    Stravinsky: The Second Exile. France and America 1934–1971 (London: Jonathan Cape, 2006).

Warden, John (ed.), *Orpheus: The Metamorphoses of a Myth* (Buffalo: University of Toronto Press, 1982).

West Marvin, Elizabeth, 'Generalization of contour theory to diverse musical spaces: analytical applications to the music of Dallapiccola and Stockhausen', in Elizabeth West Marvin and Richard Hermann (eds.), *Concert Music, Rock, and*

Jazz since 1945: Essays and Analytical Studies (Rochester, NY: University of Rochester Press, 1995), 135–71.

Whitesell, Lloyd, 'Britten's dubious trysts', *Journal of the American Musicological Society*, 56/3 (Fall 2003), 637–4.

Whittall, Arnold, 'A public–private partnership: Wagner's voices in *Die Meistersinger*', *Wagner Journal*, 2/3 (2008), 39–57.

'Birtwistle's *Last Supper* and Adams's *El Niño*: Echoes of old beliefs', *Musical Times*, 143 (Winter 2002), 16–26.

'Comparatively complex: Birtwistle, Maxwell Davies and modernist analysis', *Music Analysis*, 13, 2/3 (October 1994), 139–59.

'First performances. London, Royal Opera, Covent Garden: Birtwistle's *The Minotaur*', *Tempo*, 246 (2008), 50–1.

'Modernist aesthetics: some analytical perspectives', in James M. Baker, David W. Beach and Jonathan W. Bernard (eds.), *Music Theory in Concept and Practice* (Rochester, NY: University of Rochester Press, 1997), 157–80.

'Orpheus – and after', *Musical Times*, 139 (Winter 1998), 55–8.

Serialism (Cambridge University Press, 2008).

'The mechanisms of lament: Harrison Birtwistle's "Pulse Shadows"', *Music & Letters*, 80/1 (1999), 86–102.

The Music of Britten and Tippett: Studies in Themes and Techniques (Cambridge University Press, 1990).

Williams, Alastair, 'Ageing of the new: the museum of musical modernism' in Nicholas Cook and Anthony Pople (eds.), *Cambridge History of Twentieth Century Music* (Cambridge University Press, 2004), 506–38.

'Swaying with Schumann: subjectivity and tradition in Wolfgang Rihm's "Fremde Szenen" I–III and related scores', *Music & Letters*, 87/2 (August 2006), 379–97.

'Voices of the other: Wolfgang Rihm's music drama *Die Eroberung von Mexico*', *Journal of the Royal Musical Association*, 192/2 (2004), 240–71.

Williams, Raymond, *The Country and the City* (London: Chatto and Windus, 1975).

Wintle, Christopher, 'A fine and private place', *Musical Times*, 137 (November 1996), 5–8.

Wolff, Janet, *Resident Alien: Feminist Cultural Criticism* (Cambridge: Polity Press, 1995).

Wordsworth, William, *The Prelude: 1799, 1805, 1850*, ed. Jonathan Wordsworth, M. H. Abrams and Stephen Gill (New York: Norton, 1979).

Wright, Patrick, 'Facing up to the subterranean stream: the challenge of Robin Blaser's libretto', in the programme booklet to the Glyndebourne premiere of *The Last Supper*, October 2000, 41–6.

'Relocating the high lyric voice', interview with Robin Blaser for BBC Radio 3's *Night Waves*. Available online at http://writing.upenn.edu/pennsound/x/Blaser.php (accessed 1 November 2010).

'The mystery of the kiosk composer', *Guardian*, 3 September 1992.

Young, B. A., 'Herod', *Financial Times*, 12 December 1978.

Zenck, Martin, 'Antonin Artaud – Pierre Boulez – Wolfgang Rihm: Zur Re- und Transritualität im europäischen Musiktheater', in Danuser and Kassel (eds.), *Musiktheater heute*, 235–61.

Zinovieff, Peter, *The Mask of Orpheus: An Opera in Three Acts* (London: Universal Edition, 1986).

  The Mask of Orpheus: Libretto, included with CD recording of *The Mask of Orpheus* (1997), NMC recordings: NMC D050.

Žižek, Slavoj, *Enjoy Your Symptom: Jacques Lacan in Hollywood and Out* (New York and London: Routledge, 2001).

  "The everlasting irony of the community', in Slavoj Žižek and Mladen Dolar, *Opera's Second Death* (New York and London: Routledge, 2002), 151–80.

  and Mladen Dolar, *Opera's Second Death* (New York and London: Routledge, 2002).

Index

Abbate, Carolyn
  on narrative and voice   156, 190, 196n.4,
    219, 219n.81, 234
Accrington Amateur Operatic and Dramatic
    Society   16
action
  physical *see* body, the; mime; pantomime
  symbolic representation of   279
Adlington, Robert   1n.1, 13, 73n.70, 88, 116,
    143, 150, 153, 203, 204, 204n.40,
    205n.43, 246, 248, 252n.37, 276, 280,
    303, 303n.88, 316n.119, 317, 317n.123,
    322, 336
Adorno, Theodor   5, 72, 153, 166, 166n.21,
    219, 239, 265, 361
Affekt   40, 73, 412
Agamben, Giorgio   376
  Coming Community, The   362, 363, 364,
    365n.52, 376n.88, 389, 400, 436
'*Agamemnon* Experiments'   143, 290–5, 303,
    304, 306
Aldeburgh Festival   168, 306n.100
Allen, Thomas   92
Almeida Opera   306n.100
Almén, Byron   220
Alpers, Paul   169–70, 172, 173, 174
  'representative anecdote' of pastoral   169,
    172, 174, 175, 183, 194, 195
Anderson, Barry   79n.17, 83–4
Andriessen, Louis   6n.14, 151
Aperghis, George   5, 286
Arendt, Hannah   363, 363n.42
  The Origins of Totalitarianism   363
Aristotle   152, 196
  'mythemes'   156
  Poetics   154
Artaud, Antonin   8, 282n.22, 280–6, 291n.60,
    293, 294n.68, 296, 297, 301, 301n.81,
    307, 314, 336, 346, 412
  between gesture and thought   280, 282
  'concrete' signs or gestures   284, 288, 305,
    316, 336
  cruelty, concept of   281, 283n.27, 341,
    354

  mechanics of signification   282, 283, 285,
    292
  scenic rhythms   284, 285
  'true' theatre   281, 354
Atherton, Elizabeth   337
Attali, Jacques   77
  on music as a simulacrum of ritual murder
    43, 72–3
Auden, W. H.   79n.4, 160, 161n.13
audibility
  of compositional schemes   57, 58, 59, 66,
    68, 117, 129, 138, 233, 233n.102, 265,
    394, 396
audience participation   26
Augustine, Saint   152, 154
Austin, J. L.   341
avant-garde dilemma   2, 5–7, 81, 197

Babbitt, Milton   40, 40n.15, 62
  Philomel   7, 145
Bach, Johann Sebastian   314, 392, 412, 439
  St Matthew Passion   39, 67n.51
Bacon, Francis   247, 281n.15
Bakhtin, Mikhail   72, 157n.219
Ballad of the Cruel Mother   5, 25, 26
Ballad of the Two Sisters   296–7
Barba, Eugenio   30
Barenboim, Daniel   355n.2
Barrault, Jean-Louis   285, 294n.68, 296
Barthes, Roland   257, 257n.61
Baudrillard, Jean   243, 253, 254
BBC   20, 159
  Night Waves   361
Beardslee, Bethany   145
Bedford, David   21n.84
  The Wheel   21n.84
Beethoven, Ludwig van   39, 219, 239
  Fidelio   64
Bell, Catherine   280, 281
Benjamin, Walter   243, 263n.75
Bennett, Richard Rodney   6n.15
Berg, Alban   10, 270
  Lulu   255n.50
  Wozzeck   79, 240

9 781316 641989